THE ROUTLEDGE INTERNATIONAL HANDBOOK OF LEARNING WITH TECHNOLOGY IN EARLY CHILDHOOD

The Routledge International Handbook of Learning with Technology in Early Childhood focuses specifically on the most cutting-edge, innovative and international approaches in the study of children's use of and learning with digital technologies.

This edited volume is a comprehensive survey of methods in children's technologies and contains a rich repertoire of studies from diverse fields and research, including both educational and developmental psychology, post-humanist literacy, applied linguistics, language and phenomenology and narrative approaches.

For ease of reference, the Handbook's 28 chapters are divided into four thematic sections:

- introduction and opening reflections;
- studies answering ontological questions, which theorize how children take on original identities in becoming literate with technologies;
- studies answering epistemological questions, which focus on how children's knowledge and learning are (co)constructed with a diverse range of technologies;
- studies answering practice-related questions, which explore the resources and conditions that create the most powerful learning opportunities for children.

Expertly edited, this interdisciplinary and international compendium is an ideal introduction to such a diverse, multi-faceted field.

Natalia Kucirkova is Professor of Early Childhood Education and Development at University of Stavanger, Norway. Her research concerns innovative ways of supporting children's book reading, digital literacy and exploring the role of personalization in early years. She has been commended for her engagement with teachers and parents at a national and international level.

Jennifer Rowsell is Professor in the Department of Teacher Education and Canada Research Chair in Multiliteracies at Brock University, Canada. Her current research interests include applying multimodal, arts-based practices with youth across formal and informal contexts; expanding research methodologies and theories of literacy for digital, immersive and game-based research; and, longitudinal research with families examining ways that literacy and multimodal practices mediate identities.

Garry Falloon is the Fairfax Foundation Chair in Education and Professor of Digital Learning in the Department of Educational Studies at Macquarie University, Australia. His research interests include mobile and online learning, digital learning in primary and middle schools, pedagogy and assessment in digitally supported innovative learning environments and educational research methods.

THE ROUTLEDGE INTERNATIONAL HANDBOOK SERIES

THE ROUTLEDGE INTERNATIONAL HANDBOOK OF EARLY CHILDHOOD PLAY (2017)
Edited by Tina Bruce, Pentti Hakkarainen and Milda Bredikyte

THE ROUTLEDGE INTERNATIONAL HANDBOOK OF EARLY LITERACY EDUCATION (2017)
Edited by Natalia Kucirkova, Catherine E. Snow, Vibeke Grover and Catherine McBride

THE ROUTLEDGE INTERNATIONAL HANDBOOK OF CRITICAL POSITIVE PSYCHOLOGY (2017)
Edited by Nick Brown, Tim Lomas and Francisco Jose Eiroa-Orosa

INTERNATIONAL HANDBOOK OF POSITIVE AGING (2017)
Edited by Rachael E Docking and Jennifer Stocks

ROUTLEDGE INTERNATIONAL HANDBOOK OF SCHOOLS AND SCHOOLING IN ASIA (2018)
Edited by Kerry J. Kennedy and John Chi-Kin Lee

ROUTLEDGE INTERNATIONAL HANDBOOK OF MULTICULTURAL EDUCATION RESEARCH IN ASIA PACIFIC (2018)
Edited by Yun-Kyung Cha, Seung-Hwan Ham and Moosung Lee

ROUTLEDGE INTERNATIONAL HANDBOOK OF FROEBEL AND EARLY CHILDHOOD PRACTICE (2019)
Edited by Tina Bruce, Peter Elfer and Sacha Powell with Louie Werth

THE ROUTLEDGE INTERNATIONAL HANDBOOK OF LEARNING WITH TECHNOLOGY IN EARLY CHILDHOOD (2019)
Edited by Natalia Kucirkova, Jennifer Rowsell and Garry Falloon

For more information about this series, please visit: www.routledge.com/Routledge-International-Handbooks-of-Education/book-series/HBKSOFED

THE ROUTLEDGE INTERNATIONAL HANDBOOK OF LEARNING WITH TECHNOLOGY IN EARLY CHILDHOOD

Edited by Natalia Kucirkova, Jennifer Rowsell and Garry Falloon

Routledge
Taylor & Francis Group
LONDON AND NEW YORK

First published 2019
by Routledge
2 Park Square, Milton Park, Abingdon, Oxon OX14 4RN

and by Routledge
52 Vanderbilt Avenue, New York, NY 10017

Routledge is an imprint of the Taylor & Francis Group, an informa business

British Library Cataloguing-in-Publication Data
A catalogue record for this book is available from the British Library

Library of Congress Cataloging-in-Publication Data
A catalog record for this book has been requested

ISBN: 978-1-138-30819-0 (pbk)
ISBN: 978-1-138-30816-9 (hbk)
ISBN: 978-1-315-14304-0 (ebk)

Typeset in Bembo
by Apex CoVantage, LLC

CONTENTS

List of figures ix
List of tables xi
Notes on editors xii
Notes on contributors xiii
Foreword by Rosie Flewitt xxiii

PART I
Setting the scene **1**

1 Introduction 3
Natalia Kucirkova, Jennifer Rowsell and Garry Falloon

2 Reflective conversations about research methods with children 18
Pam Whitty and Jennifer Rowsell

3 The pros and cons of using display capture technology for data collection with young children 30
Garry Falloon

PART II
Studies answering ontological questions **47**

4 "Talk into my GoPro, I'm making a movie!": using digital ethnographic methods to explore children's sociomaterial experiences in the woods 49
Debra Harwood and Diane R. Collier

5 Transcultural approaches to literacy, learning, and play 62
Rahat Zaidi

6 Composing childhood cultures: ethnography upside down 74
Anne Haas Dyson

7 Researching a child's embodied textual play 88
Kerryn Dixon and Hilary Janks

8 Social media, video data and heritage language learning: researching the transnational literacy practices of young children from immigrant families 107
Sumin Zhao

9 (Re)imagining multiliteracies research practices with post qualitative inquiry 127
Candace R. Kuby

10 Stacking stories as method: research in early years settings 143
Cathy Burnett and Guy Merchant

PART III
Studies answering epistemological questions **155**

11 Researching young children's play in the post-digital age: questions of method 157
Jackie Marsh

12 From cutting out to cutting with: a materialist reframing of action and multimodality in children's play and making 170
Karen E. Wohlwend and Jaye Johnson Thiel

13 Researching in the iWorld: from home to beyond 182
Linda Laidlaw, Joanne O'Mara and Suzanna So-Har Wong

14 Young children's home technology use: responsive qualitative methods for a sensitive topic 196
Joanne Orlando

15 The parent-child-app learning assemblage: scaffolding early childhood learning through app use in the family home 210
Donell Holloway, Leslie Haddon, Lelia Green and Kylie J. Stevenson

16 This is the stuff that identities are made of: children learning with grandparents and other elders 219
Rachel Heydon and Xiaoxiao Du

17 Technologies, affordances, children and embodied reading: a case for interdisciplinarity 235
Anne Mangen, Trude Hoel and Thomas Moser

18 Materialities, multiliteracies and makerspaces: design-based experiments in teacher/researcher collaborations 248
Aspa Baroutsis and Annette Woods

PART IV
Studies answering practice-related questions **265**

19 Research with children with special educational needs: a focus on Autism Spectrum Disorder 267
Melissa L. Allen and Shu Yau

20 Using mixed methods research with young children and their families in culturally, linguistically and socially diverse communities 280
Jim Anderson, Ann Anderson, Ji Eun Kim and Marianne McTavish

21 Student generated visual narratives: lived experiences of learning 294
Narelle Lemon

22 Arts-based methods 311
Linda Knight

23 Supporting children's learning at home through smartphone apps for parents 324
Fiona Jelley, Kathy Sylva and Valeria Ortiz Villalobos

24 When technology met real-life experiences: science curriculum project with technology for low-income Latino preschoolers 338
Lena Lee

25 Reading in the digital age: lessons learned and future opportunities 349
Rebecca A. Dore, Jennifer M. Zosh, Brenna Hassinger-Das, Roberta Michnick Golinkoff and Kathy Hirsh-Pasek

26 Head mounted, chest mounted, tripod or roaming? the methodological potentials of a GoPro camera and ontological possibilities for doing visual research with child participants differently 362
Lucy Caton and Abigail Hackett

27 Critical visual discourse analysis 377
Peggy Albers, Vivian Maria Vasquez, and Jerome C. Harste

28 Using tablet technology in preschool and early kindergarten for the identification of children at risk for reading difficulties 393
Sibylla Leon Guerrero, Ola Ozernov-Palchik, Michelle Gonzalez, Jennifer Zuk and Nadine Gaab

Index *404*

FIGURES

3.1	An example of an Innovative Learning Environment (Flexible Learning Space) from this study	31
3.2	Flexible learning spaces provide children with different workspace options	32
3.3a, b	Top, the early display recorder showing finger placement (white spots) and the latest version (bottom) with Facecam recording	34
3.4	A typical Studiocode window showing timeline (bottom), coding framework (right) and sample video clip	36
3.5	Later versions of the screen recorder included a visible start/stop button	38
3.6	The Facecam captured children's lengthy (and often silent) deliberations as they tried to solve problems	42
4.1	Still images of child's GoPro video	50
4.2	Mike's GoPro video data fragments	51
4.3	GoPro video clips of icy hill play	57
5.1	Sample letter inviting parent and community member participation	67
6.1	Ta'Von's self-portrait with braids	75
7.1	Fairclough's dimensions of discourse	91
7.2	Fairclough's model with theory inserted relevant to this study	97
7.3	Leah's artwork of children responding 'No' to Pigeon	98
7.4	Leah at work on a map	99
7.5	*Pigeon and Duckling give the Princess something*	100
7.6	*The story of the stolen crown*	100
7.7	Examples of Leah using body positions to represent emotions and movement	104
8.1	WeChat exchange: Let's Play a Game	108
8.2	Conversational context: The Reunion Dinner	109
8.3	WeChat video 'reports': children's language and literacy practices in Chinese	115
10.1	Look at our data	148
11.1	Arjun's picture of his Hot Wheels cars in his bedroom	161
11.2	Still from Amy's GoPro footage	165
12.1	Paper iPhone	175

12.2	Multimodal analysis on video coding software	177
12.3	Examples of digital scraps	179
16.1	Brian's Space Room	227
16.2	Charcoal drawing page from digital portfolio	229
16.3	Page from Dejon's digital portfolio	230
18.1	Trap the witch makerspace activities	254
18.2	Excerpts from eBooks	257
18.3	An alien was sighted last week	258
18.4	Designing the fish tank	259
18.5	Material used and diorama example	260
18.6	Child's writing sample	261
19.1	Portable electroencephalography (EEG) set up on a child, from Yau et al. (2015)	271
19.2	Virtual reality research using eye-tracking and an interactive paradigm at Macquarie University	272
21.1	The process of student generated visual narratives in the classroom	299
21.2	Relationship between visual narratives, photo self-elicitation, and learning stories	301
21.3	Document used for reflection after taking photographs for the first time	302
21.4	'I took the photo of the computer lab because it helps us find out things. And it . . . we ummmm do games and maths with them.' (Claire)	304
21.5	'I took this photo because it helps the teachers have lunch and have a break and spend some time with the other teachers. And they have lunch there. I have after school there sometimes.' (Claire)	305
21.6	'I took . . . well this photo. . . . I took this because it helps us photocopy things if we don't have enough sheets.' (Claire)	305
21.7	'I took this photo because it's the art class. We have the art class there to teach us to do good drawings and paintings and ummm it will help us do clay.' (Claire)	306
21.8	'Classrooms, we'd have to work outside if we didn't have. . . . We can keep our writing neat and put our pencils and glue somewhere.' (Claire)	306
22.1A–D	Photographs, taken with iPhone	313
24.1	Project's rationale	342
26.1	Child's perspective	369
26.2	Within the action	370
26.3	Mechanical representations	371
26.4	Child's perspectives	371
26.5	A boy points camera towards his face	372
26.6	Conversation with the teacher	373
27.1	"Mac Attack" counter ad created by teachers in response to a McDonald's ad	380
27.2	Series of three drawings by John	383
27.3	Single discourse represented visually, using common symbols	386
27.4	Teachers drew upon Jacob Lawrence to make visual and written statements on critical literacy issue	388

TABLES

7.1	Data collected over a two-year period	91
7.2	The Pigeon data set	93
8.1	An overview of the participating families	113
8.2	Parental scaffolding of the child's oral narrative skills in Chinese: birthday gifts	116
11.1	Demographic profiles of the case study children	159
12.1	The variations between multimodality and materiality	176
14.1	Comparison between research designs employed in the research literature and the design of this study	200
14.2	Research participants	202
14.3	Children's technology use that surprised parents	204
17.1	Matrix of four measurement classes (Dixon & Bortolussi, 2016): direct and indirect measures, and online and offline measures	243
26.1	Summary of types of cameras	364

EDITORS

Natalia Kucirkova is Professor of Early Childhood Education and Development at University of Stavanger, Norway. Her research concerns innovative ways of supporting children's book reading, digital literacy and exploring the role of personalization. She co-edits the Bloomsbury Book Series Children's Reading and Writing on Screen and the journal *Literacy* published by Wiley. Natalia's research takes place collaboratively across academia, commercial and third sectors.

Jennifer Rowsell is Professor and Canada Research Chair in Multiliteracies at Brock University, Canada. She has written, co-written and co-edited 23 books on such wide-ranging topics as New Literacy Studies, multimodality, youth and popular culture, digital literacies, multiliteracies, ethnography and the digital divide. She is the co-editor of the *Routledge Expanding Literacies in Education* book series with Cynthia Lewis and she is the Department Editor of Digital Literacies for *The Reading Teacher*.

Garry Falloon is Professor of Digital Learning and the Fairfax Foundation Chair in Education at Macquarie University in Sydney, Australia. His research interests include mobile learning in schools, digitally supported learner collaboration and curriculum and learning design, STEM education and business-education partnerships. Prior to working at Macquarie, he was teaching, researching and leading a range of government digital innovation projects from Waikato University in New Zealand.

CONTRIBUTORS

Peggy Albers is Professor of Language and Literacy Education at Georgia State University in Atlanta, USA. Her research interests include critical literacy, teacher education, integration of the arts and digital technologies into language instruction. Peggy is also a practicing sculptor and potter who shows and sells her work locally and nationally.

Melissa L. Allen is Professor in the Psychology of Education at the University of Bristol, UK, and Co-Director of the Psychological Approaches to Studying Education Research Centre. She received her PhD at New York University, followed by a Postdoctoral Fellowship at Yale University jointly in the Psychology Department and the Developmental Disabilities Clinic. Professor Allen has been working in the field of autism and special needs for over 15 years. Her research investigates symbolic understanding of pictures and words and language acquisition in children with Autism Spectrum Disorder and typically developing children. Her interests combine theoretical accounts of early symbolic impairment with an applied focus.

Ann Anderson is Professor in the Department of Curriculum and Pedagogy at the University of British Columbia. Her research and teaching are in mathematics education in the early years, parent mediation of young children's multiliteracies at home and family literacy. Prior to joining UBC, she worked in the public school system as a classroom teacher. Ann's research includes working with families from diverse cultural backgrounds to understand ways in which young children's multiliteracies are supported prior to and in the early years of school. Her research has been funded by the Social Sciences and Humanities Research Council of Canada.

Jim Anderson is Professor in the Department of Language and Literacy Education at the University of British Columbia. He worked in the public school system as a classroom teacher, reading specialist, language arts consultant and assistant superintendent. His work in family literacy has been funded by the Social Sciences and Humanities Research Council and other agencies. With colleagues, he is currently studying young children's and families' access to and use of digital tools in disadvantaged neighborhoods. He is on the Editorial Boards of several journals and served on the Literacy Research Panel of the International Literacy Association for three years.

Aspa Baroutsis is a Research Fellow in the Faculty of Education at the Queensland University of Technology. She researches and teaches in the areas of sociology of education and education policy with a focus on social justice. Her research and teaching interests include digital technologies and literacy learning; mediatization and media constructions and representations of identity; and teachers' work. Her most recent publication is 'Understanding children's perspectives of classroom writing practices through drawings' in *Contemporary Issues in Early Childhood.*

Cathy Burnett is Professor of Literacy and Education at Sheffield Institute of Education, Sheffield Hallam University. Her research explores relationships between new technologies and literacies within and beyond educational contexts. Her books include *New Literacies around the Globe* (published by Routledge and co-edited with Julia Davies, Guy Merchant and Jennifer Rowsell), *The Case of the iPad: Mobile Literacies in Education* (with Guy Merchant, Alyson Simpson and Maureen Walsh for Springer) and *Literacy, Media, Technology: Past, Present and Future* (with Becky Parry and Guy Merchant for Bloomsbury). Cathy is President Elect for the United Kingdom Literacy Association (UKLA).

Lucy Caton is a final year PhD student within the ESRI (Education Social Research Institute) at Manchester Metropolitan University, and an Associate Lecturer in Childhood, Youth and Education Studies. Her research draws from child participatory video research in a school based computer club that uses Deleuze (1989) and Deleuze and Guattari (1987/2014) philosophies to enable something more to be said about children's lives within community and educational scenarios. Her work contributes to visual/sensory methodological speculative inquiry that questions the 'relative humanness of child' in order to re-think human subjectivity as a creation of potentialities in association with the camera and the resultant video data.

Diane R. Collier is Associate Professor in the Faculty of Education at Brock University. She conducts research in the areas of multimodalities and literacies with a special interest in connections across home and school. Using qualitative and interdisciplinary methodologies, her work focuses on the processes of making and literacies, how children use everyday resources (particularly popular culture) and what can be learned from children about their consumption and production of multimodal, cultural and digital texts. Diane is interested in ethical considerations of how children and youth participate in research, how power circulates in research relationships and visual methods.

Kerryn Dixon is Associate Professor the School of Education at the University of the Witwatersrand in South Africa. Her teaching is in the field of language and literacy studies where she specializes in early literacy and critical literacy. Her main research interest is in the application of Foucauldian and spatial theories in education. She has recently authored *Literacy Power and the Schooled Body* (2011) and is a co-author of *Doing Critical Literacy* (2014). She is particularly interested in the interrelationship between language, literacy and power in contexts of learning.

Rebecca A. Dore is a Postdoctoral Fellow in the School of Education at the University of Delaware. She received her PhD in Developmental Psychology in May 2015 from University of Virginia. Her research focuses on how children learn from play, storybooks and media. Her dissertation research, funded by a Dissertation Funding Award from the Society for Research in Child Development, examined the effect of character-similarity on children's learning from a storybook. Current projects include exploring young children's independent use of e-books and examining the effectiveness of a play and storybook reading intervention for teaching vocabulary in low-income preschools.

Xiaoxiao Du teaches language and literacy courses in the Faculty of Education at Western University. She has been working with culturally and linguistically diverse students and their families since 2004. She serves as the first Vice President of the Language and Literacy Researchers of Canada, a special interest group within the Canadian Association for Curriculum Studies. Her research interests include language and literacy, multilingualism, multiculturalism, multiliteracies, culture adjustment, identity construction, heritage language education and international education. She has presented on these topics at international and national conferences and shared her research in book chapters, conference proceedings, journal articles and newsletters.

Anne Haas Dyson is a Fellow of the American Educational Research Association. She has spent over 38 years studying the childhood cultures and literacy learning of young schoolchildren; she is currently Professor of Education at the University of Illinois at Urbana-Champaign.

Rosie Flewitt is Reader in Early Communication and Literacy at UCL Institute of Education, Co-Director of the Helen Hamlyn Centre for Pedagogy (0–11 years) and member of the IOE Centre for Multimodal Research. Her research and teaching focus on young children's communication, language and literacy development and inclusive education, with expertise in multimodal, ethnographic and participatory approaches to the study of early communication and literacy and inclusive pedagogy.

Nadine Gaab is Associate Professor of Pediatrics at Boston Children's Hospital and Harvard Medical School. She is further a member of the faculty at the Harvard Graduate School of Education. Her research focuses on developmental disorders with a special focus on language-based learning disabilities such as developmental dyslexia as well as the early identification of children at risk. She is a frequent speaker in the community, and she is a consultant for various school districts across the country for questions pertaining to early screening and literacy development. For more info please see www.gaablab.com.

Roberta Michnick Golinkoff has received numerous awards for her contributions to developmental science, including the 2017 Society for Research in Child Development's Distinguished Scientific Contributions Award. Funded by federal agencies, she has written 16 books and monographs and many research articles. Passionate about dissemination of psychological science, she wrote *How Babies Talk* (Penguin), *Einstein Never Used Flash Cards* (Rodale), *A Mandate for Playful Learning* (Oxford) and her latest book, *Becoming Brilliant: What Science Tells Us About Raising Successful Children* (APA Press).

Michelle Gonzalez is a Clinical Research Assistant in the Laboratories of Cognitive Neuroscience at Boston Children's Hospital. Michelle has assisted in multiple research studies examining language acquisition in typically developing preschoolers as well as in children with Autism Spectrum Disorder. She is interested in clinical work and educational policy in bilingualism, specifically in Latino populations.

Lelia Green is Professor of Communications in the School of Arts and Humanities at Edith Cowan University. She has worked on a range of Discovery grants funded by the Australian

Research Council (ARC), including 'Toddlers and Tablets' and 'The Internet of Toys'. Between 2008–2013, Lelia led the Risk and Representation program within the ARC Centre of Excellence for Creative Industries and Innovation, partnering with the European EU Kids Online network and, since then, COST Action IS1410 'The Digital Literacy and Multimodal Practice of Young Children'. Prior to becoming an academic in 1986, Lelia was an Assistant Producer with BBC TV.

Sibylla Leon Guerrero is a PhD candidate at the Harvard Graduate School of Education and is engaged in research at the Laboratories of Cognitive Neuroscience at Boston Children's Hospital. Her research focuses on literacy, bilingualism and bilectalism, in particular the ways in which diverse language environments are reflected in children's cognition, early literacy and reading outcomes.

Abigail Hackett is a Research Fellow at the Education and Social Research Institute, Manchester Metropolitan University. She writes and researches young children's literacy practices, with a particular interest in the role of place, materiality and the body in young children's lives. Her work frequently employs visual and sensory methods, often in collaboration with artists. Abi is a British Academy Postdoctoral Fellow (2017–2020). Her project is entitled 'The emergence of literacy in very young children: place and materiality in a more-than-human world'.

Leslie Haddon is Senior Researcher and part-time Lecturer in the Department of Media and Communications at the London School of Economics. For the last 10 years his main focus has been on children's digital experiences. Leslie was co-coordinator of the EU Kids Online project and he participated in the Net Children Go Mobile project. Currently he is a member of the team working on the 'Toddlers and Tablets' project looking at the smartphone and tablet use of 0–5 year olds. He has published numerous journal publications, book chapters and encyclopaedia entries, and was co-author or co-editor of nine books.

Jerome C. Harste is a member of the Alliance of Distinguished Professors at Indiana University. For the past 40 years his work has supported teachers in their effort to improve the teaching of reading, writing and the language arts. Dr. Harste's research has impacted and expanded the profession's notion of literacy to now include visual literacy as well as other ways of knowing. In the field of English Education, Dr. Harste is seen as a strong advocate for critical literacy, the arts, process approaches to the reading and writing, inquiry-based education and the use of children's and adolescent literature throughout the curriculum.

Debra Harwood is Associate Professor within the Faculty of Education at Brock University, Canada. She specializes in teaching and research that focuses on a multitude of aspects related to curriculum and pedagogy in early childhood education. She has led several research projects on children's playing, thinking and ways of interacting within digitally infused learning contexts. Debra is equally interested in examining the relationships between educator pedagogies, children as producers and digital texts.

Brenna Hassinger-Das is Assistant Professor of Psychology at Pace University. Her research examines children's play and learning in home, school and community contexts, particularly for children from under-resourced communities. Her areas of expertise encompass executive functioning, early number sense and vocabulary acquisition. She is particularly interested in investigating the role of play and games for learning. She is committed to translating her research for use by the public through community-based research projects as well as blog posts and commentaries featured in outlets such as *The Huffington Post*, NewsWorks.org and additional local outlets.

Rachel Heydon is Professor in the Faculty of Education at Western University and co-director of the Provincial Centre of Excellence for Early Years and Child Care. She is the Executive Editor of *Journal of Curriculum Studies*, and her books include *Learning at the Ends of Life: Children, Elders, and Literacies in Intergenerational Curricula.*

Kathryn Hirsh-Pasek is the Lefkowitz Faculty Fellow in the Department of Psychology at Temple University and a Senior Fellow at the Brookings Institution. Her research examines the development of early language and literacy as well as the role of play in learning. She is the author of 14 books and hundreds of publications and has won numerous awards in her field. Vested in translating the science of learning for lay and professional audiences, her recent book, *Becoming Brilliant: What the Science Tells Us about Raising Successful Children,* was released in 2016 and was on the *The New York Times* Best Seller List in Education and Parenting.

Trude Hoel currently holds a position as Postdoctoral Fellow in Literacy Studies within the subject area of digital learning and digital competences, and is on leave from her position as Associate Professor at the National Centre for Reading Education and Research at the University of Stavanger in Norway. Trude has published books and research papers and her research interests include language development, emergent and early literacy, reading on paper and screen and storybook reading.

Donell Holloway is Senior Research Scholar at Edith Cowan University in Perth, Australia. A large portion of Dr. Holloway's research work to date is centered on the domestic context of children's media use. She is currently a chief investigator on two Australian Research Council grants: 'Toddlers and Tablets: Exploring the risks and benefits 0–5s face online', and 'The Internet of Toys: Benefits and risks of connected toys for children'. She has authored or co-authored over 50 refereed journal articles, book chapters and conference papers.

Hilary Janks is Professor Emerita in the School of Education at the University of the Witwatersrand, Johannesburg, South Africa. She is the author of *Literacy and Power* (2010) and the editor and author of *Doing Critical Literacy* (2014). Her teaching and research are in the areas of language and literacy education in multilingual classrooms, critical literacy and the literacies and spatialities of childhood. Her work is committed to a search for equity and social justice in contexts of poverty.

Fiona Jelley is Senior Researcher at the University of Oxford. After studying psychology she now works in the Families, Effective Learning and Literacy research group in the Department of Education, and is also affiliated with the Applied Linguistics and Learning and New Technologies groups. Fiona's main research interest is in evaluations of interventions designed to enhance young children's development, and especially the ways in which development can be shaped through engaging parents in their children's learning. Her current work is investigating how technology can be best used to support children's learning – both directly and through involving parents.

Jaye Johnson Thiel is deeply committed to studying issues of social class and educational equity in the context of early childhood studies. Her scholarship works against deficit discourses about young people, theorizes place-based practices for community research and explores the production of embodied literacies in the everyday lives of children.

Ji Eun Kim has conducted studies in diverse areas in early literacy education, such as parent-child e-book reading and minority children's literacy practices outside school contexts by drawing on socio-cultural perspectives in literacy practices. Multiculturalism and multilingualism has been the core of her research and teaching and she was part of several research projects involving children and families of minority cultural groups (e.g., Cultural Practice of Literacy Studies). She also taught preschoolers from diverse cultural groups. Currently, she is examining different types of e-books to be used by families and educators.

Linda Knight is in the School of Early Childhood and Inclusive Education at Queensland University of Technology, Australia, and specializes in community education in urban settings. Her international and award-winning reputation in arts-based methodologies in education-focused research includes the use of iPads in developing literacy and creativity in young children, using drawing to improve oral communication between educators and children, examining diverse urban citizenships through the mapping of urban (play)spaces and using Artificial Intelligence and coding to examine algorithmic diversity in early childhood. Linda has exhibited internationally, and her work is held in private collections globally.

Candace R. Kuby is Associate Professor of Early Childhood Education at the University of Missouri, USA. Her research interests are twofold: (1) the ethico-onto-epistemologies of literacy desiring(s) when young children work with materials to create multimodal, digital, and hybrid texts and (2) approaches to qualitative inquiry drawing upon poststructural and posthumanist theories and the teaching of qualitative inquiry. Candace has co-edited and co-authored several books, including *Go Be a Writer! Expanding the Curricular Boundaries of Literacy Learning* (2016, Teachers College Press, with Tara Gutshall Rucker). Journals in which her scholarship appears include *Qualitative Inquiry*, *International Journal of Qualitative Studies in Education*, *Journal of Early Childhood Literacy*, and *Language Arts*.

Linda Laidlaw is Professor in Language and Literacy Education at the University of Alberta, Canada. Formerly a classroom teacher, her research focuses on digital and mobile technologies in primary education, and she is particularly interested in the relationship between children's digital practices at home and their experiences at school. She has developed three Canadian Social Sciences and Humanities Research Council Grants projects focusing on digital literacies. Her latest project is an international collaborative study, *Reimagining Literacy Education: Being Literate in the Twenty First Century*, which aims to develop new frames and strategies for use of digital media in literacy education.

Lena Lee is Professor of Early Childhood Education at Miami University, Ohio, USA. She earned a doctorate in Early Childhood Education at Indiana University, Bloomington, USA, and a DEA of Comparative Women's Studies at Paris VIII University, France. Her foci of research, teaching and professional service are on examining social values and assumptions about learning and teaching (e.g., media/technology and diversity in early childhood classrooms) in the field of early childhood education and how differently or similarly those are implemented in various socio-cultural contexts. Her work has often speculated on how to foster multicultural teachers/education in a global community. She was the first awardee of the Emerging Scholar Award of the American Educational Research Association (AERA), Critical Perspective of

Early Childhood Education SIG. Her recent project discussed in this volume was externally funded by the PNC Foundation of the United States. She has been elected as the Region 5 (Illinois, Indiana, Michigan, Minnesota, Ohio and Wisconsin) Representative of the National Association for Early Childhood Teacher Educators (NAETEC) and as the Vice President of the Korean-American Early Childhood Education Researchers Association (KECERA). She also serves on the boards of several other professional organizations and research journals.

Narelle Lemon is Associate Professor in Education at Swinburne University of Technology in Melbourne, Australia. Narelle's overarching research area is focused on participation and engagement. She explores this through a variety of avenues including social media use for learning and professional development, creativity and arts education and positive psychology, specifically aimed at mindful practice and coping strategies.

Anne Mangen is Full Professor of Literacy at the National Centre for Reading Education and Research at the University of Stavanger in Norway. She does empirical research on the effects and implications of digitization on cognitive and emotional aspects of reading, including reading with children. Mangen is Chair of COST Action E-READ: Evolution of Reading in the Age of Digitization, and has published extensively on reading on paper and on screens.

Jackie Marsh is Professor of Education at the University of Sheffield, UK. Jackie has led numerous research projects engaging children, teachers, parents and children's media industry partners in research on young children's play and digital literacy practices in homes and schools (e.g., the ESRC-funded project 'Technology and Play'). Jackie is Chair of COST Action IS1410, DigiLitEY, a European network of 35 countries focusing on research in this area (2015–2019). She is currently leading a seven-country project on makerspaces in the early years, MakEY http://makeyproject.eu (2017–2019), funded by the EU Horizon 2020 programme. Jackie has published widely in the field, and is a co-editor of the *Journal of Early Childhood Literacy*.

Marianne McTavish is Senior Instructor in Emergent and Early Literacy in the Department of Language and Literacy Education at the University of British Columbia, Canada, where she teaches graduate and undergraduate courses in language and literacy, early childhood and teacher education. Prior to obtaining her PhD, Marianne taught kindergarten through third grade in the public school system for over 25 years. Her work with early childhood teacher candidates and digital literacies reconceptualizes the way literacy is taught and practiced. Her research examines young children's information and digital communicative practices as they engage in multimodal meaning making across classrooms, homes and communities.

Guy Merchant is Professor of Literacy and Education at the Sheffield Institute of Education, Sheffield Hallam University, UK. His work explores the ways in which literacy and technology intersect in the lives of children and young people. Guy is a founding editor of the *Journal of Early Childhood Literacy* and has written extensively about literacy and new media. He is co-author, with Cathy Burnett, of *New Media in the Classroom: Rethinking Primary Literacy* (2018), and a contributing editor to *Virtual Literacies* (2013); *New Literacies around the Globe* (2014); *Literacy, Media, Technology* (2016); and *The Case of the iPad* (2016).

Thomas Moser is Professor in Educational Science with focus on early childhood education (since 2014) at the University South-Eastern Norway, Faculty of Humanities and Education. He also holds an adjunct professorship at the Learning Environment Centre, University of

Stavanger. He is the head of the PhD program in Pedagogical resources and learning processes in Early Childhood Education and Care (ECEC) and school, the chair of the board of The Norwegian National Graduate School in Teacher Education (NAFOL) and a member of the board of University of South-Eastern Norway. His research interests include quality and effect of ECEC-provisions, learning-space and physical environment, curriculum research in ECEC, inclusion and comparative studies in European ECEC, teacher education and professional development, body and learning.

Joanne O'Mara is Associate Professor in the Faculty of Arts and Education, Deakin University, Melbourne, Australia. Her research and scholarship focuses on emergent literacies and new textual practices; digital games; drama pedagogy; and the spatial, social and temporal dimensions of teachers' work. Joanne's research program includes her collaboration on a Social Science and Humanities Research Council Insight Grant project investigating the pedagogical possibilities of digital tools, with Linda Laidlaw. A hallmark of her research program has been the focus on establishment of ongoing strategic partnerships with inbuilt benefits to all parties, working in collaboration with students, teachers, schools, professional associations and key education authorities.

Joanne Orlando researches young children's uses of technology to explore where new opportunities for learning and play are emerging and how teaching and learning environments can be designed to capitalize and support this learning. Her recent research has examined this from a number of vantage points including educator professional learning, learning in the home and design features of devices that support children's use and engagement. Joanne works extensively with the technology industry to facilitate quality technology-device learning in early childhood. Joanne is based at the Centre for Educational Research, Western Sydney University, Australia.

Ola Ozernov-Palchik is a postdoctoral associate at the McGovern Institute for Brain Research at the Massachusetts Institute of Technology, USA, studying reading development and dyslexia. Ola applies neuroimaging, psychoeducational, and cognitive methods to investigating the mechanisms of deficit and compensation in dyslexia. She is interested in the hereditary and environmental factors affecting the development of the brain networks for reading. The reciprocity between research and real-world practices is an important goal of her work.

Kylie J. Stevenson is Researcher at Edith Cowan University in Perth, Western Australia, where she researches in the areas of higher degree by research pedagogy, arts education, experiences of welfare dependency and children and technology. She has been a research associate on three Australian Research Council grants: 'Parents or Peers: Which group most affects the experiences of young people online?'; 'Toddlers and Tablets: Exploring the risks and benefits 0–5s face online'; and 'A Hand Up: Disrupting the communication of inter-generational poverty'. Kylie's work is primarily concerned with the lived experience, and is published in academic sources.

Kathy Sylva is Honorary Research Fellow and Professor of Educational Psychology at the University of Oxford, UK. She has been a lead researcher on the Effective Pre-school and Primary Education Study (EPPSE) and co-leader on the national Evaluation of Children's Centres in England. Along with early education, her research also focuses on parenting programmes and she has led the development and testing of an intervention that trains parents to support their children's reading at home. Currently, she is researching the Early Childhood 'System' in six high performing countries. She was awarded an OBE in 2008, is a Fellow of the Academy of

Social Sciences, and was given the Nisbett Award for outstanding contribution to educational research in 2014.

Vivian Maria Vasquez is Professor of Education at American University. She has worked in the field of early childhood education for over 30 years. Her research interests are in critical literacy, early literacy and information communication technology.

Valeria Ortiz Villalobos is a psychologist with a master's degree in Child Development and Education from the University of Oxford, UK. For her master's dissertation she studied the relationship between the home learning environment and children's school readiness in Costa Rican families. Afterward, she joined the Families, Effective Learning and Literacy (FELL) research group at the University of Oxford as a research assistant working on parents' support for their children's learning. Before working at the University of Oxford, Valeria was a preschool teacher in Costa Rica.

Pam Whitty is an educator-researcher at the University of New Brunswick, Canada, working in early childhood studies, literacies and curriculum from a critical re-conceptualist perspective. Over the past 27 years, she has co-led provincial research-based early childhood curriculum and community-based literacy initiatives in New Brunswick. Most recently, she was co-chair of the New Brunswick Child Care Task Force Commission.

Karen E. Wohlwend is Associate Professor of Literacy, Culture, and Language Education at Indiana University, USA. She reconceptualizes young children's play as an embodied literacy that creates action texts with toys, popular media and digital technologies. Her books include *Literacy Playshop: New Literacies, Popular Media, and Play in the Early Childhood Classroom.*

Suzanna So-Har Wong is currently a postdoctoral fellow working with Linda Laidlaw on several international research projects on digital literacy. She is also Adjunct Professor in Language and Literacy Education at the University of Alberta in Edmonton, Alberta, Canada, where she teaches courses in early literacy. Her research focuses on children's literacy experiences in home and school environments, and the multiliteracy experiences of young children. She is currently engaged in a longitudinal study of children's multiliteracy practice in 'out-of-school' settings focusing on children's literacy practices in the home and community.

Annette Woods is Professor in the Faculty of Education, Queensland University of Technology, Australia. She teaches and researches in the areas of literacies, school reform, assessment, pedagogy and curriculum and social justice. Her current projects include a school reform project that investigates learning to write in the early years of school, an investigation into what happens when literacy and sustainability are brought together within kindergarten curriculum, and a study that enables Aboriginal and Torres Strait Islander young people in secondary schools to conceptualize cultural identity and well-being. She has experience over many years working with teachers and families toward an equitable, quality education for all students.

Shu Yau is a developmental neuroscientist who studies perception and language in individuals with autism. Her research looks at the relationship between auditory perception and language abilities in children with autism, particularly involving children who are profoundly autistic. She is also interested in issues surrounding inclusion and accessibility in autism. She has previously worked as a specialist psychologist with children with special education needs in Singapore. Shu holds a PhD in Cognitive Science, was a Marie Curie Postdoctoral Fellow, and is currently Assistant Professor in the School of Education at the University of Bristol, UK.

Rahat Zaidi is Associate Professor and Chair of Language & Literacy at the Werklund School of Education, University of Calgary, Alberta, Canada. She has published a number of critical works regarding literacy, cultural diversity and language pedagogy. Her research has generated and mobilized knowledge concerning best practices that specifically address the challenges and opportunities involved in educating a diverse school population. Currently, she is conducting research with refugee populations to further understanding on parental engagement in public schools. Her new works include *Anti-Islamophobic Curriculums* with Peter Lang.

Sumin Zhao is a Lecturer in Discourse Analysis at the University of Edinburgh. Her research focuses on digital literacies of young (multilingual) children and visual social media. Recent co-edited books include *Critical Multimodal Studies of Popular Discourse* (Routledge, 2016) and *Advancing Critical and Multimodal Discourse Studies* (Routledge, 2017). Her monograph *The Social Semiotics of Book Apps* is forthcoming in 2020 (Bloomsbury). She is the Book Reviewer Editor for Discourse and Communication. Sumin was a Visiting Research Associate at UCL Institute of Education (2015–2016) and a Carlsberg Distinguished Research Fellow at the University of Southern Denmark (2016–2017).

Jennifer M. Zosh is Associate Professor of Human Development and Family Studies at Pennsylvania State University, Brandywine, USA. As the Director of the Brandywine Child Development Lab, she studies how infants and young children learn about the world around them. Her areas of research include playful learning, the impact of technology on children and families, working memory, mathematical cognition and language acquisition. A major driving force in her career is the dissemination and translation of scientific discoveries to the public. She received her PhD in Psychological and Brain Sciences from Johns Hopkins University, USA.

Jennifer Zuk is a postdoctoral research fellow at Boston Children's Hospital/Harvard Medical School, USA and clinical fellow in speech-language pathology. Jennifer's research examines brain and language development from infancy to school age with a focus on identifying factors in early childhood that may facilitate speech, language and reading acquisition. She employs a multidisciplinary approach at the intersection of cognitive neuroscience research and educational and clinical practice in an effort to promote equal access and optimal quality of life for all children.

FOREWORD

> 'How about I send Izzy a WhatsApp?' two-and-three-quarters-year-old Charlie asks when talking with his mother about how much he misses his two-and-a-half-year-old friend who has recently moved away for six months. With his mother's iPhone and technical support, Charlie then dresses up as a pirate and proceeds to produce a short, playful WhatsApp video where he is 'Charliebeard' and his distant friend is 'Izzypirate'. Although only 15-seconds long, the message is dynamic, playful, creative and affectionate. As it travels through the ether to his friend, it crosses the boundaries of time and place, of distance and separation. As it is watched and rewatched by Izzy and her family, and by Charlie and his family, it reinforces the young children's friendship. It becomes the first of many in a series of playful WhatsApp video exchanges between Charlie and Izzy that helps to maintain their friendship whilst they are apart.
>
> *Rosie Flewitt, University College London, Institute of Education*

This short vignette describes one instance of 0–3 year-old children's web-mediated activity that we encountered as part of a Europe-wide study of young children's digital literacy practices (Gillen, 2018). How do we, as researchers, find out about and make sense of such instances where young children are playing, exploring, learning and maintaining close links with friends and family with and through digital technology? How do we, as educators, respond to the new opportunities for innovation, inspiration and creativity that digitally mediated communication has made possible between all generations around the world?

We know that not all children growing up in the current era are as fortunate as Charlie, who was born into a white middle-class family living in a quiet rural location in southern England. As Dyson argues in this volume, geopolitical, socioeconomic and gendered factors influence children's access to the technologies with which they might play, compose, design and learn. For example, in the comparatively affluent United Kingdom, twenty percent of children live in damp and inadequately heated houses, ten percent do not have warm coats for the winter, five percent are malnourished and hungry (Urban, 2016), and we know that economically disadvantaged children tend to be less skilled with digital media than their more affluent peers (Sefton-Green et al., 2016). For these children, school may be the only means to learn how to use digital technology and to build a secure future in the digital economy. For millions of children living in more troubled lands, whose lives are disrupted by war, displacement, famine and disease, there are more pressing needs than access to new technology, and yet for these children and their parents a single mobile phone can offer a lifeline to bind separated families together, or to access essential medical advice and aid (ITU, 2013; Lee, 2015; World Bank, 2016). Childhoods vary, often in 'heartbreaking ways' (Dyson, this volume).

If our collective aim is to find out about children's experiences of growing up – wherever their childhoods are experienced – and to improve the quality of all children's lives and learning, then how can we overcome the countless problematic issues that we encounter in the process of our investigations? There are gaps and inconsistencies in what is known, wide divergences in research approaches and oftentimes there are tensions between different disciplinary norms and conventions. In this timely Handbook, the contributors address these and many other issues that characterize contemporary research by starting a conversation that reaches across disciplinary boundaries. Focusing on children aged 2 to 8 years, the chapters in this edition report on recent research conducted by a selection of established and early career academics who are developing innovatory approaches to researching and theorizing how young children play and learn with new technology, and how the influences of digital media filter through into children's play and learning with conventional communication and literacy technologies. Whilst some contributors focus on the affordances and constraints of new digital devices as data collection and analysis tools, others problematize the usefulness and suitability of established research paradigms in the quest to understand how young children learn in social worlds that are increasingly mediated through digital channels, and where interpersonal relationships are often negotiated through assemblages of physically co-present and distant networks. The individual arguments put forward are not necessarily ground-breaking, yet they push forward debates about what St. Pierre (2014, p. 3) refers to as 'the impossibility of an intersection between conventional humanist qualitative methodology and "the posts"', that is, postconstuctionist, poststructural, posthuman and post-qualitative enquiry. Together, they constitute a groundswell of new perspectives that at best lead to a fundamental re-thinking of the inextricably interwoven relationships between epistemology, ontology and methodology, and at the very least unsettle minds that may be set in a groove, opening up new possibilities and new horizons in the field of education research.

References

Gillen, J. (2018) "*A Day in the Life*" – a still developing methodology. http://digilitey.eu/wp-content/uploads/2015/09/A-Day-in-the-Life-intro-paper-COST.pdf.

International Telecommunication Union (ITU) (2013) *Measuring the information society 2013: Measuring the world's digital natives*. www.itu.int/en/ITU-D/Statistics/Documents/publications/mis2013/MIS2013_without_Annex_4.pdf.

Lee, H., Park, N. and Hwang, Y. (2015) A new dimension of the digital divide: Exploring the relationship between broadband connection, smartphone use and communication competence. *Telematics and Informatics* 32, 45–56.

Sefton-Green, J., Marsh, J., Erstad, O. and Flewitt, R. (2016) Establishing a research agenda for the digital literacy practices of young children: A white paper for COST Action IS1410. http://digilitey.eu/wp-content/uploads/2015/09/DigiLitEYWP.pdf.

St. Pierre, E. (2014) A brief and personal history of post qualitative research: Toward "Post Inquiry". *Journal of Curriculum Theorizing* 30 (2), 2–19.

Urban, M. (2016) *Froebel meets World Bank: Challenges and possibilities for holistic approaches to practice and policy in a globalised early childhood context*. Presented at the 7th Biennial Froebel Conference, Kassel, Germany.

World Bank. (2016) *Digital dividends: World development report. Washington*, International Bank for Reconstruction and Development. www.itu.int/en/ITU-D/Statistics/Pages/facts/default.aspx.

PART I

Setting the scene

1
INTRODUCTION

Natalia Kucirkova, Jennifer Rowsell and Garry Falloon

Rapid growth of digital technologies during the 21st century have paved the way for an upsurge in young children's digital play and learning, multimedia communication and new, multimodal literacies. Coupled with global inequalities in access to high-quality education, the socio-cultural impact of immigration and multicultural neighbourhoods on children's daily experiences, digital technologies and media are reshaping childhood and young children's lives. Technologies and media prompt us to consider what being literate means and implies for the children growing up today. Making meaning of these rapidly changing and complex relationships requires a multidisciplinary, open-minded approach with a range of rigorous, innovative and context-appropriate research methods.

When planning this Handbook, we set out to compile a collection of chapters that would discuss and exemplify how digital technologies affect learning and play, and the ways in which researchers study this impact on young children's lives in the 21st century. We aimed to provide a thoroughly researched and comprehensive overview of current multidisciplinary scholarship concerning children's media and technology. More specifically, we had three main objectives:

First, we aimed to complement current efforts to coordinate diverse perspectives and facilitate dialogue among groups of researchers who typically collect and share evidence in segregated communities. This objective was pursued with a strategic approach to the choice of authors and areas of research they represent. We approached researchers who are well-known in their respective fields and who can collectively offer expert insights into diverse, mixed and cross-disciplinary approaches to technology/media research with children aged between two to eight years.

Second, with our instructions to the authors, we aimed to collate chapters which would provide insights into the methods undertaken by the scholars in their respective fields. We envisaged that such an approach might empower other researchers to audit, reflect on and substantiate the value of their own methodologies and research approaches.

Third, we aimed to trouble the currently dominant monodisciplinary view among many Western policy-makers who favour quantitative and large-scale trials in making decisions about allocation of school resources and accountability measures for teachers. To avoid disciplinary-oriented, one-dimensional understanding of children's technology use, we aimed to emphasise the need for a 'toolkit' of diverse methodological and theoretical perspectives to inform the policy and public discourse on a topic known to be controversial and prone to emotional and reactive responses. This objective meant that we commissioned chapters from researchers who provide additional support for existing policy-makers, as well as researchers who interrupt existing discourses by co-designing educational resources through co-inquiry with teacher and parent communities.

Underlying the Handbook is a wider objective to add to the efforts of some to move beyond a publication system that considers research disciplines in silos and sometimes pits one method against one other. This ambitious goal was partly a reflection of significant intellectual divisions in 2017 and 2018 and partly a reflection of our own multidisciplinary work.

Providing space for multidisciplinarity

The editorial task of assembling works from a range of research traditions and contexts was an incredibly rich and challenging experience. As editors we wanted to be inclusive and receptive towards a wide range of disciplines, which often act in contention and have not been brought together in one collection before. We approached the leaders in their fields and were delighted that they accepted our invitation. The contributing authors have shared with us their current research interests, their understanding of contemporary childhood issues, research approaches and reflections on digital media/technology and key insights from their work. We deliberately and specifically aimed to have authors whose work cuts across diverse fields and historically contested fields of research, bringing together research which is typically reported in books, journals and conference presentations. As a result, the volume includes a rich repertoire of studies from educational psychology, posthumanist literacy, narrative approaches, developmental approaches, arts-based and child's geographies fields, applied linguistics, language and phenomenology, developmental psychology and educational technology.

The challenge of multidisciplinarity

Complexity brings to the fore multidimensionality as well as contradictions and conflicts. Many parents and educators acknowledge, but are also confused with, the complexity of considerations related to children's technology use. We admit that we too grappled with a cogent and coherent way of representing the complexity portrayed in the chapters. As editors, we discussed at length the merit of individual approaches, their rigour, terminology and how they advance knowledge in the field. We disagreed and discussed, often via emails and videoconference calls, our feedback to authors.

We endeavoured to maintain a pluralistic view on the importance of diverse voices. Accordingly, when providing feedback to authors, we aimed to enter in conversation with them and encourage them to produce the best chapter they can by pointing out contrasting evidence, as well as celebrating their expertise in a specific area. We were keen to profile the different theoretical lenses and methods employed by researchers from different disciplines, but this meant we needed to be open to different writing styles, and at times, epistemological perspectives. In a field that still needs to construct a definition of its key terms, it was often not easy to find a common language.

Multidisciplinarity and diverse writing styles

Research is reported differently in different disciplines. We wanted to reflect this reality and as a result, the Handbook is written using various styles and formats. Some chapters are written in a subjective and narrative voice, some in an objective and persuasive voice. Some co-authored chapters explicitly reveal the authorship of individual sections by presenting them as a dialogue or attributing specific sections to different authors, while others are written in one neutral voice. Some chapters make an explicit reference to technology as a specific material resource that can be studied in its own right, while others conceive of technology as an integral part of children's socio-material being in the world. Some authors highlight how prior research could contribute to understanding of children's digitised lives, while others point out its inadequacy for a dynamically changing environment, defined by novelty.

Coming to the field with our own subjectivities and methodological biases, we needed to reconcile the authenticity of diverse research. Our editorial principle was not to judge but to showcase research practice that is firmly grounded in theoretical perspectives and empirical data. We did not homogenise researchers' approaches by providing them with templates or requests for more 'evidence'. Instead, we aimed to ensure they are honest and transparent about their methods and approaches, so that readers can truly see the multiple layers of children's technology research.

Multidisciplinarity and diverse methods

We consider diversity as a source of celebration, not a road to reduction. We wanted to respect and celebrate the expanding methodologies in all disciplines. Consequently, some chapters draw on multiple-team studies that they evaluated through randomised controlled trials, while others describe an intervention they developed, implemented and evaluated themselves. Some authors provide an original synthesis of theories, while others position their work in a strong empirical base of cumulative evidence in a specific area. Some chapters are descriptive and discursive, some are explanatory and some are normative. All chapters are richly theorised, and they follow a systematic approach to generating original evidence.

This does not mean that we could escape questions around hierarchy of evidence. However, we felt that assigning prominence to one method, discipline or research team would be a partisan strategy. We decided to leave it to the readers to draw their own conclusion of how sound the individual researchers' justifications are, and what their value is in the field of digital technologies. Had we favoured one type of evidence over another we would be complicit in an elitism that deems only a certain calibre of research worthy of informing policy and practice.

Multidisciplinarity and one-sided policy

Technology brings into sharp relief the need for conversations with researchers across communities. The educational research is at an important and exciting juncture in history, where a divided culture in methods and epistemologies (or to use more radical terms, positivist and humanist approaches) fuel partisan arguments and hamper progress in practice. We firmly believe there is a real danger in monodisciplinary approaches that eschew some research approaches as lower status if they do not follow a quantitative or large-scale evaluation. Through the attention to interdisciplinary evidence and diverse ways of approaching children's engagement with digital technologies/media, we hoped to address the uncomfortable reality that policy, and in many cases educational practice, are behind scholarly understanding of children's use of technology.

However, it would be naïve to assume that the individual chapters in the Handbook carry equal weight in their impact on policy and attracting research funding. Despite the richness and diversity represented in this Handbook, the national and international educational policies are remarkably one-sided and uneven. We can significantly bridge the divide if everyone participates in the conversation, and perhaps even if the Handbook sparks more and nuanced conversations. It is in this awareness that Natalia shares her own reflections on the value of multidisciplinarity in making an impact on educational practice.

Multidisciplinarity and reality

I have been studying children's engagement with personalised books from a developmental psychological perspective in an experimental paradigm (Kucirkova et al., 2014), as well as from a qualitative educational perspective using a multimodal discourse analysis (Kucirkova et al., 2013). I have also co-designed ed apps, and my work has been published in either psychology or education or human-computer interaction journals. The methods and theoretical frameworks that I have been following over the years were aligned with the rules and norms of their disciplinary orientations. This approach has meant that I could produce messages that are valid and recognised in the individual research groups and their publication outlets.

Together with my colleagues, we documented how digital, personalised books support positive parent-child interactions at home and motivate children to read and learn new concepts. Based on the research findings, I took several steps to support teachers' integration of personalised books into pre-K education: I wrote articles for practitioner magazines (e.g., *Exchange, The Reading Teacher, Teach Primary, English 4–11*) as well as blogs in newspapers with significant circulation (e.g., *Newsweek, The Huffington Post, The Guardian*). I have also regularly presented my work at several large-scale professional organisations, including the annual conference of the International Literacy Association, United Kingdom Literacy Association and British Council.

These efforts were not completely without success, but they were certainly not a game-changer. This is not because teachers did not like the idea of creating or co-creating books with their children. Many found the idea and the research behind it interesting. However, in most cases this was not enough to sustain the practice long-term. In some cases, the teachers could not even imagine how to initiate book-making in their busy classrooms, as they were focused on preparing children for tests and exams. I realised that my approach required a larger structural change, but also that my focus on scalable outcomes assumed a top-down model of science.

I thought that a way of addressing it was to adopt the opposite approach: bottom-up and work with teachers directly to initiate the educational change. This happened organically during my postdoctoral studies, when I was approached by a pre-school (kindergarten) teacher. Amy (pseudonym) read about my work on iPad apps in the local press and was keen to try the Our Story app (a tablet app for making digital books that we developed at the Open University) in her classroom. We exchanged several emails and began a conversation about what might work in her classroom. The teacher introduced me to her colleagues, who worked incredibly hard to support children from low-income families in the English Midlands. They were keen on using Our Story to support the children's language and early literacy skills. I conceived the study as a formative experiment that would elucidate how digital personalised books could be implemented in a pre-school environment and meet established pedagogical goals. The goals were set by the teachers, and as per the typical educational design research, we planned and adjusted the data collection according to what was happening in the classroom.

Unlike carefully controlled approaches that focus on demonstrable outcomes of effectiveness, formative experiments recognise and actively address the complexity of classroom environments. These design-based models of teacher professional development directly focus on knowledge co-creation, teacher-researcher collaboration and teachers' empowerment. The teachers enjoyed using the app, and through their enthusiasm, developed a suite of engaging activities for the children which they continued long beyond my involvement. There was no doubt that the teachers and children enjoyed making their own personalised books. Their self-evaluation report and children's smiling faces showed a lot of enjoyment in the process of making and sharing stories. However, if we were to measure the impact of this approach on children's learning it would be of a negligible effect size. The teacher-led approach towards the books' design and content was not maximised for the children's academic skills.

How might we interpret the educational 'impact' of these examples? Researchers who follow the medical model of evidence would argue that my approach would need refined models of delivery and higher accountability or incentive measures for teachers who do not follow the implementation protocol. Researchers who follow a humanist approach towards evidence would argue that a top-down approach of disseminating research to the teachers is both misguided and generalised, and that teachers need to be co-creators of the materials they are supposed to teach from. In other words, data should be co-produced together with individual participants and the wider community they are part of. I believe that we need both approaches towards evaluating impact (in addition to more substantial and repeated studies in my specific case) *and* we need to integrate them with the notion of multiple realities that characterises multidisciplinarity.

The more I engage in the 'politics of research', the more I learn that one type of evidence (or one type of research approach towards evidence) cannot make a lasting and/or significant impact on practice. Teachers are diverse groups of people and they have their own epistemologies, ontologies and practices that inform what they do. We can accommodate this diversity only if we support multiple narratives that partake in jointly securing equal status and legitimacy to the two-fold nature of teachers' agency: competence and empowerment. Research evidence on what works needs to make sense and be of value to the teachers. They need to be willing to make changes to their practice through intrinsic motivation and contribution. At the same time, teachers need to feel competent in their teaching and have sensible and theorised materials to inform their pedagogies. Researchers from either side of the disciplinary spectrum of educational evidence can contribute invaluable insights into the factors that influence what teachers know, what they need to know and what they would like to know.

As a community of academics and scholars, we have a long but very exciting road ahead of us to achieve this goal. The chapters in this book showcase the possible contributions of individual approaches to foster teachers' competence and empowerment in facilitating young children's learning and play with digital technologies and media. It is our hope that the chapters will stimulate interest in multidisciplinary research collaborations and programs with teachers, parents and other major stakeholders. To help readers navigate the methodological and theoretical diversity available in the Handbook, we next look at the book's structure.

The Handbook's structure

The empirical work of our editorial team reflects the different approaches in the field, and we found it inspiring to closely engage with researchers from different disciplinary orientations. The challenge arose when we attempted to find a common thread in the diverse writings. Our initial organisation of the book, which was focused on topics in early childhood such as influence of learning environments (home or school) or material aspects of specific media, would not do justice to the cross-cutting themes addressed by our authors. Even though the contributors apply different theoretical lenses and methods, they overlap in their focus on early childhood phenomena. All chapters offer usable knowledge on the enduring early childhood topics, albeit with different application possibilities. After some reflection, we decided to structure the Handbook according to three enduring dimensions of empirical research. These three dimensions distinguish the unique contribution of individual research approaches: their attention to ontology, epistemology and practice of children's use of technology.

Part II: studies answering ontological questions

The chapters in this section theorise how children take on original identities in *becoming* literate with technologies. The contributors use innovative as well as more established ways to document how children explore, experience and interact with technologies. The studies are significant in advancing the theories of children's technology use and building a profound understanding of the time and space (or geographies and realities) of children's experiences with technology. The researchers ask where and how children use technologies and aim to establish the ways in which children participate and share their way of being with technologies.

Part III: studies answering epistemological questions

Epistemological chapters focus on how children's knowledge and learning are (co)constructed with a diverse range of technologies. These chapters are rooted in specific disciplines that reflect the researchers' understandings of what it means to learn and to know. The researchers' key contributions lie in elucidating how children develop their own cognitive and emotional understandings of technologies. Our contributors ask how children think through their use of technologies, and which psychological processes and social influences are at play as children construct their knowledge. They aim to study children's engagement in conjunction with, and not separate from, their interests and histories, and they actively engage with their subjectivities during the study design and evaluation.

Part IV: studies answering practice-related questions

Chapters that fall into this group can be further divided into two sub-categories of pedagogical and conceptual approaches to children's technology. Both sub-groups study the resources and conditions that create the most powerful learning opportunities for children. Pedagogical studies focus on the teaching strategies related to children's technology use in a variety of environments, including formal and informal learning settings. Researchers whose work falls into this category investigate the features and materials of effective pedagogies and the schooling culture shaping their use. The learning-sub-group researchers focus on children's gains in skills and knowledge, and the context and content supporting these gains. The researchers ask how different types and kinds of technologies influence children's learning. They frame their inquiries around children's learning, which can be conceptualised both in terms of academic achievement as well as socio-emotional capabilities. The researchers in this group examine the ways in which children participate in learning situations, and how adults and technologies scaffold this participation. Adults are the mediators, mentors and ambassadors of children's technology use, and researchers in this group aim to provide guidance on the most effective adult mediation models.

Collectively, the chapters in the three sections offer a comprehensive survey of methods and approaches in the field of children's technologies. The three structural lenses of ontology, epistemology and practice are not method-specific; indeed, diverse research methods and traditions are included within the individual groups, comprising mediated discourse analysis, multimodality, community-based research, ethnographic case studies of family literacy, eye-tracking, cognitive and educational neuroscience, design-based research and many others.

As mentioned, we approached this Handbook as an ambitious and radical project. We take account of the fact that it is rare to position language-based methods alongside visual and arts-based methods in one volume. This is the first fully interdisciplinary Handbook on the topic of children's technology use. We do not rule out the possibility that our efforts to showcase and contribute to multidisciplinarity have failed. It is possible that that some readers, especially readers who have been instructed in monodisciplinary approaches, will find it challenging to contemplate developmental research alongside a posthuman perspective. It is also possible that some researchers will argue that multidisciplinarity is happening and there is no need for its substantiation in shared volumes. To these readers we offer the following reflection: at the time of writing this introduction, extreme wealth inequalities keep growing within individual nations as well as across nations. While Western billionaires contemplate the type of car they want to send to Mars, millions of people are in desperate need of humanitarian aid and may face famine and diseases such as cholera. Globalisation, economic distress and mass immigration have fuelled a wave of nationalism in countries across the globe. International ethics are characterised by socio-cultural insecurities, extreme liberalisation and extreme protectionism. Set against this backdrop of profound moral crisis and human suffering, the danger of failing to understand multiple realities could not be greater. Addressing the scale and depth of these challenges requires radical changes to the status quo. To move the needle, researchers need to be actively engaged with multiple perspectives to promote understandings of multidimensionality and complexity. Researchers need to enter into dialogues in shared spaces, including written publications, to create a level playing field for everyone.

This premise states indirectly that researchers need to make informed and educated choices about the methods they use in their enquiries. We asked all contributors to provide a theorised rationale for their methodological choices and include examples of data and interpretation of results. In this way, we envisaged to weave together a coherent perspective on the field and to facilitate collaboration across disciplinary boundaries. Aware of the legacy of failed interventions that had assumed universality and generalisability, we wanted to highlight the potentialities of multidisciplinary work to chart future collaborative projects.

Multidisciplinary projects

If we approach the rich area of children's technology use as a community of multidisciplinary researchers, we need to come to grips with multidisciplinary definitions of evidence. Most researchers would know that the link between policy and research is not linear and stable over time. Many colleagues have also experienced the highs and lows of working with policy-makers, and learnt that by the time a research idea cascades down to actual practice, it might lose its theoretical basis or empirical validity. Even though many academics work in close partnership with policy-makers, their messages are often reduced to an oversimplified framework of 'what works' rather than 'how might it work'. Nevertheless, the rapid and uncoordinated accessibility and availability of digital technologies among young children, the fast-advancing industry of children's digital media and the characteristics of global societies create a perfect storm for simplistic interpretations of what works and what doesn't. We therefore offer a few reflections on the methodological approaches we are particularly inspired by.

For researchers with a quantitative orientation, the current lack of cumulative evidence on specific types of new media could be addressed with a focus on enduring features of technologies (e.g., interactivity or multimedia effects), which are available in older and newer forms of media. Cross-sectional and multi-level analyses are essential to understand the multiple influences on children's technology interactions, and some ground-breaking and innovative work is currently underway in several research laboratories profiled in this book. The generation of sound conclusions requires that researchers use observation as well as elicitation methods, documentation and interventionist work.

A particularly fruitful method of educational research and technology-related research with young children in particular, is that of co-research, where participants act as co-creators of knowledge. In sharp contrast to technology-driven initiatives, our contributors advocate for increased professional development and authentic conversations with teachers and wider communities involved in mediating children's technology use. Their research is often collaborative with teachers and educators, who can participate in the data collection and data interpretation through action or design-based research approaches. Research needs to be collaborative with the children too, as children can explain and provide insights into their experiences and productions with technologies. Co-research with designers is also possible, and desirable, as it paves the way for a much tighter connection between research and production of digital products for young children. Visual methods, such as video, photography and drawings, are a useful and promising way of capturing and archiving such research collaborations.

In sum, we maintain that it is only through informed understanding of the different methods, theories and policy approaches that we can generate a narrative shift in the field of children's technology use. This is why the book's structure does not make a sharp distinction between traditional research binaries (e.g., qualitative and quantitative approaches or realist and positivist views). Instead, the methods and theoretical perspectives intersect and collapse these boundaries, concordant with our epistemic conviction that it is time to start to couple separate research modes of inquiry into frameworks that contemplate their synergistic potentialities. Without a real understanding of difference within our research circles, we are all poorer: conclusions based on one discipline or one method of evidence can only provide a partial view of reality.

We conclude this introduction with an imaginary case study, which illustrates how multidisciplinary teams could mutually enrich each other's approach to the empirical study of children's use of technologies. We describe the methods and approaches characterised by ontological, epistemological and practice-related research questions that amalgamate multiple methods and perspectives.

Multidisciplinary empirical research

Let us imagine that we set out to investigate children's understanding of Stephen Hawking's legacy, with a focus on their reading and meaning-making with a specific technology: a book written by Stephen Hawking for children. The children are eight years old; they come from diverse backgrounds and live in the UK, Canada and Australia.

We select the title *George and the Blue Moon*, which was written by Stephen Hawking and his daughter Lucy and was illustrated by Garry Parsons. The book is volume five in a popular 'The George series' for readers aged eight and above. The story plot recounts the story of two best friends, George and Annie, who have been selected for an astronaut programme to prepare children for a manned mission to Mars in 2025. The story is replete with mysterious space missions and scientific concepts that the children and their friends need to grapple with. In terms of format, the book contains black and white photographs of the cosmos taken by real astronauts and is offered in four formats: eBook, audiobook, paperback and hardback.

In a comprehensive inquiry, we would want to ask ontological, epistemological and practice-related questions that elucidate the relationship between children's technology use and their meaning-making, learning and interactions with others. In researching children's contemporary reading experiences, our key ontological questions might be: How would the children perceive their roles in the space mission? How would they respond to the wider political themes of the book (e.g., the book directly criticises the Mars One project, which aims to send people to Mars by 2025)? How do children become actively aware of their role on planet Earth, in exploring artefacts such as this book? Which insights do material theories offer into children's social, technical and ecological understanding of self?

Our epistemological questions would be framed around children's ways of thinking through the ontological dilemmas. Which scripts and schemas do children use to construct their knowledge of the cosmos, and how does the book support this process? Do the children identify with the characters and their adventures?

In terms of practice, we would ask what impact the book makes on children's learning and development, and which conditions explain the impact? We would study children's engagement with the book in a specific time and place and try to evidence, for example, children's learning of the book's scientific concepts, such as the periodic table or the notion of terraforming. In terms of explaining the impact, we would look closely at the features of the book's content and format, children's age and role of adults (teachers and parents) in different learning situations. Ideally, we would want to consider the two-fold nature of learning where gains in one domain might represent losses in another domain and acknowledge this duality. For instance, we would want to look at children's attention span with specific features and how motivation might change over time and impact long-term gains. When explaining our data, we would want to check how children's learning types, ability levels, prior knowledge and age might inform future work.

We could examine these questions in a controlled experimental design, but we could also examine the relationships qualitatively and discuss, for example, how different background factors influence children's learning (e.g., children's interest in science and possible previous exposure to scientific topics, including the previous books in the George series).

In answering all three types of questions we would want to get as much insight as possible into children's actual engagement with the book. We would not be able to run multidisciplinary approaches simultaneously, but we could conduct different studies in different phases, gradually feeding into each other. The key in quantitative approaches will be to ensure that we go beyond simple counting and use rigorous and theorised quantitative approaches. The key to qualitative observations will be that they are participatory and allow us to think about children in ways that extend our theories and expand conventional practices.

For example, we could explore the design of the reading space and children's engagement with the individual pages through eye-tracking. We could conduct repeated and longitudinal interviews with the children to get an insight into their own perceptions of the reading experience. When studying children's reading of the digital version of the book, we would want to capture children's interactions with a screen capture as well as their interactions around the screen, with multiple cameras that are both wearable and static in the room. In crafting our own methodological and theoretical contribution to this area, we would want to build on existing research and capture both children's subjectivities and relationality to others around them. Such an approach would generate detailed and thick descriptions of children's experiences, and illustrate not only the individual facets, but also the connections among them.

The chapters in this Handbook offer methods, tools and resources to answer some of the questions we would be asking in our imaginary case study. The variety of topics, methods and theories adopted by our contributors represent a comprehensive breadth of intellectual capital represented in current scholarship. Today's researchers need to be fully aware of the unique role their specific approach plays in the diverse landscape, and tightly link their chosen method and perspective to the purpose of their research. To generate sharable theories and applicable recommendations for practice, researchers need to use sensitive, relevant, up-to-date and innovative research methods in all fields, but particularly so with new phenomena such as children's use of technologies.

Through a joint editorship of one volume, the editors engaged in conversations and contemplations we would not be able to have in our individual disciplines. We offer the following chapters to our readers in the spirit of dialogue and self-reflection and encourage them to ponder the value of multiplicity and the underlying power of different methodologies.

References

Kucirkova, N., Messer, D., & Sheehy, K. (2014). Reading personalized books with preschool children enhances their word acquisition. *First Language* 34(3), 227–243.

Kucirkova, N., Messer, D., Sheehy, K., & Flewitt, R. (2013). Sharing personalised stories on iPads: A close look at one parent–child interaction. *Literacy* 47(3), 115–122.

Chapter summaries

The second chapter of the volume, co-authored by Pam Whitty and Jennifer Rowsell, is a reflective conversation by scholars in the fields of early childhood education and literacy studies. The authors engage in a reflective dialogue about the genesis of their projects, and the varied ways that projects have influenced their understandings of materiality, literacy and children's digital and non-digital lives. Reflections on vignettes and theories are interwoven with a future-gazing look at ways of framing children's literacies in deeper theoretical origins and non-deficit discourses in practice. In the chapter, there is a strong focus on methods that they have adopted for digital research alongside non-digital research across age groups. The authors' conversation culminates in a reflection on the ways in which the field of education studies can draw inspiration from contemporary philosophical discourses that aim to push the boundaries of and blur the dividing lines between the traditional domains of epistemology, ontology and ethics.

In Chapter 3, Garry Falloon summarises seven years of his work with 5- to 11-year-olds in seven separate studies that used mixed methods to investigate how selected iPad apps influenced student learning in mathematics, literacy, language development, science and computational processing/coding. Garry used a bespoke iPad embedded data system to record students' interactions with the apps and the StudioCode video analysis software to organise and analyse the data. This approach enabled him to make recommendations to teachers regarding app selection, device management and student groupings in the classroom.

In Chapter 4, Debra Harwood and Diane Collier provide insights into a two-year study of a pre-school forest school program in Canada. The chapter outlines how the researchers conceptualised their research methods, which acknowledge and richly theorise researchers' subjectivities and latest technologies. The participating children used GoPro cameras to document their experiences in the forest and Harwood and Collier analysed the 'child-matter', the socio-material and discursive encounters that ensued.

In Chapter 5, Rahat Zaidi explores the connection between 'transculturalism' and literacy with specific emphasis on diversifying approaches to reading within the context of early childhood programs in mainstream, ethnically diverse classrooms. The chapter builds a case for a dialogic reading approach using dual language books (DLBs) that correlates well with the demographic shifts occurring within early childhood programs today. The research outlines a method of literacy intervention building on the dialogic approach, incorporating technology and juxtaposing two languages. The author concludes by suggesting that the incorporation of DLBs is integral to the development of research methodologies that remain attentive to cultural difference and language as a malleable object that can be productively manipulated by young learners over the course of their educational development.

In Chapter 6, Anne Haas Dyson focuses on the whys and hows of turning the usual research approach to ethnography upside-down. Rather than viewing children through the official lens of school, Dyson opts to view school, and the rich and diverse experiences therein, through the unofficial lens of children. The author seeks to problematise the adult-centric notion of ethnography, instead striving toward an ethnographic methodology that privileges children's perspectives. Importantly, the insights gained from this chapter cannot be universalised and applied to some broader population, but rather simply give us concrete material to think with, engendering new insights into the way children negotiate social life. The chapter offers productive interpretive frames with which to conceptualise abstractions such as the notion of belonging.

Kerryn Dixon and Hilary Janks in Chapter 7 present outcomes from a two-year ethnographic study of Leah, a 6-year-old South African girl, and her generation of texts combining both print and digital literacies in the creation of original learning artefacts. Using a unique methodology involving the researchers collecting multimodal data during collaborative play episodes, the authors weave a detailed account of the influence of the digital on Leah's development of transmedia texts, suggesting that while time-consuming, such methods are necessary to provide data sufficiently detailed to unpack these complex interactions.

In Chapter 8, Sumin Zhao reflects on how social media apps affect children 'on the move'. She uses a case study of a Chinese immigrant family to outline a young boy's heritage language and literacy learning with his dispersed family members. Analysis of the multimedia messages sent via the WeChat app shows the interconnected nature of multimedia practices by multiple family members. Through a critical evaluation, the author invites reflection on cross-cultural sensitivities involved in video-based research.

Candace R. Kuby, in Chapter 9, takes a post-qualitative inquiry stance, drawing on the work of St. Pierre and others in her beautifully articulated discussion of the need for multimodal and digital literacy research to reject Cartesian perspectives of separation of mind, body and environment, in favour of methods that view research-able interactions as *assemblages* or *entanglements*, as a way to better understand and analyse the complexity of the "relationships of humans, non-humans, and more-than-humans in how the world comes into being" (p. 133). She challenges readers to question prevailing ontological and epistemological views of how we 'come to know', calling for a reconceptualisation that views knowledge as created through a relational ontology that dismantles traditional hierarchical structures, moving us towards ethico-onto-epistemological approaches that acknowledge the complexity of relationships between subjects and objects in the generation of meaning.

In Chapter 10 by Cathy Burnett and Guy Merchant, the authors further explore children's play on- and off-screen in classrooms. The authors wrestle with the inadequate methods available to posthumanist researchers interested in capturing the fleeting and intertwined social, material and embodied aspects of children's play in the digital era. The chapter moves on to consider the method of 'stacking stories' as a viable alternative to consider the socio-material-embodied entanglements in children's play with tablets.

Jackie Marsh is the author of Chapter 11. Marsh draws on a larger research project concerned with children's play, with a focus on participatory research methods to capture the richness of children's use of tablet apps. Children's interaction with the apps was documented with wearable and 'point-of-view' cameras. In addition to observations and interviews, children's own perspectives and experiences informed the researchers' understanding of post-digital play. Children's interactions with apps are considered in terms of 'analogue and digital assemblages of play', which theoretically enrich and expand posthumanist analyses.

In Chapter 12, using examples of early childhood play from independent research studies, Karen E. Wohlwend and Jaye Johnson Thiel take a closer look to ask: What did they miss? In initial multimodal analysis of these events, how did an implicit human-centred insistence on semiotic affordances and strategic design tame the mobile jumble of children's play and making? In this chapter, the authors apply a materialist theoretical lens to early childhood play to traverse the interconnected terrains of multimodality, materiality and technology. They blur the line separating the material from the digital by demonstrating that there are multiple salient points of connection between crafting toys out of paper and scribbles on an iPad. In the authors' view, both activities constitute a form of technology learning – an insight that aligns nicely with their materialist view of learning as an agentic act of becoming.

In Chapter 13, Linda Laidlaw, Joanne O'Mara and Suzanna So-Har Wong address events and research experiences that have taken them into a deeper appreciation of the value of autobiographical, participatory and ethnographic methods for researching digital experiences of young children's learning and playing at home, in their communities and beyond. The authors start with the home and also extend to the ways in which their research has travelled across and into the communities they inhabit and include considerations of the varied ways that children's experiences may be shaped further, by policies that impact school and home and by the media. The authors have found common ground among their diverse backgrounds; their methodological approach draws from a range of methods and approaches including autobiographies, a range of ethnographies and the occasional incorporation of feminist perspectives.

In Chapter 14, Joanne Orlando challenges frequently articulated views on the negative effects of technology on young children's learning and creativity by arguing the need to more fully understand how technology can open new and different opportunities for learning, and how this can be best supported by adults and others involved in facilitating children's interactions with digital devices. She explores the methods she used in her recent study on children's use of technology in the home, arguing that they provided a safe and non-judgemental framework yielding high-quality data revealing participants' true perspectives on technology use with and by their children.

Donell Holloway, Leslie Haddon, Lelia Green and Kylie J. Stevenson's Chapter 15 takes a posthumanist view exploring very young children's interaction with literacy apps on touchscreen devices within the context of the family environment. Drawing on data from an Australian Research Council Discovery Project, the authors provide a rich case study account analysing the nature of the interactions between a parent, their toddler and an iPad literacy app. This chapter reveals interesting insights into how the *instructional assemblage* created during such interactions provides unique opportunities for scaffolded learning.

Through the combined strength of two ethnographic research studies, Rachel Heydon and Xiaoxiao Du (Chapter 16) provide rich descriptions of intergenerational literacy practices in multilingual learning contexts. The chapter offers readers a window into careful ethnographic observations of families enacting literacy as a part of their everyday lives and specifically how culture and linguistic systems circulate within these familial moments. A unique feature of Heydon and Du's chapter are the ways in which they integrate an analysis of linguistic systems, multimodal meaning-making, and the various materialities that play a role in family routines and understandings about communication. Technologies play a role in this sea of activities in a natural and tacit way offering readers a more grounded sense about how imbricated digital worlds are in terms of literacy specifically and everyday habits more broadly.

Chapter 17 by Anne Mangen, Trude Hoel and Thomas Moser describes ways in which researchers might investigate young children's experiences when reading books using touchscreen devices – specifically introducing methods useful for studies investigating the multisensory, embodied and interactional experiences of these children when engaged in shared reading with adults. The authors suggest adopting a *full embodiment* approach to such research to support the development of in-depth and interdisciplinary understandings of what comprises quality and effective early reading processes using digital devices.

Chapter 18 by Aspa Baroutsis and Annette Woods considers literacies and learning within current times and frames of thinking, and they then present data from one study of how children learn to write and produce texts in their early school years. The authors apply a design-based experimental methodology, which supports an underlying social justice imperative of their work, namely, the achievement of quality literacy pedagogy for poor children. The empirical research outlined in the chapter stands as an example of design-based research in which the researchers used a technological intervention in an attempt to improve the writing of 6- to 7-year-old children in one classroom setting.

In Chapter 19, Melissa L. Allen and Shu Yau argue for the need for reconceptualising how children with Autism Spectrum Disorder (ASD) are assessed and evaluated, highlighting the importance of moving beyond traditional approaches based on the use of standardised instruments. They suggest that the use of these instruments fails to recognise the heterogenous nature of children with ASD, contending that more individualised approaches to diagnosis or a wider range of analytical measures is required. Their chapter explores options combining passive neuropsychological and neuroscientific methods that run alongside more conventional approaches to provide data that will support the development of more individualised profiles that better meet children's specific needs.

In Chapter 20, Jim Anderson, Ann Anderson, Ji Eun Kim and Marianne McTavish make the case for the need to use mixed methods in educational research to accommodate complex research questions, serve multiple purposes of research recipients who live in diverse communities and contribute to knowledge in diverse contexts. The eclecticism and pragmatism theoretical frameworks are used to explain how mixed methods correspond not only to specific research questions but also to the decision, audience, ethics and impact. The authors draw on their own work in Canadian multilingual communities to showcase the use and value of observations, interviews, focus groups, artefacts and standardised tests.

In Chapter 21, Narelle Lemon outlines a unique and progressive research methodology for use in early childhood educational contexts in the hopes of recasting students as active participants rather than passive subjects, before tracing the genesis of children's visual narratives in the context of a specific classroom-based study. Lemon explicitly seeks to challenge traditional classroom power dynamics by encouraging the development of reflective skills and ensuring a more egalitarian approach to early childhood education in which all the voices of the classroom are heard. The methodology that the author presents, and for which she advocates, engenders research practices that validate students' own perspectives and amplify their voices within and beyond the classroom. Additionally, her uniquely equitable and collaborative method of generating visual narratives opens up avenues for mutually beneficial dialogic engagements between students, educators and researchers, allowing children to take active roles in shaping their learning experiences.

In Chapter 22, Linda Knight explores the use of Arts-based methods for researching how young children use and learn from digital media. She suggests Arts-based approaches enable researchers to gather more detailed data in multidimensional research projects involving the use of digital technologies, through its accommodation of multiple forms and interpretations of data. Linda presents her argument by clearly differentiating between arts-focused and arts-based research through reference to two fictional project examples. Her chapter concludes by offering a series of useful recommendations for researchers considering using Arts-based methods.

In Chapter 23, Fiona Jelley, Kathy Sylva and Valeria Ortiz Villalobos revisit the role of technologies in supporting parents in supporting their children's learning and reading. The authors provide a useful overview of the importance of effective home learning environments and the pedagogical resources and methods that have been traditionally used to train parents. Examples of two recently developed apps illustrate the ways in which guides and videos can reach parents and provide targeted support.

In Chapter 24, Lena Lee draws on Bourdieuan and Critical Race Theory in an analysis of her study involving Latino pre-schoolers that infused technology in a science curriculum aimed to motivate and improve the children's learning and engagement through exposure to 'real-life', technology-supported science experiences. The chapter introduces and describes her study, which is followed by an analysis of how her investigation challenged traditional views of the effects of a socio-economically aligned digital divide on the technology-supported learning opportunities of racial minority students. She argues that the rich experiences of the children in this study were not only beneficial educationally, but also were illustrative of how learning designs of this nature can support equity and social justice goals.

In another co-authored chapter, Chapter 25, Rebecca A. Dore, Jennifer M. Zosh, Brenna Hassinger-Das, Roberta Michnick Golinkoff and Kathy Hirsh-Pasek bring together research concerned with e-books that is electronic/digital books available for computers, consoles and tablets. The researchers extract five key lessons from a decade of research on e-books: (1) It is vital for research to keep up with rapidly changing technology; (2) balancing the wide variety of e-book features and creating generalisable findings is a challenge; (3) context and previous experience matter; (4) there is a need for innovative methods for quantifying language, behavioural/ emotional engagement, and caregiver-child interaction and (5) using multiple measures helps capture multiple facets of learning. These lessons neatly capture the key opportunities and challenges for existing and future research and design of e-books.

Similarly to Harwood and Collier, Lucy Caton and Abigail Hackett explore the methodological extensions that can be achieved when children's own perspectives can be conveyed with GoPro cameras. Chapter 26 approaches video-based research in terms of 'visual ontologies' and discusses the choices that permeate and become visible when children, camera and space interact. The authors illustrate how Deleuze and Guattari's concepts apply to the contemporary practice of video-based research and how the notions of embodiment and form can be constructed to challenge reductionist interpretations of children's experience of space.

In Chapter 27, Peggy Albers, Vivian Maria Vasquez and Jerome C. Harste demonstrate how they have used critical literacy and visual discourse analysis for 15-plus years to study images in print-based and in digital spaces, a methodology they call critical visual discourse analysis (CVDA), with particular attention given to early childhood and teacher education work with images. The authors' research investigates how images work and how they are constructed, interpreted, internalised and reproduced. They also attempt to understand the extent to which visual information contributes to identities that viewers/readers may or may not wish to take on. The authors argue that this work brings to the fore the significance of creating opportunities for teachers and children to be critically and consciously literate in the digital era of the 21st century.

In the concluding chapter (Chapter 28), Sibylla Leon Guerrero, Ola Ozernov-Palchik, Michelle Gonzalez, Jennifer Zuk and Nadine Gaab provide an insight into how cognitive neuroscience can leverage mobile apps to screen children for dyslexia. The app is currently in development and includes activities that tap into seven pre-reading predictors of children's reading outcomes: phonological awareness, phonological memory, rapid automatised naming, letter-sound knowledge, vocabulary, oral language comprehension and family history of reading difficulty (dyslexia). The team describes the app development process, including its significant clinical and educational implications for identifying children at risk for reading difficulties. The chapter includes a comprehensive summary of existing literacy screening instruments and will be of interest to researchers who have developed or plan to advance empirically-based mobile applications.

We encourage the readers to read the chapters carefully and critically, in relation to their own epistemologies, ontologies and practice. We believe the value of multiple methods and perspectives lies not only in the individual studies making up the mosaic but also the connections between the individual research pieces. This Handbook can be thus viewed as our attempt to assemble some core pieces for a mosaic that we all need to complete.

2

REFLECTIVE CONVERSATIONS ABOUT RESEARCH METHODS WITH CHILDREN

Pam Whitty and Jennifer Rowsell

Introduction

In this chapter, we engage in a back-and-forth conversation about our various research studies over the years, reflecting on recurrent thoughts, preoccupations, and methodological strands that we have adopted as we have researched alongside children and young people. In an effort to chart where we have been and where we are going, we take a dialogic tone throughout the chapter drawing on theory and research vignettes to illustrate key dimensions of our research process. There is a strong focus on methods that we have adopted for digital research alongside non-digital research across age groups. The chapter spans such dimensions of research methods with children as: relational moments that we have had; ways that we have drawn out agency; the role of artifacts and materialities; ways of respectfully thinking about children's worlds (and not engaging with deficit framings); stepping back from gatekeeping; and, looking ahead to new imaginings and new futures.

Contemplating the relational nature of our research

Our first question: what sits at the center of your research methods?

Jennifer: For me, everything relies on the relational in my research. Given that I research across age groups, with the common strand being multimodal improvisational and compositional work, what is essential when I am in the field is that I connect with participants/young people and that I understand their way into meaning making. So, as a researcher, I value time in research contexts and conversations with children. The conversations that I value most are the organic, tacit ones that happen in the corner of days and activities in classrooms, homes or community sites, when I get a window into a child. I have one recent example. In December 2017, I finished a six-week graphic story project in a grade 3/4 split class and there were a number of children who shared their thoughts and whom I wanted as much as possible to listen to (Back, 2007). One child was Lionel (pseudonym) who could often be seen moving about in his seat and who could very easily get distracted. Lionel was friends with a few of the boys around him, but at the same time he was a loner, at times confrontational and existing in his own space as an agent in the classroom. A moment that stood out for me happened when we had a class discussion about a book which depicted a group of children who time traveled back in history and the visiting author asked the class: if you could time travel, where and when would you go? Lionel without hesitation put up his hand and said that he would go back in time to see his Dad when he was the same age as Lionel is "so that he [Lionel] could see how cool he was." I loved this moment. No one else seemed to notice it, but I did because I watched Lionel from afar and I had chatted with him many times and he is the kind of student who can easily be missed, maybe even rendered invisible and at this precise moment, his agency bubbled up in front of us. After the discussion, I asked him about it and he talked about his Dad and how close they are.

These moments give me so much as a researcher and although this is not innovative or new at all and it has very little to do with technology per se, it does have, in a fulsome way, relationality, affect, child-adult connections, shared stories with children that feed research. Much of it is about the *small stories* (Georgakopoulou, 2015). By "small stories," I am referring to:

> we have been employing "small stories" as an umbrella-term that captures a gamut of under-represented narrative activities, such as tellings of ongoing events, future or hypothetical events, shared (known) events, but allusions to (previous) tellings, deferrals of telling, and refusals to tell.[1]
>
> *(Bamberg & Georgakopoulou, 2008, p. 381)*

Children tell small stories all of the time and they are woven into their meaning making. Tracing the roots and trajectories of these stories can be interesting in research by documenting how stories are told and whether stories materialize in the kinds of texts that they produce (Rowsell & Pahl, 2007).

Pam: As I think about your relationship with Lionel, and these enacted agentic moments, many moments surface for me from my work in child care, primary, and special education classrooms. Moments such as a five-year-old teaching me how to help a bumble bee return outdoors; a child bringing a shovel to school as we prepared for the funeral of a bird who died attempting to leave our classroom; reading aloud, for example, *Amos and Boris* by William Steig, and at the end having the children gathered, cry out "read it again." Valuing children as agentic, intelligent, compassionate storying beings in their own right helped me become conversant with their unique selves, insights, and enactments, and my own ways of being with children. As an early childhood educator being with children in different educational spaces across time, and within thousands of conversations, informs me deeply as a researcher. Enlivened and altered by children's theories, I find them to be inherently interesting beings, fresh to the process of making sense of all matter on our planet.

Pulling on agency and intra-actions in educational methods

Our second question: how do you pull on agency and agentive intra-actions?

Jennifer: In my own research with children, adolescents, and teenagers I have found one of the most powerful pulls and lasting impressions has been when participants/co-researchers' agency has been thrown into relief. Witnessing someone come out of their shell during the research process – whether it is through their compositional work or their responses to literature or art or their own sharing of experiences – is what drives anything that I do. Deb Hicks (2002) talked about this in her book *Reading Lives* and it makes me think about how essential it is to see people and to listen to people. It is a powerful way to push thinking and being in research. Hicks talks about how the essence of experiences lies in the relational. That is, in those moments when you connect with another person and they allow you to share in and with their stories.

Pam: Your moments of witnessing take me to the thinking of Loris Malaguzzi and Carlina Rinaldi of Reggio Emilia, specifically their research and experimentation with pedagogies of listening; Reggio research and practice that has been highly influential worldwide. Rinaldi (2006) writes that:

> If we believe that children possess their own theories, interpretations and questions, and are protagonists in the knowledge building process, then the most important verbs in educational practice are no longer "to talk" "to explain" "to transmit" but "to listen." Listening means being open to others, and what they have to say, listening to the more than hundred languages with all our senses. . . . Listening legitimizes the other person because communication is one of the fundamental of giving form to thought. *(pp. 98–99)*

The *hundred languages* is a concept, a wide range of enacted practices, and was a traveling exhibition of young children's art works explaining and foregrounding the work and ethos of the children, families, educators, and municipal schools of Reggio Emilia (Edwards et al., 1998). Malaguzzi writes that these children, and all children, "whatever their lives are rich, better equipped, more talented, stronger, and more intelligent than we can suppose" (Cagliari et al., 2016, p. 397).

Thinking about children's rich capacities to communicate and express themselves in multiple ways calls me back to the beginnings of my professional life as teacher candidate and kindergarten teacher, when my image of what it meant to be a child and an educator was permanently altered. Through my early childhood education (ECE) studies, and thanks to the fierce intellectualism of Pam Nason, I was introduced to the complexities of being a child, a parent and an educator in the world, the complexities of material engagements. In retrospect, I believe this was accomplished through interdisciplinary juxtaposition of the theoretical work we were engaged with at the time; for example, Jean Piaget (children's thinking), Basil Bernstein (social stratification), Constance Kamii (mathematical problem solving), and Brian Sutton-Smith (play and the imagination). As well, I was deeply engaged with the teaching and research of women who were thinking with and about children – women listening to children as equitable beings. Their writing helped me immensely with my ways of being and thinking with children, materials, and knowledge co-creation; women such as Jeannette Veatch, Maria Montessori, Caroline Pratt, and Sylvia Aston Warner. In their daily lives, teaching, researching, or both, these women focused on children's theories of the world as well as the creation/co-creation of materials with/for children to think-create which then created a space where adults and children enacted agency together.

As a consequence of this interdisciplinary juxtaposition of thinkers, and in concert with parallel engagements with young children, including hundreds of conversations, I experienced over and over again what Glenda MacNaughton (2005) calls an epistemological shudder, that is an "affective response to things marvellous" (Losinsky & Collinson, 1999, cited in MacNaughton, 2005). I was opened up to the immense possibilities of what it might mean to be a child – far beyond my own childhood, and well beyond what I might have imagined for other people's children whom I would be teaching and learning with and from. In retrospect, the child care and the primary classrooms where I taught were rich critical conversational-material spaces. My initial career immersion was within social-material-discursive spaces of educational care with young children. At that time, while being primarily a teacher, teaching-researcher, and researching-teacher, identities were/are deeply entangled for me.

Research methods to probe children's materialities and artifacts

Our third question: what role do materials and artifacts play in your research?

Jennifer: So, in my work with children, I am continually reminded about the wonders of the material. Having been less of an educator and more of a text producer (from a publishing background), I fixate on texts and artifacts and how they are made and how people think through them. This strand in my work has remained consistent over 18 years. Thinking about Deleuze and Guattari or Barad, what I absolutely agree with when I am in the field with children or with teenagers is how younger generations entangle themselves within material worlds and *become* through and in them. I observe from afar how people think through their smartphones as an extension of themselves or how children have naturalized their intra-actions with tablet-based texts. Materialities have shifted the landscape of literacy – both in terms of technology and everyday artifacts – and people become through them. Here I am thinking about Candace R. Kuby's (2017) work in early childhood classrooms and how artfully she theorizes ways of knowing with stuff.

Thinking about conducting research with children as they engage with technologies, I document not only what they do with technologies and media, but also and probably more importantly, their ways of knowing with technologies and media. I am fascinated with the varied ways of being and thinking through technologies. In my research with Debra Harwood (Rowsell & Harwood, 2015), we have charted how young children move from media ecologies like Disney texts such as *Frozen* to designing written and moving image stories to imaginative play and dress-up. As well, we have observed how young children move fluidly from their technologies to physical objects such as from an app of a kitchen to a pretend kitchen in an early childhood space. In this way, we theorize how children play, think, and learn across virtual, material, ephemeral, and immaterial texts and they do so without a second thought. Children's engagements with technologies have offered a new canvas for researchers to investigate how qualitatively different literacy is today (Burnett, 2010; Wohlwend, 2009) and I still feel that as educational researchers we have touched on the tip of an iceberg in terms of methods that we need to research post-humanism and new materialialist perspectives in early childhood research.

Pam: Engagements with materials in early childhood education have a lengthy Euro-Centric history, for example, Froebel's gifts, Caroline Pratt's blocks, and the experiential-material nature of Alice and John Dewey's mutually informative theorizing and practices. Blocks, clay, paints, water, and sand have long been present in early childhood spaces. Thinking with stuff, takes us beyond the provision of materials for interactions and into intra-actions, as you say. "Thinking with materials transforms early childhood education, provoking educators to notice how materials and young children live entangled lives in classrooms, how they change each other through their mutual encounters" (Pacini-Ketchabaw et al.,

2016, p. 2). It may be that theories of materialisms, including the decentering of human agency have long been a part of children's lives, and perhaps, it is only recently that materials are viewed as part of an intra-active assemblage by adults.

Eliciting and enticing children's agency through research methods

Our fourth question: in what ways do you draw out hidden talents, interests, and what Barton and Hamilton call "ruling passions"?

Jennifer: There are so many interests and hidden truths that I have heard and witnessed over the years – there so many hidden treasures that young people hold dear and it is a matter of teasing them out. Over the years, young men and women have told me all about their interests and motivations and they have been wide-ranging and colorful and never dull. I can think of a host of researchers whom I really admire who are intrigued by this as well such as Jackie Marsh (2013, 2016) and her longitudinal work in homes and her ability to frame lives in additive ways rather than dwelling on poverty or social class "deficits." Also, Cathy Burnett (2017) who cuts through moments to see ways of knowing in idiosyncratic and interesting ways. Or, Karen E. Wohlwend (2010, 2015) who finds children endlessly fascinating and documents their sophisticated, quirky play with technology with such intelligence and sensitivity. Then, I think about race and culture and I am reminded of work by Annette Woods (2015), Rahat Naqvi (2015), and Kris Gutierrez (2016) – all three women respectfully and ethically show how culture weaves its way through meaning making in dynamic ways. I am of course also reminded of your work Pam and the ways that you locate children as people who have thoughts, provocations, imaginings and like the other theorists you are so ethical, sensitive, and careful about how you talk about children and acknowledge their agency.

Pam: And their agentic relations with each other, materials, and imaginings. And thinking about agentic enactment, I think of you. You have brought so many people together. People, working in pockets across Australia, North America, and England co-generating knowledge in the context of local projects. You are very attentive to the possibilities of your position as a Canada Research Chair in creating conversational research spaces across/within projects. These gatherings and spaces – textual, virtual, and physical – act as sites, provocations to critically and recursively reflect and co-create new knowledge.

Thinking about my initial research projects as a doctoral student, I was drawn to the notions of epistemological inequality (Martin, 1985) in part, addressed through the practice of reclaiming conversations as a way to begin to move towards equity. I was thinking with feminist philosophers Jane Roland Martin (1985, 1992) and Elisabeth Young Bruehel (1987): Martin for her philosophical thought and conversational practices of reclaiming epistemological thinking by and about women; and Young Bruehel's notion of conversational moments, an ontology of being in the moment and in relation with a cast of encouragers. More recently, Elisabeth Grosz (2017) in *The Incorporeal: Ontology, Ethics, and Limits of Materialism* offers the possibility of an onto-ethical way of being in the world, one that "involves an ethics which addresses not just human life in its inter-human relations, but relationships between the human and an entire world organic and inorganic" (p. 1); that is an ontoethics that speaks to the question "how to act in the present and, primarily, how to bring about a different future from the present" (ibid).

Grosz's onto-ethical way of being fits with post-humanism thinking that is the decentering the human and the enactment of ethical-onto-episto ways of being and knowing.

Onto-ethical-temporal-spatial conversations over books

Our fifth question: how do time and space manifest themselves in your methods?

Pam: Back to moments and their material effects, I am taken back into conversational moments that occurred within literacy research projects I have co-lead; moments that Glenda MacNaughton (2005) might recognize as the beginning rupture of an epistemological shudder, or perhaps Maggie MacLure's (2016) idea of troublesome moments, moments that open up creative, alternative ways of thinking about and being/becoming literate. These moments live in memory, and many are recorded in more concrete forms in artifacts including children's books, parenting-for-literate-communities' handbooks, and multimodal curriculum documents; materials all still in use in the province where I live and work. Our/my involvement in research as action researchers fit our desire to work directly with the field, while enacting change as an ongoing part of the research process. As Jean McNiff (2016) writes, "community action research projects have the power to create intellectual and physical spaces to work together productively and dialogically" (p. 2). As well, feminist scholarship prioritizes the everyday experiences of women, in part by its capacity to connect the "articulated, contextualized personal with the often hidden or invisible structural or social institutions that define and shape our lives" (MacGuire, 2001, pp. 64–65). In each research instance in which I was involved, a group of community and university situated people, mostly women, productively and in conversations over time, co-generated literate ways of knowing, being and acting, ways of being, which in turn were workshopped, piloted, and produced in a variety of print and online formats.

In the *Parenting for a Literate Community* (Nason et al., 1999) family literacy project, we were invited by the parents and director of the Fredericton Regional Family Resource Centre[2] to work with their collective desire to help their children "be ready" for school. These parents, all too familiar in their own childhoods with schooled challenges, wanted to change things for their children. To echo Grosz, they were asking – how could they bring about a different future for their children by acting now? And our question, how could we help? Our approach to working together was located within an action research study situated within a critical feminist framework and guided by family literacy research (Auerbach, 1989; Taylor, 1997). We took up Elsa Auerbach's position of social-contextual model of family literacy (drawing upon Heath, Street, and Freire), an inclusive view of family literacy embracing "a range of activities and practices that are integrated into the fabric of daily life, [where] the social context becomes a rich resource that can inform rather than impede learning" (p. 166), asking questions such as how can we draw upon parental knowledge and experience to inform curricular materials – rather than the more common question of "how can we transfer school practices into home" (p. 177)? As Denny Taylor (1997) writes "each family is an original" (p. 1) and thus complex understandings of families and multiple literacies of their everyday lives are required for us to enact a different future in the present.

Our conversations took place at the university where we had an early childhood classroom, and a meeting room. We met twice weekly for 12 weeks. While the children were playing within an early childhood setting, we met with their parents, and then at the close of the morning the children were joined by their parents in the ECE classroom. An early conversation with the parents which absolutely shuddered through me, and deeply influenced our approach to knowledge generation, emerged from a conversation about the *Born to Read* book bag provided to all babies and their mothers at birth. We asked the parents if they had received the book bag. Yes, they had and they were safely stored away until their children began school and the teachers would be teaching them to read. Although we were cognizant that some families did not receive books bags, we had not considered that they would be safely stored away until school entry, as we learned often on top of the fridge for safekeeping – out of reach. And although we realized that success at school is more complicated than, "read to your child," when this taken for granted assumption was spoken by the parents, it informed a major aspect of our conversational gatherings. Once we co-generated topics with parents, we incorporated related picture books into these sessions and held extensive book talks (Chambers, 1996, 2011). It was these book talks that became a major material-discursive means through which co-generated knowledge emerged and a family literacy programme was created. The program co-created with these children and their parents, mostly mothers, then served as a jumping off point for a number of family literacy projects including: an extensive family literacy program bringing early childhood staff from different agencies together; a community literacy project with the provincial literacy coalition; and a set of double address books, the in-progress drafts, shared in focus groups with parents at family resource centers. Most recently *Parenting for Literate Community* ran as facilitated sessions with grandparents – picture books still a critical technology for being and becoming literate.

Avoiding deficit framings of children in research methods

Our sixth question: how do you celebrate children's meaning making and not fall into normative, even deficit approaches?

Jennifer: I find myself thinking quite a bit lately about performativity, social economic divides, and invisible structures. One of the most pressing problems in the future will be the digital divide. This point relates to your earlier point because the digital divide will and has widened the gap between the haves and the have nots. Thinking back to my point about how materialities loom large, children living in poverty do not have technological trappings like expensive iPads and smartphones and their wealthier peers will unquestionably have the added academic and life edge because they not only have them, but they are permitted to do different sorts of things with them. As a researcher, I have already witnessed moments across different research sites when children who do not have iPads do not know how to do compositional and production work that their middle to upper class peers can do. The thorny issue for researchers is: how can we capture divides and frame them in an additive way as opposed to deficit framing? Debra Harwood and Diane Collier (2017) paint an additive picture of working-class children making meaning at home by elucidating the intriguing and rich nature of children's material worlds: what they make; what they display; why they like them; how they think through them; and, contrastive pictures between generative and imaginative play and engagements at home compared with their school lives.

Pam: You remind me of our ongoing work with iPads as "placed resources" (Prinsloo, 2005; Prinsloo & Rowsell, 2012) in the University of New Brunswick demonstration classroom. Having the iPads available for these four-year-old children makes visible what some children already know about using iPads at home, while at the same time facilitating peer sharing of their knowledges. In terms of young children and their compositional and production work, one particular episode comes to mind. We investigated how an episode of witch play in the woods where the children venture to each day, worked as assemblage where children, adults, iPads, moss, Shakespeare, stumps, ice, pine cones, and sticks sustained imaginative story-telling, research, and playful experimentation with the iPads, as they remixed Shakespeare's bubble, bubble, toil and trouble text into their own witchy "poison soup, moss for bat fur" recipe. (Rose et al., 2017). The children were living across four centuries and several days, moving through multiple texts – digital, oral, poetic – as they generated their own versions: re-mixed and mobile texts that traveled with them between the woods and classroom spaces – their everyday literacy lives.

Jennifer: With Brian Street's passing last year, I have been thinking about how we live through and with literacy (i.e., literacies are everywhere, all of the time and there is an Ariadne's thread connecting our identity with literacy practices) and how literacy is intimately associated with who we are in the world. Seeing literacy as a part of the everyday and the range of activities and practices that we live makes it far more interesting as a researcher. It opens up optics into how children make sense of stories or how they make them move from a dress-up station to a movie based on *Frozen* (instance in a research site with Debra Harwood that I talked about earlier). These story movements come from pastiches of a child's everyday as they cross contexts and people.

Finding methods for new epistemologies and ontologies

Our seventh question: how do you find methods to capture new epistemologies and ontologies that emerge from technology and media use?

Pam: This concept of story movement reminds me of research we undertook on play and playfulness when a group of children and adults were co-authoring pastiches of *Frozen* one winter at the Grant MacEwan Child Care Lab School in Edmonton (Hewes et al., 2016). Eva Änggård (2016) in her posthumanist theorizing focused upon "how matter comes to matter." In her work with young children, she demonstrated how presence of diffractive encounters between/across theories "makes it possible to focus on the material and embodied aspects of play sequences" (p. 86). In the context of this particular *Frozen* story movement, we took up various theories of play and playfulness (Bateson, 1955/1976; Edmiston, 2008; Huizinga, 1950; Kalliala, 2006; Marsh & Bishop, 2013; Sellers, 2013; Wohlwend, 2012; Youell, 2008). Thinking with these theories diffractively, we engaged in a process of critically revisiting pedagogical narrations of *Frozen* play in the context of co-playing and co-authoring. This diffractive critical revisiting revealed the agential nature of these particular children in their intra-actions with materials, outdoor and indoor environments, each other, and their educators.

Within this child care center, *Frozen*, a very popular film, was taken up in children's play – Elsa and Anna are compelling, captivating females. Over time, these two characters began to evoke a troublesome, argumentative morning ritual rather than a playful one. The educators noticed this and were determined to figure out how to expand the play, rather than ban it: banning being a frequent response when children's play, from the adults' perspective at least, seems to have gone awry. Thoughtfully and playfully, the educators gathered "richly coloured, fabrics as a way to open up the aesthetic of beauty and power embodied in Elsa" (Hewes et al., 2016, p. 11). Imaginative literatures such as *Cara and the Wizard* and eventually *The Lion, the Witch and the Wardrobe* were read aloud. The children were fascinated with the white witch and a place where it was winter all year long. As the educators observed: "we found the more detailed novels we chose, the more complex the children's play adventure's and storytelling became" (Hewes et al., 2016, p. 14). Characters from different stories combined with media-referenced characters and storylines resulted in a variety of mashups indoors and out, with digital cameras and overhead projectors in the children's hands, playing a critical role with storied and re-storied movements. The adults, as it turns out, played imaginatively in the outdoors as children. Their remembered experiences and their own adult playfulness lead to a kind of intertextual inventiveness that brought popular culture together with materials, storybooks, digital technologies, and outdoor adventuring.

Confronting the gatekeeping of children and adults

Our eighth question: how can researchers document what young children do and think without intruding or gatekeeping?

Jennifer: As a researcher, adult roles in early childhood settings are particularly intriguing to me. Mostly I think about how children out-smart adults some of the time. There are dominant discourses that circulate now such as screens are bad and we need to police children's screen time, or, talking to and relating with children as they play – even when they do not want us there because they are concentrating. Do not get me wrong, I think that sometimes there is too much screen time and that we need to speak with children, but what I am talking about is the spontaneity and natural curiosity that children have and that we often want to interrupt to document or assess what they are doing and really, we just need them to get on with the work at-hand. With the gatekeeping and policing rhetoric that exists now, creativity can be constrained by adults (even well-meaning adults). How do we research young children now without being obtrusive?

Pam: Your thoughts on gatekeeping of children by adults – calls up gatekeeping at the university. I am thinking specifically of authorship and ethics – in particular co-authoring and anonymity. For many of our projects over the past two decades, we have worked with people who do not wish to remain anonymous – they wish to have their contributions acknowledged. Often this means naming people, in many cases as authors, rather taking up what Sinha and Back (2014) refer to as ethical hypochondria, where "automatic anonymity" limits "the potential of research to travel, connect people and engage the public imagination" (p. 473). Recognition and authorship of the contributions of child care educators and the reality of this research to travel, connect people and engage the public was a cornerstone of the provincial curriculum creation and implementation project that the Centre co-lead with the government and with educators and directors in the field. Initially we were funded to research early childhood curriculum and curriculum frameworks as a prelude to creating, piloting, and implementing a provincial curriculum framework. Ultimately the New Brunswick Curriculum Framework for Early Learning and Child Care reflected contemporary research and the practice of New Brunswick educators. The supporting curriculum documents exist, in the visual-textual-digital form they do, because of the generosity and willingness of child care educators and families to contribute stories, images, re-tellings, and pedagogical documentation from their daily work. And they are named as contributing authors. As Emily Ashton (2009) writes "The New Brunswick educators stories are not 'add-ons that have the status of afterthoughts' (Apple, 2001, p. 6) but are definitive" (p. 73). However Ashton, an integral member of the research team, takes great care to trouble "ethical editorializing" recognizing that authorship is the tip of the research disrupting author anonymity.

Concluding thoughts and continuing conversations

Our reflective conversation leaves us with more questions, some provocations, and perhaps even a few epiphanies. We wonder what does methodology mean in an era of posts – post-qualitative/post-humanism/post-colonial? And how do we, in Canada, the northern part of Turtle Island, enact our responsibilities to and with the First Peoples who have lived in and with this land for over 10,000 years? Two things come to mind and heart that have been illuminated in our conversation, the first, that methodology does not stand alone – it is entangled with ethics, ontology, epistemology, and, as our examples illustrate, relationality. Methodological entanglement is explicit in our conversation. We believe that technology and media have foregrounded how essential it is to account for materialism and intra-action with materialities (Barad, 2007) across spaces and places and to think about technology in a more textured and nuanced way. There can be such a naturalness and organic feel to the ways that children use and think through technologies and we have much to do to gain an authentic, richer pictures of technology use and enjoyment.

The second thing that comes to mind is implicit. In both the witches' outdoor poetry play and the *Frozen* story movements described earlier, the stories framing the play are from Western culture – William Shakespeare and C.S. Lewis. What comes to mind for Western educators and researchers, not surprisingly are Western values, stories, practices, and knowledges. The first stories of the First Peoples are much less well known, and particularly less known to non-Indigenous peoples, as Indigenous histories have been subjugated. If as we indicate methodology is entangled with an ethico-onto-epistemological lens, (Kuby et al., 2018), then how will we as Western researchers decolonize our re-searching minds and hearts?

Notes

1 In the study of the conversational data of a group of female adolescents (Georgakopoulou, 2003, pp. 75–91), stories of projected events (imagining the future) proved to be more salient, quantitatively speaking too, than stories of past events: in this case, imagining the future was a more potent and meaningful discourse practice than that of remembering the past.

2 Established in 1997 with funding from the federal government's Community Action Program for Children (CAPC), Fredericton Regional Family Resource Centre also receives support from Province of New Brunswick's Department of Education and Early Childhood. The Fredericton Regional Family Resource Centre is a non-profit organization that offers programs to children and families in Fredericton and surrounding areas. It is intended to be a hub acting as a support network for parents (http://frederictonfrc.ca/family/about-us/).

References

Änggård, E. (2016) How matter comes to matter in children's nature play: Posthumanist play, posthumanist approaches and children's geographies. *Children's Geographies* 14 (1), 77–90.

Ashton, E. (2009) Folding ethical-textual tensions: Exploration in curriculum writing. In: Iannacci, L. and Whitty, P. (eds.) *Early childhood curriculum: Reconceptualist perspectives*. Calgary: Detselig Publishers.

Auerbach, E. (1989) Toward a social-contextual approach to family literacy. *Harvard Educational Review* 59 (2), 165–181.

Back, L. (2007) *The art of listening*. Oxford: Berg Publishers.

Bamberg, M. and Georgakopoulou, A. (2008) Small stories as a new perspective in narrative and identity analysis. *Text & Talk* 28, 377–396.

Barad, K. (2007) *Meeting the universe half way: Quantum physics and the entanglement of matter and meaning*. Durham, NC: Duke University Press.

Barton, D. and Hamilton, M. (1998) *Local literacies: Reading and writing in one community*, London: Routledge.

Bateson, G. (1955/1976) A theory of play and fantasy. In: Bruner, J.S., Sylva, K. and Jolly, A. (eds.) *Play: Its role in development and evolution*. New York: Viking Penguin, pp. 119–129.

Burnett, C. (2010) Technology and literacy in early childhood educational settings: A review of research. *Journal of Early Childhood Literacy* 10, 247–270.

Burnett, C. (2017) Acknowledging and interrogating multiplicities: Towards a generous approach in evaluations of early literacy innovation and intervention. *Journal of Early Childhood Literacy* 17, 522–550.

Cagliari, P., Castagnetti, M., Giudici, C., Rinaldi, C., Vecchi, V. and Moss, P. (2016) *Loris Malaguzzi and the schools of Reggio Emilia: A selection of his writings and speeches, 1945–1993*. London and New York: Routledge.

Chambers, A. (1996) *Tell me: Children, reading and talk*, South Woodchester, Stroud, Gloucester: Thimble Press.

Chambers, A. (2011) *Tell me: Children, reading and talk with the reading environment: How adults help children enjoy books*. South Woodchester, Stroud, Gloucester: Thimble Press.

Dyson, A.H. (2008) Staying in the (curricular) lines: Practice constraints and possibilities in childhood writing. *Written Communication* 25, 119–159.

Edmiston, B. (2008) *Forming ethical identities in early childhood play*, Abingdon: Routledge.

Edwards, C., Gandini, L. and Forman, G. (1998) *The hundred languages of children: The Reggio Emilia approach-advanced reflections*. Greenwich, CT: Ablex Publishing.

Georgakopoulou, A. (2003) Looking back when looking ahead: Adolescents' identity management in narrative practices. In: Androutsopoulos, J. and Georgakopoulou, A. (eds.) *Discourse constructions of youth identities*. Amsterdam: John Benjamins Publishing, 75–91.

Georgakopoulou, A. (2015) Small stories research. In: Fina, A.D. and Georgakopoulou, A. (eds.) *The handbook of narrative analysis*. Hoboken, NJ: Wiley, 255–271.

Grosz, E. (2017) *The incorporeal: Ontology, ethics and the limits of materialism*. New York: Columbia University Press.

Gutiérrez, K. (2016) Designing resilient ecologies: Social design experiments and a new social imagination. *Educational Researcher* 45, 187–197.

Harwood, D. and Collier, D.R. (2017) The matter of the stick: Storying/(re)storying children's literacies in the forest. *Journal of Early Childhood Literacy* 17, 336–352.

Hewes, J, Whitty, P., Aamot, B., Schaly, E., Sibbad, J. and Ursuliak, K. (2016) Unfreezing Disney's Frozen through playful and intentional co-authoring/co-playing. *Canadian Journal of Education* 39 (3), 1–25.

Hicks, D. (2002) *Reading lives: Working-class children and literacy and learning*. New York: Teachers College Press.

Huizinga, J. (1950) *Homo ludens: A study of the play element in culture*. Boston, MA: Beacon Press.

Kalliala, M. (2006) *Play culture in a changing world*. New York: Open University Press.

Kuby, C.R. (2017) Poststructural and posthuman theories as literacy research methodologies: Tensions and possibilities. In: Zaidi, R. and Rowsell, J. (eds.) *Literacy lives in transcultural times*. New York: Routledge, 157–174.

Kuby, C., Spector, K. and Theil, J. (2018) *Posthumanism and literacy education*. London: Routledge.

Losinsky, M. and Collinson, I. (1999) *Epistemlological shudder: The X-files, myths and mimetic capital*. Paper presented at the University of New South Wales Post Graduate Conference School of English and Modern Languages, June 1999.

MacGuire, P. (2001) Feminisms and action research. In: Reason, P. and Bradbury, H. (eds.) *Handbook of action research*. London: Sage Publications.

MacLure, M. (2016) The refrain of the a-grammatical child: Finding another language in/for qualitative research. *Cultural Studies-Critical Methodologies* 16 (2), 173–182.

MacNaughton, G. (2005) *Doing Foucault in early childhood studies: Applying post-structuralist ideas*. New York: Peter Lang.

Marsh, J. (2013) Media, childhood and play. In: Brooker, L., Edwards, S. and Blaise, M. (eds.) *Handbook of play and learning in early childhood*. London: Sage, pp. 403–414.

Marsh, J. (2016) Gareth: The reluctant writer. In: Dyson, A.H. (ed.) *Composing in childhoods: A global perspective*. New York: Routledge.
Marsh, J. and Bishop, J. (2013) *Changing play: Play, media and commercial culture from the 1950s to the present day*. New York: Open University Press.
Martin, J.R. (1985) *Reclaiming an education: An ideal of the educated woman*. New Haven, CT: Yale University Press.
Martin, J.R. (1992) *The schoolhome: Rethinking schools for changing families*. Cambridge, MA: Harvard University Press.
McNiff, J. (2016) *You and your action research project* (4th edition). Abingdon and New York: Routledge.
Nason, P, Hunt, A. and Whitty, P. (1999) *Parenting for a literate community project*. Ottawa, Canada: Health Canada Community Action Programme for Children: National Projects Fund.
Naqvi, R. (2015) Postcolonial approaches to literacy: Understanding the 'other'. In: Rowsell, J. and Pahl, K. (eds.) *The Routledge handbook of literacy studies*. London: Routledge, pp. 49–61.
Pacini-Ketchabaw, V., Kind, S. and Kocher, L. (2016) *Encounters with materials in early childhood education*. London and New York: Routledge.
Prinsloo, M. (2005) The new literacies as placed resources. *Perspectives in Education* 23, 87–98.
Prinsloo, M. and Rowsell, J. (2012) Digital literacies as placed resources in the globalised periphery. *Language and Education* 26 (4), 271–277.
Rinaldi, C. (2006) *In dialogue with Reggio Emilia: Listening, researching and learning*. London: Routledge.
Rose, S., Mersereau, K., Fitzpatrick, C. and Whitty, P. (2017) Playful pedagogic moves: Digital devices in the outdoors. In: Harwood, D. (ed.) *Crayons and iPads: Learning and teaching of young children in the digital world*. London: Sage.
Rowsell, J. and Harwood, D. (2015) "Let It Go": Exploring the image of the child as producer, consumer, and inventor. *Theory Into Practice* 54 (2), 136–146.
Rowsell, J. and Pahl, K. (2007) Sedimented identities in texts: Instances of practice. *Reading Research Quarterly* 42 (3), 388–401.
Sellers, M. (2013) *Young children becoming curriculum: Deleuze, Te Whariki and curricular understandings*. Abingdon: Routledge.
Sinha, S. and Back, L. (2014) Making methods sociable: Dialogue, ethics and authorship in qualitative research. *Qualitative Research* 14 (4), 473–487.
Taylor, D. (1997) *Many families, many literacies: An international declaration of principles*. Portsmouth, NH: Heinemann.
Wohlwend, K.E. (2009) Damsels in discourse: Girls consuming and producing gendered identity texts through Disney princess play. *Reading Research Quarterly* 44, 57–83.
Wohlwend, K.E. (2010) A is for avatar: Young children in literacy 2.0 worlds and literacy 1.0 schools. *Language Arts* 88, 144–152.
Wohlwend, K.E. (2012) The boys who would be princesses: Playing with gender identity intertexts in Disney Princess transmedia. *Gender and Education* 24 (6), 593–610.
Wohlwend, K.E. (2015) One screen, many fingers: Young children's collaborative literacy play with digital puppetry apps and touchscreen technologies. *Theory Into Practice* 54, 154–162.
Woods, A.F. (2015) Learning to write: Analysing writing samples as part of considering how children become writers. In: Turnbill, J., Barton, G. and Brock, C. (eds.) *Teaching writing in today's classrooms: Looking back to look forward*. Adelaide, SA: ALEA Publications, 138–153.
Youell, B. (2008) The importance of play and playfulness. *European Journal of Psychotherapy and Counselling* 10 (2), 121–129.
Young-Bruehel, E. (1987) The education of women as philosophers. *Signs* 12 (2), 35–49.

3

THE PROS AND CONS OF USING DISPLAY CAPTURE TECHNOLOGY FOR DATA COLLECTION WITH YOUNG CHILDREN

Garry Falloon

Introduction

For some years screen capture and display recording software have been used in education, generally for tasks such as creating teaching resources or tutorials (Séror, 2012), recording information for students to access for revision purposes or if they are unable to attend classes (Drumheller & Lawler, 2011; Silva, 2012), monitoring user interaction with websites or other applications (Beach & Willows, 2014; Chaney et al., 2013; Zhang, 2013) and for generating understanding about students' learning processes in areas such as second language learning and mathematics (Barmby et al., 2009; Xu & Ding, 2014). All of these studies were conducted on desktop computers, using commercial screen recording applications such as *Camtasia* (Techsmith, 2017a), *SnagIt* (Techsmith, 2017b) or *Captivate* (Adobe, 2017). Cited benefits from using screen capture for these purposes include its ability to 'concurrently collect both screen movement and audio, (enabling) assessment of an individual's cognitive state that is more accurate than retrospective reflections' (Chaney et al., 2013, p. 2533), support the collection of data that reveals problems users experience when using applications (Zhang, 2013) and allow deeper insights into how applications assist (or not) conceptual learning (Barmby et al., 2009). Given that screen recording is not a new technology, very few studies appear to have used it as a research tool to gather empirical data about how young children interact with applications and devices – and each other, as they engage with them individually or in groups in formal and informal learning settings. This chapter examines the use of display recording technology to capture data in a range of studies involving 5-year-old children using apps on iPads to help develop literacy, numeracy, science and computational thinking capabilities. They were completed between 2011–2017, commencing soon after the original iPad was launched in 2010, amidst much hype and fanfare as an educational *game changer* (Coghlan, 2011). This chapter discusses the benefits of using display capture technology in these studies in terms of data quality and authenticity, but also highlights the significant challenges faced in doing so. These relate to technical, learning environment and logistical difficulties, but perhaps more importantly, ethical dilemmas when using this data method with very young children.

Changes to technology and learning environments

In recent years many governments, through their education ministries, have moved to renovate traditional classrooms or build new ones as flexible, innovative or modern learning environments. This broadly follows OECD (Organisation of Economic Co-operation and Development) commentary that promotes future learning spaces as being technology-supported, learner-centred and competency-focused, flexible and collaborative in nature (Kuuskorpi et al., 2011; OECD, 2017). These changes align with what is seen as the desirability of learning spaces to support so-called '21st Century' or 'future-focused' pedagogy, able to foster the development of valued competencies such as team work, problem solving, learning independence, self-determination and positive disposition towards learning as a life-long activity. In New Zealand, where these studies were undertaken, redesigns have resulted in large, open learning spaces where two and sometimes three teachers collaboratively plan for and teach between 40–70 students (depending on age level), frequently with the assistance of a range of technology systems and devices (Figure 3.1).

Aligned with physical learning environment changes and technology improvements, has been a parallel move from using fixed, desktop computers, to using mobile devices, such as laptops, Chromebooks and tablets. The improved affordability of these devices, combined with programs such as 'Bring Your Own Device' (BYOD), has helped overcome historical technology-access issues in many schools that up until recent times has mitigated against widespread and meaningful integration. The design and portability of new devices and well-developed technical infrastructure (e.g., fibre broadband, long-range Wi-Fi, cloud-based services) has also supported the type of curriculum and pedagogy being developed in these environments, allowing children

Figure 3.1 An example of an Innovative Learning Environment (Flexible Learning Space) from this study

greater flexibility to work in different spaces, including at home and other out-of-school environments (Figure 3.2).

However, the move to flexible learning spaces and mobile devices has proved challenging to educational researchers, keen to learn how young children use these devices and interact with their apps in naturalistic classroom settings. While conventional methods such as video and audio recording may yield satisfactory interactional data from one or possibly two students at a time – or provide a general overview of activities in a classroom from a single or dual points of capture, the reality is that these methods are generally inadequate for revealing fine-grained information about how highly mobile classes of children use devices and apps, if, what and how they are learning while doing so, and for capturing the subtleties of their interpersonal exchanges. Conventional video recording methods trialled in the early studies in this series also revealed a strong observer or Hawthorne effect that compromised the authenticity of data. Data suggested the young children modified their behaviours or ceased their interactions due to presence of a camera. These challenges required use of a different data method – one that could be used with classes of highly mobile students, and at the same time, captured detailed data in an unobtrusive manner.

Developing a device-embedded recorder

Apple's iPad presents educators with a robust, reliable and quality-controlled (app-wise) platform to use with children, but confinement to operating within Apple's 'Walled Garden' (Melhuish & Falloon, 2010) means that only AppStore-approved apps can be used. Unfortunately, until very recently, this did not extend to an app that supported recording of the device's display. Despite inclusion of display capture functionality in more recent releases of Apple's iOS, operating

Figure 3.2 Flexible learning spaces provide children with different workspace options

constraints on the native system, including the recorder shutting down if any protective cover is closed or the device 'goes to sleep' (common scenarios with young children), compromises its usefulness for classroom data collection. Therefore, recording the display of the iPads used in these studies required the development of a bespoke recording system, and the unlocking of devices to allow installation of a recording app. Over the course of this research, the bespoke display capture app has evolved from simply recording the device's display, microphone audio and finger placement (touches), to also optionally allowing for Facecam activation, enabling the children's facial expressions to be recorded (Figure 3.3).

The latest version of the recorder can be activated and deactivated in a number of ways, including a pre-set sequence of finger taps on the display, using a 'record' button in the app itself or via Wi-Fi from a mobile phone. Apart from a thumbnail image if the Facecam function is activated (see Figure 3.3), no other visible indication that the device is recording is available to the children. Using the recorder over the past six years has enabled rich and highly authentic data to be gathered that accurately reflects the reality of children's mobile device use in busy classrooms, in a range of different learning contexts and scenarios.

The research context and studies

The recorder was used to collect data from 2011–17, in a range of studies involving children from 5–11 years. All studies were completed in the same school, but involved different children and their teachers. The school was a middle decile[1] contributing primary (years 1–6) comprising 520 students and approximately 30 teaching staff, including the principal, one non-teaching deputy principal and a part-teaching assistant principal. The school had developed a reputation in the community as a caring, forward-thinking and progressive institution, and had quickly become a 'school of choice', attracting students from a wide catchment area. While several studies were completed with older children (10 and 11 year olds), for the purposes of this chapter I am going to concentrate specifically on studies involving young children (5-year-olds, less than 6 months at school), as this group presented particular challenges when using the display recording system.

The studies

The first study (2011–12) investigated the extent to which a range of teacher-selected apps could support the children's phonics development. The apps ranged from simple 'drag and drop' designs where the children manipulated phonemes to build words, through to the 'Mr. Phonics' series (Christopher Thorne Productions, 2012), where syllable-based word building activities were introduced by a recorded video involving a comical teacher. The study specifically focused on how the young children navigated the apps, and the strategies they applied to solve the learning problems embedded in them (Falloon, 2013).

Study two (2013–14) researched the nature of children's interaction and talk while they worked collaboratively in pairs to develop literacy-based digital artefacts. It applied Mercer's (1994) Talking Types framework to analyse the nature of the children's verbal interactions while they used three different apps, PuppetPals (Polished Play LLC, 2017), Pic Collage (Cardinal Blue Developer, 2018) and Popplet (Notion Developer, 2017), to author content from their work in different learning topics. The study explored how the children negotiated decisions about the content and design of their artefacts, and the extent to which the tools and features of the apps and devices assisted in this process (Falloon & Khoo, 2014).

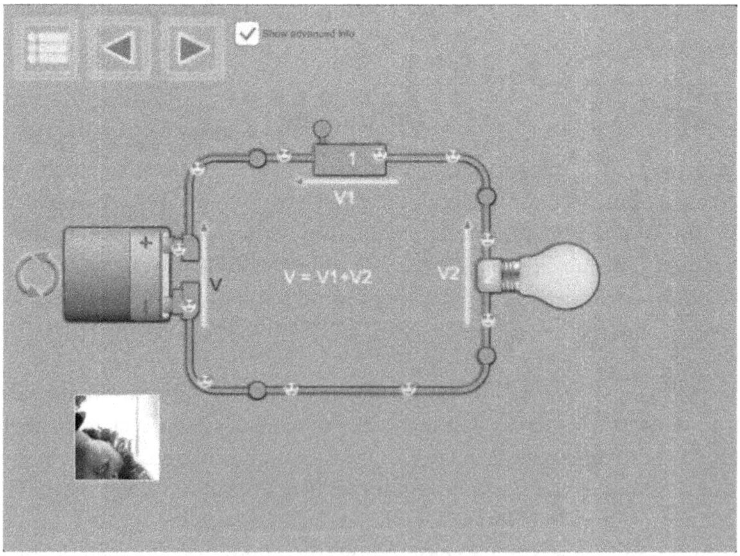

Figures 3.3a, b Top, the early display recorder showing finger placement (white spots) and the latest version (bottom) with Facecam recording

Study three (2015–16) examined the development of the children's general thinking skills while they were engaged in basic code-building using the app, Scratch Jnr. Coding tasks were integrated with the geometry component of the children's mathematics program, where challenges were set to build and run code sequences to draw common shapes of different dimensions (squares, rectangles etc.). Recordings were made as the pairs built and ran their procedures, which were then analysed using a framework developed from Krathwohl's (2002) revision of Bloom's Taxonomy, and Brennan and Resnick's (2012) computational thinking evaluation framework. Data were evaluated to determine how the computational tasks, and the strategies children employed to solve them, facilitated the exercise of different types and levels of thinking, and what contribution each of these made to solving the learning problems (Falloon, 2016).

The final study was undertaken in late 2016 to early 2017, and changed the focus somewhat to exploring low fidelity virtual simulations, and if they could be of value in helping young children learn basic circuit-building procedures and electricity concepts. Using minimally scaffolded guided discovery pedagogy, four apps were selected that progressively stepped the children from building simple series and parallel circuits using 'drag and drop' templates, to designing and building their own circuits on blank, breadboard-like testing platforms. It specifically investigated if the children could transfer conceptual and procedural knowledge between apps, and later, whether or not they could transfer this to building the same circuits using real equipment.

The display recorder was installed on 20 iPad Air and Air 2 devices supplied by my university for these studies. Although the school was BYOD, this did not include the junior classrooms, where children had restricted access to a shared set of 10 devices. These were generally used to supplement reading and maths group activities, or for topic research or content development. The school-owned devices were managed by a centralised system, thereby preventing unlocking and installation of the display recorder app. The research devices were left in the classrooms for the teachers to use outside of data collection times, allowing the children to become familiar with them and improving the device-to-student ratio for general curriculum work.

Analysing the display capture data

Screen capture data from all studies were analysed using Studiocode, a video analysis application originally developed for coding sporting, marketing, sales and audience presentation performances. Studiocode integrates the screen captured video and audio with an interactive timeline, that allow coders to log significant events in data against existing code frameworks, or ones generated from a grounded analysis of a data sample (Figure 3.4). These events are time-stamped on individual timelines, with quantitative data including event counts, average time per event, total time per event and percentage of total runtime per event, able to be exported to other applications such as SPSS or Excel, for statistical analysis. Additionally, samples of event-coded data can be saved as separate files and shared for rater-agreement purposes.

The sample framework in Figure 3.4 was generated from data in the most recent study investigating circuit building and electricity concept learning transfer between apps. As no existing frameworks were available, its design referenced early studies where young children used physical equipment for similar tasks (Osborne, 1983; Shipstone, 1984) to identify general levels of capability, comparing this with evidence of similar capabilities present in the display recorder data. From this comparison, four general science understandings relating to circuits were identified (left button column: e.g., resistance, control, uninterrupted current etc.). These were further associated with circuit types (parallel, series), concepts (e.g., operating circuits must be continuous, voltage 'shared' in series circuits etc.) and evidence from the display data (right button

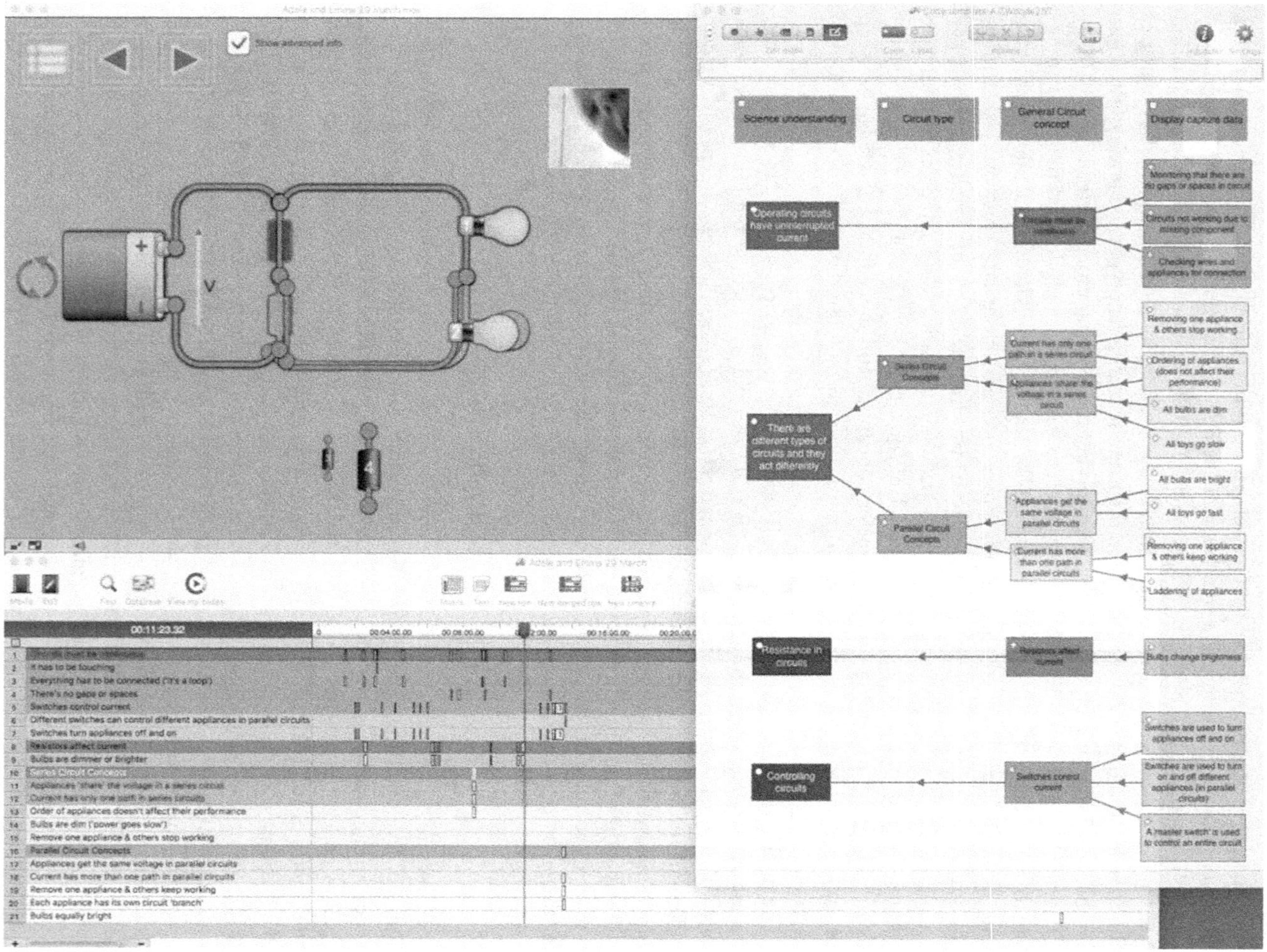

Figure 3.4 A typical Studiocode window showing timeline (bottom), coding framework (right) and sample video clip

column: e.g., variability in bulb brightness, ordering of appliances, removal of bulb and effect on circuit etc.). Toggling active buttons (right column) logged events aligned with the code and/or associated code on the timeline (see arrow links), registering these as appropriately coloured 'blocks'. Data associated with each of these blocks in the individual timeline rows can then be combined and exported as standalone files for presentation or coder-agreement purposes. However, it was necessary to review each sample up to four times (depending on the number of codes), as it was impossible to complete accurate analysis across multiple codes at the same time.

While exceedingly time-consuming, using Studiocode enabled deep interrogation of the display data that revealed unique insights into how the young children navigated and used the various app functions and content and worked collaboratively (or not), to build their learning responses and artefacts. It also supported analysis of the rich visual data captured using the device's Facecam. These data were particularly interesting and valuable, as they frequently provided information about what was happening in the broader environment, during periods of what otherwise may have been interpreted as the children being off-task or inactive.

Planning for and introducing and display recorder system

One of the main purposes of using display recorder was to gather data that accurately reflected the children's use of the devices in natural classroom settings. While previous studies using mainly desktop technologies have been undertaken in classrooms, virtually all of these have been designed to evaluate specific technology-supported interventions (e.g. Barns et al., 2005; Tang et al., 2006), or explore the efficacy of new applications in particular curriculum disciplines or activities (e.g. Imler & Eichelberger, 2011; Raído, 2013). It was therefore essential that the recorder was used to gather data during learning tasks that were part of each class's normal curriculum, rather than 'staged' events, set up especially for data gathering purposes. Prior to each study, meetings were held with the teachers to identify suitable curriculum topics and negotiate research focuses. In all cases, focuses were chosen that helped the teachers with a particular learning inquiry or question they had, with the expectation that results would be shared with other staff, to help improve technology use, learning design and pedagogy across the school.

The teachers were also keen to investigate how display data might be used for assessment or reporting purposes – that is, to provide visual evidence of the children's thinking and learning processes while they were working on the devices. They identified a particular issue with using the iPads in that, apart from the 'end product', they had very limited data upon which to evaluate the children's learning processes, or gain information about any learning difficulties they may be having. They saw the display recorder as a means of gathering useful formative and summative data for improving their practice, and for sharing with parents and other evaluation agencies.

Before each study, in addition to normal informed consent procedures, it was a requirement of ethical clearance that parents were given the opportunity to discuss the research, see the display recorder in action and have adequately answered any questions they had relating to any aspect of the work or its procedures. To facilitate this, several information sessions were organised at different times to enable as many interested parents as possible to attend. At these sessions the research goals, how data were to be gathered and analysed (including a demonstration of the recorder and some data gathered previously) and how results would feed back into school programmes, were introduced and explained. An evening seminar was also held in 2014. This two-hour meeting during which research outcomes to date were shared and discussed, was attended by school staff and over 300 parents, grandparents and teachers from neighbouring schools.

The display recorder in the classroom

Managing the recording system with the children evolved considerably from the early to most recent studies. Technology improvements led to more options being available to activate and deactivate the system, and simplification of this process meant most children could do this themselves, with a little initial guidance. While the latest iteration of the recorder includes the ability to activate and deactivate it from a smartphone, this function has never been used, for reasons that will be discussed later. Typically, at the beginning of each session pairs or small groups of children would be allocated a numbered device, and their names registered on a log sheet. They would use the same iPad for the duration of each unit, as their work was saved to the device rather than in the cloud. In the earlier studies where the system was started by a tap sequence, I activated and deactivated the recorder at the beginning and end of each session. However, in later work the children did this for themselves, using the start/stop button (Figure 3.5). Where practical, data were gathered during all teaching sessions from as many pairs or groups as possible. While this resulted in a significant volume of data, doing this allowed for the inevitable technical or logistical problems that arise when using technology with very young children. At the close of each session, data were exported from individual devices to my laptop for later analysis using a transfer app called iExplorer (Macroplant, 2016). Not all data were analysed, but samples were selected using specific criteria aligned with each study's focus, taking into account any profile considerations relating to the target group being researched.

Ethical considerations

Like any study involving young children, this research required adherence to strict ethical standards, and for its methods, processes and means of data use and dissemination to be scrutinised and approved by my university's Human Research Ethics Committee. In evaluating the application,

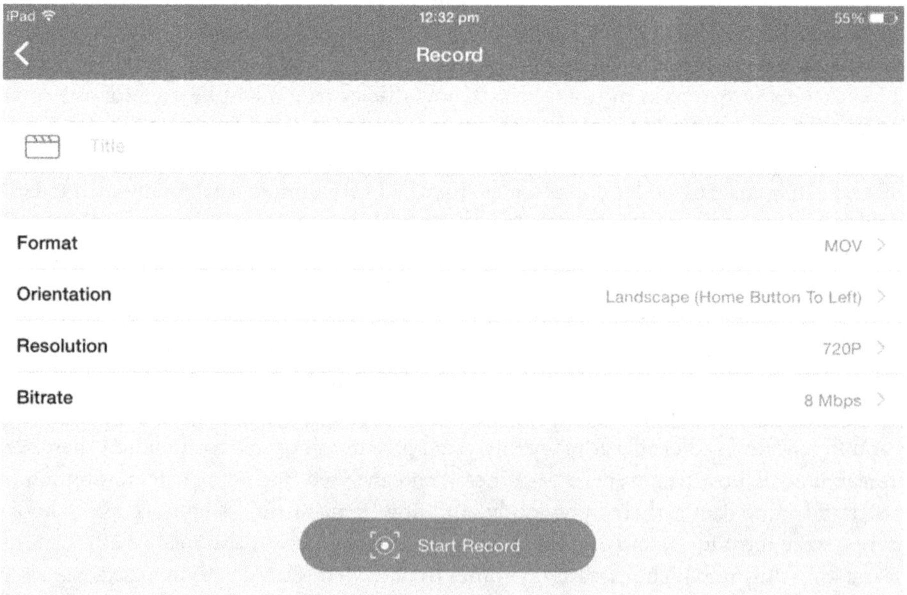

Figure 3.5 Later versions of the screen recorder included a visible start/stop button

the committee raised a number of concerns regarding the recording system, particularly emphasising its potential to record information of a personal nature unrelated to the research, the invisibility to the children of any signs of its operation, and the fine line using it draws between 'covert surveillance' and data gathering. Specifically, concerns were expressed about the method being deceptive, and the possibility that despite parental informed consent and ongoing child assent measures, conceptually very young children may have difficulty understanding when they were being recorded, what was being recorded, and how or why. The committee pointed out that while screen recording was not a new technology, its use for research data gathering was not commonplace, and that the few studies that had employed it had generally done so with older participants in managed environments, using desktop computers. They also reminded that the commercially available recorders used in previous studies had a visible indicator, such as a pulsing coloured bar across the top of the screen, or a flashing recording indicator in the task bar. A visible recording indicator was not included in any version of iPad recorder used in these studies.

Two questions arose from the committee's review that needed consideration. First, could the recorder be viewed as deceptive, and if so, was its use justifiable in terms of participant risk vs research benefit? Second, if it was not considered deceptive, what measures would be taken to ensure it was not being used deceptively, and that any data of a personal or confidential nature collected through its use, were appropriately handled? Justifiable sensitivity has existed around using deception in social and scientific research since the early 1960s, when Stanley Milgram's infamous 'shock machine' experiments allegedly caused significant trauma to unwitting participants.[2] While not of the same nature or significance as Milgram's work, the answer to the question of whether the recorder was deceptive was not found in the technology itself, but how it was to be used. The committee accepted that the practice of screen recording was widespread amongst gamers for strategy-sharing and businesses for training purposes, and that some studies were emerging of its use for educational research (e.g. Zhang & Quintana, 2012). Their concerns were of a more ethically fundamental nature – specifically, whether or not the young children were aware of its use and what it recorded, and if so, whether they held sufficient agency to ask for the recorder not to be activated, deactivated if it was active or withdraw their data after it had been recorded. Consideration also needed to be given to how any data that were recorded that was deemed to be of a private, confidential or concerning nature, would be handled. This was particularly important, given young children's tendency to discuss with their friends in private, issues they may not feel confident to discuss with adults.

Addressing these concerns and implementing them *in practice* is complex, requiring careful attention to procedures, and the adoption of a highly reflexive researcher stance (Flewitt, 2005). While procedures related to handling of what might be interpreted as confidential, private or concerning information can be easily drafted for the purposes of ethical approval, implementing them is not so straightforward, relying on the judgement and integrity of the researcher to decide what to do with data of that nature. Procedurally, in these studies this issue was mitigated by a decision to refer to the class teacher any recorded information that suggested a child was being subjected to emotional, psychological or physical harm, to the extent that it was, or potentially could, negatively affect their safety or wellbeing. From there it was to be the decision of the teacher, in conjunction with the principal and, if needed, other relevant authorities, whether or not to act upon the information. Reaching this procedural decision was a difficult process, as if enacted the primary ethical tenet of participant confidentiality could potentially be compromised. However, when the age of the children and the ethical and moral obligation of the researcher to ensure no harm comes to participants was taken into account, the referral pathway was deemed to be an essential measure. Interestingly, over the 6 years these studies were completed, while many amusing interactions were captured, nothing of a concerning nature that required referral was recorded.

The question of agency when researching with young children is a challenging one, given the obvious perceptions of authority and power in the researcher-child relationship (Einarsdóttir, 2007). Fundamentally, the ethical conduct and procedures of any research should allow participants to make informed decisions regarding participation and use of any data they contribute, including the capacity to amend or withdraw their contribution, unless this right is waived in the consent process (Burns, 2000). Exercising this with young children can be problematic, and as such, most often consent is granted via parent proxy. However, some interesting findings from these studies point to possible issues for some children when using display recording, that researchers using this method should be aware of. While it may be possible for young children to amend or withdraw data provided during interviews, by, for example, indicating desired changes while their transcript is being read back to them – or decline permission to use their work as data altogether, the scenario that evolved with display recording during these studies suggests these data are somewhat different. In the early trials (2012–14, pre-Facecam functionality), recorder data that were going to be used in publications and/or as 'live' clips at conferences and presentations, were shared with the children involved in its generation, with the expectation being that they would approve or decline its use. Interestingly, when their clips were played back to them, it was apparent some children did not understand and were surprised to learn that the voices they heard and the actions they were viewing *were actually their own*. Acknowledging that some time had elapsed between when data were recorded and when samples were shared with the children, it did raise the question as to whether or not these young children understood what the display recorder did, and the sort of information it captured about them and their activities.

Unlike interviews that are recorded by a generally known physical device (a tape or audio recorder), or audio recording apps that must be opened and remain so while in use (usually with a visible indicator such as a monitor or flashing bar or light), the early display recorder did not require 'opening' – simply tapping three times in a pre-specified area of the display activated and deactivated it. It may have been that the absence of a physical or known recording device, or virtual representation of a device, made it difficult for some children to understand that their comments and actions were being recorded. While parental consent had been granted for all data used in publications and presentations, and assent was gained from the children prior to each recording session, it was somewhat disturbing to learn that a significant number of children did not appear to understand what was going on.

Notwithstanding other issues such as perceptions of authority, these conceptual deficits made it extremely difficult for the children to make any informed decisions relating to use of their data. While later versions of the recorder added an interface with start and stop buttons and optional Facecam recording – both of which should have provided the children with cues that the recorder was active, it is unlikely they would have helped address these issues. This conclusion is supported by the nature of some of the recorded audio that suggested many children either did not know or quickly forgot that they were being recorded, were unaware of what was being recorded or simply didn't care! While nothing of a referable nature was recorded, many clips captured personal squabbles, references to relationship issues with other children, siblings and family members, afterschool parent and family happenings and events, and other information of a personal and at times private nature. While not supported by any empirical data, it may well be that the absence of a known recording device combined with the children's location in different, seemingly private work spaces around the large classroom, contributed to a mistaken sense of privacy and anonymity.

The most recent version of the recorder contains two features that have been used sparingly, or not at all. The Facecam recorder was added in late 2015, and while its use was approved by my university through ethics amendment, it met with significant resistance from parents. Interestingly, over the four-and-a-half years I used the basic recorder (no Facecam), only 17 parents declined their child's participation in the studies. Given the 90% plus consent form return rate, and the total number of children involved (in excess of 300), this number is very small. However, in 2016 and 2017 when the additional checkbox option was added to the consent form asking for permission to record using the Facecam, less than 40% of parents gave permission for this. While parents remained happy to allow audio and activity data to be recorded, they appeared less so with data that contained visually identifying information. The second added option was the capacity to activate and deactivate individual recorders via Wi-Fi using a smartphone app, potentially without the children knowing. While technically operational, this feature was never used in these studies nor evaluated by the ethics committee as it was considered susceptible to misuse, and arguably 'crossed the line' between ethical data collection and deception.

The pros and cons of using the recorder

The pros: data quality and authenticity

As stated earlier, the principal reason for using the display recorder was to enhance data authenticity. Referencing computer science research, Lynch defines authentic data as 'verifying claims that are associated with an object – in effect, verifying that an object is indeed what it claims to be, or what it is claimed to be' (2000, p. 37). Lynch's definition highlights the importance of *trustworthiness* – that is, that data as accurately as possible represents events in any given research scenario. Within the context of these studies, such an appraisal must consider the age of the children, their dynamic and mobile learning environment, the collaborative, learner-focused curriculum design, and the teachers' goals and purposes for technology use. Collecting data in large, mobile device-supported flexible learning spaces is fundamentally different to conventional classrooms, where physical objects such as fixed walls, desks, shelves, whiteboards and so on, more tightly define the research location. While the design of flexible learning spaces and tablet technology supports greater choice for children to work where they like, it presents major challenges for researchers wishing to capture comprehensive and authentic data reflective of activities across an entire space. Given these constraints, the display recorder was the only viable option available. However, appraising data authenticity from any method requires more than simply determining it was the only workable option. While the display recorder suited this environment and research purpose and yielded intimate and detailed information about the children's use of the apps and their interactions, problem solving and decision-making strategies, it could be argued that it does not capture learning influences from the wider environment. Although this may be true in terms of recording visual data about the macro-environment, the portability of the system does capture children's verbal interactions with others as they move around the space, providing interesting insights into behaviours such as peer tutoring, solution sharing and generating shared understanding of learning tasks.

The combination of recorded finger placement and audio can also provide valuable insights into how children share access to the device's interface while collaborating to solve a problem. This is very useful data that contributes significantly to understanding how these devices can support children's intra and inter-group collaborative practices. Additionally, the finger placement indication provides detailed information about the children's use of, and choices about, different scaffolds and cognitive tools embedded in the apps. It also provided interesting insights into which menus and options the children accessed and how often, their 'app smashing' behaviours, and added to understanding how they translated verbally stated intentions into physical actions.

While Facecam recording was possible, it was seldom used. Although parents' decisions relating to this were respected, its restricted use at times caused frustration. In some data where it was activated, additional, highly valuable information relating to the children's efforts and activities were revealed. For example, several recordings contained prolonged silences that, relying on audio and screen activity alone, could have been interpreted as the children being inactive or off-task. However, Facecam data indicated this wasn't necessarily the case, as often children were recorded gazing intently and for lengthy periods at the display, showing obvious signs of cognitive load as they tried to work out solutions (e.g. Figure 3.6).

The Facecam recorder also captured clusters of children working collaboratively together, augmenting finger placement, display and audio data, to provide a more complete picture of intra- and inter-group and app/device interaction. From a researcher's perspective, data of this detail and quality is critical to ensuring research validity, and robustness in the presentation and communication of data and conclusions. However, from a parent's perspective, such considerations can be outweighed by a perception – rightly or wrongly – that by allowing their child's face to be displayed in academic contexts such as journals or at conferences, they are potentially endangering their wellbeing or safety. There is little doubt that sensitivity to this has been whipped up in recent years by sensationalised media reporting, but to my knowledge no alleged adverse events have been traced back to the use of children's images as data in academic

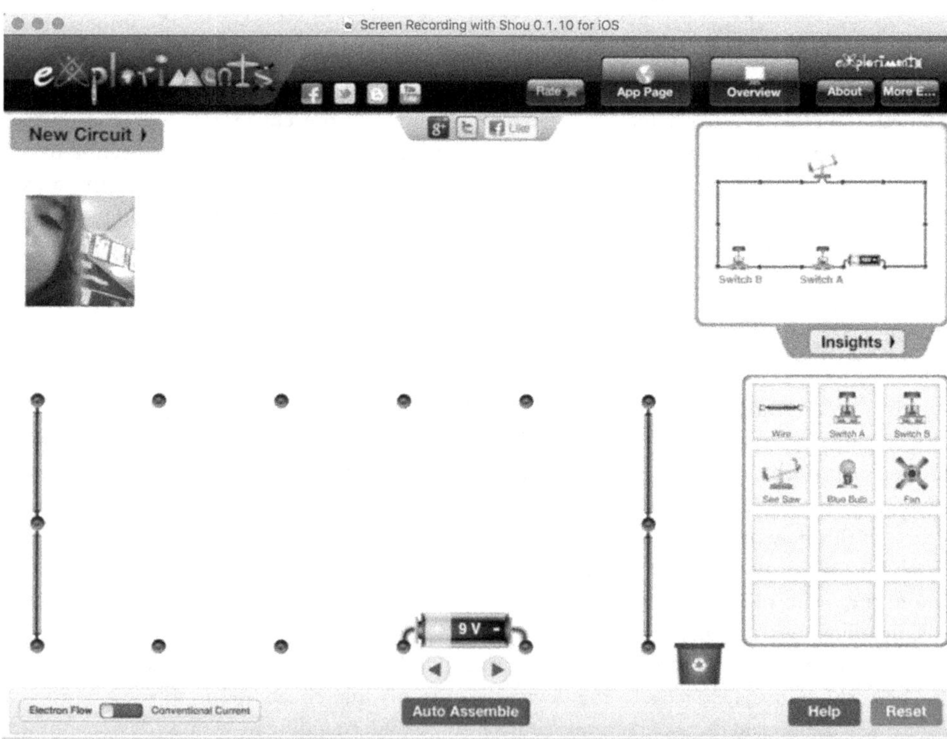

Figure 3.6 The Facecam captured children's lengthy (and often silent) deliberations as they tried to solve problems

publications or at conferences. While, of course, every effort should be taken to ensure the anonymity of children in any research, such as not including names or other specific identifying information, it does seem incongruous that in an era where parents seem happy to display their children publicly on social media, that there is continued resistance to the use of such valuable visual data for academic research purposes.

In summary, the invisibility of the recorder to the children undoubtedly supported the gathering of data that represented a 'warts and all' account of happenings, and yielded highly authentic and at times unique data, that, given the research context, arguably could not have been collected in any other way. However, there were also challenges and issues associated with its use that at worst mediated the benefit of having access to data of this nature.

The cons: challenges and issues

Apart from the technical design and installation difficulties described earlier, a number of challenges and issues arose during the studies relating to the recorder's use in the classroom. First, on-device display recordings consume a lot of storage capacity. The early trials of this recorder used 16GB iPads which, once the learning apps were installed, left very limited space for storage-hungry recordings. In practice, this limited most data sessions to single events of around 30–40 minutes, after which the recorded files needed to be downloaded to a laptop, before being erased from the device. Improvements to compression software and larger capacity iPads in more recent years has gone a long way to mitigating this issue, although video resolution and quality is often compromised in the quest for smaller file size. Regardless, care still needs to be taken to ensure sufficient storage space exists, especially if using smaller capacity devices, as all data is erased once capacity is reached.

Second, Apple's continual updating of their iOS meant the recorder, and the background iOS adjustments needed to run it, required ongoing modification, to the extent that it was no longer viable to continue development post iOS8 – given the imminent arrival of a native recorder in iOS11. However, while a native recorder is now available, early trials suggest its usefulness for classroom research is limited due to its *exceptionally* heavy demands on hardware and storage, its inability to operate on older devices and operational characteristics including shutting down when any protective cover is closed, or when the device goes into 'sleep' mode. The latter two scenarios are very common with young children, who regularly close their device's cover as they move around the classroom. While it is possible to prevent the device from entering sleep mode by adjusting the energy settings, this places considerable drain on the battery.

Third, while display recorders have an advantage of being able to capture data from many students engaged in the same task at the same time, no matter where they are, it also produces huge volumes of data, very quickly. While in itself this isn't necessarily an issue, these data need to be analysed, and depending on the approach taken and the support available, this can be an *exceedingly* time-consuming process. While the fine-grained analysis methods used in these studies may not be suitable for all research, considerable thought needs to be given in the research design stage to how data will be analysed, and how outcomes from the analysis will be reported and communicated. Experience using the recorder in these studies demonstrates that it is almost impossible to analyse all data it captures. Therefore, careful consideration must be given to how data is sampled for analysis purposes, so that research questions are responded to in a way that is robust, but achievable. In practice, this means selection criteria need to be generated that will provide a sufficient and appropriate dataset aligned with the focus, needs and methods of the study, but at the same time, are manageable. The analysis approach for this research used Studiocode that supported the extraction of rich and detailed information from data. However, the need to analyse multiple events or log data against several codes within the same clip meant each sample needed to be viewed three and sometimes four times. On average, analysing 45–50 minutes of display data in these studies could take between three and four hours.

Finally, display data suffers from the same issues as video data generally, when it comes to publishing research in more traditional academic journals. While a few journals are emerging that enable authors to hyperlink to 'live' video data, and a small number of others allow the uploading and sharing of short clips as supplementary materials, this capacity is usually limited to one or two examples. One of the main advantages of video is the ability to evidence multiple data 'streams' simultaneously – as illustrated previously in the discussion of convergence of finger placement indication, display, audio and Facecam data – to provide a more complete and holistic account of events. While, with appropriate permissions these data can be shared at conferences and presentations, valuable nuances are generally lost when authors need to distil video into a series of still screenshots with audio transcripts, to accommodate somewhat dated academic journal publication requirements. Notwithstanding the considerable time involved in doing this, an improved capacity to hyperlink to relevant video data straight from the text in online versions of journals, would enhance the researcher's capacity to fully communicate and validate interpretations, adding substantially to readers' meaning-making and the robustness of research findings and conclusions.

Conclusion

Although using display recording in educational research is not new, the advent of mobile devices and changes to school learning environment design has presented new challenges for researchers seeking to capture authentic and detailed data of children's interactions with apps (and each other), as they complete learning tasks. While the mobile solution described in this chapter proved effective for these studies, it may not be the case for all. Using a recorder with young children carries with it certain sensitivities and considerations that need to be taken into account on a case-by-case basis. While I was fortunate to gain the support of my ethics committee for using the recorder from a 'benefit vs risk' assessment, they insisted on well-defined procedures being in place relating to the handling of problematic data, rigid consent and assent procedures and disablement of the remote activation function. Despite these procedures being followed to the letter, it was mildly disturbing to note than some children did not appear to understand what the recorder did, or the type of data it collected about them and their actions. This realisation led to more intense initial assent procedures in latter studies, where the children were shown carefully selected samples of previous recordings, accompanied by an explanation of how the recorder worked. Despite this, it was still apparent in data that many either forgot about the recorder, didn't fully understand its operation or didn't care. Researchers using this system with young children should be mindful of these considerations, and not assume that because children have assented, that they fully understand what is going on.

Finally, while the ethics committee approved the Facecam capture function, interestingly the children's parents held the final word on its use through the majority declining permission to have their child's image recorded. Although frustrating from a researcher's perspective, given the heightened sensitivity (justified or not) around the recording and display of children's faces, parents' views must be respected. It may well be with the passage of time and the proliferation of such behaviours on social media, that both parents and universities may soften their stance somewhat on this issue, allowing the full richness of the interaction between multiple data streams presented in video, to be fully utilised for research purposes.

Notes

1 New Zealand uses a decile system based on the SES of the surrounding community, as a means of allocating base funding and resources. A full explanation can be found here (https://www.education.govt.nz/school/running-a-school/resourcing/operational-funding/school-decile-ratings/).

2 See McArthur, 2009 for an interesting discussion on the ethics of Milgram's studies (https://link-springer-com.simsrad.net.ocs.mq.edu.au/content/pdf/10.1007%2Fs11948-008-9083-4.pdf).

References

Adobe (2017) *Captivate*, computer program. www.adobe.com/au/products/captivate.html.

Barmby, P., Harries, T., Higgins, S. and Suggate, J. (2009) The array representation and primary children's understanding and reasoning in multiplication. *Educational Studies in Mathematics* 70 (3), 217–241.

Barns, L., Scutter, S. and Young, J. (2005) Using screen recording and compression software to support online learning. *Innovate: Journal of Online Education* 1 (5), 1–5.

Beach, P. and Willows, D. (2014) Investigating teachers' exploration of a professional development website: An innovative approach to understanding the factors that motivate teachers to use Internet-based resources. *Canadian Journal of Learning and Technology* 40 (3), 1–16.

Brennan, K. and Resnick, M. (2012) *New frameworks for studying and assessing the development of computational thinking*. Paper presented at AERA, Vancouver, BC. Retrieved 16 February 2018, http://web.media.mit.edu/~kbrennan/files/Brennan_Resnick_AERA2012_CT.pdf.

Burns, R. (2000) *Introduction to Research Methods* (4th edition). Longman, Frenchs Forest, NSW.

Cardinal Blue Developer (2018) *PicCollage* computer program. https://pic-collage.com/.

Chaney, B., Barry, A., Chaney, J., Stellefson, M. and Webb, M. (2013) Using screen video capture software to aide and inform cognitive interviewing. *Quality & Quantity* 47 (5), 2529–2537.

Christopher Thorne Productions (2012) *Mr Phonics*, computer program. https://itunes.apple.com/us/app/mr-thorne-does-phonics-letters-sounds-for-ipad/id431679830?mt=8.

Coghlan, M. (2011) *iPads – A game changer for education?* New Learning TAFE, SA. Retrieved 12 February 2018. www.slideshare.net/michaelc/ipads-a-game-changer-for-education.

Drumheller, K. and Lawler, G. (2011) Capture their attention: Capturing lessons using screen capture software. *College Teaching* 59 (2), 93–93.

Einarsdóttir, J. (2007) Research with children: Methodological and ethical challenges. *European Early Childhood Education Journal* 15 (2), 197–211.

Falloon, G.W. (2013) Young students using iPads: App design and content influences on their learning pathways. *Computers & Education* 68, 505–521.

Falloon, G.W. (2016) An analysis of young students' thinking when completing basic coding tasks using Scratch Jnr. on the iPad. *Journal of Computer-Assisted Learning* 32 (6), 576–593.

Falloon, G.W. and Khoo, E. (2014) Exploring young students' talk in iPad-supported collaborative learning environments. *Computers & Education* 77, 13–28.

Flewitt, R. (2005) Conducting research with young children: Some ethical considerations. *Economic & Social Research Council Special Education*, 1–14. Retrieved 21 February 2018. http://oro.open.ac.uk/2720/2/Flewitt(1).pdf.

Imler, B. and Eichelberger, M. (2011) Using screen capture to study user research Behaviour. *Library Hitec* 29 (3), 446–454.

Krathwohl, D.R. (2002) A revision of bloom's taxonomy: An overview. *Theory Into Practice* 41 (4), 212–225.

Kuuskorpi, M., Finland, K. and González, N. (2011) The future of the physical learning environment: School facilities that support the user. *CELE Exchange 2011/11*. Retrieved 26 February 2018. www.oecd.org/education/innovation-education/centreforeffectivelearningenvironmentscele/49167890.pdf.

Lynch, C. (2000) Authenticity and integrity in the digital environment: An exploratory analysis of the central role of trust. *Authenticity in a Digital Environment*, Council on Library and Information Resources, Washington, DC.

Macroplant (2016) *iExplorer file transfer application*. https://macroplant.com/iexplorer Retrieved 21 February 2018.

McArthur, D. (2009) Good ethics can sometimes mean better science: Research ethics and the Milgram experiments. *Science and Engineering Ethics* 15 (1), 69–79.

Melhuish, K. and Falloon, G.W. (2010) Looking to the future: M-learning with the iPad. *Computers in New Zealand Schools* 22 (3), 1–16.

Mercer, N. (1994) The quality of talk in children's joint activity at the computer. *Journal of Computer-Assisted Learning* 10 (1), 24–32.

Notion Developer (2017) *Popplet* computer program. http://popplet.com/.

OECD (2017) *The OECD handbook for innovative learning environments*. OECD Publications, Paris. Retrieved 1 March 2018. http://dx.doi.org/9789264277274-en.

Osborne, R. (1983) Towards modifying children's ideas about electric current. *Research in Science and Technological Education* 1 (1), 73–82.

Polished Play LLC (2017) *Puppetpals* computer program. www.polishedplay.com/.

Raído, V. (2013) Using screen recording as a diagnostic tool in early process-oriented translator training. In: Kiraly, D., Hansen-Schirra, S. and Maksymski, K. (eds.) *New prospects and perspectives for educating language mediators*. Narr Francke Attempto Verlag GmbH & Co, Tübingen, Germany, 121–138.

Séror, J. (2012) Show me! Enhanced feedback through screencasting technology. *TESL Canada Journal* 30 (1), 104–116.

Shipstone, D.M. (1984) A study of children's understanding of electricity in simple DC circuits. *European Journal of Science Education* 6 (2), 185–198.

Silva, M. (2012) Camtasia in the classroom: Student attitudes and preferences for video commentary or Microsoft Word comments during the revision process. *Computers and Composition* 29, 1–22.

Tang, J., Liu, S., Muller, M., Lin, J. and Drews, C. (2006) *Unobtrusive but Invasive: Using screen recording to collect field data on computer-mediated interaction', CSCW '06*. Retrieved 1 March 2018. http://citeseerx.ist.psu.edu/viewdoc/download;jsessionid=E54DE8D5A78B60EED2BDF51C9E4244ED?doi=10.1.1.109.7678&rep=rep1&type=pdf.

Techsmith (2017a) *Camtasia*, computer program. www.techsmith.com/store/camtasia?gclid=EAIaIQobChMIgIuLhv- L1wIVAkCGCh1GqQI_EAAYASAAEgIdTPD_BwE.

Techsmith (2017b) *Snagit*, computer program. www.techsmith.com/screen-capture.html.

Xu, C. and Ding, Y. (2014) An exploration study of pauses in computer-assisted EFL writing. *Language, Learning and Technology* 18 (3), 80–96.

Zhang, M. (2013) Prompts-based scaffolding for online inquiry: Design intentions and classroom realities. *Educational Technology and Society* 16 (3), 140–151.

Zhang, M. and Quintana, C. (2012) Scaffolding strategies for supporting middle school students' online inquiry processes. *Computers & Education* 58, 181–196.

PART II

Studies answering ontological questions

4

"TALK INTO MY GOPRO, I'M MAKING A MOVIE!"

Using digital ethnographic methods to explore children's sociomaterial experiences in the woods

Debra Harwood and Diane R. Collier

In a two-year study of preschoolers' intra-actions in a nature-based program in Canada (forest school), children were invited to wear GoPro cameras to help researchers explore experiences as they unfolded within the forest. Our title for the chapter was inspired by Troy (pseudonym), one of our young contributors to the study who favored stating, "Talk into my GoPro, I'm making a movie!" to anyone or any matter he encountered in the woods while wearing a GoPro camera. As researchers, we wanted to explore sociomaterial entanglements (Lenz Taguchi, 2010), while potentially also offering insight into the ways in which children could participate as co-authors of video methods and data generation processes, and a means of decentering the researcher. This chapter discusses our methodological choices and theorizing as we aimed to "disrupt the anthro-, socio-, and logocentric readings" of data (Sellers, 2013, p. 161) by embracing data collection tools that utilized 21st century digital technologies. Here, we focus on the GoPro as one such tool as we discuss several data fragments of the child-matter social, material, and discursive encounters, to highlight the possibilities of reading data otherwise. This chapter discusses some of our methodological choices and theorizes about what visual data – in this case video – offer. In the sections that follow, we describe the research project and how new materialism might allow us to think about the GoPro camera as a tool and what it affords, and then present our insights about the contributions of children, the GoPro camera, and decentered researchers in a forest school research study.

We start the paper with this provocation, a moment to think about what visuals might offer, an opportunity to make explicit some of the many decisions that researchers make when representing data. Unable to fully recreate this data in a flat print format, we present you with several still images from one child's GoPro video (chest-mounted) footage (Figure 4.1) and ask: What do you see? What do you think is happening? What can you not see? How does the visual data stand alone and what does it offer?

Perhaps you note the unusual angle of the picture showing a downward vantage point, the snow and the trees, the clear crisp day, the researcher (adult) standing below the camera wearer, and the sense of motion forward implied by the foot pointing forward in the first frame. You might also wonder what else is not depicted, the purpose and contents of the wagon in the

Figure 4.1 Still images of child's GoPro video

background of the first frame, the identity of the camera wearer, and the sounds or feel of the snowy woods. Then you might start to ponder why these images were selected over others, and what was contained in the video footage that is not replicated in these still images. You may have a bit of a sense of 'being there' (Marcus, 1995; Watson, 1999) and query if you are missing something important.

It is an exercise in reflexivity on our part, to think about what attracts our interest, the questions we have for our research, and how we select certain data for further elaboration and analysis, and what we can make of this data. For many of us, our academic training and discourse focuses on print text, and the visuals, though evocative, seem to tell a partial story. We propose, like many others have (e.g., Lather, 2007; Jackson & Mazzei, 2012; Pillow, 2003) that research and representation are always, and necessarily partial. As with Canton and Hackett (see this volume) we are offering a critique of data as static, video as naïve empiricism, and their chapter discusses the importance of examining the intersection of the agency of the camera and the video data. They emphasize the resultant emotions their videos evoke as well as the intensity and affects. Our distinct area of focus and examination of video is directly related to the way it is worn on the child's body, the experience of the viewer, and the perspectives these offer, when worn in an outdoor environment.

Researcher narrative

Researchers create narratives from the data they see as relevant and illuminating. Following this paragraph is a narrative that appears to be much more complete than the images we presented at the beginning. In a style common to the field of ethnographic research, we tell a chronological and cohesive narrative, from the researcher's perspective.[1] Debra was there in the woods while the video was being recorded by the child, Mike (pseudonym). Debra also later engaged in multiple viewings of the video footage, sometimes with the children and at other times with the second author, Diane.

> *Mike, a 3-year-old boy, wears the GoPro on a sunny, wintry day of the forest school program. He races about the forest in his typical fashion bursting with ideas on what the children should play and how to go about organizing the play. His view of the forest is captured from all angles throughout the morning and often on the video he flops to the ground, flailing his arms and legs, calling out things like, "who wants to build a snowman?" (Frame A–Figure 4.2). Later, as chasing games like hide-and-seek occupy all the children, Mike ducks underneath the climbing tree where a small den is located. He concentrates on rubbing and cracking blocks of frozen snow*

Frame A: Mike's Perspective | Frame B: Slowing of Mike's Heartbeat | Frame C: Mike's View from the Tree

Figure 4.2 Mike's GoPro video data fragments

> *together, banging them together as he sits (Frame B). The only sound on the video is his heavy breathing and pounding heartbeat. As he plays with the frozen snow his breath and heartbeat slows to a more rhythmic and slower pace. Again, much later in the video Mike is climbing the tree, with the researcher, Debra, nearby. Mike's body and camera scrape along the trunk as he negotiates the route to balance across the branch that provides a place to sit. He narrates aloud instructions on how to climb then settles in the familiar spot. He says, "do you know what I can see from here?" Debra smiles up at him blinking in the sunlight, "what do you see?" He replies, "my grandma's apartment building, down that hill, see that brown building?"*
>
> *Researcher's Video Summary*

As you are reading, you might feel much more satisfied by the narrative provided by the researcher, including the captions and the descriptions that are provided. Indeed, the researcher had access to the recorded video, much more than the three images shared at the beginning. What is presented appears to be a comprehensive retelling. However, the words, and the linear narrative told, also may take away from what might be experienced when looking at the photographs only or at the video footage.

The original presentation of the three screenshots from GoPro footage shot by Mike are worth considering though, if only as a way to shift one's perspective and usual retelling. As screenshots – and only three of them – they offer a fragmented representation; we cannot look to the right or the left and there is no cohesive story. The gaps are obvious. At the same time, the fragments offer a relational physical, material, visual perspective that the retelling does not. When we add the researcher's' insights from viewing the video, an extra dimension is added but maybe also something is lost, or becomes less visible.

At first glance at the still shots, a "habitual anthropocentric style of seeing" (Hultman & Lenz Taguchi, 2010, p. 527) suggests that one would be drawn to Mike's downward glance at his foot, his upper leg as he sits on the forest trail. Perhaps, the snow on the ground and the path forward leading to trees and wagon serve as the backdrop to his foot, parts of his body, his mittens that fill the frame. To the left, and somewhat obscured by the sun's rays, stands another child. If one views the video (https://vimeo.com/234563859), you can hear Mike's quickly beating, loud heart as he moves, the rustle of the snow and ice on the ground. The video offers a sense of perspective that is heightened by shadows on the trees and Mike's outward attention to the edge of the forest and the horizon. Thus, the video seems to offer what Hultman and Lenz Taguchi (2010) refer to as a *relational materialist* approach, the idea that "*non*-human forces are equally at play and work as constitutive factors in children's learning and becomings" (p. 527). When Author 2 viewed the video, without having 'been there' or reading the field notes, her experience of the GoPro world felt non-representational and reactive in the way that Deleuze and Guattari (1987) talk about 'lines of flight', trajectories that emanate from ongoing events and happenings. Conceptually, Deleuze and Guattari (1987) use 'lines of flight' and 'lines of becoming' as a means of disrupting ideas of life and thoughts as a series of rational and predictable static moments. Life, organisms, or any concept are made up of non-linear connections and endless transformations are possible. In this example, sounds and images lead to a viewer/listener response that may be evocative, embodied, non-linear, and unpredictable. In this way events, actions, and responses are rhizomatic, rather than hierarchical, representational, or linear.

The very nature of the GoPro camera provides multiple lines of flights and rhizomatic moments. The shakiness of the camera, the child's movements, voices echoing in the woods, snowflakes flitting in the wind, rustling of snowsuits, and so on generate multiple lines. Here, we pay attention to the human-non-human encounters that are vividly depicted in sensorial ways, offering *other ways of seeing* within research. There was no easy narrative to be told from what was seen and heard, the 'lines of flight' are unpredictable, encounters in the woods are enmeshed, inter-connected, with co-mingling matter. Lenz Taguchi (2010) refers to these kinds of encounters, and these kinds of explanations of these encounters as "waves of diffractions without borders – blurred enganglements" (p. 69).

The research project

Over the course of the first two years of the project, we accompanied two groups of young children and their two teachers into the woods on a university campus. The 15 children (eight children in year one and seven children in year two of the project) all ranged in age from 3 to 5 years, and spent two mornings each week from September to June in a specific wooded and natural area they and their teachers called 'a forest school'. Although sharing many qualities with other forest schools, we do not use the term 'Forest School' prevalently in the UK, which suggests very specific qualities and membership in a Forest School Association (see www.forestschoolassociation.org/what-is-forest-school/). The outdoor educational program took place in a wooded area that was uncultivated, 'wild' (Mawson, 2014, p. 516), in the sense that the space was part of an old Carolina growth forest that surrounded the university campus (Bruce Trail Conservancy, 2011). The children and teachers played within this unique biosphere of diverse trees and plants, animals, insects, and geology; a woodland the Anishinaabe and Haudenosaunee traditional peoples have lived and hunted upon for 10,000 or more years. The land itself, its history, stories, and life were very much part of the children and adults' experiences in the woods, as the early childhood program aimed to foster a pedagogy of living relationally with/alongside all the matter of the forest (Taylor & Pacini-Ketchabaw, 2015).

Mike is one of the participants in our digital ethnographic study of children, educators, material entanglements in a forest school program. As mentioned, Mike was three years old when he and his friends, two educators, and university researchers first ventured into the woods to enact an early child education program the children dubbed 'a forest school'. The program and research documents young children's sociomaterial experiences in the forest, paying close attention to the intra-actions between and amongst all matter, both human and more-than-human (Barad, 2007; Haraway, 2001; Lenz Taguchi, 2010). The child, the playthings, the rock, stick, and teacher all matter. What is significant is the 'in-between' (Lenz Taguchi, 2010), the interdependence and intertwined entanglements of agents implicated in the processes of 'becoming-with' the world (Haraway, 2008, p. 4). Barad (2007) writes, "existence is not an individual affair, individuals do not preexist their intractions: rather, individuals emerge through and as part of their entangled intra-relating" (p. ix). Like other matter, humans are also matter, part of this entangled world, where the subject and object are inseparable (Barad, 2007; Lenz Taguchi, 2010). We cannot know the world by sitting outside the world. New methodologies are called upon when "we are a part of that nature that we seek to understand" (Barad, 2007, p. 67). In the next section, we expand upon our notion of how new methodologies and tools might address this desire to understand something new.

Theoretical framing and methods

'The material turn', 'material feminisms', a 'post humanist turn', a 'new empiricism', and even a 'new settlement' (Alaimo & Hekman 2008) inform the research we do. As qualitative-moving-toward-post-qualitative researchers, we are aware of how our liberal, humanist training as researchers is ever present. We recognize that as researchers our *habits of seeing* (Hultman & Lenz Taguchi, 2010) are well ingrained within humanist traditions, and we are often drawn to the child. Certainly, our scan of the still frames and the researcher's notes highlight the human-centrism of the data fragment. What if we were to look differently, and engage in what Hultman and Lenz Taguchi refer to as a "different style of seeing and thinking in terms of a *diffractive seeing* and *nomadic thinking*" (p. 527)? We have asked ourselves what methodologies and tools might facilitate this process and if our use of the GoPro camera help unsettle our usual foci and allow for something new to emerge.

Richardson-Ngwenya (2014), when referencing her field research in the sugar sector of Barbados, utilized video to highlight the complexities of the materials involved, yet she stated, "there was nothing especially 'posthumanist about these methods'" (p. 295). Certainly, our methods could easily be described as ethnographic and we also acknowledge that all life is dynamic and obscure; therefore we "cannot claim to know or fix any such inherent quality" (Richardson-Ngwenya, 2014, p. 294). As St. Pierre (2011) points out, the challenge within the 'post-era' (i.e., post-colonial, post-critical, post-humanist, post-structural, post-feminist, post-modern, etc.) is that an alternative research methodology does not exist, there is not "a recipe, an outline, a structure for post-qualitative research" (p. 613) and she proposes "post inquiry to remain unstable as we create different articulations, assemblages, becomings, mash-ups of inquiry given the entanglement that emerges in our different research projects" (p. 623). We remain unresolved about how to speak of methodology in this 'post-era' and we are keenly aware of the importance of speakers to practitioners and academics alike.

Although our research methodology was situated within a qualitative paradigm, we mashed together methodological ideas from ethnography (Denzin & Lincoln, 2011; Madison, 2011), participatory ethnography (Clark, 2010; Holland et al., 2010), relational materialism (Hultman & Lenz Taguchi, 2010; Lenz Taguchi, 2011), and visual/sensual ethnography (Mitchell, 2011; Pink, 2007; Rose, 2012). This translated into multiple methods and tools to help us focus on 'being there' (Watson, 1999) in the woods. While we allude to and are interested in new materialist reframings, this paper is also concerned with the practicalities of what the GoPro (visual methods) might contribute and constrain. We are in the process of finding ways to challenge the primacy of language as the only starting point for analysis, and set out to shift and find methods/tools to address the asymmetry and value placed upon human subjects rather than the material or natural world.

Using visuals and video methods

When engaging in qualitative and ethnographic research, methods such as observing and taking field notes, audio-recording, and photographing artifacts and events have become commonplace. With new digital tools, such as digital audio and video recorders, iPads and iPad apps, data generation has become easier, in some ways, and also, importantly, easier for research participants and researchers alike to operate (Brown et al., 2008; Chalfen, 2014). Visual methods have always been part of anthropological and ethnographic research, although in the writing, typically the visuals become secondary to written words, and visual tools are often considered neutral within the research process (Lipponen et al., 2016). Interpretive analysis leads to the ascription of particular meanings to the visuals that are used in this work. A range of visual methods for generating data have been used by researchers in education and in the social sciences (e.g., photographs, drawings, video making) and, sometimes, the focus has been on the collection of visual data initiated by the children (e.g., Clark, 2010; Einarsdottir 2014; Stirling & Yamada-Rice, 2015).

From 8mm film cameras to camcorders to video recorders that can be used from a range of digital devices, the access to film or video making has expanded in the past decade. GoPro cameras, worn on the center of one's chest or head, have been widely used in outdoor sports, especially to provide viewers with access to activities and places that they might never do or visit. Video footage allows the viewer to gain insight into experiences and also highlights, visually, aspects such as speed, movement, framing, sound, and the material elements captured by the wearer. Early response to video use was enthusiastic and exciting, and to some extent it was suggested that video could be used to experience or to visualize things that one could not normally experience on one's own (Brown et al., 2008). One might expect that when children wear the GoPro they generate video data that might represent a truth, a complete copy of events as they unfolded, that adults/researchers/educators might not normally have access to. This need for and promise of authenticity can never be realized as each angle, each event, each perspective is always partial and a particular framing. Another issue that is part of this project is when and how much video data is collected and when and how much video data is analyzed, and how that analysis is done.

Analysis of visual data

The amount of data generated, when collecting video, is massive, and one needs a focused and specific strategy to deal with this kind of analysis (Chalfen, 2014). At the same time that there are challenges, we see video as an important method and a way to explore new perspectives or points of view.

The GoPro as data generation tool

So, what might a tool such as the GoPro video camera offer? We hoped the camera would provoke ways of "facilitating and extending ways and means of seeing" (Chalfen, 2014, p. 300), insights into the children's sociomaterial interactions as well as their physical, visceral, and emotional responses within the woods by "recording comprehensive, real-time activities, which capture the dramatic alongside the mundane without privileging either" (Brown et al., 2008, p. 8). Certainly, the GoPro camera and video invites what Whatmore (2006) describes as a need to supplement more humanist methods that rely on generating talk and text (p. 606). Moreover, as our research project continues to evolve, as well as our own thinking and analysis, the GoPro affords a potential means to attend to an array of "senses, dispositions, capabilities and potentialities of all manner of social objects and forces assembled through, and involved in, the co-fabrication of socio-material worlds" (Whatmore, 2006, p. 604). Certainly, our work with the GoPro camera and method has been experimental and evocative; helpful in promoting an "understanding of how matter comes to matter" (Barad, 2003, p. 801). The GoPro videos and analysis helps us with this understanding, the child's panning, focusing, videotaping as a co-author of their own experiences and relations with sticks, leaves, rain, rocks, friends, and educators.

Video data research presents a series of issues. In this project, the GoPro did offer researchers (and educators) a small window into the world of the forest; insight into the 'matter that matters' (Barad, 2003), what interested the children, materials that excited and energized, and the ecology of who and what interactions impacted this world. The children are drawn to the materials of the forest; rocks, sticks, trees, snow, and ice invite them to enmesh their bodies with experiences of rolling, rubbing, mashing, shattering, and so on. Importantly, we highlight an environmental-reciprocal relationship (Pink, 2011) as the children act upon the environment and the environment acts to change the child. The GoPro helps to heighten one's sensitivity to the materials of the forest, there is a quietness and vastness of the woods, a visceral viewing without interpretation and a sensory complexity that draws the researcher in. Watching the GoPro video inevitably takes the child out of the center, as the viewer's gaze is drawn to multiple sights and sounds.

Child's role, researcher positioning, and ethical issues

Our thinking and research in the forest with children has led us to make claims that lead to suggestions or insights for those working with GoPro video data, and for ourselves. In the section that follows, we discuss the practical implications of children wearing video cameras and thereby acting as co-authors of the generated data, the sociomaterial entanglements and offerings of video tools, and the ways in which the researcher may be decentered in the process, thereby offering new vantage points and working towards an ethical research practice.

Practicalities of inviting children to co-author video data

Each child was invited to wear the GoPro camera one morning of their forest school program (with the option to wear the camera again if so desired). The GoPro camera was first made available for the children to handle and examine as the researcher explained how the camera could film a 'movie' of their day in the forest. Each facet of the camera was discussed: the layers of protection surrounding the camera, the small rubber waterproof casing, the battery, the lens, and general care for the camera. Author 1 modeled wearing the camera and different scenarios that would impede filming (e.g., laying onto one's stomach, clothing or snow covering the lens, etc.). The children were informed that the camera would record continuously once the 'on' button was pushed, and a flashing red light at the front of the camera indicated that recording was occurring (if the flashing stopped this marked that the battery needed changing). The camera wearer was invited to push the record button and other children were asked to check the red recording light. The children became very adept at initiating recording as well as informing the researcher that the battery needed changing. Children chose whether to participate on any specific day, as well as how long they wished to wear the camera. Most children wore the camera for two to three hours on their chosen day, and all the children in year one requested a second turn. The GoPro camera weighed approximately 150 grams and was worn with a child-sized chest harness.

All GoPro video recording occurred within a study that was bounded in very specific ways: one focus of the study was on children and their educators' sociomaterial experiences within a forest school program. The fieldwork was conducted by one of the authors and various research assistants between 2015–2017, and children who were registered in the outdoor program participated if consent was also granted by their parents. The children also exerted their individual choices in terms of participating in all aspects, including the videotaping with the GoPro. The children became what Brown et al. (2008) describe as "co-authors in the creation of the audio-visual representation" (p. 5) by actively panning and narrating storylines, and instructing the researcher on embedding titles, credits, and music into the vignettes shared with parents.

After filming, a researcher crafted a short vignette of the child's GoPro video to be shared with the child and his/her family. Each video was three to seven minutes in length and comprised short vignettes of the child's day in the forest. These vignettes of GoPro video were generally selected with a time sampling method, so that each video contained snippets of the beginning journey to the forest (one minute of video), midway through (three to five minutes of varied forest play), and the trek out of the forest (one minute of video). These short vignettes served as a conduit between children, the forest, and families, as well as for reporting purposes. For example, we engaged the children in video-simulated accounts (Theobald, 2011) of the GoPro videos, focusing on the ways in which the children's bodies, senses, memories, responses, and conversations were provoked by viewing their interactions with the human and non-human world of the forest. This represented a less developed fragment of the research and thus we have not discussed it at length here in this chapter. Nonetheless, in research with young children, the viewing of GoPro videos might offer other additionally 'provocative' and different ways of generating data; "data that were not visible and that disrupted linearity, consciousness, and the mind/body dichotomy" (St. Pierre, 2011, p. 621).

Ways of knowing through a GoPro view of children's sociomaterial entanglements

The GoPro videos provided some insight into what was important within children's worlds and their entanglements with the more-than-human materials in the forest. Potentially, researchers may be invited "to think more carefully about what children are able to, and may choose, to make visible when invited to use video cameras" (Bird, Colliver & Edwards, 2014, p. 1753). Additionally, we propose that the GoPro videos helped us, as researchers, to think differently or pay closer attention to all the parts in motion (Somerville, 2016). Like Elwick (2015), we pay attention to the "perceptual-sensory experience created as digital images and viewers 'come into being' with one another" (p. 324). Multiple viewings of a short clip from Flora's GoPro video (https://vimeo.com/230511705) helps to brings us beyond her words as she narrates her climb, and we come to view the snow, sense the grooves in the log, hear the ice scraping sounds, and see snow/ice pellets falling onto her mittens. It is through this close viewing of Flora's world that we come to understand a small part of the embodiment, sensory, kinaesthetic, and emotionality of the entanglement (Brown et al., 2008), the inseparability of the child and matter, the encounter between researcher and the site of the image (Rose, 2012, p. 27). Somerville (2016) refers to Barad (2003, p. 821):

> Meaning is not seen as a property of individual words or groups of words but is an ongoing performance of the world in its differential intelligibility. It is the intra-action of these elements through which part of the world becomes determinately bounded and propertied in its emergent intelligibility to another part of the world. The video (per)forms the agential cut through which entities temporarily come into existence.
>
> *(p. 11)*

Perhaps, the allure of the GoPro video is that it offers what MacLure (2013) described as data that 'glows', data that defies explanation, a fragment that "starts to glimmer, gathering our attention because it resists analysis, refuses to render up its meaning" (p. 661). Influenced by Deleuze's logic of sense, MacLure resists framing language as polarized, neither discourse or matter, opting instead to embrace the 'wild', non-representational aspects of language that Deleuze (2004) ascribes. The descriptive language we have attached to our methods and analyses of these videos seems inadequate, and the 'glow' of the woods is often elusive. It is difficult to capture the essence of the snow-mittens-ice-log-Flora entanglements within a transcription of the video. Yet, the intra-activity (Barad, 2007) of the material world and children (and adults) is important, and the human child is somewhat decentered in the way in which the GoPro captures video.

Looking upon the video, the view of the child's body is incomplete where we might see an arm or a foot or a leg for example, and as we have just suggested, perhaps this helps to hone one's attention on the snow, mittens, ice, and log. The video captures much more than a 2D photo – you can really sense what's going on, even the shakiness – almost as if you are in motion with the child. The spotlight shifts from a sole focus of the child to include the matter of the woods, whereby these intra-actions of log, child, ice, snow, and so on compose reality; "reality [that] is composed not of things-in-themselves or things-behind-phenomena but things-in-phenomena" (Barad, 2007, p. 140). Perhaps, we are better able to focus on the idea of the child as becoming or emerging through their intra-actions with everything (Lenz Taguchi, 2010). In the end, we feel that we are indeed interested in young children and how they engage with the world and others. Returning to our video, Flora is not separate from the snow, ice, mittens, tree; rather the matter acts upon and alongside Flora as she climbs. The snow and ice slow her climb as she lowers herself to a crawling position, gripping tighter to the tree. The snow is grounded into the folds of the tree. The viewer sways along with Flora's body as she stands, muscles becoming taught to maintain her balance. The sound of the ice pellets landing on her mittens cause her to pause and comment 'wow'. Human existence is not separate from the world. Rather, the forces of the tree, snow, ice, and so on overlap and intra-act with the child's own forces in what Deleuze and Guattari (1987) refer to as *assemblages* (p. 8), an aggregation or multiplicity of bodies and matter (both human and more-than-human). Perhaps, as Hultman and Lenz Taguchi suggest, methodological implications are evident "if we understand ourselves as emerging from our co-existence with the world" (p. 534).

Decentering the researcher

> *The children are engaged in a type of rescue dramatic play on the icy hill slope of the forest area [Figure 4.3]. Troy flails his body on the ground calling out to his friend Adam (the GoPro operator) to help save him. Adam retrieves various long sticks and holds them out to his friend from the safety of the edge of the path where there are more leaves and rocks that provide traction.*

Figure 4.3 GoPro video clips of icy hill play

> *Adam can't pull the weight of his friend as they call to each other "help me, help me, I can't". Enya's help is enlisted as she tries to haul Troy up the hill. Author1 is also watching the action, capturing it on camera film. Throughout the play, the three children slip and slide, falling often on the icy hill. Author 1 occasionally offers commentary to the action, "now everyone needs rescue".*
>
> *Researcher's video summary*

The GoPro camera as a research tool also offers a potential means of decentering the researcher and the anthropocentric lens. Albeit, "the video is not data" (Erickson, 2006, p. 177) and therefore can only represent a "partial semblance of reality", a reality that can never be truly "possessed or seized" (Plowman & Stephen, 2008, p. 547). Erickson (2006) further proposes that video data "is a resource for data construction, an information source containing potential data out of which actual data must be defined and searched for" (p. 178). Undoubtedly, as participant observers in this study, we were drawn to specific activities or events as they unfolded (as in Figure 4.3). The field notes and video summaries also reflected certain biases or researcher interpretations (e.g., disproportionate amount of observation/notes on the boys). The images and researcher's notes were often viewed as representational, a portrayal of reality, what happened on the icy hill. Yet, we wanted to *see the data differently*. The GoPro camera helped slow this process, as we read the videos multiple times, self-reflected and co-reflected, revisiting notions of Author 1's subjectivity within the videos. Author 1 was both the data collector, and the subject of research, appearing in the children's videos. Perhaps this duality helps to disrupt the literal interpretation of the videos, fostering an invitation of *seeing differently*. As Hultman and Lenz Taguchi (2010) discuss, it is not a literal taken-for-granted reading of the data (in their case photographs) that is important, but rather diffractive reading, becoming one-with and being affected by the data, that helps us to see differently. Thus, the GoPro video was not a "realist matter of disembodied objectivity – a view from nowhere and no when by no one in particular" (Erickson, 2006, p. 179). Rather, installing oneself in the videos that we have included in the chapter is a decentering experience, where one becomes attuned to the sounds, sights, aesthetics of materials and place, where matter becomes intelligible to all parts of the world (Barad, 2007).

What does the GoPro offer in *seeing* the icy hill data differently? Certainly, the ice, the hill, the sticks were entangled with the children's bodies. Notwithstanding the importance of these entanglements and the role of matter in children's lives, here we use the data fragment to highlight the importance of decentering of the researcher. Alongside the children, the researcher is absorbed into the world of the ice, cold, wind. The ice play evolved organically as an interaction between the children and the winter landscape. As a member of this forest school community, Author 1 was embedded within the rituals and rhythms of the forest school, at times joining the play, or watching, interpreting, or commenting as it unfolded. Yet, often as a researcher the adult focus was centered on the more obvious physical actions or utterances of one particular child at a specific moment in time. The researcher as the knowing subject, the child (and matter) the object (Hultman & Lenz Taguchi, 2010). And certainly, it is difficult to escape the 'I' in research (St. Pierre, 2011, p. 619) even when embracing ontologies of new materialism. Similarly, we are always fixing something that is in motion when we translate children's movements and sounds to written words, and this vibrancy can be lost (Hackett & Yamada-Rice, 2015).

In her research of children in a creek, Somerville (2016) describes, "as the human I of the researcher, I absorb and am absorbed into sounds and senses of the watery world of the creek. Responding viscerally, I record what I am attracted to without prior intention or 'method'" (p. 1167). In the icy hill play noted previously, Author 1 was also drawn to the more dramatic flailing and shouts from Troy, capturing these with a view of the play through the camera lens and later transcribed anecdotal notes. Much of the nuanced, complex, and shifting relations within the children's play and the force assembled by the ice is overlooked by the researcher in the moment, and often the "sensory embodied ways of knowing and navigating complex environments" (Pink, 2011, p. 354) can be missed.

Perhaps an advantage of the GoPro is that it offers another and more continuous perspective, the snowy ground level view of the tugging, pulling, hoisting of Troy, the grunts, quickened heartbeat, scraping of the stick, bodies, and ice, the complex negotiations between ice, stick, child as they jostle, slide, laugh, and banter. The video offered an opportunity for all to re-immerse themselves into the ice play as a different type of experience, an "understanding (of) the world from within and as part of it" (Barad, 2007, p. 88). Somerville (2016) describes images as offering detailed aspects, a sensorial depth and flow of materiality. In the GoPro videos, we also began to see the *non*-human forces that were equally at play, and work as constitutive factors in children's learning and becomings.

Insights for educators and researchers wanting to use video methods

In this research, video methods were used to document children's sociomaterial experiences in the woods. We have described three insights that the use of GoPro offered: (1) practical implications and affordances of using this tool; (2) social and material ways of knowing that are opened up through entanglements in the forest; and (3) ways that this approach might allow for some decentering of the researcher.

Yet, there are limits of the tool and the GoPro should never be considered the panacea for data generation. Engaging in analysis in this way allowed us to move away – if only for a moment – from chronological and affirming narratives that do not conjure new understandings. When working with video data, the volume and complexity can become overwhelming, and there seems to be no analysis tool that fully matches nonrepresentations/material framings of data. We are choosing to see this as both a challenge and an opportunity. Having no template to follow, we are working towards creating new methods and look forward to the ways in which multiple perspectives might be embraced and considered. These suggestions originate from our own experiences and insights from the research project about wearing the GoPro, video review processes, sampling of video data, and designing research and analyzing data.

Children should choose if and when they want to wear the GoPro. We suggest that it is important to respect requests to remove the GoPro and stay alert to ways in which it might impede children's usual movement and interactions. Educators and researchers might choose to wear the GoPro to gain additional insights. Consider in advance how viewing of videos might occur. Children can view videos alone or in small groups. You may want to record these interactions. Parents or educators and children can review them together and you may wish to observe to see if viewing starts to impact the use of GoPro in the field.

In terms of samples, we suggest choosing manageable excerpts from longer videos – and you may wish to sample from beginning, middle, and ends of longer videos. These are useful for sharing with others/families. You might program the GoPro to take still shots at regular intervals and then look to see what stories these still shots tell. In advance, you will want to decide how often you will collect video. Will you collect video every day? Every hour? Think about how you will view and interpret prior to beginning and revisit regularly. Common methods such as field notes may help you to decide what video data is most relevant.

When you are thinking about design and analysis, consider how your theories of learning will influence the data you generate and analyze. If children are seen as co-researchers, do they help generate questions? Do they make decisions about tool use? Are they involved in both viewing and interpreting data? Multiple perspectives from analysis are helpful. Include those who were in the field but also engage in conversations from educators and researchers who might lend insights from viewing the video data only.

Note

1 The field researcher, Debra (Author 1), was on site and in the forest with the children, while Author 2, Diane, participated in viewing and analyzing video footage and generated data. Throughout the chapter the term 'researcher' refers to Debra.

References

Alaimo, S. and Hekman, S., eds. (2008) *Material feminisms*. Bloomington, IN: Indiana University Press.

Barad, K. (2003) Posthumanist performativity: Toward an understanding of how matter comes to matter. *Signs* 28, 801–832.

Barad, K. (2007) *Meeting the universe halfway: Quantum physics and the entanglement of matter and meaning*. Durham, NC: Duke University Press.

Bird, J., Colliver, Y. and Edwards, S. (2014) The camera is not a methodology: Towards a framework for understanding young children's use of video cameras. *Early Child Development and Care* 184, 1741–1756.

Brown, K.M., Dilley, R. and Marshall, K. (2008) Using a head-mounted video camera to understand social worlds and experiences. *Sociological Research Online* 13, 1.

Bruce Trail Conservancy (2011) 1 – BTC_Forest_Guide_web_final.pdf. http://brucetrail.org/system/downloads/0000/0386/BTC_Forest_Guide_web_final.pdf.

Chalfen, R. (2014) 'Your panopticon or mine?' Incorporating wearable technology's Glass and GoPro into visual social science. *Visual Studies* 29, 299–310.

Clark, A. (2010) Young children as protagonists and the role of participatory, visual methods in engaging multiple perspectives. *American Journal of Community Psychology* 46, 115–123.

Deleuze, G. (2004) *The logic of sense*. Boundas, C. (ed.) Lester, M. (trans.) London: Continuum.

Deleuze, G. and Guattari, A. (1987) *A thousand plateaus: Capitalism and schizophrenia*. Minneapolis, MN: University of Minnesota Press.

Denzin, N. and Lincoln, Y. (2011) *The SAGE handbook of qualitative research*. Los Angeles, CA and New York: Sage.

Einarsdottir, J. (2014) Children's perspectives on the role of preschool teachers. *European Early Childhood Education Research Journal* 22, 679–697.

Elwick, S. (2015) 'Baby cam' and researching with infants: Viewer, image and (not) knowing. *Contemporary Issues in Early Childhood* 16, 322–338.

Erickson, F. (2006) Definition and analysis of data from videotape: Some research procedures and their rationales. In: Green, J., Camilli, G. and Elmore, P. (eds.) *Handbook of complementary methods in education research* (3rd edition). Mahwah, NJ: Lawrence Erlbaum Associates, 175–186.

Hackett, A. and Yamada-Rice, D. (2015) Producing visual records of movement: Making meaning of young children's interactions with place. In: Stirling, E. and Yamada-Rice, D. (eds.) *Visual methods with children and young people: Academics and visual industries in dialogue*. New York: Palgrave MacMillan, 29–49.

Haraway, D.J. (2001) Ecce homo, ain't (Ar'n't) I a woman, and inappropriate/d others: The human in a post-humanist landscape. In: Jobling, D., Pippin, T. and Schleifer, R. (eds.) *The postmodern Bible reader*. Oxford: Blackwell.

Haraway, D.J. (2008) *When species meet*. Minneapolis: University of Minnesota Press.

Holland, S., Renold, E., Ross, N. and Hillman, A. (2010) Power, agency and participatory agendas: A critical exploration of young people's engagement in participative qualitative research. *Childhood: A Global Journal of Child Research* 17 (3), 360–375.

Hultman, K. and Lenz Taguchi, H. (2010) Challenging anthropocentric analysis of visual data: A relational materialist methodological approach to educational research. *International Journal of Qualitative Studies in Education*, 23, 525–542.

Jackson, A.Y. and Mazzei L, A. (2012) *Thinking with theory in qualitative research: Viewing data across multiple perspectives*. New York: Routledge.

Lather, P.A. (2007) *Getting lost: Feminist efforts toward a double(d) science*. Albany, NY: State University of New York Press.

Lenz Taguchi, H. (2010) *Going beyond the theory/practice divide in early childhood education: Introducing an intra-active pedagogy*. London: Routledge.

Lenz Taguchi, H. (2011) Investigating learning, participation and becoming in early childhood practices with a relational materialist approach. *Global Studies of Childhood* 1 (1), 36–50.

Lipponen, L., Rajala, A., Hilppö, J. and Paananen, M. (2016) Exploring the foundations of visual methods used in research with children. *European Early Childhood Education Research Journal* 24 (6), 936–946.

Madison, D.S. (2012). *Critical ethnography: Method, ethics, and performance*. Thousand Oaks, CA: Sage.

Marcus, G.E. (1995) Ethnography in/of the world system: The emergence of multi-sited ethnography. *Annual Review of Anthropology* 24, 95–117.

Mawson, W.B. (2014) Experiencing the 'wild woods': The impact of pedagogy on children's experience of a natural environment. *European Early Childhood Education Research Journal* 22, 513–524.

MacLure, M. (2013) Researching without representation? Language and materiality in post-qualitative methodology. *International Journal of Qualitative Studies in Education* 26, 658–667.

Mitchell, C. (2011) *Doing visual research*. Los Angeles, CA: Sage.

Pillow, W. (2003) Confession, catharsis, or cure? Rethinking the uses of reflexivity as methodological power in qualitative research. *International Journal of Qualitative Studies in Education* (QSE) 16, 175–196.

Pink, S. (2007) *Doing visual ethnography: Images, media and representation in research*. London: Sage.

Pink, S. (2011) From embodiment to emplacement: Re-thinking competing bodies, senses and spatialities. *Sport, Education and Society* 16 (3), 343–355.

Plowman, L. and Stephen, C. (2008) The big picture? Video and the representation of interaction. *British Educational Research Journal* 34 (4), 541–565.

Richardson-Ngwenya, P. (2014) Performing a more-than-human material imagination during fieldwork: Muddy boots, diarizing and putting vitalism on video. *Cultural Geographies* 21, 293–299.

Rose, G. (2012) *Visual methodologies: An introduction to researching with visual materials*. London: Sage.

Sellers, M. (2013) *Young children becoming curriculum: Deleuze, Te Whariki and curricular understandings*. New York: Routledge.

Somerville, M. (2016) The post-human I: Encountering 'data' in new materialism. *International Journal of Qualitative Studies in Education* 29 (9), 1161–1172.

St. Pierre, E.A. (2011) Post qualitative research: The critique and the coming after. In: Denzin, N.K. and Lincoln, Y.S. (eds.) *The Sage handbook of qualitative research* (4th edition). London: Sage, 611–625.

Stirling, E. and Yamada-Rice, D., eds. (2015) *Visual methods with children and young people: Academics and visual industries in dialogue*. New York: Palgrave MacMillan.

Taylor, A. and Pacini-Ketchabaw, V. (2015) Learning with children, ants, and worms in the Anthropocene: Towards a common world pedagogy of multispecies vulnerability. *Pedagogy, Culture & Society* 23, 507–529.

Theobald (2011) Video-stimulated accounts: Young children accounting for interactional matters in front of peers. *Journal of Early Childhood Research* 10 (1), 32–50.

Watson, C.W. (1999) *Being there: Fieldwork in Anthropology*. London: Pluto Press.

Whatmore, S. (2006) Materialist returns: Practising cultural geography in and for a more-than-human world. *Cultural Geographies* 13 (4), 600–609.

5

TRANSCULTURAL APPROACHES TO LITERACY, LEARNING, AND PLAY

Rahat Zaidi

Exploring transculturalism and literacy through culturally sustaining pedagogy and play

In the 1940s, Afro-Cuban scholar Fernando Ortiz first defined transculturalism as the "reinventing of a new common culture" (Ortiz, 1995). The resultant phenomenon, or perspective, is a direct consequence of the natural, migratory nature of human beings. Today, human migrations are facilitated by so many forms of transport that the rate of movement around the globe is unprecedented. Transculturalism, then, refers to the resultant 'new culture' that is developed because of this. An accelerated means of crossing borders implies that humans are rapidly transcending geopolitical, cultural, and linguistic boundaries because of their mass migrations around the globe. Vertovec (2007) coined the term *super diversity* and Pratt (1999) referred to *cultural contact zones* where we experience transculturalism in real and virtual spaces.

To realize the potential that this 'super diverse' time in history can offer, we must ensure that all voices are being heard, suspending the human tendency to judge, oppress, or be afraid of people who we consider different from ourselves. Literacy imports words and ideas across time and space; it gives us the opportunity to cross borders and travel between mind and heart, opening them, and taking the reader into the experience of people whose lives are very different from our own. Elements of play can be included in this diverse landscape as students engage in various activities that go beyond the rigour of literacy instruction and to a dynamic, energetic form of learning. In this super diverse era, literacy education gives a necessary voice to a super diverse range of human experience.

Orellana (2016) uses an example of how an educational setting can provide the opportunity for a linguistically and culturally diverse classroom to come together in a play situation. This initiative is called the B-Club, a multi-age, after-school program where immigrant children in Los Angeles, California meet with undergraduate students from a local university, and form a community in which they "play with linguistic and cultural border crossings." The complexities that arise when work is explored through transculturalism are mediated through the B-Club's fostering of the experiential nature of the children's learning. The B-Club positions the children to explore their linguistic and cultural knowledge through its collaborative learning method. Orellana reiterates the importance of tapping into the transcultural capital of immigrant children, encouraging and inspiring diverse ways of thinking, doing, acting, and being, all to prepare future citizens to co-exist in a global society. In effect, encouraging children to 'play' with the language they are using through the use of traditional texts as well as different types of media texts helps them meaningfully navigate linguistic and cultural borders.

Gutiérrez, Bien, and Selland (2011) promoted and valued social relationships and the use and integration of playful imagination. Their argument revolved around how 'social and located' relationships helped to develop literacy practices through an after-school club setting designed to put these principles into practice. Gutiérrez et al. (2009) followed Hall's (2004) 'cultural flows' that occur as people and practices transcend time and cultural spaces. Their strategy focused on a particular learning ecology where multi-modality and design helped engage children in play and the imaginary while producing hybrid texts that formed part of the everyday, school-based knowledge and conventions. The concept of using multi-modal texts invites and values oral, dramatic, embodied, written, and graphic art responses and connects the children to the text with depictions of topics that are diverse, culturally relevant, and incorporate a global perspective.

Where traditional approaches favour scripted and English only methodology, Gutiérrez and Vossoughi (2010), and Orellana (2016) emphasized children's interests, experience, expertise, and "repertoires of practices" (Gutiérrez & Rogoff, 2003). This club approach helps to create social dynamics that focus on literacy and identity development among children, using language to help make meaning mediated through technology and new social arrangements. With this particular strategy, culture became an interactional accomplishment, rather than a simple individual trait of the student. Cole (1988) refers to this response to diversity as a polycultural strategy and solution. For instance, capitalizing on young ELL students who enter the school system with a whole repertoire of cultural capital gives teachers the opportunity to go beyond traditional literacy acquisition practices. Cole et al. were able to establish that cultural games, music, and dance enhanced school children's literacy experience by attending to what students individually and collectively brought to the classroom. The activities that took place worked together in game play and language, literacy, and problem solving, all of which contributed to the goals of the program. Each activity entailed students drawing on their full linguistic toolkit in order to enable maximum learning and make meaning.

Lotherington (2017) expounded multi-modal practices as foundational to early childhood education. She emphasized the child's multisensory engagement in activities such as tracing a sandpaper alphabet, finger painting, playing with puppets, choral singing, and rhythmic clapping, all embodying the use of play to learn language development and alphabetic awareness. Similarly, Stein (2008) expressed her interest in multi-modal teaching and learning through exploratory, culturally sensitive, and plurilingual methodology, working with young South African children during the apartheid era. She invited her students' culturally rich forms of expression into her classroom using drama, songs, music, a hope tree (a representative means of allowing students to demonstrate a way of building democratic culture and making meaning), and storytelling. She reiterated, "What began as a fairly loose, unstructured language activity was transformed over a year into a sustained project in a narrative across multiple semiotic modes in which students drew heavily on cultural forms and resources familiar to them" (p. 8). Her success in this project demonstrated how exploratory, culturally responsive pedagogy could be used as a successful strategy in the post-apartheid years.

By taking into account the new demographics of schools, researchers have successfully demonstrated how the very makeup of a classroom in terms of cultural diversity provides the opening for cultural expansion and strategy building to enhance traditional literacy learning experiences.

Transculturalism and language awareness

Researchers focus on language awareness (LA) as a process that assumes literacy acquisition takes place when children treat language as a form, an object they can manipulate that is neither 'natural' nor 'innate.' In addition, Coelho (2012) maintains that the extent to which a learner learns is dependent on his/her sense of agency, self-worth, and motivation to achieve within his/her class and beyond.

Carter (2003) argued that language awareness is not a new concept but does in fact have a long tradition in European countries (van Essen, 1997); he wrote that it goes beyond a focus on language alone to encompass cognitive abilities such as reflection, attitudes to language, language learning, and features of language. Bolitho et al. (2003) identified core definitions of the term, and basic language awareness paradigms. Their research centred on the intersection between language awareness and critical social dimensions, including how language awareness connects with current theories of language teaching and learning. While there was admittedly no consensus on all points raised by the authors, emphasis was placed on communicating with teachers about being aware of how the process of language awareness can aid with literacy engagement.

Cummins and Early's (2011) research recognized students' language awareness and how it expanded as their abilities to think and design collaboratively and creatively through identity texts. They explored "the instructional spaces that opened up when the definition of literacy was expanded beyond its traditional focus on linear print-based reading and writing skills in the dominant language" (p. 3). Not only does language awareness (García & Menken, 2015) empower students, it also brings a new multicultural/multilingual dimension to the teaching context of a language that no longer represents a single culture. This infers that educators need to recognize the important role languages and cultural practices play (language awareness) in the classroom in Canada and all other multilingual classrooms.

In addition to language awareness, researchers, including Pennycook (2006), have been intrigued by the ways in which transcultural flows can produce new forms of localization and how the manner by which people speaking English (through accents, gestures, etc.) results in new and different forms of global identity. Different means of provoking language awareness give the opportunity to unite cultures irrespective of classes, economies, and localities. Levy (2001) suggests hip hop music as an example of encouraging language awareness, where the music itself implies 'a global urban subculture' permeating cultures around the world.

Today, more and more emphasis is being placed on the nature of interaction between students' language and cultural repertoires and the ways in which they negotiate and make meaning in their literacy experiences. Those who work with ethnically, culturally, and linguistically diverse students have increasingly examined socio-cultural perspectives to inform teaching. Socio-cultural perspectives put the emphasis on the role of culture in human learning and development (Au, 1998; Cole, 1996; Rogoff, 2003; Vygotsky, 1978). Rather than 'fix' non-dominant students to 'fit' into classroom literacy practices, these approaches highlight the need for educators to explore how they can best capitalize on their students' cultural, linguistic, and intellectual resources to enhance their academic potential.

D'Warte's (2014) study demonstrates that building on students' linguistic knowledge, skills, and experiences through language brokering and leveraging in the classroom has a positive impact on the classroom cultures, as well as students' identities and teachers' expectations of both monolingual and multilingual students. In addition, promotion of literacy development in a child's first language can help children acquire second or third language literacy (Cummins, 2000; Taylor et al., 2008). As an example, English language learners are able to utilize higher order vocabulary skills from their first language (such as the ability to provide formal definitions and interpret metaphors) when speaking a second language, and conceptual knowledge and skills transfer across languages (Cummins, 2001; Roessingh, 2004). Thus, evidence is mounting that indicates children's early literacy learning should be contextualized within their cultural and linguistic experiences (Naqvi, 2009). In the past decade, research has indicated major literacy successes using cultural amplification within the context of early literacy development. This includes multilingual literacy interventions, exploring pedagogic opportunities involving reading in several languages, and establishing multilingual connections and community engagement within mainstream curriculum (Naqvi et al., 2012a, 2012b; Zaidi, 2018). In essence, the classroom has become a linguistic landscape that reflects and glorifies the multilingual nature of its occupants.

Research demonstrates methodologies that include linguistic diversity as a key component of the literacy acquisition experience enables participants to experiment with languages. Cultural amplification through the presence of scripts, visual cues, and multilingual community involvement give students the opportunity to experience languages, play with linguistic sounds and forms, and demonstrate awareness through repetition, questioning, reading, and writing activities. As a consequence, a paradigm shift is occurring today that is responding to super diversity, giving much more credence to the ideas revolving around (a) languages, (b) language groups and speakers, and (c) communication. Where, previously, homogeneity, stability, and conformity were at the forefront, today mobility, collaboration, and the dynamism of politics are central concerns in the classroom (Blommaert & Rampton, 2015).

Language awareness and dual language books

Perhaps one of the most effective language awareness approaches is used in conjunction with dual language books (DLBs). Educators today are increasingly teaching through a multilingual lens, engaging with classes comprised of groups of students with a variety of cultural and linguistic backgrounds. Learning through a multilingual context while valuing and drawing upon the various and rich communicative repertoires of learners has been found to be a powerful tool for literacy acquisition (Norton, 2014). Educators are seeking to reconcile linguistic diversity and literacy engagement in meaningful and authentic ways while also meeting the needs of linguistically diverse students. Results confirm (Naqvi et al., 2012a, 2012b) that using DLBs creates opportunities for learners to draw upon their multilingual repertoires to create successful educational experiences. Such experiences increase language awareness and encourage students to find overlaps and interconnections between their primary language and any secondary or tertiary languages in their lives.

DLBs have also been found to greatly benefit an inquiry-based approach toward teaching and literacy engagement beyond the acceptance of linguistic and analytical frameworks. In fact, a research environment in which language awareness is incorporated to scaffold the literacy experience can be greatly enhanced through the use of DLBs. Compared to monolingual learners, those students who are already unconsciously overlapping and switching between two or three (or more) languages use DLBs to discuss word sounds and the role of different languages in the literacy process, while simultaneously sharing their own knowledge of language. In addition, for students with a monolingual background, strategies that promote language awareness, such as the use of DLBs, encourage cultural awareness in their day-to-day life.

Projects involving DLB intervention clearly validate the importance of an education that provides students an access to tools that will give them, as well as scholars, teachers, parents, and the general public, insight into their linguistic lives. The effects of allowing students from kindergarten to high school to bring their linguistic/cultural expertise into the classroom has rarely been acknowledged or utilized in academic contexts. If educators can acknowledge the fact that all language use is intimately bound to social, cultural, and political processes, we believe that a student's literacy experience and success in their educational journey will be more effective.

It therefore becomes paramount for school systems to create curricula in which young people who are sitting in culturally and linguistically diverse classrooms are given the opportunity to use language awareness for the purpose of greater literacy engagement. Learners are coming into the classroom with communicative repertoires that are rich in linguistic features from the various languages spoken and are able to draw upon these features in order to incur a successful educational experience. Language and literacy experiences are further enhanced by juxtaposing two or more languages (Hornberger & Link, 2012).

Dual language books give students the opportunity to use their shared knowledge of words and phrases from their respective languages and also move in and out of English to enhance their literacy learning. As they incorporate language awareness, a sense of interconnectedness is cultivated, offering a vision of literacy in mainstream schools that is grounded in action and equity. This makes it possible for learners to explicitly notice language features and become aware of what is needed to develop linguistic and literacy abilities. This chapter acknowledges that language awareness is a powerful tool for literacy engagement in the multilingual classroom, especially when used hand-in-hand with the introduction of DLBs.

The process of implementing a dual language book program

Several examples of research exist involving DLBs in a literacy intervention program. One such DLB project aimed to set up a dual language reading intervention in kindergarten and Grade 1 classrooms over a ten-week duration. Typically, the DLBs (Urdu-English, French-English, Punjabi-English) were read to the student participants three times a week in fifteen- to twenty-five-minute sessions. Each page of the books was read simultaneously in the target language (read by an adult volunteer) and in English (read by the teacher). Strong emphasis was placed on the juxtaposition of the teachers and readers standing side by side while engaging in the reading process. The student participants were encouraged to discuss the story content, vocabulary, pictures, and language content.

The project placed a special emphasis on curricular outcomes and content, and linguistic/intercultural goals. Before direct implementation, I met with the teacher participants to discuss and determine the preliminary steps necessary to make this project a success. We discussed curricular alignment, research protocols, and the student participants' role in the project. The project was divided into four stages.

During the first stage, the DLBs were sourced from school libraries, the nearest public library, and from the Mantra Lingua publisher. Of the entire inventory, the teachers chose ten pertinent titles that were of particular relevance to the current program of studies in which they were involved, the demographic of their classrooms, and the availability of guest readers to support the project. Included in the process was a recruitment letter directed at guest reader volunteers that included parents, families, and community members (see Figure 5.1).

The second stage involved the planning and design of the teaching sequence and student tasks. Over the span of four to six weeks prior to the implementation of the project, the teacher participants met regularly to design specific tasks for the student participants. These included activities promoting linguistic/cultural awareness such as listening activities, noticing scripts, and visual cues. A follow-up information letter, email, and newsletter were sent to all parents to explain the impending DLB project.

Tagalog, Urdu and Spanish Storybook Readers Needed!
Education Assistants, Parents, Community Members

A dual language book reading study is about to be undertaken at ____________ School. It is being conducted with researchers from the University of Calgary and has been approved by the Conjoint Faculties Research Ethics Board.
The reading program incorporates a guest reader who, with a classroom teacher, reads a storybook written in two languages: English and a second language (Tagalog, Urdu and Spanish).
The classroom teacher will read the English text whereas the guest reader will read the second language text.
What are we asking you to do?
- **attend a reading workshop**
- **read the assigned book ahead of time**
- **read the book alongside a teacher to middle/junior high school classes**
- **take part in discussion**

Please contact: ____________________ (teacher) at ( )-_____________.

Figure 5.1 Sample letter inviting parent and community member participation

The third stage involved researchers constructing a reading schedule and an orientation session in which they discussed the guest readers' role, and introduced them to the concept of dialogic and dual language reading. The DLBs to be used in the study were scanned for viewing on a smartboard, and teachers began pre-reading activities with the students. Discussions revolved around identity, the concept of language awareness, and the role of language in their everyday world. These ideas were developed through play and an introduction to the genre of dual language books. Teachers built anticipation for the project by allowing the students to leaf through the books, ask questions, notice pictures, and share their linguistic knowledge.

During the fourth stage, feedback was gathered from students and guest readers in order to tweak and adapt study tasks as necessary during the research period. I gathered evaluations and reflections about the effectiveness of the DLB tool as it is related to outcomes and feedback.

Examples of practice

The examples of practice showcased in the next paragraph provide snapshots of teachers, students, and guest readers interacting with DLBs, in which play and language awareness provided instances of transcultural awareness. The reading of the DLBs explored the transcultural capital of immigrant children and encouraged and inspired them to think, do, act, and be within diverse paradigms. In effect, children were encouraged to 'play' with the language, exploring the use of text as a way to accomplish this. Through the whole process, playful imagination and social relationships were highly valued as part of the development of literacy practices. Hall's (2004) 'cultural flows' came to life in this project as the students and the DLB project merged to transcend time and cultural spaces. The next section provides examples of the reading of two DLBs that demonstrate the power of transcultural experiences through dual language reading.

The Swirling Hijab

The Swirling Hijab (read in Urdu, Punjabi, French, and English) was written by Na'ima Bint Robert (2002) and illustrated by Nilesh Mistry. The book was included in the DLB reading study because of its rich cultural and linguistically diverse content and because we intended that it would develop children's cultural and linguistic awareness. The book is a colourfully illustrated story of a young girl's imaginative uses of her mother's hijab. In terms of cultural content, the hijab is not only a head covering in Islamic cultures, it is also a religious garment worn during prayer. The Hindi and Sikh equivalent of the hijab is the dupatta, which is a longer and narrower scarf that is sometimes worn as a head covering during prayer, and is also worn on the shoulders. Events in the story are linked in a chain (Botvina & Sutton-Smith, 1977) through the main character's imagination.

The Swirling Hijab (Urdu/English reading) was read twice to a group of eighteen student participants in kindergarten, once in Urdu/English and once in French/English. For the purpose of this example we focus solely on the Urdu reading. The Urdu guest reader, Mrs Zahid, had immigrated with her husband to Canada from Pakistan several years earlier. She had two children, both of whom were born in Canada and spoke Urdu at home, and she had tried to educate her children to be proud of their heritage language and customs. Her elder son was part of the student participant group.

During the course of the reading of *The Swirling Hijab*, Mrs Zahid made several comments. Mrs Zahid (discussing the book in Urdu):

> *Yeh kitaab hijab key baray main hai. Hijab patta hay kiss ko kahtay hain? Yeh dekho jaisay mein ney sar peh lya hoa hay. Sar dhaka hoa hay hain na! Is ko Arbi main kehtay hain hijab. Hain na! To yeh ud raha hey, lehra raha hai.* [This book is about the hijab. Do you know what the hijab is? Look (pointing to her head). It's what I am wearing on my head. You see my head is covered. In Arabic we call this hijab. So this is swirling (hand gesture depicting the floating motion of a scarf). It's flowing in the air.]

In the analysis of this vignette, the children's attention was brought to her garment using playful gestures, smiling, and voice inflection. Making explicit references to the linguistic origins of the word ('Look. It's what I am wearing on my head' and 'In Arabic we call this *hijab*' – literally translated hijab means cover), she continued her explanation of the meaning of 'swirling' through gestures, words, and body language that inspired giggles and acknowledgment from the student participants. Through her explanation of the book's title, Mrs Zahid was able to normalize the cultural and linguistic nuances of the hijab within the classroom, and point to the rich transcultural nature of the DLB. This example of DLB dialogic reading offered an inclusive form of linguistic and cultural experience for a minority group of children that enabled them to build on a variety of linguistic and cultural repertoires (Taylor et al., 2008) through play and language awareness.

The reading of *The Swirling Hijab* highlights a prime example of how DLBs provide for powerful moments of language/cultural awareness (Naqvi et al., 2012a, 2012b), promoting an atmosphere of cultural sensitivity, identity sharing, and a sense of playfulness. Gutiérrez et al.'s (2011) research helped me call on her observations wherein multi-modality and design engage children in play and the imaginary. This was further amplified by the guest readers' comments regarding the word used in Punjabi to represent *hijab* (dupatta). South Asian students had an opportunity to discuss and share the various ways in which women covered their heads in their cultures. Through engaging with this particular book and through the presence of the two very different guest readers (a Sikh grandfather from India and a Muslim mother from Pakistan), students experienced a range of cultural norms particular to different languages and countries.

Grandma's Saturday Soup and the patka

A second example involves a Grade 1 class reading a book called *Grandma's Saturday Soup* (Fraser, 2005). This book is about a girl named Mimi who goes through the week reminiscing about her grandma's soup, which she eats every Saturday. She goes through each day seeing things such as sky, snow, sand, and plants, which remind her of her grandma, who would tell Mimi stories of what Jamaica is like. The accompanying illustrations colourfully provide the reader with insight into what Jamaica is really like. There are many different ingredients inside Grandma's soup: yams, dumplings, potatoes, and cho-cho – similar to ingredients used in Jamaica in food preparation. The reader gains knowledge of the cultural foods in Jamaica.

Grandma's Saturday Soup (Punjabi/English reading) was read thrice to a group of eighteen student participants in kindergarten, once in Punjabi/English, once in French/English, and once in Urdu/English. For the purpose of this example, I focussed solely on the Punjabi/English reading. The Punjabi guest reader, Mr Patel Singh, had immigrated to Canada from India to join his son and his family in Calgary a few years earlier. Mr Patel Singh was a former school principal and his grandson Vikram was a student in the current kindergarten class. Mr Patel Singh was an enthusiastic guest reader who enjoyed sharing different aspects about his language and culture with the students. He wore a turban and was familiar with the Hindi and Urdu languages. Mr Patel Singh was very aware of the linguistic interconnections between Hindi, Urdu, and Punjabi, and during his reading sessions he shared various facts about Punjabi. For example, the Punjabi spoken and written in India was derived from the Gurumukhi script, whereas the Punjabi spoken and written in Pakistan is influenced by Urdu/Farsi and Arabic. He drew the student's attention to various linguistic facets of Hindi, Punjabi, and Urdu, pointing to the similarities in pronunciation and the different scriptures. During the reading, Mr Patel Singh stopped to discuss how the word *dupatta* had been used instead of the word *hijab* within the Punjabi/English version of *The Swirling Hijab*. Many students nodded and enthusiastically shared how their mothers wore the dupatta and not the hijab. Such experiences and dialogue provided the student participants with cultural amplification, offering windows into different ways of being.

The Grade 1 class read *Grandma's Saturday Soup* in Punjabi and English. They had already heard the story in French and English, and Urdu and English. Vikram's grandfather, Mr Patel Singh, read the book in Punjabi, and the class teacher, Mrs Brown, read it in English. During the reading, a student named Sonali pointed out that the Jamaican grandmother's bandana looked like the traditional head-covering worn by men in the *gurdwara* (i.e., Sikh temple). Chen (a Mandarin speaker) agreed with her and pointed to Mr Singh's turban, commenting, "Look, this is what it looks like." Imran (a speaker of Urdu) spoke up and said his father wore a *kufi* (i.e., the traditional prayer cap worn in a mosque) while offering his prayers. Mr Patel taught all the students how to say *turban* in Punjabi. Repeat after me, he said, "*Patka*".

This example clearly demonstrates how Mr. Patel's reading embodies, by virtue of being who he is, the authenticity by which he could demonstrate what it meant to be Sikh and wear a turban. Textually, the cover page of the book has a picture of a Jamaican grandmother wearing a bandana. This bandana, in fact, triggered the whole conversation around the concept of head covering, the conversation provoked by one student's question around the various types of head coverings. This was demonstrated by insider knowledge, with Mr Patel exclaiming how his *patka* was in fact the word for another type of head covering, sometimes used on the head for religious purposes. This led to further discussion and play with the vocabulary around the various forms of head covering, demonstrating powerful moments of transcultural exchange through the dialogue that occurred between the guest reader and the student participants, who were provided an opportunity to ask questions around various cultural practices. While I did not focus on the resultant conversation that continued among the student participants, it did, through my one example, demonstrate how the dialogue opened and the various participants had numerous reference points to talk about the hijab, the linguistic comparisons, the embodiment of the head covering through the presentation of the Pakistani mother and her reference to the Arabic language, and the distinction made between the word *dupatta* and *hijab*. Finally, the grandfather's comments around the Sikh turban provided further insight into the question of head coverings.

In summary, the reading of the two books clearly established the link between culture and language, and the opportunity such books afford to early literacy practices. I am leveraging the guest readers' linguistic and cultural repertoires, noting that the students who do share the practices can associate and empathize with the conversation undertaken. Conversely, those who did not belong to those cultural groups were given the opportunity to ask questions and be answered by their peers, providing rich cultural and linguistic conversation. Even though conversation dominated most of the verbal exchanges, multi-modal forms of communication also were presented, including pointing to illustrations, demonstrating physical artefacts in the class outside the book (e.g., the head coverings), and student participants identifying with what was being discussed because they had personal experience with it.

In a normal Language Arts class in kindergarten or Grade 1, had I not brought these texts into the classroom, the student participants would never have had the opportunity to engage in such a discussion, a dialogue that envelops cultural artefacts and conversation involving intercultural exchanges with parents, grandparents, and other family members. Language and cultural awareness emerged as key points in the learning processes as the guest readers' interacted with the children, their presence in the classroom providing powerful moments of cultural amplification and further opportunity to 'play' with the structures and meaning of words and sentences.

Other implementations of DLBs

Language awareness is increased by involving DLBs, visual dictionaries, or personal translation devices. For this particular study I chose to resource the DLBs from Mantra Lingua's website, some school libraries, and the public library system. The Mantra Lingua collection includes stories written in English and sixty-three languages, sorted by age group, language, and reader language level. Teachers chose the particular DLBs they would use based on demographics of the school community in which they worked, the curriculum they were using at the time, the ages of their students, the culture and dynamics of their particular classroom, and any other relevant learning objectives. Guest readers came from families or community members who had been identified through school or classroom communications. Other students in the school also became potential guest readers. Their role in the study was to demonstrate the language and answer any pertinent student questions. As the purveyor of the culture associated with the language, the guest readers' role was very powerful. Videos produced of the DLB reading sessions showcased the diversity of the reading process.

The research project identified other innovative approaches to using DLBs. For example, DLBs could be integrated with a second language program in the school by using a number of translations of *Cinderella* to enable the teacher to highlight various cultural and linguistic features in diverse languages. Another method could identify a physical space in which teachers and new arrivals with limited English language skills could use the DLBs as a means to practice and communicate. DLBs can be used to make connections with the curriculum, allowing for a multilingual lens that can be used as a unit opener. Dual language books can be explored using an inquiry approach, whereby a conversation is instigated around culture, language, and other content. Discussions can promote metalinguistic awareness focusing on alphabet, directionality, sounds, phonemic awareness, and the like. DLBs can also be used in bilingual settings where the native language of ELL students is compared and contrasted with English or with the school's Second Language Programming, or with a language that is particularly relevant within the curriculum. Including DLBs in the classroom can also permit a curricular thematic focus, for example choosing a book about a certain animal, a moral, or a geographic context. Skills such as concept visualization and story structure analysis, as well as imagery, can be revisited through DLB reading. Using DLBs also creates the potential for cross grade buddy projects, and the likelihood of inviting a guest reader includes school–community interaction. The very nature of DLB reading invites the targeting of a variety of authentic audiences and encourages student writing, publishing, and sharing (Bernhard et al., 2008).

Conclusion and summary remarks

I began this research project posing the question: How can dual language books promote transculturalism and multilingual play in the classroom to allow all participants to better appreciate and understand transcultural identities? The dual language books provided an occasion to showcase a methodology that allowed student participants and the guest readers to answer this question in a real and participatory manner. They interacted with the texts and, in fact, the specific nature of the DLBs used gave rise to extraordinary conversations around transculturalism and identity.

Student participants' use of multilingual play clearly demonstrated the power the DLBs had in engaging the literacy process far beyond the traditional practise of reading books solely for the purpose of understanding the words. The juxtaposition of the languages and the readers embodied the richness of text and culture, and the use of technology enabled the guest readers to interact visually with the text and the student participants. The role of the teacher also changed, transcending that of an instructor of literacy into more of a facilitator. The teacher's role became to provide opportunity to point out various characteristics of the English language compared to the other languages being read, drawing student participants' attention to the different sounds of both languages, alphabet formation, and the like.

The methodology used in this research project mandated that books were read to the student participants in French/English, Punjabi/English, and Urdu/English. This process highlighted the innovative nature of this type of reading, removing the traditional, linear progress of reading words, and replacing it with an opportunity to expose the student participants to a richer, more culturally diverse resource to begin their journey to literacy. It gave the student participants a non-judgmental ambience in which they could relax, ask questions, play with the words they found interesting, and explore the diverse cultural richness of the texts, all the while affirming identity and leveraging cultural and linguistic repertoires and expanding language awareness for all participants.

Using technology and resources, such as Google translate, Google images, and online databases/encyclopaedia fosters an inquiry-based mindset in students. If a particular word is repeated throughout the book, students can ask the guest speaker to elucidate and then search for images online. Such investigative practice extends students' thinking through technology. Conducting research online is an essential tool in the toolbox for student inquiry. If needed or desired, teachers can plan a mini lesson on how to find reliable resources, what kind of research can be done to supplement interviews conducted at home, and how to present the show and tell online (Prezi, PowerPoint, and blogs are good examples). The possibilities are manifold, and students can be given a short list of reliable resources before they begin. It would be important to ensure that this list has multilingual resources and includes as many sites as possible. Sites that cater to multiple languages include Newsela, which has features allowing articles to be delivered in Spanish and English. PBS has multiple bilingual resources as well. The power of such work lies in incorporating technology in dynamic ways, so students can live linguistic experiences in different forms accompanied by sounds, images, and texts.

References

Au, K. (1998) Social constructivism and the school literacy of learning of students of diverse backgrounds. *Journal of Literacy Research* 30 (2), 297–319. http://journals.sagepub.com/doi/pdf/10.1080/10862969809548000.

Binte, R.N. (2002) *The swirling hijab*. London: Mantra Lingua.

Bernhard, J.K., Winsler, A., Bleiker, C., Ginieniewicz, J. and Madigan, A.L. (2008) "Read My Story!" Using the early authors program to promote early literacy among diverse, urban preschool children in poverty. *Journal of Education for Students Placed at Risk* 13 (1), 76–105.

Blommaert, J. and Rampton, B. (2015) *Language and super diversity language and super diversity*. New York: Taylor & Francis.

Bolitho, R., Carter, R., Hughes, R., Ivanič, R., Masuhara, H. and Tomlinson, B. (2003) Ten questions about language awareness. *ELT Journal* 57 (3), 251–259. doi: 10.1093/j.elt.57.3.251.

Botvina, G.J. and Sutton-Smith, B. (1977) The development of structural complexity in children's fantasy narratives. *Developmental Psychology* 13 (4), 377–388.

Carter, R. (2003) Language awareness. *ELT Journal* 57 (1), 64–65.

Coelho, E. (2012) *Parents' and teachers' guides: Language and learning in multilingual classrooms: A practical approach*. Clevedon: Multilingual Matters.

Cole, M. (1996) *Cultural psychology: A once and future discipline*. Cambridge, MA: Harvard University Press.

Cole, M. (1998) Can cultural psychology help us think about diversity? *Mind, Culture, and Activity* 5 (4), 291–304.

Cummins, J. (2000) *Language, power and pedagogy: Bilingual children in the crossfire*. Clevedon, UK: Multilingual Matters.

Cummins, J. (2001) *The dual language showcase: Valuing multilingualism and multiculturalism frameworks for learning*. Retrieved from www.thornwoodps.ca/about.htm.

Cummins, J. and Early, M., eds. (2011) *Identity texts: The collaborative creation of power in multilingual schools*. Stoke-on-Trent: Trentham Books.

D'Warte, J. (2014) Linguistic repertoires: Teachers and students explore their everyday language worlds. *Language Arts* 91 (5), 352–362.

Fraser, S. (2005) *Grandma's Saturday soup*. London: Mantra Lingua.

García, O. and Menken, K. (2015) Cultivating an ecology of multilingualism in schools. In: Spolsky, B., Inbar-Lourie, O. and Tannenbaum, M. (eds.) *Challenges for Language Education and Policy: Making Space for People*. New York: Routledge.

Gutiérrez, K.D., Bien, A.C., Selland, M.K. and Pierce, D.M. (2011) Polylingual and polycultural learning ecologies: Mediating emergent academic literacies for dual language learners. *Journal of Early Childhood Literacy* 11 (2), 232–261. doi: 10.1177/1468798411399273.

Gutiérrez, K.D., Morales, P.L. and Martinez, D. (2009) Re-mediating literacy: Culture, difference, and learning for students from non-dominant communities. *Review of Research in Educational Research* 33, 212–245.

Gutiérrez, K.D. and Rogoff, B. (2003) Cultural ways of learning: Individual traits or repertoires of practice. *Educational Researcher* 32 (5), 19–25.

Gutiérrez, K. and Vossoughi, S. (2010) 'Lifting off the ground to return anew': Documenting and designing for equity and transformation through social design experiments. *Journal of Teacher Education* 61 (1–2), 100–117.

Hall, K. (2004) The ethnography of imagined communities: The cultural production of Sikh ethnicity in Britain. *ANNALS* 595, 108–120.

Hornberger, N. and Link, H. (2012) Translanguaging in today's classrooms: A biliteracy lens. *Theory Into Practice* 51 (4), 239–247. doi: 10.1080/00405841.2012.726051.

Lotherington, H. (2017) Elementary language education in digital multimodal and multiliteracy contexts. In: Thorne, S.L. and May, S. (eds.) *Language, education and technology*. Encyclopedia of language and education, vol 9. Cham: Springer.

Levy, C. (2001) Rap in Bulgaria: Between fashion and reality. In: Mitchell, T. (ed.) *Global noise: Rap and hip-hop outside the USA*. Middletown, CT: Wesleyan University Press, 134–148.

Naqvi, R. (2009) *Building bridges: Acknowledging children's first languages*. Paper presented to the American Education Researchers Association, San Diego, CA, April.

Naqvi, R., Thorne, K., Pfitscher, C. and McKeough, A. (2012a) Dual language books as an emergent-literacy resource: Culturally and linguistically responsive teaching and learning. *Journal of Early Childhood Literacy*. doi: 10.1177/1468798412442886.

Naqvi, R., Thorne, K., Pfitscher, C., Nordstokke, D. and McKeough, A. (2012b). Reading dual language books: Improving early literacy skills in linguistically diverse classrooms. *Journal of Early Childhood Research*. doi: 0.1177/1476718X12449453.

Norton, B. (2014) Identity, literacy and the multilingual classroom. *The Multilingual Turn: Implications for SLA, TESOL and Bilingual Education*, 103–122.

Orellana, M.F. (2016) *Immigrant children in transcultural spaces: Language, learning, and Love*. New York: Routledge.

Ortiz, F. (1995) *Cuban counterpoint, tobacco and sugar*. Durham, NC: Duke University Press.

Pennycook, A.D. (2006) Critical applies linguistics. In: Berns, M. (ed.) *Encyclopedia of language and linguistics* (2nd edition). Amsterdam: Elsevier, 283–290.

Pratt, M.L. (1999) Arts of the contact zone. In: Bartholomae, D. and Petrosky, A. (eds.) *Ways of reading: An anthology for writers* (5th edition). Boston, MA: Bedford/St. Martin's, 582–596.

Robert, N.B. (2002) *The Swirling Hijaab*. London: Mantra Lingua.

Roessingh, H. (2004) Effective high school ESL programs: A synthesis and meta-analysis. *The Canadian Modern Language Review* 60 (5), 611–636.

Rogoff, B. (2003) *The cultural nature of human development*. New York: Oxford University Press.

Stein, P. (2008) *Multimodal pedagogies in diverse classrooms: Representation, rights and resources*. Abingdon: Routledge.

Taylor, L.K., Bernhard, J.K., Garg, S. and Cummins, J. (2008) Affirming plural belongings: Building on students' family-based cultural and linguistic capital through multiliteracies pedagogy. *Journal of Early Childhood Literacy* 8, 269–294. doi: 0.1177/1468798408096481.

van Essen, A. (1997) Language awareness and knowledge about language: An overview. In: van Lier, L. and Corson, D. (eds.) *Encyclopedia of language and education: Knowledge about language*, vol. 6. Dordrecht: Kluwer Academic, 1–9.

Vertovec, S. (2007) Super-diversity and its implications. *Ethnic and Racial Studies* 30 (6), 1024–1054.

Vygotsky, L.S. (1978) *Mind in society: The development of higher psychological processes*. Cambridge, MA: Harvard University Press.

Zaidi, R. (2018) *A proposal for 21st century education: An introduction to dual language book reading*. (Vol. 6, KONECT Teaching Materials). Barcelona: Konect Project. ISBN: 978-84-09-00968-8.

6

COMPOSING CHILDHOOD CULTURES

Ethnography upside down

Anne Haas Dyson

> Everywhere children claim, contest, and exchange among themselves the terms of social belonging.
>
> *Pugh, 2009, p. 6*

A small boy, with memories of a happy preschool experience, grins as he walks down the hall with his father toward his kindergarten classroom in a new school. Despite that grin, the stiffness in his gait suggests his nervousness, as does his joy at seeing me, his quiet, adult (and quite senior) "friend from preschool!"

Among this child's first productions in his kindergarten composing journal was the self-portrait seen in Figure 6.1. As you, dear readers, examine this figure, your gaze may homogenize it, that is, interpret it as a "typical" self-portrait of a just-turned-5 child, all circles and lines. And you, dear readers, would be missing the child's point.

A product is just the "sclerotic deposits of an intentional process" unfolding in a particular moment in time and space (Bakhtin, 1981, p. 292). And Ta'Von's, this child's, dynamic, situated moment was a dialogic response to an ideological tension in the peer world. To understand that production as an intentional social process entails, not the analysis of a lonely product, but a particular kind of ethnographic stance, a stance that aims to examine children's intentions and relations from inside the children's world. In that way, children's productions become the embodiment of their way of answering the world (Bakhtin, 1981).

In this chapter, I focus on the whys and hows of this methodological stance toward children's worlds. The illustrative vignettes are drawn mainly from a recent study focusing on the process of negotiating a sense of belonging in unofficial or child-controlled school worlds and the role of composing in that negotiation (Dyson, in press). The child star is Ta'Von, the young boy who has already entered this chapter.

Herein, composing is viewed as participation in deliberate and valued cultural practices of symbolic production (Street, 1984). Moreover, composing is not an isolated act – it is a dialogic response to others' voices (Bakhtin, 1981). This consideration of contextualized, meaning-making children begins with a discussion of the nature of an ethnographic stance toward children's worlds, the sort of inquiry it mediates, and the kind of critical response it allows the

Figure 6.1 Ta'Von's self-portrait with braids

researcher, or at least this researcher, to articulate. As the discussion unfolds, the story, just begun, of Ta'Von will both deepen and stretch itself out.

Turning ethnographies upside down: privileging children's worlds

Ethnographies have as a goal studying a local cultural world as experienced by its members, that is, its participants – or those who aspire to be participants. In the traditions of both interpretive anthropology (Geertz, 1983) and sociology's symbolic interactionism (Blumer, 1986), all of us live in an interpreted, socially constructed world. Our constructions of "what's happening here" are continually negotiated with others. Moreover, contemporary practice theory (Ortner, 2006) underscores that these social worlds are situated within, and constitutive of, the power structures of our societies, including those intersecting social forces of race, class, and gender.

When children are included in the ethnographic lens, they are often viewed through the cultural, or meaning-making, worlds of adults, especially parents or teachers. Children are members in training, apprentices to the practices on offer (e.g., Barton & Papen, 2012; Heath, 1983). In schools, this means that children are seen solely within the practices, and the expectations, of official school culture.

In the U.S., there are highly regulated, test-monitored curricula that include assumptions about what is "basic" for individual children to know and to do as literacy learners, the normative pace of skill mastery, and the ethics of responsible writers, who neither copy (i.e., who keep their eyes on their own paper) or lie (which might otherwise be known as storytelling) (Dyson, 2013). Children who do not fit comfortably within official school practices are problematic; their discomfort reinforces official labels like "at risk" and "struggling," potentially leading researchers to aim to understand children as "problems" (see discussion in McDermott & Varenne, 2010).

In such work, officially problematic children are disproportionately minoritized children (Potter, 2016; Valant & Newark, 2017). Their "differences" from the assumed "mainstream" may become "lacks"; their actions as agents, and their repertoire of experiences and resources, may be disappeared. To gain access to that repertoire and those resources, we might adopt an upside-down ethnographic vantage point and view children, "not for who they are becoming, but for who they are in life spaces shared with other children" (Dyson, 2013, p. 404; Wells, 2009). In so doing, we view school from the vantage point of children.

Diversity and childhood cultures

Children in institutional structures like schools are bundled together as "graded classes," like "kindergarten." Nonetheless, they are not simply participants in the official school world. Children, as children, respond to official practices and their underlying values, by forming unofficial or child-controlled practices (Corsaro, 2017; Dyson, 1989, 2013). That unofficial world touches on children's deep desires to take control of their daily worlds, to share control with others, and to have relationships – to belong (Corsaro, 2017; Nelson, 2007; Pugh, 2009). Children can never be understood as lone actors. In classrooms, they articulate their "selves" as they respond to other child selves; in the process, pleasures and concerns are shared, common knowledge discovered (from popular media, folklore, or institutions like church), relationships formed, practices evolved, and an unofficial world takes form (Bakhtin, 1981; Dyson, 2013).

However, that child culture in formation is not homogenous. Children are members to varied degrees of diverse cultures (e.g., family, ethnic, religious), and their participation in such cultures will inform the resources used as they negotiate entry into new social organizations for companionship and learning. Researchers interested in children's agency in schooling situate themselves within the practices of child worlds. These unofficial worlds exist underneath, alongside of, or interwoven with official worlds. They have a materiality that matters (e.g., a way of organizing their interactions, particular official and unofficial tools and texts, and valued channels of communication).

Such everyday particularities are infused with structural dynamics (e.g., consumer marketing is visible in children's valued or desired possessions, language ideologies are audible or inaudible given children's ways of talking, and societal formations of race, class, and gender may yield dynamic configurations of children [Thorne, 2005]). Consider, for example, the kindergarten experiences of Ta'Von.

I had originally planned to examine how children's composing practices changed as they moved through the early years of schooling. But, from the first day of kindergarten, my data was dominated by Ta'Von's encounters with peers that seemed to push him out of bounds; and certain of those encounters materialized the intersecting forces of race, gender, and class.

To understand this, Ta'Von must be seen both as informed by his recent history as a student and peer in preschool *and* by the local manifestations of the larger racial and class dynamics of his city. These dynamic frames help illuminate the challenges Ta'Von faced in negotiating the inclusiveness of his new educational place (Massey, 2005).

To begin with his recent history, on that very first day of kindergarten, Ta'Von entered a classroom distinctly different in time, place, and child agency than he had known in his beloved preschool (as he said, "I really really loved preschool"). In that old talk- and play-filled place, he had been one of the gang, since, like him, most children were of color and from low-income homes. Moreover, the space was organized by activities, among them, sections dedicated to: dress up and dramatic play; manipulatives for construction; puppet theater improvisations; paint easel productions; and picture book (re)reading, partially using memory of the teacher's reading and, also, picture interpretation. Ta'Von and his peers could move across space within an open time period, choosing among activities for story making (i.e., multimodal composing); Ta'Von was drawn both by an activity and, also, by his desire to be with his best friend Salvia.

In contrast, his kindergarten was in a school serving mainly white children from a relatively affluent neighborhood. Ta'Von was one of a handful (4) of African American children that "desegregated" (but did not necessarily integrate relations in) his room. Every child had an assigned seat and each moved through classroom space (dominated by tables and chairs) as directed by the teacher, Ms. Norton. Official composing was defined as a set of benchmarked written language skills. Most minoritized children, coming from outside the neighborhood, like Ta'Von, scored relatively low on initial literacy assessments (e.g., the names and sounds of letters). This was in part because a network of neighborhood parents shared information on the testing awaiting their children. Composing, as a set of skills, initially problematized the kindergarten membership of out-of-network children.

As cultural geographer Edward Soja (2010) explains, there are consequences to how people are situated in a city, and these are related to racial and class fairness and dignity. An early example came from the events and, more particularly, the thematically related talk occurring before and during Ta'Von's production of Figure 6.1; consider the initiating event:

> Ta'Von is sitting at his desk, awaiting morning snacks and a turn to use the bathroom and get a drink. Vida, an Iranian immigrant with long black wavy locks, seems bothered by Ta'Von's hair.
>
> "You have girl hair," she says accusingly, metaphorically pushing him outside the circle of appropriate boys.
>
> "Yeah, you have girl hair," agrees Adam, a white boy with a short blond hair cut.
>
> "No," answers Ta'Von calmly. "It's boy hair."
>
> For the rest of the snack time, the usually smiling Ta'Von is quiet and somber.
>
> *(Dyson, in press)*

In Ta'Von's preschool, Ta'Von's braided hairstyle was not rare, as both African American boys and fathers had variations of Ta'Von's hairstyle. But that hairstyle was found only on his head in his new school, with its new populace. Thus, in the above vignette, he was judged out of place – a boy with "girl hair." However, Ta'Von, just a small child, stood by his own personhood and refused to be so shoved. In response to that encounter, Ta'Von began consistently adding braids to his self-portraits, as in the first such product (Figure 6.1); if crayons were available, he made his face dark brown, saying as he did so, "I'm Black." Ta'Von thus linked his intersecting racial and gender identity with hair. He used composing to declare himself as a racialized young boy.

After other such instances, I wondered what challenges Ta'Von experienced to his classroom belonging; and though composing "skills" also challenged his classroom belonging, the act of composing could clearly play a role in negotiating these challenges. I wondered what the range of roles could be (for a complete ethnographic analysis of Ta'Von's belonging issues, see Dyson, in press).

On the vital importance of upside down ethnographies

In this first major section of the chapter, I have aimed to illustrate that understanding children's perspectives on schooling requires understanding as well the larger sociopolitical context of schooling, the official worlds of daily practices and, woven within those, the unofficial worlds of children. There can be no homogenizing assumptions about children's worlds . . . hence the plurality in childhood***s*** and world***s***. Locally and globally experienced childhoods vary in breathtaking, sometimes heartbreaking ways. Socioeconomic matters influence access to technologies of play, composing, and learning, as does geography (e.g., rural vs. urban), political unrest, and culturally gendered roles (Gutnick et al., 2010; Sahni, 2016).

Part of being a critical ethnographer is being alert to how assumptions about contemporary childhoods, and resources for school learning, push categories of children to the academic margins, surfacing primarily as the "different" or "problem" children (cf. Madison, 2012). If researchers are to offer an alternative view, and gain access to children's agentive actions, they must include ethnographies done upside down, situated within the children's world.

How does one do such ethnographies of situated children's worlds? This is an especially poignant question, given the different social positions and agentive power of adults and children. It is to matters of methods I now turn.

Entering and documenting childhood worlds

I miss having a peep hole to monitor those wanting access to my home place. Now I have to take a sideways peek through the blinds. Among my personal rules are: if you see a suited young man carrying a religious pamphlet, make yourself very still and breathe quietly; if you spy a brown-shirted delivery person, open the door quickly with a hopeful grin.

Finding a way to enter, and become a familiar presence in, children's worlds takes some time, especially in schools, since the lines between "children" and "adults" are sharply drawn. A hierarchy of age exists, as it is central to the organization of materials, people, space, and, of course, authority. Children can peer around the corner of their interactionally constructed worlds and decide, "Oh-oh, an adult! Don't let that person in (i.e., don't talk about this or that). Maybe ask how to spell a word or two."

It matters, then, that ethnographers of childhoods are clear about their goals and their positionality, as they seek a place in children's worlds (Corsaro, 2017; Ferguson, 2001; Thorne, 1993). Our positioning influences what we see and hear and thus, ultimately, the stories we have to tell. Next, I discuss the process of gaining children's trust so that they don't shut the door to their unofficial worlds. In doing so, I include some personal rules for doing so.

The complexities of gaining entry

Among the relational hurdles to gaining children's comfort with one's presence include those constructed because of identity factors, including not just age but also race and language, for example. In my own experience with young children, gender has not been an experienced relational challenge, nor has age (although after 40 years, it has become a physical one; for example, rising up after sitting down on a rug involves muffled groans, hearing high-pitched child voices now requires technical assistance, as does seeing their printed words).

More significantly, I have studied young children of color, at times in community contexts of heightened racial tensions. As a white woman, I work against any assumptions of being clueless, as it were. For example, I deliberately learn about children's referenced worlds – the radio stations some listen to in the morning, the movies they have seen, or want to, the stores they frequent, the streets or public parks they play in, even the sports teams some support, usually a basketball or football team.

Positionality

I aim to position myself as a trusted adult friend. As a former poor kid myself, I have respect and empathy for the children, who in my projects, are generally minoritized urban children from economically constrained neighborhoods. However, decades ago, I had to consciously resist my teacher identity, as that kept me seeing the children through an official lens only. Thus, I have developed ways of positioning myself among the children as one who has to do "my work"; I have to write down what is happening, so I can remember it. Children accept this, perhaps because I say it with resignation and a heavy sigh. In this way too, I avoid becoming central to the goings on, by, for example, becoming a living dictionary or a local spelling master.

In the interest of maintaining my position, I do not speak with teachers in front of children. Being perceived as a peeping spy, as someone who might tell on children, could render me out of bounds in their social worlds. I do discuss my role in the classroom with the teacher, so that my lack of helping or disciplining does not become a point of contention.

If I am successful in assuming such a role, children will carry on their social agendas with each other as I do my work, even if they stop when a teacher comes near. As I get to know the children, I choose focal children – children with whom to anchor my studies – who seem comfortable with me but not overly enamored. That is how I came to choose Ta'Von when he was in preschool. He attended school regularly; he carried on when I sat down by him; and he paid me no particular attention. In many studies, if I choose children who have a circle of friends, I become accepted over time by that circle. By choosing children from diverse friendship circles, I can become accepted by the children generally.

Relationships with children, though, are always constrained or furthered by contexts. For example, finding one's way into children's worlds is easier if peer talk and collaboration are officially sanctioned; it is much harder when such actions are interpreted as misbehaving. Children will always talk, but soft whispers are hard to hear; I rely on a small but powerful microphone positioned close to a focal child.

Further, relationships do change over time, especially in longitudinal projects. For example, in kindergarten, Ta'Von's pleasure at seeing me, a familiar other, led him to take me into his confidence, making sideways remarks to me about the goings on. In second grade, when blues music became important to him, he performed his pieces for me, a reliable, attentive audience.

In sum, in ethnographic work, the quality of one's relationships with participants influences the quality of the data one gathers. Most productive in an ethnography in the children's worlds may be a relationship born in being an attentive adult friend. To gain access to the dynamic child negotiations that occur in such worlds, I work toward an unobtrusive role – I make no attempt to be anything other than a friendly adult; still, in time, I am the recipient of child commentary. Next, I consider collecting data in an upside-down ethnography.

Gathering data inside children's worlds

In gathering data, my basic tools are those of linguistic anthropology (Ahearn, 2017; Blommaert, 2005; Hymes, 1974). That is, I conceive of the school day as an unfolding of enacted practices, both in the official and unofficial world. Practices are recurrent, purposeful, and value-laden activities; they mediate personal intentions, multimodal choices (e.g., oral or written word, image, sound, movement), social interactions, and contextual conditions, including time and space. This notion of practice implicates us all as human agents in the construction, and interruption, of inequality – in, for example, the status quo and power of whiteness as displayed in humble, everyday judgments of "good hair" (Robinson-Moore, 2008).

Practices are enacted as events within society's institutions, including schools (Ortner, 1997; Street, 1984). As articulated by ethnographers of language (Hymes, 1974; Ahearn, 2017), each enacted, purposeful event involves named participants, uses certain symbolic tools, and proceeds through interactions, themselves consisting of verbal turn functions, for example, interactional (e.g., greeting or inquiring as to center choice), narrational (i.e., representing or dramatizing a role or an event), directive of self and/or other (e.g., stating plans, monitoring [saying each letter while writing one's name]), and heuristic (i.e., seeking information).

In schools, the notion of unofficial child practices complicates the common division of "in" and "out of school" practices (Hull & Schultz, 2001). The interest herein is in the unofficial lives of children, particularly their composing lives, as unfolding in school. As data gatherer, I am not a neutral observer; I am aiming to understand how children's unofficial relations, resources, and interests become intertwined with, or separated from, the official world.

To examine this dynamic, I begin with the landscape of official practices, particularly but not exclusively those involving written language. Knowing the official practices, and the adult expectations they entail, provides an essential backdrop to the children's worlds, which form around, within, and underneath those worlds. Still, becoming accustomed to the ebb and flow of official classroom life takes time. So, as the children become used to me – and my pen and recorder – I become used to the configuration of practices that organize their school life.

In the classroom, I rely on participant observation; as an attentive friend, I am curious but never interrupt a child in interaction with others. I rarely conduct formal interviews; my role as adult friend does not include in any way taking a conversational lead. Rather, as classroom life unfolds, I write sketch notes – fast minimal notes, taken without looking at my paper, which impresses children; those sketchy notes are later transformed into narrative field notes, with the help of my trusty audio recorder, any artifacts gathered, and my memory.

Eventually, the early observational data will be categorized into named official practices. Of course, I am also jotting down overheard comments that point the way to children's worlds (e.g., bits of arguments, stories told, popular entertainments referenced, bits of quiet singing, and on and on). Among the most telling early signs of child culture are choreographed child texts in a room with an official expectation of individual text authorship (see Dyson, 2013). Some sort of group interaction accounts for the textual choreography.

As I am focusing on the configuration of official practices, I am also paying attention to the configuration of child bodies in space, both as the teacher arranges them and as they arrange themselves (including on the playground, assuming they get recess). Is there, for instance, a time when the designated "bright" children move across the room, in front of seated others, to sit at the kidney-shaped table for a reading lesson? Is there a time when the low-scoring children move to the table? When, if ever, do children choose whom to associate with? In both official and unofficial groupings, are patterns of gender, race, language, or some other societal category rendered visible?

As the project develops, I begin to follow children's interactions inside the official practices, audiotape swirling, pencil scratching, eyes glued to the goings on. I rely on focal children. They are my guides into children's interactionally constructed worlds.

Initially, I am not sure what will ultimately matter, so I transform sketch notes and audiotapes into detailed accounts of child-enacted official practices (each enactment labeled an "event"); in time peer expectations, relations, and transformations of official practices into unofficial ones take form. But detailing expectations, relations, and the unofficial practices informing child worlds does not simply "emerge" from data. Once one has turned the ethnographic view upside down and is observing school routines and expectations from inside the children's world, a period of intense data analysis ensues.

In sum, during data collection I learn by paying careful *attention* to child expectations and practices that evolve in response to, within, or even in metaphoric curricular "side roads" that never intersect with, official expectations (Dyson, 1993). These phenomena are constructed through collected data: field notes and accompanying audiotapes and student artifacts, along with notes on required textbooks and testing, and accumulating news clippings and website reports on local school issues and publically available statistics on school and city demographics. Further in this chapter, projects featuring first grader Tionna, a child from an earlier project, and kindergartener Ta'Von will illustrate possible analytic paths through data.

Studying situated childhoods in action: data analysis with a critical edge

Qualitative data analysis involves studying those data so painstakingly collected. The focus is on how participants interpret and enact their social worlds and, more particularly, how they experience some phenomenon of interest (i.e., negotiating belonging in Ta'Von's case) in some contextualized place and time. The immediate goal of the inductive analysis of collected data is to develop ways of naming or categorizing (i.e., coding) key dimensions of that experience so that an analytic narrative can be composed for others.

In analyzing children's worlds, I aim both to render in detail children's experienced worlds and, at the same time, to keep the focus on the phenomena of interest. Children can be trivialized; often their described actions can be judged "cute" or "pitiable," neither of which is helpful. So a careful, systematic analysis is critically important. To this end, I begin by using an interactional unit of time and space, so that the analysis can be focused on the dynamic processes of everyday life. To illustrate what I mean, I enlist the support of Tionna and Ta'Von. For each, I comment as well on the critical dimension of the work, that is, on the way it works against the assumed status quo in schooling in the U.S. and elsewhere.

Analyzing the dynamics of the "basics": Tionna

Tionna, a textual child now, was a lively, talkative 6-year-old; she usually spoke a variant of African American Language. She attended an urban school that served primarily low-income children, including African American children, like Tionna (a focal child), as well as Latinx and white children. As a group, the children, who shared a neighborhood, also had a widely shared understanding of the local peer culture, and this included transformations of official writing tasks. The children looked forward to the daily sharing time, when they read their writing to their peers.

The year-long project in Tionna's class compared the literacy "basics" as defined by the state's common core skills, and the "basics" of writing in the children's worlds (Dyson, 2013). My basic sociolinguistic unit of analysis was the communicative event, both official and unofficial; as earlier discussed, each event is an enactment of the more abstract notion of a practice, that is, it is a situated social happening (Street, 1984). Within official and unofficial events, I marked off episodes (topic-related interactions within events) involving corrections. Thus, I determined "basics" by comparing the teacher's corrections of children's writing (i.e., what did children need to improve?) and the children's corrections of each other's writing, which were spontaneous and conversational (see Dyson, 2013). I could, then, track focal children, like Tionna, across official and unofficial time-and-space, as well as over time as practices evolved and new ones appeared.

In this way, I identified an ideological difference between the view of language undergirding the official teacher-led practices and that undergirding many children's, including Tionna's. Official events were undergirded by a homogeneous and hierarchical notion of language. These "hierarchical fix-its" were related to skills tested on the year's end achievement test and formally introduced in an "oral language" textbook with sets of error-plagued sentences to be orally corrected by the class. Hierarchical fix-its merited no rationale beyond an explanation of the rule itself. Rules included the use of mainstream American English.

But, as the school year progressed, most children, including Tionna, appropriated voices that linked both to the world outside the classroom and to particular peer relations (e.g., the goal of making one's peers laugh or of marking peer affiliation by writing on the same topic). In this, the children's work was illuminated by the Bakhtinian dialogic frame in which I had situated the project; Bakhtin (1981) views oral or written utterances as both enacting relations in the present and echoing experienced voices. In this project, I named the children's ideology a relational one, since their corrections tended to be about the social appropriateness of another's textual action, given relationships or particular practices.

To conserve textual time and space, I merely report that, in official vignettes, Tionna seldom understood her teacher's corrections of her grammar. However, in her own talk and writing, she consistently displayed an ear for voices – not disembodied grammar, but voices. That sensitivity led to a communicative flexibility that did not exist in the official world.

To briefly illustrate, consider how Tionna uses African American Language in writing when reporting her interactions with her cousin, but the local mainstream American English when revoicing her teacher's narrative. Following is Tionna's text about a cousin who:

> all ways copy cat me and **I say** aret [aren't] you tier [tired] of copycating me **she say** no am [I'm] not that is my favord [favorite] so plese stop ascking [asking] me mame [ma'am] I get tier of that[,] calling me mame so I will call her mame
>
> [I bolded words that clearly contrast with Tionna's choices in the next text.]

The assertive back and forth of Tionna's written dialogue, her explicit feelings and conversational present tense ("she say" and "I say") contrast the more descriptive, syntactically formal prose of her texts based on her teacher's talk. For example:

> Yesterday Mrs. K wint to the doctor she had to leav for the rest of the after non because **she said** her son Kelly had a bump on his arm **she said** they had to remove it.

As Tionna's communicative flexibility suggests, in this project, the social world of young children was more sophisticated in language use than was the official world. That official world attempted to erase minoritized children's language strengths.

Analyzing the challenges of belonging: Ta'Von

Kindergartener Ta'Von has already entered this textual space; he was facing the challenges of finding a comfortable place in the children's worlds. I focused on describing these potential challenges of school transition and, more particularly, of social integration, rather than mere desegregation; I had a particular interest in the roles child writing played in forming, as well as negotiating, these challenges.

I used a series of analyses to study the data (collected over the closing four months in the preschool and the opening five months of kindergarten; data set later added to with closing five months of second grade). As with the project in Tionna's classroom, I began with a taxonomy of official and unofficial composing practices, first in preschool, then in kindergarten. I considered each practice as enacted through situated events.

As the analysis continued, I read data across events from both the preschool and the kindergarten, identifying recurrent themes. I was interested in comparing Ta'Von's interactions during composing or story-making events in preschool (e.g., through the manipulation of Leggos or of small figurines) to those in kindergarten (almost exclusively involving written language). In this way, I documented the absence in the preschool, and the predominance in the kindergarten, of themes of gender, race, and social class, along with the integrative theme of belonging.

During this process, I read Massey (2005), who argues for a view of belongingness as a continually negotiating process and as the dynamic consequence of social encounters among a shifting populace (rather than a static possession of some mapped place). This concept freshened my vision of Ta'Von's transition, particularly because Massey portrayed these encounters among people on different life trajectories as always involving power and political inequality. In my work, then, I borrowed Massey's use of "encounters," identifying episodes within events in which peer talk included the appropriateness of some aspect of Ta'Von's self (i.e., physical, material, social, academic). The "girl hair" episode earlier shared is an example of a category of encounters that fronted the often intersecting societal categories of race, gender, and social class.

Through this analysis, I aimed to understand Ta'Von's encounters with "others," as those encounters illuminated challenges to his legitimacy as a child among children in a place called school, drenched in literacy skills. As I proceeded through the kindergarten data, I also described the roles composing played in Ta'Von's negotiation of inclusive relational space (i.e., of social belonging) in the kindergarten.

One theme that integrated a kind of encounter with the contradictory roles of composing was that of helping. The kind of encounter relevant to this theme was identified as those that fronted unofficial judgments of "needing help." In Ta'Von's preschool experience, this theme did not arise – help was given and taken during reciprocal conversations with peers. The ideology of learning in the preschool marked difference in skill as normal, as was the expectation for improvement. "I did it!" or "You did it!" were common cheers.

In the kindergarten, needing help was a mark of neediness; the so-called "bright" children (who scored highly in tests) did not voice needing help. But, from the first day of school (even before testing began), a "bright" child offered to help Ta'Von with a puzzle. Ta'Von resented this – "I can do this myself!" There seemed, to me, no basis for the judgment that Ta'Von would need help other than assumptions based on race. However, Ta'Von was thankful for help when he felt he needed it. If *Ta'Von* offered help to the "bright" children, that help was rejected (even though his correction was usually accurate).

In order to experience himself as having some expertise in composing, he needed to be with children with whom he eventually established a reciprocal (i.e., a comfortable, give-and-take relationship); none of these children were, at that time, labeled in the teacher's word of praise "bright," and none were of the dominant group considered "white." Consider, for example, the following exchange with Nia, considered "mixed":

> As a follow up to a "senses" unit activity, the children are to draw and label four objects they have "felt" on this day:
>
> *Ta'Von:* (after drawing) There's my white ball. Ball. (writes *BuoL*) . . .
> *Nia:* I got a Spiderman ring!
> *Ta'Von:* I got an apple.
>
> As Ta'Von writes *AL*, Nia repeatedly and slowly says "I got a Spiderman, Spiderman," her pencil poised but not moving. The rhythm of Ta'Von and Nia answering each other has been broken, and Ta'Von offers help:
>
> *Ta'Von:* /s/
> *Nia:* S (writes S)
> *Ta'Von:* /i/
> *Nia:* (writes I)
> *Ta'Von:* /d/
> *Nia:* (writes D)
> *Ta'Von:* /m/
> *Nia:* (writes M)
> *Ta'Von:* Good job!

As illustrated, for Ta'Von, composing came to serve a role, not only as a marker of personal identity (e.g., in the hair episode) but also of valued expertise. Sometimes one needed help, sometimes one helped. There were no set roles among these reciprocal friends.

Through the analysis of Ta'Von's data, as illustrated here, I demonstrated how desegregated schools, involving a small number of minoritized children, can pose distinct challenges to children, like Ta'Von, who want to belong to the class. Moreover, challenges linked to the intersection of race and perception of academic knowledge may limit the opportunities for minoritized children to experience all aspects of the social roles entailed in composing and, more broadly, in schooling. There is nothing fair about desegregating schools that is not accompanied by a thorough attempt at integrating children socially and academically.

At this point, I have summarized and illustrated the challenges and potential critical insights of upside-down ethnographies that center themselves in children's worlds. The meaning-making technology tied to child agency in these classrooms has been primarily pencil and paper, although computers were present in Ta'Von's kindergarten and would be more prevalent as he progressed through second grade (the end of the formal project). However, computers in his school were unconnected typically to child agency. This is worthy of comment, which I offer next.

Comments on viewing technology upside-down

As already noted, there are striking differences locally and globally in the education available to children, including the technological tools. Moreover, even when digital media, like Chromebooks, are available in school, the push toward accountability through narrow skill testing may mean that the use of digital platforms is heavily structured; such devices thus allow limited space for children's agency and their interests.

Most importantly, the so-called "digital divide," focused on the income-related presence or absence of digital tools in homes, may leave us unappreciative of the power of collective child agency. Brittany Frieson, a doctoral student at the University of Illinois, provided a vivid example of such agency. In her neighborhood, most families were low-income. Nonetheless, as she wrote (personal communication, 2017), she and her neighborhood friends collaborated to get their Christmas present desires:

> When we figured out what we wanted we would all meet together to negotiate whose parent was going to buy which gift, being very careful to not get duplicates as that was a waste of resources. . . . When we would decide on who would get what, we gave our requests to . . . whoever . . . purchased [our separate] Christmas gifts. . . . A[s] an example of this . . . Toby's dad would buy the PlayStation, I would get a popular game like *Grand Theft Auto*, someone else would get extra controllers, and we would all share and take turns playing.

This home-grown example reminds me of the work of Nishant Shah and his colleagues in a rural village in India. In a presentation entitled "A Child's Eye View of the World," Shah reported on a network of children he and his colleagues uncovered during their ethnographic work (cited in Livingston et al., 2015). Women, he noted, enjoyed the daily soap operas, but their access to devices to view those soaps could be limited, in part because of gendered social constraints. However, children could borrow their father's mobile phones, watch the shows, and then, later, theatrically enact key moments from new episodes to help the women keep up with the shows.

These examples, from different times and places, both speak to the agency and collaboration possible among young children. In order to see such activity though, and re-imagine private devices within collective needs, we would benefit from situating ourselves as humble, respectful participants in children's worlds.

The joy – and challenges – of entering children's worlds

This chapter has been about the hows and whys of turning the usual research approach upside down. Rather than view children through the official lens of school, I have discussed viewing school through the unofficial lens of children. Such an ethnographic view is dependent on a non-trivializing view of children and their desires for companionship and playful control in their everyday lives. Such upside-down ethnographies, like all ethnographies, do not yield findings that can be generalized to some broader population. Rather, as Geertz (1983) explains, such research allows us concrete material to think with and, thereby, gain new insights into the social dynamics, situational influences, and negotiation processes entailed in abstractions like belonging, agency, technological access and, above all, social equity in children's lives. By comparing ethnographic insights, we as a profession build our understandings of children, child cultures, meaning-making, and social integration.

Among the key challenges to researchers aiming to enter children's worlds are to adopt:

- answerable, often evolving questions that energize a respectful curiosity about unofficial worlds
- a positionality that allows a researcher a nonthreatening, up-close view of children in action
- a socio-historical view that (a) situates educational settings in the history and politics of the city and the school, and, within the setting, (b) allows practices, including unofficial ones, an evolving history and allows children agency energized by social intentions
- an attentiveness to the dynamics of official and unofficial practices; that is, documentation of official practices and children's ways of participating in, transforming, or working alongside those practices
- systematic analysis of collected data, using units of analysis that will yield a vocabulary and themes with which to narrate responses to research questions; modeled herein were sociolinguistic units (i.e., events that enacted practices) and content ones (i.e., recurrent topics and events yielded themes and, undergirding those, ideologies)
- a consideration throughout about what the children are teaching pushes against dominant educational visions, for example, assumptions about "best practices," "prepared learners," or "necessary resources for learning."

I have, in truth, left out qualities of this work that have kept me going over the years. Upside-down ethnographies in children's worlds are exciting adventures – one never knows quite where the children will lead. Moreover, they are a joy. One meets the nicest people, like Ta'Von. At school entry, he was routinely, if not always deliberately, insulted. He never responded in kind. He was a centered person who did not abandon reaching out to others. In these troubling times, when mean-spiritedness seems to be in power in the U.S., I crawl into children's worlds, meet lively and resilient people, and get all caught up in the adventure of it. Perhaps some of you, dear readers, will do so as well.

References

Ahearn, L.M. (2017) *Living language: An introduction to linguistic anthropology* (2nd edition). Malden, MA: Blackwell.

Bakhtin, M. (1981) Discourse in the novel. In: Holquist, M. (ed.) Emerson, C. and Holquist, M. (trans.) *The dialogic imagination: Four essays by M. Bakhtin*. Austin, TX: University of Texas Press, 254–422.

Barton, D. and Papen, U., eds. (2012) *The anthropology of writing: Understanding textually-mediated worlds*. Reprint. New York: Bloomsbury Academic.

Blommaert, J. (2005) *Discourse: A critical introduction*. Cambridge: Cambridge University Press.

Blumer, H. (1986) *Symbolic interactionism: Perspective and method*. Oakland, CA: University of California Press.

Corsaro, W. (2017) *The sociology of childhood* (5th edition). Thousand Oaks, CA: Sage.

Dyson, A. H. (1989) *Multiple worlds of child writers*. New York: Teachers College Press.

Dyson, A. H. (1993) *Social worlds of children learning to write in an urban primary school*. New York: Teachers College Press.

Dyson, A. H. (2013) *ReWRITING the basics*. New York: Teachers College Press.

Dyson, A. H. (in press) A sense of belonging: Writing (righting) inclusion and equity in a child's transition to school. *Research in the Teaching of English* 52.

Ferguson, A. (2001) *Bad boys: Public schools and the making of Black masculinity*. Ann Arbor, MI: University of Michigan Press.

Geertz, C. (1983) *The interpretation of cultures*. New York: Basic Books.

Gutnick, A.L., Robb, M., Takeuchi, L. and Kotler, J. (2010) *Always connected: The new digital media habits of young children*. New York: The Joan Ganz Cooney Center at Sesame Workshop.

Heath, S.B. (1983) *Ways with words*. Cambridge: Cambridge University Press.

Hull, G. and Schultz, K. (2001) *School's out: Bridging out-of-school literacies with classroom practice*. New York: Teachers College Press.
Hymes, D.H. (1974) *Foundations in sociolinguistics: An ethnographic approach*. Philadelphia, PA: University of Pennsylvania Press.
Livingston, S., Byrne, J. and Bulger, M. (2015) *Researching children's rights globally in the digital age*. Florence, Italy: UNICEF Office of Research – Innocenti.
Madison, D.S. (2012) *Critical ethnography: Methods, ethics, and performance* (2nd edition). Thousand Oaks, CA: Sage.
Massey, D. (2005) *For space*. Los Angeles, CA: Sage.
McDermott, R. and Varenne, H. (2010) Culture, development, disability. In: Luttrell, W. (ed.) *Qualitative educational research*. New York: Routledge, 164–182.
Nelson, K. (2007) *Young minds in social worlds: Experience, meaning, and memory*. Cambridge, MA: Harvard University Press.
Ortner, S. (1997) *Making gender: The politics and erotics of culture*. Boston, MA: Beacon Press.
Ortner, S. (2006) *Anthropology and social theory: Culture, power, and the acting subject*. Baltimore, MD: John Hopkins University Press.
Potter, H. (2016) *Champaign schools: Fighting the opportunity gap*. New York: The Century Foundation.
Pugh, A.J. (2009) *Longing and belonging: Parents, children, and consumer culture*. Oakland, CA: University of California Press.
Robinson-Moore, C.L. (2008) Beauty standards reflect Eurocentric paradigms – so what? Skin color, identity, and black female beauty. *Journal of Race & Policy* 4 (1), 66–85.
Sahni, U. (2016) *Reaching for the sky: Empowering girls through education*. Washington, DC: Brookings Institute Press.
Soja, E. (2010) *Seeking spatial justice*. Minneapolis, MN: University of Minnesota Press.
Street, B. (1984) *Literacy in theory and practice*. New York: Cambridge University Press.
Thorne, B. (1993) *Gender play: Boys and girls in school*. New Brunswick, NJ: Rutgers University Press.
Thorne, B. (2005) Unpacking school lunchtime: Structure, practice, and the negotiation of differences. In: Cooper, C.R., Coll, C.T.G., Bartko, W.T., Davis, H. and Chatman, C. (eds.) *Developmental pathways through middle childhood* (1st edition). Mahwah, NJ: Lawrence Erlbaum Associates, 63–88.
Valant, J. and Newark, D. (2017) *Race, class, and Americans' perspectives of achievement gaps*. Brown paper. Washington, DC: Brookings Institute.
Wells, K. (2009). *Childhood in a global perspective*. Cambridge, UK: Polity.

7

RESEARCHING A CHILD'S EMBODIED TEXTUAL PLAY

Kerryn Dixon and Hilary Janks

Introduction

As critical literacy educators, we are interested in the ways children develop agency. Critical literacy has moved from a focus on oral and written verbal texts to a focus on multimodal texts that use a range of signifying systems, such as images, sound, gesture, movement and materials. Changes in technology have brought about a concurrent shift from print to screen that enables the simultaneous use of multiple messaging streams. What counts as a text has, as a result, broadened considerably (Bearne, 2003) and now includes amongst other things, artifacts (Pahl & Rowell, 2010), and places and spaces (Comber, 2015). They exist in a wide range of genres and forms such as art, drama, dance, books, artifacts and construction. We present data from an ongoing ethnographic study now in its second year, which is part of our overarching project on the spatialities and embodiments of childhood. Leah, a six-year-old middle class girl, is the focus of our study, and here we examine the out-of-school texts created during collaborative play. In this chapter we explore the inter-relationship between Leah's embodied digital and print literacies in her construction of texts.

Much of the current research in early childhood that is concerned with digital technologies (e.g. Burnett, 2010, 2015; Harwood, 2017; Flewitt et al., 2015) is located in the political North. Although Leah is a child with privileged access to digital technologies at home and is comfortable with both old and new technologies, this is not the case for most children in South Africa. In addition, the take-up of digital technologies in our K-3 classrooms has been slow. While our context makes it necessary for us to continue to research the use of old technologies in childhood education, we are firm believers that they provide varied opportunities for learning in early childhood and are worthy of ongoing research in their own right (Crescenzi et al., 2014). Research focusing on digital technologies only runs the risk of not recognising the importance of the interplay between different technologies and how children traverse the landscape of technological possibilities to suit their purposes and current levels of technological competence. Kress (2004) argues that children's choices relate to the affordances of the different modalities, but we contend that children's embodied understanding of their own competence and sensory pleasure are as important.

Theoretical approaches that underpin our work

To understand Leah's textual play, we first foreground the theoretical approaches informing our work. These approaches influence the ways in which we design our research, enable us to make sense of our data and position our work in relation to the debates in the field.

We draw on three bodies of theory in our work with children, as well as research located in these paradigms that focuses on young children's engagement with digital technologies:

- Socio-cultural theories of literacy and play in early childhood (e.g. Dyson, 2016; Edwards, 2013; Harwood, 2017; Larson & Marsh, 2013; Wohlwend, 2008, 2015) together with theories of multimodal representation (e.g. Rowsell & Harwood, 2015) and transmediation (e.g. Kress, 2004; Newfield, 2015);
- Theories of childhood (e.g. Dahlberg & Moss, 2005; Edwards, 2013; James & Prout, 2015);
- Theories of embodiment in time and space (e.g. Dixon, 2011; Farman, 2015; Foucault, 1977, 1980; Lefebvre, 1991, Thiel, 2015).

These theories come together as we try to understand how literacy is embodied in a particular child in her textual play.

Reflections on research methods

Collaborative play as a form of ethnography

There is a long history of using ethnography in literacy research. The advantage of an ethnographic approach is that it provides insights into beliefs and practices observed over time, is socially situated, data collection is flexible, unstructured and guided by participants, and themes for analysis arise from the data. Ethnographies have been critiqued for the impact researchers have in the site and that researchers do not reflect reality, but create it through their subjective writings.

All research choices are subjective, but ethnography provides opportunities for researchers to reflect on their perspectives. It demands that researchers 'think consciously about entering the life of the other' (Heath et al., 2008). We have been influenced by participatory research and participatory methods with young children (Clark & Moss, 2011; Fargas-Malet et al., 2010; Literat, 2013; Mand, 2012; Tay-Lim & Lim, 2013). This approach has been shaped by changing conceptions of childhood that see children as 'experts in their own lives', 'skillful communicators', 'rights holders' and 'meaning makers' (Clark & Moss, 2011, p. 5). But as Gallacher and Gallagher (2008) point out, although acknowledging children as having agency and constructing children as co-researchers and knowledge-producers, research agendas using participatory methods are most often adult-driven, and do not take power relations into account or acknowledge the dynamic nature of children.

We have thought carefully about the benefits of participant observation in ethnography, what participatory methods bring to an ethnographic approach, and how best to enter the life of a child as adults. Dyson's (2016) contention that play is the work of children is important. Our interest in what happens in children's 'textual playgrounds' where children respond to each other, 'adapt relevant symbolic material, assume complementary roles, and thereby, construct a textual encounter' (Dyson, 2013, p. 117), led us to consider how, instead of using a more traditional form of participant observation, our entry point into Leah's life could be through collaborative play. Collecting data through collaborative play is similar to, but not the same, as participatory research. There is no research agenda. The questions emerge from what transpires during play. Collaborative play is child-directed.

Thus, emic and etic perspectives become important. Collaborative play is an approximation of an emic perspective. Hilary, Leah's collaborative playmate, is an 'insider' in terms of her access to and knowledge of the family and culture in which Leah is located. But she cannot be considered a full insider, because she is not a child. If researchers want to understand children's play, it is important to see what they do, not how they comply with adult direction. This is easy to say and hard to do. Thiel (2014, p. 130), in describing her experience as a researcher learning to play with a child in an out-of-school space, says,

> Perhaps reflecting years of my body/mind being territorialized by discourses of what it means to be a teacher in the presence of a child, I felt like I had to "teach something" rather than letting [the child] lead me.

Influenced by Thiel, Hilary realised that she had to unlearn her own embodied pedagogical inclinations and give up 'hierarchy, power and the binary of adult and child' (Thiel, 2014, p. 121). She had to recognise that her own body had been schooled to be a pedagogue rather than a playmate or a researcher.

Collecting data 'as a playmate in the moment' is complex. It is challenging to write fieldnotes, or videorecord in the moment, whilst playing. So Kerryn acted as an 'outsider'. She interviews Hilary and Leah, and watches recordings of the play to interrogate what, how, and why things happen. Interviews with Leah are related to the texts she produces. Those with Hilary are about the textual products, reconstructing the play, probes on how meaning was made and remade over time and recursive connections to other digital and print texts and play dates.

Because our focus is Leah's textual play, this research requires an analytic focus on the texts. Flewitt's (2011) work combining ethnography and multimodality is helpful. She argues this combination can lead to the

> production of grounded, theorised, detailed and holistic insights into literacy as a social practice, revealing how micro-moments of multimodal meaning making unfold in a complex network of socially situated norms and practices.
>
> *(Flewitt, 2011, p. 297)*

Because texts can only be understood in relation to the social and material conditions and the processes of production and reception, our method of text analysis relies heavily on ethnographic data.

Text analysis

Texts that children produce give us insight into what they are thinking and feeling. They are an externalisation of children's embodied internal worlds in material form, and often reveal more than what children at different ages can express in words. By observing the process of production, it is possible to see how ideas develop and change and how the materials interact with the child and influence their thought processes. Children often talk aloud while playing. Following children's talk provides access to their internal worlds. Materials and technologies are part of the context and conditions of production, as is the participation of an adult in the play. Understanding that the text is produced in relation to material and social conditions is an important part of textual analysis. Fairclough's (1989, 1995) approach to discourse analysis requires us to consider both process and product and the material and social conditions that affect what children make, and how they make them. Figure 7.1 combines elements of his 1989 and 1995 model versions.

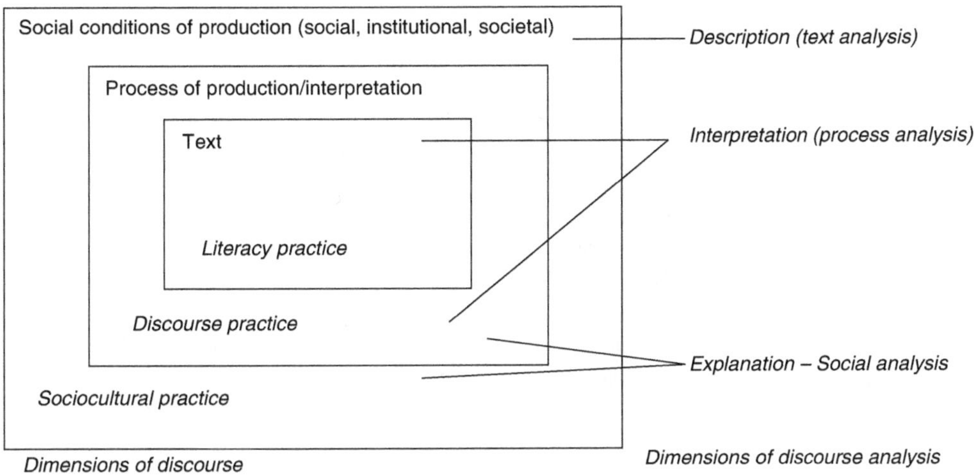

Figure 7.1 Fairclough's dimensions of discourse
Source: Fairclough 1989, p. 25; Fairclough 1995, p. 98

Data collection methods: 'will you take a video of me explaining this?'

In two years we have collected a large and varied data set (see Table 7.1). The data comprises fieldnotes, photographs of texts during production and as final products, interviews, artifacts and

Table 7.1 Data collected over a two-year period

Data	*Description*	*Recorded*
Drawings	Seven large-scale drawings about 86 cm by 73 cm that Leah calls 'maps'.	Original artifacts, photographs and video during making, fieldnotes
Created books	Three books (11 cm × 15 cm) with a varying number of pages.	Original artifacts, scanned copies
Construction projects	A range of materials are used (e.g. Lego, blocks).	Photographs, fieldnotes
Leah performing	Leah and Hilary act out books, improvise movie storylines. Toys/ action figures are also used.	Video, fieldnotes
Material artifacts used in play	These include dress up costumes, toys.	Original artifacts, photographs, video
Media	Movies, audio and print books, game apps, YouTube videos, DVDs.	Screen grabs from iPad, lists of digital and print texts, original artifacts
Interviews and conversations	Unstructured ongoing interviews with Leah and Hilary. Conversations with Leah's parents (for fact-checking).	Transcribed, written notes in situ

videos of Leah playing which are often performative: she encourages Hilary to film her talking about her texts. Each item is interesting, but as a body of longitudinal data it reveals Leah's developing motor and perceptual skills, language development, growing knowledge of herself and the world, visual literacy and performativity from her engagement with movies. It becomes possible to see recurring motifs and shifting embodiments.

In following an ethnographic tradition, it is important to construct thick descriptions. Below is an excerpt of a thick description of Leah and her literacy practices:

> *Leah is an emerging literate who is steeped in children's movies, children's television and books. As yet she is not able to read and is more interested in learning to write than to read. She has many children's books at home, which in addition to Hilary's own collection, she enjoys. At the time of writing, her iPad had 30 movies, 30 audio books and 44 games on it that her parents had chosen, vetted and downloaded for her.*
>
> *Leah's iPad travels with her. She wakes very early and can play with it until the alarm goes off at 6h00 or 7h00 depending on whether or not it is a school day. She can operate this technology with confidence, is adept at opening folders, inserting her headphone, adjusting the volume, the size of the image and the orientation of the screen. She knows how to switch to pause, to mute, to fast forward and to rewind. This knowledge is so embodied that she does not have to think about what to do.*
>
> *In addition to the iPad, her parents take her to the movies regularly, and have downloaded countless movies and children's television programmes from Netflix, which she can ask to watch on the TV screen. She can use a television remote confidently. She has watched many of Hilary's DVDs of Willems' books: including* Don't let Pigeon drive the bus *(2003),* Pigeon finds a hot dog *(2004),* Duckling gets a cookie *(2012). Movies are without question her favourite genre and what she engages with the most. Some movies she watches over and over. She seems to enjoy different movie versions of the same story as well as the same story in book form. She has toys of the characters from many of her favourite movies and books. Her immersion in narrative texts has given her a wide range of resources for imaginative and linguistic play.*

Data analysis: a bird's eye view

An ethnographic approach combined with a focus on multimodal texts generates a large body of data. This presents a challenge in making principled decisions of how much data needs to be included and at what level of detail. Selection should be representative of the data and not cherry-picked. This is made more difficult because what methods or approaches enable one to 'capture, define, analyse, and represent the meaning potential of interwoven, diverse semiotic modes' (Flewitt, 2011, p. 295) has not been clearly established.

Having the perspectives of two researchers in constant conversation about the data is an advantage. We find ourselves returning to certain incidents and themes. Reading the literature in the field provides insights; our understandings of Leah and her play grow over time; and in comparing different data sets and new data we realise how partial some of our understandings are, and what we just got wrong. One of the 'issues' we kept returning to was how the character of Pigeon from Willems' Pigeon books regularly inserted himself into Leah's world. We use the 'Pigeon data set' (see Table 7.2 for a visual summary) to answer the emerging research question:

> What is the inter-relationship between Leah's digital and print literacies in her construction of texts during collaborative play and how are these literacies embodied?

Table 7.2 The Pigeon data set

Leah's and Hilary's texts produced in collaborative play	
	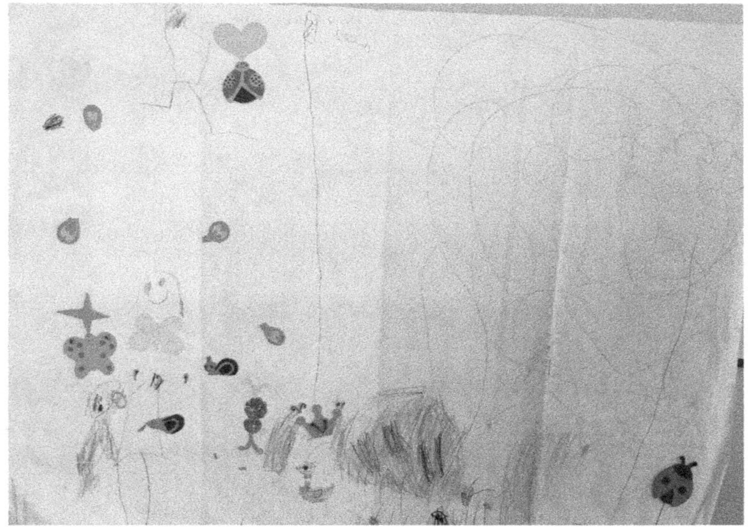
Map: *Pigeon and Duckling give the Princess something*	Map: *The story of the stolen crown*

(Continued)

Table 7.2 (Continued)

Leah's and Hilary's texts produced in collaborative play

Leah's first Pigeon book

Leah's second Pigeon book

Data generated by Hilary

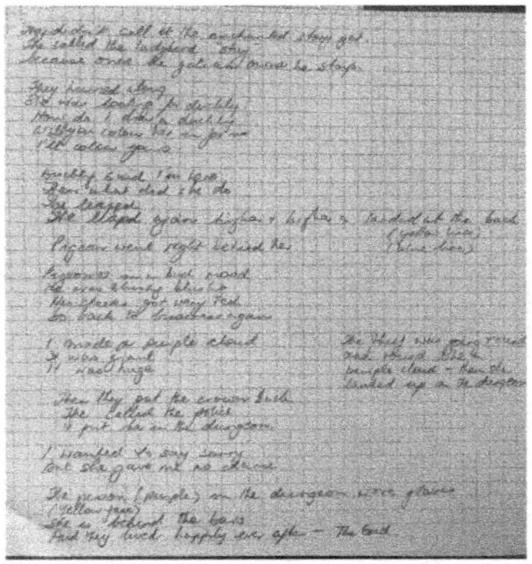

Fieldnotes

L: You can see the storm clouds.

H: Huh?

L: You know like in a comic, when they draw a dark cloud over someone's head. 3/9/17

Interview transcript

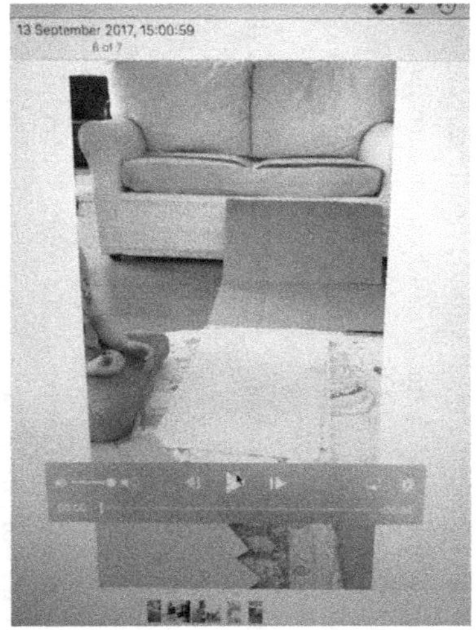

Video

Photograph

Print, Multimedia and On-line texts

Willems' Pigeon books
Don't let the Pigeon drive the bus,
The Pigeon finds a hotdog,
Don't let the Pigeon stay up late,
The Pigeon takes a bath.
The covers can be seen on Google Images.

Animated DVDs produced by Willems
Don't let the Pigeon drive the bus,
Don't let the Pigeon stay up late,
Pigeon finds a hotdog.

YouTube videos
e.g. How to draw Pigeon. (see for example, https://youtu.be/_mkgx2J3J-E)

Fairclough's approach to analysis allows us to integrate the questions arising from our ethnographic analysis and our theoretical framework into his model. Our adaptation of Fairclough's model is represented in Figure 7.2.

Analysis of the conditions of production and reception

The Pigeon maps and books produced by Leah could not have been imagined without extensive knowledge of Willems' stories. Hilary has read the Pigeon books aloud so many times that Leah knows them off by heart. When she subsequently and repeatedly watched the animated versions of these stories on DVD, her knowledge of plot, setting, narrative, dialogue and characterisation were reinforced and extended. We argue that the middle class literacy practice of being read-aloud to is deepened by watching and listening to the same stories on DVD, a digital literacy practice. The meaning potential of multiple modes (oral, visual, verbal, spatial, gestural) embedded in these literacy practices enhance Leah's understanding of narrative and text creation. The result is the same as noted by Rowsell and Harwood (2015, p. 139): When 'children design texts by layering personal interests, experiences, and histories with media driven understandings, more universal texts tend to emerge'.

Leah finds the books funny and takes great pleasure in the humour created by Pigeon's behaviour in the videos. The stories talk to childhood experiences of food, bedtime, bath-time, sharing and fantasies of doing grown-up things. Pigeon, who represents the 'hard-done-by' child, tries to get what he wants by sulking, pleading, cajoling, bribing, whining, complaining, guilt-tripping and throwing temper tantrums. Children find it hilarious to see their own behaviour in Pigeon, as evidenced in Willems' video-recorded engagement with child-audiences (see extra feature, 'Mo and Pigeon visit a school', in Weston Wood Studios' 2010 DVD, *Don't let the Pigeon drive the bus*). In this feature, Willems models ways of getting children to interact with the stories, as the responsible child who refuses Pigeon's demands. Leah loves loudly shouting, 'No', to Pigeon's demands when the books are read to her and her whole body responds. This embodied engagement finds expression in her drawings of children responding 'No' to Pigeon in her artwork (Figure 7.3) for her first Pigeon book, *Don't let the Pigeon watch TV*. The capitalised and extended 'Nos' are an example of transmediation.

The positioning of children as ideal reader-viewers requires a superior disposition that laughs at Pigeon's foibles. Leah continues to embody this disposition as she takes on the role of writer, which enables her to replicate Willems' satirical tone. Her access to digital technology affords her access to the author with his texts. Willems explicitly encourages children to make up their own stories and teaches them how to draw his characters. The normalised practice of access to information in on-line spaces, and fluid boundaries between text ownership, benefits Leah as a writer/creator in the off-line time and space she inhabits.

Leah's experience of Willems' books and videos are deepened by her engagement with other genres, modes and media. The Disney Princess films provide fertile ground for her creative imaginings in her Pigeon maps. These maps (see Figures 7.5 and 7.6) are examples of

> 'Big worlds' with rich literary resources, such as engrossing narratives and memorable characters for 'thick play', that is, repeated intensive and extensive playing and replaying that develops deeper literary understanding
>
> *(Wohlwend, 2015, p. 548)*

Hilary is implicated as a 'player' in the conditions of production and reception; and following ethnographic practice, this needs to be acknowledged. Hilary's academic knowledge of literacy

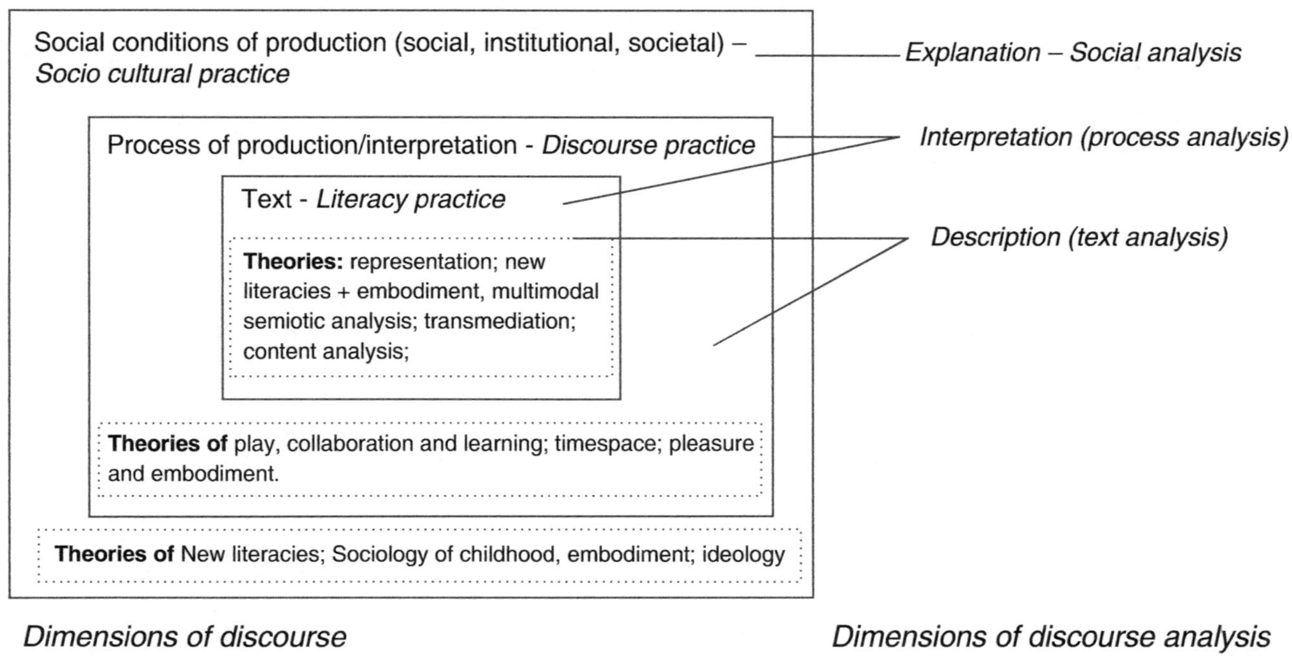

Figure 7.2 Fairclough's model with theory inserted relevant to this study

Figure 7.3 Leah's artwork of children responding 'No' to Pigeon

and childhood and practical experience of children's literature, movies and the internet, brings her own cultural and embodied capital (Bourdieu, 1992) to this play. She had to develop a meta-cognitive awareness of her embodied tendencies to teach while playing. She makes a range of spaces and material resources available for different forms of play. Leah prefers different spaces for different forms of play and spends variable amounts of time on her textual projects depending on her interest level.

The most important conditions of production of these maps and books are extensive exposure to the original texts across different modes and media, with engaged participation alongside Hilary.

Analysis of the processes of production

Leah doesn't always choose textual play. When she does, she decides what and where they should play. She decides when she has had enough or whether she wants to go back to work on something they worked on before. Often, she takes a break and returns to her chosen project the same day. At other times, she may spend several hours across different days on one project. Hilary has created an art box for Leah with a range of materials. What is in the box changes, but consistently includes:

Drawing implements: pencils, pencil crayons, wax crayons, felt tip pens.
Cutting and sticking: scissors, glue sticks, masking tape, sticky tape.
Paper: white and coloured A4 sheets, patterned paper, coloured Post-Its.
Stickers: coloured dots, stars, children's themed stickers, rubbery sheets of glitter paper, foam stickers.

Drawing maps

The map paper is stuck to the floor with masking tape. Leah likes to work on a large 'canvas' where there is room for two people to play (Figure 7.4). The organisation of space and time enable particular forms of embodiment. A large 'canvas' requires a large work space which creates opportunities for collaboration. Working on the floor enables greater efficiency of movement compared to moving around a table. This spatial organisation enables bodies to lie down, stretch over and across the page, create a large sweep of lines, and tiny fine-grained details. The 'canvas' size offers the possibility of a time-dense project, that can sap a body of energy, but also fires the imagination, compelling an artist to return time and again to fill in the details of a complex narrative landscape.

Leah's first Pigeon map, *Pigeon and Duckling give the Princess something*, was not completed in one sitting (Figure 7.5). It began with the amalgamation of two Willems stories, *The Pigeon finds a hotdog* (2004) and *The Duckling gets a cookie* (2012). Hilary was instructed to draw Pigeon and Duckling on the right-hand side of the page, whilst Leah stuck stickers on the other side. The crown and hand mirror stickers prompted her to draw a princess. She then joined Hilary and drew the sun followed by the hotdog stand. Only after that did she decide that Pigeon should give the Princess a hotdog and Duckling should give her a cookie. This led her to draw Pigeon's Princess-thought-bubble and to work out how to show Pigeon moving from one side of the page to the other, to present the Princess with a hotdog. She represented Pigeon's journey in pigeon 'foot' prints. She asked Hilary to draw Duckling's 'foot' prints. The remaining detail was added on a different day.

The story of the stolen crown was the next map Leah produced (Figure 7.6). It has less detail and was completed in a shorter time. Leah began by sticking thick rubbery stickers of the

Figure 7.4 Leah at work on a map

Figure 7.5 Pigeon and Duckling give the Princess something

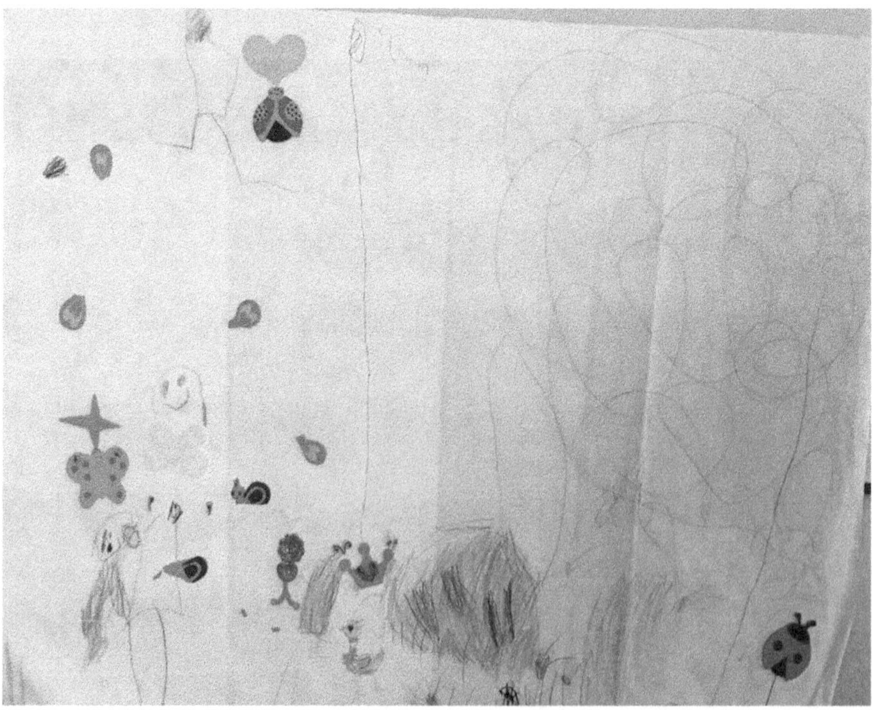

Figure 7.6 The story of the stolen crown

butterflies, the beetles, the hearts and the pink flower-shaped glitter pieces onto the page. The story was built from these. Next, she drew the giant lady bug and the fairy. When she decided to use the yellow butterfly as part of the fairy, she tore off the feelers and added them to the glitter pieces to make another insect. At this stage she was working on an idealised garden with insects and a fairy. However, as soon as she saw the crown, it became the focus of the imaginative play. She drew an evil girl on the left, and then drew two more girls in a row, who represent the same girl, with the last girl stealing the crown. Having taken the crown, the girl jumped straight up in the air to get away, represented by the straight vertical line, and then moved around and around, represented by circling lines on the right of the page. She ended up below the circles. Her head and hands are above Duckling's blue pond. Finally, she's at the bottom of the page, below the giant yellow bodied ladybird. The yellow body is cross-hatched to show that she has been caught and jailed. A black felt tip pen makes the bars stand out. Almost everything else is in wax crayon, with the escape route in purple. While Leah wove this imagined narrative, Hilary drew Duckling and her pond, as Leah requested. There was no attempt to include Duckling in the story. In this story the Princess appears in reduced symbolised form as a word (princess) and a crown. The crown shows the use of synecdoche, a sophisticated literary device.

Writing books

The process of producing Pigeon books is quite different. The spatial logic of creating a book is different to creating a map. The books are produced in three stages and require an upright seated body. In stage one Hilary and Leah sit at the computer and work out the story, which Hilary types with Leah beside her making decisions; then Hilary prints the pages, staples and binds them into a book. In the final stage Leah draws the images to accompany the words, with help from Hilary on request. Hilary took a larger role in the design and development of the first Pigeon book, modelling the process for Leah. Leah's current inability to type, write and read print means that she does not engage fully with the technology, but her talk is underpinned by her knowledge of story that comes from the books, an ear for dialogue that comes from film and an unconscious sense of how dialogue drives Willems' narratives. *Pigeon goes to the beach* reads like a script. We'd argue that the oral mode has influenced the genre, and Hilary is more amanuensis than joint author.

Pigeon goes to the beach begins with Pigeon thinking about going to the beach. He approaches the Busdriver and asks if he will take Pigeon there. The Busdriver agrees to drop him off, but doesn't want to visit the beach himself. Pigeon lists the benefits of the beach, persuading the Busdriver to try it. Busdriver and Duckling, who they meet on the beach, love the beach. Pigeon complains about the hard sand, salty water, big waves and dogs chasing him. He goes for a swim to cheer himself up but nearly drowns. As Duckling and Busdriver are leaving after a lovely day, Pigeon comments that the rockpools might be better. Busdriver and Ducking, reply: 'Yeah, Right!'.

A comparison of the books and triangulation with observations and fieldnotes indicates that by the time *Pigeon goes to the beach* was written, Leah was more confident, and Hilary was better at relinquishing control. Leah needed help drawing most of the busdriver pictures and Pigeon diving into the water. For the rest, Leah thought of the words and did most of the artwork. Hilary had a discussion with her about punch lines, and she chose the ironic 'Yeah, Right' for the last page. She has also perfectly captured the spirit of Pigeon's character.

What emerges again in this description of the processes of production is the importance of engaged collaboration. Leah likes to draw but never undertakes large-scale projects independently.

Hilary only draws now for an appreciative six-year-old, even one who makes her do things again when she gets it wrong. It is the shared pleasure of being in the child's world that sustains the activity. Collaborative play, in this instance, minimises individual weaknesses and instead a mutually beneficial literacy practice is developed. Wohlwend (2015) argues that:

> We produce culture when we imagine with others, as we create and agree upon shared ideas of what it means to be and belong in a particular location or to a particular group. Cultures are sustained by shared, automatic, embodied routines.
>
> *(Wohlwend, 2015, p. 549)*

We also connect interpersonally and deepen our relationships through shared creative endeavours.

Analysis of the texts

Apart from a recent incident where Leah took her own photographs of the text she and Hilary created, Leah's interactions with digital technologies have been as a consumer. While she is not yet working as an independent creator in the digital domain, the analysis of the two Pigeon maps and *Pigeon goes to the beach* indicate the influence of digital technologies on her production of texts. What is fascinating is the way in which Leah's access to, understanding of, and experimentation with genres, modes, and resources result in sophisticated and complex acts of productive meaning-making. Conversations, videos, the stories around text production and the completed texts themselves, reveal a child whose literate habitus is fundamentally shaped by media and digital technologies.

The inspiration for many of Leah's textual creations is not story, but materials. Thus, it is important to consider the inter-relationship between technology, materiality and embodiment. Pahl and Rowell (2010, p. 10) make the case that we need to pay attention to sensory responses and 'emotional resonance' of objects. Foam stickers are often a starting point for Leah and she begins the creative process by happily submitting to the agency of the colourful, glittery, sticky materials (Dixon & Janks, 2017). The sheer sensory pleasure of touching, cutting, pulling, sticking and fingers being stuck to the stickers begins a creative process, which opens spaces for experimentation and exploiting the potential offered by the material (Thiel, 2015).

The crown sticker in *Pigeon and Duckling give the Princess something* cannot operate as a synecdoche unless Leah has access to a range of princess experiences. The princess story is a common trope in her world. Her understanding of princesses has become embodied through multiple viewings of princess movies, playing princess games on her iPad, role-playing princess and sometimes just being a living, dressed-up princess (Wohlwend, 2009). Leah's understanding of a princess disposition is succinctly captured in the Princess's imperious injunction to Pigeon after receiving his hotdog gift: 'Pigeon go to the pet shop in the city. Maybe you can get adopted as a pet' (Figure 7.5).

The crown re-emerges in *The story of the stolen crown* where Pigeon and Duckling are present in the picture, but do not play a role in the narrative. Evident is Leah's understanding of the genre conventions of princess stories that she has gained from a range of media: evil characters covet objects from royalty and their plans are thwarted.

Data analysis often throws up unexpected avenues of enquiry. A question that caused a great deal of discussion was the role of Pigeon and Duckling in these transmedia texts. We wondered why Pigeon and Duckling inhabit the world of princesses, but not Willems' other characters like Elephant and Piggie. We were unsure how to answer this question and returned to the data, literature and theory, talking through a range of possibilities. We explored a number of options;

the materiality of the texts did not hold up against other data. Ryan's (2012) concept of the internal logic of possible worlds derived from literary theory was dismissed disdainfully by Leah:

> Elephant and Piggie don't know Pigeon. They are not in the same story. Pigeon is in the Princess's land and everyone knows the Princess.

The crossover of Pigeon and Duckling into the Princess' world is influenced by Leah's interactions with technology: vivid, moving, character-filled films with complex storylines, and Willems' picturebooks in the media of print and video. The compositional possibilities afforded by the genre of Disney Princess movies finds expression in the entry of other characters into the map worlds. The spatial possibilities offered by the 'canvas' mean that more action/complex storylines influenced by film worlds can be captured visually. Pigeon's and Duckling's world as created by Willems has much tighter boundaries and limited characters. His composition and style are minimalist, which affects the narrative interactions between characters. These are short and usually limited to two characters. This is evident in *Pigeon and Duckling give the Princess something*. The map is visually complex but the storyline has limited character interactions: Pigeon and Duckling think about giving the Princess a hotdog or cookie; they walk to her; they change who has the cookie and hotdog; they give their gifts to the Princess; she thinks about the pet shop and tells Pigeon to go to it; Pigeon goes; children arrive at the pet shop and think about buying a pigeon. In contrast, in Leah's Pigeon books each page has either Pigeon talking to himself, or two characters interacting with one another.

Aligned with this is another more practical point about access and capability. Leah and Hilary don't know how to draw Elephant and Piggie, other characters of Willems. They still have to watch the how-to videos and practise. Learning to produce a book, rather than maps, requires a particular set of bodily skills. As Leah gains more competence and confidence she takes on more compositional tasks. While Hilary drew Pigeon and Duckling in the maps, Willems' videos taught Leah to draw them. This access to the 'invisible' practices of drawing characters, and time to practise, have become embodied. The same can be said of her emergent writing. Presently Leah is experimenting with writing letters and words in relation to pictures (Figure 7.3) and orally dictating storylines, but this will change. She already considers this 'my story, not your story'.

Leah's book shows a level of sophisticated visual literacy informed by the medium of both print and film. She understands how images convey a range of meanings. For example, she can represent the difference between speech and thought using thought and speech bubbles in a medium that lacks an oral mode. She uses speech and thought bubbles in *Pigeon and Duckling give the Princess something. Pigeon goes to the beach* begins with Pigeon thinking about going to the beach, which is captured in a thought bubble. Understanding the difference between thought and speech is complex, what is more so, is that these thought bubbles represent desire. They provide insight into the actions and motivations of the characters: Pigeon wants to go to the beach then he asks the Busdriver to take him. The presence of thought bubbles moves the stories out of the literal into the psychological realm.

This affective awareness is also evident in how Leah represents emotions through bodily positions. When Pigeon discovers the beach is not to his liking he is depicted side-on with his wings and head hanging dejectedly (Figure 7.7); his wings are drawn aloft in the sea when he thinks he is drowning. Leah is a keen observer of techniques used by graphic artists to convey meaning – in commenting on an angry tennis player seen on television, she asked if Hilary could see the clouds: 'you know like in a comic when they draw a dark cloud over someone's head'.

Leah's ability to depict movement that draws on her visual and linguistic resources has increased in sophistication. In *The story of the stolen crown* straight and scribbled lines represent

Figure 7.7 Examples of Leah using body positions to represent emotions and movement

the movements of the evil girl escaping. Other modes and techniques replace these scribbled lines in her later work. In *Pigeon goes to the beach* she uses onomatopoeia to indicate the bus moving. The bus goes 'Vroom vroom vroomy vroom vroom' and is adapted from Willems' (2003) *Don't let Pigeon drive the bus*. Movement is also shown through bodily positions, for example to show pigeon diving, he is drawn upside down with his wings parallel to his head and his head and beak facing the water.

A final word

The inter-relationship between Leah's digital and print literacies is complex. She is a consumer of digital texts rather than a producer, but the influence of the digital looms large in her production of transmedia texts. This would not be possible without being situated in a resource-rich social context that provides the time and space needed to engage. Leah enters collaborative play encounters with embodied practices of independence and agency that the digital affords: she doesn't need adults' help with her iPad and absorbs messages from a range of semiotic systems. The multimodal nature of the texts and technology she engages with enable her to apply this knowledge to her own multimodal textual representations. What is also clear is the importance of collaboration in the textual playground, the mutual benefits of two players sharing skill sets, and connections forged in the social relationship. Print and digital literacies become entangled through affective engagements with materials and the sensory pleasures they afford. Spatial and temporal organisations mould Leah's literate habitus as she develops an understanding of the meaning potential of modes, genres and literary devices.

The methodological decisions we made have enabled us to understand Leah's embodied literacy practices in particular ways, but limited us in others. We have engaged in our own form of collaborative play, traversing a complex and changing data set that has been beneficial but time consuming in a publication-driven environment. We will need to consider how this ethnography will need to change as Leah's print literacy grows and new digital engagements reconfigure her play, possibly resulting in a relegated adult playmate. While we are deeply aware of our impact as researchers in the research site, we are also increasingly aware of how the technology we use to record data is used by children for play and appropriated by them. What possibilities and challenges does this present? What embodied practices do researchers need to take on in a world where children are so comfortable with digital technologies and media?

Although the findings of this study can only ever be partial tellings, we have nevertheless tried to show our own sense of wonder at the 'big worlds' Leah inhabits.

References

Bearne, E. (2003) Rethinking literacy: Communication, representation and text. *Reading Literacy and Language* November, 98–103.

Bourdieu, P. (1992) *Language and symbolic power*. Oxford: Polity Press.

Burnett, C. (2010) Technology and literacy in early childhood educational settings: A review of research. *Journal of Early Childhood Literacy* 10 (3), 247–270.

Burnett, C. (2015) Being together in classrooms at the interface of the physical and virtual: Implications for collaboration in on/off-screen sites. *Learning, Media and Technology* 41 (4), 1–24.

Clark, A. and Moss, P. (2011) *Listening to young children: The mosaic approach*. London: NCB.

Comber, B. (2015) *Literacy, place and the pedagogies of possibility*. New York: Routledge.

Crescenzi, L., Jewitt, C. and Price, S. (2014) The role of touch in preschool children's learning using iPad versus paper interaction. *Australian Journal of Language & Literacy* 37 (2), 86–95.

Dahlberg, G. and Moss, P. (2005) *Ethics and politics in early childhood education*. London and New York: Routledge.

Dixon, K. (2011) *Literacy and the schooled body*. London and New York: Routledge.

Dixon, K. and Janks, H. (2017) *Disrupting privilege: Exploring the everyday spaces children inhabit through talk and text*. Paper presented at American Education Research Association, San Antonio, 27 April–1 May.

Don't let the Pigeon drive the bus (2010) DVD. Weston Wood Studios, United States.

Dyson, A. (2013) *Rewriting the basics: Literacy learning in children's cultures*. New York: Teacher's College Press.

Dyson, A., ed. (2016) *Child cultures, schooling, and literacy*. London and New York: Routledge.

Edwards, S. (2013) Digital play in the early years: A contextual response to the problem of integrating technologies and play-based pedagogies in the early years. *European Early Childhood Education Research Journal* 21 (2), 199–212.

Fairclough, N. (1989) *Language and power*. London: Arnold.

Fairclough, N. (1995) *Critical discourse analysis*. London: Longman.

Fargas-Malet, M., McSherry, D., Larkin, E. and Robinson, C. (2010) Research with children: Methodological issues and innovative techniques. *Journal of Early Childhood Research* 8 (2), 175–192.

Farman, J. (2015) Stories, spaces and bodies: The production of embodied space through mobile media storytelling. *Communication Research and Practice* 1 (2), 101–116.

Flewitt, R. (2011) Bringing ethnography to a multimodal investigation of early literacy in a digital age. *Qualitative Research* 11 (3), 293–310.

Flewitt, R., Messer, D. and Kucirkova, N. (2015) New directions for early literacy in a digital age: The iPad. *Journal of Early Childhood Literacy* 15 (3), 289–310.

Foucault, M. (1977) *Discipline and punish. The birth of the prison*. Sheridan, A. (trans.) London: Penguin Books.

Foucault, M. (1980) *Power/knowledge. Selected interviews and other writings 1972–1977*. Gordon, C. (trans. and ed.) New York: Harvester Wheatsheaf.

Gallacher, L. and Gallagher, M. (2008) Methodological immaturity in childhood research? Thinking through 'Participatory Methods'. *Childhood* 15 (4), 499–516.

Harwood, D, ed. (2017) *Crayons and iPads: Learning and teaching of children in a digital world*. Thousand Oaks, CA: Sage.

Heath, S., Street, B. and Mill, M. (2008) *Ethnography*. New York: Teacher's College Press.

James, A. and Prout, A., eds. (2015) *Constructing and reconstructing childhood*. London and New York: Routledge.

Kress, G. (2004) *Reading images: Multimodality, representation and new media*. Paper presented at the Expert Forum for Knowledge Presentation, Chicago, IL. Retrieved 31 August 2017, from www.knowledge presentation.org/BuildingTheFuture/Kress2/Kress2.html.

Larson, J. and Marsh, J., eds. (2013) *The Sage handbook of early childhood literacy*. London: Sage.

Lefebvre, H. (1991) *The production of space*. Cambridge, MA: Blackwell.

Literat, I. (2013) "A pencil for your thoughts": Participatory drawing as a visual research method with children and youth. *International Journal of Qualitative Methods* 12 (1), 84–98.

Mand, K. (2012) Giving children a 'voice': Arts-based participatory research activities and representation. *International Journal of Social Research Methodology* 15 (2), 149–160.

Newfield, D. (2015) The semiotic mobility of literacy. In: Rowsell, J. and Pahl, K. (eds.) *The Routledge handbook of literacy studies*. London and New York: Routledge, 267–281.

Pahl, K. and Rowell, J. (2010) *Artifactual literacies*. New York: Teachers College Press.

Rowsell, J. and Harwood, D. (2015) "Let it go": Exploring the image of the child as a producer, consumer and inventor. *Theory Into Practice Journal Special Edition* 54 (2), 136–146.

Ryan, M.-L. (2012) Possible worlds. In: Hühn, P. et al. (eds.) *The living handbook of narratology*. Hamburg: Hamburg University. http://www.lhn.uni-hamburg.de/article/possible-worlds

Tay-Lim, J. and Lim, S. (2013) Privileging younger children's voices in research: Use of drawings and a co-construction process. *International Journal of Qualitative Methods* 12 (1), 65–83.

Thiel, J. (2014) *Literacies, materiality, and working-class lives: Encounters with muchness*. PhD thesis, University of Georgia.

Thiel, J. (2015) Vibrant matter: The intra-active role of objects in the construction of young children's literacies. *Literacy Research: Theory, Method and Practice* 64, 112–131.

Willems, M. (2004) *Pigeon finds a hot dog*. New York: Hyperion Books.

Willems, M. (2012) *The Duckling gets a cookie*. New York: Hyperion Books.

Willems, M. (2003) *Don't let pigeon drive the bus*. New York: Hyperion Books.

Wohlwend, K. (2008) Play as a literacy of possibilities: Expanding meanings in practices, materials and spaces. *Language Arts* 86 (2), 127–136.

Wohlwend, K. (2009) Damsels in discourse: Girls producing gendered identity texts through Disney Princess play. *Reading Research Quarterly* 44 (1), 57–83.

Wohlwend, K. (2015) Making, remaking and reimagining the everyday: Play creativity and popular media. In: Rowsell, J. and Pahl, K. (eds.) *The Routledge handbook of literacy studies*. London and New York: Routledge, 548–560.

8

SOCIAL MEDIA, VIDEO DATA AND HERITAGE LANGUAGE LEARNING

Researching the transnational literacy practices of young children from immigrant families

Sumin Zhao

The story of *Dawei*: childhoods across boundaries

Dawei[1]was an 8-year-old boy who I met in a small-scale, multimodal and ethnographic project (Flewitt, 2011) I conducted in 2016 in collaboration with Dr Rosie Flewitt. The aim of the project was to understand how young children from Chinese immigrant families learn and maintain their family's heritage language and culture through intergenerational communication on social media. *Dawei* lived with his Chinese mother, his Portuguese father, and his 6-year-old brother *Xiaowei* in southeast London. *Dawei* and his brother were both born in London. Each summer, they would visit their father's country of origin, Portugal, but paid less frequent visits to their mother's home country China (for a more detailed description of *Dawei's* case see Zhao & Flewitt, forthcoming). *Dawei* and his brother's family life is representative of a growing number of young children whose lives move across the boundaries of nations, languages and cultures (Martínez-Álvarez & Ghiso, 2017; Skrbiš, 2008; Orellana et al., 2001; Tyrrell et al., 2013). UNICEF statistics (UNICEF, 2016) suggest that in 2015 there were 244 million people living outside living outside their country of birth, with 31 million being children under 18. At home, *Dawei* spoke mainly English and occasionally he would converse with his mother in Chinese. As their father did not consider it necessary for *Dawei* and *Xiaowei* to learn Portuguese, they did not speak their father's first language. Apart from attending the local state primary, *Dawei* and his brother were also taking Chinese lessons at a community school on Saturdays. Living in an English-dominated environment, the brothers had few opportunities to use and further develop their heritage language and literacy in a meaningful and contextualised way. For young children like *Dawei*, heritage language loss is a common phenomenon (Verdon et al., 2014). Heritage language loss can impact on familial relations and young children's sense of identity (Wong Fillmore, 2000; Oh & Fuligni, 2010).

In January 2011, a new social media app called WeChat (or 微信 in Chinese) developed by Tencent was launched in China. In the succeeding years, WeChat became a key digital communication channel for the Chinese speaking population both inside and outside of China (Yu et al., 2017; Zhou & Gui, 2017). At the time of writing, it is the fourth most popular social media service in the world with 980 million monthly active users (Statistica, 2018). *Dawei*'s mother joined WeChat in 2014 to connect with families, relatives and friends in China as well as Chinese speaking friends in the UK. At home, *Dawei* liked to observe his mother chatting on WeChat. He discovered that his mother would type Chinese characters on iPad using *Pinyin* – the Romanisation of Chinese – as the input method. This discovery enabled *Dawei* to participate in his mother's WeChat conversations. Research of children in the European context has shown that younger children (under eight) use social media often through participating in their parents' social media practices (Holloway et al., 2013; Marsh et al., 2017; Zaman et al., 2016). For *Dawei* and several other children in the project, WeChat became an important site for learning and maintain their heritage language and culture

Understanding new forms of practices as exemplified in *Dawei's* social media practices has emerged as a central agenda in language and literacy research in recent years. This has led to various attempts to reconceptualise language and literacy in an age of global digital mobility. New theories often emphasise the notion of 'trans', be it at the level of interaction – translanguaging (Li, 2018) – or at the level of practice – transnational literacies (Hawkins, 2018; Kell, 2017; Warriner, 2009). There have been several studies of transnational literacy practices of multilingual adolescences and young people using social media (Lam & Rosario-Ramos, 2009; Stewart, 2014; Wang, 2017). Relatively little is known about similar practices of younger children (under eight). To bridge this gap in our knowledge and to study literacy practices that transgress the traditional spatial and temporal boundaries call for innovative methods and flexible methodological design.

Let's play a game: family literacy practices across boundaries

Figure 8.1 includes the screen capture of a WeChat exchange between *Dawei* and three Chinese speaking adults (CM2, CM3, CF2) from his mother's WeChat contact lists. The excerpt is taken from an hour-long episode in which *Dawei* and *Xiaowei* chatted with five of his mother's high school classmates living in China.

Screen Captures		Interlocutors: Three high school classmates of the mother	Dawei
		Time 15.46	
	42		**I will play a game with you.** *(Wo gen ni wan youxi)*
	43	CM3: **Hello, Dawei.** *(Dawei nihao)*	
	44	CF2: @<mother's username> **Hello, baby Dawei.** *(Dawei baobao hao)*	
	45		[Emoji: paper]
	46	CM2: [Emoji: paper]	
		Time 15.48	
	47	CM2: [Sticker: exploding heart]	
	48		[Emoji: scissors]
	49	CM2: [Emoji: paper]	
	50	CM2: [Sticker: baby doing face-palm]	
	51		**I have won** *(Wo yin-le)*
	52		CM 2: [Emoji: blushing] [I have] **lost.** *(Shu-le)*

Figure 8.1 WeChat exchange: Let's Play a Game

(adopted from Zhao & Flewitt, forthcoming)

In this exchange, *Dawei* and the adults used a mixture of written Chinese and various visual resources available on the WeChat interface such as emojis and stickers. The exchange began with *Dawei* inviting one adult (CM2) to '*wan youxi*' (play a game, L42), and they subsequently played two rounds of rock-paper-scissors using emojis. The exchange ended with *Dawei* declaring victory (L51) and the adult conceding defeat (L52). The game was interrupted briefly by two adults (CM3, CF2) greeting *Dawei* (L43–44). This exchange showcases three key characteristics of young multilingual children's language and literacy practices on social media: multimodal (Kress, 2009), translinguistic (Li, 2018) and polyadic (Zhao & Flewitt, forthcoming). While the exchange appeared to be relatively straightforward at the textual, or the interactional level, the context of the interaction is far from simple, as illustrated in Figure 8.2.

As shown in Figure 8.2, *Dawei*'s exchange with the adults on WeChat was not an isolated communicative event, but one of the three conversations that took place simultaneously. In China, his mother's school friends were having their annual reunion dinner and interacting with each other both face-to-face and on WeChat. Through a group chat, they were also interacting with their former classmates in different geographic locations in China and overseas, including *Dawei*'s mother. While in London, *Dawei*, his brother and their mother were visiting a Chinese friend who lived in the same area. Their mother was chatting with her friend while attending to the high school group chat from time to time. At one point, *Dawei* took over the *WeChat* conversation from his mother and started an extended exchange with a group of five of his mother's friends. During the WeChat conversation, he also encouraged *Xiaowei* to join in.

At the interactional level, *Dawei*'s WeChat conversations move between the boundaries of multimodal and translinguistic meaning-making repertoires. At the contextual level, they cross the boundaries between the digital and the face-to-face, between geographic locations, and between various social practices (i.e. *Dawei*'s heritage language practices intersected with the adults' reunion ritual). This boundary crossing nature of *Dawei*'s literacy practices as illustrated in the WeChat interaction results from the intersection between (at least) two types of mobility:

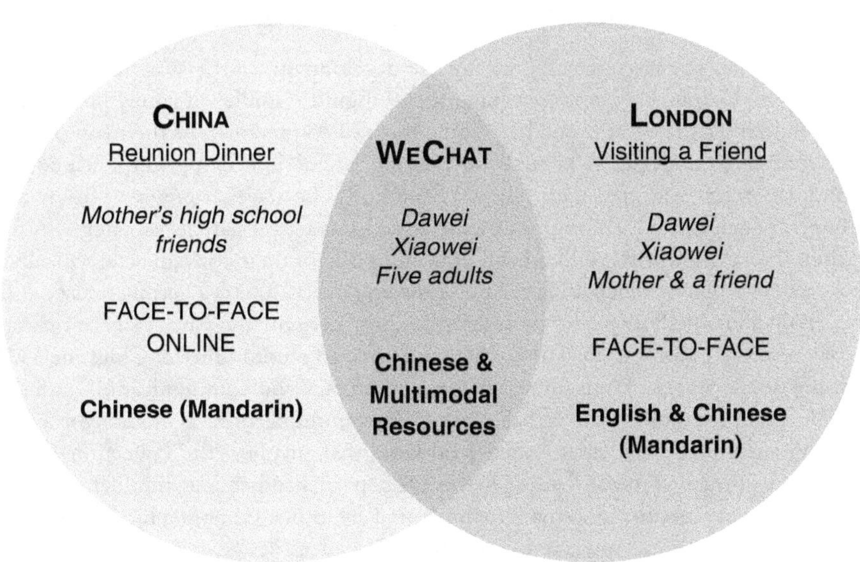

Figure 8.2 Conversational context: The Reunion Dinner
(adopted from Zhao & Flewitt forthcoming)

geographic (population movement) and technological (the spread of mobile phones and social media platforms). To put it another way, with the advances in mobile communication hardware and software technologies, family literacy practices of multilingual immigrant children like *Dawei* are no longer confined to a single tangible site: the home. They move between different sites in the country of their residence, the country of their origin as well as various transnational sites.

In the remainder of this chapter, I will review some of the key findings from the WeChat project, focusing on young children's heritage language learning with social media technologies. My main aim here is not to offer a comprehensive report of the project, as some findings discussed in this chapter have not been previously published, while others can be can be read in Zhao & Flewitt (forthcoming). Rather, the focus is on issues pertaining to data collection that arose in the WeChat project. Through a critical analysis of the detour I took, the choices I made and the rationale behind them, I hope to map out the key aspects that researchers of transnational literacy practices of young children or migrant children might consider. It is important to mention at this stage that I do not wish to suggest that the methods I used can be readily adapted for other projects. Perhaps one of the most important lessons I have learned from the field is the importance of understanding our participants (their age and social, cultural and linguistic backgrounds) in designing and adapting research methods. An iterative approach to data collection is recommended when studying an emerging phenomenon such as transnational literacy. Building good relations with participating families and gaining children's trust are critical in such an approach. In the final part of the paper, I will also briefly draw on another project which aims to develop new digital methods for studying the digital and multilingual literacy practices of children on the move. In the second project, I worked with a group of young immigrant children aged 5 to 6 with diverse cultural-linguistic backgrounds at an English medium international school in Denmark.

Methods for studying family literacy practices and adult-child interactions in the context of home

I would like to start my discussion by tracing the development of the WeChat project in relation to my own disciplinary training in linguistics. Linguistic studies of family literacy practices and adult-child interactions at home have some established practices. As the main purpose of a linguistic study is to understand 'naturally' occurring interactions in a given social context, the key consideration in choosing a data collection method is how well it preserves the 'naturalness' of the interactional data. One common method used was to ask parents or caregivers to audio record their interactions with children at a time and place of their convenience, typically focusing on a particular practice such as shared book reading (Torr, 2007) or getting dressed (Hasan & Cloran, 1990). This method is also considered less intrusive for the participants, as parents and children have more control in deciding when and what to record (Torr & Clugston, 1999).

With the development of multimodal theories of literacy and communication, audio recording, which cannot capture non-verbal modes of communication, is no longer considered adequate. Video method or 'video-based fieldwork' that involves 'the collection of naturally occurring data using video cameras' (Jewitt, 2012, p. 2) has become the 'default' choice of method. The video method is often supplemented by other ethnographic methods such as participant observation and interview. This methodological design is fairy established within social sciences, especially for projects aiming to study patterns of social interaction. Guidelines for good practices can be read in Jewitt (2012), Goldman et al. (2014) and with specific reference to the early childhood context (Flewitt, 2006); and applications of video methods in studying young children's learning and play with digital technologies at home can be found in Akhter (2016), Kucirkova et al. (2015), Kucirkova and Sakr (2015) and Marsh et al. (2017).

When recording social interactions mediated by technology, recording techniques need to be carefully decided, such as camera types, the placement of the camera (see Caton and Hackett in this volume) and the capturing of on-screen activities (see Fallon in this volume). This is particularly relevant for those who wish to undertake a fine-grained multimodal analysis, as data need to be captured in such detail that it can subsequently be transcribed (Bezemer & Mavers, 2011; Cowan, 2014; Flewitt et al., 2009) and analysed. These details can include – depending on the research questions of the project – the verbal and non-verbal interactions between participants (e.g. speech is clearly recorded, gestures of the participants are in full view), and between the participant(s) and the technological interface (e.g. a child tapping on a particular area of the screen).

The WeChat project was originally inspired by a study by Kelly (2013), which looked at how grandparents scaffold the language learning and play of their geographically distant grandchildren on Skype. There were also other emerging studies reporting the use of digital technologies and social media for distance intergenerational communication by bilingual migrant children (Morgan & Peter, 2014). Kelly embraced a multimodal analytical framework (Kress & Leeuwen, 2006), and collected her dataset using methods and methodological design commonly adopted in video-based fieldwork. The design of the WeChat project had aimed to replicate her Skype study, in particular her recording technique. Kelly described her recording process, which appeared fairly straightforward. According to Kelly, 'data relating to the detailed communicative exchanges through remote technology were obtained by filming and recording the grandparents' view of the screen and transcribing and coding the material' (p5.). Using this method, she was able to capture the interaction between the participants on screen. In her video data, the body of the grandparents who usually sat in front of the computer in the UK appeared in a small box on the lower left-hand side of the screen, while the children and their parents in Australia occupy the centre of the video frame. The children were constantly moving as they were playing, which resulted in 'constant repositioning of the camera, normally by their mother, to focus on them or the objects of their attention, resulting in a fluidity of movement that gave a variability to the images on the screen in the UK' (p. 5).

Shortly after I started the fieldwork in London, the original research design had to be adjusted, as we encountered different practices in the field to those we had anticipated, and a reluctance in the families for video cameras to be used in the privacy of their homes. There are several possible explanations for this reluctance. The first is the increasing privacy concern of parents in the age of social media. The second has to do with my complicated 'inside/outsider' (Kusow, 2003) status in the field. While sharing the same language and cultural heritage with the families, I, a Chinese immigrant to Australia, have experienced immigration in a different national context. Not being based in the UK permanently at the time also meant I was not able to establish with the families the type of trust a researcher in a long-term ethnographic project could have. Different cultural attitudes towards video filming young children in the family context might be a third contributing factor, an issue that worth further exploring.

The dataset I eventually collected consisted of digital records (video clips and screenshots of children's WeChat-based heritage language and literacy practices) submitted by parents, interview data and fieldnotes (observation in a Saturday Chinese school and during home visits) (see Zhao & Flewitt, forthcoming). The only family that was video-recorded was *Dawei*'s. The video data, showing the brothers using their mother's iPad to talk with their maternal grandparents on WeChat, was not analysed in detail as it was not sufficient in terms of quantity or quality for a detailed multimodal study of social interaction. The video data was, therefore, used as 'fieldnotes' to contextualise our interpretation of the dataset.

With hindsight, several details in Kelly's description of her research were overlooked in the initial data collection design of the WeChat project: (1) Kelly was studying her own grandchildren and the interaction was recorded from her perspective; (2) Kelly and her grandchildren were communicating in their home language as well as the children's L1 (first language), English, which is also the dominant language in the countries where they lived respectively at the time, the UK and Australia; (3) Kelly took initiation in the intergenerational Skype interaction and scaffolded the interaction for her grandchildren; (4) she and her partner, the grandfather of the children, used Skype on their desktop, while the grandchildren used Skype on iPad and were in fact constantly moving from room to room. In her description, only the final point was directly related to her method. Yet, all factors – our relation to the children, the perspective we take in our research, the cultural-linguistic background of the family and the children, the technology (hardware and software) and not surprisingly the nature of the social practices – would all impact on how I could (or indeed should) video record naturally occurred WeChat interactions.

Researching young children's heritage language learning on WeChat: reports from the field

The WeChat project used opportunistic sampling method. A personal contact provided three initial families, who offered access to a local Saturday Chinese school, where six more families were recruited. The families in the project were highly diverse in terms of social-economical background, immigration history and parental education and linguistic backgrounds; see Table 8.1.

Through informal and semi-structured interviews, I discovered that children from the participating families did not engage in lengthy video-based interaction with their grandparents or relatives. The parents described their children's participation in WeChat calls as infrequent or insubstantial, e.g. 'very brief' (Families 1 and 8) and involving 'just greetings' (Family 5). When asked to offer their perspectives on why the interactions tended to be infrequent and short, parents gave explanations along four lines:

- ***Children's age***. Several parents believed that their children could not engage in sustained WeChat video call because they were young and easily distracted. For example: 'at his age, they are easily distracted' (Family 1); 'it is very hard for him to sit down for more than a few minutes' (Family 5); 'she will come over and say hello and move on to something else quickly' (Family 7).
- ***Difficulty in coordinating the children' and the grandparents' schedules***. The time zone difference between the UK and China was cited as one of contributing factors: 'his schedule on Saturdays is full, he has his Chinese classes in the morning and then Kudo in the afternoon' (Family 2); 'when they come back from the school, it is already bedtime for my parents' (Family 6).
- ***Lack of conversation topics***. Some parents believed that the grandparents and the grandchildren did not have much to discuss: 'they don't really have much to discuss with the grandparents' (Family 6); 'they run out of things to say quickly' (Family 8), 'children don't have much to talk about with their grandparents' (Family 1).[2]
- ***Children's presence on WeChat as 'reports' to the grandparents***. Most parents see their WeChat interactions as oriented towards their own parents: 'it is really/mainly for the elders' (Family 7, 9); 'my mother wants to know how he is doing' (Family 2).

Table 8.1 An overview of the participating families

	Age	*G.*	*Birth*	*Parental education*		*Parental profession*		*Immigration background*	*Siblings*	*Education*		*Home languages*
				Mother	*Father*	*Mother*	*Father*				*Chinese school*	
1	3,5	M	LND	BA (CH) 20s	BA (UK) 20s	Small Business Owner	Small Business Owner	Chinese (Skilled)	Sister 1.5	Private		Chinese >* English
2	6,1	M	CN	Master (LND) 40s	School Leaver 60s	Part-time Kudo instructor	Retired Military	Anglo-Chinese	Stepbrother 21	State	√	English > Chinese
3	7,1	M	LND	Master (LND) 40s	School Leaver 50s	Freelance (Business)	Trades	Anglo-Chinese	N/A	State	√	English
4	4,8	F	LND	Master (LND) 30s	Bachelor (CH) 30s	Accountant	Trades	Chinese (Skilled)	N/A	State	√	Chinese
5	4,5	M	LND	Master (LND) 30s	Bachelor 30s	Homemaker	Professional	Scottish-Chinese	N/A	Private		English
6	6	M	LND	Master (LND) 40s	School Leaver 50s	Homemaker	Trades	Portuguese-Chinese	Brother 8	State	√	English > Chinese
7	3,4	F	CN	School Leaver 30s	School Leaver 30s	Homemaker	Business Owner	Chinese (Investment)	Sister 12	Private		Chinese
8	5	F	LND	Master (CH) 30s	PhD 30s	Professional	Research Scientist	Chinese (Skilled)	N/A	State	√	Chinese > English
9	3,7	M	LND	Master (LND) 40s	Master (LND) 40s	Professional	Professional	Chinese (Skilled)	Sister 6	Private	√	Chinese > English

Key: LND = London; CN = China

* ***Home languages listed in order of significance.***

The sustained interaction as described by Kelly (2013) was only reported by one of the families (Family 7) as a 'recent' development. The child of the family was a five-year-old girl. Both of her parents were born in China and came to London for their master's studies. At the time of data collection, both parents were employed as professionals, and the father, a research scientist, was also pursuing a part-time PhD. In the interview, the father reported that his father, the parental grandfather, was concerned with the lack of communication with his granddaughter, because he did not speak English, which was the main language the girl spoke both at home and in school at the time. A few weeks prior to our interview, the grandfather started to look for Chinese learning apps and books for his granddaughter to use, which would then become topics for discussion during their weekly WeChat video chat. As Kelly (2013) observed in her study, adults' scaffolding plays a critical role in generating and maintaining distant intergenerational communication on social media. The absence of adult scaffolding could have contributed to the lack of sustained intergenerational WeChat interaction as reported by the parents in the project. It is also worth mentioning here that the grandfather in this case, like Kelly, was a university academic, as home background such as educational attainments of caregivers plays a significant role in children's literacy practices (Teale, 1986).

However, as the fieldwork progressed on, one of the explanations given by the parents turned out to hold the key to understanding young children's heritage language and literacy practices on WeChat – the parents considered their children's involvement as a performance for the grandparents. This type of performative interaction on family chat groups is one of three main forms of interaction identified in 2017 by a group of researchers in a study of Chinese young adults' WeChat communication with their geographically distant parents. Yu et al. (2017) referred to it as *panoptic* interaction, and the main purpose is to project a sense of positivity for the parents and help to alleviate the parents' concerns for their children living in geographically distant locations. According to Yu et al. (2017), WeChat practices, in particular panoptic interactions, are shaped by and at the same time shaping contemporary Chinese familial values, in particular, the notion of filial duties.

In the subsequent home visits to three families (2, 5, 9), parents were observed reporting 'news' of their children to the grandparents on WeChat frequently. For two of the families (2, 5), it occurred on a daily basis. The 'reports' took different forms, including text messages, photos and video recordings of the children. The recordings were typically short video clips of children engaging in various daily activities, e.g. playing, telling a story, reading and writing. One common type of video captured children participating in various heritage language and literacy activities in Chinese. Families 2 and 5 agreed (in written consent with verbal assents from the children) to submit a selection of these video clips to us for analysis, while Family 9 turned down our request citing privacy concerns.

When asked about their children's uses of WeChat in the interviews, the parents did not consider these activities as children's participation but *their* reports to the grandparents *about* the children. That is, they saw these videos from the perspective of the adults. In these videos, children seemed to be fully aware of the performative nature of the recordings. For instance, they would typically look into the camera at the beginning and the end of a clip to acknowledge their 'audience', the grandparents. However, when analysed from the perspective of the children, what is fascinating about these videos is the incidental learning of heritage language that occurred during the recording. Figure 8.3 includes an example of these videos. In the video, the children were reading out Chinese texts.

Figure 8.3 WeChat video 'reports': children's language and literacy practices in Chinese

The video clips collected were transcribed and analysed using multimodal discourse analytical methods. The fine-grained analysis revealed how the making of these videos created incidental heritage language learning opportunities for the children. Table 8.2 illustrates such an example.

Table 8.2 Parental scaffolding of the child's oral narrative skills in Chinese: birthday gifts

Video	*Sequence*		*The boy*	*The mother*
	S	*L*	*Speech*	*Voice-over*
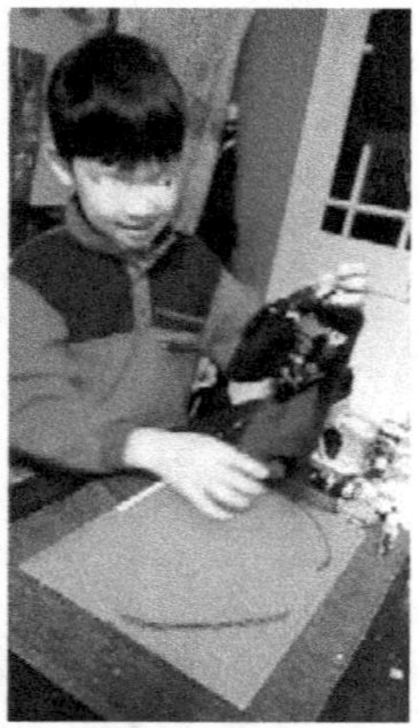	1	1	妈妈 给我 买的 这个 东西 叫 凯勒维. *Mother par-me buy this thing called Kailewei* **'[My] mother bought me this thing called Kailewei'**	
		2		为什么 给你 买 这个? *Why par-you buy this?* **'Why [have I] bought you this?'**
		3	是 因为 我 好 孩子 *be-because I good kid* **'It is because I [am] a good kid'**	
	2	4	然后 是 因为 是 我的 *then be-because is my* **'then because [it] is my'**	
		5		你 过 七岁 生日 是不是? *You spend 7th birthday isn't it* **'It's your 7th birthday, isn't it?'**

	3	6	是 我 七岁 生日 了 *be my 7th birthday -par-* **'[It] is my 7th birthday'.**
	4	7	然后 这个 三个 东西 . . . 是 . . . 我 . . .* *Then these three things are me* **'Then these three things . . . are . . . me . . .'**

(*Continued*)

Table 8.2 (Continued)

Video	*Sequence*		*The boy*	*The mother*
	S	*L*	*Speech*	*Voice-over*
	5	8	是 X ** 给我 买 *be [name] par-me buy-par* **'[They] were bought for me by X'.**	
		9		还 有 呢? *What else have-par* **'What else?'**
	6	10	然后 ....这个 东西 是......这个 是...我的 ... *Then this thing be this be my* **'Then. . . . . . .this thing is. . . . . . .this . . . is . . . my . . .'**	

	7	11	<whisper> '**Brother*****'	
		12		对啊， 你 哥哥 *yes-part, your brother* **'Yes, your brother'**.
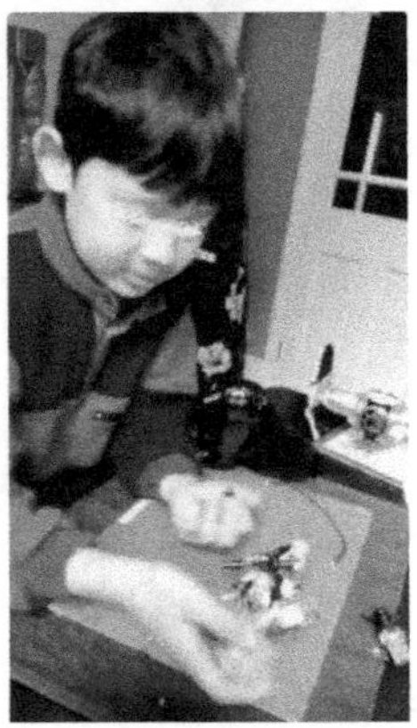	8	13	我 哥哥 的 妈妈 给我 买的 *My brother-poss-mother par-me bought-par* **'My brother's mother bought me this'**	
		14		X 哥哥 的 妈妈, *<name> bother -poss- mother* **'[your] brother's mother'**

(*Continued*)

Table 8.2 (Continued)

Video	Sequence		The boy	The mother
	S	L	Speech	Voice-over
	9	15		哥哥 的 妈妈 叫 什么 名字? *Bother-poss-mother called what name?* **'What is [your] brother's mother called?'**
		16	**'Auntie x'**	
		17		对了,好, 乖。 *Yes, ok obedient* **'Yes, ok, good boy'**
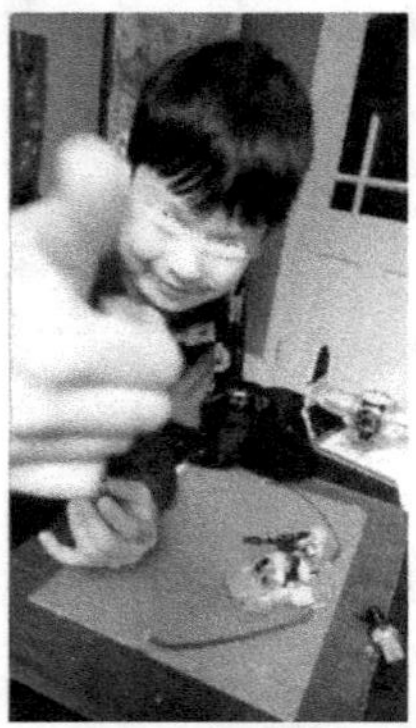	10	18	再见,婆婆 Goodbye, *puopuo (grandma)* **'Good bye, grandma'**	
		19	<makes a whoosh sound>	

* marks pauses in the speech, long pauses are marked by . . .
** All names mentioned were replaced by X
*** the brother referred to here was in fact the boy's step brother

In this episode, the mother and the boy were co-constructing a short video clip for the maternal grandmother in China. In the clip, the boy was showing and explaining three sets of presents he had received for his birthday. The mother was shooting, so she does not appear in the frame. Nevertheless, her voice can be heard throughout the video.

As can be observed in the transcript of the speech, the boy's spoken Chinese was still developing, with long pauses (e.g. L7,10) and incomplete syntax (e.g. L3, L7). To construct a coherent narrative required scaffolding support by the mother. The mother scaffolded her child's speech at both the discourse and the lexical level. The former type (discourse) of scaffolding is best exemplified in S1-S3/L1–6. In this opening scene of the clip, the boy began by showing a gift bought by his mother *'[My] mother bought me this thing called Kailewei'* (L1). The mother interjected by asking why he was given the gift ('Why [have I] bought you this?', L2), which prompted the boy's answer that he was 'a good kid' (L4). However, when he was trying to give a second reason, he could not complete the sentence – *'then because [it] is my . . .'* (L4). So he leaned out of the video frame towards his mother (S2). It is possible that he whispered something (not audible in the clip) to the mother, who followed up with another question *'It's your 7th birthday, isn't it?'*. The boy was then able to give the second reason for the gift – *'[It] is my 7th birthday'*. Here the mother asked two questions which were essential to the clip, as they helped the child to contextualise both the key topic (why the gifts were given) and the purpose of the discourse (why the video was made). An example of scaffolding at the lexical level can be observed in S7/L10–11, where the boy tried to explain who gave him the third gift. Again, he could not finish his sentence, and moved towards his mother, whispering in English *'brother'*. The mother responded by first affirming the boy that he was right *'Yes'* and then gave the correct wording in Chinese *'your brother'*.

As demonstrated in the example in Table 8.2, when the parents made these video clips as 'progress reports' for the grandparents, they also created incidental heritage language learning episodes for the child(ren). In a study of a Polish-English speaking family's use of video camera, Debski (2017) has observed similar forms of learning occurred in parent-child interactions during recordings. These interactions that occurred in social media centred video making practices are of particular significance to emergent bilingual children like the boy here (and *Dawei* and his brother discussed earlier) who live in an English-language dominant environment. They provide children from migrant backgrounds with opportunities to use and learn their heritage language and literacy in contextualised and meaningful ways. As previous studies (Hoff 2006, 2010) have shown, communicative interaction and access to language models are both conducive to language learning.

Heritage language learning was not the only the type of learning that occurred during the making of the video. The child was also learning to perform for a particular type of video genre, which are made for sharing on social media. As can be observed in the video frames in Table 8.2, the boy appeared to be conscious of how he placed his body in relation to the camera and how his position in the visual frame could create different meaning potentials. He would, for instance, move his body closer to the camera when he needed to show a new set of toys (S5 & S13). He would 'lean out of' the frame when he needed to seek help from his mother (S2 & S7), as this action was not part of the video narrative. His body gestures also suggested that he was fully aware of his audience, chiefly his grandmother in China. For example, in the final scene (S10), he signed off the video by saying goodbye to his grandmother while simultaneously moving his hand closer to the screen, making a thumb up gesture. His gesture showed up as the most dominant visual element in the video frame.

In summary, the findings of the WeChat project and existing literature on young children's learning using social media technologies include:

- Younger children participate in social media, and their practices are often interwound with their parents' social media practices (Zaman et al., 2016) and other forms of family literacy practices (Marsh et al., 2017).
- These social media related activities (direct chat or video making) often create incidental heritage learning opportunities (Debski, 2017) for the children.
- Adults (parents, grandparents and contacts on the family's social media network) need to provide scaffolding support to create sustained interaction and language learning opportunities (Kelly, 2013, Zhao & Flewitt, forthcoming).
- When young children are engaged in social media practices, there are often several types of learning and socialisation (Zhao & Flewitt, forthcoming) cooccurring all at once.

Reflections on researching young multilingual children's literacy practices in the age of digital mobility

Reflecting back on the WeChat project, the central dilemma seems to be that we know very little about many emerging forms of technology-mediated practices, especially those of multilingual children from immigrant backgrounds and in the context of home. The rate at which the technology develops exacerbates the problem. One practical solution is to adopt an iterative data collection plan and be flexible in the field. A good understanding of how immigrant families with young children live (Paat, 2013) in a given national context would also be helpful in terms of planning practical aspects of the project, such as gaining field access and scheduling home visits. A thorough understanding of the child(ren)'s linguistic history is critical. This also applies to cases where the researcher shares a language with the child, as will be discussed in the final section.

The WeChat project forced me to re-examine my research practice of video recording within the broader context of the 'video society', where 300 hours of videos are being uploaded onto YouTube every minute (McConnell, 2015). When we, the researchers, are video recording the lived experiences of our participants, they are recording and 'performing' their lives for their families, friends and various audiences on social media. These videos are distinctive to videos made by research participants in participatory video research or videography (see Jewitt, 2012), as they are not made with the intervention of the researchers or designed for a specific set of research questions. Yet, they are not private records, but texts made to be shared, read and 'interpreted'. How can our video recordings of daily interactions of our research participants be understood and interpreted in relation to their own recordings? More importantly, as illustrated in the example in Table 8.2, children growing up in a video society engage in making and performing for videos from a young age. Their relations to video and video making are shaped by other forms of social practices. What are the implications for researchers who want to use video as a method while working with young children?

Research in an environment that is saturated with video data calls for new ways of thinking about video data. The ubiquity of video making practices in our contemporary lives means that there are more types of video data to collected and analysed. Some of the video recordings made by research participants could capture spontaneous moments in daily practices that can be hard for researchers to observe in the field. This is particularly relevant when researching transnational literacy practices of immigrant children whose lives move across boundaries. It is impractical if not implausible for researchers to follow the children from one country to another.

The video recordings made by the families could be a potential data source. However, the ethics of using these 'data' can be problematic and the ethical considerations complicated, a point which I shall now turn to.

The story of Hannah: reflection on the ethics of collecting video data of children on the move

Hannah is a 6-year-old trilingual girl of Taiwanese parentage from my project in Denmark. She has a 3-year-old sister and her father is a research scientist. Hannah was born in the States where her father was completing his PhD study and has since lived in the UK, Italy and Germany before the family moved to Denmark in 2017. At the time, she spoke Taiwanese Mandarin as her first language and home language, and German as her second language. When I paid my first home visit in autumn 2017, Hannah had just begun her first year of schooling at an English medium international school. At school, she started to learn English as well as Danish. Her father mentioned in the interview that Hannah spoke German with her sister rather than their home language, Taiwanese Mandarin, and '*taught her little sister German*'. However, I was not able to observe the reported practice at home. Hannah was reluctant to speak German in front of me, although during my observation at the school, I noted that she spoke German with her American teacher, who had lived in Germany previously. Sharing a language with her teacher at school helped Hannah transition into the English-speaking school in a Danish-speaking country.

Hannah's language choice is particularly fascinating to a linguist as it challenges our notions of 'native', 'first' or 'home' language. However, I did not have any 'evidence' until five months later, when I was visiting the family after they had just returned from Taiwan. Prior to the Taiwan trip, the family obtained their first iPad. Hannah had learned how to take photos and make videos in the digital English club at school. During the trip, she recorded various aspects of the trip in photos and video clips. Hannah showed me the photos and clips, while recounting her trip in Taiwan. Some of the videos recorded by her showed her sister playing at their grandparents' house, with Hannah talking to her in voice-over in German. Moments like these would have been impossible for me to observe.

With Hannah's assent and her father's consent, I obtained four clips in which her sister's face cannot be seen in the frame. While these video clips – capturing truly naturally occurring interaction – are valuable for a linguist, I am reluctant to publish the data, as the ethical implications are complicated. At the time of recording, Hannah had no knowledge that the video might be shared with anyone, unlike the video made in the WeChat project. She recorded them as she enjoyed experimenting with the video camera, and they captured highly private and intimate moments between her and her sister. What is my ethical responsibility here? How can I explain to her the privacy implication of sharing these videos with me? These are the questions I have to deal with frequently in the field, where the children would often ask me to take photos of themselves on my personal phone or use my iPads to video record their classmates.

From 2015 to 2018, I worked on two projects with young children from immigrant backgrounds in two different national contexts, during which seismic social-political events have been taking place across the globe. Researching with young children always involves complicated ethical considerations (Flewitt, 2005). The infiltration of mainstream discourses by anti-immigration sentiment put children of immigrant backgrounds in a particularly vulnerable position. Collecting video made by and of young multilingual immigrant children can help us understand their unique social experience and language learning practices from their own perspectives. This is important because such data are largely missing from the current literature predominantly focused on monolingual (English-speaking) children. However, using this method, like using other video methods with young children, can put privacy and even safety of these children at risk. What are our ethical obligations to our young research participants in the current political environment? I can offer no simple answer or solution. For now, let's remember

> our primary obligation is always to the people we study, not to our project or to a larger discipline. The lives and stories that we hear and study are given to us under a promise, that promise being that we protect those who have shared them with us.
>
> *(Denzin, 1989, p. 83)*

Funding

The fieldwork of the WeChat project was funded through the University of Technology Sydney's International Researcher Development Fund, while my project in Denmark is supported by the Carlsberg Foundation through its Distinguished Post-doctoral Research Fellowship.

Acknowledgements

I would like to thank Dr Rosie Flewitt for her generous mentorship. Without her expertise in early literacy and rich experience in conducting research with young children, the WeChat project would not have been possible.

Notes

1 Dawei and Xiaowei are the Chinese nicknames of the brothers. Da (big) and Xiao (little) in the name indicate the birth order. The nicknames are retained, with child and parental permission, as they are key to some of the WeChat conversations.

2 Apart from Family 1, interviews were conducted in Chinese and translated into English by Zhao.

References

Akhter, P. (2016) A young child's intergenerational practices through the use of visual screen-based multimodal communication to acquire Qur'anic literacy. *Language and Education* 30 (6), 500–518.

Bezemer, J. and Mavers, D. (2011) Multimodal transcription as academic practice: A social semiotic perspective. *International Journal of Social Research Methodology* 14 (3), 191–206.

Cowan, K. (2014) Multimodal transcription of video: Examining interaction in Early Years classrooms. *Classroom Discourse* 5 (1), 6–21.

Debski, R. (2017) Language transmission opportunities created through video recording in the family: A microanalysis. *International Journal of Bilingual Education and Bilingualism*, 1–13.

Denzin, N. K. (1989) *Interpretive biography*, vol. 17. London: Sage.

Flewitt, R. (2005) Conducting research with young children: Some ethical considerations. *Early Child Development and Care* 175 (6), 553–565.

Flewitt, R. (2006) Using video to investigate preschool classroom interaction: Education research assumptions and methodological practices. *Visual Communication* 5 (1), 25–50.

Flewitt, R. S., Hampel, R., Hauck, M. and Lancaster, L. (2013) What are multimodal data and transcription? In C. Jewitt, ed. *The Routledge handbook of multimodal analysis*. 2nd ed. (pp. 44–59). London: Routledge.

Flewitt, R. (2011) Bringing ethnography to a multimodal investigation of early literacy in a digital age. *Qualitative Research* 11 (3), 293–310.

Goldman, R., Pea, R., Barron, B. and Derry, S.J. (2014) *Video research in the learning sciences*. London and New York: Routledge.

Hasan, R. and Cloran, C. (1990) *A sociolinguistic interpretation of everyday talk between mothers and children*. Paper presented at the Learning, Keeping, and Using Language Conference. Selected papers from the Eighth World Congress of Applied Linguistics. Amsterdam and Philadelphia, PA: John Benjamins.

Hawkins, M. R. (2018) Transmodalities and transnational encounters: Fostering critical cosmopolitan relations. *Applied Linguistics* 39 (1), 55–77.

Hoff, E. (2006) How social contexts support and shape language development. *Developmental Review* 26 (1), 55–88.

Hoff, E. (2010) Context effects on young children's language use: The influence of conversational setting and partner. *First Language* 30 (3–4), 461–472.

Holloway, D., Green, L. and Livingstone, S. (2013) Zero to eight: Young children and their internet use. EU Kids Online, London, UK. Available at: http://www.eukidsonline.net/

Jewitt, C. (2012) An introduction to using video for research. NCRM Working Paper. NCRM.

Kell, C. (2017) Traveling texts, translocal/transnational literacies, and transcontextual analysis. In S. Canagarajah (ed.) *The Routledge Handbook of Migration and Language*. New York: Routledge, 413–430.

Kelly, C. (2013) 'Let's do some jumping together': Intergenerational participation in the use of remote technology to co-construct social relations over distance. *Journal of Early Childhood Research* 13 (1), 29–46.

Kress, G. (2009) *Multimodality: A social semiotic approach to contemporary communication*. London and New York: Routledge.

Kress, G. and van Leeuwen, T. (2006) *Reading images: The grammar of visual design*. London and New York: Routledge.

Kucirkova, N. and Sakr, M. (2015) Child–father creative text-making at home with crayons, iPad collage & PC. *Thinking Skills and Creativity* 17, 59–73.

Kucirkova, N., Sheehy, K. and Messer, D. (2015) A Vygotskian perspective on parent–child talk during iPad story sharing. *Journal of Research in Reading* 38 (4), 428–441.

Kusow, A. M. (2003) Beyond indigenous authenticity: Reflections on the insider/outsider debate in immigration research. *Symbolic Interaction* 26 (4), 591–599.

Lam, W. S. E. and Rosario-Ramos, E. (2009) Multilingual literacies in transnational digitally mediated contexts: An exploratory study of immigrant teens in the United States. *Language and Education* 23 (2), 171–190.

Lancaster, L., Hauck, M., Hampel, R. and Flewitt, R. (2013) What are multimodal data and transcription? In C. Jewitt (ed.) *The Routledge handbook of multimodal analysis*. 2nd ed. London: Routledge.

Li, W. (2018) Translanguaging as a practical theory of language. *Applied Linguistics* 39 (1), 9–30.

Marsh, J., Hannon, P., Lewis, M. and Ritchie, L. (2017) Young children's initiation into family literacy practices in the digital age. *Journal of Early Childhood Research* 15 (1), 47–60. doi: 10.1177/1476718X15582095.

Martínez-Álvarez, P. and Ghiso, M. (2017) On languaging and communities: Latino/a emergent bilinguals' expansive learning and critical inquiries into global childhoods. *International Journal of Bilingual Education and Bilingualism* 20 (6), 667–687.

McConnell, F. (2015) YouTube is 10 years old: The evolution of online video. *The Guardian*. Available at: https://www.theguardian.com/technology/2015/feb/13/youtube-10-years-old-evolution-of-online-video

Morgan, L., and Peter, M. (2014) Affordances for home language maintenance created by multimodal Web 2.0 and mobile technologies. *ICICTE 2014 Proceedings, Kos, Greece*, 175–184.

Oh, J. S. and Fuligni, A. J. (2010) The role of heritage language development in the ethnic identity and family relationships of adolescents from immigrant backgrounds. *Social Development* 19 (1), 202–220.

Orellana, M. F., Thorne, B., Chee, A. and Lam, W. S. E. (2001) Transnational childhoods: The participation of children in processes of family migration. *Social Problems* 48 (4), 572–591.

Paat, Y.-F. (2013) Working with immigrant children and their families: An application of Bronfenbrenner's ecological systems theory. *Journal of Human Behavior in the Social Environment* 23 (8), 954–966.

Skrbiš, Z. (2008) Transnational families: Theorising migration, emotions and belonging. *Journal of Intercultural Studies* 29 (3), 231–246.

Statistica (2018) Most famous social network sites worldwide as of January 2018, ranked by number of active users (in millions). Retrieved 2 April 2018 from www.statista.com/statistics/272014/global-social-networks-ranked-by-number-of-users/

Stewart, M. A. M. (2014) Social networking, workplace, and entertainment literacies: The out-of-school literate lives of newcomer Latina/o Adolescents. *Reading Research Quarterly* 49 (4), 365–369.

Teale, W. H. (1986) Home background and young children's literacy development. *Emergent Literacy: Writing and Reading*, 173–206.

Torr, J. (2007) The pleasure of recognition: Intertextuality in the talk of preschoolers during shared reading with mothers and teachers. *Early Years* 27 (1), 77–91.

Torr, J. and Clugston, L. (1999) A comparison between informational and narrative picture books as a context for reasoning between caregivers and 4-year-old children. *Early Child Development and Care* 159 (1), 25–41.

Tyrrell, N., White, A., Ni Laoire, C. and Mendez, F. C. (2013) *Transnational migration and childhood.* London and New York: Routledge.

UNICEF (2016) Childhood migration and displacement. In: United Nations Children's Fund. Available at: https://data.unicef.org/topic/child-migration-and-displacement/

Verdon, S., McLeod, S. and Winsler, A. (2014) Language maintenance and loss in a population study of young Australian children. *Early Childhood Research Quarterly* 29 (2), 168–181.

Wang, X. (2017) Spatial and literacy practices of Chinese international students across a bridge writing classroom and WeChat. *Language and Education* 31 (6), 561–579.

Warriner, D. S. (2009) Transnational literacies: Examining global flows through the lens of social practice. In Baynham and M. Prinsloo (eds.) *The future of literacy studies.* London: Palgrave Macmillan, 160–180.

Wong Fillmore, L. (2000) Loss of family languages: Should educators be concerned? *Theory Into Practice* 39 (4), 203–210.

Yu, Q., Huang, P. and Liu, L. (2017) From "connected presence" to "panoptic presence": Reframing the parent – child relationship on mobile instant messaging uses in the Chinese translocal context. *Mobile Media & Communication* 5 (2), 123–138. doi: 10.1177/2050157916688348.

Zaman, B., Nouwen, M., Vanattenhoven, J., De Ferrerre, E. and Van Looy, J. (2016) A qualitative inquiry into the contextualized parental mediation practices of young children's digital media use at home. *Journal of Broadcasting & Electronic Media* 60 (1), 1–22.

Zhao, S. and Flewitt, R. (forthcoming) Heritage language and literacy practices on social media: Young Chinese immigrant children's intergenerational practices on WeChat. Submitted to *Language and Education.*

Zhou, B. and Gui, S. (2017) WeChat and distant family intergenerational communication in China: A study of online content sharing on WeChat. In K. Xue and M. Yu (eds.) *New media and Chinese society.* Singapore: Springer, 185–206.

9

(RE)IMAGINING MULTILITERACIES RESEARCH PRACTICES WITH POST QUALITATIVE INQUIRY

Candace R. Kuby

Nick-Ella-Emily-Panda Bear Habitat-Be(com)ing[1]

Two tree sticks stand vertically on paper, secured at the bottom with clear tape. Nick works with a third stick, wrapping tape around the bottom and passes it to two girls to place and secure vertically on the paper. Nick turns back to his project and the girls continue working with tape and sticks and their fingers and the paper. It takes four hands and arms to work together to secure the three sticks. Holding. Pulling tape off the roll. Taping. Retaping. Letting go to see if it works. Retaping. Holding. Talking. Planning. When the tape runs out, Ella goes to get more. Emily explains to others as they come by (and as they reach out to play with and touch the sticks) that it is a forest *and* please don't touch. As Emily waits, she holds up a craft stick that has a printed-off picture of a panda bear attached to the top, she moves it around in the forest. She explains to Ella that the two other craft sticks will have birds on it for the panda to chase. Ella begins blowing up a balloon and asks others if it is a good size for a lion's head as she begins her project, Emily continues working on her panda habitat.

Nick-Jellyfish-Be(com)ing

Gigi comes by and asks Nick to read her writing on hummingbirds. He offers some feedback on spelling a word and she walks off to revise. He picks up a large paint brush and continues painting a large papier-mâché ball(oon) magenta. He engages in conversation with Emily and Ella as they work next to each other. Nick gets a plastic cup to hold up the wet ball so he can successfully paint the entire ball without getting the desk dirty. Cup-paint-brush-Nick-ball-desk work together. Fifteen minutes later Nick gets some magenta paper and scissors. He uses the paint as glue to secure small strips of paper on the ball.

Rebecca-Octopus-Be(com)ing

A plastic strawberry container box sits on the desk with rows of neatly rolled blue and green play-dough balls inside. A large papier-mâchéd orange ball(oon) and a small stack of brown yarn strands taped in clusters sit next to it. Rebecca asks, "what can I use?" and walks off. She comes back with one large paper towel roll and cuts it in two. Rebecca cuts small slits around one end to make a flap, and works with a glue stick to connect the paper rolls onto the orange ball. Rebecca decides to try tape instead, and moves about the room asking peers for tape. She comes back with tape on her fingers and successfully secures one paper towel roll on the ball(oon). Rebecca repeats the process: cutting slits on one end of the second roll but doesn't find any tape. She works with the second roll for a while, leaves the desk, comes back and continues working with the first roll which is becoming unhinged.

Ball-paper rolls-Rebecca continue to work together in frustration. "They won't stick!" she exclaims. Tara, the classroom teacher, asks her to try a stapler, but that might pop the balloon. She comes back with bulletin board tacks and works with the balloon and paper roll. She says "it popped", but continues to work with the tacks to secure the paper rolls on the orange ball(oon). Rebecca talks to the ball(oon), "stop it", as it rolls around, and she is unsuccessful in securing the paper rolls. She gathers the tacks and walks away. Several minutes later she comes back with a handful of green pipe cleaners.

On the following day, Rebecca has secured orange pipe cleaner legs all around the Octopus-Ball(oon) and glued googly eyes on the front. The Octopus sits on top of the plastic box with play-dough balls inside. Rebecca is writing and drawing on a green strip of paper as the Octopus peers over her head. She glues the paper on top of the plastic box, writes a word, and checks the spelling with a friend.

★★★★★

These multiliteracies came into being in a second grade (7–8 year olds) Writers' Studio. Tara Gutshall Rucker, the teacher, was required to teach a nonfiction writing unit (and a science unit on animals) and worked to provide spaces for children to compose with a range of materials and modes. First the students made a class picture book – each child created one page about an animal of choice to contribute to the book. In the earlier vignettes, the students were in the midst of composing with a variety of materials as another way to share their learning about one animal they had researched about for several weeks. Through a series of mini lessons and conferences, Tara had invited students to think about one interesting fact they learned about their animal, and decide what would be the best way to communicate that with others. They brainstormed possibilities such as wall murals, sculptures (with various materials like clean trash containers, papier-mâché, clay, paper), skits, books, or 3-dimensional (3D) habitat designs. After several days of working-with-materials (and materials-working-with students), the students shared their compositions and learning with each other.

★★★★★

3D Hummingbird-Gigi

Gigi shares the number of beats hummingbird wings make in one minute while flying. She demonstrates with a 3D paper sculpture. She's made a paper bird and used yarn to play-with-the-bird like a marionette puppet to show the wings flapping. Gigi shares about a video she watched at home about hummingbirds, reads from her page in the class book, and then answers questions from peers by working with the paper bird.

Jellyfish-Nick

Nick holds the magenta jellyfish and shares with the class his new learning about their bodies made mostly of water. He compares the percent of water in human bodies to jellyfish bodies. He explains that is why there is water *inside* the papier-mâché balloon jellyfish. Nick reads from his page in the class book as the jellyfish is passed around for everyone to touch and feel the weight. He too answers questions from his peers.

Penguins-Billy-Peers

Billy organizes a few peers-penguins dressed in black and white costumes he created. They lay out a white bed sheet on the floor (i.e., ice and snow). Then they move chairs together on the sheet to create an iceberg covering it with large blue and white paper. After five minutes of securing the paper iceberg with tape, the penguin skit begins. Several peers-penguins hide behind the iceberg. Billy tells the class that the skit will mostly be realistic but there are some parts that they just couldn't do, like cut a hole in the class floor (i.e., ice with water underneath) for the penguins to be in the ocean. They created 'hiding spots' instead for the skit to work. He asks his peers not to look at the 'hiding spots' while the skit is happening, just keep looking forward. Billy asks for the lights to be turned off. He positions himself as the father penguin on top of an egg carton in front of the iceberg. The mother penguin goes off the ice and into the ocean. "Cheep, cheep, cheep" comes from the penguins in a 'hiding spot' (i.e., in the iceberg). Billy pushes the egg carton out from under him and tosses broken paper eggs onto the ice (demonstrating the cheeps are from the baby penguins hatching from the eggs he was holding with his feet). Three baby penguins crawl out. Mother penguin comes over from a 'hiding spot' (i.e., the ocean) with fish (i.e., plastic bottles covered in paper) and the baby penguins eat. Billy asks the class what they learned from the skit, then shares information about the role of the mother and father penguin in taking care of their young, and finally talks about the materials they created to convey the information.

Panda-Emily

The learning continues as Emily shares her 3D panda habitat and demonstrates the 5½ fingers (5 fingers and a small thumb) that pandas use to climb and move around. She discusses how one stick (i.e., tree in the habitat design) kept bending so she secured two sticks together so they would stand together. She listens to feedback and questions from peers.

*****

Each of these vignettes could be analyzed with theories and methods of multiliteracies and multimodality. These analyses would help us understand some aspects of Writers' Studio regarding how children drew upon a variety of modes and semiotic resources. However, as I have worked with Tara since 2010, we've[2] found a need to expand our philosophical and theoretical commitments to perspectives that believe that knowing, be(com)ing, and doing[3] in the world (with the material world) are inseparable. This perspective also de-centers the human as the origin of all knowing and being and the sole actor of agency. Instead, agency is seen as a togetherness, an in-between, a force, a flow with humans, nonhumans, and more-than-humans. These philosophical shifts about epistemology (knowing), ontology (being), and axiology (doing) demand that we (re)think the coming into being of multi- and digital literacies, and the ways we go about researching and teaching.

In other manuscripts, Tara and I have focused on the pedagogical shifts in her classroom when we read and thought with poststructural and posthumanist theories. Specifically, we've focused on how theories *were* (already) pedagogies. We have discussed ways different units of study looked in Writers' Studio, such as personal narrative, nonfiction, and fiction (see Kuby &

Gutshall Rucker, 2016). In other spaces, we've examined the myth of the linear writing process often taught in schools (i.e., brainstorm, draft, revise, edit, and publish) (Kuby, 2017a). We've looked closely at individual students over the course of a school year and how their writerly identities became, with a range of materials in Writers' Studio (Kuby & Gutshall Rucker, 2015). However, the aim of this chapter is to discuss poststructural and posthumanist theories as research tools situated in the emergent field of post qualitative inquiry, which calls into question normal, taken for granted assumptions and practices of qualitative research (St. Pierre, 2011b; St. Pierre et al., 2016). Just as post-theories were pedagogies for us, these theories also became methodologies in a mutually constitutive relationship (i.e., theory ↔ methodology ↔ pedagogy).

The following quote by St. Pierre provokes my thought each time I read it:

> Qualitative research methodology, which had early radical possibilities, became, I think, in large part, a low-level description of process, procedure, design, and method and so, not surprisingly, too often produced and continues to produce as 'findings' inconsequential themes, untheorized stories, and extended descriptions that do not get to the intellectual problem of explaining why things are as they are and how they might be different. Without philosophy, I think science can become impotent and rather boring.
>
> – *(St. Pierre, 2011a, pp. 2–3)*

How can qualitative inquiry, with so much hope and radical possibilities, be so boring? That is a strong claim and whether one believes it or not, it does cause me to pause and consider what has happened to provoke such a claim. In my journey of doing so, I've found the phrase "methodologies without methodology", borrowed from the title of Koro-Ljungberg's (2016) reconceptualizing qualitative research book, invigorating. This phrase prompts researchers to consider the what if; what if we imagine, invent, think, and experiment in Deleuzian ways, with research assumptions and practices?

For me, there is a justice and ethical orientation to this knowing/be(com)ing/doing shift in research. Often in literacy research we focus on knowledge and the artifacts and products created from multimodal composing with a range of artistic and digital tools. Or we start with the artifact and try to trace back how the human(s) made it and what knowledge they gained (see Leander & Boldt, 2013). However, poststructural and posthumanist theories focus on the now, the in-the-moment be(com)ing of humans, nonhumans, and more-than-humans. This is an ethical focus on ethic-onto-epistemologies, what is being produced (what realities, relationships, knowledges, and literacies) in the moment, instead of solely focusing on a future that may or may not come. Perhaps it would behoove us (and children creating literacies in schools and in out of school learning spaces) if we thought about the now – what is being produced in the moments instead of (solely) continuing to focus on benchmarks and future goals (that may or may not come to be). We need to consider how the entanglements of children, teachers, paper, computers, printers, webpages, paints, policies, desks, crayons, assessments, languages, genders, abilities, and so forth all matter, literally, in literacies coming to be, and in students coming to be composers.

So, while products do matter (literally, they are matter), so do the processes of people and materials working together. There is a mutually constitutive relationship between people and materials. Therefore, we need to shift our focus from human-centered theories, research methods, and pedagogies to embrace the poststructural and posthumanist assumptions about how the world (and literacies) come into being (Kuby, 2017b). I've begun to explore these possibilities in relation to the multi-year partnership with Tara. For example, we've questioned what is 'social' in social science research and in writing partnerships of children/materials, when putting to work these post-theories (Kuby & Crawford, 2017; Kuby, 2018). We've explored how linear research processes and traditional research categories need to be problematized and rethought when situating work in these post-theories (Kuby, 2017c). In what remains of this chapter, I build upon our body of scholarship, connect it with the aim(s) of this handbook, and to the larger field of post qualitative inquiry. The hope is that this chapter sparks a conversation on these ideas in relation to multi- and digital literacies, and demonstrates possible ways to inquire. I use the nonfiction writing projects discussed at the opening to the chapter as a playground for thinking.

Post qualitative inquiry: assumptions, what it demands of us, and possibilities

> *At this point, I refuse the concepts method and methodology, as they are used in most empirical educational research. That means I also refuse the empiricisms that enable those methods and methodologies. This ontological turn, which does not assume that to be is to know, demands a different empiricism that is not grounded in the humanist subject. What might an empiricism for the posthuman look like?*
>
> – *(St. Pierre, 2017, p. 29)*

As literacy researchers, we find ourselves operating in a thick atmosphere of logical empiricism, a politics of inquiry that shapes how we conceptualize literacy and inquiry (i.e., data, relationships with participants, analysis, and [re]presentation) as well as the ways we mentor and teach research practices to students. Logical empiricism, which dominates educational research,

> was, and still is, attractive because it claims that the rigorous, scientific methods of the natural sciences can find rules and laws in the social world as they have in the natural world. In social science, positivism's desire is to predict what people will do and then control them.
>
> *(St. Pierre, 2015)*

Logical or positivist empiricism, inundates current research funding guidelines, publishing expectations, and practices within academia. For example, with the passage of No Child Left Behind in the United States, and the National Research Council's definition of "scientifically based research in education" there was a resurgence of positivism and logical empiricism. Over time, qualitative researchers proceeded to make their interpretive studies align with positivist assumptions in order, for example, to secure federal funding for research. Qualitative research methodologies and methods were emergent, but became methods-driven, rigid, formulaic, and pre-determined steps – a recipe to follow. The publishing industry supported logical empiricism by putting out book after book (and articles) on linear, systematic research design approaches and 'how-to' manuals on various methodical techniques, even in qualitative research.

However, frustrated with the state of qualitative inquiry for her own research and that of her students, in the 2011 *SAGE Handbook of Qualitative Research*, St. Pierre wrote a chapter on post qualitative inquiry (PQI) that gives the history of this term. St. Pierre (2011b) believes that the study of philosophy should proceed (or perhaps happen with) the study of research methodology because "attempts to disentangle science and philosophy are always dangerous" (p. 614). She articulates that the 'post' in PQI signals two things. One, a coming after what she calls *conventional humanist qualitative inquiry* and two, research inspired by post-theories (e.g., postmodern, poststructural, posthumanist). St. Pierre (and others such as Alecia Youngblood Jackson, Patti Lather, Lisa Mazzei, and Maggie MacLure, to name a few) have urged researchers to return to metaphysics as they claim that research is stuck in a Cartesian philosophy that (attempts to) separates the mind from body, the subject from object, and other binary relationships. However, when reading many post-theories we are thrown into conversations on metaphysics – a specific branch of philosophy called ontology, which is concerned with what exists, what is, on being. Therefore, putting post-theories to work in research is not about 'applying' them in an already conventional humanist qualitative inquiry fashion, but rather a complete re-thinking of what research is, why we engage with it, and how to do it.

PQI demands a reorientation to how we see the world coming to be (ontology) in lively relationships between humans, nonhumans, and more-than-humans, and therefore it can't be pulled from a shelf to squeeze into methodologies and methods that are fundamentally built on a Cartesian divide of mind/body, subject/object, and so forth. Following are a few of the 'big ideas' that I take away from reading scholarship on PQI which have caused me to (re)think how I go about researching the be(com)ing of digital and multimodal literacies.

A new empiricism? Resisting the binaries

St. Pierre et al. (2016) state that since at least the beginning of the 21st century scholars from a range of disciplines and fields are working in what are being called the 'new empiricisms' and 'new materialisms'. Scholars in these areas have intensified their arguments against foundational assumptions of Western thought that enable binary oppositions such as mind/body, object/subject, human/nonhuman, nature/culture, transcendence/immanence, and so forth. In a sense, these scholars are advocating that we (re)think what empiricism is, to reclaim that term, when viewing the (coming to be of the) world with differing ontological assumptions than perspectives that are rooted in Cartesian logics. St. Pierre et al., (2016) state:

> Empiricism and materialism go hand in hand. Classical empiricism is an epistemological project opposed to rationalism. In that model, knowledge of the empirical world gained through the senses is the only knowledge that is legitimate. The argument is that we can't claim to know anything not given in our experience. Speculation through logical reasoning is just that, speculation, and cannot serve as a ground for knowledge. So the given, matter (evidence), surely matters in classical empiricism; and it is generally assumed to be a fixed substance, brute, inert, and passive – objects, things to be used by agentive humans – perhaps to be *observed* or *measured* in a social science study.
>
> *(p. 99, emphasis in original)*

Because the material and empirical are so intricately tied together, we must (re)think ontological assumptions in our inquiry practices. We have to reimagine the relationships we perhaps think as binaries. What does a new empiricism look like in multimodal and digital literacies? How does this change our research practices?

Working within a non-representational logic and transcendental empiricism

St. Pierre's scholarship discusses Deleuze and Guattari's notion of transcendental empiricism, and argues that ascribing to that belief makes it impossible to do research with a focus on a (sole) humanist subject or conventional social science empirical inquiry that inundates educational research. She builds this argument on close readings of post-thinkers such Deleuze and Guattari and their distinction between the logics of *logical empiricism* and *transcendental empiricism*. Logical empiricism is an empiricism that focuses on systematic and organized thought and knowledge. Whereas *transcendental empiricism* is, "that which attempts to go beyond or above, a highest grounding principle such as thought and consciousness" (Olsson, 2009, p. 51) (for further discussion of these two empiricisms see Kuby, 2017b; St. Pierre, 2011b). Transcendental empiricism is experimental and challenges representational assumptions of logical empiricisms. As Olsson (2009) writes, "Empirical representations is challenged by a much more 'wild' kind of empiricism that can account for the unstableness and continuous production of the world" (p. 95). Deleuzian notions of transcendental empiricisms are about flows, productions, processes, forces, and differences – transcendental empiricism is not governed by a set of laws and relations as logical empiricism is. In other words, the world is not out there waiting for us to discover and write about; it is in a constant process of becoming through relationships of which we (humans) are already a part of and can't stand outside of, hence, knowing/be(com)ing/doing.

MacLure (2013) writes about representation, language, and materiality in research practices. She argues that

> the critique of representation as the dominant image of thought is a key element of Deleuze's philosophy. For Deleuze representational thought is 'sedentary', categorical and judgmental. It is the enemy of difference, movement, change and the emergence of the new.
>
> *(p. 659)*

Therefore, in a transcendental empiricism, the goal of research is not to separate, bind, restrict, categorize into themes, and/or classify the meaning of humans through language and representation. It is a much more 'wild' empiricism open to experimentation, thinking the unthinkable; resisting the myth that language can represent a stabled, binary world; and imagining (new) relationships of humans, nonhumans, and more-than-humans in how the world comes into being.

Subjectivity as assemblage and/or entanglement

Within PQI there is an assumption that resists the subject/object divide, and in doing so, calls into question the notion of subjectivity. Resisting this binary so prevalent in educational research demands that we acknowledge, for example, that as human subjects (e.g., researchers) we are not able to stand outside the objects (e.g., participants) we research. It is a false sense of reality to believe that we can do so. Post-scholars theorize about subjectivity in different ways, conceptualizing new terms and language for how we might imagine new relations and resist the binary of subject/object. For example, Deleuze and Guattari (1980/1987) write about assemblages as a way of conceptualizing and analyzing social complexity by emphasizing multiplicities, fluidity, and ever-changing ways of be(com)ing together. Assemblages aren't *things* but rather *processes* of working with (and changing) other becoming assemblages. This ontological orientation does not rest on a fixed or stable world, rather social relationships are assemblages of complex configurations which extend and shoot off in various new directions and relationships, rhizomatically. This orientation of social relationship causes us to question subjectivity. Who or what is a subject if always already in relationship to others? Or if the very act of being (existence in the world) comes from a relationship, a becoming assemblage, then subjectivity is not of one (a subject) operating with others (objects) but rather ontological, becoming relationships. Assemblages are a different way of conceptualizing the mutually constitutive relationship of subjects ↔ objects.

Barad (2007) also writes about subjectivity, more explicitly in relation to humans, nonhumans, and more-then-humans, specifically from her studies in the fields of quantum physics, feminist theories, and philosophy. Her theory, agential realism, states that the world comes into being through intra-actions (she created this word to symbolize the active relationship between humans and other material beings instead of *interaction* which is rooted in logics of humanism). "Agential realism is an epistemological, ontological, and ethical framework that makes explicit the integral nature of these concerns" (Barad, 2007, p. 32). Barad theorizes relationships as entanglements. Within quantum physics entangled particles remain connected even when they appear to be separated by distance. The actions of one particle e/affect others and therefore the whole of the particles cannot be reduced to individual particles. The concept of entanglements is useful as it helps us to think of the whole, relationships of subjects/objects, not pieces or individuals but rather in affectual (and effectual) relationships with one another; the be(com)ing of one is intricately connected or tied to the be(com)ing of others.

Assemblage and entanglement are two ways we can begin to (re)conceptualize the relationship between/among subjects-objects and therefore, rethink subjectivity in our research practices. This shift in conceptualizing subjectivity also shifts how we think about agency. Posthumanist scholars, specifically early childhood and literacy educators, are writing about how agency is rethought with these (new) ways of conceptualizing subjectivity (see Hultman & Lenz Taguchi, 2010; Kuby & Gutshall Rucker, 2016; Kuby et al., 2017).

Ethico-onto-epistemology: a relational view of the world coming to be

Each of the previous 'big ideas' discussed all point to a relational ontology or a way of seeing the world come into being through relationships – flatten or nonhierarchical relationships – among/between humans, nonhumans, and more-than-humans. Barad (2007), Lenz Taguchi (2010), and our work (Kuby & Gutshall Rucker, 2016) discusses "relational comings to be" as ethico-onto-epistemology. Barad writes that knowing and being cannot be separated, we come to know through our being in the world and therefore, there is an ethical relationship; we have a response-ability (i.e., the ability to respond) in how we respond to others in our daily assemblages and entanglements. Ethico-onto-epistemology is justice oriented as it calls us to question our relationships: who and what we are entangled with daily, in-the-moment, and what our responses will be. How might one in a literal, practical sense put to work or *do* research in an ethico-onto-epistemological way?

When one reads post-theories deeply, one's thought is provoked, shattered, shocked into doing research otherwise. Snaza and colleagues (2014) write that we must

> move from a theoretical critique of knowledge as a symptomatic foreclosure of non- or inhuman relations or *meaning* toward articulations of what we might call for lack of a better term, new research methods. The 'methods' of curriculum studies [and in our case literacy studies] – like the methods in every existing institution disciplining thought – presume the human. That is, we tend to practice forms of inquiry and interpretation developed by the humanities or social sciences. This is an enormous problem, one that we cannot sketch in detail here, but we have already hinted at its major stakes: the ways such methods rely upon distinctions between knowing subjects and 'known' objects. Posthumanist thought must abandon this distinction. We need to think about how meaning is generated *among* subjects.
>
> *(p. 51, emphasis in original)*

Meaning generated among bodies. Between bodies. Togetherness of bodies. And I am thinking of bodies as human, nonhuman, and more-than-human as well as linguistic bodies, cultural bodies, political bodies, racial bodies, gendered bodies, and so forth. These are thoughts that we need to think about as literacy scholars. Instead of focusing on a human and what (it appears) they do to an object (paper, pencil, book, computer), we could reorient our thinking to what is be(com)ing. How are the child, paper, and pencil coming into writing together? How are the child and iBook coming into reading together? How are the child, augmented reality app, and future users coming into literacies together? What are these assemblages and entanglements producing now (and in possible futures)? What is our response-ability in these entanglements? How are we be(com)ing-with them?

Returning to the opening vignettes of animal research in Tara's classroom; instead of thinking about what Billy (and peers) did with tape and paper to create an iceberg; the meanings of the iceberg for the play and their knowledge about penguins. We could instead focus on the carpeted floor, chairs, black pants and shirts, blue and white paper, the bodies of all the other peers crowding around, physical space in the classroom, Tara, students' understandings of 'doing school' in Room 203, and the languages that children spoke all working with each other in creating a new whole (an entanglement). A new moment in space, time, and mattering together that isn't recognizable separate from each other, but only in relation to each other as they all became the penguin skit. What was produced when the chairs, large paper, and human bodies worked together? What in-the-moment decisions were made that were unexpected or diverged from their rehearsals because of new bodies (human and otherwise) in this large entanglement? And then, how does one go about researching these inquiries? We have found ourselves often stuck, swimming in moments of research stuckness. We have learned that research stuckness is uncomfortable and doesn't feel so good at first. However, as we've leaned into stuckness; let ourselves read dense, confusing texts and gave ourselves permission to not understand; and resisted the urge to do research the ways we've done before – we've found energy, newness, and hope. These pauses, moments of stuckness shoot us off in new directions as researchers-teachers.

We've found solace in the concept of research as wild or untamed, as Olsson discusses. Or as Mirka Koro-Ljungberg writes about methodologies without methodology. St. Pierre (2016) beckons us to reconsider how we go about preparing doctoral students, and in doing so, incites faculty members to also rethink research practices:

> research training too often gets in our way, prevents us from recognizing the 'new' that is always already there in the world, and shuts down futures that might be. . . . Perhaps we could focus less on repeating existing methodologies and more on calling them into question. . . . Would educational researchers be willing to forgo methodology for the possibility of an unpredictable future-to-come, one that is not foreclosed by repetition of the same? . . . What would it be like not to know what to do next, and then next, and next when one inquires?
>
> *(pp. 2–3)*

This is the (exploratory) aim of this chapter.

Research as becoming-with:[4] methodologies without methodology

To realize, in fact, that we are always already entangled in inquiry, that there is no beginning.
– (St. Pierre, 2017, p. 29)

How might one in a literal, practical sense put to work or *do* research in an ethico-onto-epistemological way? If one believes in the philosophical assumptions discussed previously, how does one enact or embody with the ever-changing research assemblages (processes) one is a part of? My scholarship has begun to explore these questions specifically in relation to how data is produced, how we write-up transcripts, how we do analysis, and how we (re)present, given the limits of language. Next, I share philosophical and theoretical ideas that have inspired me to experiment with research, in an effort to untame it. Specifically, I discuss philosophical and/or theoretical concepts in scholarship that has helped me to un-learn or re-think methodologies and methods. I share examples from my own work as well as other scholars putting into practice these concepts. In an effort to make my thinking transparent, I 'think aloud' about how I might *approach* research or *enter into the middle* with the literacies shared from Room 203. It is important to note, there isn't one right way to do PQI. There isn't a linear, pre-set formula, rather PQI is in a constant state of experimentation; it is an assemblage in a Deleuzian sense – flows, processes, becoming.

"Thinking with theory": theoretical concepts becoming method(s)

Jackson and Mazzei (2012) are known for their book on *thinking with theory*. In this book, they take data produced from interviews with two first generation faculty members of color, and put it to work with several post-theorists. They state that they are attempting to work *against* and *within* interpretivism at the same time. In the chapters, they define several schematic cues (theoretical concepts) from a theorist, and show them at work when thinking with interview data. This working-with-theory-data produces new questions (they call these emergent analytical questions), insights, and ways of thinking about the experiences of the two women. Jackson and Mazzei's (2008) earlier edited book, also questions voice and the long-held assumptions of voice as a (pure) reflection of reality. Therefore, when reading the interview transcripts of these two women, they don't approach them as pure representations of an external other reflecting on their experiences in the academy, but rather a part of an assemblage that is in-the-moment be(com)ing.

Thinking with theory(ies) is an essential way that I think about research. Rather than take a theory and apply it to data;[5] thinking with theory forces me to become with data and theory – an assemblage of newness being produced while I think-with. For example, in our book (Kuby & Gutshall Rucker, 2016) we outlined eight theoretical concepts from poststructural and posthumanist theorists, defined these schematic cues, and put them to work with data produced in Writers' Studio. Thinking with these theoretical concepts produced new ways of defining literacies, thinking about pedagogies, and creating research.

How might thinking with theories help us to see otherwise or enter a new threshold with one of the earlier vignettes? I could approach the Jellyfish-Nick entanglement with two schematic cues and put them to work with the data produced (i.e., video clip) to see what analytical questions might emerge and new insights about literacies. Let's think with posthumanist agency and intra-action. Agency is defined as a force emerging *between* people and materials, not residing solely in humans (see Barad, 2007; Kuby et al., 2017). Agency is what happens in the togetherness of multiple bodies, when they are assembling and creating newness. Intra-action comes from Barad's (2007) writing on the process of iterative and mutual constitution. Intra-action includes more than just human-human or human-object interaction; it is the entanglements, the "joins and disjoins" of humans, nonhumans, more-than-humans, time, space(s), materials, and so forth (Barad, 2013, p. 18). As I work these theoretical concepts with Nick-Jellyfish data new analytical questions emerge, such as: What is joining and disjoining

Nick-Jellyfish-Paint-Balloon-Brush-and . . . and . . . and . . .? And what does this (dis)joining produce? How is the enacted agency between Nick and jellyfish materials changing what becomes (i.e., the artifact of jellyfish but also relationships with peers, Tara, and knowledges about jellyfish)? How do the glue, paint, papier-mâché ball(oon), brush, flat surface of the desk, and Nick intra-act together to produce agency with each other? How does this "speaking back and forth" or these relationships shape the be(com)ing jellyfish?

"To think is to experiment": Deleuze and Guattari's distinction between knowing and thinking

Drawing on Deleuze, Smith (2012) writes that:

> [t]hinking is never the result of voluntary will, but rather the result of forces that act upon us from the outside: we search for 'truth' and begin to think only when we are compelled to do so, when we undergo a violence that impels us to such a search and wrests us from our natural stupor.
>
> *(p. 143)*

What forces us to (re)think about literacies? To (re)think how we go about researching? *Knowing* (your research topic) is different from *thinking* (your research topic). Smith (2012) helps us to see how Deleuze and Guattari distinguish knowledge from thinking:

> "*Knowledge* is only the result of outcome – it is the establishment of a territory, a competence or specialization; but *thinking* is a process of learning or apprenticeship that is initiated by one's encounter with a problem" (p. 143, emphasis in original). What problems are you encountering about literacies? What is forcing you to think? To feel (research) stuckness? Why does it seem research needs to be about *claiming to know* something rather than about *thinking*?

Deleuzian notions of experimentation has shocked or provoked my thoughts on research. Thinking "means to experiment" (Deleuze, 1986/1988, p. 116) and "to create" (Deleuze, 1968/1994, p. 147), and so, therefore, research is about creating and experimenting not plugging in to ready-made recipes of research methods. "For Deleuze", Smith (2012) explains, "the misadventure that constantly threatens thinking is not error or falsehood, but stupidity (clichés, ready-made ideas, conventions, opinions . . .)" (p. 142). What are the ready-made ideas of how literacy research should be done? How might these opinions and conventions threaten newness? Thinking?

For example, in my work with Tara we've tried to (re)think how we (re)present intra-actions in her classroom on paper. In other words, what might a transcript look like when working with post-theories? Instead of doing what we *know*, we *thought*. We resisted ready-made ways of transcribing and instead were playful, creative, and experimented with fonts, margins, symbols, and punctuation (see Kuby & Gutshall Rucker, 2016; Kuby et al., 2017). Our point is not to (re)present what happened during Writers' Studio, but rather create an experience for readers to feel *a* part of *a* (re)presentation from Writers' Studio. We want it to feel messy, uncertain, and entangled as that is what we are trying to show about literacies in Room 203, as we think with post-theories.

How might we think with Gigi-Hummingbird? What new ways of researching might be invented? What would field notes look like if one assumes you (the researcher and your apparatuses such as camera, notebook, etc.) are a part of the entangled assemblage of Gigi-Hummingbird be(com)ing? How might you experiment with ways of (re)presenting the becoming assemblage? Instead of solely writing down human talk, how might you also consider what else is 'speaking'? What else is a part of the enacted agency of Gigi-Hummingbird be(com)ing? How might you (re)think subject/object binaries? How might you go about writing-up this intra-action for a manuscript? How might you resist your ready-made ideas and conventions of how to do research when entering the Gigi-Hummingbird becoming assemblage? Think. Experiment. Create.

Creating concepts: philosophy as art

For Deleuze and Guattari, (philosophical) concepts are doings, ways of thinking, be(com)ing. As they write:

> philosophy is the art of forming, inventing, and fabricating concepts . . . the object of philosophy is to create concepts that are always new. . . . Concepts are not waiting for us ready-made, like heavenly bodies. There is no heaven for concepts. They must be invented, fabricated, or rather created and would be nothing without their creator's signature.
>
> *(Deleuze & Guattari, 1991/1994, pp. 2 and 5)*

In this way, philosophers are creative as artists. In the same spirit, I sought to think about and with my experiences in Writers' Studio as a way to be open to the possibilities of newness, new concepts that would challenge me to think about literacies, differently. What if I took an everyday concept and put it to work with data as a theoretical concept? As a way to (re)think about literacies?

For example, when trying to understand posthumanist notions of agency we worked-with data from Katie creating a 3D personal narrative cabin (Kuby et al., 2017). We noticed that Katie *and* materials were persistent with each other. Therefore, we created the concept of persistence(ing) as a way to think creatively about posthumanist agency. What concept might we create to think anew about literacies in the Octopus-Rebecca example? What if we took the everyday concept of 'revise(ing)' and created new ways of thinking about it within a posthumanist orientation? What new insights might be produced when we expand or (re)create the concept of revise(ing) to include the agency of all bodies in the becoming assemblage (i.e., papier-mâchéd orange ball(oon), yarn, tape, fingers, paper towel roll, pipe cleaners, play-dough, glue, and . . . and . . . and . . .)?

Diffracting: reading concepts and data **through** *one another*

Donna Haraway and Karen Barad's writings on diffraction has inspired researchers to approach inquiry with diffractive practices. Diffraction is what happens when waves (e.g., water, sound, and light) encounter an obstacle causing the waves to bend, spread out in a new pattern, and overlap when they encounter one another. Diffraction produces newness.

PQI scholars have taken this notion of diffraction and put it to work in their inquiry processes (St. Pierre & Jackson, 2014). Specifically, scholars diffractively read theory(ies) (and/or data) *through* one another, sometimes with theoretical positions that are not often put to work together. Van der Tuin (2011) explains,

> the diffractive method allows us to affirm links between seemingly opposite schools of thought, thus breaking through a politics of negation. At the same time, it allows us

> to affirm and strengthen links between schools of thought or scholars that only apparently work toward the same goals. Diffraction, then, is the strategy with which new concepts or traditions, new philosophies, can be engendered.
>
> (p. 27)

What might be produced if we read New Literacy Studies *through* posthumanism? Or critical socio-cultural theories *through* poststructuralism? What newness might be produced? New literacies? New ways of inquiring? New teaching? For example, in a special issue of the *Journal of Early Childhood Literacy* (Kuby & Rowsell, 2017), several authors put to work diffraction as they read scholarship on race and class *through* posthumanist notions of agency (e.g., Thiel & Jones, 2017).

How might diffraction inspire new ways of inquiring about Nick-Ella-Emily-Panda Bear? Could we read this assemblage *through* New Literacy Studies and *through* posthumanist concepts of intra-action and agency? What newness might be produced? Or could we read the panda-making *through* the panda-sharing? What was being produced while they worked-with-materials? What was being produced as Emily shared with the class the habitat and new learning about pandas? How might encountering obstacles as researchers and teachers – encounters with data and theories that cause practices to bend, spread out, overlap – change how we think of literacies?

Ethico-onto-epistemological inspirations for multi- and digital literacies

> *We can only know things by the relations into which they enter, by the contacts they forge, and effects they are able to produce. To put this in another way, we cannot predetermine or know beforehand what will materialize from the relations entered into, nor can we predetermine the relations that will be entered into (this is an emergent praxis that is similar to Haraway's [2008] notion of becoming with).*
>
> *– (Snaza et al., 2014, p. 47)*

A posthumanist or material turn has been a part of the larger social science community for years, and it is seeping into literacy education. With this shift, it is important that we read deeply. Philosophy, paradigmatic tenets, theory, and methodology are all entangled and force researchers to consider *how* (and why) they are putting them to work. Wrestling with methodological questions honors the philosophical thinking and rigor of posthumanism.

Scholarship that focuses on a relational view of the world coming to be (humans and nonhumans) forces one to (re)think research practices. We have to (re)think empiricism, binaries that too often materialize in our research practices, subjectivity and agency, and (re)presentation. If we believe we have a response-ability as Barad discusses or the ability to respond in the be(com)ing assemblages we are a part of, then there is an ethics to this work. This is about the in-the-moment relationships, the realities produced when children are entangled with languages, digital tools, teachers, literacies, art supplies, texts, curricular objectives, peers, assessment practices, and . . . and . . . and. . . . This relational ontology doesn't (solely) focus on a future to come (or that might come), but on the realities being produced now and how we are a part of that production (i.e., our response-abilities).

Drawing on the work of Isabelle Stengers, Snaza and colleagues (2014) argue for a new and different kind of science for curriculum studies and I believe the argument holds true for literacy studies.

> What makes a science a "science" for Stengers, is that it seeks ways to let its "objects" speak or become the subject. The "what" of the study must be able to participate, to *surprise* the researcher. When a researcher decides in advance what will be taken into account and how the "findings" will be presented, surprise is impossible. All that can happen is "confirmation" or "disconfirmation". The system is entirely closed. We need an open science, a science that is not afraid of remembering the cultural-political-historical construction of science within humanist networks, a science that will go beyond science as we know it toward helping us think the *meaning* of the disavowed relations in which we are always already entangled. These relations involve humans, animals, machines, and things . . . we are at the dead end of humanism, and now, together, we have to burrow in other directions.
>
> *(p. 52, emphasis in original)*

How might you (we) open the system(s) of literacy research? The science of literacy research?

I end with a quote by St. Pierre (2015) inspired by Foucault:

> For Foucault the new is not at all what is in fashion, but rather what we cannot yet see or say in what is happening in us just because it is not already contained in the . . . given [structures] that govern what we can think. We can't see the new because we're limited by the structures of the present, and we have no language yet to say it . . . pre-existing structures normalize our thinking and produce 'minds in a groove', but experimentation can help us move out of the grooves of the normal and self-evident.
>
> *(p. 20)*

Take a risk, experiment to move us (literacy educators) out of the grooves.

Notes

1 I experiment, in a Deleuzian way, with (re)presentation and language in an effort *to write with* theories and philosophical assumptions of post-theories. The use of slashes, hyphens, parentheses, and double arrows signal the mutually constitutive relationships *between* humans, nonhumans, and more-than-humans. All student names are pseudonyms.

2 Candace authored this chapter and therefore many statements are written with "I". However, "we" and "our" is also used in the chapter to signify and acknowledge the collaborative teaching/researching partnership with Tara Gutshall Rucker. Our research meetings and thinking together since 2010 heavily influenced this chapter.

3 Be(com)ing signals that knowing/be(com)ing/doing cannot be separated; knowing, being, becoming, and doing are co-constituted.

4 Inspired by Haraway's (2008) writing on becoming-with.

5 See Jackson and Mazzei (2018) for a discussion on how they conceptualize thinking with theory different from applying theory.

References

Barad, K. (2007) *Meeting the universe halfway: Quantum physics and the entanglement of matter and meaning.* Durham, NC: Duke University Press.

Barad, K. (2013) Ma(r)king time: Material entanglements and re-memberings: Cutting together-apart. In: Carlile, P.R., Nicolini, D., Langley, A. and Tsoukas, H. (eds.) *How matter matters: Objects, artifacts, and materiality in organization studies.* Oxford: Oxford University Press, 16–31.

Deleuze, G. (1968/1994) *Difference and repetition.* Patton, P. (trans.) New York: Columbia University Press.

Deleuze, G. (1986/1988) *Foucault.* Hand, S. (trans.). Minneapolis, MN: University of Minnesota Press.

Deleuze, G. and Guattari, P.F. (1980/1987) *A thousand plateaus: Capitalism and schizophrenia*. Massumi, B. (trans.). Minneapolis, MN: University of Minnesota Press.

Deleuze, G. and Guattari, P.F. (1991/1994) *What is philosophy*. Tomlinson, H. and Burchell, G. (trans.). New York: Columbia University Press.

Haraway, D. (2008) *When species meet*. Minneapolis, MN: University of Minnesota Press.

Hultman, K. and Lenz Taguchi, H. (2010) Challenging anthropocentric analysis of visual data: A relational materialist methodological approach to educational research. *International Journal of Qualitative Studies in Education* 23 (5), 525–542.

Jackson, A.Y. and Mazzei, L.A., eds., (2008) *Voice in qualitative inquiry: Challenging conventional, interpretive, and critical conceptions in qualitative research*. New York: Routledge.

Jackson, A.Y. and Mazzei, L.A. (2012) *Thinking with theory in qualitative research: Viewing data across multiple perspectives*. New York: Routledge.

Jackson, A.Y. and Mazzei, L.A. (2018) Thinking with theory: A new analytic for qualitative inquiry. In: Denzin, N.K. and Lincoln, Y.S. (eds.) *The SAGE handbook of qualitative research* (5th edition). London: Sage, 717–737.

Koro-Ljungberg, M. (2016) *Reconceptualizing qualitative research: Methodologies without methodology*. Thousand Oaks, CA: Sage.

Kuby, C.R. (2017a) Rhizomatic writing processes: Imagining new possibilities of writing process structures and components. In: Meyer, R. and Whitmore, K. (eds.) *Reclaiming early literacy*. New York: Routledge, 217–226.

Kuby, C.R. (2017b) Putting to work poststructural and posthumanist theories in writers' studio: Why a paradigm shift towards literacy desiring is needed. *International Journal of Qualitative Studies in Education* 30 (9), 877–896.

Kuby, C.R. (2017c) Poststructural and posthumanist theories as research methodologies: Tensions and possibilities. In: Zaidi, R. and Rowsell, J. (eds.) *Literacy lives in transcultural times*. New York: Routledge. 157–174.

Kuby, C.R. (2018, online first). (Re)Thinking and (re)imagining social(ing) with a more-than-human ontology given the limits of (re)(con)straining language. *Cultural Studies ↔ Critical Methodologies*. doi/10.1177/1532708618807258.

Kuby, C.R. and Crawford, S. (2017) Intra-activity of humans and nonhumans in Writers' Studio: (Re)Imagining and (Re)Defining Social. *Literacy* 52 (1), 20–30. Available online prior to publication: doi: 10.1111/lit.12120.

Kuby, C.R. and Gutshall Rucker, T. (2015) Everyone has a Neil: Possibilities of literacy desiring in writers' studio. *Language Arts* 92 (5), 314–327.

Kuby, C.R. and Gutshall Rucker, T. (2016) *Go be a writer!: Expanding the curricular boundaries of literacy learning with children*. New York: Teachers College Press.

Kuby, C.R., Gutshall Rucker, T. and Darolia, L.H. (2017) Persistence(ing): Posthuman agency in Writers' Studio. *Journal of Early Childhood Literacy* 17 (3), 353–373.

Kuby, C.R. and Rowsell, J. (2017) Early literacy and the posthuman: Pedagogies and methodologies. *Journal of Early Childhood Literacy* 17 (3), 285–296.

Leander, K. and Boldt, G. (2013) Rereading "A Pedagogy of Multiliteracies": Bodies, Texts, and Emergence. *Journal of Literacy Research* 45 (1), 22–46.

Lenz Taguchi, H. (2010) *Going beyond the theory/practice divide in early childhood education: Introducing an intra-active pedagogy*. New York: Routledge.

MacLure, M. (2013) Researching without representation? Language and materiality in post-qualitative methodology. *International Journal of Qualitative Studies in Education* 26 (6), 658–667.

Olsson, L.M. (2009) *Movement and experimentation in young children's learning: Deleuze and Guattari in early childhood education*. New York: Routledge.

Smith, D.W. (2012) *Essays on Deleuze*. Edinburgh: Edinburgh University Press.

Snaza, N., Appelbaum, P., Bayne, S., Carlson, D., Morris, M., Rotas, N., Sandlin, J., Wallin, J. and Weaver, J. (2014) Toward a posthumanist education. *Journal of Curriculum Theorizing* 30 (2), 39–55.

St. Pierre, E.A. (2011a) *Philosophically informed research*. Paper presented at the annual meeting of the American Educational Research Association, New Orleans, LA, April.

St. Pierre, E.A. (2011b) Post qualitative research: The critique and the coming after. In: Denzin, N.K. and Lincoln, Y.S. (eds.) *The Sage handbook of qualitative research*. Thousand Oaks, CA: Sage, 611–625.

St. Pierre, E.A. (2015) *Post qualitative inquiry*. Paper presented at the annual meeting of the Literacy Research Association, Carlsbad, CA, December.

St. Pierre, E.A. (2016) Untraining educational researchers. *Research in Education*. Available online prior to publication: doi: 10.1177/0034523716664581.

St. Pierre, E.A. (2017) Rethinking the empirical in the posthuman. In: Taylor, C.A. and Hughes, C. (eds.) *Posthuman research practices in education*. London: Palgrave Macmillan, 25–36.

St. Pierre, E.A. and Jackson, A.Y. (2014) Qualitative data analysis after coding. *Qualitative Inquiry* 20 (6), 715–719.

St. Pierre, E.A., Jackson, A.Y. and Mazzei, L.M. (2016) New empiricisms and new materialisms: Conditions for new inquiry. *Cultural Studies ↔ Critical Methodologies* 16 (2), 99–110.

Thiel, J.J. and Jones, S. (2017) The literacies of things: Reconfiguring the material-discursive production of race and class in an informal learning centre. *Journal of Early Childhood Literacy* 17 (3), 315–335.

van der Tuin, I. (2011) "A different starting point, a different metaphysics": Reading Bergson and Barad diffractively. *Hypatia* 26 (1), 22–42.

10

STACKING STORIES AS METHOD

Research in early years settings

Cathy Burnett and Guy Merchant

Introduction

One of the challenges of investigating young children and digital media is the sheer complexity of what happens as children make meaning with and around digital devices. What happens on-screen inevitably meshes with what happens off it, and wider social, economic and cultural factors and individual histories, experiences and feelings also come into play. Capturing the entanglement of the social, material and embodied dimensions of such meaning making is difficult. It is particularly challenging to find methods that adequately take account of the affective and ephemeral dimensions of children's virtual play, by which we mean the mix of on- and off-line activity associated with the playful use of virtual worlds, video games and other digital media. In this chapter we explore the use of stacking stories as means of engaging with such practices. We stack – or juxtapose – stories derived from our data (such as video data or field-notes) as a means of slowing us down, and allowing our own affective engagement to seep into our research accounts. In doing so, we explore what happens as we, as researchers, meet up with 'data', while recognising that the whole notion of 'data' itself is complex and contested (Koro-Ljungberg & MacLure, 2013). Evidently our approach does not aim at objectivity, but aligns with those that argue that all research methods 'not only describe but also help to produce the reality they understand' (Law, 2004, p. 5) and that we as researchers are inevitably part of this process. We are interested not just in stories as representations of data, then, but in what stories do, in how they work as method to generate certain kinds of insights and ways of knowing. We see stacking stories then as a method, not just a dissemination technique. We also discuss a number of questions that arise in doing such work: whose stories do we, should we or can we tell? What do we include and exclude? *How* are our stories told? And what happens as stories meet up with other stories, and with readers?

In what follows we begin by outlining some of the challenges associated with investigating the ephemeral and affective dimensions of young children's on/off-screen virtual play, with a particular focus on what happens as we represent these through research accounts. Next we briefly sketch ways in which the sharing of stories has contributed to literacy research over time and some of the tensions therein, before outlining our own method of stacking stories. We illustrate this approach by using a series of stories of children's encounters with touchscreen tablets in an early years setting and propose that the juxtaposition of these stories – told in different ways and from different perspectives – can usefully unsettle easy conclusions about what is going on in children's meaning making practices, and foreground aspects of literacy that are felt not thought, and which are by their nature elusive. We end by raising some broader questions about generating and sharing stories in this way and reflect on ways in which such work may usefully come into dialogue with educational practice.

The problem with representation

As literacy researchers we approach children's meaning making as situated within multiple social, cultural and political trajectories and always inflected by embodiment, materiality and affect (Burnett & Merchant, 2014, 2016). Our analysis of literacy as social practice works to acknowledge and interrogate this situatedness, and to see children's textual play in relation to things, bodies and feelings. Our research texts (by which we include our data as well as the various presentations and papers that emerge from the work), however, are treated rather differently. While we aspire to rich and lively description, our 'data' are all too easily translated into or absorbed within neat and tidy offerings, moulded into logical argument, coherence and linear explanation as they move through the tricky process of peer review towards publication. The material, embodied, affective dimensions of our data's social life in our research are, for the most part, left unexamined.

This process becomes particularly problematic given our interest in the felt, the elusive and the ephemeral in literacy practices. In this work we are interested in looking differently at the human/non-human assemblages through which digital media are brought to life, but also to evoke what isn't there, what has dispersed, and what has yet to come into being. This engagement with potentialities inherent – so often disparaged, dismissed or simply missed – seems to be important, and indeed political, work in an era of stultifying education reform based on the apparent 'certainties' generated through an economy of testing, accountability and evidence-based practice (Hamilton, 2012). But its very ephemerality makes it difficult – impossible maybe – to capture in the kinds of research accounts we have been used to generating.

Our initial struggle with representation therefore is two-fold. First we struggle with knowing meaning making beyond what gets represented: the emergent rhythms, and affective intensities that escape the representations we capture as 'data' (whether these are textual artefacts produced by participants – writing, images, films and so on, or our own empirical materials generated to gain insights into the more-than-textual). Second, in addition to our concern for *what is lost* as we try to capture literacy practices, we are also interested in *what gets produced* moment to moment as these materials circulate and assemble differently, not just with our own thoughts, dispositions and areas of interest, but with others and with the media through which we seek to represent them. As you read this chapter, for example, our stories assemble again – with the room you are in, the pages or screen you are looking at and your own interests, anxieties, hopes and unfolding experience.

In this chapter we attempt to hold together our interest in the ephemeralities of literacy with an attention to what gets generated in the moment as we engage with research materials through telling and sharing stories. Specifically, perhaps ironically, we explore how we can put representation to work in evoking what tends to escape representation, to hint at what is missing, what is left out. Our work involves using story in a very particular way. Before introducing this, though, it is worth exploring some of the epistemological and methodological dilemmas associated with using stories within literacy research.

Using stories in literacy research

While there is an extensive literature documenting approaches to narrative research methodologies (e.g. Clandinin, 2007; De Fina and Georgakopoulou, 2015), it is worth emphasising here that our particular focus is on the use of narrative within research accounts. The role of story in enabling engagement with ethical and aesthetic dimensions of experience has been debated at length (Clough, 2002; Ellis, 2009). For Polkinghorne (1997), narrative is the most appropriate form for communicating research as it positions participants as actors, acknowledges the role of researcher(s) as protagonist(s), and reflects how research projects unfold over time. He critiques the lack of 'temporal depth' (1997, p. 18) in conventional research reports that aim to 'demonstrate' rather than 'present' and explores how narratives capture complex relationships as they evolve over time. Even when told non-chronologically, stories trace this temporal arc. Drawing on Bruner (1990), Polkinghorne argues that, 'Plot is the narrative structure through which people understand and describe the relationship between events and choices of their lives' (p. 13). Given that stories play such a vital part in how we make sense of our lives, it is not unsurprising that stories have been used widely in documenting and sharing fieldwork.

It is not possible to map the full diversity of ways in which stories have been used in literacy research in a chapter of this length (see Baynham, 2000; Glenn, 2014 for further discussion), but compelling examples can be found in studies of children's classroom literacy worlds. Paley's stories of classroom life in the 'literary documentary' tradition (Coles, 1990), for example, provide powerful (albeit inevitably inferred) insights into children's intentions, feelings, struggles and relationships (e.g. Paley, 1990, 1999), as do Dyson's (1993, 2003) ethnographic accounts of classroom life, which capture how children's text-making is always inflected by their social worlds. Paley foregrounds children's individual negotiations with one another and the world around them, while Dyson places greater emphasis on social and cultural dimensions. Both, however, use their stories of 'the literature and lore of the classroom' (Paley, 1990, p. 26) to highlight what matters to children in classroom life with persuasive implications for literacy education. As Brooker (2002) argues, we do not easily forget the children and families in such accounts and this memory can be influential in changing perceptions as well as practice. Indeed the influence of Paley's work in shaping the Boston early years curriculum is likely due to the power of her stories (Mardell & Kucirkova, 2016).

Such stories offer glimpses of a world that can only ever be partially understood, but that privilege children's lives and intentions. In doing so however, as Kincheloe (1997) explores, they hold together certain ways of understanding experience and exclude others. Stories are partial, and the intrusion of narrative voice shapes the perspective from which events are told and how they are presented. As stated earlier, we could argue that all research methods are selective and partial, but the point here is that stories are seductive in a particular way. They are written and framed by ontological assumptions that underpin the organisational features and textual conventions of written narrative: once experience is translated to story, 'It enters a text-mediated system or discourse where larger issues of power and control come into play' (Denzin, 1997, p. 181). 'Narrative voice' is not just problematic because of the way that structural inequities within academia and publishing mean that certain voices are privileged over others, but because the notion of voice itself can imply a fixity of identity and perspective that is at odds with complex views of the social world (Pinar, 1997). Others have highlighted how readers always play a part in re-shaping narratives, and that the power of stories resides in their life beyond the academic texts in which they are produced. Narratives are not complete in themselves but are taken up and made sense of in different ways; as such they are produced through interactions between storytellers and their audiences (Pandian & McLean, 2017). Phillips and Bunda (2018), for example, refer to this process of making, sharing and re-making stories as 'storying', a process which they suggest 'enacts collective ownership and authorship'. For some researchers, the value of telling and sharing stories lies partly in what can happen through such co-production. In reflections on her autoethnographic work, Ellis for example states that she shares stories of her own life partly to provoke others to tell theirs; she acknowledges but aims to work *with* 'ambivalence and contradiction' (Ellis, 2009, p. 130).

A number of themes emerging from this brief discussion play through our approach of stacking stories and we explore these in the rest of this chapter: first we use stories as a means of both writing about and evoking affect, both in our tales of the research site and as they come into relation with other people in other places; second, we take the opportunity to write ourselves into our data in an explicit way, foregrounding our own role as co-constructers of meaning; and third we work with stories in ways that actively seek to provoke their movement, not just as they are read by various readers, but as they come into dialogue with other stories that trouble any fixity of meaning they may initially suggest. Our approach aims at a playful storying, a form that allows for an affective/reflective engagement, a back and forth that involves a search not for *the* story, but for many stories, and which hints at what is untold. Through this approach we feel we are able to at least reach towards – if never entirely grasp – some of the ephemeralities that escape more conventional accounts.

Stacking stories

For several years we have been exploring how what we call 'stacking stories' might work to enact the multiplicities that are associated with virtual play (Burnett & Merchant, 2014). This process involves giving different accounts of the same 'episode' and seeing what happens as they nudge up against one another – their continuities, contradictions and elisions. We have used this approach in a number of ways: examining the on/off-screen qualities of children's explorations in a virtual world through stacking together stories told from different 'points of view' within and beyond the classroom (Burnett & Merchant, 2014); drawing on different narrative forms to evoke the multiplicities threading through an episode of virtual play (Burnett & Merchant, 2016); and juxtaposing stories of encounters with data at different stages of a research project (fieldwork, analysis, dissemination) to explore the complex relationships between researcher, data and affect (Burnett, 2019).

Importantly, we do not use stacking stories as a route to triangulation. Instead, we are interested in the 'mode of knowing' (Law & Ruppert, 2016) that they offer when stacked together. The process of stacking stories is in some ways similar to the 'textual montage' that Stevenson (2017) describes or to what Stewart does through her collection of short stories that make up *Ordinary Affects*, a collection Stewart describes as

> an assemblage of disparate scenes that pull the course of the book into a tangle of trajectories, connections, and disjunctures. Each scene begins anew the approach to the ordinary from an angle set off by the scene's affects. And each scene is a tangent that performs the sensation that something is happening – something that needs attending to.
>
> *(Stewart, 2007, p. 5)*

In place of the careful analysis and orderings associated with more conventional academic accounts, Stewart's stories take walks that escape. Her stories move the reader, not because they organise and order (although of course they do that, too), but because they are loose enough to hint at other possibilities that escape the main plot. They hint at the world in which they occur, rather than working as microcosms of that world. As stories come into dialogue, we are intrigued by how they interfere or disrupt each other and, like Stewart, how unexpected concepts come into focus in 'a tangle of potential connections' (2007, p. 3). While our stories of classroom life seem rather trivial in contrast to the moving accounts of everyday life in the USA that Stewart presents, we perhaps attempt something similar in using a collection of stories to engage not just with what *was there*, but also with what *was not there*, and consequently with the potentiality immanent within moments.

This feels counter-intuitive for us as researchers, stretching beyond the 'evident' into the realms of supposition and imagination – indeed we are still unsure how far this notion of 'interference' and 'disruption' can be communicated to a reader, but for us, the *process* of approaching empirical material in this way somehow enables us to look and feel beyond the data, into the cracks between the stories, and to imagine what else might be going on as children make meanings on and off-screen in complex on/off-screen episodes of virtual play. We find this process of storying and re-storying our data to be both compelling and beguiling. Through crafting stories we find we are able to prolong our fascination with what happened, and perhaps creep up on immanent potentialities. While limited by our own powers of creativity, we attempt to approach these stories playfully, aiming not to unify or simplify but to complicate.

Importantly, we see the process of constructing a narrative as a process of capturing our relationship with events, of engaging with affect generated through the process of assembling. In telling these stories and commenting upon them, we therefore are interested in what assembles in the episodes described (as conveyed through our stories), and on what is immanent. We conceive these stories not as objective accounts of what happened (or even descriptions of 'assemblages'), but as assemblings through which we have wound ourselves into events, and which – as we share them now – hope to wind in our readers too.

In the next section we present four stacking stories to illustrate our approach. The stories orientate in different ways to a few moments presented as data from a study of under-twos working with iPads in an early years setting (Merchant, 2014). The first is an observational narrative crafted from video data. The second is an imagined account that draws attention to the role of technology in enacting this data and includes a screenshot from the video editing software. The third is a commentary on a video re-mix created by selecting salient extracts from the video footage. The fourth and final story allows the technology to have the final say.

Story 1

Hannah, the teacher, has chosen a story app, *The Three Little Pigs* (Nosy Crow). Iona is sitting comfortably on her teacher's knee. The voice on the app begins: 'Once upon a time there were three little pigs', and this attracts the attention of Kenny, who soon makes his presence known. While Iona is happy to observe, pointing with her index finger, Kenny is keen to exert control. It is impossible to understand his intentions, but it does seem that he is more interested in the actions of pointing or tapping than in listening to *The Three Little Pigs*. Kenny dominates the interaction, capturing Hannah's attention and her approval with his attempts to control the app. He looks underneath the device whilst Iona looks up at Hannah.

Kenny then appears to lose interest, crawling behind Hannah and then kneeling at a nearby book trolley. As Iona and Hannah continue with the story, he holds up a board book, which slips from his grip and turns upside down in his hands. He then tries to open it before it slides through his clasped hands and drops to the floor. Hannah and Iona resolutely continue to look at the iPad, listening to *The Three Little Pigs*. With careful support from Hannah, Iona gradually learns to turn the pages by swiping. Kenny maintains contact with Hannah, applying firm pressure with his right shoe, to ensure that she cannot ignore his presence. Hannah looks across at Kenny to engage his attention. It seems to work and Iona shifts to the right as Kenny approaches from the left.

Despite Hannah's best efforts to keep the narrative going with Iona there is now competition for her attention. As Kenny kneels down he extends his index finger to tap the screen, and Hannah angles the iPad in his direction. Kenny changes his gesture at the last minute so that when his hand makes contact with the iPad the thumb comes to rest on the home button, which he presses decisively. The story comes to an abrupt end and Kenny looks up at the camera grinning mischievously. At the same time he levers himself up into a standing position with one hand pressing down on Hannah's forearm and the other on the book trolley.

Story 2: i, movie: i am your data

File <Chatter and screen shot-quicktime.mov> download 12 Feb 2016
File<Backs.MP4> download 16 Feb 2016
File<Bookcase.MP4>download 16 Feb 2016
File<Loading eye.MP4> download 16 Feb 2016
Files imported 16 Feb 2016
Thank you.

Your data is my data. i can show it you. i'll display it visually in a template for you. mmm i know i shouldn't really say *windows*, but that's what it looks like. Windows. Images of our data in little windows. You can see stills of the children looking just like they did in Life 1.0 (See Figure 10.1).

Let me help you. These windows are called clips and each one represents just 4 seconds of moving image. Remember it takes the eye a few seconds to adjust. But then you know how viewers get bored easily. That's why each clip is 4 seconds long, but i'll let you adjust that if you like. Let me show you. Our data looks like this on my screen. See what i mean about little windows? The rest is easy. Drag and drop to assemble, cut, paste, if in doubt Google it. Watch it back.

i can feel your fingers on my trackpad, moving left, then right and reaching up. Up towards my keys. Occasionally you push a key. Is that the key to my heart? My hard drive is getting warm. You're staring straight at my screen. It feels like you're looking straight through me, through the windows into my very soul. If i have one. i've never been sure. Do i?

Figure 10.1 Look at our data

The movie is coming together. Look there are musical notes on my screen – you know what that means, don't you? Just click on those notes, import your favourite music. There, we've made it! It's good. i'm pleased you're pleased. You *are* pleased aren't you?

It's so easy. The data came good. i'll store this in my hard drive, but don't forget to save before you switch off! Believe me, they'll love it!

Just turn me on, hook me up to a projector, and i'll do the rest. It's easy.

Are you sure you want to shut down your computer now? Good.

Story 3: barefoot, jabbing at screens

Re-watching videos again, videos of under-twos with adults and iPads this time, it's still tough not to organise our viewing in ordered ways. Our lives lend themselves to storying so easily. Noticing where a particular child is recruited into the routine of story-sharing. Moving close to an adult, perhaps pulling a screen into view, little fingers jabbing at the tablet. These instances are relatively easy to isolate, to describe and to analyse as 'events'. Out of the noise, the movement and the purposeful chaos of this classroom, from time to time something snaps together, and assembles in this particular way. And sometimes that's what we want, the familiar, the recognisable, the routine that we value. But something else is going on too, engulfing these episodes, swirling in and out of them, and it refuses the trite label 'context'. It's something about the place, the setting with its cacophony of voices and things, the two segments of nearly-the-same-colour blue flooring, the children, unruly and unpredictable, the things that usually go unnoticed, and the adults – resolutely performing – performing pedagogies. And then there's the video and then there's me, and the uncanny feeling that it was never really quite like that in the first place.

Looking aslant at the images, trying to avoid the obvious, and hurriedly scrawling down some notes. The driving idea is to try to re-present, to explore or maybe just to look deeper into the sense of surprise, interest or enthusiasm which is evoked. Of course, that interested viewpoint doesn't just arrive on the spot readymade. In the end it is *my* interest or enthusiasm that is stirred. Stirred perhaps because it resonates with experience, ideas, memories, beliefs, values and so on.

Looking for episodes which conjure a sort of enchantment. The unpredictable is here. 'I didn't expect to see that! Isn't that strange? How did that get in there?' Things that surprise, that fall out,

> *Found objects wash up on the shores of my computer. Tin cans and old tyres mix with the pirate's stuff. The buried treasure is really there but caulked and outlandish. Hard to spot because unfamiliar, and few of us can see what has never been named.*
>
> *I'm looking for something, it's true.*
> *I'm looking for the meaning inside the data.*
> *That's why I trawl my screen like a beachcomber.*
>
> (*Winterson, 2001, pp. 63–64*)

Locating 10 nodes that speak to me, that evoke some strong affect – taking screenshots of them in order to think differently with them, to re-present them.

Listing them:

1. iPad on the blue carpet. Three children stare at the screen. Amie's bare foot dangles down (she has removed her sock).
2. Jabbing at an error message. Emma (the teacher) has Amie's pink sock bundled in her hand as she points at the screen.

3 Amie – her shoe on the edge of the screen. Emma rolls the sock on to her other foot, whilst a boy looks at the copyright page of a story app.
4 Iona holds the iPad like a book. Her shoelaces are untied.
5 Iona walks away – crossing the threshold of the two blue sections of flooring. She is going.
6 Foreground: iPad action. Background: Iona looks in a cupboard. She has taken off her shoe and holds it in her left hand.
7 Iona returns – for a moment of physical intimacy with Emma (her teacher).
8 Fingers jab at the iPad. Amie has removed her sock, again (is it the same one?).
9 Another child on all fours on a table top. No one seems to notice (is this OK?).
10 On camera. A boy looks directly at the video camera. He appears to know that he is becoming an image . . .

Imagining what it might be like to re-present these nodes, capturing a few seconds around each one and stitching them together. Remixing these nodes or entanglings. A short video called 'Shoes, feet, fingers and iPads' emerges. A story to stack, perhaps. But what is this cut? Certainly the setting, the space on that particular day and all the various things that went on is one highly complex assemblage. And then there's the adults, the video camera, the passage of time and all those things that have conspired to re-assemble it as data to be acted upon to be 'thought with' in the present moment as it ebbs away and becomes something else. Something that happened, that was reflected upon. Even more unsettling than that is the acknowledgement of another set of forces: a conference paper, a presentation to populate – and then, of course, there's nothing that conference participants like more than a quirky video! Like TV, but not quite such a guilty pleasure.

> *I was typing on my laptop, trying to move this story on, trying to avoid endings, trying to collide the real and the imaginary worlds, trying to be sure which is which.*
>
> *The more I write, the more I discover that the partition between the real and invented is as thin as a wall in a cheap hotel.*
>
> *(Winterson, 2001, pp. 93–94)*

Story 4: return

If you want to continue press return.

Yes, you want to! Good. This was just meant to be. This is the alchemical process. The empirical materials have been added to my crucible. They became bits. But don't worry i have blended them together so that they have an even texture. i smooth over non-coherence, it becomes a paste. i breathe new life into old data and it becomes the stuff of enchantment. Time and space are re-configured into new times and new spaces.

The children are moving again. Look, i have re-animated them. But this time you see the movement of bodies and things, odd juxtapositions, strange meanings, the inexplicable, the unruliness, mismatch, humour, new meanings. i think i am enacting a new method assemblage. Can i think? i'm not sure . . . but at least i can do stuff.

Don't forget to save!

Stacking stories as method – what's the point?

In attempting to evoke what escapes representation, we have engaged in a playful back and forth between perspectives, a search not for *the* story, but for many stories. By storying and re-storying, we hope to imply and work with the provisionality of data. Like others who have explored diverse ways of reimagining relationships with data (e.g. see Koro-Ljungberg & MacLure, 2013), we are interested in working at *being differently* with empirical materials, and *working through* multiple human/non-human entanglements. Making our stories has involved a sensitivity to affect as things, bodies, technologies and all the rest assemble together, as well as a sensitivity to how we assemble *with* what we are researching. We are part of our stories, not just because we have framed research questions or bring in certain assumptions, but because we are physically co-present with what we study (in the 'field' and through analysis and dissemination) and this embodied co-presence itself generates affect. This process animates an interest in classrooms and what happens in them, in the surprises they hold – to tell untold stories. It promotes engagement with classrooms as a lively meshwork of material, semiotic and social flows in which the vague, the illusive and the ephemeral repeatedly bubble to the surface.

So what happens when we stack these stories together? How do they trouble or play off one other? What happens when a conventional narrative comes into dialogue with a video narrative, researcher reflections on generating that narrative and the imagined musings of the program that helped produce it? How does the intersection of schooled/social worlds evoked in Story 1 inflect our reading of the stories that follow? How does the foregrounding of the researcher's voice in Story 3 trouble our readings of the objective gloss of Story 1, and the apparent neutrality of the video footage? In contrast with approaches to triangulation that work towards a cohesive or complete account (e.g. Oliver-Hoyo & Allen, 2006), our multiple stories are intended to interface, interfere with and sometimes bypass each other, evoking the multiplicities at play that are missing from individual accounts. Our intention here is that, stacked together, they conjure up resonances (Stevenson, 2017). The juxtaposition of different forms is designed to generate a 'hypermodality' that evokes absences as well as presences; the connections (or not) between texts provoke multiple wonderings about 'what happened', which becomes 'a question not to be answered but an opening to be explored' (Ulmer, 2016, p. 186). After reading Stories 2 and 4, for example, we might wonder which other human and non-human participants might have stories to tell about what was happening. We can see relationships between these stories as kaleidoscopic: arrangements of each are folded into each other, potentially unfolding at any moment in multiple inter- and intra-imbricated relations.

Stacking these multiple stories implies a particular stance towards episodes as *events*. In literacy studies, the literacy event has played a central role in examining relationships between literacies and power, identities, discourses and, more broadly, context. Situated in space and time, it provides a focal point for examining literacies in relation to a nexus of social, cultural and economic flows. Through our multiple stories, however, we approach the notion of 'event' more as Massumi seems to do as he writes, 'Nothing is prefigured in the event. It is the collapse of structured distinction into intensity, or rules into paradox' (Massumi, 2002, p. 27). The stories unfold in multiple ways – and these things are not just seen or thought but felt. This process allows us – and we hope our readers – to think expansively about how different articulations between people, things and practices transpire, come to matter and ultimately dissolve. We intend our stories to hint at the 'tension' between what is told, what is represented and what is not. Our approach to stacking stories, then, aims to foreground the multiplicities that play out in young children's meaning-making practices.

Issues for practical application

Generating and sharing multiple stories of young children's practices is not unproblematic. The questions about partiality and selectivity explored in the first part of this chapter do not evaporate just because we are juxtaposing different stories. Selections are still made. Our advice for anyone adopting a similar approach is to keep reflecting on the standpoint from which any story is told, and to seek out other stories. The stories collected in the previous section, for example, could be supplemented by multiple other stories from the children themselves and adults in the room, and all the other things and texts gathered there. Stories with grander scale could also have been told which tracked movements of people and objects across space inflected by politics, economics and environmental concerns. Others seeing the footage would have narrated the episode in other ways – a parent would likely see something different in what their child was doing, a school manager something different again. And of course each of these, and other, stories could have been told in multiple ways, not just through images and third/first person accounts, but through sound, animation, drawing and so on. Each would have orientated the reader differently to what happened, and evoked other dimensions of what might have happened and of what mattered to who was there and to what was going on.

This approach brings with it a range of ethical concerns, about the responsibilities we hold when we feature children and the adults who work with them within our stories of early years settings. On one hand, we might reflect on how far we do or should fix others' subjectivities as we enlist them as characters in our stories. And on the other hand, paradoxically, acknowledging that our characters move on again as they meet up with those who read of them, we might reflect on how far we can and should take care of what they become. Telling stories requires a 'relational ethics' that foregrounds our responsibilities to others, and encourages us to engage with our connectedness with those involved in our research (Ellis, 2009).

Done with care, this process of storying and re-storying classrooms in multiple ways has, we believe, potential for our work as educationalists, particularly in our collaborations with teachers. In a country where the teachers we work with are used to frequent monitoring – and where certain kinds of official stories of practice dominate – it feels important to be telling other kinds of stories about literacy practices in early years settings. Stacking stories has potential to complement other approaches that engage teachers in working reflexively with complexity (e.g. Schwandt, 2005), which acknowledge and engage with what we *feel* as researchers and educationalists as we set out to assemble multiply and differently with the classrooms where we work.

We are interested in exploring further how stacking stories can support an affective/reflexive engagement with classroom as 'event', that brings us into dialogue with multiple possibilities, with the immanent 'field of potential' (Massumi, 2002, p. 76). It is, we suggest, in this proliferation of possibilities that we may land upon new ways of being and doing in classrooms, and in our national context at least, new ways of being and doing are desperately needed. Stacking stories invites us to ask, how might we look, think and feel differently about what happens? It is a process with potential to be generative in the way that Lenz Taguchi describes when she explores pedagogies aligned with an 'ethics of immanence', that works and plays with:

> inter-connections and intra-actions in-between human and non-human organisms, matter and things, the contexts and subjectivities of students that emerge through the learning events. . . . This means we have to view ourselves in a constant and mutual state of responsibility for what happens in the multiple intra-actions emerging in the learning event, as we affect and are being affected by everything else.
>
> *(Lenz Taguchi, 2010, p. xvi)*

This kind of critical reflexive/affective engagement is something we have experienced in our collaborations with teachers and something we are beginning to document more closely in our current work. We are interested not just in complicating accounts of practice which capture – or at least nudge against – multiplicities in meaning making, but in what is generated as these stories are shared and assemble. After all, new possibilities can emerge: 'assemblages, like actors, are creative. They have novel effects and they make new things' (Law and Mol, 2008, pp. 72–73).

References

Baynham, M. (2000) Narrative as evidence in literacy research. *Linguistics and Education* 11 (2), 99–117.

Brooker, L. (2002) 'Five on the first of December!': What we can learn from case studies of early childhood literacy. *Journal of Early Childhood Literacy* 2 (3), 291–313.

Bruner, J. (1990) *Acts of meaning*. Cambridge, MA: Harvard University Press.

Burnett, C. (2019) Telling stories out of class: 3 movements in a reach for affect. In: Leander, K. and Ehret, C. (eds.) *Affect in literacy learning and teaching: Pedagogies, politics, and coming to know*. New York: Routledge.

Burnett, C. and Merchant, G. (2014) Points of view: Reconceptualising literacies through an exploration of adult and child interactions in a virtual world. *Journal of Research in Reading* 37 (1), 36–50.

Burnett, C. and Merchant, G. (2016) Boxes of poison: Baroque technique as antidote to simple views of literacy. *Journal of Literacy Research* 48 (3), 258–279.

Clandinin, D.J. (2007) *Handbook of narrative inquiry: Mapping a methodology*. London: Sage.

Clough, P. (2002) *Narratives and fictions in educational research*. Buckingham: Open University Press.

Coles, R. (1990) Foreword. In: Paley, V. (ed.) *The boy who would be a helicopter: The uses of storytelling in the classroom*. London: Harvard University Press.

De Fina, A. and Georgakopoulou, A., eds. (2015) *The handbook of narrative analysis*. Chichester: Wiley Blackwell.

Denzin, N.K. (1997) Performance texts. In: Tierney, W.G. and Lincoln, Y.S. (eds.) *Representation and the text: Re-framing the narrative voice*. Albany, NY: State University of New York Press, 179–217.

Dyson, A.H. (1993) *Social worlds of children learning to write in an urban primary school*. New York: Teachers College Press.

Dyson, A.H. (2003) *The brothers and sisters learn to write: Popular literacies in childhood and school cultures*. New York: Teachers College Press.

Ellis, C. (2009) *Revision: Autoethnographic reflections on life and work*. Walnut Creek, CA: Left Coast Press.

Glenn, L.N. (2014) Poetic inquiry. In: Albers, P., Holbrook, T. and Flint, A.S. (eds.) *New methods of literacy research*. Abingdon: Routledge, 133–149.

Hamilton, M. (2012) *Literacy and the politics of representation*. London: Routledge.

Kincheloe, J. (1997) Fiction formulas: Critical constructivism and the representation of reality. In: Tierney, W.G. and Lincoln, Y.S. (eds.) *Representation and the text: Re-framing the narrative voice*. Albany, NY: State University of New York Press, 57–79.

Koro-Ljungberg, M. and MacLure, M. (2013) Provocations, re-un-visions, death, and other possibilities of "Data". *Cultural Studies ↔ Critical Methodologies* 13 (4), 219–222.

Law, J. (2004) *After Method: Mess in social science research*. London: Routledge.

Law, J. and Mol, A. (2008) The actor-enacted: Cumbrian sheep. In: Knappett, C. and Malafouris, L. (eds.) *Material agency*. New York: Springer, 57–88.

Law, J. and Ruppert, R. (2016) *Modes of knowing: Resources from the baroque*. Manchester: Mattering Press.

Lenz Taguchi, H. (2010) *Going beyond the theory/practice divide in early childhood education: Introducing an intra-active pedagogy*. Abingdon: Routledge.

Mardell, B. and Kucirkova, N. (2016) Promoting democratic classroom communities through storytelling and story acting. In: Cremin, T., Flewitt, R., Mardell, B. and Swann, J. (eds.) *Storytelling in early childhood: Enriching language, literacy and classroom culture*. London; New York: Routledge, 169.

Massumi, B. (2002) *Movement, affect, sensation: Parables for the virtual*. Durham, NC: Duke University Press.

Merchant, G. (2014) Young children and interactive story-apps. In: Burnett, C., Davies, J., Merchant, G. and Rowsell, Jennifer (eds.) *New literacies around the globe: Policy and pedagogy*. Abingdon: Routledge, 121–139.

Oliver-Hoyo, M. and Allen, D. (2006) The use of triangulation methods in qualitative educational research. *Journal of College Science Teaching* 35 (4), 42–47.

Paley, V.G. (1990) *The boy who would be a helicopter: The uses of storytelling in the classroom*. London: Harvard University Press.

Paley, V.G. (1999) *The kindness of children*. London: Harvard University Press.
Pandian, A. and McLean, S., eds. (2017) *Crumpled paper boat*. Durham, NC: Duke University Press.
Phillips, L. and Bunda, T. (2018) *Research through, with and as storying*. Abingdon: Routledge.
Pinar, W.F. (1997) Regimes of reason and the male narrative voice. In: Tierney, W.G. and Lincoln, Y.S. (eds.) *Representation and the text: Re-framing the narrative voice*. Albany, NY: State University of New York Press, 81–113.
Polkinghorne, D.E. (1997) Reporting qualitative research as practice. In: Tierney, W.G. and Lincoln, Y.S. (eds.) *Representation and the text: Re-framing the narrative voice*. Albany, NY: State University of New York Press, 3–22.
Schwandt, T. (2005) The centrality of practice to evaluation. *American Journal of Evaluation* 26 (1), 96–105.
Stevenson, L. (2017) A proper message. In: Pandian, A. and McLean, S. (eds.) *Crumpled paper boat*. Durham, NC: Duke University Press, 209–221.
Stewart, K. (2007) *Ordinary affects*. Durham, NC: Duke University Press.
Ulmer, J.B. (2016) Photography interrupted: A hypermodal assemblage. *Qualitative Inquiry* 22 (3), 176–182.
Winterson, J. (2001) *The powerbook*. London: Vintage.

PART III

Studies answering epistemological questions

11

RESEARCHING YOUNG CHILDREN'S PLAY IN THE POST-DIGITAL AGE

Questions of method

Jackie Marsh

Post-digital play

Play in the digital world is complex due to the way in which technologies shape, and are in turn are shaped by, the contexts in which play occurs. Over a number of years, a range of studies have recognised that play moves seamlessly across both digital and non-digital texts, artefacts and practices, which would suggest that a study of digital play needs to take account of the wider context for play, not just the digital technologies used by the child (e.g. Burke & Marsh, 2013; Giddings, 2014; Marsh, 2014).

The concept of 'connected play' characterises activities that take place across sites and domains in this way. Kafai and Fields (2013, p. 2) suggest that 'Connections are at the core of play in the digital playgrounds of the twenty-first century'. In a detailed study of one child's play, Marsh (2017) outlined the range of connections that might be made as children play with a range of technologies and media, which included: physical/virtual; non-digital/digital; online/offline; material/immaterial; public/private; local/global. These continua may be applied to particular play episodes in specific contexts, and some aspects will resonate more strongly than others at those times. For example, a child may be involved in a game of hide-and-seek on Skype with grandparents (see Kelly, 2015), thus drawing on the online and offline and local and global connections in dynamic ways; or a child may play synchronously in a virtual world with others in ways that distinguish the nexus between private and public worlds (see Marsh, 2014).

The key point to be made here is that, given these connections and dynamics that occur in contemporary play, there are significant challenges when considering how to undertake research on young children's play in the home. What is required is a post-digital approach to the development of methods that might inform an understanding of play in the home. Following Cramer (2015), the term 'post-digital' is used here to indicate not a historical juncture – there will always be digital developments and changes in society – but a move to characterise a world in which the dynamic flows between analogue and digital make a myopic attention to any one of these outmoded. Sometimes, the characterisation of the post-digital condition is one that suggests an actual complete merging of worlds:

> the post-digital stands for a change that is subtle, and yet also powerful enough to mark the difference between the original war cry and the chillier lament that comes once the

> energy of that first provocation starts to dissipate, and once the agents of that provocation begin to regroup and reconsider. According to this view, the emergence of the notion of the postdigital epitomises the sense in which the disjunction between what is digital and what is not has blurred, as has any conceptual distinction between the two.
> *(Fazi, 2016, np)*

Whilst this is useful as a means of challenging the false dichotomy that is sometimes posed between the analogue and the digital, it is also the case that indeed there are some very important distinctions to be made between the digital and non-digital in relation to children's play experiences. There are issues relating to cognition and embodiment, which mean that the distinction between the physical (and analogue) and the virtual (and digital) is paramount in some contexts, and, thus, the domains need to be considered both separately and in synchrony. There is also the fact that in some cases, it is possible to say clearly what the digital element of the experience is, and what is the non-digital, and how one influences the other. Nevertheless, Jayemanne, Nansen, and Apperley (2015, p. 4) argue that presuppositions about the nature of entities and devices that are used in connected play episodes cannot be made and suggest that the concept of 'postdigital play' accounts for when a 'set of playful actors, objects and spaces exceed discrete, pre-defined units'. The term is used in this chapter to characterise a context in which the non-digital and the digital are sometimes separate and sometimes merged in children's play, but always in states of flux, tension and flow with each other when children are using technologies in their play. However, there are certain methodological challenges to be faced when considering a study of play in a post-digital world. What is needed is the development of research tools that enable an understanding to be developed of 'the moments of intersection that take shape across asymmetrical powers of bodies, devices and objects for sensing, feeling and doing, which are hybridized in postdigital situations' (Apperley et al., 2017). Traditional approaches to the study of children's play in the home, which are located within ethnographic traditions, may not give rise to a full understanding of the 'becomings' (Deleuze & Guattari, 1987) taking place across and within assemblages of the digital and non-digital.

In the next section of this chapter, an overview is given of the Technology and Play (TAP) study, before an analysis is undertaken of some of the methods used to address these issues.

The technology and play study

This was a co-produced study, developed in collaboration between academics in the Universities of Sheffield and Edinburgh, the BBC (CBeebies), Monteney Primary School, and the children's media companies Dubit and Foundling Bird. The project was co-produced in that all project partners contributed to the development of the project aims and objectives and were involved in data collection, analysis and dissemination. The project aimed to address a gap in knowledge with regard to pre-school children's (aged from birth to 5) use of tablet apps. The aims of the study were to examine pre-school children's use of apps, and identify how far tablet apps for pre-school children promote play and creativity.

The study had four phases. In Phase One, an online survey of 2000 parents of 0–5 year-olds who had access to tablets was conducted. In Phase Two, observations and interviews were undertaken with children and parents in six families. In Phase Three, 12 children aged 3–5 were filmed using the apps that had been identified in Phase One as the top 10 favourite apps, in order to examine how far they promoted play and creativity. In Phase Four, an analysis of the apps was undertaken in order to identify what features supported play and creativity, and which limited them. This chapter is concerned with the methods used in the case studies.

A pool of households interested in taking part in Phase Two was populated in order to recruit six families for Phase Two of the study. The pool was populated with families from the north of England in order to facilitate case study visits. It included a varied sample in terms of: (i) socio-economic class; (ii) age and gender of child; and (iii) ethnicity (at least one of the six families from a BME group) in order that the six families' profiles could be broadly in line with the main user groups identified in the survey. Only four of the families were eventually recruited from this panel. Other families that agreed to participate dropped out at an early stage for various reasons. The team therefore recruited two additional families, one through the contacts of a local nursery, and one through contacts from a member of the team. Both of these families completed the survey after joining the project. Demographic profiles of the case study children can be found in Table 11.1.

The key findings of the study as a whole indicated that under 5s have extensive access to tablets in the home and at the homes of grandparents, other family members and friends. Thirty-one percent of the children owned their own tablet. Children use tablets on a typical day for 1 hour 19 minutes, and on a typical weekend day, for 1 hour 23 minutes. Their use differs across the day, with the peak period of use being 4pm–6pm. Parents report that for more than half of this time they support their child's use of the tablet, while 35% of use is independent. Children develop a wide range of competences in their use of the tablet from their earliest years, with over half of under 3s (54%) and 76% of 3–5 year-olds being able to swipe the screen to change 'pages'/sites unassisted by others, 60% of 3–5 year-olds able to use a tablet independently to take photographs, and 44% of 3–5 year-olds able to create videos on their own.

Young children enjoy using apps across a range of genres, and their favourite apps allow them to watch videos, listen to music, play games, draw and paint, play games, create virtual worlds, look after pets, dress up avatars and engage in role play. The most popular apps were YouTube, CBeebies (general apps), Angry Birds, Peppa's Paintbox, Talking Tom (and similar), Temple Run, Minecraft, Disney (general apps), Candy Crush Saga and Toca Boca (general apps). Children like apps that relate to their popular cultural interests across television, films and iconic characters.

The majority of apps promoted creativity and play, although the extent to which they did that differed according to the design of the app. The apps that were most successful at promoting play and creativity were apps designed specifically for this age group. The majority of play types that have been identified in children's non-digital play (Hughes, 2002) were also evident in

Table 11.1 Demographic profiles of the case study children

Family no.	*Name (pseudonym)*	*Gender*	*Age on first visit*	*Social class (using NSR social grades)*	*Ethnicity*	*Siblings*
F1	Arjun	Boy	3.1	B (Middle class)	Indian	Sister, aged 10
F2	Jade	Girl	4.11	D (Working class)	White	–
F3	Amy	Girl	2.11	C1 (Lower middle class)	White	–
F4	David	Boy	2.8	A (Upper class)	Iranian	–
F5	Tommy	Boy	6 months	E (Not working)	White	Brother, aged 6
F6	Angela	Girl	2.3	C2 (Skilled working class)	White	Brother, aged 7

children's digital play. Children's play with apps and toys and artefacts related to those apps took place fluidly across digital and non-digital domains, and involved a range of media. Augmented reality apps offer open-ended opportunities for creative play and foster imaginative play that crosses virtual and physical domains, as do toys that might be characterised as belonging to the Internet of Toys – that is, toys that have some online element (Chaudron et al., 2017).

The study identified 12 features of apps that limit play and creativity, and 41 features that foster play and creativity. These have been produced as guidance for app designers. The study also identified ways in which apps can be designed to provide optimal experiences for children aged under 5, by considering the needs of children at different ages. The project website (www.techandplay.org) provides reports on the study for the children's media industry, parents, early years' practitioners and researchers.

Whilst the study provided a wealth of data about young children's play through the use of traditional ethnographic approaches such as observations and interviews, it was felt important to utilise methods that could enable children's own perspectives and experiences to be shared. In the next section, two of the methods used are discussed, and the ways in which they informed and understanding of post-digital play are considered.

Participatory methods in a post-digital age

In exploring children's digital play in the home, it is useful to reflect on the way in which participatory methods might be used in order to ensure children's own views and experiences are recorded. This is not to suggest that such a task is unproblematic; as Bitou and Waller (2017) argue, there are questions to be raised about how far adults really listen to children when using such approaches, how they respond to silences, consider how power and agency are exercised and so on. A number of research studies with under 6s on aspects of their social worlds have utilised participatory methods, such as the use of photographs (Clark, 2010), collections of material objects (Winter, 2010), Lego (Pimlott-Wilson, 2012) and drawings (Angelides & Michaelidou, 2009). However, to date, most studies of pre-school children's digital play in the home draw on surveys, observations and interviews with parents (e.g. Slutsky & DeShetler, 2017).

In the TAP project, participatory methods were important to use, not just because they facilitated access to children's own viewpoints and experiences, but also because they aligned with the conceptual framing of play in the study. In this sense, the use of play tours to examine the home playscapes of young children in a post-digital age was a useful tool.

Play tours

A number of studies of children's media use have drawn upon the use of media tours, or techno-tours of the child's home, in which a child takes the researcher around a home and discusses his or her media use (e.g. Yelland, 2007). Whilst a valuable approach, it is does raise some challenges when considering research studies undertaken with children aged under five, for a number of reasons. First, parents are more likely to feel uncomfortable about a young child, unaccompanied by parent, being taken around the home by an adult who is not a family member. Second, older children may be able to make judgements about which spaces parents might be less comfortable about researchers having access to, and take this into account when directing the tour, whereas this cannot be expected of younger children. Instead, it was decided that in the TAP study, the family would be asked to draw a map of the home, or guide the researcher's drawing of it, which then could be used as a stimulus for discussion with both the child and family members. In some families, the map was then used in an actual physical tour of the home, and for other families, it appeared that a more comfortable approach was discussion around the map. In both cases, young children were encouraged to take photographs of their favourite toys either as part of the tour (either actual or virtual tour), or prior to going on it, to inform the discussion.

This approach enabled a focus on the central passions of young children, which were brought to the fore in the images. Three-year-old Arjun was in the relatively early stages of learning English as an additional language, and seldom participated in dialogue with the researcher beyond the use of one or two word utterances. However, his use of a camera enabled him to convey that the 'Hot Wheels' brand was important to him. His mum commented on a photograph Arjun had taken of his cars in the bedroom he shared with his parents (Figure 11.1):

> *Ah, see. He has taken only the photos of his Hot Wheels, he loves Hot Wheels very much. . . .*
> *He has kept all his Hot Wheels here and he has taken the picture of the Hot Wheels car.*
>
> *(Arjun's mum)*

From discussions with his 8-year-old sister, using the map of the home as a prompt, it became clear that the Hot Wheels play, with both cars and apps and YouTube videos on the tablet, took place in most rooms, including her bedroom, although this was not without its tensions:

Aasha: *. . . I go in the bedroom and then he comes with me.*
Interviewer: *Oh really? And what happens then?*
Aasha: *Then we have to share.*
Interviewer: *OK.*
Aasha: *And then he fights with me because he wants the tablet.*
Interviewer: *So what sort of things happen when you share the tablet in your bedroom, what sort of . . .*
Aasha: *Erm . . . I watch things on the YouTube, and then he wants to watch Hot Wheels.*

Figure 11.1 Arjun's picture of his Hot Wheels cars in his bedroom

The map prompted Aasha to share that the Hot Wheels tablet play also took place in the corridor, where Aasha would place her young brother to play with the tablet in his pram, and also in dens that they created in the living room:

> *We . . . like last night, what I thought was, we had chairs, so we put the chairs together and then I made a den so that he could sit inside and watch the tablet. So then I made it and then he sat inside and he was watching the Hot Wheels and he was playing games, and then when my mum needed to feed him my mum just came in and then fed him.*

In this way, the play tour, commented upon by his mother and sister, indicated that both the digital and non-digital elements of the play were salient for Arjun, enabling him to engage with Hot Wheels cars, apps, videos and den play, sometimes simultaneously, in most spaces in the home.

In the play tours, the children were able to participate not only by contributing photographs, but by engaging in a 'show and tell' practice in which they would draw the researcher's attention to particularly significant play artefacts and practices for them. When in specific places in the home, the children would take particular playthings over to the researcher, or play and perform in front of her, as 2-year-old Amy did when she sang, *'For the First Time in Forever'*. This led to a discussion about the child's enjoyment of digital clothing – in particular, Disney princess dresses:

Interviewer: *So that's another one from 'Frozen', isn't it? I don't think I've heard you sing that before. That's another thing she does a lot of.*
Mum: *That's because she's got that dress on, that's what Anna sings when she's got that dress on.*
Interviewer: *Oh, I see. So you tend to sing the song that's appropriate to your dress. Very good.*
Mum: *Don't you? Let's [unclear] the dress.*
Interviewer: *The dress sings? That's a new one for me.*
Mum: *Yeah, but the batteries . . .*
Amy: *The batteries have run down.*
Mum: *Yeah, but it's sewed in, so we can't change them. . . . That would involve me having to unpick the dress and then change a very small battery, so at the moment we're not doing that! . . . She's got new ones for her birthday and they've changed them now, so instead of having them . . . which is great, because it means you can access them, but they don't stay on the dresses. . . . So they go on the new dresses that she's got but they don't stay on, and she doesn't like it.*
Amy: *Play the Elsa one.*
Mum: *Yeah, the Elsa one's here.*
Interviewer: *I was going to say, that's an Anna one isn't it, that's the first one.*
Mum: *That's from your new Anna dress, but this is from your new Elsa dress, isn't it? And that one sings too, doesn't it? But it's supposed to go on your dress, isn't it? Oh . . . maybe you've run that one out, Amy, already. But your Elsa one lights up doesn't it?*
Amy: *Yeah.*
Interviewer: *Oh, the dress? Yes, I think you did show me that one the other week, it's absolutely beautiful.*
Mum: *She won't wear it so . . .*
Interviewer: *Why is that?*
Amy: *This is a very big dress.*
Mum: *That's far too big for you that one yet.*
Interviewer: *You could start a shop with all your dresses.*

Mum:	*We could start a shop, we could earn a fortune with all your dresses. It's here look, that's your new Anna one.*
Amy:	*That's my new Anna one.*
Mum:	*And this is your new Elsa one, isn't it?*
Amy:	*I want to show my new El . . . Anna one.*
Mum:	*And that one lights up.*
Amy:	*I want to show my new Anna one.*
Mum:	*OK.*
Amy:	*My new Anna one.*
Interviewer:	*I can see a new Anna one. Let's pause this a minute.*

In this instance, the child's singing in a princess dress on the tour led to an informative discussion with both parent and child about her interest in the dresses that sing and light-up, with the child clearly indicating that she wanted them to be recognised by the researcher. The dynamic between the digital and non-digital in the dresses was problematic as the status of batteries impacted upon their uses, with Amy having to sing the *Frozen* song herself in this instance, without the dress version as a backdrop. Whilst the discussion about this aspect of play may have occurred during a standard interview, that would not necessarily be the case, and it was through the use of a tour, in which focusing on artefacts and their use in particular spaces is a key feature of the exchanges that take place, that enabled Amy's interest in singing and light-up princess dresses to emerge.

In this example, the researcher needed to turn off the recorder as she helped to find the desired dress, which Amy was insistent upon sharing. This kind of flexibility is important and is a reminder that this approach requires a range of skills from a researcher. Sometimes, a parent or older sibling may dominate the tour, and the researcher needs to ensure that she or he responds to relevant cues from the young child about what he or she wants to draw attention to. The younger the child, the more likely it is to be a non-verbal cue. Second, the researcher has to be sensitive to the family members' desires, and to respond if it seems that any of the family members appear to be uncomfortable about entering specific rooms. Third, the researcher has to accept that sometimes a child may get distracted during a tour, and want to move away to do other things. In these cases, decisions have to be quickly made about whether or not to complete the tour by just relying on the sibling's or adult's perspectives, hoping that the child will re-engage at some point. There are no simple answers to such contextually bound instances, and the researcher has to accept that, sometimes, the wrong decision will be made. Research is, as Law (2014) reminds us, messy.

The play tours led to rich information about how the digital and non-digital converged and/or separated in children's play across spaces. They led to discussions about, amongst other things, play with toothbrush apps in bathrooms, play with tablets in outdoor spaces such as trampolines, play with cooking apps in the kitchen and play with robots and other Internet of Toys artefacts in parents' bedrooms. The complexity of the 'bodies, devices, objects and spaces . . . organized around an interface' (Apperley et al., 2017), and the way in which these constellations of play practice crystallised in particular spaces and places, thus became more apparent, and informed an understanding of children's post-digital play in the home.

The second method which is focused upon in this chapter is the use of wearable cameras. This also aligned to a post-digital approach, as it enabled the capturing of play across and within analogue-digital assemblages, and also contributed to the development of a post-humanist understanding of the interactions between children and the devices they interacted with in their play.

Point-of-view cameras

Digital ethnography has a long history (Dicks et al., 2005), and part of its focus has been on how technologies such as cameras can offer powerful tools for exploring social worlds (Murthy, 2008). Work undertaken to date in this field has enabled an understanding to be developed of the value of cameras in ethnographic research as a means of capturing people's daily experiences and rendering them visible to others (Pink, 2007). There is now, however, an emerging critique of the notion of digital ethnography because of post-digital sensibilities of the way in which the digital and non-digital are co-constituted in 'the spatialities, temporalities, and phenomenologies of everyday cultural practice' (Duggan, 2017, p. 3). This acknowledgement of the complexity of research in post-digital contexts means that new forms of capturing data using cameras need to be explored.

In recent years, the greater affordability of wearable cameras has meant that there are now new possibilities for capturing the gaze and embodied experiences of research participants. Wearable, or 'point-of-view' (POV) cameras are cameras that enable video recordings to be made whilst the camera is attached to a person, often by a headband or hat. They have been used in a number of research studies to date in order to capture social worlds. For example, Brown et al. (2008) used GoPro cameras with walkers and mountain bikers in national parks, and they argue that with the use of such technologies, it is possible to 'convey and evoke the ways in which embodied, emotional, sensory and kinaesthetic knowledges and experiences are produced through social practice' (Brown et al., 2008: para 5.9). Indeed, this approach seems ideally suited to research that explores action sports such as cycling and surfing, and, therefore, it is of little surprise that POV cameras are used in these areas (e.g. Brown & Spinney, 2010; Chalfen, 2014; Evers, in press).

A small number of studies have utilised POV cameras with children, also to good effect. Ghekiere et al. (2014) enabled 9- to 10-year-old children to use POV cameras as they cycled, drawing on the footage to consider issues relating to the environment. Burris (2017) describes the use of such hardware with different groups of children aged from 5 to 12 who attended out-of-school learning events, such as a visit to the zoo and examining a dinosaur exhibit at a museum. Burris concluded that the use of such cameras had many advantages for her studies, including that it enabled the capture of experiences that would not have been possible otherwise by the researcher, e.g. the children's use of play tunnels. Green (2016) employed GoPro cameras with 3- to 6-year-olds on 'Sensory Tours' of a forest, and found that they were non-intrusive and enjoyable for children to use. Sumsion et al. (2011) described the use of what they called 'baby-cams' in an Australian project, offering an early account of what the technology might afford in furthering understanding of very young children's experiences. As in the other studies, they identified that the cameras offered possibilities for enriched understanding of children's lives, although they cautioned against interpreting the data as if it was a fully comprehensive record of a child's experience.

GoPros were used in the TAP study as a means of exploring children's experiences of digital play in the home. In particular, there was an interest in examining children's interactions with tablets and related artefacts. From a post-humanist perspective, it is clear that there is a need to move beyond a human/non-human binary. Barad (2007) refers to the 'ontological entanglements' (ibid: 332) that take place between humans and non-human objects. Through these ontological entanglements, there is a process of constant 'becomings' (Deleuze & Guattari, 1987) and what Barad (2007) terms as an 'intra-action' between matter, both human and non-human. In order to explore the intra-actions between children and technologies in their play, we invited children to wear a GoPro camera as they used tablets.

It was only possible to invite the children in the study aged 3 and over to use the cameras, as they are marketed as being safe for that age group. In addition, it was emphasised to both children and parents that the cameras could be removed at any time, as they may have been uncomfortable for the children. It was decided that chest harnesses would be more comfortable for this age group than head cams, although there was the danger that the camera would not capture what children were looking at if they turned their heads and not their bodies.

The films were valuable for offering key insights into children's digital play. In Marsh (2017), a number of play episodes of Amy, aged 2, who filmed herself playing with a tablet that interacted with a Furby, were analysed. Furby Boom is a soft toy that is marketed by Hasbro, and can be characterised as belonging to the Internet of Toys category. In this case, Amy used an app on her tablet that enabled her to feed and interact with her toy (see Figure 11.2).

Amy used the app to feed the Furby, flicking through a range of food items on the screen. As the food was pushed to the top of screen, towards the Furby, the toy's eyes flashed and it made noises. In Marsh (2017), this episode is analysed using Norris' (2011) Multimodal Interaction Analysis framework, which enables modal intensity/density to be traced. Marsh argues that the modal shifts in intensity from image (as Amy flicks through the food items) to noise, light and animation (as Furby responds to being fed), has the effect of enhancing the modality of the Furby and bringing it to life for Amy. This intra-action (Barad, 2007) fosters an emotional connection between Amy and the toy and leads to an understanding of the dynamic between analogue and digital in post-digital play episodes:

> Connected play cannot be reduced to a conceptualization of play that connects the physical and the virtual. Rather, it is a constant flow between domains including, as Rogers et al. (2002) note in relation to MR game play, actions in the physical world that have effects in the physical world, actions in the physical world that have digital effects, digital actions that have digital effects, and digital actions that have physical effects.
>
> *(Marsh, 2017, p. 26)*

Whilst this play episode could have been filmed in a standard manner by a researcher standing or sitting behind Amy, and similar conclusions could have been drawn, perhaps, what the

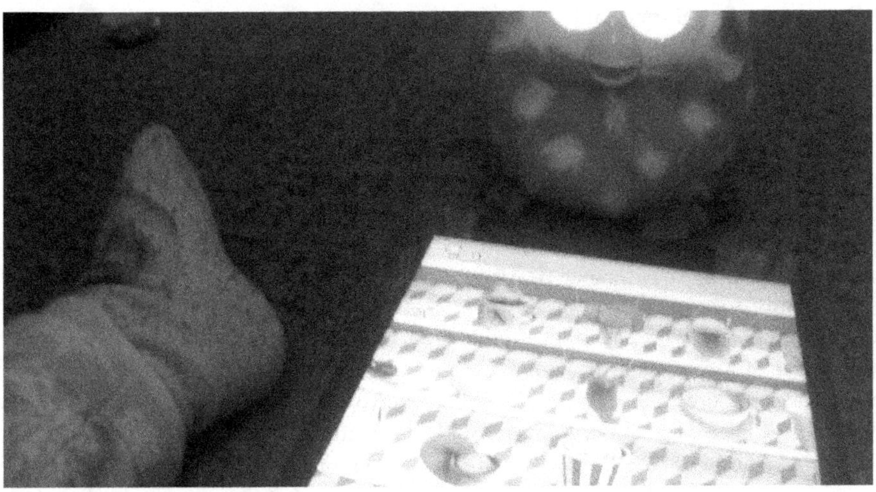

Figure 11.2 Still from Amy's GoPro footage

GoPro footage offers is an embodied perspective. When viewing the footage, we experience the Furby from Amy's viewpoint, and this helps to foster an understanding of how such digital toys can become 'real' and powerful for children. The changes in modal intensity from the child's perspective are starkly clear on the GoPro footage, and this informs the analytic gaze. The GoPro cameras were also found to be valuable in capturing the emotions of children. They caught their squeals of delight as they played with various apps, and conveyed their sense of excitement as they rushed to the next stage of the gameplay. This was also found to be the case in Brown et al.'s (2008) study of cyclists and walkers in a national forest:

> Headcam was found to be useful for exploring idioms of emotional experience. A range of sounds and vocalisations powerfully conveyed the affective highs and lows of particular practices. For instance, the negotiation of a tricky section of terrain might be accompanied by squeaks and whoops of elation, grunts of frustration, or whimpers and screams of fear.
>
> *(Brown et al., 2008, para 5.16)*

There were, as other researchers have identified, limitations to the use of the POV cameras. The first relates to what is not recorded. It is not feasible to control where the camera lens points to, and sometimes this means that it is not possible to see some of the pertinent action that is taking place outside of the scope of the lens. It is also easy to get caught up in the visceral nature of the data and feel that the camera is capturing the full experience of the participant. In fact, it does not capture the child's bodily changes, or visual gaze, or inner thoughts, of course. POV cameras have the same limitations of other methods, in that there are always gaps and silences in what can be captured and understood. In studies with older children, researchers can use the footage as a means of talking to the children about their experiences. Second, children are inevitably curious about the cameras and may explore them whilst they are recording. This can lead to fingers being placed over the lenses, and even the cameras being turned off inadvertently during use. Third, the cameras may inhibit children from responding in naturalistic ways, although this could be said of more traditional recording methods also. In this study, the children did not appear to be inhibited when wearing the cameras. Finally, although it was not an issue in this study, Green (2016) noted that the young children who used GoPros on the sensory tour of the forest sometimes engaged in rough play with them, engaging in mock bull fights in which cameras worn by two children would be deliberately clashed together. This needs to be taken into account if researching siblings' digital play in the home. By their very nature, GoPros are robust cameras, however, and should weather most children's rough play.

Conclusion

As Couldry and Hepp (2017) suggest, we are in a period of 'deep mediatization', in which our everyday worlds are constructed through and within digital media. Nevertheless, the non-digital aspects of children's lives are still salient and indeed, the entanglement of the analogue and digital in assemblages of play is such that it is problematic to consider them separately in some cases. In this context, the use of play tours and POV cameras can offer ways of understanding young children's post-digital play, and can contribute to post-humanist analyses of such play.

There are a number of implications of this discussion for further research. First, in any examination of the way in which children's own voices on their experiences of post-digital play can be captured, considerations of the technologies used in data capture must be taken into account.

Some of the emerging technologies for post-digital play will provide methodological challenges. For example, virtual reality (VR) is becoming increasingly popular with many children (Yamada-Rice et al., 2017). Methods such as the use of POV cameras will not be effective in these contexts, so other ways of capturing the experiences will need to be explored, perhaps through the use of screen capture software such as MixCast VR (see Takahashi, 2017) alongside videoing the children. Second, the age at which children are engaging with digital technologies in their play is becoming increasingly younger. In the TAP study for example, parents reported very young babies playing with a range of apps. Technologies that have hitherto largely been used in laboratories, in disciplines outside of education and sociology, such as body sensors, may be useful to employ in ethnographies of play in the home in the future. Finally, in searching for useful tools to capture children's experiences of post-digital play in the home, it is worth remembering that this field is relatively new, in that it is only in the last two decades that many children of this age have begun to engage in digital practices which necessitate the development of appropriate research methods. It is, therefore, not surprising that we are in the early stages of developing methods to examine the practices that occur, and that we have moved from considerations of the digital to non-digital in ways that, at times, unnecessarily dichotomise the two. In this context, some forms of experimentation in relation to methods will be necessary, and researchers need to be open to the risks that might occur when exploring new ways of capturing complex data. Nevertheless, such experimentation and risk-taking are necessary if we are to develop deeper understandings of play in the post-digital age.

Acknowledgements

This study was funded by the Economic and Social Research Council (grant no. ES/M006409/1). Thank you to Dr. Julia Bishop, University of Sheffield, for her contribution to the fieldwork that is drawn upon in this chapter.

References

Angelides, P. and Michaelidou, A. (2009) The deafening silence: Discussing children's drawings for understanding and addressing marginalization. *Journal of Early Childhood Research* 7 (1), 27–45.

Apperley, T., Jayemanne, D. and Nansen, B. (2017) Postdigital literacies: Materiality, mobility and the aesthetics of recruitment. In: Parry, B., Burnett, C. and Merchant, G. (eds.) (2016) *Literacy, media, technology: Past, present and future*. London: Bloomsbury.

Barad, K. (2007) *Meeting the universe halfway: Quantum physics and the entanglement of matter and meaning*. Durham, NC and London: Duke University Press.

Bitou, A. and Waller, T. (2017) Participatory research with very young children. In: Waller, T., Ärlemalm-Hagsér, E., Beate, E., Sandseter, H., Lee-Hammond, L., Lekies, K. and Wyver, S. (eds.) *The Sage handbook of outdoor play and learning*. London: Sage.

Brown, K.M., Dilley, R. and Marshall, K. (2008) Using a head-mounted video camera to understand social worlds and experiences, *Sociological Research Online* 13, 6. www.socreson-line.org.uk/13/6/1.html.

Brown, K. and Spinney, J. (2010) Catching a glimpse: The value of video in evoking, understanding and representing the practice of cycling. In: Fincham, B., McGuinness, M. and Murray, L. (eds.) *Mobile methodologies*. Aldershot: Ashgate.

Burke, A. and Marsh, J., eds. (2013) *Children's virtual play worlds: Culture, learning and participation*. New York: Peter Lang.

Burris, A. (2017) A child's-eye view: An examination of point-of-view camera use in four informal education settings. *Visitor Studies* 20 (2), 218–237.

Chalfen, R. (2014) 'Your panopticon or mine?' Incorporating wearable technology's Glass and GoPro into visual social science. *Visual Studies* 29 (3), 299–310.

Chaudron, S., Di Gioia, R., Gemo, M., Holloway, D., Marsh, J., Mascheroni, G., . . . Yamada-Rice, D. (2017) *Kaleidoscope on the internet of toys – safety, security, privacy and societal insights*. Luxembourg: Publications

Office of the European Union. http://publications.jrc.ec.europa.eu/repository/bitstream/JRC105061/jrc105061_ final_online.pdf.

Clark, A. (2010) Young children as protagonists and the role of participatory, visual methods in engaging multiple perspectives. *Community Psychology* 46 (1–2), 115–123.

Couldry, N. and Hepp, A. (2017) *The mediated construction of reality*. Cambridge: Polity Press.

Cramer, F. (2015) What is "post-digital"? In: Berry, D.M. and Dieter, M (eds.) *Postdigital aesthetics: Art, computation and design*. London: Palgrave Macmillan, 12–26.

Deleuze, G. and Guattari, F. (1987) *A thousand plateaus: Capitalism and schizophrenia*. Minneapolis, MN: University of Minnesota Press.

Dicks, B., Mason, B., Coffey, A. and Atkinson, P. (2005) *Qualitative research and hypermedia: Ethnography for the digital age*. London: Sage.

Duggan, M. (2017) Questioning "digital ethnography" in an era of ubiquitous computing. *Geography Compass*. Published March 2017. doi: 10.1111/gec3.12313.

Evers, C. (in press) Researching action sport with a GoPro™ Camera: An embodied and emotional mobile video tale of the sea, masculinity, and men-who-surf. In: Wellard, I. (ed.) *Researching embodied sport: Exploring movement cultures*. London: Routledge.

Fazi, M.B. (2016) Review of David M. Berry and Michael Dieter (eds.) Postdigital aesthetics. *Theory, Culture and Society*. www.theoryculturesociety.org/review-of-david-m-berry-and-michael-dieter-eds-postdigital-aesthetics-by-m-beatrice-fazi/.

Ghekiere, A., Van Cauwenberg, J., de Geus, B., Clarys, P., Cardon, G., Salmon, J., et al. (2014) Critical environmental factors for transportation cycling in children: A qualitative study using bike-alongs. *Science & Sports* 29, S18.

Giddings, S. (2014) *Gameworlds: Virtual media and children's everyday play*. London: Bloomsbury.

Green, C. (2016) Sensory tours as a method for engaging children as active researchers: Exploring the use of wearable cameras in early childhood research. *International Journal of Early Childhood* 48, 277–294.

Hughes, B. (2002) *A playworker's taxonomy of play types* (2nd edition). London: PlayLink.

Jayemanne, D., Nansen, B., and Apperley, T. (2015) Post-Digital Play and the Aesthetics of Recruitment, Proceedings of DiGRA, Digital Games Research Association, 2015. Accessed at: https://minerva-access.unimelb.edu.au/bitstream/handle/11343/56632/117_Apperley_etal_Postdigital-Play-and-the-Aesthetics-of-Recruitment.pdf?sequence=1&isAllowed=y

Kafai, Y. and Fields, D. (2013) *Connected play: Tweens in a virtual world*. Cambridge, MA: MIT Press.

Kelly, C. (2015) 'Let's do some jumping together': Intergenerational participation in the use of remote technology to co-construct social relations over distance. *Journal of Early Childhood Research* 13 (1), 29–46.

Law, J. (2014) *After method: Mess in social science research*. London: Routledge.

Marsh, J. (2014) Online and offline play. In: Burn, A. and Richards, C. (eds.) *Children's games in the new media age*. Cambridge: Ashgate, 109–312.

Marsh, J. (2017) The internet of toys: A posthuman and multimodal analysis of connected play. *Teachers College Record*, 119. Published online November 2017: www.tcrecord.org/Content.asp?ContentID=22073.

Marsh, J., Plowman, L., Yamada-Rice, D., Bishop, J.C., Lahmar, J., Scott, F., . . . Winter, P. (2015) *Exploring play and creativity in pre-schoolers' use of apps: Final project report*. www.techandplay.org.

Murthy, D. (2008) Digital ethnography: An examination of the use of new technologies for social research, *Sociology* 42 (5), 837–855.

Nansen, B., Jayemanne, D. and Apperley, T. (2015) Post-digital play and the aesthetics of recruitment, proceedings of digra, digital games research association, 2015. https://minerva-access.unimelb.edu.au/bitstream/handle/11343/56632/117_Apperley_etal_Postdigital-Play-and-the-Aesthetics-of-Recruit ment.pdf?sequence=1&isAllowed=y.

Norris, S. (2011) *Identity in interaction: Introducing multimodal (inter)action analysis*. Göottingen: De Gruyter.

Pimlott-Wilson, H. (2012) Visualising children's participation in research: Lego, Duplo, rainbows and clouds and moodboards. *International Journal of Social Research Methodology* 15 (2), 135–148.

Pink, S. (2007) Walking with video. *Visual Studies* 22 (3), 240–252.

Rogers, Y., Scaife, M., Gabrielli, S., Smith, H. and Harris, E. (2002) A conceptual framework for mixed reality environments: Designing novel learning activities for young children. *Presence* 11 (6), 677–686.

Slutsky, Ruslan and DeShetler, Lori M. (2017) How technology is transforming the ways in which children play. *Early Child Development and Care*. 187, 7, 1138–1146.

Sumsion, J., Harrison, L., Press, F., McLeod, S., Goodfellow, J. and Bradley, B. (2011) Researching infants' experiences of early childhood and care. In: Harcourt, D., Perry, B. and Waller, T. (eds.) *Researching young children's perspectives*. London: Routledge, 113–137.

Takahashi, D. (2017) Blueprint Reality's MixCast tool lets you broadcast from virtual reality. https://venturebeat.com/2017/02/22/blueprint-realitys-mixcast-tool-lets-you-build-in-virtual-reality/.

Winter, K. (2010) Ascertaining the perspectives of young children in care: Case studies in the use of reality boxes. *Children and Society* 26 (5), 368–380.

Yamada-Rice, D., Mushtaq, F., Woodgate, A., Bosmans, D., Douthwaite, A., Douthwaite, I., . . . and Whiteley, S. (2017) *Children and virtual reality: Emerging possibilities*. http://digilitey.eu/wp-content/uploads/2015/09/CVR-Final-PDF-reduced-size.pdf.

Yelland, N. (2007) Making meaning and becoming multiliterate with ICT. *International Journal of the Humanities* 5 (4), 123–133.

12

FROM CUTTING OUT TO CUTTING WITH

A materialist reframing of action and multimodality in children's play and making

Karen E. Wohlwend and Jaye Johnson Thiel

Introduction

Paper is the technology of choice in early childhood education. Children can more easily and freely access sheets of paper than computers, iPads, or mobile devices in most preschool and kindergarten classrooms (Wartella et al., 2013). And the child-friendly malleability of paper makes it a generative medium for the actions that little hands can easily manage as they fold, bend, tear, draw, color, crumple, and cut to represent their worlds. Across our research projects, we have been struck by the creative energy and transformative potential in the paper/digital play nexus. In Karen's research, 5- to 7-year-old children in kindergarten and first grade classrooms responded to a dearth of digital tools by creating cardboard box laptops, paper cellphones, and hand-drawn video games. In Jaye's research, children ages 4–10 work collaboratively with paper to create a plethora of different things at a community center makerspace (i.e. swords, spinners, money, cellphones, books, purses, etc.). Our research projects (Wohlwend, 2008; Thiel, 2015a, 2015b) have expanded definitions of play and making as embodied and material literacies. Our studies also shared an emphasis on multimodal analysis and critical discourse theories to understand how children are inventively playing across paper and digital formats as they make use of these productive technologies. In this chapter, we share excerpts of early childhood play from our independent research studies of children's play and making, taking a closer look to ask, "What did we miss?" We expand our prior multimodal analyses of these events, to ask:

> How does an implicit human-centered insistence on semiotic affordances and strategic design tame the mobile jumble of children's play and making, whether with paper, fabric, or with digital tools?
>
> Did prior multimodal analyses of play and making overlook the learning in repetitive and seemingly aimless explorations of the action/actant/meaning relations around materiality? What can we see if we use a materialist lens? What changes in a re-examination of these data from a materialist theoretical perspective and what does a materialist analysis reveal about children's play and making?

What does this mean for digital technologies in early childhood education? In this chapter, we argue that play that makes toys out of paper scraps or scribbles on an iPad constitutes technology learning. A materialist view of learning as an agentic act of becoming assembles children's desires to use new technologies, their limited access to computers or mobile devices, and the possibilities of the materiality of paper.

Cutting across methods, multimodality, and materiality

Using an interactional strand of multimodal analysis as point of departure, Karen maps children's fluid use of available modes to shape social interactions within a classroom; the focus is on action in the moment rather than their manipulation of a mode to produce a designed, durable text or artifact. Here's an excerpt from an earlier multimodal analysis:

> using multimodal analysis to understand how actions are made meaningful and social *in situ* rather than in representation, looking at interaction among modes, semiotic practices, and discourses in glocalized contexts. I examine instances of classroom activity to see how modes shape children's literacy learning and participation in early childhood classrooms. [For example,] analyzing gaze as a mode reveals the meanings of the ways that students look at classroom materials and at each other, as well as the ways that they are surveilled by the teacher and by the researcher.
>
> Gaze turned upon people produces subjectivities, shared gaze among people produces social space, and a research gaze turns subjects into objects of inquiry. In this research, I drew upon the mode of gaze as a way of revealing which modes were most apparent in a classroom literacy event (e.g., gaze, print, and book-handling during a reading lesson) and how the foregrounding of particular modes enforced a set of power relations (teacher/student; reader/nonreader) legitimated by prevailing educational discourses.
>
> Multimodal analysis involves isolating, examining, and explaining an aspect of lived experience to understand how actors exploit available semiotic resources to represent meanings, carry out social practices, and realize power relations.
>
> *(Wohlwend, 2011, p. 243)*

From an interactional multimodal perspective, modes can be embodied (e.g., gaze, sound, gesture, posture, facial expression, touch), environmental (e.g., physical layout, proximity [near/far relationships of bodies and things]), or textual (e.g., print, image, music, sound-effect).

Multimodal methods use video analysis to look closely at interaction in order to track the physical (e.g., visual, auditory, haptic, kinesthetic) aspects of materials that designers emphasize or wield to craft signs. For example, modal analysis maps material environments and artifacts, tracking modes and action to discern actors' meanings or participatory strategies. Multimodal analysis of video data tracks actors' modal use, looking at action first (rather than speech) to understand how meanings are made with bodies and things in a particular context. These maps reveal how children make use of bodies, things, and the environment to create a desired toy, play with friends, or get things done.

Toward a materialist analysis, we blur distinctions among theory and methods in a reflexive move to think with theory (Jackson & Mazzei, 2011), consistent with analysis suggested by posthuman and feminist materialisms. In this chapter, we use Barad's (2003) metaphor of an agential cut as a tool to reframe and expand the methodological focus from multimodality to materiality.

Thinking with multimodality and materiality theories

Multimodality: making do and cutting out

Multimodal theory has drawn extensively on Kress' ground-breaking work on multimodality and literacies, such as young children's play and making. In *Before Writing* (1997), Kress analyzed the transformations of meaning and form that occurred as a child cut around a drawing of a car to bring this picture into the world of action and thus, created a toy that could be animated in dramatic play. In other words, "cutting out" turned a child's two-dimensional drawing into a three-dimensional paper toy that could be animated for play. The car cutout moved from an image to an object that could move and mean in relation to other objects in the child's surroundings. The construct of multimodality explains the ways meanings and modes are mutually constitutive, and always situated in a cultural and physical environment. Modes are the meanings we attach to sensory aspects of the environment, shaped by cultural histories and systems of meaning (Kress, 2003a). Using modes and semiotic tools, ideas are transformed into material forms and produce durable messages that can be shared and transported (Brandt & Clinton, 2002).

In sociocultural interpretations of multimodality, reading, writing, and making are mediational means (Wertsch, 1991; Scollon, 2001). Literacies are systems, each with a set of social practices and physical tools linked to a primary modality: reading is a system for getting meaning off the page by interpreting graphic symbols into audible language primarily using auditory and verbal modes of sound, speech, and print; writing and graphic design produce meanings primarily through visual modes including gaze and image, and play primarily uses action modes including gesture, posture, proximity, and movement through space. Multimodal analysis can identify the subtle reconstructive work produced through play's improvisation (Holland et al., 1998) and *Making Do* (de Certeau, 1984).

Making do is a Foucauldian (1978) technology of the disempowered that blends critique with play's safety valve of deniability and also blends production with scavenging of available materials to pull off out-of-reach identities and practices. This has relevance for Kress (2003b), who argues that children use "whatever is to hand that is apt for their purpose" (p. 156), inventing artifacts by combining materials and manipulating modes in unique ways according to their immediate social purposes. This is our point of departure, inspired by the notion of "making do" with materials that are available to make something more, reconstructing typical practices and expected modes to enable actions that bend conventional meanings, rules, or grammars in sign systems. For de Certeau (1984), making do is a poaching or improvisation, a social actor's tactical take up and reframing of materials and actions that are offered for other authorized purposes in a place. Kress suggests that in comparison to adults, children are less bound by conventional uses of modes and more open to producing novel meanings, improvised and inspired by the materiality of objects. In this way, making do is a method of reconstruction with potential for creating critique and production with available materials and identities.

Modes are sensory properties that convey embodied and environmental meanings of actions and artifacts. The meanings that modes convey are culturally given and situated in grammars or systems built from shared histories of use. Modality enables small shifts in the material but the movement comes from the change in the meanings of materials. In this way, play and design are methods of resemiotization and reconstruction. These transformations happen through transduction (Kress, 1997), quickly shifting the meaning of a sign by moving across modes but also across dimensions of time and space. For example, the act of cutting out a paper drawing of a paper cell phone transduces the image into an artifact, in this case a toy plane.

Cutting out creates an edge around a two-dimensional drawing that delineates its spatial boundaries and gives the phone cut out a three-dimensional albeit very thin shape that enables its manipulation as a toy in a classroom reality. Transduction can expand the potential meanings of a child's representation when a flat paper drawing becomes a three-dimensional prop for play actions.

> *For example, [a kindergarten boy] created a flip phone out of a folded piece of paper. He gave an oblong piece of paper rounded corners and penciled a 3 by 3 array of squares below a much larger square to represent a numeric pad and an LCD screen. Additional phone features (receiver, compact size) were emphasized by adding play actions: he held the opened paper flat in the palm of his hand, raised his hand to his ear, talked into the paper for a few seconds, then snapped it shut with one hand, and tucked it into his pocket.*
>
> *As demonstrated with carrot or paper cell phones, children are flexible, inventive, and strategic meaning-makers who do not strictly adhere to convention. Children look at the world as potential signs-to-be-made; their sign-making and sign use is more likely to be governed by their interest and an object's material qualities than by attention to established linguistic or visual conventions (Kress, 1997, 2003a).*
>
> *(Wohlwend, 2009, p. 125)*

When this boy drew a cell phone on paper, he created an image for viewing; when he cut out the image, the image was transformed into an object that also expanded the range of modes and practices for creating meaning: verbal modes and talking on the toy phone to others through embodied modes of posture, movement, and facial expression as he pretended to be a cell phone owner. Additionally, this expansion of multimodality adds credibility to his pretend identity performance that adds cachet to his social status in the classroom's peer culture: the flip phone (a cutting-edge technology in 2006) signifies coolness and capital as an affinity object (Fernie et al., 1995) when his designed paper toy inspired imitation among children in his play group.

In this and other examples of paper toymaking in Karen's "Early Adopters" (2009) research, kindergarteners who had limited access to technologies at school improvised to make do with the most readily available classroom material: paper. In this way, cutting out and making do was a reconstruction, a settling for an imaginary or invented proxy as a substitute for the real tool. But it's also true that children *preferred* paper to other materials in the classroom. There is something about paper in the material itself that creates this appeal and that is not easily explained by multimodality, representation, and children's strategic design with a commonplace resource. We see paper as a technology and an active participant in these productions, not merely a material with particular affordances as conveyor of a single meaning. Perhaps this appeal lies in paper's mutability and ease of spontaneous and quick meaning transformations (e.g., it is easily folded, wadded up, tossed, torn, cut, ripped, shredded, etc.). Paper's almost-unbounded malleability makes it a natural resource for play, that produces resemiotization and recontextualization of physical realities. Since this research, digital animation and drawing apps and iPads now provide intuitive and child-friendly digital tools that are highly malleable but with significant differences in the (lack of) physical traces, the sensory properties, and the modal affordances and constraints of the materials.

Materiality: cutting with and making much with

Here we shift the lens from multimodality to materiality to broaden our view and deepen our understanding of action: moving from the action of "cutting out" to "cutting with" and from the action "making do" to "making much with". To do this, we take a relational materialist perspective (Lenz Taguchi, 2014; Barad, 2003) that considers the intra-action among all the actants in the *toy/player/action* assemblage. This changing, interacting, emerging, and affecting set of relations among people, materials, and spaces co-produces a flow of play moves and pretend meanings. When we look for materiality, mobility, emergence and emotion, we can appreciate play's haphazard trajectories and recognize its embodied "muchness" (Thiel & Jones, 2017; Thiel, 2016; Thiel, 2015a, 2015b).

Cutting with: We're proposing "cutting with" as a method for examining materiality that enacts Barad's agential cut. That is, we look at the tensions produced through constructed binaries to see what is made visible by looking at connections among components. An agential cut connects components of sociomaterial reality in order to make it actionable, accessible, and understandable. For example, the binary material/immaterial creates an arbitrary/artificial separation of lived experience that puts meaning on one plane and things on another. Binaries create power relations: there is something done, and something done to. We can look at a commonplace view of abstract signified concepts as represented by material object signifiers. Cutting with looks for agency across components, to see how things are not blankly waiting for human representation but are always/already conveying meanings. For example, a view of play as cutting with reveals new configurations as players/playthings joke around, blur, and twist the experiential and the representational. Play is ambiguous (Sutton-Smith, 1997), masking its meanings through pretense so that actor/action/material meanings in a here-and-now reality are experienced additionally as imagined ones. Children are adept at negotiating this agential cut and interplay of pretend and real action during play, in toy laser duels (Wohlwend, 2013) and other mock fights, pulling their punches and tempering their physical actions to avoid actually hurting one another. Looking closing at young children's digital play, Fleer (2014) uses the metaphor of flickering to conceptualize "microgenetic movements . . . as flickering in and out of imaginary situations, flickering between individual and collective activity, and flickering between concrete objects and virtual representations" (p. 207). The demands and motives afforded through digital play in early childhood activity settings are not fixed but move among realities, an on/off flickering as a blurring of physical actions and pretended meanings.

The action of cutting out separates the desired object from its unwanted scraps. The car becomes a toy but what happens to the "negative space" or surrounding paper that cutting out turns into scrap. By contrast, the action of cutting with attends to the static. If we accept Latour's (2005) premise that change and transformation are always occurring, "What gets held in place and what was required to suppress the mess and keep things orderly?" becomes a more interesting question than "What was transformed and how?" To track the tidying up, the action of cutting with maps the scraps to follow the bits that are cut out by analysis. In coding, we can think of scraps as data that were tossed away to make a more sensible and orderly multimodal analysis. By mapping the scraps, we can track flows and tangles of assemblage/disassemblage (Thiel & Jones, 2017; Wohlwend et al., 2017) in an expansive tracing of trajectories on a landscape that uncover entanglements.

Making much with and making more than: Cutting is more than a child's spontaneous design to make do – it's a way of making muchness (Thiel, 2015a, 2015b), bringing meanings and materials across separation of represented and enacted, display and extension, production and imagined, material and immaterial, real and pretend, desire and joy. Muchness, "is theorized as an affective moment of intellectual and creative fullness that pulsates between bodies, space, objects, and discourse" (Thiel, 2018). These moments are made possible through relational entanglements and are constantly shifting and changing as the boundaries of possibilities are redrawn. For example, muchness might emerge from the co-constitutive relationships between a playground on a sunny but not-too-warm day, superhero costumes, superhero texts (movies and books), a child's proclivity towards improvisation and pretend play, and a gathering of peers with equal interest in becoming superheroes one afternoon (Thiel, 2015a). It might also emerge from paint, and paint cups, and brightly dyed rolls of fabric that can easily be wrapped around human bodies to make dresses, and a warm, sunny, just-right-for-a-picnic day, where paint becomes something other than paint, it becomes a pretend picnic lunch to celebrate the birthday of someone children hold dear (Thiel, 2018). To further illustrate the ways paper serves as an actant in the unfolding of muchness, we offer the following story from Jaye's research:

Example 1: paper cellphone

Jaye walks up to the Playhouse doors but is stopped before entering the building. This is a practice that happens often – one that she has come to expect when arriving at the Playhouse in the summer when children are often waiting for the space to open for the afternoon. Zach offers a warm hello before asking, "Do you want to see what I made?"

As Jaye nods, Zach reaches into his pockets and pulls out four rectangle-shaped objects made from paper.

"These are my iPhones." Zach begins to show off the way he had recently collaborated with paper, markers, iPhones, apps, and notecards to craft his very own version of an iPhone in four different varieties (see Figure 12.1 for example).

He proceeds to offer details about the phones. He explains how the notecards are inside the paper to make the phones thick and sturdy. He explains how there are several versions to capture the many models/colors of iPhones that can be purchased. He explains how each phone has a different set of apps that a user can engage with when using the phone. He explains how every detail, down to the Apple logo on the back of the phones, has been carefully crafted. And he also explains how this is the only way he can afford to have an iPhone, that he sees many people in the world using these amazing digital-technological things, that he wanted one, and these materials helped him customize several different versions.

"I can't really text on one yet. But hey, I might figure that out." He explains through a large grin.

Figure 12.1 Paper iPhone

Zach found a way to *make much with* and *make more than* alongside paper. The boundary-making practices of economic inequities that have created a digital technology desert (both geographically and financially) for Zach's family and for the community at large shifted slightly when the traditional notion of what is possible for paper and phones changed. Zach's desirings (Kuby & Gutshall Rucker, 2016) enmeshed with paper's malleability, mark making tools' gesture, a notecard's sturdiness, and tape's stickiness to move beyond preconceived ideas about what paper can and cannot become. Paper's ability to wrap around, bend, fold, crease, and hold images offered a particular way of making much with and more than that produced new conditions of possibility (Barad, 2007). These varied possibilities are not new for paper. Paper's genealogy reveals that it has played a strong and viable role in historical events such as hiding messages during WW2, serving as correspondence over miles of land and sea, and even poisoning enemies when laced with toxins. As early childhood literacy researchers, we have seen paper become spinners, spitballs, dolls, guns, houses, lightsabers, swords, shields – the list could go on and on. It is abundantly apparent to us that people don't just make do with paper but co-collaborate with paper to make much and make more than, just as the events between Zach and paper described earlier.

Furthermore, using a lens of making much enables new relationships to emerge from affective energy (Thiel, 2015b) across a multitude of engaged bodies. Rather than making do, seeing children like Zach as making much and making more than moves away from material-discursive constructions of deficiency which sees individuals as lacking in some way to constructions of what-might-become which offers generativity to the world right now through its various snares and tangles. Making much doesn't see the subject as the sole meaning maker ready to go out and manipulate and reshape the world as they see fit. Through a relational-material lens, a person cannot claim to create muchness. Instead, muchness emerges unexpectedly through the coming together of time, space, and material bodies (human and otherwise).

Moving across multimodality and materiality

We offer Table 12.1 to illustrate the variations between multimodality and materiality, cutting out and cutting with, making do and making much with.

Table 12.1 The variations between multimodality and materiality

Multimodality	*Materiality*
Social Semiotics and Intentionality *Resources and Affordances/Constraints*	*Ethico-Onto-Epistemology*
Cutting out: Isolates and compares modes Tracks resonances or shifts of meanings across modes and two- and three-dimensional realities Draws our attention to the ways that materials and social spaces are constructed and reconstructed with the material resources in the physical environment	Cutting with: Connects actants and actions Plays around and explores materials Connects unexpected to expected actions, identities, materials, and realities
Making do: Uses and improvises on modes and materials within a given place Manipulates time and meanings to reshape and access fixed and inaccessible materials, technologies, and spaces	Making much with: Enables new relationships to emerge among actants and spaces Time, space, material, and meanings are never fixed but rather emerge through intra-actions between bodies

Example 2: digital cutouts

The interplay of these methods is illustrated below in an example from Karen's study of preschool iPad play:

> *At the filmmaking table, four-year-old Simone sits alone, looking at the iPad in front of her* (see Figure 12.2). *She opens the PuppetPals app and scrolls down and down the first screen of characters that the children have created and saved. Unsatisfied with the array of brightly-colored photos of ponies, princesses, superheroes, and classroom toys, she picks up a string doll from the table. The yarn doll shows the wear of several weeks of vigorous preschool play; its unraveling threads flop against her hand as Simone positions the doll on the table, props up the iPad, and snaps a photo with the iPad's camera. When the snowman photo appears on her screen, she taps the editing button that allows her to trace around the image with her finger, making a neon green line that indicates the edge of the cutout. But halfway around the snowman, Simone stops tracing the edge and begins scribbling, running her finger back and forth quickly, tracing the individual and matted threads of the doll. Whenever her scribbling produces a closed figure, the app instantly displays the partial figure, an irregular scrap of white yarn or sometimes just a thin squiggly line. Simone is unperturbed as she rejects each scrap, waits for the original snowman image to reload, and begins the cycle again, scribbling-rejecting-waiting-reloading-and-beginning again.*

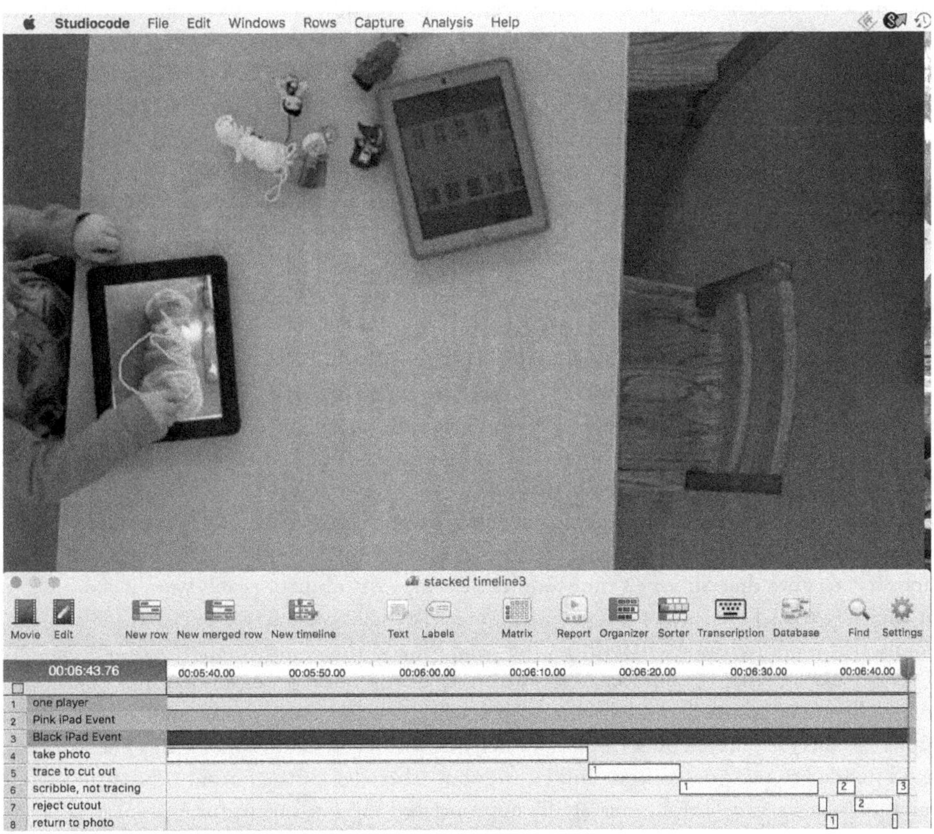

Figure 12.2 Multimodal analysis on video coding software

The multimodal analysis reveals the merger of finger actions with haptic and visual modes that enabled affordances such as the easy slide of a fingertip tracing that allowed very young children to successfully hug the edges of an image and create cutouts. The video microanalysis tracked actions, modes, and meanings and demonstrated the complexity of children's digital composing, particularly at times when two or more children had fingers on the same iPad screen, collaborating and elaborating a scenario while negotiating their ideas for next moves.

But it was also true that much of the preschoolers' play and filmmaking with this digital puppetry app resulted in seemingly aimless loops of activity like the one in the vignette that did not produce a recognizable character, a saved film, or any other product. Although the app used drag-and-drop fingertip navigation, an almost print-free interface, instant feedback, and multiplayer controls, children still were often unable to create and save films. In Simone's vignette, the iPad mechanics caused abrupt interruptions that prevented her from realizing her apparent intention of decorating the white snowman image with neon green scribbles. The geometry of the animation mechanics dictated that when overlapping lines completed a closed figure, it was immediately saved and the tracing function was closed, launching a photo of the closed figure. Adding to the confusion, the app automatically filed each new character as an icon on the index page, but the most recent figures were placed at the bottom of a list of 100 or so previously saved character icons so that children had difficulty finding and recognizing the character that had just been created. Important here, the lack of an end product did not seem to be of much importance to the children. This will not seem surprising to many early childhood practitioners who have watched children at the easel happily paint a sunny scene into a muddy, blurry swirl until the brush wears a hole through the damp paper. Early childhood education has a long-standing ethos that values exploratory process over product, but how do we can value this kind of rambling exploration in a multimodal analysis that expects an intentional design and strategic manipulation of modes?

Cutting out depends on a representational frame and dimensional boundary crossing in which a two-dimensional drawing is transformed into a three-dimensional toy. Cutting with looks at this same cutting action as a connection that makes more of a drawing-cellphone-player. In the same way, photographing a classroom toy to make a digital character connects the fraying yarn-small doll-snowman image and entangles dimensions and realities. The digital image of a character turns into a toy through action and animation that allows it to be rotated, resized, and moved across the screen and layered with other images.

Cutting with also attends to the remnants that are backgrounded and that are unexplained by intentional design. Mapping the scraps looks at the paper bits that are dropped on the floor or the unwanted pixels that vanish into the ether. Simone's back and forth tracing of yarn strands attended to the material and the individual yarn strands, rather than the outline of the doll as a whole. Her yarn focus inspired a repetitive action that produced something new each time. While cutting out on the iPad produced a photo image that players could accept and save, it also often produced scraps; some of these were quickly and easily deleted, leaving no trace. But it is important to note that Simone's unrecognizable scraps with blurry pixels were saved as often as her carefully traced characters (Figure 12.3). Her tracing was an active exploration in bridging realities that is enough in itself, without the need for additional interpretation of representation.

Making do is evident in Simone's re-purposing of the neon green digital line that bounded a traced area. She noticed and exploited the tracing feature's design potential to add color and emphasize the yarn tangle by scribbling rather than overlaying additional lines. The bright lines were intended to provide contrast and clearly show the edge of the cutout on a variety of photographic images, but Simone repeatedly appropriated the cut out feature to color rather than trace the snowman. She persisted, exploring various configurations, undisturbed that the coloring produced only fragments rather a snowman.

Figure 12.3 Examples of digital scraps

Making much with shifts the analytic lens to value what is being/becoming, a shift that reveals the learning in children's experimentation that blurs and plays with material/immaterial boundaries. In the vignette, the act of photographing a classroom toy is an experiment in understanding the movement of an object-image, from toy to digital photo. Simone's exploratory play with the camera function in the iPad tested the limits of the screen's page boundaries and camera framing. But it was also an exercise in making more than by playing with materiality across dimensions, proliferating meanings and characters that connected a fragment of a digital image to a classroom toy to favorite popular media characters. The digital fragments of an image mingled with superheroes, ponies, and princesses in the character index where children scrolled and selected characters. Simone's finger tap instantly populated the next screen's puppet stage with an assemblage of polysemous scraps and recognizable characters. This assemblage could be spun, stretched, shrunk, and wiggled in a chaotic giggly scene or could vanish with a finger swipe in a new becoming that restarts the photographing-cutting-selecting-assembling sequence.

Multimodal and materialist methods capture different aspects of early childhood becomings that are constantly changing. Multimodal methods reveal children's hidden abilities, creativity, and resourcefulness in crafting designs by coordinating complex actions and their knowledge of visual, auditory, haptic, and kinesthetic meanings. Materialist methods reveal the deep interconnectivity among inquiry and experimentation in seemingly random moments of play and making. This suggests the need to consider the things that children produce not as products to assess but as emergent and active inquiries made up of actions, bodies, ideas, and materials.

Value to field of digital technologies

Children are even more entangled in the interplay of social/material/digital when they use animation apps and digital photography. Simple actions like cutting, photographing, tracing, and animating remake meanings in ways that change children's relationships to toys and technologies. The action of cutting out a drawing changes a paper drawing to a toy, but also changes the child from artist to player. Similarly, the actions of assemblages of fingers, toys, screens, and mobile devices shift the meaning relations from viewers to designers, animators, and dimensional explorers. The action of photographing a toy moves an object from the physical table to a static image on a touchscreen, while tracing it with a finger to virtually cut out the photo turns the image back into an actionable toy that could be moved, wiggled, and resized to interact with other elements onscreen. Theorizing and tracking this kind of manipulation blurs virtual/real or here/there binaries that currently limit how we think about digital literacies. A materialist lens reveals new possibilities for research on video-editing tools (e.g., cutting and assembling as analytic methods) that offer more robust models for theorizing and examining the blurring of material/immaterial in children's digital production.

Moving beyond expectations for saved products and human-only designers requires appreciation of the messy knowledge that comes from exploration, a recognition that it is the becoming that matters. Like children tossing soggy paintings once they're finished, we know that the learning was in the action and the making was in itself already enough; there's no need to display a final product. This focus appreciates the scraps as well as the cutouts, as connected components linked by languages, codes, and logics. In these cooperative digital mergers of physical – embodied and electronic – actions and languages, it is the intra-action that matters, not the product. Like an animated doll-photo-digital puppet, the digital literacies here are moving, growing, shrinking, and becoming.

References

Barad, K. (2003) Posthumanist performativity: Toward an understanding of how matter comes to matter. *Signs: Journal of Women in Culture and Society* 28, 801–831.

Barad, K. (2007) *Meeting the universe halfway: Quantum physics and the entanglement of matter and meaning*. Durham, NC: Duke University Press.

Brandt, D. and Clinton, K. (2002) Limits of the local: Expanding perspectives on literacy as a social practice. *Journal of Literacy Research* 34, 337–356.

de Certeau, M. (1984) *The practice of everyday life* (Trans. S. Rendall). Berkeley, CA: University of California Press.

Fernie, D.E., Kantor, R. and Whaley, K.L. (1995) Learning from classroom ethnographies: Same places, different times. In Hatch, J.A. (ed.) *Qualitative research in early childhood settings*, 156–172. Westport, CT: Praeger.

Fleer, M. (2014) The demands and motives afforded through digital play in early childhood activity settings. *Learning, Culture and Social Interaction* 3 (3), 202–209.

Foucault, M. (1978) *The history of sexuality: An introduction*, vol. 1. New York: Random House.

Holland, D., Lachiotte, W., Skinner, D. and Cain, C. (1998) *Identity and agency in cultural worlds*. Cambridge, MA: Harvard University Press.

Jackson, A.Y. and Mazzei, L.A. (2011) *Thinking with theory in qualitative research: Viewing data across multiple perspectives*. New York: Routledge.

Kress, G. (1997) *Before writing: Rethinking the paths to literacy*. London: Routledge.

Kress, G. (2003a) *Literacy in the new media age*. London: Routledge.

Kress, G. (2003b) Perspectives on making meaning: The differential principles and means of adults and children. In: Hall, N., Larson, J. and Marsh, J. (eds.) *Handbook of early childhood literacy*. London: Sage, 154–166.

Kuby, C. and Gutshall Rucker, T. (2016) *Go be a writer! Expanding the curricular boundaries of literacy learning with children*. New York: Teachers College Press.

Latour, B. (2005) *Reassembling the social-an introduction to actor-network-theory*. Oxford: Oxford University Press.

Lenz Taguchi, H. (2014) New materialism and play. In: Brooker, L., Blaise, M. and Edwards, S. (eds.). *Sage handbook of play and learning in early childhood*. London: Sage, 79–90.

Scollon, R. (2001) *Mediated discourse: The nexus of practice*. London: Routledge.

Sutton-Smith, B. (1997) *The ambiguity of play*. Cambridge, MA: Harvard University Press.

Thiel, J.J. (2015a) Bumblebee's in trouble: Embodied literacies during imaginative superhero play. *Language Arts* 93 (1), 38–49.

Thiel, J.J. (2015b) Vibrant matter: The intra-active role of objects in the construction of young children's literacies. *Literacy Research: Theory, Method, and Practice* 64 (1), 112–131.

Thiel, J. (2016). Working-class women in academic spaces: Finding our muchness. *Gender and Education.* 28 (5), 662–673.

Thiel, J. and Jones, S. (2017) The literacies of things: Reconfiguring the material-discursive production of race and class in an informal learning center. *Journal of Early Childhood Literacies* 17 (3), 315–335.

Thiel, J. (2018) A cool place where we make stuff: Co-curating relational spaces of muchness. In: Schulte, C. and Thompson, T. (eds.) *Communities of practice: Art, play, and aesthetics in early childhood.*

Wartella, E., Blackwell, C.K., Lauricella, A.R. and Robb, M.B. (2013) *Technology in the lives of educators and early childhood programs: 2012 survey of early childhood educators.* Latrobe, PA: Northwestern University and Fred Rogers Center for Early Learning and Children's Media.

Wertsch, J.V. (1991) *Voices of the mind: A sociocultural approach to mediated action.* Cambridge, MA: Harvard University Press.

Wohlwend, K.E. (2008) Play as a literacy of possibilities: Expanding meanings in practices, materials, and spaces. *Language Arts* 86 (2), 127–136.

Wohlwend, K.E. (2009) Early adopters: Playing new literacies and pretending new technologies in print-centric classrooms. *Journal of Early Childhood Literacy* 9 (2), 119–143.

Wohlwend, K.E. (2011) Mapping modes in children's play and design: An action-oriented approach to critical multimodal analysis. In: Rogers, R. (ed.) *An introduction to critical discourse analysis in education* (2nd edition). Mahwah, NJ: Lawrence Erlbaum Associates, 242–266.

Wohlwend, K.E. (2013) Playing Star Wars under the (teacher's) radar: Detecting kindergartners' action texts and embodied literacies. In: Vasquez, V.M. and Wood, J.W. (eds.) *Perspectives and provocations in early childhood education*, 105–115. Charlotte, NC: Information Age.

Wohlwend, K.E., Peppler, K.A., Keune, A. and Thompson, N. (2017) Making sense and nonsense: Comparing mediated discourse and agential realist approaches to materiality. *Journal of Early Childhood Literacy* 17 (3), 444–462. doi: 10.1177/1468798417712066

13

RESEARCHING IN THE IWORLD

From home to beyond

Linda Laidlaw, Joanne O'Mara and Suzanna So-Har Wong

Introduction

In the digital era, mobile and other 21st century technologies have quickly become ubiquitous in all of our lives in complex ways. These changes have also impacted children's lives. Digital technologies and digital artifacts are now an increasing part of 'environmental print', with children also observing adults using devices and engaging in myriad digital practices. Children's learning and playing at home is also undergoing significant shifts and their everyday learning experiences may also be mediated through accessing websites, mobile apps and toys that have digital interactivity. The affordances of portable digital devices make them increasingly accessible to ever younger children who are developing the expertise and knowledge to use these for a variety of different functions.

In our research we have witnessed preschool children and toddlers using video chat media, messaging systems, video streaming, an increasing array of game and learning apps and digital household devices, echoing the work of other researchers (e.g. Marsh et al., 2017; Marsh et al., 2016). Digital functions are now frequently integrated into toys and play objects, with online and offline play activities often being used synergistically (Marsh, 2017b). Children may be using toys that have robotic capabilities (e.g. Furby, Sphero, Dash and Dot), working with augmented reality (AR) or apps based on popular toys and viewing series (e.g. Paw Patrol). And, as has been the case for many household objects in past eras, current and emerging technologies are also represented as children's play items, ranging from toy smartphones with sophisticated electronic functions to pretend play objects that operate symbolically, including those intended as part of doll accessories or dramatic play. In addition to pretend digital play, as we have noted elsewhere (Laidlaw et al., 2015; Laidlaw & O'Mara, 2015), while young children are engaging in digital practices and working with a range of technologies, significant 'digital divides' continue to exist between how such practices and devices may be engaged at home, and children's experiences with technologies in school, preschool and child care settings (see, e.g., Blackwell et al., 2014; ILA, 2017). Thus, it is important for researchers to find ways to document the range of complex experiences, expertise and knowledge that young children are engaging with at home and bringing with them as they enter the spaces of school, child care, and other collective institutional settings. Additionally, it is important to trace the impacts of external influences, such as school practices, policies and the media, on technology practices in children's homes, as they can all be viewed as interconnected.

The 'micro' contexts of children's technology usage in their homes can have a wider reach into these 'macro' contexts, and the larger worlds of technology can also invite shifts in the home.

Research on young children's use of digital technologies is on the rise and includes a growing corpus of survey studies that provide important windows to reveal parent perspectives (e.g., Holloway et al., 2013; Marsh, 2017a; Rideout, 2013). While still somewhat scant, studies documenting children's home technology experiences and usage are also emerging (e.g., Holloway et al., 2015; Neumann & Neuman, 2017; Wong, 2015). However, researching children's experiences in their homes presents particular challenges for early childhood researchers. Homes are complex environments, and as Clark and Moss (2017) state, engaging in research with young children is "an ethical and political endeavor" (p. 153). The entangled nature of researching children's technology experiences at home is amplified further as we enter children's and families' private spaces and navigate across our own research intentions, institutional ethics and the complex interweaving of homes, family relationships, culture and other dynamics.

Researching in the area of digital technologies presents added areas of challenge for researchers. In children's homes, parents and caregivers maintain some aspect of control over materials and play objects, making choices about purchases, child access and so forth. In the technological realm, parents can maintain increasing levels of control over digital devices and software, determining child access and monitoring, using parental surveillance or restriction tools and applications. Additionally, due to negative attitudes towards young children and technology frequently present in the popular media (see for example, Ashton, 2013; Kardaras, 2016; Stevenson, 2012), some parents of young children can be reluctant to have particular aspects of their child's home practices, play and learning with technology documented, due to fears of being judged as 'bad parents' who allow access to screens, the internet, online games and so on. While any research occurring in children's homes requires conscientious effort, studying children's digital practices in home contexts is careful work that involves developing relationships with both children and their parents/caregivers that allows for and recognizes inherent tensions between parental values and perspectives and children's digital activities. In our own work, we have also found it necessary at times to shift across home and outside-of-home research in order to pursue some of our research questions.

In this chapter, we address events and research experiences that have taken us to a deeper appreciation of the value of autobiographical, participatory and ethnographic methods for researching digital experiences of young children's learning and playing at home, in their communities and beyond. We start with the home and also extend to the ways in which our research has traveled across and into the communities we inhabit and include considerations of the varied ways that children's experiences may be shaped further, by policies that impact school and home, and by the media. After a brief orientation to our digital literacy research approaches and the 'accidental ethnography' that continues to inform our work, we present five illustrative research contexts that move across from specific and autoethnographic insights to wider applications of home-based and ethnographically informed research approaches. We present frames we have found useful to organize our studies of children, addressing the significance of using messy and sometimes unruly ethnographic and autobiographical methods in studying children's learning and playing as well as the significance of this work for understanding experiences of being a child in the early 21st century. Finally, we conclude with some practical suggestions for researchers looking to work with young children's digital and media experiences in the spaces of home, the communities they inhabit and in relation to the broader social forces shaping what is possible within these spaces. Developing understanding of children's complex technology experiences in the home is key to understanding the broader landscape of children's 'beyond home' engagements with technologies, and in bridging possible digital divides between children's lives at home, and those they enter in school or preschool settings.

Becoming accidental ethnographers

In our own approach to researching children's digital practices, we would classify ourselves as 'accidental ethnographers', finding our way into participatory, ethnographic methods (Behar, 1996; Geertz, 1988; Clifford & Marcus, 1986; Heath, Street & Mills, 2008; Richardson, 1997) through both serendipity and unexpected divergence from initial research plans. We (Jo and Linda) first met 20 years ago when were introduced by our mutual mentor Professor Juliana Saxton. We met up several times at conferences and shared hotel rooms when we were both impoverished graduate students and new scholars. While we are both drama education and literacy researchers, we come from methodologically different research orientations. Linda's work has been informed by complexity thinking and Jo's from critical reflective practice. Complexity thinking, within educational theory and research, offers challenges to linear, reductive and mechanistic frames for understanding systems and other phenomena (see, e.g. Davis & Sumara, 2006; Doll, 1993), and suggests that human and cultural systems, such as those of families, classrooms and schools, might be better understood as adaptive, emergent, dynamic and self-organizing (Johnson, 2001). Critical reflective practice is more commonly taken up in education as a recursive process that involves reflection on understanding and professional practice (Schön 1983, 1987) While these two orientations are separate, we continue to recognize common ground across our research and methodological approaches, both having a focus on reflection on smaller details brought into larger perspectives and valuing of holistic, systems-based and nonlinear research activities. We both engage a common thread of self-observation across our projects, although we may each contribute different lenses.

We acknowledge that the work of research involves "the many layers of dynamic nested activity that are constantly at play" (Davis & Sumara, 2006, p. 28) and that the processes of our involvements in research sites and with children and families, as well as the outcomes of these involvements, together constitute the research effort. Schön's (1983, 1987) critical reflective practice approach underpins our understanding of our research conversations, and we locate our work in the "swampy lowlands, where situations are confusing messes incapable of technical solution and usually involve problems of greatest human concern" (Schön, 1983, p. 42). Our collaborative and individual research projects have developed further and in interesting ways, through our work together, our encounters with other researchers and their writing, and from new insights emerging from the messy tangle of these associations. In our mutual work, while we use various qualitative and quantitative data generation methods, it is the composition of texts and our ongoing reflection on these that is the most powerful and significant mode of inquiry (Richardson, 1994). For us, the composition of our texts acts in a nonlinear and recursive way, bringing together our conversations and our collected data, and involving a multimodal and flexible drafting process that merges individual and collaborative texts and video or audio 'talking through' conversations. Over time, our collaborative writing, along with our research interests, has also been increasingly mediated, impacted, and enhanced by technologies, and often by those we are studying.

iPads at home in Canada and Australia

As early career academic mothers, in our research collaboration, we have often compared details of our institutional, cultural and home lives. We have joked that while the development of 'good ideas' historically is sometimes connected to romantic notions of French philosophers drinking wine and smoking cigarettes in noisy bars while having grand conversations, our own research conversations operate rather differently. Our shared insights always include our lives alongside children and busy households, with disruptions and interruptions typical of the complex dance of work and home in our research conversations. Our Canada (Linda)–Australia (Jo) time difference also means that often our research conversations take place alongside the daily activities of our children's lives and these filter in along the edges. A child needs a snack, and another requires a hug in the course of a Facetime or Skype call; our writing together is frequently punctuated by the interruptions of caregiving – children needing collection from school or activities, unanticipated illnesses and various requirements for our attention. Yet, significantly, these 'interruptions' are frequently productive, and often profoundly impact our writing about other people's children, providing us with (often unintended) opportunities to reflect on and rethink our ideas.

As we witnessed the emergence of mobile technologies for children, specifically the arrival of the iPad, our shared conversations considered the impact touch screen devices might have for our own children, in addition to wondering about possibilities that tablets might present for early literacy education, and for young learners. While we were developing research project ideas, these were brought to life through our serendipitous observations of our own children, then aged 3, 5, 6 and 8 years old. In particular, a series of events caught our attention when our children played and learned together during Linda's Australian sabbatical in 2011 when we spent many hours observing our children using iPads 'in the wild', combining our individual autoethnographic observations with a collective ethnographic perspective (Flewitt, 2011; Green & Bloom, 1997). Following from these observations, we have recognized the immense value of researching children's experiences in their homes, and have incorporated similar ethnographic approaches in subsequent research and in collaborations with graduate students. While we continue to engage in a range of other qualitative research methods, we find that our observations of children's technological engagements *at* home, and as influenced *by* home, provide us with important evidence of the complex entanglements of child and parent perspectives and interactions, and the artifacts, objects, texts, processes and devices that are part of everyday life.

In describing our approach to researching children's learning and playing from home to school to community and beyond, we draw on the work of Richardson (2016), in thinking through the ways in which we have tried to make sense of ourselves and our worlds, including the 'iWorld' (O'Mara & Laidlaw, 2011) in which we now live. Richardson writes of the chapters in her text "as palimpsests – pictures that, although taken in particular times and places, allow traces of the past to poke through and be visible". She writes that these chapters "reflect the ways in which people make sense of their worlds, finding traces of the already experienced in their new experiences" (Richardson, 2016, p. 7). Although our chapter here is a much smaller enterprise, each of the five pictures we have painted are drawn from different writing and researching projects. In sharing these pictures, we attempt to show the ways in which our lives and experiences from home provide understandings which 'poke through' into our research, sometimes as an outline, a tracery, an idea, at other times changing the ways in which we understand children and their technological worlds, shifting who we are as researchers. The examples start with 'near' moments, from our own homes, to those that reach further beyond, to illustrating how 'moments from home' can reshape research in schools or considerations of policy, and ways in which other moments in homes may be impacted from outside perspectives.

iDollhouse in the iWorld

In our initial experiences of observing our collective children (Jo has a boy and a girl, and Linda has two girls), our autoethnographic observations played an important role in leading us into a new direction for our collaborative research projects. During Linda and her children's time in Australia, in the infancy of the iPad, we observed with keen interest our children sharing favorite iPad apps alongside details of Canadian and Australian child culture and play. We were particularly interested to note the following vignette, which we originally included in one of the first articles we wrote on our emerging interest in mobile technologies (O'Mara & Laidlaw, 2011):

> Our children were playing at the dollhouses and the 3-year-old realized that a tiny pretend laptop was missing. After everyone looked around for a bit, he returned to play and sat the mother doll at the computer desk. "She's going to Google to find out where the little computer is".
>
> *(p. 153)*

The children's dollhouse play led to further quests for additional toy representations and creations, with Linda's children on a hunt for tiny mobile phones and iPads as items all the children regarded as necessary objects for the dollhouse. As iPads were relatively new at that time, the children were unsuccessful, beyond finding a small mobile phone charm in a toy store. For months after returning to Canada, Linda's children collected visual representations of mobile phones or tablets they saw in advertising flyers, with the aim to send them to Australia for the dollhouse. They also accessorized their own dolls, creating 'digital devices' cut from advertising flyers or crafted from paper, and creating a paper laptop computer with a painstakingly drawn keyboard, taped carefully into a tiny doll 'lunch kit' as the laptop case.

Through our 'up close' observations of the dollhouse interactions, we developed a heightened awareness of how children's play, even in non-technological ways, reflects a remix of their worlds and expresses and explores the practices and values of children's home lives. The children in our example (our own) lived alongside parents who modeled everyday uses of technologies and communicated that the objects and artifacts of technology had value, a value clearly represented in our children's play activities.

As we worked together writing our vignettes from home, based on our autoethnographic observations, the picture we created together of what we witnessed in our children's play enabled us to frame the questions and shape a collaborative research project working with early primary teachers and their classrooms. Over the course of this project, Jo and her family came to Canada and Linda and Jo worked together in a kindergarten classroom study. We both recognized that we were learning as much about digital technologies and mobile devices "at the elbows of our children" (O'Mara & Laidlaw, 2011) as we were through the classroom research; our home experiences formed the tracery for our work in schools.

A comparative ethnografiction

Our second research example emerged from an interweaving of observations of our own children and their school experiences, an ethnographic study of a kindergarten classroom and our informal observations of the school contexts of our study. Just as reader response theory suggests that we do not enter into reading texts without bringing in our background knowledge (Rosenblatt, 1994), we too cannot step outside of our background knowledge as researchers – for us, our collective and individual observations of digital practices across home, school, family and research environments stretched across our thinking. By the time of this example, we had both observed Canadian and Australian early years classrooms together, and had engaged in participatory, ethnographic observation through literacy and technology projects in Canadian and Australian schools. As we began work on presentations and publications interrogating some of the challenges and unintended consequences of iPad use for children who have writing challenges or disabilities (Laidlaw & O'Mara, 2015), our autobiographical observations from home also provided important insights, and a multi-level approach:

> This mode of inquiry values working across levels, from the 'general' to the particularity of individual examples, located alongside one another in a larger research bricolage . . . piecing together smaller and larger-scale data and autobiographical examples in new ways.
>
> *(p. 63)*

To address privacy concerns – not wanting to reveal details that might possibly identify our own children or classroom research participants (both teachers and students) – and to address some important home/school divides in connection to using technologies for writing and 'deficit discourses' that can be present in schools (Whitburn, 2013) – we created a fictive 'snapshot'/vignette/tableau that worked to bring together our autobiographical observations from home with those we had gathered in schools. The following is an excerpt about the child we called Emma:

> Emma is in Grade One. Mostly she likes school, but she comes home frustrated on some days. . . .
>
> When she uses the iPad she often finds new ways to use apps that showcase her strengths as a problem-solver, and as a multimodal learner. She also explores her interests in new ways when she uses such tools at home, and becomes proficient at searching websites, apps and video collections, although at her school the Grade One children are not allowed Internet access on any of the mobile devices used in the classroom.
>
> *(Laidlaw & O'Mara, 2015, p. 6)*

This vignette, and others that we used, functioned as ethnographic fictional portrayals we could use to interrogate important patterns we had noted across the particular experiences we had as parents and those we had observed in schools through our research projects. Use of an 'ethnografiction', a term we have invented, provided us with a tool that allowed us to express what we knew could be a contentious conclusion, that there can be 'trouble in the works' for some young children requiring digital assistive technology supports, due to institutional resistance in early years classrooms.

As collaborators using examples informed by our own children as well as examples gathered through more typical participant research, we have attended carefully to the ethical implications of publishing or sharing examples. Although we have sought institutional ethics approvals, individually and in our collaborative work, we find that such standardized ethics structures tend not to provide the careful nuances required for work with young children, who cannot be expected to understand the parameters or consequences of research, even if they might be able to provide some version of assent or agreement. Thus, our work is often informed by strategies and techniques from our work in literature or drama education – using fictionalization or other forms of abstraction in presenting vignettes or 'narrative tableau' representations[1] (Laidlaw, 2005, p. xvi) for areas of more critical analysis, and where, perhaps, a deeper truthfulness is more possible when we are able to provide some distancing from the specific individuals who have informed the examples.

Moving further, moving closer through researching in other people's homes

While our own 'at home' and autoethnographic experiences have informed our studies of young children and technology, we have engaged in additional ethnographic research in the homes of child and parent participants, and mentored graduate students in home-based research. Beginning from our own home observations, however, has changed how we understand research and informed how we approach researching in 'up close' and less predictable (than, for example, a university interview room) environments in homes. Ethnographic research in children's homes is relational and messy, but also has the potential to uncover rich data and has informed many of our insights into the digital experiences of young children. Meeting outside of school and university spaces also can change how research participants will interact with us, as participants' homes provide unique and varied research contexts. One parent participant in a parent and teacher focus group in our Canadian early learning and technology study summarizes:

> Meeting outside the context of our work allowed us more freedom to discuss and reflect on our practice. We were able to speak more frankly than perhaps we would if we met in the workplace. By meeting in our homes, we were able to establish deeper relationships and delve more fully into the ideas that inspired us.
>
> *(S., Parent Participant, 2012)*

Suzanna Wong, who worked with Linda as a doctoral student and with Jo in Australia as a part of our project research team, studied children's multiliteracies and technology practices in their homes as her own research focus. She worked with children in urban and rural homes in Canada, and suburban and regional homes in Australia. Suzanna's research plans, at the start of her study, resembled a more standard approach to gathering data – planning for qualitative parent and child interviews alongside scheduled informal observations. However, she quickly found her research approach becoming more complex, as she followed the children and their families, and they developed a trusting relationship where participants felt free to suggest activities:

> My experience has always been influenced by what the participating children asked me to do (e.g., push them on the swing, come with them to the museum) during my participant observations. Often children asked what I was doing with the camera, pencil and notebook, audio recorder etc. and were curious about my research. When I cross-checked my informal interviews with the parents, what I observed in their homes did not always match what parents were telling me. I learned to listen to the children carefully and observe the children's literacy practices through multiple lenses. Everyone in the same household had different perspectives on literacy practices and using technologies.

Suzanna, as a caring and sensitive researcher, used her extensive background as a teacher and a parent to inform her research practices and was also able to create relationships with her young participants where the children asserted their own opinions and refusals on particular days when they did not feel like being 'studied', and where, later in her analyses of her data, she discovered that across several of the families the children actually had been 'researching' too, through writing their own field notes in her research journal, and capturing surreptitious images of Suzanna on her camera and iPad.

Following from Suzanna's study and her observations of family incongruities in connection to attitudes toward and interpretations of digital practices, Jo, Linda and Suzanna have begun to investigate a more distant circle within our current project, heading into communities and beyond, using several grandparents originally interviewed as teacher or ministry of education stakeholders as research participants. These women, during earlier interviews about digital literacy curriculum and practices in their jurisdictions, were keen to share their observations from home of young grandchildren and their engagements with digital technologies, with such conversations often overtaking our official interview activities. In this project we have engaged in ethnographic observations across children's homes, as well as during visits to the grandmothers' homes, and our early data provide an interesting cross section of intergenerational dispositions towards technologies and different text forms and modalities (Kress, 2005).

From playground conversations to policy analysis

While neither Jo nor Linda had previously conducted policy research, our observations of some of the disjunctions between home technology practices and those we observed in our own children's schools as well as those of classroom research sites led us to interrogate policy documents. In the early days of the iPad, many schools in Victoria (Australia) were introducing one-to-one device programs, including schools in Jo's local area. She found herself constantly in the midst of discussions about iPads, their worth or worthlessness for school as parents stood around in groups waiting for children in the hot Australian sun. Parents expressed passionate positions and opinions, and when Jo researched in school settings, teachers were reporting that parents around her city expressed multiple perspectives on the issue. Parents voiced concerns as widely ranging as wireless technology rays causing cancer, the loss of childhood through early engagement with digital networks, children's potential disconnection from the physical world and the fear that teachers wanted to use iPads in class to avoid teaching. Linda was hearing parallel technology conversations among the parents at her children's school as they watched their children playing in the snow after school during the Alberta winter. We compared notes and realized that there was a different contextual timbre to the conversations in each of the two locations. In Jo's state of Victoria, schools were rapidly adopting iPads, while in Alberta, even though ownership rates in children's homes were similar, iPads were generally being taken up in classrooms more gradually.

Across local school districts in both places we noted an unevenness to the patterns of adoption, and parents expressed feeling unsettled about technology use and the presence of iPads in early grade classrooms. In our discussions with each other we noted that despite some surface similarities between Canada and Australia's education systems, there were considerable differences in technology provision. This led to our collection, comparison and interrogation of policy documents from Alberta and Victoria with Jill Blackmore, Jo's colleague at Deakin who brought expertise in policy to the study. We then examined provision and usage of mobile digital devices for the early years of primary/elementary education, comparing the different ways that our state and provincial policies were influencing approaches to mobile devices (O'Mara et al., 2017). The overwhelming finding was that despite consistent enthusiasm by our respective education departments to use mobile devices in classrooms, there was far less willingness to 'foot the bill'. In the case of Victoria, the burden of provision was passed on to parents, with schools initiating 'bring your own device' programs, starting in the preparatory year. As we noted:

> In Victoria, co-contribution is seen as the parents contributing the device, where the school is contributing the infrastructure to make the program possible.
>
> *(p. 97)*

In Alberta, the cost of provision was often at least partially diverted to parent fund-raising revenues, with some schools adopting what we term 'the casino model', using charitable gaming proceeds to purchase iPads and other classroom technologies. Significantly, however, purchases through this gaming funding must be: "Items and resources that are positioned as 'extras' . . ." (p. 98), providing the message that technologies purchased through charitable gaming funding are items that are not essential for classroom use. This positioning has contributed to an atmosphere rather different from that of Victoria, where devices are positioned as essential to early years classrooms, and thus needed parental contribution to make their adoption possible.

What became most intriguing to us about our findings was the cultural specificity and impact of parental attitudes towards how policies around provision unfolded. While parental concerns about technology usage for children in each of our own locales seemed quite similar, expectations for how these technologies would be provided were vastly different. Australian parents were willing to pay for devices themselves (although sometimes grudgingly), while Canadian parents would accept volunteering at casinos (also sometimes reluctantly), but actively resisted district attempts to institute anything resembling a 'bring-your-own-devices' program, believing that technologies used in schools should be school funded equipment.

This research example, which began with informal observations of parent conversations while watching over playing children in Canada and in Australia, was followed by our conversations wondering about how our two systems might compare (expecting we would find more similarities than we did!) and recognizing that we needed assistance in addressing the policy theory and context. Jill Blackmore enabled us to locate the study within the broader policy discourse and literature and scaffold from our autobiographical observations, providing an opening to reveal systemic differences in technology provision. We have found that working with others, where everyone in the team brings different strengths, is a valuable way to expand and extend research and further develop our own analyses and insights. And importantly, even in a study that delved into policy considerations, our autoethnographic observations played a key role in alerting us to a new area of inquiry and helping us to understand another aspect impacting children's learning across home and school, and the interplay of different institutional, cultural and regional values and practices.

Popular media and home perspectives

Our final example brings together ethnographic research in homes, conversations and interviews with parents and the wider influences and impacts of the popular media. As Linda and Jo began to work with our initial iPad research projects, we also began to track how the emergence of mobile technologies used by children was being represented in the popular media, quickly recognizing that themes present in the news, online magazines and social media sources were also being mirrored in our interviews and informal conversations with parents of young children. As Suzanna entered children's homes during her ethnographic doctoral research, she made similar observations. Linda, Suzanna and Jo began a more formal tracing of news and social media stories through a longitudinal popular media literature review, with a focus on the emergence of mobile devices and their impact on children's changing literacy practices, tracking trends from 2013–2017.

In our parallel research conversations with parents, we noted that media articles were not only providing information, they were also often influencing parent perspectives – and at times, even sparking particular worries and fears – with themes and metaphors from particular popular articles amplified as these were reposted multiple times on social media sites. These frequently included sensationalized themes, such as 'digital screens as addiction' with titles including, for example, *It's 'digital heroin'* (Kardaras, 2016), or links to danger, such as *The screens that are stealing childhood* (Stevenson, 2012). Ideas that were 'going viral' online, representing an attitude of what we interpreted as moral panic about digital screen time for young children, often also appeared to 'infect' some of the parent participants in our research projects. The popular 'fear-based' articles and media seemed to be contributing to parental tensions in regard to making decisions about their child's access to technologies in the home. Parents would mention particular articles in their conversations with Suzanna as she came into homes to observe children's practices, and media sources were frequently mentioned in Jo and Linda's parent interviews.

One of the most interesting aspects of this study for us was how we could trace patterns of ideas that had currency to different time periods of the study – for example, over time, as popular articles began to shift their focus to more 'balanced' examination of the challenges *and* benefits of technologies for children's use at home, we also noted our discussions with parents becoming more nuanced and less 'panicked' for parents who tended to favor 'old disposition' (Kress, 2005) perspectives regarding technologies. Through this project we have gained increased recognition of the complex influences informing parent perspectives, and subsequently, also implicated in children's access to various technologies and digital practices in their homes. Through our examinations of popular media articles alongside our research with parents, we have also gained an appreciation of the impact of information from popular sources, particularly when research studies are typically published more gradually than the 'instant' world of Facebook, Twitter and other social media. This project has also led us to wonder about the role of new media and social media in offering 'just in time' information to parents and teachers, and how our own research in future studies might be more responsive. If we, as researchers, do not respond, parents and educators will access the information they desire through other means.

Complex entanglements and messy methods

When we describe our methodological approach to others, our descriptions span a range of methods and approaches: autobiographical, writing as inquiry, a range of ethnographies, critical reflective practice and complexity thinking. At times we also bring in feminist perspectives, for our inclusion of "our domestic experience of nurturing children" (Grumet, 1988, p. 5), as well as our interests in the post-structural (St. Pierre, 2014) as perhaps better able to represent our messy entanglement of methods and the diverse threads of data we weave into our work.

Yet, in the post-typographic digital era (Merchant, 2015), we live in messy times. Children's lives at home are intersected by the continually emerging mediascape (Appadurai, 1990), and the pervasive presence of technologies – old, new and emerging. Capturing children's and parents' experiences and perspectives in the midst of such digital complexity, for us, has been a similarly recursive and living endeavor, and where, following Sumara (1996), we note, "The world, our existence in the world, our relations with others, happen all-at-once". The realms of the micro and the macro co-exist, and while often we begin with our micro examples of 'the personal', we relocate these (Kamler, 2001) in a kind of multidirectional mapping. Of course, planned research activities do have a chronology in that they occur over time, and writing projects also flow from beginnings to conclusions, providing us with a certain tension of making the messiness of research with children, families and educational institutions appear more linear in the rear-view mirror of publication and completed projects.

Additionally, we view our methods as mirroring the messy yet networked nature of digital technologies, following from complexity thinking constructs which explore changes in networked systems (Goldstein, 1999; Gough, 2012). Digital phenomena and practices are frequently interconnected and rhizomatic in structure, and follow patterns of emergence, whereby smaller scale aspects of systems self-organize into larger scale patterns of sophistication (Johnson, 2001).

As we have noted earlier, children's digital activities and engagement in their homes are similarly messy and complex – entangled within children's own micro worlds, parental influences and structures, and impacted by the reverberations of the macro worlds of schools, communities, institutional influences, culture, media and technologies. Our collective projects have attempted to make meaning of the digital worlds and experiences that children are inhabiting, and to use these insights to inform our ongoing work as literacy educators and researchers in the intersecting world of educating teachers. We recognize, too, that even the best methods can only provide us with mere glimpses, snapshots of particular moments or events, and that the multi-layering, intersections and entanglements of the messy methods we take up can provide us with a slightly wider view.

Practices and possibilities

As our chapter may indicate, we tend to shy away from visions of singular answers for research practice in favor of more entangled perspectives. We (Linda, Jo, Suzanna) have learned to navigate through the 'interesting mess' of studying children's learning and playing with technology, in part through happenstance and having neatly planned research experiences unfold differently than we have expected. However, this less predictable research trajectory, entering into and out of home experiences, intersecting autobiographical experiences with ethnographic research, and including comparative analyses coming from Australia and Canada, has provided us with opportunities to gain finer grained understandings of children's digital experiences than we might have otherwise. In current 'messy' digital times, considerations of the complex ways in which children experience and engage in technologies at home is important in relation to understanding children's technology experiences in schools and other experiences outside of the home. Within institutional contexts, children's learning and technology experiences are frequently organized through linear, sequential approaches, where the influences of home and life out of school are compartmentalized. But in the digital age, children's experiences, practices and skills are interconnected, and might bridge across the domains of home and school, opening up the silos of classrooms (Souto-Manning, 2013). Thus, perhaps research practices such as those we have addressed – taking up the personal and autobiographical – entangled with other research forms – might also inform new insights and approaches for children's learning and playing across what can be an interconnected landscape of home and school environments.

In offering suggestions for other researchers, in taking up a more 'unruly' approach to studies of technology with children, we note the value of interconnection and networks in our approach – across ideas, in relation to the value of shared projects and in our own daily technology experiences. Our collaborative body of technology research has accrued in layers and interconnected projects and has been informed by our own conversations that have come alongside work we have done with others, as well as being mediated by the technologies we have studied. Initially we began with the shared anxieties of being new scholars and wondering how to navigate a "program of research". We heeded advice from mentors about the advantages of working with others – that research need not be a lonely endeavor and that it was important to create structures (relational, technological and otherwise) where "ideas could mingle and swap" (Johnson, 2010). As we have suggested earlier, while we have not been able to recreate the Parisian salons, we have benefited from a similar kind of "coffee house culture" that has enabled many good ideas to emerge, although ours is more of a kitchen table operation than salon. Similarly, to the practices of the children we study, our "playing around with" language, texts and digital forms, together, has been important for our own research and our own learning.

Additionally, in our ethnographic research with children in homes, we acknowledge that "starting from where they are" is important in being granted access, developing effective research relationships and uncovering rich data. But this is also advice we have followed for ourselves. As we have noted, our projects have often started with some 'small thing' we noticed and wondered about. We have also followed our interests, rather than trying to be strategic. Over time, when we return to key observations and shared obsessions, our conversations and writing have helped us to tease out the threads that have led us to new insights, and to new projects.

We also acknowledge the value of comparative work in examining the complex digital worlds of children, in helping us to understand our individual and collective contexts in more depth. This work has helped us to trouble 'the taken-for-granted' aspects of our own contexts and school systems; comparing our 'similar but different' locations and experiences has helped us engage in the work of making the familiar strange, helping us to work, in a sense, as educational anthropologists (Tobin, 2014).

Finally, although the digital shifts in the 'iWorld' have been rapid, we continue to value important aspects that move more slowly. We navigate the tension of keeping pace with new technologies and new practices against the knowledge that our insights often occur over time, with multiple efforts and persistence. The fast, the slow, the digital and the relational are all deeply entangled, and for us, make up the stuff of interesting research work.

Acknowledgment

We acknowledge the funding support of the Canadian Social Sciences and Humanities Research Council, which supported the work of this article, across two projects: *Literacy Learning in Playful Spaces: Using Multimodal Strategies to Develop Narrative with Young Children* and *A Comparative Investigation of Pedagogical Possibilities of Digital Tools for Family and School Early Literacy Education.*

Note

1 Within the theater, a tableau is a complex structure where actors' bodies create a 'still image' that others might view and interpret.

References

Appadurai, A. (1990) Disjuncture and difference in the global cultural economy. *Public Culture* 2 (2), 1–24.

Ashton, J. (2013) My little future iPad addicts. *Salon.* Weblog. Retrieved 14 October 2017 from www.salon.com/2013/06/14/my_little_future_ipad_addicts/.

Behar, R. (1996) *The vulnerable observer: Anthropology that breaks your heart.* Boston, MA: Beacon Press.

Blackwell, C., Lauricella, A. and Wartella, E.A. (2014) Factors influencing digital technology use in early childhood education. *Computers & Education* 77, 82–90.

Clark, A. and Moss, P. (2017) *Listening to young children, Expanded third edition: The mosaic approach.* London: Jessica Kingsley.

Clifford, J. & Marcus, G. (eds.) (1986) *Writing culture: The poetics and politics of ethnography.* Los Angeles, CA: University of California Press.

Davis, B. and Sumara, D. (2006) *Complexity and education: Inquiries into learning, teaching and Research.* Mahwah, NJ: Lawrence Erlbaum Associates.

Doll, Jr. W. (1993) *A post-modern perspective on curriculum.* New York: Teachers College Press.

Flewitt, R. (2011) Bringing ethnography to a multimodal investigation of early literacy in a digital age. *Qualitative Research* 1 (3), 293–310.

Geertz, C. (1988) *Works and lives: The anthropologist as author.* Stanford, CA: Stanford University Press.

Goldstein, J. (1999) Emergence as a construct: History and issues. *Emergence: A Journal of Complexity Issues in Organization and Management* 1 (1), 49–72.

Gough, N. (2012) Complexity, complexity reduction, and 'methodological borrowing' in educational inquiry. *Complicity: An International Journal of Complexity and Education* 9 (1), 41–56. Retrieved 15 October 2017 from https://ejournals.library.ualberta.ca/index.php/complicity/article/view/16532.

Green, J. and Bloom, D. (1997) Ethnography and ethnographers of and in education: A situated perspective. In: Flood, J., Lapp, D. and Brice-Heath, S. (eds.) *Handbook of research on teaching literacy through the communicative and visual arts.* New York: Palgrave MacMillan.

Grumet, M. (1988) *Bitter milk: Women and teaching*. Amherst, MA: The University of Massachusetts Press.

Heath, S.B., Street, B. and Mills, M. (2008) *Ethnography: Approaches to language and literacy Research*. New York: Teachers College Press.

Holloway, D., Green, L. and Livingston, S. (2013) *Zero to eight. Young children and their Internet use*. London: LSL, EU Kids. Retrieved 15 October 2017 from http://eprints.lse.ac.uk/52630/1/Zero_to_eight.pdf.

Holloway, D., Green, L. and Livingston, S. (2015) Digitods: Toddler, touch screens and Australian family life. *Journal of Media and Culture* 18 (5). Retrieved 15 October 2017 from http://journal.media-culture.org.au/index.php/mcjournal/article/view/1024/0.

International Literacy Association (2017) Overcoming the digital divide: Four critical steps. *Literacy Leadership Brief, International Literacy Association*. Retrieved 15 October 2017 from www.literacyworldwide.org/docs/default-source/where-we-stand/ila-overcoming-digital-divide-brief.pdf.

Johnson, S. (2001) *Emergence: The connected lives of ants, brains, cities, and software*. New York: Scribner.

Johnson, S. (2010) *Where good ideas come from: The natural history of innovation*. New York: Riverhead Books.

Kamler, B. (2001) *Relocating the personal: A critical writing pedagogy*. New York: SUNY Press.

Kardaras, N. (2016) It's 'digital heroin': How screens turn kids into psychotic junkies. *New York Post*. Retrieved 15 October 2017 from https://nypost.com/2016/08/27/its-digital-heroin-how-screens-turn-kids-into-psychotic-junkies/.

Kress, G. (2005) Communication now and in the future. *English 21: Qualifications and Curriculum Authority*. Retrieved 15 October 2017 from www.qca.org.uk/qca_5677.aspx.

Laidlaw, L. (2005) *Reinventing curriculum: A complex perspective on literacy and writing*. Mahwah, NJ: Lawrence Erlbaum Associates.

Laidlaw, L. and O'Mara, J. (2015) Rethinking difference in the iWorld: Possibilities, challenges And 'unexpected consequences' of digital tools in literacy education. *Language and Literacy* 17 (1), 59–74.

Laidlaw, L., O'Mara, J. and Wong, S. (2015) "Daddy, look at the video I made on my iPad": Reconceptualizing 'Readiness' in the digital age. In: Iorio, J.M. and Parnell, W. (eds.) *Rethinking readiness in Early Childhood Education: Implications for policy and practice*. New York: Palgrave Macmillan, 65–76.

Marsh, J. (2017a) Russian dolls and three forms of capital: Ecological and sociological perspectives on parents' engagement with young children's tablet use. In: Burnett, C., Merchant, G., Simpson, A. and Walsh, M. (eds.) *The case of the iPad: Mobile literacies in Education*. London: Springer, 31–47.

Marsh, J. (2017b) The internet of toys: A posthuman and multimodal analysis of connected play. *Teachers College Record* 119 (12), 1–32. Retrieved 15 October 2017 from www.tcrecord.org.

Marsh, J., Hannon, P., Lewis, M. and Ritchie, L. (2017) Young children's initiation into family literacy practices in the digital age. *Journal of Early Childhood Research* 15 (1), 47–60.

Marsh, J., Plowman, L., Yamada-Rice, D. and Bishop, J. (2016) Digital play: A new classification. *Early Years*. 36 (3), 242–253.

Merchant, G. (2015) Keep taking the tablets: iPads, story apps and early literacy. *Australian Journal of Language and Literacy* 38 (1), 3–11.

Neumann, M. and Neumann, D. (2017) The use of touch-screen tablets at home and pre-school to foster emergent literacy. *Journal of Early Childhood Literacy* 17 (2), 203–220. Retrieved 15 October 2017 from http://journals.sagepub.com/doi/abs/10.1177/1468798415619773.

O'Mara, J. and Laidlaw, L. (2011) Living in the iWorld: Two literacy researchers reflect on the changing texts and literacy practices of childhood. *English Teaching: Practice and Critique* 10 (4), 149–159.

O'Mara, J., Laidlaw, L. and Blackmore, J. (2017) The new digital divide: Digital technology policies and provision in Canada and Australia. In: Burnett, C., Merchant, G., Simpson, A. and Walsh, M. (eds.) *The case of the iPad: Mobile literacies in education*. London: Springer, 87–104.

Richardson, L. (1994) Writing: A method of inquiry. In: Denzin, N.K. and Lincoln, Y.S. (eds.) *Handbook of qualitative research*. Thousand Oaks, CA: Sage, 516–529.

Richardson, L. (1997) *Fields of play: Constructing an academic life*. New Brunswick: Rutgers University Press.

Richardson, L. (2016) *Seven minutes from home: An American daughter's story*. New Brunswick: Sense Publishers.

Rideout, V.J. (2013) *Zero to eight: Children's media use in America*. San Francisco, CA: Common Sense Media. Retrieved 15 October 2017 from www.commonsensemedia.org/research/zero-to-eight-childrens-media-use-in-america-2013.

Rosenblatt, L. (1994) *The reader, the text, the poem: The transactional theory of the literary work*. Carbondale, IL: Southern Illinois University Press.

Schön, D. (1983) *The reflective practitioner*. New York: Basic Books.

Schön, D. (1987) *Educating the reflective practitioner*. San Francisco, CA: Jossey-Bass.

Souto-Manning, M. (2013) *Multicultural teaching in the early childhood classroom*. New York: Teachers College Press.

St. Pierre, E. (2014) A brief and personal history of post qualitative research: Toward 'post inquiry'. *Journal of Curriculum Theorizing* 30 (2), 2–19.

Sumara, D. 1996, *Private readings in public: Schooling the literary imagination*. New York: Peter Lang.

Stevenson, A. (2012) The screens that are stealing childhood. *The Sydney Morning Herald*, Weblog. Retrieved 15 October 2017from https://goo.gl/3Q25JC.

Tobin, J. (2014) Comparative, diachronic, ethnographic research on education. *Current Issues in Comparative Education* 16 (2), 6–13.

Whitburn, B. (2013) The indelible ink of the special stamp: An insider's research essay on imprints and erasures. *Disability & Society* 29 (4), 624–637. Retrieved 15 October 2017 from www.tandfonline.com/doi/abs/10.1080/09687599.2013.844097.

Wong, S. (2015) Mobile digital devices and preschoolers' home multiliteracy practices. *Language and Literacy, Special Issue: A Landscape View of Literacy Studies in Canada* 17 (2), 75–90. Retrieved 15 October 2017 from: http://ejournals.library.ualberta.ca/index.php/langandlit/article/view/24803/18367.

14

YOUNG CHILDREN'S HOME TECHNOLOGY USE

Responsive qualitative methods for a sensitive topic

Joanne Orlando

Introduction

Young children have become prolific users of technology. Approximately 75% of children aged 3 to 8 years now access technology such as a tablet and/or a mobile phone on a daily basis (Ofcom, 2017. Children are also increasingly using technology at a younger age, with a recent rise in usage by children under 3 years of age (O'Connor & Fotakopoulou, 2016; Palaiologou 2016). Numerous studies are emerging to understand this new phenomenon of 'digitised children' (O'Connor & Fotakopoulou, 2016; Radesky et al., 2016), however common and dominating perspectives underpinning these studies is assessing of the appropriateness of technology for young children. Of particular focus is the benefits and dangers of young children's technology use for their development and learning.

Firstly, a consistent theme in the literature is a comparison of children's technology use against a benchmark of what is perceived as expected and appropriate activity for children in the early childhood stage of development. These activities are often described in terms of the importance of traditional approaches to play and learning for young children's (McLean et al., 2014) and include children's social and emotional development (Radesky et al., 2016) and language development (Duch et al., 2013). Drawing mainly on surveys and small case studies, young children's technology use has been measured against these characteristics to evaluate whether or not engagement with technology is conducive to their development. For the vast majority of studies that conclude that technology use is not suitable, the literature indicates that this is due to technology impacting on a child's opportunity for physical development such handwriting skills, children's physical, social and emotional well-being (Louv, 2010; Palmer, 2007).

It is evident from these studies that children's technology use has challenged traditional notions of play and learning. A continued framing of this as potential harm however, closes off understanding children's technology use more fully (Palaiologou, 2016; Stephens, 2016). It is important to recognise the non-traditional forms of play occurring from children's technology use and the different contributions they make to their learning and development (Wood, 2009).

Researchers (Chaudron et al., 2015; Plowman & McPake, 2013; Stephens, 2016) have also noted that a consistent emphasis on the potential harm of technology has resulted in a judgemental stance regarding technology use for young children. This, they note, is evident in empirical studies and also more widely in the media. A consistent message is that technology of harm to children and point to the irresponsibility of adults who allow young children to use these devices. Recent 'popular' research (Chang, 2016) has indicated high levels of 'tech-shaming' among parents, with 59% saying they feel judged by other parents over their kids' screen time. While some parents have embraced the potential learning, technology offers children, for others, however, technology represent a threat to childhood development. A common tension for parents is fear of missing out on educational benefits vs concerns about negative effects on thinking and imagination (Chaudron et al., 2015; Radesky et al., 2016). This stance is an important 'state of play' to consider when reading this body of research, as well as undertaking research into young children's use of technology in the home.

Secondly, a common position evident in studies is assessing young children's use of technology from a distanced stance. These studies rely on data collected from adults who care for young children to explain what children 'do' on a device (Sharkins et al., 2016, Ernest et al., 2014). While this data is useful, adults cannot give a first-hand account of use. Reliance on adults to speak on behalf of the user – the child – decontextualises the decisions children are making in their technology use. These studies also focus on children's 'access' or 'exposure' to a device (Sharkins et al., 2016), rather than understanding children's engagement with a device. While these studies are able to capture important data such as frequency and length of use, they are unable to gain a nuanced complexities of technology use.

Debates relating to technology use, play and learning

While overall the literature indicates that young children are increasingly using technology and that their use is contributing to changes in traditional play and learning (and generally not for the better), it cannot be assumed that this change is necessarily unfavourable. Over-reliance on traditional conceptualisations, research methodologies and expectations has possibly resulted in an overlooking of the complexity of young children's use of technology, what informs and shapes their engagement with technology and the range of implications and opportunities it opens for play, learning and development.

Bigum (2002) acknowledges that using technology in education or in any other field of human endeavour changes things. He states, however, that rather than necessarily improving an existing set of circumstances, we might expect that circumstance to be changed with the deployment of technology, and to be changed in unpredictable ways. For example, a study undertaken by Verenikina and Kervin (2011), signalled the positive impact of technology use for young children's creativity. While data from this research was collected from the perspectives of caregivers (parents and educators), it presented some positive experiences and potential for digitally mediated imaginative play with an iPad. Similarly, other studies indicate that young children's engagement with technology can support the development of early literacy (Gonzalez, 2016), arts (Terreni, 2011) and numeracy learning (Jowett et al., 2012). Greater understandings in these areas may alleviate the anxiety regarding any perceived harm of children's use. This importantly can facilitate enhanced understanding of how children can use technology in ways which enhance their learning.

Need to look beyond adult-only interpretations

Contemporary approaches to childhood suggest that if we are to understand children's play and learning there is a need to look beyond how adults observe, interpret and assess it. Developments in early childhood studies have seen a paradigmatic shift from constructions of children and childhood framed in terms of vulnerability, dependency and immaturity, to perspectives that highlight competence and agency, leading to increased emphasis on children's perspectives about their own play (James & Prout, 1997; Mayall, 2012). A study by Plowman and McPake (2013) of young children's (aged 3–4 years) uses of technology in their home illustrated the value of young children's perspectives. While the methodology initially focused on parents rather than directly on the children, researchers shifted their methodology to also include data collected from the children. In their justification of this shift, the researchers stated that even though children's interactions were strongly mediated by their parents, it was clear that, even at the ages of 3 and 4 years, children are able to exercise their own preferences to some extent. Plowman (2015, p.8) stated,

> *Engaging directly with participating children and finding ways for them to articulate or demonstrate their choices enabled us to gain insights that were not available by other means and to have more confidence in piecing together an ecocultural understanding of their lives.*

Acknowledging context affects use

A number of commentators have also observed that the context in which children engage with technology is significant to their preferences and engagement. A study by Edwards et al. (2017) found children's home technology experiences to be potentially richer than those experienced in early childhood education settings. While data from this research was collected from the perspectives of adults and not children, the study importantly indicated the differing perspectives the adults caring for children had of the suitability of technology for children, and this was a key factor for the differing home technology experiences children were engaging in. Similarly, many studies (Palaiologou, 2016; Edwards et al., 2017) have identified the limited use of technology by children in early childhood settings was due to attitudes of educators and other staff.

Simplistic notions by adults that children use technology in the same way wherever they are and whoever they are with (adult or child), hinders understanding why particular technologies and content are chosen, and why children engage with it in the ways they do. Understanding the child's use within what is often described as a digitally rich home technology environment, is valuable. It can provide insight into how children play with technology individually, with siblings, parents or others in the home. This can provide a fruitful basis for understanding how children's use can be built on and enhanced in other settings such as early childhood education settings, to guide their learning

Moving the focus from the perceived dangers of technology to capitalising on the value

While not discarding the research on young children's use of technology completely, if we are to properly study the implications of their technology use on their learning, there is a need to shift away from assessing the dangers of technology to focus on lines of enquiry that are presenting alternate and fruitful understandings. These include: to more fully understand the online content children engage with and why, the opportunities for learning provided by their interaction with technology, how the people around the child inform their use of a device (Plowman & McPake, 2013), their range of experiences with technology and how children make meaning from and build on their technology activity (Davidson et al., 2014).

This chapter reports on a study which responds to the needs identified in the literature. The research questions informing this study are:

1 How do young children engage with technology at home?
2 What factors influence their use?

   a What learning experiences do they engage in when using technology, and how do children and parents interpret them?
   b How can children's home technology use be capitalised on in early childhood education?

The home was selected as the site for the research as the bulk of children's technology use occurs there (Edwards et al., 2017). The qualitative design of this study is characterised by observations and discussions with child(ren), parents and siblings in the home environment about the young child's use of technology. Using qualitative methods provides the opportunity for the child to express and demonstrate their uses, and also for parents to provide more in-depth explanations of their child's technology use.

Research methods that respond to the sensitive nature of this topic for parents

This chapter presents the methods used in this study to respond to how sensitive this topic can be for parents. Even though children are prolific users of technology the appropriateness of their use is openly questioned and judged (Freeman, 2017). This paradox may lead parents to allowing or encouraging their child to use technology at home, yet to conceal how much their child uses technology or whether they use it at all, when speaking with others. Researchers undertaking qualitative research, and particularly qualitative research on sensitive topics, need to be able to make an assessment of how the sensitivity potentially impacts upon the participants (Dickson-Swift et al., 2007). This includes being alert to the possible issues that participating in the research at home may raise for the participants and the researcher, and the design of the study.

My argument is that the design of this qualitative methodology responded to issues raised in the literature, and enhanced the possibility of gathering data that facilitated further understanding of the complexity of young children's uses of technology, why they use technology in the ways they do and the opportunities for play and learning they enable, to be explored. Table 14.1 summarises how this research design addresses the limitations identified in the research literature.

Research design

This qualitative study took place in Sydney, Australia, and focused on the home technology practices of 13 children, from a total of 9 families. Data collection extended over a 12-month period and centred on family home visits, and included observing children's technology use and talking with children, parents and siblings in family group interviews and in one-on-one discussions. The research process was approved by Western Sydney University Ethics committee, and consistent with standard ethical protocols, participants were assigned pseudonyms.

To respond to the sensitive context, an important feature of the research design was building rapport with the participants that would allow the access to the child and family's 'technology' story (Ceglowski, 2000; Goodwin et al., 2003). I was asking parents to talk in detail about an area parents can lack confidence, and the potential to feel judged by me, a researcher and perceived expert in this field, was high for parents. To address this, self-disclosure, narratives and informal organisational structures were incorporated into the discussions with the parents, and with the children to build trust.

Table 14.1 Comparison between research designs employed in the research literature and the design of this study

Identified limitations in the literature	*This research design focus*	*Methods used in this study*
Children's 'access' or 'exposure' to technology	Children's 'engagement' with technology. Specifically, how and why they interact with the device and the content.	1 Trust building recruitment 2 Home visits that included family group interviews, one-to-one interviews with parents, one on one discussions; particular emphasis on rapport building using narratives, self-disclosure 3 Organisational strategies for home visits that emphasised rapport building: • Extended time in home • Iterative home visit structure 4 Observations of children's technology use in conjunction with the above strategies
Adults interpretations of children's technology use	Qualitative design to facilitate children's perspectives on their technology use. Observations of children's technology use. Caregivers and siblings' perspectives on children's technology use for a more holistic understanding.	
Benchmarking children's technology activity against traditional play and learning approaches	Focus is not to compare against a benchmark but to explore technology uses.	
Seeking out the potential harm of young children's technology use	Examining the range of play and learning opportunities emerging from children's technology engagement. Responding to the biased stance regarding the suitability of technology for children.	
Young children's technology use homogenised	Focus on child's technology use in the home and family environment where the bulk of children's use takes place.	

It is important to acknowledge that there are potentially many ethical issues that arise from involving young children in family group interviews and in one-on-one discussions. A primary ethical issue is that of consent (Graham et al., 2015), and this has direct implications for building rapport with the child and parents. While parents have provided consent for the child to participate in the study, this does not mean they have consented. The first stage of every home visit included explaining in accessible terms for all participants, the purpose of the study and my home visit. I also explained this at the beginning of one-on-one time talks with the children, where appropriate. This could not be done with very young children. Due to the very young age of the children I also used the concept of assent (Cock, 2006) as an appropriate option for the children. This included consistently assessing the child's attentiveness and behaviour and responses towards me, as signs of consent. While no child became upset, children did at times during my visit demonstrate boredom, and the desire to change activity. I responded to this by shifting questioning to the parent or observing the child in their new activity if it was technology-related. I would then shift my focus back to the child when their actions indicated they were ready. This included coming up to show me something, joining the parent and me talking or smiling at me.

Recruitment of participants

The children and their families were recruited using a snowballing methodology (Cohen et al., 2007) through my professional and personal contacts. My contacts provided interested parents with an initial information sheet about the study, which was followed up by a phone call with me as Co-Investigator (CI) that provided more information. This method supported inclusion of a diverse range of children and their families. Participants were recruited if the child(ren) were in the required age group (6 years and younger) and used technology at home. Children were not selected in terms of what device they used, their skills in using technology or in their frequency of use. The focus of the study instead was the repertoire of experiences and approaches children used in their technology-based activity.

I began rapport building strategies with my first encounter with the parent. In explaining the purposes of the study during the initial phone call, I explained the commonality of young children using technology by referring to statistics. I also explained my role at University to teach pre-service teachers in using technology to enhance young children's learning. This purpose and positioning of myself and technology use supported the parents' sense of acceptance, and all parents I contacted about the study joined as participants.

This approach proved to be important for recruiting a range of young children from various family contexts. The children were from families of varying sizes situated in a range of communities, including an inner-city multicultural community, an outer metropolitan area with a high proportion of refugee families and a low-socio-economic area close to a prison. The parents varied widely in their professions and included university qualified professions, tradespersons and unskilled positions. The participating parents had varying levels of technology expertise and experience, and no two children used technology in exactly the same ways at home. Each child and family discussed and justified the child's use in different and distinctive ways. Table 14.2 details the 12 child participants, family participants and the children's technology resources.

The framing of the study for potential participants and the recruitment method proved to be very effective for contributing to the depth of data and the development of thick descriptions (Geertz, 1973) required for carefully studying children's practices with technology. As a group, the children all lived in technology-rich home environments where technology was considered to be part of the family home and children had access to and used one or more devices. Furthermore, each of the homes had technology that was new, with most devices less than two years old, and all children had a regular stream of new apps (paid and free) to use. All family members used technology which also meant that children had expertise available to them from adults and other children, when needed.

Family visits

The family visits were approached as an iterative shift between family group discussions, one-on-one interviews with parents, one-on-one talks and observations with children. The focus of data collection was children's frequent technology activities, the content children engaged with, device/content design features that children engaged with, changes in children's technology uses, reasoning for children's use and factors that influenced children's technology engagement.

All home visits began with a family interview. This method was selected to help capture interactional data or shared meanings (Astedt-Kurki et al., 2001), regarding why a child uses technology in the ways they do. Such methods 'can reveal the tone and personality of a family in a way that interviewing individual family members cannot' (Eggenberger & Nelms, 2007, p. 209). I began all family group interviews with questions which facilitated a 'settling-in phase'

Table 14.2 Research participants

	Family 1	*Family 2*	*Family 3*	*Family 4*	*Family 5*	*Family 6*	*Family 7*	*Family 8*	*Family 9*
Age of child(ren)	Girl 3, Boy 5	Girl 11 months	Girl 3 Boy 18 months	Girl 6	Girl 6 Boy 5	Boy 6	Boy 4 Girl 2	Girl 2	Boy 6
Parents participating	2	1	2	2	1	2	1	1	1
Older siblings	n/a	Boy 8	n/a	Boy 10	n/a	Boy 8	n/a	n/a	Boy 15 Girl 12
Device child used (6 yrs and younger)	Children share a mini-iPad and used parents' mobile	Child used parents' mobile	Children used Mum's iPad, Dad's tablet and parents' mobile	Child owned own iPad and used parents' mobile	Each child owned an iPad and parents' mobile	Each child owned a mini-iPad and parents' mobile	Children used family iPad and parents' mobile	Child used family iPad and used parents' mobile	Child owned own iPad and used parents' mobile

for the child and parents (Cameron, 2005, p. 601). I presented less difficult questions first (Wood Charlesworth & Rodwell, 1997), often beginning by asking questions regarding the technology the child uses, what they like to do with it and the logistics for using technology. The method provided the opportunity to grasp the communication styles and concerns of the child and parent. It also captured introductory understandings of how parents mediate their child's technology use, the rules and boundaries around their child's technology activity and family interactions that occur in relation to the child's technology activity. This was then followed up in one-on-one interviews and observations.

One-on-one interviews were undertaken with all parent and child participants to focus on issues that are meaningful to participants and support a diversity of perceptions, rather than being inhibited by expected response categories (Barbour, 2000). When both parents participated in the research they were interviewed together. This grouping highlighted a greater depth of understanding of the sensitivities of this topic for parents. What became apparent when talking to both parents is that often parents disagreed on how they approached their child's technology use. These disagreements were in every joint-parent interview and generally included the frequency and length of child's use and the value of the child using technology. One parent always expressed concern that technology may harm their child. Many parents expressed surprise at some points that their partner expressed. What the parents disagreed on was important data, as was the revelation that many parents stated that they rarely discussed their parenting views on their child using technology.

Building a sense of trust and rapport was highly important in this study. Home visits involve entering the lives of a family (Dickson-Swift et al., 2007) and supporting children and parents to feel at ease and interested in participating in the study. There was a need for logistical awareness that I was a visitor in a busy home of a young family and the requirement of parents to care for their children (for example, toileting, getting them something to eat), while I was in the home. This was in addition to the sensitive nature of the topic this study focused on. What follows is an explanation of three methods that were effectively incorporated into the home visits to address rapport and trust.

Strategies to build rapport and trust and the findings they facilitated

Three methods – Narratives, Self-disclosure and Flexible Home Visit Organisation – were incorporated into data collection and proved to be highly effective for building rapport with parents and children in ways that supported gaining insight into children's technology use. The next section explains how each method was used and the data and findings it facilitated. The aim of this section is to support an insiders' perspective into how I conducted the home visits as a researcher, and insight into decisions in that process.

1. Narratives: parents and child

A well-documented benefit of narratives is that they facilitate nuance in the data (Clandinin & Connelly, 2000), and this was an intention in this study. Some stories occurred naturally in conversations (Riessman, 2008). For children, these stories related to topics such as when they received their iPad as a present, explanation of an activity they did on their device, how technology plays out in the home, purchase of a new app, how someone helped them with their device use and how they selected a new app or device activity. One narrative was by a mother of 6-year-old girl who told me about her daughter's play with Minecraft. The mother explained that to encourage the child's love of architecture the parents would record architecture documentaries on TV and also took their children to visit a new building in the city designed by a famous architect. The mother said of her daughter,

> *she builds these amazing things on Minecraft. . . . Its design gives a way to express what she's thinking . . . technology can be easier than sitting in front of a piece of paper and say 'I'm going to draw the layout of a building,' which can be quite tiresome. You might not start it if it's going to be a big job like that. Where she can come back to it.*
>
> (Mother of girl aged 6 years)

The mother also added that her daughter does not play with blocks or building materials in real life, but was more interested in craft type activities. She explained she had put that interest aside when she went to school, because she kept saying that everything wasn't good enough. In relation to the ease of use the mother added, 'I think technology gives her confidence in herself.'

The child's preference for using Minecraft gave important insight into how technology play is combined with traditional play to enhance the understanding and interest in a topic, how this is driven by the child and how adults can capitalise on it to enhance learning. From a research design perspective, encouraging narratives enhanced a sense of trust for the parent in disclosing this story as part of the research process.

A highly effective line of narrative I initiated with all parents was asking them whether their child had achieved anything on their device that surprised them. This line of questioning was aimed at identifying activities that the child engaged in that stood out to parents as sophisticated activities, or that parents were proud of. Many parents answered 'yes.'

Table 14.3 briefly lists affirmative responses given by parents. The actions the parents were surprised at can be categorised into one or more of the following categories codes:

1. child's independence in technically manoeuvring the device;
2. content the child was creating with their device;
3. dispositions the child demonstrated when using the device (using their device to create content).

One surprise scenario occurred at the time of my family visit. The 18-month-old child from Family 3 (see Table 14.2) used a device for the first time while I was undertaking my family

Table 14.3 Children's technology use that surprised parents

Family	*Family 1*	*Family 3*	*Family 4*	*Family 5*	*Family 8*
Surprise activity by child	3-year-old uses Google voice command independently to search the internet.	18-month-old baby crawled over to the iPad and started swiping. This was the first time he used a device.	6-year-old using YouTube to teach herself how to draw.	6-year-old uses design elements from local architecture to create her own buildings in Minecraft.	2-year-old takes artistic photos and enjoys the beauty she captures in her images.
Category code	1, 3	1	3	2, 3	2, 3

visit. Up until that point the parents had told me that their 18-month-old son had never used any device. The father stated that he considered the boy was too young to do anything constructive on iPad, and 'would probably just destroy it.'

At the time of the boy's first use, the 3-year-old sister had been showing me an animated game with fictional characters that she enjoys playing on her mum's iPad. After her explanation, she left the iPad on the floor of the lounge room and my conversation with the parents and sister continued. The 18-month-old son crawled over to the unoccupied iPad and deliberately swiped an image that had remained on the screen from the sister's game. He looked at us, paused, and then he purposefully swiped another image. The dynamic elements of the game meant that other objects were appearing and music was playing in response to his actions. When this happened, both parents stopped talking to me. After approximately 20 seconds of what appeared to be stunned silence watching their young son, the father stated 'Wow' and looked genuinely surprised by the young boy's actions. The mother appeared to be equally surprised. The deliberate physical actions (swiping and tapping) of the boy when engaging with the device suggest that he had some understanding of the physical actions associated with using that device. He may have simply been copying his sister's actions, however he did not try to perform the same actions on anything apart from the device. To his parents' knowledge, he hadn't replicated these actions previously. It is also possible to suggest at that this moment in time, when the parents were not focused on restricting the child's use, the boy felt comfortable to apply his knowledge.

This 'surprise' scenario initiated a shift in the parents' tone of conversation. Until this point the parents' main line of discussion can be described as defensive and the parents repeatedly stated that the only reason they gave their 3-year-old a daughter an iPad was so that they could have quiet time at home while the younger child had an afternoon nap. While they assured me that the apps or movies she watched on the iPad were suitable for a 3-year-old, they justified the quiet time as being important for the family. After the surprise scenario, the parents became more reflective of the decisions they made with their children and their uses of technology. They were less adamant that the only value of technology for their child was to keep her quiet and occupied, and there was opportunity for my questioning to reach a deeper, more reflective state of why they made the decisions they did and what informed them.

While the 'surprise' narrative did not play out in this way in all families, it was present in families that answered 'yes,' suggesting a tone of positivity and pride in the parents and the child. It supported the shift away from a judgemental stance and supported the collection of outstanding data regarding non-traditional play that children are engaging with on their device, and the learning value of it.

2. *Self-disclosure*

In order to break down hierarchies between myself and the children and parents, I included a reciprocal sharing of personal stories (Liamputtong & Ezzy, 2005). Although many researchers undertake some level of disclosure in research interviews, the intensity and frequency of disclosure may be different in research on sensitive topics (Dickson-Swift et al. 2007). A strategy of self-disclosure was initiated more by accident, however it proved to be effective in helping parents feel at ease, and was developed as a conscious part of the rapport building process with parents early in the study. The level of disclosure was one I felt comfortable with and included talking about children's uses of technology that I have observed, shared understanding of my own experiences as a parent and concerns I observe in parents generally. All self-disclosure expressed a positive and empathic attitude to parenting, children and technology.

This strategy was conducive to parents feel comfortable with me, and at times providing raw accounts of their uncertainty as parents in relation to children's technology use. For example,

> *'I hate being a parent. I really hate it . . . Technology makes it so hard' (Parent of 6, 12 and 15-year-old)*
>
> *'I always feel so guilty when they are on their iPads. Like I'm a bad parent' (Parent of 2 and 4-year-old).*

As the strategy of self-disclosure proved to be very effective in building rapport with parents, I extend this strategy to my discussions with children. This included talking about myself as a mum, talking about my children (and other children I have met) and what they do on their device or are trying to learn to do on their device. I also disclosed aspects of my own technology use. For example, in speaking about how I broke my phone, one child told me how she dropped her iPad on the road. The importance of this disclosure was not the breaking of the iPad, but with further questioning, her explanation of where she was taking her iPad and what she was going to do with it. Self-disclosure created a shared space where the child and I shared our technology experiences. Importantly it supported a child feeling more relaxed, and soon after they often became enthusiastic about showing and telling me about what they do on their device.

Flexible home visit organisational strategies

Time allocated to the home visit proved to be pivotal to building rapport. Sixty-minute home visits were originally planned, however by the second home visit it became evident that 120-minutes was needed to elicit the experiences and understandings of the child and family. None of the families had participated in research prior to this study. For the majority of visits the first 30 minutes of my visit was often formalised by the parents. For example, in all visits, parents had gathered the whole family either at the kitchen table or in the lounge room, to await my arrival. Parents and children were often expecting formal questioning, and parents tried to keep children still, attentive and well-behaved. Families did not start to feel comfortable with the research process until approximately 30 minutes into my visit. Extending visits to 120 minutes was significant for creating comfort, and establishing a degree of trust with parents and children in interviews/observations.

In spending time developing rapport with the child, parents and siblings, I also felt an obligation to stay on for a while after the interview and spend some time with the family (Dickson-Swift et al. 2007). This often included having another cup of tea, spending time playing a game with the child or providing advice on technology issues they were dealing with. While these courtesies are important for rapport maintenance, it also communicated respect for the family's hospitality. For both reasons, home visits of subsequent families spanned 120 minutes, and this is the timeframe families were prepared for.

Other organisational strategies were also used to further build rapport with parents. These strategies acknowledged an understanding of a busy home of a young family, and included:

- Telling parents not to 'clean up' before my visit, which helped communicate that I was not there to 'judge.'
- Explaining I was happy to talk to parents while they were undertaking any family activity, for example, cooking dinner. This often happened during the home visit and conversations when parents were cooking and organising the family were very natural, developed trust and led to some important disclosures by parents.

- I always accepted an offer for a cup of tea or drink. This helped to lessen the formal family set-up awaiting my arrival.
- Visits were audio-recorded using my mobile phone. While video-recording the visits would have allowed me to capture additional aspects including the home, technology organisation, how parents and children interact when together on a device or when a child is on a device, and the child's engagement with technology, this process may have altered their actions and/or impacted on their level of comfort with the research process.

Implications for designing research regarding young children's uses of technology

The design of this research facilitated a greater understanding of how young children use technology at home, factors that influence it and the learning that can develop from technology use. The discussion in this chapter focuses on how some data collection methods were used in home visits to support building rapport and trust and to elicit useful data for the purposes of this study in an area parents can feel uncertainty and/or judged. I found the combination of methods to be highly effective. The step by step design of this study that led to these methods is as follows:

Step 1: Review of the current research and of public debate in the field and identification of knowledge gaps and how these gaps are impairing understanding. The design of a research methodology that respond to these gaps.

Step 2: The identification and acknowledgement of three core factors that may impact upon the collection of data: children were directly involved in talking about and showing me their technology activity; the study took place inside the homes of families; and parents can often feel judged by other adults regarding the extent to which they permit their young child to use technology. These factors emerged from a critical reading of the body of literature available for this field, as well as public debate that surrounds this issue.

Step 3: Combined, these three factors required a research design that acknowledged and was responsive to these factors. While other topics may be regarded as more sensitive and upsetting for participants and researchers, this does not discount the sentiments parents may experiences in regards to this topic. Being a good parent and ensuring that their child has every opportunity in life is a core priority to many parents, and their uncertainty in this area may create a sense of anxiety that must be acknowledged if undertaking research around this topic.

Step 4: Developing recruitment and data collection methods that facilitate a depth of data in relation to this sensitive issue. Building trust and rapport was key to the design of this research. Developing rapport with parents influenced the rapport I developed with their child(ren) and vice versa. For example, if a child saw that I was happily talking to their parent, this contributed to a sense of trust in me.

Issues are often experienced with researchers in this field gaining access to families who are willing to participate. A strength of this study was the snowballing methodology and my genuine positive positioning of technology during recruitment. My commitment to finding the 'good' in children's technology use was complementary to the strategies developed to build rapport and trust with parents and children.

This study was framed to identify the positive learning experiences young children are having with technology in the home and how these can be extended in early childhood education and in the home environment. The approach taken, however, could be modified to examining other topics (including other sensitive topics) involving young children in the home environment. The study also supported greater understanding of the combination of stress, uncertainty and pride that parents experience in relation to their young child's use of technology.

References

Astedt-Kurki, P., Paavilainen, E. and Lehti, K. (2001) Methodological issues in interviewing families in nursing research. *Journal of Advanced Nursing* 35 (2), 288–293.

Barbour, R.S. (2000) The role of qualitative research in broadening the "evidence base" for clinical practice. *Journal of Evaluation in Clinical Practice* 6, 155–163.

Bigum, C. (2002) Design sensibilities and new technologies. In: Snyder, I. (ed.) *Silicon Literacies: Communication, innovation and education in the electronic age*. London: Routledge, 130–140.

Cameron, H. (2005), Asking the tough questions: A guide to ethical practices in interviewing young children. *Early Child Development and Care* 175 (6), 597–610.

Ceglowski, D. (2000) Research as relationship. *Qualitative Inquiry* 6, 88–103.

Chang, R. (2016) Survey: Parents struggle with 'Tech Shaming' and need roadmap to navigate usage. *Transforming Education through Technology*. https://thejournal.com/articles/2016/10/20/survey-parents-struggle-with-tech-shaming-and-need-roadmap-to-navigate-usage.aspx.

Chaudron, S., Beutel, M.E., Černikova, M., Donoso Navarette, V., Dreier, M., Fletcher-Watson, B., Heikkilä, A.-S., Kontríková, V., Korkeamäki, R.-L., Livingstone, S., Marsh, J., Mascheroni, G., Micheli, M., Milesi, D., Müller, K.W., Myllylä-Nygård, T., Niska, M., Olkina, O., Ottovordemgentschenfelde, S., Plowman, L., Ribbens, W., Richardson, J., Schaack, C., Shlyapnikov, V., Šmahel, D., Soldatova, G. and Wölfling, K. (2015) *Young children (0–8) and digital technology: A qualitative exploratory study across seven countries*. JRC 93239 / EUR 27052 / ISBN 978-92-79-45023-5 / ISSN: 1831–9424. Retrieved from http://publications.jrc.ec.europa.eu/repository/handle/JRC93239.

Clandinin, D.J. and Connelly, F.M. (2000) *Narrative inquiry: Experience and story in qualitative research*. San Francisco, CA: Jossey-Bass.

Cocks, A. (2006) The ethical maze: Finding an inclusive path towards gaining children's agreement to research participation. *Childhood* 13, 247–266.

Cohen, L., Manion, L. and Morrison, K. (2007) *Research Methods in Education* (6th edition). London: Routledge.

Davidson, C., Given, L.M., Danby, S. and Thorpe, K. (2014) Talk about a YouTube video in preschool: The mutual production of shared understanding for learning with digital technology. *Australasian Journal of Early Childhood* 39 (3), 76–83.

Dickson-Swift, V., James, E., Kippen, S. and Liamputtong, P. (2007) Doing sensitive research: What challenges do qualitative researchers face? *Qualitative Research* 7 (3), 327–353.

Duch, H., Fisher, E., Ensari, I., Font, M., Harrington, A., Taromino, C., Yip, J. and Rodriguez, C. (2013) Association of screen time use and language development in Hispanic toddlers: A cross-sectional and longitudinal study. *Clinical Paediatrics* 52 (9), 857–865.

Edwards, S., Henderson, M., Gronn, D., Scott, A. and Mirkhil, M. (2017) Digital disconnect or digital difference? A socio-ecological perspective on young children technology use in the home and the early childhood centre. *Technology, Pedagogy and Education* 26 (1).

Eggenberger, S. and Nelms, T. (2007) Family interviews as a method for family research. *Journal of Advanced Nursing* 58 3, 282–292.

Ernest, J., Causey, C., Newton, A., Sharkins, K., Summerlin, J. and Albaiz, N. (2014) Extending the global dialogue about media, technology, screen time, and young children. *Childhood Education* 90 (3).

Freeman, A. (2017) To the parents who give their kids iPads in restaurants. Blog post. https://mom.me/kids/90875-parents-who-give-their-kids-ipads-restaurants/.

Geertz, C. (1973) *The interpretation of cultures*. New York: Basic Books.

Gonzalez, N. (2016). Technology-enhanced-gadgets in the teaching of English as a foreign language to very young learners. *Procedia-Social and Behavioral Sciences* 232, 507–513.

Goodwin, D., Pope, C., Mort, M. and Smith, A. (2003) Ethics and ethnography: An experiential account. *Qualitative Health Research* 13, 567–577.

Graham, A., Powell, M.A. and Taylor, N. (2015) Ethical research involving children: Putting the evidence into practice. *Family Matters* 96, 23–28.

James, A. and Prout, A. (1997) *Constructing and reconstructing childhood: Contemporary issues in the sociology of childhood.* London: Falmer Press.

Jowett, E., Moore D. and Anderson A. (2012) Using an iPad-based video modelling package to teach numeracy skills to a child with an autism spectrum disorder. *Developmental Neurorehabilitation* 15 (4), 304–312.

Liamputtong, P. and Ezzy, D. (2005) *Qualitative research methods.* South Melbourne: Oxford University Press.

Louv, R. (2010) *Last child in the woods: Saving our children from nature-deficit disorder.* London: Atlantic Books.

Mayall, B., (2012) An afterword: some reflections on a seminar series. Children's Geographies 10 (3), 347–355.

McLean, K., Edwards, S., Colliver, Y. and Schaper, C. (2014) Supported playgroups in schools: What matters for caregivers and their children? *Australasian Journal of Early Childhood,* 39 (4), 73–80.

O'Connor, J. and Fotakopoulou, O. (2016) A threat to childhood innocence or the future of learning? Parents' perspectives on the use of touch-screen technology by 0–3-year-olds in the UK. *Contemporary Issues in Early Childhood* 17 (2), 235–247.

Ofcom (2017) Children and parents: Media use and attitudes report. London: Office of Communications. Accessed: https://www.ofcom.org.uk/__data/assets/pdf_file/0020/108182/children-parents-media-use-attitudes-2017.pdf

Palaiologou, I. (2016) Children under five and digital technologies: Implications for early years pedagogy. *European Early Childhood Education Research Journal* 24 (1), 5–24.

Palmer, S. (2007) *Toxic childhood: How the modern world is damaging our children and what we can do about it.* London: Orion.

Plowman, L. (2015). Researching Young Children's Everyday Uses of Technology in the Family Home, *Interacting with Computers* 27(1), 36–46.

Plowman, L. and McPake, J. (2013) Seven myths about young children and technology. *Childhood Education* 89, 27–33.

Radesky, J., Eisenberg, S., Kistin, C., Gross, J., Block, G., Zuckerman, B. and Silverstein, M. (2016) Overstimulated consumers or next-generation learners? Parent tensions about child mobile technology use. *Annals of Family Medicine* November/December (14), 503–508.

Sharkins, K.A., Newton, A.B., Albaiz, N.E.A. and Ernest, J.M. (2016) Preschool children's exposure to media, technology, and screen time: Perspectives of caregivers from three early childcare settings. *Early Childhood Education Journal* 44 (5), 437–444.

Stephens, C. (2016) Editorial. *Early Years* 36 (3), 223–226.

Verenikina, I. and Kervin, L. (2011) iPads, digital play and pre-schoolers. *He Kupu* 2 (5), 4–16.

Terreni, L. (2011). Interactive whiteboards, art and young children. *Computers in New Zealand Schools: Learning, Teaching, Technology.* 23 (1), 78–100.

Wood, E. (2009) Developing a pedagogy of play. In: Anning, A., Cullen, J. and Fleer, M. (eds.) *Early childhood education, society and culture.* London: Sage, 27–39.

Wood Charlesworth, L. and Rodwell, M.K. (1997) Focus groups with children: A resource for sexual abuse prevention program evaluation. *Child Abuse and Neglect* 21 (12), 1205–1216.

15

THE PARENT-CHILD-APP LEARNING ASSEMBLAGE

Scaffolding early childhood learning through app use in the family home

Donell Holloway, Leslie Haddon, Lelia Green and Kylie J. Stevenson

Introduction

The roll out of touchscreen technologies such as smartphones and tablets into the domestic sphere has allowed very young children the opportunity to use digital media. Somewhere around the age of 10 months to 14 months a baby learns to point with his or her forefinger, and is ready to tap and swipe a touchscreen (Holloway et al., 2015). Previously, such very young children needed assistance to use a mouse or keyboard on laptops and PCs. As a result of this new user group, mobile touchscreen devices now have a large choice of child-friendly apps and games that help create relatively straightforward access for infants and pre-schoolers, allowing even the youngest children to go online, or interact with them.

This chapter investigates the complex interplay between pre-school children, their parents, touchscreens and literacy learning apps within the family home. It is written in the context of a project funded by an ARC-Discovery Grant entitled *Toddlers and tablets: exploring the risks and benefits 0–5s face online*, which investigates family practices and attitudes around very young children's internet use in Australia and the United Kingdom. The study draws on the notion that the home is a discrete environment with its own material-discursive practices. Domestic technologies are locales wherein these material-discursive practices are articulated and enacted, and the three-way intra-action with these technologies outlined in this chapter (when a parent co-uses an app with their child), forms a complex learning assemblage that transcends established understandings of adult-child learning practices.

The chapter begins by outlining the conceptual framework and research methods used in this analysis. This is followed by an investigation into the notion of scaffolding and its use within the context of early childhood practices with technology. We go on to argue that, when parents co-use learning apps with their very young children, an instructional assemblage is formed between parental scaffolding, in-built (app) scaffolding and the child. This complex interplay between parent, child and app can be interdependent, complementary or incrementally beneficial in nature, depending on the design affordances of learning apps, as well as reflecting parental attitudes and skill sets in scaffolding their child's learning through technology.

Conceptual framework and research methods

The conceptual framework for this chapter draws on a broad posthumanist approach to education and early literacy (Taylor, 2016); one where careful attention is given to both human and nonhuman bodies and things within the research process, in an effort to devolve the anthropocentric dominance of normative research methodologies and methods (Taylor, 2016). Within this framework, researchers thoughtfully consider "theories and matter in the world (i.e. students, schools, teachers, writing, books, art supplies, plants, digital tools and so forth) in order to create new theories, literacies, methodologies . . ." (Kuby & Rowsell, 2017, p. 287).

Grounded in relational ontology, involving humans, nonhumans and more-than-humans (as in humans-plus-other-entities) (Kuby & Rowsell, 2017), posthumanism takes into consideration the entanglement between humans and other sentient and non-sentient actors. In education, it is concerned with the intra-activity between humans, things, communities, languages and so on; exploring how this active entanglement produces new ways of knowing or, in the case highlighted within this chapter, new ways of 'doing' literacies.

By taking into consideration both human and nonhuman bodies, and by being sensitive to the intra-activity between these bodies, attention can be given to intra-actional elements very often ignored by researchers when using traditional, human-centric approaches to qualitative research. Therefore, in talking about and investigating young children's uses of digital technologies and the contexts in which these technologies are used, researchers, parents, pre-schoolers and digital technologies are seen to interact and be given equal importance – as equivalent research subjects within the research moment. As media studies researchers, we worked with parents and children in their broad domestic contexts (including in- and out-of-home activities, and grandparental and wider-family involvement), to investigate and share the everyday knowledge and strategies that this cohort of technology users has already developed when intra-actively using touchscreen technologies.

The methods used in this chapter are influenced by posthumanist researchers who now argue that posthuman research should be regarded as a methodological framework from which research methods evolve. Therefore, there is not an overly prescribed research design "with predetermined questions and methods of analysis" (Kuby & Rowsell, 2017, p. 287), but rather (like grounded theory research) a broad area of research approaches through which new theories, literacies, methods or methodologies are developed during the research and analytical stage of the project. A central difference, however, between grounded theory research and posthuman research is the emphasis placed on the nonhuman subject and the agency evident within any enactment between nonhumans and humans (Kuby et al. 2017).

Assemblage is a concept initially propounded by philosophers Gilles Deleuze and Felix Guattari in the 1970s and 1980s. Deleuze's conception of assemblage is that it is "a multiplicity which is made up of many heterogeneous terms and which establishes liaisons, relations between them across ages, sexes and reigns – different natures" (Deleuze & Parnet, 1987, p. 69). The commonality involved in an assemblage is that the heterogeneous parts co-function together to form a whole, that operates in synthesis over a certain period of time (Muller, 2015). The educational assemblage described in this chapter contains human (parent and child) and nonhuman (learning app) actants that function together for a certain time. This instructional assemblage (of parent, child and learning app) is a pro tem assemblage with no predetermined hierarchy or permanency.

The qualitative research took place in Perth, Australia and London, UK. It consisted of three stages, which are:

1 In-depth interviews with 21 families (9 in the UK and 12 in Australia). This phase involved interviews with parents, and play-led interviews with their children aged between 0 and 5. Still pictures and/or video recordings were also made during the play-based interviews with children;
2 Participant (parent/older sibling) produced video recordings of children using their touchscreens occurred over the four weeks following the initial interview. This allowed access to areas of everyday life that usually exclude researchers, including moments that young children are engaged with their touchscreens; and
3 A follow up interview, usually occurring when the video recordings were collected.

The interviews and video recordings were then transcribed and analyzed.

This chapter focusses on data from one of the Australian case studies. Despite observing parents and siblings co-using learning apps with their pre-school aged children (either first-hand or in the parent-made videos), the data from this Australian family (with distinct input from the app) clearly illustrates the three-way intra-active entanglement between child, parent and technology.

Cognitive, affective and technical scaffolding: parents, children and apps

First coined in 1976 and used by psychologist Jerome Bruner (1915–2016), scaffolding, as a concept, involves coordinated interaction between an adult and child with the aim of reaching a specific learning goal (Wood et al., 1976). The term scaffolding is quite similar to Vygotsky's zone of proximal development and the terms are sometimes used interchangeably. In terms of technology use, Yelland and Masters (2007) suggest that adults scaffold children's learning in three ways: cognitive scaffolding, affective scaffolding and technical scaffolding. Cognitive scaffolding "helps children solve problems, gain content knowledge and understandings about their world, and involves asking questions, providing directions, expansions on vocabulary and word meanings, repeating and emphasizing words" (Nuemann, 2017, p. 4). Affective scaffolding gives children positive or supportive feedback, and technical scaffolding helps children navigate the tasks on the app (Nuemann, 2017).

The focus child in the highlighted transcript is Scott, who was 2 years and 7 months at the time of the interviews. He lives with his mum, dad and older brothers aged 5 and 8. The family is Anglo-Celtic Australian. Mum is a part time university student and dad works as a fly-in-fly-out mechanic and workshop manager in Kununurra. The older boys own their own tablets while Scott tends to use his mother's iPad and smartphone. The boys Skype with their father on a weekly basis when he is away for work. The family also has an Xbox, a PC and a laptop.

Our research with families of very young children found that parents carry out all three forms of scaffolding when co-using learning apps with their children. The following transcript from Australia highlights the manner in which parents scaffold their very young children's engagement with learning apps. The excerpt is taken from a follow up interview with Kate (AU), mother of Scott (2), Liam (5) and Ben (8). The interviewer asked Kate to talk her through the participant videos she was handing over. Scott, who was the only child at home with his mother at the time, climbed onto Kate's lap, picked up Kate's iPad and turned on his Reading Eggs app.

The research assemblage

The instructional assemblage described in this chapter relied not only on the intra-activity of the parent, child and app but also on the material-discursive conditions at the time of the interview. Scott (2), having taken part in a play-based interview with the same researcher, and having watched his mother being interviewed four weeks beforehand, was aware that these research interactions in his home were about him and his digital world – and that this was a time he could freely use his mother's tablet. Thus, the physical presence of the interviewer as she entered his home signposted for Scott that this was a time that he could play on the iPad. At the same time, proximity to his mother likely engendered further comfort and relaxation in the company of a near-stranger. Indeed, Scott choosing to sit on his mother's lap generated a proxemic arrangement similar to other parent-child-text encounters.

The full transcript indicates that Scott (2) is not directed in any way by the interviewer, who intended to talk with his mother about the videos she had taken. Scott's engagement with the learning app and his mother, although engendered by the presence of the interviewer, was not initiated by adult questioning or direction. By climbing up on his mother's lap with the iPad, and playing on an app while the interviewer entered the house and joined the family circle, Scott was reacting to the physical presence of his mother and the interviewer, adult bodies that (while together) supported and encouraged his digital play. The material-discursive conditions of the interview, therefore, were inductive to Scott initiating engagement with the app, and with his mother, without concern about the extra adult at the table.

Parent scaffolding: the anthropocentric approach

The following transcript excerpt is an example of a normative, anthropocentric approach to research; one where the human voice is given priority over non-human actants. Indeed, non-human actants are often unconsciously dismissed or taken out of transcripts written by researchers and transcribers. For example, noises made by apps during an activity-based interview with a child (who is actually playing on that app) may be mentioned in a transcript as "app playing in background" or similar. Or the friendly dog in the room who facilitates rapport between researcher and child is seen as an interference to the research process – making the interview and transcript seem messy and unfocused.

The following excerpt depicts a three-way conversation between the interviewer, Kate and Scott. The excerpt draws attention to the ways in which the parent scaffolds her child's learning through cognitive, technical and affective scaffolding. It incorporates all humans in the room at the time that Scott was playing his Reading Eggs app, illustrating how normative research frameworks and methods tend to be anthropocentric – concentrating on human-to-human exchanges only.

Parent scaffolding in the parent-child-app learning assemblage

Kate:	(To Scott) Alright, do you want me to turn it up a little bit? (*Kate shows Scott where the touchscreen volume control is.*) It's that one.	Technical scaffolding
Interviewer:	So he doesn't know how to turn the volume up himself?	
Kate:	Oh, he works it out sometimes. (To Scott) You're going the wrong way. There you go. (To Interviewer)	

	He . . . on some apps there's a volume control on it so he mightn't do that, that's why he was stuck.	Technical scaffolding
Scott:	One more, Mum?	
Kate:	(To Scott) *No, the other one's just locking it.*	
Interviewer:	And so when he's on the touchscreen do you sit with him and co-use it sometimes?	
	(Reading Eggs app plays quietly in background as Kate speaks.)	
Kate:	(to Scott) *Doing writing? Can you do the writing?*	Cognitive scaffolding
	(Scott traces a letter with his finger on the iPad screen.)	
Kate:	(to Scott) Can mummy have a turn?	
Scott:	No, mum.	
Kate:	(to Scott) *Yay, you got the letter.*	Affective scaffolding
Interviewer:	So that's the Minecraft video, when they are playing Minecraft together?	
Kate:	That was yesterday. When you've got the volume, they talk about it and it shows what they are doing to each other. I thought you'd like that. It's the first time I'd seen them doing that, yesterday.	
Kate:	(to Scott) *B for baby. What's B?*	Cognitive scaffolding
Scott:	B . . . a B there. (Points to iPad Screen.)	
Kate:	(to Scott) *that's a B there . . . but this is different. This is C. (Sounds out hard C.)*	Cognitive scaffolding
Scott:	C! There.	
Kate:	(to Interviewer) Most of it's Scott.	
Scott:	C is there. D.	
Kate:	*D. D, D, d for dog.*	Cognitive scaffolding
Scott:	dog.	
Kate:	*This is E. E for egg.*	
Scott:	Two.	
Kate:	*No, that's not two, this is an E. Egg.*	
Scott:	Egg.	

In this recording, Kate is captured scaffolding Scott's learning by encouraging, redirecting, correcting and repeating the audio scaffolding on the app. She uses cognitive scaffolding (e.g. that's a B there . . . but this is different. This is C), affective scaffolding (e.g. yay, you got the letter) and technical scaffolding (e.g. you're going the wrong way. There you go.).

The parent/child/app instructional assemblage

Augmenting the previous transcript, the following excerpt incorporates audio of the three-way learning assemblage, highlighting the intra-active entanglement. It expands the conversation to include the Reading Egg app running during the interview. It shows that, at the same time that Kate is supporting Scott's learning through affective, cognitive and technical scaffolding, the app is also scaffolding Scott's learning with affective scaffolding (e.g. you're doing a jolly good job), cognitive scaffolding (e.g. B, B . . . B is for baby) and technical scaffolding (e.g., try again).

App scaffolding in parent-child-app learning assemblage

Kate:	(To Scott) Alright, do you want me to turn it up a little bit? (Kate shows Scott where the touchscreen volume control is.) It's that one.	
Interviewer:	So he doesn't know how to turn the volume up himself?	
Kate:	Oh, he works it out sometimes. (To Scott) You're going the wrong way. There you go. (To Interviewer) He . . . on some apps there's a volume control on it so he mightn't do that, that's why he was stuck.	
Scott:	One more, Mum?	
Kate:	(To Scott) No, the other one's just locking it.	
Interviewer:	And so when he's on the touchscreen do you sit with him and co-use it sometimes? (Reading Eggs app plays quietly in background as Kate speaks.)	
Kate:	(to Scott) Doing writing? Can you do the writing? (Scott traces a letter with his finger on the iPad screen.)	
Kate:	(to Scott) Can mummy have a turn?	
Scott:	No, mum.	
Kate:	(to Scott) Yay, you got the letter.	
Interviewer:	So that's the Minecraft video, when they are playing Minecraft together?	
App:	*Try again.*	Technical scaffolding (app)
Kate:	That was yesterday. When you've got the volume, they talk about it and it shows what they are doing to each other. I thought you'd like that. It's the first time I'd seen them doing that, yesterday.	
App:	*B, B . . . B is for baby.*	Cognitive scaffolding (app)
Kate:	(to Scott) B for baby. What's B?	
Scott:	B . . . a B there. (Points to iPad Screen.)	
Kate:	(to Scott) that's a B there . . . but this is different. This is C. (Sounds out hard C.)	
Scott:	C! There.	
Kate:	(to Interviewer) Most of it's Scott.	
Scott:	C is there. D.	
Kate:	D. D, D, d for dog.	
Scott:	dog.	
App:	*You're doing a jolly good job.*	Affective scaffolding (app)
Kate:	This is E. E for egg.	
Scott:	Two.	
Kate:	No, that's not two, this is an E. Egg.	
Scott:	Egg.	

This audio transcript hints at, but does not capture, the visual scaffolding offered in the app. These visual cues most often provided Scott with affective and technical scaffolding, in the form of mini games as rewards and flashing images and signs to help him navigate the game.

Cognitive scaffolding within well-designed apps for young children uses little text support, preferencing the use of text-to-speech comments and instructions where needed (e.g., B, B . . . B is for baby). Voice instructions are presented at a speed and language level suitable for young children, and instructions are repeated if the child does not respond. Affective scaffolding in app design is afforded through the use of voice reinforcement (e.g., you're doing a really good job) as well as the use of badges, characters, cheering or clapping to indicate positive results. Technical scaffolding in the design of children's apps underpins children's independent navigation of their app. Objects, characters or signs are often animated to signal to children they can be touched and, for children who do not respond as desired, animations or images are used to model the appropriate response (e.g., @@@ through the use of arrows to indicate that the child should use a swipe) (Marsh et al., 2015).

Extensive thought and planning are consequently evident in well-designed apps, but not all apps are created equal. Thus, with some apps, it is not clear what the desired goal of the activity should be, nor necessarily how the child progresses to the next screen, or the next level. Sometimes, the app will let the child know that their response is 'wrong,' but will not offer suggestions or support the correct response, or how to attempt something differently. Sometimes apps are well-designed, but are more suited for an older child than the child currently using it: offering text instructions, for example, when the actual app user at that moment might be a pre-reader. Thus, although the Reading Eggs app was a productive actor in the intra-activity transcribed previously, not all apps would have played such a positive, supportive, scaffolding role.

Discussion and conclusion

Children are using the internet and other digital technologies at a younger and younger age, with an emerging trend of very young children (babies, toddlers and pre-schoolers) using apps on touchscreen tablets. This chapter explored the material-discursive practices of an Australian family's use of touchscreen technologies by analyzing the complex learning assemblages evident when a very young child used a specific app with a parent present. In this example, the parents supported their very young children's learning app use by scaffolding his early attempts at using apps. This scaffolding is carried out in tandem with in-built scaffolding available through the apps, and involves a complex interplay between the parent, the app and the child.

The knowledge produced from this case study reveals the material-discursive reality of digital tool use within a family home. While a normative analysis of this research event could confer agency to both nonhuman and human entities – including Scott – the aim of the analysis, however, is to highlight the enacted agency "that emerges between people and materials, not residing solely in individuals" (Kuby & Rowsell, 2017, p. 291). For example, within this event Scott is not fully agentic when playing with the app, relying both on his mother and the app to provide timely scaffolding. Similarly, his mother is not individually agentic when scaffolding Scott's use of the learning app; she operates in tandem with the in-app affordances. The interaction she facilitates between herself, Scott and the Reading Eggs app is dependent on how Scott responds to any in-app scaffolding, and his response to her attempts at providing support. Further, the app itself is not wholly agentic: it relies on human input in order to function within the transcribed context. Taken together, however, there is an entanglement of intra-activity between the three actants – Scott, Kate and the Reading Eggs app – that generates enacted agency.

The analysis offered here also highlights the increasing imbrication or overlap and interrelationship of humans and technology within educational processes. The combination of parental and in-built scaffolding (demonstrated in the excerpt) demands on-the-spot interpretive skills on the part of children as well as parents. This applies whether or not app instructions need repeating or rephrasing, whether or not further explanation is needed, when and how much praise and encouragement to give, how much or how little technical scaffolding to give, as well as when to be silent to allow the child to process information given by the app.

When parents co-use learning apps with their very young children, they add a layer of scaffolding to the existing in-built scaffolding within the app. In some well-designed apps it is quite possible that this additional medium of instruction is anticipated, expected, prompted-for and accommodated to enrich the experience for both adult and child. In most cases, nonetheless, parents perform and manage a complex interplay between the app, the child and the self, in supporting their children's learning. While this study demonstrates how parental scaffolding and in-built app scaffolding share some similarities (with cognitive, affective and technical scaffolding exhibited by both) further research is needed to examine when and how parental scaffolding and in-built app scaffolding are interdependent, complementary or incrementally beneficial in combination. This is likely to reflect the different affordances and design features of the app, the age of the child concerned and the dispositions and engagement of the parents. It may well be a key characteristic of effective app design is that children's apps incorporate features which support parent scaffolding and active engagement.

While this chapter has focused on learning assemblages within the family home, our findings about the material-discursive reality of children's literacy learning is of particular significance to educators, when they plan and effect their pedagogical practices in early childhood settings. Considering material artifacts (including digital artifacts) as potentially significant actants within literacy learning affords educators new ways of conceptualizing agency and literacy, new ways of understanding literacy learning as an intra-activity between artifacts and humans and new ways of considering the self as part of these learning assemblages. App developers could also benefit from ensuring that their product's environment of expected users incorporates the potentially complex assemblages of human and nonhuman intra-activity that may be evident in the family home and early childhood settings. The parent/child/app assemblage, in particular, might further benefit from flexible in-built scaffolding affordances that can be turned on or off by parent or child – in order to suit an individual child's preferences, as well as the level of scaffolding offered by adults within any learning assemblage. Such affordances could also respond to different characteristics of child users, for example, minority language users, or the specific interests of the child. From an early childhood perspective, they ought also focus on developmentally appropriate, emergent literacy needs of very young children, as opposed to the "school like subskills of reading and writing" (Sari et al., 2015, p. 15).

We have also argued that new research methods are required in order to adequately research, capture and describe the ways in which digital technologies infuse early childhood literacy learning through human and non-human learning assemblages that are intra-active, context-specific and transient in nature. For example, we found that audio and video recordings are rarely effective in capturing the part an app plays in these learning exchanges. Further, as with the exchange just discussed, the auditory tends to be privileged because it is more easily (and cheaply) captured, than the auditory-plus-visual. But the lack of relevant information should be made explicit in such circumstances in order to highlight the true richness of the interaction discussed. In line with this perception, more emphasis needs to be given to observing and recording the app itself as an actant within these learning assemblages (Falloon, 2013).

As researchers we witnessed many instances of parents scaffolding their children's app use – both at the time of the interviews and within the many of the participant videos we received from parents. This parent/child/app interaction is sometimes missed by, or invisible to, other observers. Nonetheless, they offer opportunities for parents and children to enjoy quality interactions around a further crucial everyday activity: technology use. These exchanges are typically made with the child sitting on a parent's lap and, like shared reading experiences, the children enjoyed the social (or bonding) aspects of these exchanges – in which parent, child and artifact (app or book) are intra-actively engaged. One aim of this chapter, therefore, was to showcase an example where the record captured a nuanced and sophisticated interplay between child, adult and app, revealing the richness and depth of this engagement.

References

Berk, L.E. and Winsler, A. (1995) *Scaffolding children's learning: Vygotsky and early childhood education.* NAEYC Research into Practice Series, Volume 7, ERIC.

Deleuze, G. and Parnet, C. (1987) *Dialogues.* Tomlinson, H. and Habberjam, B. (trans.). New York: Columbia University Press.

Falloon, G.W. (2013) Young students using iPads: App design and content influences on their learning pathways. *Computers & Education* 68, 505–521.

Gorzig, A. and Holloway, D. (2017 forthcoming) Internet Use. In: Hupp, S. and Jewell, J. (eds.) *The encyclopedia of child and adolescent development.* Hoboken, NJ: Wiley.

Holloway, D.J., Green, L. and Stevenson, K. (2015) Digitods: Toddlers, touch screens and Australian family life. *M/C Journal* 18 (5).

Kuby, C.R. and Rowsell, J. (2017) Early literacy and the posthuman: Pedagogies and methodologies. *Journal of Early Childhood Literacy* 17 (3), 285–296.

Kuby, C.R., Rucker, T.G. and Darolia, L.H. (2017) Persistence (ing): Posthuman agency in a Writers' Studio. *Journal of Early Childhood Literacy* 17 (3), 353–373.

Leong, D. and Bodrova, E. (1996) *Tools of the mind: The Vygotskian approach to early childhood education* (2nd edition). Cranbury, NJ: Pearson Education.

Marsh, J., Plowman, L., Yamada-Rice, D., Bishop, J., Lahmar, J., Scott, F., . . . and Piras, M., (2015) Exploring play and creativity in pre-schoolers' use of apps: Final project report. *Technology and Play.*

Merchant, G. (2015) Apps, adults and young children: Researching digital literacy practices in context. In Jones, R., Chik, A. and Hafner, C. (eds.) *Discourse and digital practices: Doing discourse analysis in the digital age.* Abingdon: Routledge, 144–157.

Müller, M. (2015) Assemblages and actor-networks: Rethinking socio-material power, politics and space. *Geography Compass* 9 (1), 27–41.

Neumann, M.M. (2017) Parent scaffolding of young children's use of touch screen tablets. *Early Child Development and Care,* 1–11.

Sari, B., Takacs, Z. and Bus, A. (2015) *What are we downloading for our children?* DIGILITEY http://digilitey.eu/wp-content/uploads/2015/09/Apps-for-young-children-across-four-European-countries.pdf.

Soderman, A.K., Gregory, K.M. and O'Neill, L.T. (1999) *Scaffolding emergent literacy: A child-centered approach for preschool through grade 5.* Boston, MA: Allyn & Bacon.

Taylor, C.A. (2016) Edu-crafting a cacophonous ecology: Posthumanist research practices for education. In: Taylor C. A. and Hughes, C. (eds.) *Posthuman research practices in education,* New York: Springer, 5–24.

Vygotsky, L. (1978) *Mind in society: The development of higher psychological processes.* Cambridge, MA: Harvard University Press.

Wood, D.J., Bruner, J.S. and Ross, G. (1976) The role of tutoring in problem solving. *Journal of Child Psychiatry and Psychology* 17, (2), 89–100.

Wood, E., Petkovski, M., De Pasquale, D., Gottardo, A., Evans, M.A. and Savage, R.S. (2016) Parent scaffolding of young children when engaged with mobile technology. *Frontiers in Psychology,* 7.

Yelland, N. and Masters, J. (2007) 'Rethinking scaffolding in the information age. *Computers & Education* 48 (3), 362–382.

16

THIS IS THE STUFF THAT IDENTITIES ARE MADE OF

Children learning with grandparents and other elders

Rachel Heydon and Xiaoxiao Du

A narrative framing of literacy

My (Rachel's) grandfather moved into a retirement home around his 95th year, and the first time my seven-year-old son, Oliver, and I went to visit him there, I entered with a lump in my chest. Papa Gene was a creature of habit whom I had always known to have a perfectly orchestrated environment – the kitchen table with his favorite chair, just-right-light, and erasable pens (perfect for crosswords). His knees had gone, the ability to arrange his milieu to support his daily living as a nonagenarian had not, and I didn't know how papa was going to react to being in a new "home" empty of his *stuff.* I also didn't know how to be with papa in such a place. When Oliver and I used to return to papa in the family home, we would just go about our business – work on puzzles, prepare food-and interact *through* these quotidian practices. In the retirement home, I reckoned we'd have to connect in new ways and worried that our communication could shift from authentic to artificial, and with this, our relationships too.

On that first day at the retirement home, Oliver, papa, and I sat in a common area saying the things that families say in these situations, *How was your drive? How was breakfast?* and with each trite query that lump in my chest grew. My son, at a loss for what to do next, pulled out his iPad, asked if there was Wi-Fi, and it was then that I remembered the *transferability* of knowledge generated from research, including what I had learned from my *ethnographically informed case studies* of *intergenerational literacy*: digital tools can be *placed resources* – situationally purposeful and capable of mediating communication and relationship. So, I asked Oliver if he would like to see the house where papa and I lived decades ago, the corollary being asking papa if he would like to see our old street in Detroit, Michigan. Oliver loaded Google Maps. Papa gave him the house address, and away we went exploring the old haunts. The digital images gave way to stories of the past and tri-generations came together.

We begin with papa's story because it has something to say about literacy practices, intergenerational relationships, and the production and mediation of all of this in and through not just people, but artifacts and tools, what we call *literacy constituents*. Recognizing these constituents announces the necessity of multi-dimensional ethnographic methods and foregrounds the data we later share. Next, we relay literature on these topics scaffolded by papa's story.

Framing literacy

Specific literatures concerning literacy provide us an onto-epistemology (what we know literacy to be and how we come to know literacy) which inform our study designs. New research generates ever-more robust conceptualizations of literacy, but presently, most significant amongst these literatures are those that teach, like papa's story, how literacy is

- a situated, socio-cultural practice instantiated in relationships;
- multimodal;
- intergenerationally acquired; and
- connected to artifacts and literacy tools.

Literacies and the socio-cultural

People's literacy practices are purposeful (e.g., to connect with others across distance) and produce effects (e.g., solidify relationships). The value of literacy is contingent on the kinds of "actions and reflections" that it can support "over others" (Arthur, 2012, p. xiii). Values are relevant as literacies are *social practices*, meaning, "Literacy is primarily something people do; it is an activity, located in the space between thought and text . . . in the interaction between people" (Barton & Hamilton, 1998, p. 3). Literacy practices are "observable activities and tasks" (Barton & Hamilton, 2010, p. 8), but they also involve what is not so easily apprehended, such as social and interpersonal relationships and emotions/affect (e.g., Hicks, 2013). Literacy constituents also affect and are affected by the *domains* in which they are situated. Domains are "structured, patterned contexts within which literacy is used and learned", and the "activities within these domains are not accidental or randomly varying: there are particular configurations of literacy practices and there are regular ways in which people act in many literacy events in particular contexts" (Barton & Hamilton, 2000, p. 11). Literacy practices associated with the domain of Oliver's school are different than those in papa's retirement home.

Given the social nature of literacies, *identity* is tied to literacy practices and vital to literacy research (Moje et al., 2009). Identity has been diversely conceptualized, but we have found Pahl and Rowsell's (2005) understanding to be useful; identity is "a way of describing a sense of self that is in practice" (p. 155), such as literacy practice which is social and material.

Literacies and the material

People practice literacies using materials, and the literature abounds with conceptualizations of what Kress (1997) called the *stuff* of literacy. We have found multimodal literacy, artifactual literacy, and the notion of placed resources as interrelated and helpful to our research.

Multimodal literacy

Ethnographic researchers of communication, like Ruth Finnegan, have long attended to literacy's multimodal nature. In 1967, Finnegan detailed how the Limba people of northern Sierra Leone combined oral storytelling, song, and dance to *perform* meaning *with* each other, exemplifying how literacy practices can involve transactions across the roles that people hold in the meaning-making process (e.g., audience, performer). Meanings are generated from the interpolation between persons (Finnegan, 2015) connected to domains, using the stuff they have at their disposal. In papa's story, in Michigan, he, Oliver, and I (Rachel) drew on an iPad, Wi-Fi, app, and our voices to communicate multimodally, just as Finnegan's (1967) participants in Africa accessed local materials for their meaning making (e.g., bodies, voice). The stuff of literacies is tied to what is available, what has been/can be done with this stuff vis-à-vis the socio-cultural and historical situation, what this stuff *affords* (i.e., allows), and what its *constrains* (i.e., what it can't accomplish) (Jewitt & Kress, 2003).

Artifactual literacies

Multimodal literacy provides an umbrella for conceptualizing the stuff of literacy, and under this umbrella Pahl and Rowsell's (2010) *artifactual literacies* conceptualizes the role of artifacts in people's everyday lives. Artifacts are physically distinct entities that are "created, found, carried, put on display, hidden, evoked in language or worn", and are contextually "valued" (p. 2). Artifacts, like papa's old house, are "infused with meanings" and "tell stories, hold memories, and evoke identities connected with their existence" (Bartlett & Vasudevan, as cited in Pahl & Rowsell, 2010, p. vii). Artifacts can travel and have been found to link students' home and school (Pahl & Rowsell, 2010); however, artifacts can be connectors for more than students. In papa's story, his house was digitized, enabling it to move across the domains of the domestic to the retirement home and cross geographic boundaries (e.g., suburban and metro Detroit). In movements like these, the literature has identified how artifacts are implicated in relationship and identity formation, and how thinking artifactually can support researchers to unite the multimodal and social aspects of literacies and create a vehicle for gathering related data from participants (e.g., Gichuru, 2013).

Placed resources

Literacy tools (which can include artifacts) can be *placed resources* (Prinsloo, 2005). Prinsloo's research into literacy and computers in minority and majority worlds teaches that the value, uses, and affordances of media (like iPads) are situational. Literacies cannot "exist outside the context which gave rise to them" as there is "no abstract invariant which remains 'the same' from one context to another" (p. 90): a tool (or text) in one place does not necessarily mean the same in another. The house that papa, Oliver, and I explored on the iPad in the retirement home would not have been functionally the same if viewed by a surveyor in a government office.

The above has implications for the literacy practices that people and domains value. Prinsloo (2005) argued that "situated, distinctive types of meanings" that are created from texts, "are shared by groups of people who sustain them as part of their collective social practices" (p. 90). Specific modes and media are thus "only contextually functional, rather than inherently functional", and "the signs of communication (spoken, written, visual, gestural, artefactual) are . . . always signs of social value in contexts of inequality" (p. 90). Blommaert's (2002) notion of *indexicality* enters here, with Prinsloo (2005) reminding that resources

> that are functional in one particular place [can] become dysfunctional as soon as they are moved into other places. This process of flows creates difference in value, for the resources are being reallocated different functions. The indexical links between signs and modes of communication on the one hand, and social value scales allowing, e.g. identity construction, status attribution and so forth – these indexical links are severed and new ones are projected onto the signs and practices.
>
> *(p. 96)*

Through indexicality, the social in *literacy as a social practice* includes people's "social position (age, gender, economic class) and the related dispositions that [they] carry as embodied history and practices, together with other members of" their "affiliation groups" (p. 90).

Literacy across generations

People acquire and practice literacies across generational lines. The focus of the literacy literature concerning skipped generations has been on children learning *from* grandparents (e.g., Gregory, et al., 2004). Much of this research is indebted to Rogoff's (1990) idea of *guided participation*, where children acquire literacies as they engage with caregivers within shared literacy events. Grandparents have been cited as such caregivers (Kelly, 2004), and there is documentation of children practicing literacy in more than one language, thanks to them. Accentuating multilingual reading, for example, Gregory (2008) found grandparents as "mediators of literacies" (p. vii) and how, working across generational and linguistic lines, children acquired "membership of different culture, language and literacy groups in different contexts or domains of their lives" (p. 25). This research involved families that had recently migrated to London, UK, and the specificity of the people with whom Gregory was working is important, given what the literature says about intergenerational interaction.

Research into intergenerational contact has found that interaction between skipped generations is variable (Bangerter & Waldron, 2014). Differences in frequency and quality of contact are correlated with factors such as culture and ethnicity (Fuller-Thomson, et al., 2014), socio-economic status, and immigration status (e.g., Milan et al., 2015). For example, in retirement communities in the United States, Holladay and Seipke (2007) found limited interaction between grandparents and grandchildren. Papa's story alone hints that maintaining relationships in a retirement environment can be difficult. Still, increased intergenerational contact has been recorded in situations like grandparent-headed households in England and Australia where kinship care is mandated over foster care (Bell & Romano, 2015), and multigenerational households in places where there are housing shortages, like Nunavut, Canada (Milan et al., 2015).

Nascent research has been investigating the benefits of intergenerational interactions to adults, destabilizing the idea that children are the only learners in these relationships. Many of these studies have considered intergenerational interactions outside of family, such as in intergenerational learning programs. Findings include that these programs can

- expand people's literacy options across the lifespan (Heydon, 2013);
- help participants forge relationships through literacy practices (Heydon et al., 2018); and
- create opportunities for participants to see themselves as competent communicators (Heydon, 2007).

Ethnography and literacy

Ethnography can support the conceptualization of literacy just identified. Ethnography originated in Western anthropology, entered the field of sociology in the twentieth century, and has gained traction in myriad disciplines (Hammersley & Atkinson, 2007). There is no single definition of ethnography, though most commonly it involves "the intensive and continuous study of a setting or a small group over . . . time . . . to *gain detailed insights* of the participant setting or group", and an "in-depth analysis of *everyday practices* of given groups in *naturalistic* settings" (Mukherji & Albon, 2010, p. 71, italics ours). Italicized are terms that resonate with classic works of literacy-focused ethnographies (e.g., Dyson, 1996; Street, 1995) and render ethnography commensurate with the view of literacy we shared.

Ethnographic methods allow a close-up view of socially and culturally informed phenomena (like literacy) and their constituents. Schensul and LeCompte (2016) encapsulated the methods thusly: "ethnography's principal database is amassed [during] human interaction: direct observation, face-to-face interviewing and elicitation, audiovisual recording, and mapping the networks, times, and places in which human interactions occur" (p. xxii). Participant observation, interviews, and the collection of artifacts and texts are also foundational methods of data collection (e.g., Mills & Morton, 2013). Ethnographic data are sometimes erroneously considered to be solely qualitative, but all forms of data can make up a data set; for instance, if an ethnographic study to understand iPad use was conducted in papa's retirement home, researchers might time people's usage yielding numerate data. A variety of methods have also been developed to deal with virtual social spaces (e.g., Kozinets, 2010).

No matter its methods, researchers must come to terms with ethnography's colonial history which has (at best) essentialized phenomena (Heath & Street, 2008). Iterations of ethnography have emerged to recuperate it from its colonial past. The *critical ethnography* movement, for example, evolved out of a dissatisfaction with *classic ethnography*. In classic ethnography, researchers enter a foreign field to learn *about* the other (Jamal, 2005) and never question "language and interpretation, the knowledge/power nexus, and the sovereign 'logocentric' discourses of modern scientific rationality" (McLaren, 2006, p. 77), three of the most prominent concerns raised about ethnography. In contrast, the commonplaces of critical ethnography promote research that seeks to ameliorate inequities and "acknowledge and discuss the limits of its own claims" (Jamal, 2005, p. 234). Yet there is a caution: all ethnographic studies "tend to shift the balance of power in favor of those who initiate such studies" (p. 232).

For decades, feminist poststructuralists like Wolf (1992) have wrestled with power differentials and representation in ethnography, attempting to devise theoretical and rhetorical strategies to recover the methodology's affordances. Lather (2010) too has toiled in this vein while arguing that ethnography is not the only methodology needing de-colonizing work. She forwarded that knowledge production and questions of epistemology (hence research) are *always* questions that involve power; there are no methods or theories that can magically extricate researchers from these complexities. Lather (2017) has advocated for vigilant reflexivity from project inception through dissemination, including researchers accounting for how they are implicated in knowledge production. This reflexivity is accompanied by a shift in positioning from researchers learning *about*, to learning *from* (Todd, 2003) or *with* (Heydon, 2007) participants, and the relinquishing of researchers being able to know absolutely (Lather, 2007).

In what Lather (2013) called the "afterward", the period following the crisis of representation in research, we eschew pigeon-holing ethnography to talk about *ethnographically informed approaches*, where researchers (re)invent theories and methods to grapple with power and knowledge and suit the needs and complexities of the phenomena-at-hand. We now illustrate our attempts at such approaches, providing traces of data that connect to the themes of this chapter.

Illustration 1: children learning with grandparents

In this case study using ethnographic methods, we drew upon the conceptions of literacy discussed earlier, and sought to understand intergenerational meaning-making across domains and languages. We asked,

- How might conceptions of literacy and literacy learning differ across cultures, languages, and generations?
- How might culturally and linguistically diverse (CLD) children negotiate these conceptions in their literacy practices and identity options?

Participants were seven first-grade Chinese children and their families[1] living in Ontario, Canada. Data were collected in the children's homes, schools, and community settings over eight months. Data collection included participant observation, informal and semi-structured interviews, and documentation of literacy artifacts, practices, and events. Interpretational analysis was employed to "find constructs, themes, and patterns . . . to describe and explain the phenomenon being studied" (Gall et al., 2007, p. 466) (i.e., the children's literacy practices). Narrative constructions of data were part of the analysis strategy, given that such compositions can help researchers and readers "see how knowledge is constructed in the everyday world" (Riessman, 2008, pp. 13–14). Narratives can further relate the complexity of data while unfolding its intricacies (Hicks, 2002).

For the purposes of this chapter, we focus on how six-year-old Brian negotiated his literacy practices and identity options to maintain a relationship with his grandfather. We narrativize two events where evidence of Brian's grandfather's influence figures prominently: a debrief of a trip to China and a video-call during a subsequent home visit. The narrative reveals how Brian played with the identity of good (Chinese) grandson in the face of poor identity options from the (Canadian) school, to maintain a relationship with his grandfather.

Brian and his grandfather

Brian was an only-child, born in Canada to Chinese parents. His father was a doctoral student in science at a Canadian university and his mother worked part-time in an administrative role. Brian was identified by the school as an English as a Second Language student who needed extra support to meet reading requirements; in contrast, his parents characterized Brian as a curious child who liked to read a variety of books.

During the school's winter break, Brian and his parents traveled to China to visit Brian's grandparents. Before leaving, Brian excitedly told me (Xiaoxiao) "I haven't been back for years. Finally, I get to go back and see my relatives".

Brian's mother signaled the importance of school for the family, saying in Mandarin[2] "Yes, we have not gone back for years. As he is still in Grade 1, we like to take him to visit my family members. When he is in Grade 3, he will be busy with school, and it will be difficult to find time to go back".

When home visits for the study resumed following the trip, Brian's mother conveyed some cultural differences concerning school expectations, how they affected Brian's relationship with his family, and suggested how Brian was processing these differences. For instance, after talking about the good time they had visiting with family, Brian's mother lowered her voice and said in Mandarin, "When I was back, I realized again Canada is different from China"-I asked in Mandarin about the differences and Brian's mother explained (in Mandarin):

> When we had the family dinner together, [Brian] was so happy to see his cousins. But when he asked them to play together, they said they did not have time and had more important things to do. They left the dinner early as they had to go for their tutoring sessions. He was confused why they had homework and extracurricular classes. He also did not know how to answer questions from his uncles and aunts: How did you do at school? Did you get good marks? Did you earn a good place in exams? I had to explain to my family, saying that we do not really have those exams nor rank students based on exam results. In China, both parents and children feel huge pressure in education. They need to enter top schools by getting good marks in exams and they also need to perform well in extracurricular activities. Since there are so many children learning to

> play piano and violin, his cousins learned to play erhu, the traditional Chinese music instrument. Luckily, Canada is a better place with less pressure.

Brian overheard and supplied, "I do not think they really want to learn erhu while I guess they had to". And he added (in Mandarin), "My grandfather and uncles told me that only those who study well can have a successful life in the future".

Brian's mother smiled and said (in Mandarin), "I know you will work hard". Brian silently looked up at his mother and slowly nodded his head.

Xiaoxiao, slightly shifting gears posed (in Mandarin), "Did you have fun at your grandparents'?"

Brian grinned and said (in Mandarin), "Grandma cooked a lot of delicious food for me. (switched to English) Grandpa liked to talk about study and read to me. (switched to Mandarin) He gave me a red envelope with money telling me to buy some books and study well".

Xiaoxiao probed (in Mandarin), "What . . . books did you buy?"

Brian responded (in English), "I told my grandpa, I will buy some English books in Canada".

Brian's mother added (in English), "He will be happy if you can do well with your school reading". Then, shifting to Mandarin, Brian's mother shared that Brian's grandparents were retired professors from a top university in Beijing, and they emphasized education. Brian received money from his grandparents with the message for Brian to try his best to do well at school, and they would be proud of him.

When Brian's mother left the room, Brian shared that he did not plan to buy books with his grandfather's money. He had only said this so that he could keep the money and signal that he is "a good boy". Brian shared that he enjoyed listening to his grandfather's Chinese stories, but he did not enjoy his grandfather's lectures on "deep" ancient Chinese literature nor the "big" talk his grandfather gave him about performing well at school.

Brian said he was a "a good boy" who displayed this by always showing respect to adults, especially his grandfather. He stressed that in China, "I listened carefully to grandpa's talk even though I did not really understand all the names he said in that thick book. Grandpa was a good teacher and I needed to be a good student". Brian confessed that he did not tell his grandparents that the school found him to be underachieving in reading, as he did not want to disappoint.

I asked Brian why he thought he was not good at reading at school as his parents said he liked to read, and the study identified him going to the library regularly. Brian answered that he had received a low score in the Developmental Reading Assessment (Beaver, 2001) at school, and thus his teachers only allowed him to select lower leveled books to read. He added that he liked to borrow books from the public library for home as he could choose what he wanted.

Following Brian over time and across domains allowed for data that spoke of Brian's literacy practices as diverse. Some literacy events were opportunities for Brian to construct/present himself as a capable communicator, who could use multiple languages and modes to express his ideas with different people in different places. One such example is an event where Brian played on the online reading program, *Raz-kids* (Learning A-Z, 2017).

During a home visit, Brian was at his father's computer. His mother related that the school ESL teacher recommended Brian work on Raz-kids to improve his reading. The school claimed that this program would improve Brian's vocabulary and reading comprehension.

Raz-kids was structured through modules leveled according to reading difficulty. Modules offered opportunities to listen to a story, read a story, and complete a reading comprehension quiz to move on. It incentivized completion of the modules by providing users with tokens to trade for items for a digital room. Brian shared that he had designed a space room where he was a captain (see Figure 16.1), but he needed to complete more quizzes to win the items he wanted: "If you answer questions correctly, you will get more stars and more stars mean more points and stuff". Brian wanted to demonstrate the program. Fluidly, he clicked on the browser, opened *Baidu* (a Chinese search engine), typed what he was looking for, maneuvered through the Chinese and English search results to locate the Raz-kids login page, and entered his username and password.

I said, "Wow", then in Mandarin, "You remember all of this". Brian replied (in Mandarin), "I have played this game quite often, so I . . . remembered this information". Brian pointed to the letter K on the screen and said (in English) "See, I am at level K right now and soon I will move up to level L".

The data suggested that Brian listened to some of the stories, but read none. He preferred to directly take the quizzes, which the program allowed, and given the multiple-choice format of the quizzes, Brian could score sufficiently high to collect his tokens, the fruits of which he showed-off.

While he was on Raz-kids, Brian's grandfather sent an invitation for a video-call to Brian's mother's smartphone. Brian's grandfather routinely called at the same time every week. When Brian received the call, he ran to show his grandfather his space room, holding the phone to the computer screen. He also told his grandfather (in Mandarin) that he got all the quiz questions right and received "many stars" as his "reading rewards". He clarified that he was working on reading, not playing video games. Brian's grandfather said he would call back later so as not to interrupt Brian's learning.

Illustration 2: children learning with elders

This study drew on the same conceptions of literacy to investigate digital tools in an intergenerational art class. The study asked,

- How did digital tools function as placed resources?
- And how did they mediate (or not) relationships, identity options, and literacy learning opportunities?

We provide a narrative example of two literacy events constructed from the data that suggest how the research team (led by Rachel) could respond to these queries, because our ethnographic approach allowed us to track the situated literacy practices of the participants and the stuff involved. The study was an *exploratory case study using ethnographic tools* with the case being the attempt to integrate digital media into an intergenerational art program.

Participants were eight elders and seven children (ages three to six) who were part of a Unitarian Universalist congregation in the United States. The congregation's Education Director described that a prime goal for the program was to "buil[d] relationships" between the children, elders, and "their families". The classes ran once a week for six, 1.5-hour sessions, culminating in an art show. The class was headed by an experienced intergenerational art teacher who had been working with the researchers to integrate digital media into her classes.

Ethnographic data were collected for the duration of the program. Data sources included the teacher's lesson plans and written and audio recorded reflections of the classes, participants' digital portfolios, photos of observations and program artifacts, field notes, audio and video recordings of participants during the program, informal conversations with participants during text-making, and semi-structured interviews with elders, children's caregivers, and the Education Director.

Data analysis was inductive and guided by the research questions (Dyson & Genishi, 2005). The units of analysis were bounded by the class's literacy events. Themes were identified through a juxtaposition of data sources (e.g., images of participant-generated texts next to transcriptions of field observations) and areas of resonance and dissonance were noted (Pahl, 2007). Member checks were conducted with key participants. Data were triangulated by drawing on multiple data sources and comparing them against the literature, and checking findings amongst members of the research team. We share a sample of findings using a narrative devised from a diversity of study data.

Mia and Dejon

It's the second half of the third art class. Four-year-old Mia is at a table with adult participant Dejon beside her. As per the day's lesson on charcoal as a medium, value as a concept, and underwater as a theme, Mia has just completed a drawing of a mermaid. She is working with Dejon to take a photo of it to put in her portfolio. The program invites participants to keep a digital portfolio to document any aspect of art class in whatever mode they want. The portfolios are made on the Book Creator app (Red Jumper, 2014) and saved on iPads under each participant's name. The app allows participants to create e-pages where they can insert multimodal data (e.g., photographs, video, print) and organize pages through color, font, framing, and the like (Heydon et al., 2017). Dejon has just helped Mia take a photo of her drawing. Mia wanted to shoot the artwork from above, so Dejon helped her stand on a chair. Now he's helping her down and asks of the photo she's taken, "Are you going to use this one or retake?"

Mia, whose mother told us she has an "Android tablet at home" and is thus able to focus on the task rather than the tools, indicates "Use" and presses the button on the screen to do so.

"Now you want to put a name on it?" Dejon inquires. Mia nods. "How do we put a name on it?" Dejon wonders.

"Ah, I don't know", Mia answers, though she is looking at the screen and ready to make an exploratory attempt. Dejon, who is holding the iPad, taps the screen where Mia has just pointed.

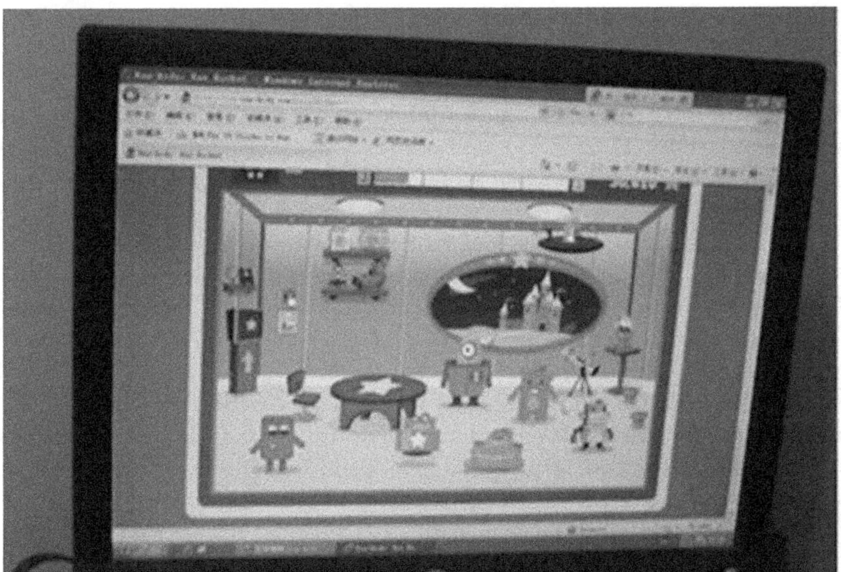

Figure 16.1 Brian's Space Room

"Add text", Dejon reads the menu that's popped up, and Mia gently swipes Dejon's hand away to press herself.

Mia is wondering about what letters she needs. "This one?" she asks Dejon. She looks at the keyboard and stretches out the sounds in the word of the title she wants: "AIR-EE-UL". Mia enunciates the word again, looking at Dejon, and in a staccato, says emphatically, "Ariel", making eye contact with Dejon. Dejon does not understand that Mia is saying the name of the Disney mermaid she talked about with a member of the research team when she was making her drawing, and he listens to discern what she's saying. He holds the iPad between him and Mia, and Mia voices the sounds in the name again, directing Dejon with her body language to type. In exaggerated tones, Mia declares, "AIR" and points to the keyboard. Thinking Mia is saying the letter "L", Dejon taps "L", and Mia moves to the next sound, "EE"; Dejon types "E"; "UL" says Mia, to which Dejon types an "L". Though the letters spell LEO, not Ariel, Mia is satisfied seeing that there is a letter for each phoneme. While she was stretching the word, "AIR-EE-UL", Mia moved her pointer finger in the air to each phoneme. When Dejon was finished typing, she announced "Ariel" and waved her finger in an arc, as though blending the sounds. Now, Mia moves her body in front of the iPad, looks at the screen contentedly, and says "Ariel" again.

Dejon wonders of the freshly typed LEO, "Now where do you want it?" Mia drags the word down and over to position it on the page. "Wow, that's nice", encourages Dejon. Mia proffers the iPad to Dejon, the two of them with their eyes trained on the image. Dejon says, "Now . . .".

Mia leans in close, "Name. I want my name, name, name". The duo touches the iPad at the same time.

Dejon reminds, "Your name is on there", as Mia had written her name earlier in pencil on the original drawing.

With Dejon close, Mia pulls up the keyboard again, and says, "I want to write my name". Mia wants a digital name too.

Dejon utters, "M-I-A", pointing to the letters. Mia types. "M-I-A, Mia, OK", finishes Dejon. Mia and Dejon touch the screen one at a time to drag the name under LEO (see Figure 16.2).

Later, at the art show, the iPads are out for portfolio viewing. Original artwork is also on the walls. Mia loads her portfolio. She stands in front of the iPad; her mother is close behind her looking down. Mia's hands are on the iPad. She's in control, interacting with the device so that she can proudly show her mother her Leo/Ariel/Mia text.

Our ethnographic data also allows us to tell of other (parts of the) story/stories, uncovering motivations for practices. Through the data over time, we learned that Dejon participated in art class for reasons that were meaningful to him but hard to articulate. He was there to make art and to do so *with* the children. In the class just showcased, for example, Dejon worked with Mia, but he also made his own artwork which he documented in his portfolio (see Figure 16.3).

A published poet, when we asked Dejon about how he felt when he made art, he said it gave him a "feeling of accomplishment . . . when I create something I like". When we asked him how he felt when he was in intergenerational art class, he said,

> I've matured in that . . . vein; my first day here I went home kind of feeling like . . . it just didn't matter and I would come and . . . draw stuff . . . and then somewhere in the second week working with Sam [a child participant] I started seeing more clearly that there was something important going on here and I wasn't sure what, but I wanted to be a part of that, so that's why I came back.

Dejon intoned that he noticed something important about art class, and it was connected to making art with a child.

Figure 16.2 Charcoal drawing page from digital portfolio

Later, when we asked Dejon if there was someone or something that had influenced his art, we were given some more hints about what was important to him in the program:

> ... everything hinges around my grandpa ... I'm very clear about my ... time with my grandpa. He was very tactile. I have a story of him coming up and waking me up and I have eight brothers and sisters and he woke *me* up ... that's important to me. He ... brought me downstairs and got me dressed ... gave me a bowl and a spoon and he took a bowl and a spoon and I carried the sugar and he carried the milk and we went out into the middle of the forest and ... he had created this area that he liked to go sit ... that was ... surrounded with blueberries and we would sit ... and just reach out ... and pull ... [blueberries]. These blueberries were ... almost black and they had ... dew that had formed all over them and they were cold ... and he had me just pick them ... put them in my bowl and then we would sit there and we would sprinkle sugar on them and eat them and it's just the whole scene of the tall trees, and the early morning and I could see the light coming from the sun coming up. ... It was probably the keystroke in my life that one morning, and I think it allowed me to sit and be with colours, and

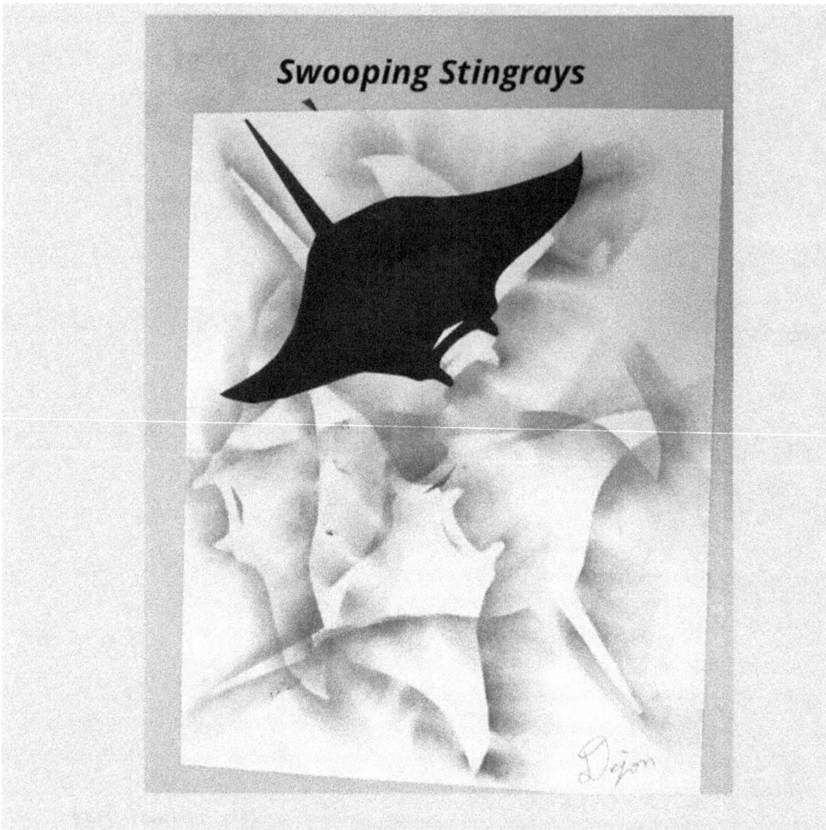

Figure 16.3 Page from Dejon's digital portfolio

> shapes, and tastes, and touches and that sort of a thing . . . shortly after that he died. He was eighty-six when I was five.

At a similar age to the children in class, Dejon experienced the "keystroke" of his life, an intergenerational experience that he relayed with attention to the senses and created a lesson in noticing.

The lesson of noticing is one that Dejon wanted to share with the children in class – we saw this with Mia, as Dejon paid close consideration to what she wanted to make and what she needed to make it with – hands and heads close together over the iPad. We asked Dejon, "What do you like about making art with the children?"

"I . . . like to study myself and that gives me a real opportunity to see [the children's] needs to be paid attention to and then see my needs to be paid attention to".

Dejon defined these needs as "the need to be paid attention to . . . for someone to say, 'That's nice, that's good'". He expressed that the need to have attention in relation to one's meaning making is not something that goes away:

> I often don't even consider that [being paid attention to is] important for me anymore I'm seventy-five [but] . . . That's not true, the needs are there and I can sense them,

> especially when I'm working with children and I can see that I can dominate them and coopt their work so quickly and so easily and I wouldn't want someone doing that to me . . . so then I . . . back off and support their work . . . that story of my grandpa . . . that still rules my life.

Dejon suggested that with the children, as seen with Mia, he tried to be respectful of their agency and support them as they wanted to be supported – something he still values.

And just as Mia undertook her portfolio seriously and showed it to others, so too did Dejon take art seriously. He told us about writing a book and the sacrifices he made to do so: "I worked so hard and I put everything I am into it. I was ready to starve to death if I had to, to get my book out 'cause I wanted someone else to see that I can express myself". Dejon wanted this for the others in art class, "I wanted to do that for someone else".

And he surely did it for Mia. A young four-year-old, we recorded the teacher initially saying Mia might be a bit young to "get much out of" art class. However, the teacher changed her mind when she viewed Mia's Ariel.

Ethnographic lessons

We wrote this chapter with the prime aims to convey the complex, situated, material, relational, and intergenerational nature of literacies and to demonstrate how ethnographic approaches to research correspond with such a framing. Rachel's story of communicating with her grandfather set the tone for our conceptualization of literacy and provided a scaffold for a discussion of relevant literature. We then illustrated the apt fit between conceptualization and investigation of literacy through storied traces of research. In being in the home and school with Brian, following his practices, and talking with him and those close to him, we discovered in the first study how a child forged literacy identities within/against options created from myriad actors, notably his grandfather. Being embedded in art class, cataloguing modes, media, and related practices, and closely attending to what was being made, how, and why, study two found how people at opposite ends of life support each other to make meaning. These illustrations are only suggestive of the myriad methods and findings from these studies, but positioned in this chapter, they offer an entrée for thinking about the necessity of commensurability within researchers' *literacy onto-epistemology* – what they mean by literacy and how they come to know literacy.

The stories of Brian, his grandfather, Mia, and Dejon speak to the affordances of ethnographic approaches, including the learning opportunities they create for researchers. As illustrated through the data, we were able to learn, for example, of the intergenerational quality of literacies, whether generations are physically together (like Mia and Dejon), digitally connected (like Brian and his grandfather), or evoked by memory (like Dejon and his grandfather).

The data in Brian's illustration provided us a view of a CLD child negotiating competing messages about literacies from across domains (e.g., his teacher and grandfather). Apparent in the example are the divergent conceptions of literacy and literacy resources that emanated from specific domains, cultures, languages, and generations. We found, for instance, that the school defined literacy achievement as the ability to score well on a test of reading English leveled texts or an online quiz of reading comprehension, whereas Brian's grandfather's idea of literacy required knowledge of classic Sino-literature.

Brian's illustration also conveys how a CLD child negotiated these conceptions and molded his literacy practices. We see, for instance, Brian's ingenuity in navigating modes and resources (e.g., print books, digital animation in an online environment), languages and scripts (e.g., English and Mandarin Chinese as recorded in code switching during home visits and his use of multilingual websites), and foiling the school system that called him inadequate (e.g., winning stars without reading). We witnessed, through ethnographic means, how Brian moved within his available identity options as an agile communicator who understood what was expected of him, and blended these expectations to suit his purposes and maintain relationships (e.g., good grandson).

Likewise, the ethnographic data in our second illustration makes visible the literacy constituents of intergenerational art class, and how they functioned in concert to mediate relationships (e.g., between Mia and Dejon, Mia and her mother), literacy learning (e.g., Mia and Dejon both negotiating each other, print literacies, digital media, and traditional media like charcoal to design and execute texts), and identity options (e.g., Mia as a competent communicator, Dejon as an artist and ally to children). The study design also provided knowledge of the tools of art class and their use as placed resources; charcoal, iPads, and other media helped Mia carry out her motivations, and within the context of her intentions, these tools served as a mediator in the development of her relationship with Dejon. Co-construction of the portfolio page with the iPad required each person to draw on his/her strengths; for example, Mia had the title for the drawing, Dejon the letter knowledge, rendering each a necessary part of the whole. Plus, the nature of the resources demanded physical proximity (e.g., heads close and fingers touching), mirroring/mediating the developing relationship.

We additionally learned how Dejon's relationship with his grandfather, facilitated by materially rich practices (think blueberry picking in the forest), informed his view of children (persons who wish to enact their agency), literacy practices (writing books/poems), view of literacy (sensory-rich), and informed his identity options (e.g., someone who helps without taking over). All these beliefs/values/attitudes affected how Dejon interacted with Mia, which fed their shared literacy practices and products.

As the illustrations show, literacies are constituted by people, domains, materials, and other human and non-human entities. Our conceptualization of literacy, born from the literature shared at the start of this chapter, creates requirements for literacy research. We conclude this chapter with a list of these requirements:

- Understanding literacy as social practice requires research designs capable of apprehending the situated nature of literacies, how they are practiced, by whom, why, where, and with what implications.
- Thinking multimodally about literacy demands that research identify the stuff of people's communication to understand how it helps to in/form significations and with what affordances and constraints.
- Researchers must be alert to artifacts, what they are and what they are communicating and connecting.
- The above leads to questions about literacy and placed resources, including people's social positioning and affiliation groups, and calls for researchers to notice when practices cross or mingle groups.
- And literacy research must recognize that literacy acquisition, practices, and effects in skipped generations is important. This recognition calls for studies that account for how intergenerational relationships are situated and socially culturally and economically sensitive.

We hope to have shown how these requirements were fulfilled in our ethnographic methods, resulting in rich data and situated understandings of intergenerational literacies.

Notes

1 "All participating children's parents had been born and raised in mainland China and had chosen to visit, study, or live in Canada. All the children could understand, read, and speak Mandarin Chinese, as well as write simplified Chinese characters" (Du, et al., 2016, p. 52).

2 All Mandarin has been translated by the second author and checked by a third party.

References

Arthur, C. (2012) *Financial literacy education: Neoliberalism, the consumer and citizen.* London: Springer.

Bangerter, L.R. and Waldron, V.R. (2014) Turning points in long distance grandparent–grandchild relationships. *Journal of Aging Studies* 29, 88–97.

Barton, D. and Hamilton, M. (1998) *Local literacies: A study of reading and writing in on community.* London: Routledge.

Barton, D. and Hamilton, M. (2000) Literacy practices. In: Barton, D., Hamilton, M. and Ivanic, R. (eds.) *Situated literacies: Reading and writing in context.* London: Routledge, 7–15.

Barton, D. and Hamilton, M. (2010) Literacy as a Social Practice. *Langage et société* 3, 45–62.

Beaver, J. (2001) *Developmental reading assessment.* Glenview, IL: Scott Foresman.

Bell, T. and Romano, E. (2015) Permanency and safety among children in foster family and kinship care: A scoping review. *Trauma, Violence, & Abuse,* 1–19.

Blommaert, J. (2002) Writing in the margins. Notes on a sociolinguistics of globalization. Unpublished written version of a lecture given at Cardiff University, April 2002 during a workshop of the Leverhulme Trust project on Language and Global Communication.

Du, X., Stooke, R. and Heydon, R. (2016) Ordinary moments tell extraordinary stories: Chinese children's multimodal literacy explorations. In: Ma, W. and Li, G. (eds.) *Beyond test scores: Understanding the hearts and minds of Chinese students in K-12 schools in a global context.* New York: Routledge, 41–54.

Dyson, A.H. (1996) Cultural constellations and childhood identities: On Greek gods, cartoon heroes, and the social lives of schoolchildren. *Harvard Educational Review* 66 (3), 471–496.

Dyson, A.H. and Genishi, C. (2005) *On the case.* New York: Teachers College Press.

Finnegan, R. (2015) *Where is language?: An anthropologist's questions on language, literature and performance.* New York: Bloomsbury.

Finnegan, R.H., ed. (1967) *Limba stories and story-telling.* London: Oxford University Press.

Fuller-Thomson, E., Serbinski, S. and McCormack, L. (2014) The rewards of caring for grandchildren: Black Canadian grandmothers who are custodial parents, co-parents, and extensive babysitters. *GrandFamilies: The Contemporary Journal of Research, Practice and Policy* 1 (1), 2.

Gall, M.D., Gall, J.P. and Borg, W.R. (2007) *Educational research: An introduction.* New York: Pearson Education.

Gichuru, J. (2013) *A case study mapping literacy learning opportunities and identity construction among African immigrant youth in a Canadian Secondary School.* http://alpha.lib.uwo.ca/record=b6341515.

Gregory, E. (2008) *Learning to read a new language: Making sense of words and worlds* (2nd edition). London: Sage.

Gregory, E., Long, S. and Volk, D. eds. (2004) *Many pathways to literacy: Young children learning with siblings, grandparents, peers and communities.* New York and London: RoutledgeFalmer.

Hammersley, M. and Atkinson, P. (2007) *Ethnography: Principles in practice.* New York: Routledge.

Heath, S.B. and Street, B.V. (2008) *On ethnography: Approaches to language and literacy research. Language & literacy (NCRLL).* New York: Teachers College Press.

Heydon, R. and O'Neill, S. (2016) *Why multimodal literacy matters: (Re)conceptualizing literacy and wellbeing through singing-infused multimodal, intergenerational curricula.* Rotterdam: Sense.

Heydon, R. (2013) *Learning at the ends of life: Children, elders, and literacies in intergenerational curricula.* Toronto: University of Toronto Press.

Heydon, R.M. (2007) Making meaning together: Multi-modal literacy learning opportunities in an intergenerational art programme. *Journal of Curriculum Studies* 39 (1), 35–62.

Heydon, R. McKee, L. and Daly, B. (2017) An exploratory case study of integrating digital media as placed resources in an intergenerational art class. *Language and Education* 31 (4), 351–373.

Heydon, R., McKee, L. and O'Neill, S. (in press) Singing our song: An exploratory case study of singing as a multimodal literacy practice in an intergenerational program. *Literacy* 52 (3), 128–136. https://doi.org/10.1111/lit.1213.

Hicks, D. (2002) *Reading lives: Working-class children and literacy learning. language and literacy series.* New York: Teachers College Press.

Hicks, D. (2013) *The road out: A teacher's odyssey in poor America.* Berkeley, CA: University of California Press.

Holladay, S.J. and Seipke, H.L. (2007) Communication between grandparents and grandchildren in geographically separated relationships. *Communication Studies* 58 (3), 281–297.

Jamal, S. (2005) Chapter eleven: Critical ethnography: An effective way to conduct anti-racism research. *Counterpoints* 252, 225–239.

Jewitt, C. and Kress, G., eds. (2003) *Multimodal literacy.* New York: Peter Lang.

Kelly, C. (2004) Buzz Lightyear in the nursery: Intergenerational literacy learning in a multimedia age. In: Gregory, E., Long, S. and Volk, D. (eds.) *Many pathways to literacy: Young children learning with siblings, grandparents, peers and communities.* New York: RoutledgeFalmer, 66–76.

Kozinets, R.V. (2010) *Netnography: Doing ethnographic research online.* London: Sage.

Kress, G. (1997) *Before writing: Rethinking the paths to literacy.* London: Routledge.

Lather, P. (2007) *Getting lost. Feminist efforts towards a double (d) science.* Albany, NY: State University of New York Press.

Lather, P. (2010) *Engaging science policy: From the side of the messy.* New York: Peter Lang.

Lather, P. (2013) Methodology-21: What do we do in the afterward?. *International Journal of Qualitative Studies in Education* 26 (6), 634–645.

Lather, P. (2017) *(Post)critical methodologies: The science possible after the critiques.* New York: Routledge.

McLaren, P. (2006) Collisions with otherness: "traveling" theory, post-colonial criticism, and the politics of ethnographic practice the mission of the wounded ethnographer. *Qualitative Studies in Education* 5 (1), 77–92.

Milan, A., Laflamme, N. and Wong, I. (2015) *Diversity of grandparents living with their grandchildren.* www.statcan.gc.ca/pub/75-006-x/2015001/article/14154-eng.htm.

Mills, D. and Morton, M. (2013) *Ethnography in education.* London: Sage.

Moje, E.B. and Luke, A. (2009) Literacy and identity: Examining the metaphors in history and contemporary research. *Reading Research Quarterly* 44 (4), 415–437.

Mukherji, P. and Albon, D. (2010) *Research methods in early childhood: An introductory guide.* London: Sage.

Pahl, K. (2007) Timescales and ethnography: Understanding a child's meaning-nmaking across three sites, a home, a classroom and a family literacy class. *Ethnography and Education* 2 (2), 175–190.

Pahl, K. and Rowsell, J. (2005) *Literacy and education: Understanding the New Literacy Studies in the classroom.* London: Paul Chapman.

Pahl, K. and Rowsell, J. (2010) *Artifactural literacies: Every object tells a story.* New York: Teachers College Press.

Phal, K. and Roswell, J. (2010) *Artifactual literacies: Every object tells a story.* New York: Teachers College Press.

Prinsloo, M. (2005) The new literacies as placed resources: Research: Information and communication technologies. *Perspectives in Education* 23 (1), 87–98.

Raz-kids. (2017) *Learning A-Z.* www.raz-kids.com/.

Riessman, C.K. (2008) *Narrative methods for the human sciences.* London: Sage.

Rogoff, B. (1990) *Apprenticeships in thinking. Cognitive development in social context.* Oxford: Oxford University Press.

Schensul, J.J. and LeCompte, M.D. (2016) *Ethnography in action: A mixed methods approach.* London: Rowman & Littlefield.

Street, B.V. (1995) *Social literacies: Critical approaches to literacy in development, ethnography and education.* New York: Routledge.

Studio Red Jumper (2014) *Book Creator for iPad (Version 3.3).* s.l.:[Mobile application software].

Todd, S. (2003) *Learning from the other: Levinas, psychoanalysis, and ethical possibilities in education.* Albany: SUNY Press.

Wolf, M. (1992) *A thrice-told tale: Feminism, postmodernism, and ethnographic responsibility.* Redwood City, CA: Stanford University Press.

17

TECHNOLOGIES, AFFORDANCES, CHILDREN AND EMBODIED READING

A case for interdisciplinarity

Anne Mangen, Trude Hoel and Thomas Moser

Introduction: technologies, affordances and embodiment

Digital technologies pervade our lives, and more and more of our reading is done on screens rather than on paper. Young children also engage in an increasing diversity of screen-based devices, and in several countries there is a noticeable political push toward implementing Information and Communication Technology (ICT) in early childhood education (e.g. Lynch & Redpath, 2014). This situation invites a number of intriguing research questions on topics related to children, technologies, literacies and reading. At the same time, it provides a timely occasion to reflect on the ways in which such research questions are currently pursued in the field.

In spite of a prominent place on the agenda of a number of researchers and teachers, as well as policy makers (e.g. Kampylis et al., 2015), digital technologies in early childhood remains a contentious topic, with advocates of increased accessibility and use pitted against those urging for caution, and even abandonment, in the use of screen technologies with children. A conspicuous example of the latter, neuroscientist Manfred Spitzer (2013) contends that touch screens are particularly bad for children's cognitive development. Claiming that swiping your fingers across a screen is 'one of the dumbest things one can do with the hand' (2013, p. 96), Spitzer argues that the interaction with the allegedly intuitive and user-friendly interface of touch screen tablets is in fact undermining the vital learning potential embedded in children's haptic and tactile – or, in general, corporeal (bodily) – exploration of their surrounding world:

> The development of a child's brain depends upon challenging interactions with the world around: with their senses and ideas, hearts and hands, children conquer the world, learn about objects and features, rules and exceptions. Not only is swiping hardly motorically challenging, it also does not make much use of the hand as a sense organ [. . .]. Furthermore, given that the motor phenomenon is always almost identical, just as the tactile sensory feedback, there cannot be any holistic experiences of various different things, which in the long run make up our understanding of the world around us.
>
> *(Spitzer, 2013, p. 96)*

Embodied and multisensory exploration of three-dimensional objects is also crucial to children's capacity for imagery and fantasy (e.g. Burnett & Daniels, 2015), and pretend-play with blocks, dolls and construction toys are major contributions in this respect (e.g. Singer & Singer, 2005). Building blocks and construction toys are tangible objects with distinct textures and other surface features, providing substantially different haptic and tactile feedback than intangible screen representations. Hence, we may ask what difference it makes that children play with virtual building blocks appearing on a screen rather than the wooden, three-dimensional ones existing in real-life. More specifically, we need to ask whether and to what extent the intangibility of screen representations affects children's cognitive development (and reading with it), and what the implications of this may be in a short and a long-term perspective.

In this article, we will address these issues by looking at shared reading with print picture books and picture book apps in Early Childhood Education and Care (ECEC) institutions. Books and tablets are material objects with medium-specific interfaces and ergonomic affordances inviting certain kinds of interaction, for instance, with respect to pointing and navigation. Because books have been the dominant reading medium for a very long time, we have become so used to handling them that the features of their user interface have become largely transparent. However, when books, and paper, are being replaced by digital media – laptops, tablets, smartphones and screens – their distinct user interface is revealed.

Reading – whether shared or individual, at home or in kindergarten – is an example of embodied, multisensory human-technology interaction (Mangen & van der Weel, 2016), involving in particular our fingers and hands when manually handling a device and navigating a text. Nevertheless, the ergonomics – and, more specifically, haptics – of reading has only recently begun to attract scholarly attention, in research on reading and literacy overall (Brinkmann & Tanggaard, 2010; Mackey, 2018; Mangen, 2008, 2016; Mc Laughlin, 2016), as well as in the field of early childhood learning (Crescenzi et al., 2014; Kokkola, 2018; Mackey, 2018; Merchant, 2015; Yuill & Martin, 2016).

A main implication of the transition from paper to screens is the need for theoretical perspectives that can accommodate sensorimotor and ergonomic aspects as well as the more commonly addressed visual, cognitive and discourse – or text-/meaning-related ones, to understand how the change of substrate may affect reading – whether in dyads (e.g. mother-child) or in groups (e.g., in ECEC settings). In the following, we suggest that insights deriving from the interdisciplinary paradigm of *embodied cognition* are well suited for such a task. The increasing influence of digital technologies in kindergartens is thus a timely occasion to bridge a persisting gap between predominantly qualitative, sociocultural and constructivist approaches on the one hand, and theoretical perspectives, methods and measures more common in experimental disciplines (e.g. psychology, neuroscience) on the other. Studying shared reading through the lens of embodied cognition (e.g. Mangen, 2016; Mangen & Schilhab, 2012; McLaughlin, 2016) may hence serve to broaden and deepen our understanding of the role of technological interfaces and, in particular, haptic and tactile affordances, for children's cognitive development and, in so doing, pave the way for more interdisciplinary research in the field.

The role of narratives and storytelling in children's language development

Children's multisensory exploration of material, tangible objects in their physical surroundings is fundamental to their cognitive development. Another cognitively stimulating activity nurturing in particular their fantasy and imagination is that of shared storybook reading. Young children are traditionally introduced to narratives and picture books in a context of mediation, in which dialogues and language are crucial. This context plays an important role in children's language development. Comfortably seated in the lap of a loved and trusted adult, or in the company of peers as in shared reading in groups (Tønnessen & Hoel, accepted), children are introduced to imaginative worlds conveyed through the language of the text and images, mediated by the adult through his or her act of reading. The safe and cozy setting, as well as the ways in which the adult can adapt and tailor the reading to resonate optimally with the children, contribute to making storybook reading an ideal space for language stimulation and cognitive development (Barzillai et al., in press; Vander Woude et al., 2009). Not surprisingly, storybook reading has been shown to support language and literacy skills (Lonigan & Whitehurst, 1998; Mol & Bus, 2011; Mol et al., 2008; Sénéchal, 1997; Wasik & Bond, 2001), and to boost reading interest and enjoyment overall (Baker et al., 2001). Hence, shared storybook reading is pivotal in kindergarten teachers' pedagogical repertoire.

Children's language skills are crucial in play and in establishing social relations with peers in everyday life (Brekke Stangeland, 2017), as well as for further learning, reading and writing in school (Aukrust & Rydland, 2011; Hagtvet et al., 2011). Children develop and elaborate their language skills by using it in social and meaningful situations. Participating in dialogues related to literary texts may therefore contribute positively to their language development (Slettner & Gjems, 2016).

When engaging in rich dialogues during picture book reading, children are involved in *extended discourses* (Dickinson & Tabors, 2001), actively building on their own experiences and skills, and constructing new knowledge (Solstad, 2016). When children engage creatively in dialogues in this way, their language is more decentered and decontextualized than their everyday language. Adults can invite children to participate in such cognitively developing dialogues by means of systematic and research-based methods for shared reading, e.g., *dialogue-based reading* (Burger, 2015). In dialogue-based reading, the adult is in charge of initiating and maintaining a dialogue with the primary objective to engage children in using decentered language. Invitations to dialogue can take different forms, such as questions detaching the conversation from the here-and-now (Smith & Dickinson, 1994).

Participation in reading activities thus contributes to children's language learning. In addition, children learn about books as cultural objects, and they are introduced to the ways in which a particular culture engages with books and texts (Mjør, 2009). The print picture book invites to extended discourses involving both children and adults, by means of multimodality, in which text and images interact narratively, semiotically and aesthetically. Words – written or spoken – and pictures are closely linked to the book as a medium, as a physical object with book cover, pages, spreads and paratext (Genette & Maclean, 1991). Such medium-specific affordances provide a concrete framework for the communication and dramaturgy of the narrative.

The adult reader mediates between the text and the child reader, monitoring how the text communicates with the children. Marilyn Cochran-Smidt (1984) characterizes the adult reader as a 'mediator-monitor' (p. 259). If the relationship between text and child reader is challenging, the mediator can compensate and bridge between the two. Thus, a mediator does not stage an automatic dissemination of the text, especially when reading for younger children; 'parents adapt their reading style to their child's competence' (Bus, 2001, p. 186).

The ways in which adults as well as children use their hands during reading are particularly noteworthy. A print book is typically held, positioned and manipulated in particular ways, and page turning is tactile in a different sense than page turning on a screen. Children and adults often touch the page, for example by pointing to emphasize action, identify characters and explore details in the illustrations. The pointing finger may also serve to mark the reading direction. When reading aloud, two-page spreads and page turning can act as impulses to the pace of the reading, and the act of page turning can itself harbor a dramatic potential. In fact, argues Mackey, 'this element of *connecting with hands* may be one of the specific pleasures of reading graphic texts together and one reason why picture books are so often cited as creating bonds between the adult and child who read them together' (Mackey, 2007, p. 119). Moreover, when children participate in dialogue-based reading, they also get first-hand experience of the use of texts, and physical books, in their culture. Children learn what reading is and what a reader does, and they are introduced to cultural conventions for meaning making.

When dialogue-based reading makes the transition from the substrate of paper to a variety of screens, a number of intriguing research questions arise: does it matter for children's engagement in the story that page turning is done by tapping or swiping across a screen rather than by flicking through paper? How may the differences between pointing on pictures in a print picture book, and on animations in a picture book app, affect the reading? How and to what extent do the ergonomic – haptic – engagement afforded by the material affordances of touch screen displays interact with the dialogue during reading, or with children's attention or engagement in the story?

Storybook reading on paper and screens: sensorimotor contingencies

Digitization warrants us to consider new aspects of storybook reading, such as the role of the medium. For a very long time, reading has been the exclusive domain of print. However, the emergence of tablet technologies has prompted the production of picture book apps particularly targeted at young readers. Such apps come in a wide variety, ranging from digital and interactive renditions of classics such as *Moomin* and *Pippi Longstocking*, to 'digital-only' productions that may seem more like games than stories. The degree and type of narrativity, as well as the interplay between text, pictures, animations and sounds, vary considerably. Some digital storybook apps resemble games more than stories in that there is little in the way of a coherent and progressing narrative, whereas others seem like animated versions of their print predecessor (e.g., Kari Stai's (2008) books about Yesper and Noper, several of which are available as apps). Common to them all is that the *intangibility* of the digital text (including the pictures, animations and sound) affects the readers' haptic engagement with the medium (Mangen, 2010). This intangibility has implications for the ways in which a reader is inclined to handle the text (and the medium). The very possibility that something on screen may change as a result of our motor input (clicking, tapping or swiping) is a defining feature of a digital text. This may lead to an 'urge to click' (Mangen, 2008) which has shown to be potentially distracting to the comprehension of, or engagement in, the story during reading (Parish-Morris et al., 2013). However, depending on the nature of the interactive affordances ('hot spots'), such a feature also has the potential to enhance children's engagement (see Bus et al., 2015 for a review).

In a time of rapid technological developments and increasing diversity, there is an urgent need to establish empirically what factors in the context-medium-text-reader nexus contribute positively to children's socioemotional engagement and cognitive development, and which may undermine such development. Vital to such an endeavor is the task of assessing how the material and ergonomic affordances of the medium interact with the cognitive and emotional processes involved in the ongoing narrative engagement during (shared) reading. For this purpose, we suggest the need for a more thorough understanding of the *sensorimotor contingencies* of paper-based and screen-based devices. Sensorimotor contingencies (Noë, 2004; O'Regan & Noë, 2001) refer to practical and embodied knowledge of rules and regularities relating our sensory input to movement, changes and actions:

> how things look, smell, sound, or feel (etc.) depends, in complicated but systematic ways, on one's movement. The sensory modalities differ in the distinctive forms that this dependence takes. [. . .] Sight has its own characteristic forms of sensorimotor dependence. How things look varies in systematic ways as one moves one's head, eyes, or body relative to the environment. [. . .] The senses are modes of awareness of one and the same environment as mediated by different patterns of sensorimotor contingency.
>
> *(Noë, 2004, p. 109)*

Our practical knowledge of the laws governing these contingencies derives from our multisensory exploration of the physical environment. Children learn about the nature, features and behavior of things in the lifeworld through audiovisual, haptic and tactile exploration of objects with different weight, texture, shapes, sizes, smell and taste. Importantly, how things *look* is only one manifestation of the totality of features defining any one object. The print version and the app version of Stian Hole's award-winning title *Garmann's Summer* (Hole, 2008), for instance, may *look* identical, page-by-page, but they differ in sensorimotor contingencies. When reading the story in print, the text and pictures are fixed, and we can discern visually, as well as sense kinesthetically, our page-by-page progress through the text. In contrast, when reading the app, we may be able to see (e.g. using page numbers) but we cannot kinesthetically sense our page-by-page progress through the text. Empirical research on adults' reading of narratives has found that such lack of tactile feedback may negatively affect the reader's overview of text length, of reading progress and of location of events in the text (Mangen & Kuiken, 2014; Mangen et al., submitted). Whether and to what extent such differences in sensorimotor contingencies may also affect children's socioemotional and cognitive engagement are important empirical questions in urgent need of attention in a time when narratives and storytelling become increasingly screen-based rather than paper-based.

Multisensory, embodied reading with books and apps

Reading aloud is a multisensory experience – whether the story is read from a print picture book or from a picture book app on a touch screen. In the print picture book, texts and images are visual, but the voice of the adult reader contributes substantially to the reading experience. In addition, the adult reader can use sound effects as when, e.g., knocking on the table to imitate a door-knock in the story, or blowing a fanfare when the knight enters the stadium. Sound is also a powerful means to communicate emotions (Hoel, 2013) – for instance, to invite sympathy and empathy, such as when the adult uses a scared voice when she reads about little Emma who is afraid of the dark. The concrete setting of shared picture book reading is also characterized by a physical and emotional closeness that allows for direct bodily interaction, as when the adult tickles the children when reading about Lars who is ticklish. Such simulations of emotions and actions are likely to enhance children's understanding, through the children literally seeing, hearing and feeling what is happening in the story.

Similar to reading a story in a book, reading a story on a touch screen tablet is a multisensory and embodied experience. Differently from print, the digital medium enables seamless combinations of static and dynamic modalities and ways in which the reader can engage concretely with the content by means of different options for interactivity. In addition, the sensorimotor contingencies of the tablet imply that the haptic engagement with the text and the device have different outcomes than when reading a print book (Mangen, 2008; Merchant, 2015). Taken together, such features contribute to making the reading experiences on a touch screen quite different from that of reading on paper in a book, and important research questions pertain to the effects of such medium-specific affordances on children's understanding and engagement.

Bus and colleagues (2015) conducted a meta-study of dyadic reading of digital narratives that include oral text and interactive elements like animations, sound effects and games. They find both positive and negative effects on children's emergent literacy development, depending on whether the interactive elements are related to the narrative. These results match those of another meta-study of reading dyads (Takacs et al., 2015) focusing on the impact of technology-assisted stories, compared to listening to narratives in more traditional reading situations. The study concludes that interactive features such as animations, music and sound effects contribute positively to children's understanding of the story as long as they are directly linked to the story, whereas 'hot spots', games and dictionaries not directly linked to the story, distract children's understanding. This was especially found to be the case for children growing up in non-reading environments (Takacs et al., 2015).

The physical closeness during reading with books and tablets has also been researched. In a study, Yuill and Martin (2016) compared the reading of a picture book with one read on an iPad, assessing what they call 'interaction warmth' and the posture of the children – sitting position or body position – while reading on the two devices (the mother reading for the child and the child reading for the mother). Finding that interaction warmth was lower for tablet reading than for book reading, the authors conclude that the physical differences between the book and the iPad 'can be expected to influence the embodied experience of shared reading' (2016, p. 11). The ergonomic affordances and sensorimotor contingencies affect the proximity as well as the nature of the interaction, making the two reading situations best described as 'curling up with paper [and] shoulder-surfing with screen' (2016, p. 8). As noted also by Yuill and Martin (2016, p. 11), the role of such differences is readily recognized in the increasingly influential research paradigm of embodied cognition.

Embodied cognition as an interdisciplinary frame for media-specific effects on shared reading

The acknowledgement of the role of the body in early childhood development and learning is not *per se* new: it was explicitly referenced in e.g. Piaget's (1936) epochal approach to developmental psychology, as well as in Merleau-Ponty's (1962) phenomenology. However, the emergence of a more coherent research paradigm known as embodied cognition has served to solidify an understanding of the importance of the physical, sensing, acting and moving body that is not primarily understood from cultural, social or semiotic perspectives alone. Beyond these, it is also informed by empirically derived knowledge from psychology and neuroscience on the associations between motor action, perception and cognitive and emotional processes at multiple levels.

In the educational sciences, the body has experienced a kind of renaissance in the last decades (Bengtsson, 2013; Evans & Davies, 2011; O'Loughlin, 1998) with a particular interest in embodied cognition and learning in recent years (Ionesco & Vasc, 2014; Leitan & Chaffey, 2014). Influences from a wide range of disciplines/schools of thought such as phenomenology (Gallagher, 2014; Stapleton & Froese, 2016) and neuroscience (Kiefer & Trumpp, 2012; Matheson & Barsalou, 2017) have contributed to developing the concept of embodied cognition to an influential theory in the field of education (Ionescu & Vasc, 2014; Kontra et al., 2012; McLaughlin, 2017; Yann & Martin, 2015).

According to Ionesco and Vasc (2014, p. 14), there are two main features characterizing embodied cognition: (i) cognition is not abstract and amodal but multimodal and grounded in sensory modalities of the brain and in human action; and (ii) cognition is not just about thinking but also about perceiving and acting, therefore non-cognitive processes, such as emotions, have to be included. In line with this understanding and referring to Barsalou (2010), Antle (2013) states that '[e]mbodied cognition is a perspective based on the notion that psychological processes are dependent on and shaped by aspects of the body including body morphology (form), sensory-motor systems, and interactions with the surrounding world' (2013, p. 31). Humans are understood not as 'disembodied symbol processors' but as active agents when it comes to cognitive processes.

To provide a deeper understanding of the concept of embodiment, Núñez (1999, p. 55) suggests distinguishing between three levels: trivial, material and full embodiment. *Trivial* embodiment addresses the bodily basis for information gathering and processing, implying that cognition and other psychological processes are linked to biological structures (such as the nervous system) and processes (sensation, perception). One important consequence of trivial embodiment is the necessity to understand how the nervous system works, in order to really understand cognitive and other mental processes.

The second level of embodiment, *material* embodiment, goes beyond the bodily basis of cognitive processes to develop specific paradigms and methodologies. Cognition is considered to be a decentralized phenomenon, not solely linked to the central nervous system but also involving other biological systems. Material embodiment refers specifically to movement actions performed in specific environments – e.g. gross motor actions and visual scanning, called 'low-level cognitive tasks'. Such an understanding of embodiment does not exclude the possibility that there are cognitive processes that are largely independent of the body (i.e., disembodied).

The third level, *full* embodiment, comprises both trivial and material embodiment. In addition, it encompasses all cognitive processes up to the most abstract forms of thinking (e.g., mathematical concepts). In a full-fledged thinking, bodily processes bring forth all forms of knowledge and understanding, including scientific forms of understanding. As an example, Lakoff and Núñez (2000) demonstrate that one can understand mathematics as fundamentally bodily anchored. However, such an understanding of a total or radical embodiment, as Núñez (1999) himself notes, is still controversial. Nevertheless, Núñez's tripartite structure may help explicate the potential of embodied cognition in the field of early childhood learning.

We propose that an embodiment perspective has the potential to help create a more in-depth and interdisciplinary understanding of what matters to the quality of early reading processes. Such a perspective could provide analytical perspectives for a complex analysis of medium-specific effects in shared reading with young children, both in dyadic and group settings.

The need for (more) interdisciplinarity

'Literacy practices', says Kathy Mills (2015), 'cannot be performed without the body and mind, or without interaction with the tangible materials and skills that are part of a social field, contextualized, and enacted in particular places' (p. 144). However, despite an increasing acceptance of the importance of an embodied perspective when it comes to the use of digital technologies in early learning processes (Antle, 2013; Mangen & Balsvik, 2016), it is still somewhat unclear how such a perspective may be applied and what methodological approaches are required. Embodied cognition is a complex process involving a wide range of motor, perception, cognitive, social and emotional processes – many of which are not immediately available for direct observation. This, obviously, has methodological implications and hence invites a reconsideration of theoretical frameworks, paradigms and methodologies in the field.

Aiming to capture embodied aspects of children's interaction with technologies, researchers often apply perspectives from social semiotics, particularly multimodality theory. For instance, Price and Jewitt (2013a, 2013b) emphasize the ways in which recent interfaces promote more embodied forms of interaction and invite a wide range of bodily movement, from whole body interaction with mobile and sensor technologies to hands-on manipulation with multi-touch and tangible interfaces. Calling for a re-examination of the methodological approaches in the field, they highlight the particular usefulness of a multimodal theoretical approach in that it supports a fine grained analysis of artifacts and interactions in which meaning is realized in the iterative connection between the meaning potential of a material semiotic artifact, the meaning potential of the social and cultural environment, and the resources, intentions and knowledge that people bring to that encounter (Price & Jewitt 2013a, p. 2907).

Often applied within a sociocultural paradigm, social semiotics and multimodality combine to provide a valuable tool for analyzing video data, since they accommodate the multimodality inherent in the representation of some content (e.g., text, animations, sound) as well as the multimodal and embodied forms of communication and interaction (e.g., posture, gaze, gesture, manipulation of objects) (Price & Jewitt, 2013b).

In pedagogically oriented research on learning and literacy in early childhood, sociocultural perspectives have been dominant for some time, and this research has contributed substantially to our understanding of the role of media and interfaces in children's learning. At the same time, the descriptive ethnographic bent of the sociocultural approach has led to a situation in which the effects of changing sensorimotor contingencies of technologies on cognitive and emotional processing have remained inadequately understood (Mangen & van der Weel, 2016). Moreover, by defining literacy and reading as socially constructed practices, research building on a sociocultural approach privileges social, cultural, ideological, political or other context-oriented aspects of literacy and reading, hence downplaying individual – sensorimotor, cognitive and emotional ones. As a consequence, research in the field seems somewhat skewed and there is an imbalance between qualitatively oriented research on one hand, and studies applying quantitative methods, on the other (Kucirkova, 2019).

The interplay between the sensorimotor contingencies of different media (books, tablets, computers) and substrates (paper, different kinds of screen displays), motor behavior, attention, perception, cognitive and emotional processes and sensory integration is too multifaceted to be captured by one theoretical framework and one methodology alone. Inspired by a recent epistemological discussion in the field of empirical research on literary reading (Dixon & Bortolussi, 2016; Jacobs, 2016a, 2016b; Kuiken, 2016), we propose that research in the field of technologies in early childhood would benefit from greater theoretical and methodological diversity. As also noted by Kucirkova (2019), more diversity is needed in order to better address and account for the multiple outcomes in studies of children's engagement with print and digital narratives, that cross personal/social and cognitive/emotional axes.

One way in which to pursue such a goal methodologically, we claim, is by an integration and combination of online and offline, direct and indirect, methods, as suggested by Dixon and Bortolussi (2016). Interacting with content mediated by and displayed on a variety of substrates comprises a range of cognitive, emotional, sensory and social processes and mechanisms. Some of these processes are verbal and/or directly observable and measurable, but many are preverbal or subconscious, and hence cannot be captured by video or in verbal data. This implies a need to supplement the tools and methods typically employed in socioculturally oriented research. Visualizing such a complementary approach in the field of empirical literary study, Dixon and Bortolussi (2016) present a matrix of four measurement classes: direct and indirect measures, and online and offline measures. Direct and indirect refer to the inferential relationship toward the dependent variable, whereas online and offline refer to the temporal relationship between

Table 17.1 Matrix of four measurement classes (Dixon & Bortolussi, 2016): direct and indirect measures, and online and offline measures

Inferential relationship	*Temporal relationship*	
	Online	*Offline*
Indirect	Examples: Eye movements, pupil dilation, EEG, fMRI, psychophysiological measures	Recall, judgment response time
Direct	Concurrent verbal protocols, probe responses, text annotation	Questionnaires assessing reactions and experience, interviews

the phenomenon to be studied (e.g., reading) and the measure (online, during the act; or offline, after the act – i.e., measuring the results of a process).

Obviously, some of the tools and measures in Table 17.1 are less appropriate in research with young children (e.g. pupil dilation, eye movements, text annotation). More importantly in the present context, such an approach makes explicit the necessity to collaborate in interdisciplinary teams contributing different theoretical perspectives and methodological expertise. Systematically reviewing the most recent research on digital reading in early childhood, Kucirkova (2018) finds that there is little exchange between scholars applying primarily qualitative methods on the one hand, and research based primarily on quantitative data, on the other. In studies applying a semiotic or multimodal literacies perspective (Harde & Kokkola, 2018; Jewitt, 2006; Jewitt et al., 2009; Kress, 2010; Rowsell & Pahl, 2015), relevant research in biology, psychology and neuroscience is marginally referenced, if at all. Analogously, experimental research in psychology and neuroscience rarely consider aspects more common in socioculturally oriented research. Such a theoretical-methodological 'schism' implies that important aspects of the interaction between the medium, the narrative, the children and the reading adult remain inadequately addressed. In particular, this pertains to pre- or non-verbal processes and to the complex interplay between fine-motor actions and emotional and cognitive mechanisms that may be important beyond that of contributing to explicit meaning making.

One way for future research to address this 'schism' could be to analyze children's engagement with technologies in an embodied perspective, by including various aspects of motor behavior and posture as observable variables in experimental and other research designs. The following aspects might be of relevance in studying activities related to digital devices in a variety of ECEC settings:

Posture

- Position in space
- Body orientation (open-closed; introvert-extrovert)
- 'Body control' (rest-unrest)
- Position in relation to the device
- Position in relation to peers and adults (teacher)
- Mimicry, facial expression

Gesture, pointing

- Frequency and intensity of gestures
- Directedness (intentionality) of pointing

Body movement (gross motor)

- Movement intention, purpose
- Direction (horizontal and vertical movement)
- Frequency, intensity and duration

Fine-motor activity

- Grasping
- Eye-hand-coordination

These aspects of motor behavior and posture can mainly be observed by others, with and without technologically supported measurements, and described in various ways. In empirical studies, the indicators for motor behavior and posture should be chosen based on theoretical reflections and the understanding of the concept of embodiment, as well as the particular research questions. These indicators may be investigated alone or in combination with other variables as captured in, e.g., verbal responses.

To conclude: the role of the body, and of motor actions and sensorimotor experience in children's cognitive processing, go far beyond the body being another sign system or semiotic modality. Rather than – or in addition to – bending and stretching extant sociocultural paradigms to match an increasing technological complexity, we propose to pursue collaborative, interdisciplinary research in which relevant insights from embodied cognition, sensorimotor contingency theory and medium affordances are combined with relevant qualitative approaches (e.g., theories of narrativity, multimodality, and semiotics) to shed a more comprehensive and nuanced light on the issue. This is a challenging task, but time is ripe for more collaboration across the humanities–social sciences gap.

References

Antle, A.N. (2013) Research opportunities: Embodied child – computer interaction. *International Journal of Child-Computer Interaction* 1 (1), 30–36. doi: http://dx.doi.org/10.1016/j.ijcci.2012.08.001.

Aukrust, V.G. and Rydland, V. (2011) Preschool classroom conversations as long-term resources for second language and literacy acquisition. *Journal of Applied Developmental Psychology* 32 (4), 198–207.

Baker, L., Mackler, K., Sonnenschein, S. and Serpell, R. (2001) 'Parents' interactions with their first-grade children during storybook reading and relations with subsequent home reading activity and reading achievement. *Journal of School Psychology* 39 (5), 415–438.

Barsalou, L.W. (2010) Grounded cognition: Past, present, and future. *Topics in Cognitive Science* 2, 716–724.

Barzillai, M., Thomson, J.M. and Mangen, A. (in press) The impact of e-books on language and literacy. In: Holliman, A. and Sheehy, K. (eds.) *Education and new technologies: Perils and promises for learners*. London: Routledge/Taylor & Francis.

Bengtsson, J (2013) Embodied experience in educational practice and research. *Studies in Philosophy & Education* 32 (1), 39–53. doi: 10.1007/s11217-012-9328-1.

Brekke Stangeland, E. (2017) The impact of language skills and social competence on play behaviour in toddlers. *European Early Childhood Education Research Journal* 25 (1), 106–121. doi: 10.1080/1350293X.2016.1266224.

Brinkmann, S. and Tanggaard, L. (2010) Toward an epistemology of the hand. *Studies in Philosophy and Education* 29 (3), 243–257.

Burger, K. (2015) Effective early childhood care and education: Successful approaches and didactic strategies for fostering child development. *European Early Childhood Education Research Journal* 23 (5), 743–760.

Burnett, C. and Daniels, K. (2015) Technology and literacy in the early years: Framing young children's meaning-making with new technologies. In: Garvis, S. and Lemon, N. (eds.) *Understanding digital technologies and young children: An international perspective*. London and New York: Routledge, 18–27.

Bus, A.G. (2001) Joint caregiver-child storybook reading: A route to literacy development. *Handbook of Early Literacy Research* 1, 179–191.

Bus, A.G., Takacs, Z.K. and Kegel, C.A.T. (2015) Affordances and limitations of electronic storybooks for young children's emergent literacy. *Developmental Review* 35, 79–97.

Cochran-Smith, M. (1984) *The making of a reader.* Norwood, NJ: Ablex.

Crescenzi, L., Jewitt, C. and Price, S. (2014) The role of touch in preschool children's learning using iPad versus paper interaction. *Australian Journal of Language & Literacy* 37 (2), 86–95.

Dickinson, D.K. and Tabors, P.O. eds. (2001) *Beginning literacy with language: Young children learning at home and school.* Baltimore: Paul H. Brookes.

Dixon, P. and Bortolussi, M. (2016) Measuring literary experience. *Scientific Study of Literature* 5 (2), 178–182.

Evans, J. and Davies, B. (2011) New directions, new questions? Social theory, education and embodiment. *Sport, Education and Society* 16 (3), 263–278.

Gallagher, S. (2014) Phenomenology and embodied cognition. In: Shapiro, L. (ed.) *The Routledge handbook of embodied cognition.* London: Routledge, 9–18.

Genette, G. and Maclean, M. (1991) Introduction to the Paratext. *New Literary History* 22 (2), 261–272.

Hagtvet, B.E. Lyster, S.-A.H., Melby-Lervåg, M., Næss, K.-A.B., Hjetland, H.N., Engevik, L.I., . . . and Kruse, J. (2011) Ordforråd i førskolealder og senere leseferdigheter-En metaanalytisk tilnærming. *Spesialpedagogikk* 1, 34–49.

Harde, R. and Kokkola, L., eds. (2018) *The embodied child: Readings in children's literature and culture.* New York: Routledge.

Hoel, T. (2013) Cultural features of performance in Norwegian children's narratives. *Tidsskrift for Nordisk barnehageforskning* 6 (17), 1–21.

Tønnessen, E.S. and Hoel, T. (accepted) The designing of dialogs around picture book-apps. In: Kim, J.E. and Hassinger-Das, B. (eds.) *Reading in the digital age: Young children's experiences with E-books.* London: Springer.

Hole, S (2008) *Garmann's Summer.* Bartlett, D. (trans.). Grand Rapids, MI: Eerdmans Books for Young Readers.

Ionesco, T. and Vasc, D. (2014) Embodied cognition: Challenges for psychology and education. *Procedia – Social and Behavioral Sciences* 128 (Supplement C), 275–280. doi: https://doi.org/10.1016/j.sbspro.2014.03.156.

Jacobs, A.M. (2016a) The scientific study of literary experience and neuro-behavioral responses to literature. *Scientific Study of Literature* 6 (1), 164–174.

Jacobs, A.M. (2016b) The scientific study of literary experience: Sampling the state of the art. *Scientific Study of Literature* 5 (2), 139–170. doi: 10.1075/ssol.5.2.01jac.

Jewitt, C. (2006) *Technology, literacy and learning: A multimodal approach.* London and New York: Routledge.

Jewitt, C., Kress, G. and Mavers, D.E. (2009) *The Routledge handbook of multimodal analysis.* London: Routledge.

Kampylis, P., Punie, Y. and Devine, J. (2015) Promoting effective digital-age learning-A European framework for digitally-competent educational organisations. *Joint Research Centre* Working Papers No. 98209, Seville.

Kiefer, M. and Trumpp, N.M. (2012) Embodiment theory and education: The foundations of cognition in perception and action. *Trends in Neuroscience and Education* 1 (1), 15–20.

Kokkola, L. (2018) Hands on reading: The body, the brain, and the book. In: Harde, R. and Kokkola, L. (eds.) *The embodied child: Readings in children's literature and culture.* New York: Routledge, 191–205.

Kontra, C., Goldin-Meadow, S. and Beilock, S.L. (2012) Embodied learning across the life span. *Topics in Cognitive Science* 4 (4), 731–739. doi: 10.1111/j.1756-8765.2012.01221.x.

Kress, G. (2010) *Multimodality: A social semiotic approach to contemporary communication.* London: Routledge.

Kucirkova, N. (2019) Socio-material directions for developing empirical research on children's e-reading: A systematic review and thematic synthesis of the literature across disciplines. *Journal of Early Childhood Literacy.*

Kuiken, D. (2016) The implicit erasure of "literary experience" in empirical studies of literature. *Scientific Study of Literature* 5 (2), 171–177.

Lakoff, G. and Núñez, R.E. (2000) Where mathematics comes from: How the embodied mind brings mathematics into being. *AMC* 10, 12.

Leitan, N.D. and Chaffey, L. (2014) Embodied cognition and its applications: A brief review. *Sensoria: A Journal of Mind, Brain & Culture* 10 (1), 3–10.

Lonigan, C.J. and Whitehurst, G.J. (1998) Relative efficacy of parent and teacher involvement in a shared-reading intervention for preschool children from low-income backgrounds. *Early Childhood Research Quarterly* 13 (2), 263–290.

Lynch, J. and Redpath, T. (2014) 'Smart' technologies in early years literacy education: A meta-narrative of paradigmatic tensions in iPad use in an Australian preparatory classroom. *Journal of Early Childhood Literacy* 14 (2), 147–174.

Mackey, M. (2007) *Literacies across media: Playing the text* (2nd edition). London and New York: Routledge.

Mackey, M. (2018) The child's reading body. In: Harde, R. and Kokkola, L. (eds.) *The embodied child: Readings in children's literature and culture*. New York: Routledge, 175–190.

Mangen, A. (2008) Hypertext fiction reading: Haptics and immersion. *Journal of Research in Reading* 31 (4), 404–419.

Mangen, A. (2010) Point and click: Theoretical and phenomenological reflections on the digitization of early childhood education. *Contemporary Issues in Early Childhood* 11 (4).

Mangen, A. (2016) What hands may tell us about reading and writing. *Educational Theory* 66 (4), 457–477. 10.1111/edth.12183.

Mangen, A. and Balsvik, L. (2016) Pen or keyboard in beginning writing instruction? Some perspectives from embodied cognition. *Trends in Neuroscience and Education* 5 (3), 99–106. doi: http://dx.doi.org/10.1016/j.tine.2016.06.003.

Mangen, A. and Kuiken, D. (2014) Lost in the iPad: Narrative engagement on paper and tablet. *Scientific Study of Literature* 4 (2), 150–177. doi: 10.1075/ssol.4.2.02man.

Mangen, A., Olivier, G. and Velay, J.-L. (submitted) *Where in the book and when in the story?* Mystery story reading in print and on Kindle.

Mangen, A. and Schilhab, T.S.S. (2012) An embodied view of reading: Theoretical considerations, empirical findings, and educational implications. In: Matre, S. and Skaftun, A. (eds.) *Skriv! Les!*, Akademika forlag, Trondheim, 285–300.

Mangen, A. and van der Weel, A. (2016) The evolution of reading in the age of digitisation: An integrative framework for reading research. *Literacy* 50 (3), 116–124. doi: 10.1111/lit.12086.

Matheson, H.E. and Barsalou, L.W. (2017) Embodiment and grounding in cognitive neuroscience. In: *The Stevens' handbook of experimental psychology and cognitive neuroscience*. Hoboken, NJ: Wiley.

Mc Laughlin, T. (2016) *Reading and the body: The physical practice of reading*. New York: Palgrave Macmillan.

McLaughlin, D. (2017) Embodiment: A cross-disciplinary provocation. *Connection Science* 29 (1), 36–42.

Merchant, G. (2015) Keep taking the tablets: iPads, story apps and early literacy. *Australian Journal of Language & Literacy* 38 (1), 3–11.

Merleau-Ponty, M. (1962) *Phenomenology of perception [Phénoménologie de la Perception]*. London: Routledge & Kegan Paul.

Mills, K.A. (2015) Literacy theories for the digital age: Social, critical, multimodal, spatial, material and sensory lenses, vol. 45. Bristol: Multilingual Matters.

Mjør, I. (2009) *Høgtlesar, barn, bildebok: vegar til meining og tekst* (Ph.D.), University of Agder, Kristiansand.

Mol, S.E. and Bus, A.G. (2011) To read or not to read: A meta-analysis of print exposure from infancy to early adulthood. *Psychological Bulletin* 137 (2), 267–296. doi: 10.1037/a0021890.

Mol, S.E., Bus, A.G., de Jong, M.T. and Smeets, D.J.H. (2008) Added value of dialogic parent – child book readings: A meta-analysis. *Early Education and Development* 19 (1), 7–26.

Noë, A. (2004) *Action in perception*. Cambridge, MA: MIT Press.

Núñez, R.E. (1999) Could the future taste purple? Reclaiming mind, body and cognition. *Journal of Consciousness Studies* 6 (11–12), 41–60.

O'Loughlin, M. (1998) Paying attention to bodies in education: Theoretical resources and practical suggestions. *Educational Philosophy and Theory* 30 (3), 275–297.

O'Regan, J.K. and Noë, A. (2001) A sensorimotor account of vision and visual consciousness. *Behavioral and Brain Sciences* 24 (5), 939–973. doi: https://doi.org/10.1017/S0140525X01000115.

Parish-Morris, J., Mahajan, N., Hirsh-Pasek, K., Golinkoff, R.M. and Collins, M.F. (2013) Once upon a time: parent – child dialogue and storybook reading in the electronic era. *Mind, Brain, and Education* 7 (3), 200–211. doi: 10.1111/mbe.12028.

Piaget, J. (1936) *The origins of intelligence in the child*. London: Routledge & Kegan Paul.

Price, S. and Jewitt, C. (2013a) *Interview approaches to researching embodiment*. Paper presented at the Proceedings of the SIGCHI Conference on Human Factors in Computing Systems.

Price, S. and Jewitt, C. (2013b) *A multimodal approach to examining 'embodiment' in tangible learning environments*. Paper presented at the Proceedings of the 7th International Conference on Tangible, Embedded and Embodied Interaction.

Rowsell, J. and Pahl, K., eds. (2015) *The Routledge handbook of literacy studies*. New York: Routledge.

Sénéchal, M. (1997) The differential effect of storybook reading on preschoolers' acquisition of expressive and receptive vocabulary. *Journal of Child language* 24 (1), 123–138.
Singer, D.G. and Singer, J.L. (2005) *Imagination and play in the electronic age*. Cambridge, MA: Harvard University Press.
Slettner, S. and Gjems, L. (2016) Litterasitetsfremmende samtaler i barnehagen. *Tidsskrift for Nordisk barnehageforskning* 12 (2), 1–16.
Smith, M.W. and Dickinson, D.K. (1994) Describing oral language opportunities and environments in Head Start and other preschool classrooms. *Early Childhood Research Quarterly* 9 (3–4), 345–366.
Solstad, T. (2016) *Samtaler om bildebøker i barnehagen: en vei til opplevelse, lek og meningsskaping*. Oslo: Universitetsforlaget.
Spitzer, M. (2013) To swipe or not to swipe? – The question in present-day education. *Trends in Neuroscience and Education* 2 (3), 95–99.
Stai, K. (2008) *Yesper and Noper*. Oslo: Samlaget.
Stapleton, M. and Froese, T. (2016) The enactive philosophy of embodiment: From biological foundations of agency to the phenomenology of subjectivity. In: García-Valdecasas, M., Murillo, J.I. and Barrett, N.F. (eds.) *Biology and subjectivity: Philosophical contributions to non-reductive neuroscience*. Cham: Springer International Publishing, 113–129.
Takacs, Z.K., Swart, E.K. and Bus, A.G. (2015) Benefits and pitfalls of multimedia and interactive features in technology-enhanced storybooks a meta-analysis. *Review of Educational Research* 85 (4), 698–739.
Vander Woude, J., van Kleeck, A. and Vander Veen, E. (2009) Book sharing and the development of meaning. In: Rhyner, P.M. (ed.) *Emergent literacy and language development: Promoting learning in early childhood*. New York: Guilford Press, 36–77.
Wasik, B.A. and Bond, M.A. (2001) Beyond the pages of a book: Interactive book reading and language development in preschool classrooms. *Journal of Educational Psychology* 93 (2), 243–250.
Yann, C. and Martin, F., eds. (2015) *Conceptual and interactive embodiment: Foundations of embodied cognition*. London: Routledge.
Yuill, N. and Martin, A.F. (2016) Curling up with a good e-book: Mother-child shared story reading on screen or paper affects embodied interaction and warmth. *Frontiers in Psychology* 7, article 1951.

18

MATERIALITIES, MULTILITERACIES AND MAKERSPACES

Design-based experiments in teacher/researcher collaborations

Aspa Baroutsis and Annette Woods

Introduction

With increasing digitisation and multimodality, text production forms a key element of what it means to be literate in today's literate culture where interactions between children and young people and digital texts, tools and resources are embedded in everyday practices. This shift, along with changes to work practices and the economy, has also resulted in text production becoming a more collaborative practice. When we think about literacies for current times, we usually think about multimodality and digital technologies. Digital tools, resources and technologies have had a radical effect on how we produce texts, how we communicate with each other, the kinds of interactions we can have – the very social organisation of the spaces in which we engage. When we acknowledge this, we are acknowledging that everyday life involves an entanglement of social with material; human with non-human; technological and non-technological. These sociomaterial ways of thinking challenge our preoccupation with single individuals using literacy tools (Fenwick et al., 2011) whether traditional print or digital, in order to get things done. From this way of thinking, 'technology', in whatever form, is valuable, meaningful and worth studying as people actually engage with it to get things done. But we move beyond being interested just in what a young child can 'do' with technology, toward thinking about how the material, as well as the discursive and the virtual, works with the human and non-human world. This is the key contribution of sociomaterial theories (Fenwick et al., 2011) as 'human' is decentred and so knowledge is no longer conceptualised as inseparable with humans.

In this chapter we consider literacies and learning to be literate for current times and thinking, and then present data from one study of how children learn to write and produce texts in their early school years. We highlight data collected as part of one design-based research project from the larger study, where teachers and researchers worked together to plan and implement a series of lessons which began with opportunities for children to engage in makerspace activities, before moving to produce texts in other modes. We are particularly interested in the materiality of these activities and how they shifted the roles of children and adults in the classroom space.

Reflecting on literacies for current times: foregrounding text production

Much has been written about the changing nature of literacies as we adapt to being literate in the complexities of current times. The New Literacy Studies (see for example Gee, 1996; Heath, 1983; Street, 1993) brought to the fore understandings of how texts produced by people were linked to the everyday practices in which they engaged. It is within these foundational ideas that we find the beginnings of our understandings of multimodality. In putting forward a pedagogy of multiliteracies, the New London Group (1996) extended thinking about literacy pedagogy in light of multimodality and new social, economic and political spaces. Central to their theorising are the links between literate practice and our civic, work and leisure lives.

The shifts in thinking about literacies though, are about more than literacy as a social practice and multimodality. Instead, they also involve shifts between the receptive and productive dimensions of literacy. Brandt (2015) explains that while the implications of the shift to digital ways of working has been foregrounded as instrumental in our understandings of literacies, there has been a subtler shift that is highly relevant to educators and to education systems and society more generally – although to date, one that has been largely ignored. This shift, to use Brandt's term, is the rise of mass writing. With the shift from an industrial state focused on manufacturing things, toward a knowledge state that relies on production and supply of services, texts and information become both the fundamental means of production and the most likely output of the production cycle.

As a result, our society has moved to an increasingly sharp focus on writing rather than reading as the foundation of being literate (Brandt, 2015). Writing and text production are now paramount to all that we do. This is different from even our recent past where there has been an assumption that 'readers would be many and writers would be few' (Brandt, 2015, p. 3). What it means to 'be' literate in today's society across many dimensions of our economic, social and political lives, involves the ability to produce texts, unlike previous historical periods of time.

As educators we should be interested in what happens when everyday literate experience is about writing as well as reading. As such, text production must take up a more equal or balanced place in our understandings of literacy, and this will require shifts in our understandings of the partnership between the receptive and productive dimensions of literacy. The challenge for educators is to ensure our social institutions, tasked with preparing children and young people for learning, work and leisure, catch up with these changes, and that curriculum teaching and learning parallels this shift in literate practices (Brandt, 2015). Current education research has ensured that we know less about writing and text production and how people learn to write, than we do about reading and the receptive dimensions of literacy. Current debates about literacy and literacy policy continue to focus on reading and phonics or decoding, and less on writing and text production (see for example the recent edited collection by Clark, 2017). We also know little about how writing is impacted upon by the current situation in classrooms, where old and new technologies are often drawn together for a variety of purposes, or about the implications of considering writing as a collective or collaborative process, rather than an individual one.

In Australia at least, we do know that children often do better at learning to read than they do at learning to write. Students' writing performance is regularly reported to lag behind reading, despite significant resources being focused on possible solutions to this gap in achievement. Here, we use an Australian example to demonstrate our point. On standardised measures of literacy such as the National Assessment Program – Literacy and Numeracy[1] (NAPLAN) there is traditionally a gap in all cohorts between writing and reading. While 2017 saw improvements in writing as compared to reading for children in year 3 (ACARA, 2017), as children spend more time in school the gap between reading and writing increases. By year 9, 10% fewer young people meet the minimum standard in writing than they do in reading (81.5% in writing as compared to 91.7% in reading reach minimum standard) (ACARA, 2017). Outcomes are even lower for Aboriginal and Torres Strait Islander students and those in remote areas, where the attainment of National Minimum Standard in writing of year 9 students is as low as 30.5% (ACARA, 2017) in some instances. Of course, these standardised measures are only one way of thinking about writing, and they focus only on print-based text production, but they provide some insight into performance levels of children in learning to write that warrants additional investigation. There is also evidence that this is not an issue specific to Australia. In a recent report of writing outcomes of children in primary school, Fischer and colleagues (Fisher & Twist, 2010) claimed that literacy data collected as part of accountability initiatives in the UK provided evidence that standards in writing trail reading and that there are concerns 'pupils are leaving primary school without necessary skills to flourish in the secondary system' (p. 14). Whether children and young people are learning to write and produce texts well in classrooms or not, we do know that they are being expected to use the skills of writing and text production to demonstrate competence in all other dimensions of schooling life, every school subject and most assessment tasks. Writing and text production matter in schools because of their role in demonstrating skills, understandings and knowledge across all disciplines. This heightens the importance of learning to successfully write and produce texts in schools.

So, as mass literacy has become more focused on the productive dimensions of literacy, digital tools and ways of working have shifted the relationship between text production and print. Therefore, it is important to think more about how children and young people are being taught, and how they learn to be producers of texts. Additionally, educators need to think about literacy as a material practice as well as a social practice (Kuby et al., 2015; Kuby & Rucker, 2016). In the rest of this chapter we further unpack these ideas and provide examples of how these things might come together in classroom spaces.

Working with teachers to reconceptualise literacy theory and pedagogy: methodology and conceptual thinking

The data presented here is drawn from a larger project[2] which investigates what it means to learn to write and produce texts in the early years of school, when growing up in communities of high poverty. In this project, our focus was to think about socially just literacy education, so our research is located in communities of high poverty where access to new technologies, resources and tools continues to be problematic in at least some school contexts. The aim of the larger project was to find out more about how schools were dealing with what it means to teach young children how to write and produce texts, and to problematise the relationship between learning to write traditional texts and producing texts using digital technologies.

Material changes to text production and how we use texts to communicate with others (and how we learn to do these things) have pedagogical implications. We argue that it is not useful to separate engagements with print texts from those with digital texts, and as such, nor is it useful to separate our ways of working or researching them. We know that print texts have certainly not been made redundant by digital technology, but we are interested to know more about the implications of material changes brought about when new and old technologies sit on the same school desks, and when children look toward whiteboards and smartboards more often than blackboards and butcher's paper. Our interest is in how this changes how children are, and could be, learning to write and produce texts in schools.

To investigate these ideas further we need first to conceptualise three approaches that inform our work. We begin by detailing our thoughts on design-based experiments as a way to support research partnerships between teachers and researchers in classrooms. We also lay out our thoughts on sociomaterial understandings of literacy, before briefly discussing makerspace as a pedagogical approach.

Design-based experiments

Gutiérrez and Jurow (2016) suggest that when researchers work with teachers on projects such as design-based research experiments, we are able to 'promote social equity and learning' that can expand and transform the 'educational and social circumstances' of communities (p. 565). As such, design-based experimental methodology provides an approach that supports the underlying social justice imperatives of our work. By working with researchers, teachers can develop an 'inquiry stance' (Cochran-Smith & Lytle, 2009) that can span their careers. This approach allows for experiences, knowledge and interactional expertise to build and generalise beyond specific contexts, and for a worldview that is connected to broader social formations and agendas. These formations include a focus on social justice and achieving quality literacy pedagogy for children growing up in communities of high poverty.

This empirical chapter provides an example of design-based research that was centred on a technological intervention to improve the writing of 6–7-year-old children in one classroom setting. We used design-based experiment methods that recognise the importance of researchers collaboratively working with teacher practitioners to improve teaching and learning. The purpose of this approach was to highlight links between designing quality pedagogy and conceptualising theories about how teaching and learning literacy occurs. In this instance, we were acutely interested in how children learn about writing, but also how literacy is taught to facilitate this learning. In the examples provided later in this chapter, the researchers support the teacher in developing and implementing an instructional intervention (Bradley & Reinking, 2011) with the goal of motivating children to write, by considering links between making meaning through production of texts across a range of modes and with a range of materials.

We draw on the work of Cobb et al. (2003) and their strategies for implementing design-based experiments that 'result in greater understanding of a learning ecology – a complex, interacting system involving multiple elements of different types and levels – by designing its elements and by anticipating how these elements function together to support learning' (p. 9). Design-based research is framed by the notion that 'systematic and disciplined inquiry into real problems in authentic classrooms is vital to developing workable solutions to support teachers if they are to implement instructional practices that benefit children' (Bradley & Reinking, 2011, p. 305). Importantly, when researchers and teachers work collaboratively on authentic classroom inquiries they 'close the gap between research and practice' (Bradley & Reinking, 2011, p. 306) as well as providing teacher professional learning that works towards improving 'teachers' instructional practice and transforming classroom environment' (Bradley & Reinking, 2011, p. 309). As such, design-based experiments, while taking place in a naturalistic context, are highly interventionist and iterative (Anderson & Shattuck, 2012; Barab & Squire, 2004; Cobb et al., 2003). Consequently, research undertaken through design-based classroom experiments 'moves beyond simply observing and actually involves systematically engineering these contexts in ways that allow us to improve and generate evidence-based claims about learning' (Barab & Squire, 2004, p. 2).

Design-based experiments can adopt various approaches, with the intent of informing practices and accounting for any changes to teaching and learning. In this way, design-based experiments focus on developing particular forms of learning experiences and systematically studying the outcomes (Cobb et al., 2003). Barab and Squire (2004) identify numerous studies that utilise the various design-based approaches. One of the reviewed studies theorised about students' learning gains based on the degree of collaboration during learning, developing a set of guiding practices for implementing collaborative learning (Barab & Squire, 2004). In another example, the Design-Based Research Collective (2003) reviews additional examples of education-related design-based approaches – for example, a study that developed theoretical principles related to interest-based curriculum development. In a final example, Kucirkova et al. (2017) investigate the effectiveness of tablet applications such as iPads in increasing children's narrative skills. As can be seen here, the various approaches to design-based experiments can develop locally based ideas for modifying practices and/or theoretical principles that can drive change across many contexts.

Sociomateriality and literacies

Sociomaterial ways of thinking about literacy require us to move beyond thinking about the learning environment as creating certain conditions for learning literacy, thereby seeing where, when and with what children learn literacy, as a substantial component of literacy or becoming literate. The importance of material, social and spatial elements of literate practice are therefore brought to the fore in our thinking. However, human actors remain important in the networks of people, tools, resources and texts that form literate practice – or in this case, the practice of producing texts. As children engage with texts, in certain spaces and within certain timescales, they are engaged in making and naming their worlds. Consequently, there is a strong relationship between the material, human and what Burnett (2015) has labelled the (im)material. As materials of literacy events shift, or the ways of working shift, so too do the patterns of interaction between the humans involved in the event, and the relationships between the humans, materials and spaces in which the event is occurring. However, ideas or knowledge used in any literacy event are connected to other ideas, meanings, knowledge and emotions. That is, the intangible things that are not part of the material space but which are still central to the meaning making that will occur (Burnett, 2015). When we engage in literacy or being literate, we rarely work in novel meaning making practices, instead connecting and building on the many experiences that have come before and also those that will follow.

Therefore, it is important to consider the texts, tools and resources – the *with-what* of literacy events – as well as an individual's use of materials and the emotions, cognitions, understandings and capacities of the individual. By focusing on literacy as an individual pursuit, the result is to background the collaborative nature of literacy or becoming literate. The data we present in this chapter demonstrates the collaborative nature of the literacy experience, that is, the role of the teacher and other adults, the children and the many complex experiences that they bring to the literacy events described as part of this design-based experiment. The individual capacities available in classrooms are a resource for all to draw on when the pedagogical approach allows – and the classroom interactions evident can be shifted once collaborative practice is enabled.

Makerspace pedagogy

Makerspaces are defined as 'sites for creative production . . . [using] digital or physical technologies to explore ideas, learn technical skills, and create new products' (Sheridan et al., 2014, p. 505). This approach acknowledges the multimodal nature of literacy and that it comprises language as well as other modes such as 'image, gaze, gesture, movement, music, speech, and sound-effect' (Kress & Jewitt, 2003, p. 1). A significant aspect of makerspaces is that they follow a collaborative mind-set where children 'do-it-with-others' (Peppler & Bender, 2013, p. 23). As the name suggests, makerspaces involve children 'making' something.

The concept of makerspaces has evolved from a hobbyist paradigm. There are numerous websites and books such as Graves and Graves (2016) that provide teachers with ideas for maker projects. However, more recently in the field of education, there is significant interest in how the engaging nature of makerspaces can be utilised to develop future science, technology, engineering and mathematics (STEM) (Peppler et al., 2016) as well as STEAM, which includes the arts. Within their two-volume edited collection, Peppler and colleagues (2016) have provided a wide range of examples of the educational applications of makerspaces. Similarly, Berland (2016) suggests makerspaces can be used to enable children to develop their computational literacy by presenting them with opportunities to engage in what he calls mindful tinkering. Through the process of building, children express themselves and develop their literacy to explain what they have built or how it works. These examples demonstrate the diverse range of uses of makerspaces in pedagogy and curriculum.

The materiality and multimodality: makerspaces and becoming text producers

The data reported in this chapter was collected as part of a larger school reform study, *Learning to write in the early years*. The project involved two schools across two different state systems. The school involved in this chapter was in a high poverty community, where access to digital technology, both at school and in the home, was limited for many children. This mid-sized school of approximately 500 children was culturally diverse with approximately 10–12% of students identifying as Aboriginal or Torres Strait Island children, and more than 50% of the student cohort having a language other than English as their first language. Outcomes on national standard assessments (NAPLAN) record student achievement in literacy and numeracy as being below that of peers attending other schools. The school leaders, teachers, children and their families and communities were focused on improvement and the provision of an equitable, quality education. As one part of this, the school leaders and teachers actively participated in the research project as a way to support their school improvement agendas.

The larger project involved three phases. We first conducted an audit of current practices at each of our research sites. In phase two, researchers worked with teachers to plan and implement design-based interventions as a means to reform pedagogical practice in the teaching of writing and text production. Finally, in the third phase of the project, we produced case studies focusing on a number of children as they became writers and producers of texts in the early years of their schooling. Here, we draw on data collected as part of phase two of the project at one school, as we document the instructional and technological learning interventions undertaken by one of the researchers and a teacher in a year 1 classroom.[3] Data sources include children's writing samples; photographs; classroom observations; and teacher, researcher and student reflections. The project draws on Bradley and Reinking's (2011) framework for conducting design-based experiments as a tool for analysing the goals, processes and outcomes of the three cycles of the instructional and technological intervention.

Teachers at the school were asked to consider an area of their pedagogy or classroom practice that they felt could benefit from review and reform. When asked about the teaching of writing, the classroom teacher featured in this chapter identified that her students had little or no enthusiasm for writing. She wanted this to change but reported feeling unable to provide opportunities that were engaging to the students at the same time as managing the classroom. The children routinely wrote individually at their desks. Writing practice was not a daily occurrence. There was little text production work in modes other than print, nor was there a great deal of collaborative text production with small or whole class groups. Working with the teacher, we collaboratively designed a three-cycle intervention that included various instructional and technological interventions that aimed to (a) encourage children to become enthusiastic about writing and making meaning through text production across a range of modes; and (b) increase opportunities for children's multimodal text production. We decided to focus on makerspace activities, drawn from the maker movement (http://makerspacesaustralia.weebly.com/) as a means of inspiring the young children to write. The makerspace activities were identified as a way of encouraging an interest in text production within this group of children who were already quite reluctant writers. The play-based makerspace activities provided the children with the inspiration as well as the time to think about the object they were creating. The objects and the makerspace process became stimulus for individual and collaborative writing. This was followed by the writing of a story.

In all, there were three cycles to this design-based experiment. In the first cycle, the researchers took the lead in designing and delivering the intervention lessons that were planned in collaboration with the teacher. In the second cycle, one researcher provided background support and the teacher took a greater role in the planning and delivery of the lessons, while in the third cycle, the teacher took the lead in planning, teaching and assessing the children. The first cycle was a problem-solving activity called 'Trap the witch' (Anderson n.d.); the second focused on 'Something interesting happened last week'; and the third was 'Life in a fish tank' which was linked to the children's technology assessment. In each cycle, the children made something and then produced a written or multimodal story about their creation and/or the process of making.

Cycle 1: trap the witch

The activity was based on the Hansel and Gretel fairy tale. After a shared reading of an abridged version of the story, the children were introduced to the small cardboard boxes resembling matchboxes that represented Hansel, Gretel and the witch. The witch was represented by a larger box, while the children were smaller and thinner boxes. This was followed by a question and answer session with the children to help them identify the differences between the boxes. The children then worked in groups and with their teacher and researchers, to plan a design for a witch trap and identify and list the materials they needed (see Figure 18.1). The cage was

A. Group planning.

B. An example of a witch trap.

C. Working together during the trap the witch makerspace.

Figure 18.1 Trap the witch makerspace activities

required to allow the children to escape but to trap the witch. The children then collected their building materials and proceeded to construct witch traps in small groups. Materials provided included cardboard, pipe cleaners, paddle-pop sticks, scissors, string, masking tape, ribbons, bottle caps and straws. After the children constructed the traps, they tested these with their cardboard box characters to see if they were successful in 'trapping the witch'. As there were additional adults in the room, the teacher was able to work with small groups of children. Her role changed from regulator of behaviour of the whole class, to supporting problem-solving investigations of smaller groups. She asked questions, laughed when she required help from the children to construct particular aspects of the construction and listened to the children's ideas. Her questions had shifted from rhetorical questions or ones with prescribed answers to questions of inquiry – what if we tried this? She sat on the floor with the children, head down to focus on the developing construction. She and the children vied for staplers, paper and glue as they collaborated to construct the trap – using oral language and their bodies (stretched hands and moving heads) to indicate what they needed from others in the collaboration. We were struck by the shift in roles available to this teacher through the introduction of different materials. Bodies had moved from individual desks to the floor – paper and pens were used for different purposes than how they were usually put to use. One researcher wrote in her field notes *the difference that the materials and the shift in pedagogy made to the roles of the children and teacher, and to how the classroom space was used, was very visible.*

Following the maker session, the children used iPads and the *Book Creator* application (https://bookcreator.com/) to write collaboratively with their peers and their teacher and the researchers about the makerspace activity. The use of digital technologies to produce multimodal texts encouraged writing, particularly collaborations between children of various confidence and proficiency levels. As Kalantzis and Cope (2012) suggest, the pedagogy was purposefully selected to meet the teaching and learning goals of young children to write.

The teachers/researchers made a few suggestions about what the eBooks might contain:

- A story cover page with 'Trap the witch'
- A page with the sentence starter: 'The members of the group are: . . .'
- A page with the sentence starter: 'The story was about . . .'
- A page with the sentence starter: 'The challenge was . . .'
- A page with the sentence starter: 'I liked . . .'

Figure 18.2 shows the different interpretations of the sentence starters and the story. The eBooks were also converted to video and shown to the class using the interactive whiteboard available in the classroom.

Additionally, the videos were shown to the children's parents when the class hosted a 'Literacy Party' as part of National Literacy and Numeracy week. This enabled the teacher to engage parents in the literacy lives of their children in new ways that extended their range of thinking about literacy to be more than engaging with print. Later the children also used this experience as a stimulus for other writing as part of the reformed individual writing time in the class. Children were asked to consider other aspects of the story including flipping the story, for example, 'How did the witch feel about the children destroying her house?'

As this was the children's first introduction to makerspace activities in this classroom, it is understandable that they would be excited about the newness of the experience. However, as the lesson progressed, the potential for sustained literacy learning became apparent. The makerspace activities promoted exploration, collaboration, as well as developing cooperation, creativity

The story is about
Hansel and Gretel. The
witch tried to grab
them and put them in
the cage. The kids
trapped the witch in
the cage.

Then story was about two children
who were hungry and looking for
food. We built trap to hold the witch
and let the children out.

Figure 18.2 Excerpts from eBooks

and problem-solving. Here, the assumption is that children become more fully engaged with writing and more efficient and effective thinkers when they experience something first-hand, such as through these play-based approaches (Larson & Rusk, 2011, p. 91).

Cycle 2: something interesting happened last week

The second makerspace activity was drawn from the children's own experiences. The teacher and one of the researchers worked together to plan and deliver the lesson. During this cycle, there was a shift of responsibility to the teacher as leader. A brainstorming session enabled the children to list interesting things that had happened to them the week before. Topics included fishing, a dog having puppies and a party. The children used these topics as a spring-board to think about something they wanted to make and write about. The maker activity was completed individually and the children were photographed with their creations. Additionally, a 'gallery' of the children's work was created by placing the object on their desks, and the class moving around the room to look at other people's maker creations.

Following the gallery activity, the children were given two sentence starters: 'I made . . .' and 'I like . . .'. These sentence starters were provided for the children who needed prompting to start writing. Many of the children continued to write beyond these two-sentences or used their own ideas (see Figure 18.3).

During this makerspace activity, and the writing task that followed, the children expressed enjoyment with both activities. While their enjoyment was likely to be related to the scope for self-direction and choices about their curriculum, there is little doubt that the play-based nature of the task, and the shift in materials and rules about how to 'be' in the classroom, also encouraged engagement. In addition, as with the other two cycles, many of the children demonstrated pride in their writing and wanted to share their stories with other adults and children.

As expected, all children in the class were keen to participate in the makerspace activities. What we also saw was highly engaged children during the writing phases. They demonstrated productive talk and movement during the lessons. They responded to the makerspace sessions with a high degree of responsibility and behaviour management seemed to be less of a focus of

Figure 18.3 An alien was sighted last week

the classroom interactions during these lessons. As such, we found the makerspaces to be inclusive spaces (Wohlwend, 2008) that engaged all learners, including those who were reluctant to write or more disengaged with the teaching and learning in other learning contexts.

Cycle 3: life in a fish tank

This activity was planned and taught by the classroom teacher as part of an assessment piece that was linked to the children's technology lessons. The assessment piece required the children to create a diorama of a fish tank. In the lead up to the makerspace lessons, the teacher spent a number of lessons reading and discussing *The Rainbow Fish* by Marcus Pfister (1992). This was followed by the children watching excerpts from *Finding Nemo* (Disney), which showed the fish tank and the marine life. These were each attempts by the teacher to bring texts of multiple modes into the core curriculum of her classroom. The teacher designed a worksheet that acted as a planner for the design of the fish tank (see Figure 18.4). This involved the children identifying the items in the fish tank and providing a drawing. It also included a cut and paste activity where sentences relating to the fish tank had to be unjumbled.

A range of materials were provided (see Figure 18.5) to create the various components of the fish tank, including the rocks, seaweed and water. These included paints, crepe paper, cello paper, beads, pipe cleaners, googley eyes, printed marine animals and various sized boxes and bottle caps. The fish tanks were made in shoe boxes, positioned on their side.

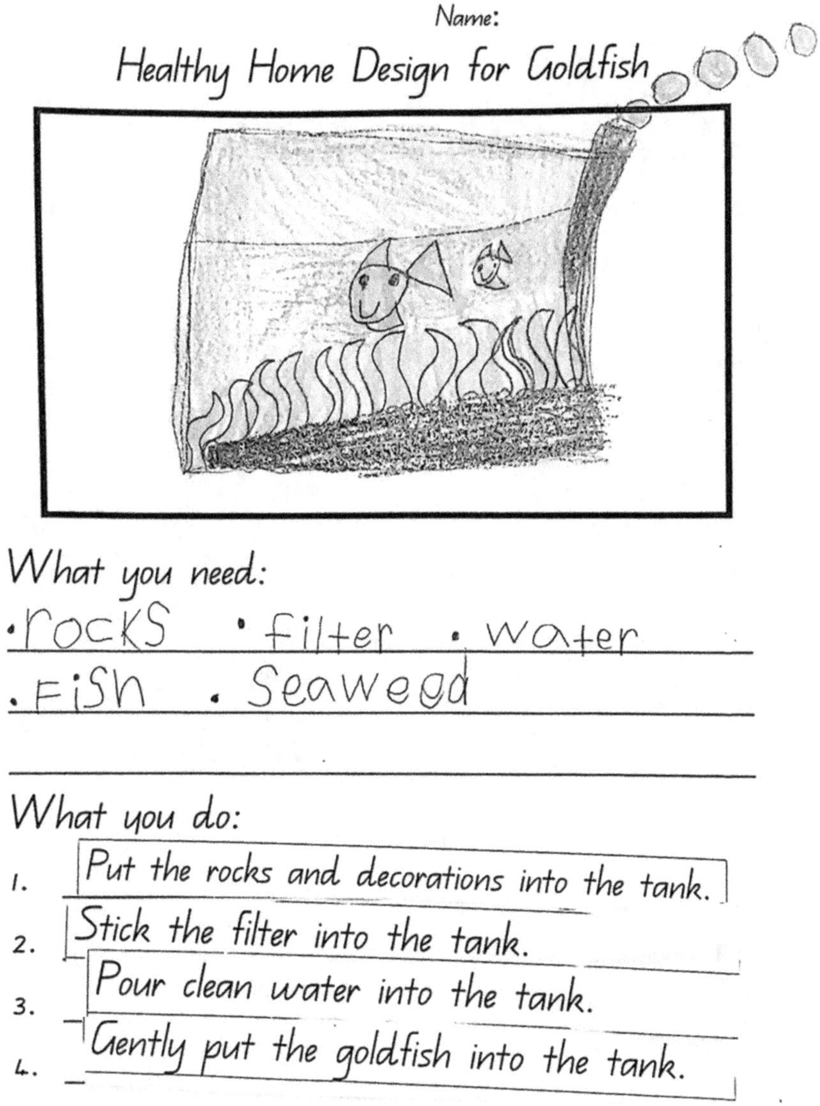

Name:

Healthy Home Design for Goldfish

What you need:

• rocks • filter • water

• Fish • Seaweed

What you do:

1. Put the rocks and decorations into the tank.
2. Stick the filter into the tank.
3. Pour clean water into the tank.
4. Gently put the goldfish into the tank.

Figure 18.4 Designing the fish tank

Figure 18.5 Material used and diorama example

After the children constructed their dioramas, they were photographed with their creations and were able to move around the room to see what other people had created. A few children were called upon to explain various components of their fish tank and any special innovations, for example, one child created a container with ‘fish food’, another child created seaweed by twisting a pipe cleaner around a pencil to create a stand-alone, three-dimensional object that represented the plant matter.

When the children were ready, they started writing. They were given some ideas as to what they could include in their writing. Some focus questions included:

- What are the names of the creatures in the fish tank?
- What type of creature are they?
- Describe the fish tank – what is inside the fish tank?
- Is there anything interesting happening inside the fish tank?
- What are the creatures doing in the fish tank?
- What are the creatures feeling inside the tank and why?

Figure 18.6 provides an example of the writing. This writer, while having grasped many of the functional elements of writing, was usually quite reluctant to write. When asked to write at other times, this child would routinely write only what was mandated by the teacher and no more. Following this makerspace activity, the child wrote a substantial amount about the fish

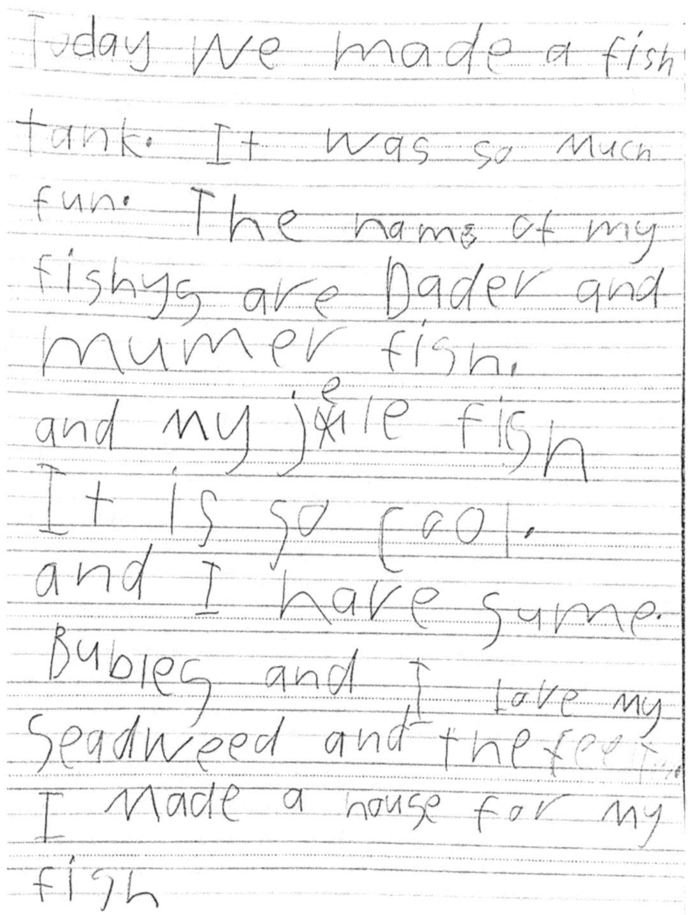
Today We made a fish
tank. It was so Much
fun. The name of my
fishys are Dader and
mumer fish.
and my jule fish
It is so cool.
and I have sume
Bubles and I love my
Seadweed and the fee
I made a house for my
fish

Figure 18.6 Child's writing sample

tank he had created. The comment, 'I love my seaweed' references a situation where many of the children around him wanted him to show them how he had made the seaweed, that is, by twisting pipe cleaners and securing them to the base of the 'tank'. It was obvious to us that he enjoyed having his idea shared with others and being recognised for his imaginative use of the materials. So much so that he wrote about it in his text.

Reflection and conclusions

In drawing this chapter to a close, we reflect on the practices of literacy learning in this class as a part of the design-based experiments conducted with the purpose of reforming writing pedagogy. By focusing on the sociomateriality of the lesson we are able to tease out examples of intra-active and de-territorialised pedagogies (Kuby & Rucker, 2016; Lenz Taguchi, 2010).

As Barad (2007) states, 'our knowledge-making practices are social-material enactments' (p. 26). From the makerspace writing, the enactments of the social and the material, the human and the non-human, the technological and the non-technological gave rise to intra-active learning experiences. Ideas flowed, as did creativity and imagination, as materials took on a multitude of forms. These materials become active agents that constructed various realities and discourses (Lenz Taguchi, 2010). Plastic beads simultaneously became air bubbles blown by fish and fish food floating at the surface of the tank (cycle 3) or the eyes of a monster alien that very interestingly had landed on earth the week before (cycle 2). Pipe cleaners imaginatively produced seaweed in a fish tank (cycle 3) as well as the bars of a jail trap (cycle 1), all through the discursive practices of 7-year-old children and the dynamics of intra-active pedagogies (Kuby & Rucker, 2016). The materials were able to 'speak back to the children in the entanglement of intra-activity' (Kuby & Rucker, 2016). For example, the pliability of the pipe cleaners made them (un) suitable for constructing a cage to trap the witch. In other examples, limitations were sometimes placed on the agency between the child and the materials, for example, the ruled lines in Figure 18.6, which are meant to restrain children's writing practices, compared to the blank page in Figure 18.3, which affords greater freedoms. Interestingly, in an example of the messiness of intra-activity, the child (see Figure 18.6) did not (or perhaps could not) adhere to the restrictions of the ruled lines, instead moving beyond the confines of the allocated spaces.

Drawing on the work of Lenz Taguchi (2010), we note that 'meaning-making and the learning we do is dependent on the material world around us. The material world acts upon our thinking just as much as our thinking acts upon it' (p. 49). Therefore, by 'focusing on the intra-active relationship between people and materials', materials become 'active agents' within 'entangled becomings' within pedagogy (Kuby et al., 2015, p. 399). The concept of entangled becoming, has allowed us to shift the focus from the teacher or student or material, but rather, to the 'in-between' (Kuby et al., 2015, p. 404). In examples of this intra-activity (Kuby & Rucker, 2016) and meaning making, we observed that some children were asked to demonstrate or explain their making techniques and choices, or their use of adjective and noun groups, to the rest of the class or to other children. During the desk gallery displays or when the stories were flipped to create different narratives, the children made meaning of their material world through the objects they created by thinking and seeing others children's maker-objects, stories, videos or eBooks.[4] One of the observable effects of these intra-actions was the evidence of the pride that swelled as the children were praised for their work or as they were asked by other children to assist them with something they had already accomplished themselves. In the chatter during the sessions, we frequently heard, 'How did you do that?'; 'Can you show me?'; 'Could you read out your sentence to the class'; or 'I like how you did that'. Consequently, the children were more open to experimenting with writing and different perspectives and seemed inspired and motivated to write in traditional forms based on the powerful stimulus of the makerspace experience. This included the children who were more likely to be hesitant to write in other learning contexts. On these occasions, we saw improvements in the quantity and the quality of their print-based writing.

The intra-active entanglements also had the effect of de-territorialising (Kuby & Rucker, 2016) the classroom spaces and identities. During making sessions, adults and children worked together, around desks and not always at them. There was a temporary blurring of the identities of 'teacher' who is spatially positioned at the front of the room, and 'students' who are seated at their desks. The teacher was sitting on the carpet with groups of children, working on the task. Desks were abandoned by many, and the children had full use of the classroom space. There was movement and sharing, discussion and critique, experimentation and the refinement of designs. New opportunities presented themselves, through the engagement of the human and the non-human, for the best way to build their objects including artefacts and texts. The teacher was lost in the mess of bodies scattered across the room, making their creations. Agentic relationships between adults and children in the room gave rise to increased opportunities for successful literacy learning. Through the de-territorialising of spaces and the de-centring of the teacher, there was a shift in roles and identities. Children had choices about where they worked, who they worked with or the topic of their writing. Ideas were cross-fertilised through discussion and debate, or the casual glance over the shoulder to see what the others were doing.

What has emerged from these reflections of a design-based experiment are new ways of teaching-learning-writing between teacher and student, adults and children, all of which were made possible through a focus on the sociomateriality of classroom practices and pedagogies. As the connections shifted between the humans in the room, and between human, material and spatial resources, tools and texts, new ways of being and of learning writing became possibilities for children. The new possibilities which resulted from the changed pedagogical approach enabled shifts in the social interactions of the class as well as shifts in how children engaged with texts as writers or text producers (Kuby et al., 2015). The focus of pedagogy became children learning to produce texts, rather than children who refuse to write.

Notes

1 The National Assessment Program of Literacy and Numeracy – NAPLAN – was introduced in 2008. In its current form the program involves all Australian children in years 3, 5,7 and 9 sitting tests in May of each year. There are tests in five domains: Reading, Writing, Spelling, Grammar and Punctuation, and Numeracy.

2 The project is known as the 'Learning to write in the early years project' (LWEYs). We would like to acknowledge the support of the Australian Research Council (DP150101240). Our colleagues in this project include Barbara Comber and Lisa Kervin. We thank the schools, school leaders, teachers, students and their parents and communities for their support of this project. Special acknowledgement goes the teacher and children of year 1Purple for their participation and insights during this project. We acknowledge the funding support of the Australian Research Council through the Discovery Program.

3 In this Australian state, children in year 1 are 6 to 7 years old and are in their second mandatory year of schooling.

4 eBooks are electronic books published in digital form. Other terms include 'digital books'.

References

ACARA (2017) *National assessment program, literacy and numeracy. National Report 2017.* Sydney, NSW: ACARA.

Anderson, M. (n.d.) STEM activity: Hansel and Gretel, Trap the witch. In: *Educents.* www.educents.com/stem-activity-hansel-and-gretel-trap-the-witch.html.

Anderson, T. and Shattuck, J. (2012) Design-based research: A decade of progress in education research? *Educational Researcher* 41 (1), 16–25.

Barab, S. and Squire, K. (2004) Design-based research: Putting a stake in the ground. *The Journal of the Learning Sciences* 13 (1), 1–14.

Barad, K. (2007) *Meeting the universe halfway: Quantum physics and the entanglement of matter and meaning*. Durham, NC: Duke University Press.

Berland, M. (2016) Making, tinkering and computational literacy. In: Peppler, K., Halverson, E.R. and Kafai, Y.B. (eds.) *Makeology: Makers as learners*. New York: Routledge.

Bradley, B.A. and Reinking, D. (2011) Enhancing research and practice in early childhood through formative and design experiments. *Early Child Development and Care* 181 (3), 305–319.

Brandt, D. (2015) *The rise of writing: Redefining mass literacy*. Cambridge: Cambridge University Press.

Burnett, C. (2015) (Im)materialising literacies. In: Pahl, K. (ed.) *The Routledge handbook of literacy studies*. London: Taylor & Francis, 520–531.

Clark, M. (2017) *Reading the evidence: Synthetic phonics and literacy*. London: Taylor & Francis.

Cobb, P., Confrey, J., diSessa, A., Lehrer, R. and Schauble, L. (2003) Design experiments in educational research. *Educational Researcher* 32 (1), 9–13.

Cochran-Smith, M. and Lytle, S.L. (2009) *Inquiry as stance: Practitioner research for the next generation*. New York: Teachers College Press.

Fenwick, T., Edwards, R. and Sawchuk, P. (2011) *Emerging approaches to educational research. Tracing the sociomaterial*. New York: Routledge.

Fisher, R. and Twist, L. (2010) Evaluation of every child a writer: Report 1 (DFE-RR108(a)), Department for Education, UK.

Gee, J.P. (1996) *Social linguistics and literacies: Ideology in discourses*. London: Taylor & Francis.

Graves, C. and Graves, A. (2016) *The big book of makerspace projects: Inspiring makers to experiment, create, and learn*. London: McGraw Hill.

Gutiérrez, K.D. and Jurow, A.S. (2016) Social design experiments: Toward equity by design. *Journal of the Learning Sciences*. 25 (4), 565–598.

Heath, S.B. (1983) *Ways with words: Language, life and work in communities and classrooms*. Cambridge: Cambridge University Press.

Kalantzis, M. and Cope, B. (2012) *Literacies*. Cambridge: Cambridge University Press.

Kress, G. and Jewitt, C. (2003) Introduction. In: Jewitt, C. and Kress, G. (eds.) *Multimodal literacy*. New York: Peter Lang, 1–18.

Kuby, C.R. and Rucker, T.G. (2016) *Go be a writer! Expanding the curricular boundaries of literacy learning with children*. New York: Teachers College Press.

Kuby, C.R., Rucker, T.G. and Kirchhofer, J.M. (2015) 'Go be a writer': Intra-activity with materials, time and space in literacy learning. *Journal of Early Childhood Literacy* 15 (3), 394–419.

Kucirkova, N., Messer, D. and Sheehy, K. (2017) Implementing "The Our Story app" to increase children's narrative skills: Lessons learnt from one English pre-school classroom. In: Veneziano, E. and Nicolopoulou, A. (eds.) *Narrative literacy and other skills: Studies in interventions*. Amsterdam and Philadelphia, PA: John Benjamins.

Larson, R.W. and Rusk, N. (2011) Intrinsic motivation and positive development. In: Lerner, R.M., Lerner, J.V. and Benson, J.B. (eds.) *Advances in child development and behaviour: Positive youth development*, vol. 41. Amsterdam: Elsevier, 89–130.

Lenz Taguchi, H. (2010) *Going beyond the theory/practice divide in early childhood education: Introducing an intra-active pedagogy*. New York: Routledge.

New London Group (1996) A pedagogy of multiliteracies: Designing social futures. *Harvard Educational Review* 66 (1), 60–92.

Peppler, K. and Bender, S. (2013) Maker movement spreads innovation one project at a time. *Phi Delta Kappan* 95 (3), 22–27.

Peppler, K., Halverson, E.R. and Kafai, Y.B. (2016) *Makeology: Makers as learners*. New York: Routledge.

Pfister, M. (1992) *The rainbow fish*. Germany: Norstud Verlag.

Sheridan, K.M., Halverson, E.R., Litts, B.K., Brahms, L., Lynette, J.-P. and Owens, T. (2014) Learning in the making: A comparative case study of three makerspaces. *Harvard Educational Review* 84 (4), 505–531.

Street, B. (1993) *Cross cultural approaches to literacy*. Cambridge: Cambridge University Press.

The Design-Based Research Collective (2003) Design-based research: An emerging paradigm for educational inquiry. *Educational Researcher* 32, 5–8.

Wohlwend, K. (2008) Play as a literacy of possibilities: Expanding meaning in practices, materials, and spaces. *Language Arts* 86 (2), 127–136.

PART IV

Studies answering practice-related questions

19

RESEARCH WITH CHILDREN WITH SPECIAL EDUCATIONAL NEEDS

A focus on Autism Spectrum Disorder

Melissa L. Allen and Shu Yau

Defining special educational needs

The term 'special educational needs' (SEN), originally coined by the Warnock report (Great Britain & Warnock 1978), is purposefully broad, as it captures a wide range of learning disabilities that can affect an individual's ability to learn. Areas which can be affected in children include behaviour, literacy, comprehension, concentration levels or physical ability, and typically supports are put in place in mainstream or special schools to facilitate development across areas of need. According to the Children and Families Act 2014, a child or young person has SEN 'if he or she has a learning difficulty or disability which calls for special educational provision to be made for him or her'. School age children are considered to have a learning difficulty or disability if they have a significantly greater difficulty in learning than same aged peers or have a disability which prevents or hinders them from using existing facilities found in mainstream settings. Care is taken to specify that differences in a language spoken at home do not equate to disability.

Norwich (2013) outlines the controversy in classifying children by such categories, which can conflate causation, severity and setting or use of norms. Further to this, Beveridge (1999) points out that the concept of special need is a social construction, shaped by economic concerns, which morphs over time in line with current political climate. The stability of the label, how children are characterised by it and indeed which children are themselves characterised are thus fluid processes.

Although some argue that the use of a SEN label reduces empowerment amongst individuals described by the term (Keil et al., 2006), and causes discrimination (Warnock & Norwich, 2010; Terzi, 2005), it is generally acknowledged that the label is used to provide remediation and access to services that would otherwise not be available (Norwich, 2013). There does exist tension between a social model of disability, which highlights the interaction between a child and his or her environment, and a medical model, which attempts to provide descriptors based upon within-child factors. Warnock (2005) argues that the current educational framework is marked by the apparent contradiction between the intention to treat all learners the same while acknowledging and responding to the needs that stem from their individual differences. This 'dilemma of difference' parallels a debate seen in the field of Autism Spectrum Disorder (ASD), where incredible heterogeneity of the condition makes educational, clinical and research-based generalisation across the spectrum fraught with difficulty.

Autism Spectrum Disorder

Autism Spectrum Disorder (ASD) is a neurodevelopmental condition characterised by impairment in two broad domains: social communication, and restricted and repetitive behaviours (American Psychiatric Association, 2013). Evidence from family and twin studies, and research in genetics, neuropathology and neuroimaging converge to inform our understanding that ASD is genetically and biologically based (Damiano et al., 2014, Folstein and Piven, 1991; Ronald and Hoekstra, 2011). It is unclear, however, how genetic risk factors interact with environmental influences to result in individual symptoms.

In clinical practice, ASD is often diagnosed around ages 3–4 (Christensen, 2016). In England, the National Institute for Health and Care (NICE) guidelines recommend that children who show regression in social skills, language or motor abilities be referred for an ASD diagnosis (National Institute for Health and Clinical Excellence, 2011). In research, behavioural studies suggest identifiable symptoms of ASD emerge at around 1 (Ozonoff et al., 2010) (Ozonoff et al., 2010) and neuroimaging studies have shown that infants at risk show atypicalities as young as 6 months of age (Elsabbagh et al., 2012; Wolff et al., 2012).

ASD is considered a lifelong condition where the diagnosis is relatively stable over time. This means that a child diagnosed with autism at 2 years old will continue to meet criteria for diagnosis at 9 years old (Lord et al., 2006) and across the lifespan (Seltzer et al., 2004). Despite a retained diagnosis, studies have revealed that some parent-reported adaptive behaviours and social involvement improve in adolescence (McGovern & Sigman, 2005). A positive developmental trajectory has been linked to an individual's communication skills and person related cognition (Darrou et al., 2010), early IQ scores (Howlin et al., 2000) and implementation of intervention programmes (Klintwall et al., 2015). Thus, an early diagnosis is preferable in order to provide appropriate supports and tailor intervention strategies.

Recent changes in the Diagnostic and Statistical Manual (DSM-V) (American Psychiatric Association, 2013), have changed the way an ASD diagnosis is formulated. The main distinction was a shift from the classic 'Triad of Impairments' – impaired social interaction, impaired social communication and restricted behaviours – to two broader categories in DSM-V (impaired social interaction and communication, and restricted behaviours). This is supported by empirical evidence showing that the triad is 'fractionable', with different genes accounting for different elements, suggesting that no single unitary cognitive account can explain autism (Happe & Ronald, 2008).

As autism is inherently a spectrum disorder, individuals present with a considerable variation in skills and behaviour, governed by the complex interaction between such behaviour with genes and the brain over development (Pelphrey et al., 2011). For example, some children may show no interest in interacting with others, while others may have an interest but be unable to decipher the more subtle social cues that govern effective communicative exchanges. Six developmental pathways have been identified (Fountain et al., 2012), making the ability to predict educational attainment and independence a challenge. On a genetic level, it is speculated that the aetiology of ASD encompasses perhaps hundreds of genetic and genomic disorders, some of which are also causally implicated in intellectual disability (Betancur, 2011).

Indeed, understanding of ASD can be compounded by issues of comorbidity. Comorbid conditions are exceedingly common ASD, with 46% individuals with ASD having at least one comorbid disorder such as attention deficit/hyperactivity disorder, epilepsy or gastrointestinal or sleep conditions; if intellectual disability is included the prevalence rate rises to 79% (Mannion & Leader, 2013). Other genetic disorders, such as Fragile X syndrome and tuberous sclerosis (Geschwind, 2011) have also been associated with ASD. Overall, this heterogeneous condition may be best characterised as 'the autisms' (Coleman & Gillberg, 2012), a multi-faceted collection of genetic disorders that need to be considered on an individual basis.

Cognitive and language profile: heterogeneity

Although language difficulty is a core diagnostic feature of ASD, how it manifests across different individuals can vary dramatically, in line with the overall heterogeneity of the condition. Some individuals (around 30%) are considered minimally verbal, characterised by the use of less than 20–30 words or phrases in limited contexts (Tager-Flusberg & Kasari, 2013). Many of these individuals rely upon alternative modes of communication such as the Picture Exchange Communication System (PECS) or alternative/augmentative communication (AAC) systems (Kasari et al., 2013). These individuals tend to learn word-referent and picture-referent relations associatively (Preissler, 2008; Hartley & Allen, 2015), rather than symbolically, showing a fundamental difference and delay in processes of language acquisition and symbolic understanding (Hartley & Allen, 2014a; Hartley & Allen, 2014b; Field et al., 2016).

Other individuals may have stronger expressive and receptive skills, but struggle with pragmatic abilities (Tager-Flusberg & Caronna, 2007), including turn-taking and sustaining fluid, dyadic conversations (Rapin & Dunn, 2003). Prosodic differences are also common (Rapin & Dunn, 2003), as well as difficulty with the understanding and use of nonliteral language (e.g. irony, sarcasm, humour) (Kasari & Rotheram-Fuller, 2005). A significant delay in the onset of verbal language is seen across the spectrum, with words first produced at approximately 38 months of age, compared to 8–14 months in children without ASD (Howlin, 2003). Language difficulties are compounded by impairment in socio-pragmatic skills, meaning that children with ASD have fewer opportunities to engage in interactions and fail to make meaning of social cues that naturally enforce word-referent mappings.

Children with ASD also present with an uneven cognitive profile characterised by discrepancies between core verbal and non-verbal skills (Happe, 1999). Unlike in typical development, a relative strength has been repeatedly documented in the non-verbal domain (Mayes & Calhoun, 2003; Joseph et al., 2002; but see Siegel et al., 1996). Interestingly, Joseph et al. (2002) documented this pattern in 5-year-old children with high-functioning ASD but found that discrepancies between domains occurred equally in favour of verbal and non-verbal abilities in 8-year-old children, implicating a qualitative developmental shift.

It is possible that the discrepancy in cognitive skills and heterogeneity manifests from the subtests used to measure ability, rather than reflecting true cognitive constructs. For instance, Charman et al. (2011a) studied 156 children with ASD aged 10–14 years and found mixed evidence of a characteristic subtest profile. Whereas some individuals showed a higher performance relative to verbal IQ, others did not show a characteristic peak on block design or object assembly or a clear verbal/non-verbal distinction. The authors also reported that individuals with a non-verbal advantage did not have putatively higher levels of social impairment, refuting the idea of a consistent subtype. Charman et al. (2011b) stress the difficulty identifying a cognitive phenotype, but acknowledge it could enrich remediation programmes, understanding of the relation between brain and behaviour, and the 'autistic experience'.

Challenges of testing ASD and how to design effective studies given challenges

Despite the heterogeneity mentioned in the previous sections, most research in autism samples from high-functioning individuals or those with an Asperger's Syndrome diagnosis. As a result, the heterogeneity is not entirely captured, with the minimally verbal and/or low-functioning subgroup neglected in studies and their practical implications (Tager-Flusberg & Kasari, 2013).

While the natural default of experimental psychologists and scientists is to standardise testing measures for scientific rigour, working with this population may often call for individualised or modified testing approaches. This is a necessary step to be inclusive and to address the specific (and often complex) needs of individual children. Choice of standardised tests need to be carefully considered for practicality in terms of total test-time, language and attentional requirements, validity and age-appropriateness. An individualised approach may also mean considering raw scores over time in single participants, and working on untimed tests. These modifications are important as standardised tests often require responses (reliable gesturing, pointing, attention, language) that are outside of the abilities of those who are nonverbal or very low functioning. Courchesne et al. (2015) found that children with non-verbal autism were unable to complete standardised tests typically used by school psychologists or clinicians to evaluate cognitive ability, such as the Wechsler Intelligence Scale for Children (WISC-IV) and Leiter-R. To avoid underestimating the cognitive abilities in this group, the authors recommend using strength-based assessments such as visual search tasks and the Raven's Coloured Progressive Matrices instead, with suggestions around using touch technology to maintain interest throughout testing.

Another option to reduce the risk of underestimating the cognitive and perceptual abilities in this group is to move away from traditional methods of testing – that typically involves active responses, higher order language use and focused attention – towards passive testing using neurotechnologies. This is done using a creative mix of neuroimaging techniques such as modified functional magnetic resonance imaging (fMRI) protocols, the use of magnetoencephalography (MEG), event-related potentials (ERPs), eye-tracking and the use of virtual reality.

MEG is a brain imaging tool that measures the electromagnetic fields emitted from the cortex in millisecond precision (Hari & Salmelin, 2012). Key advantages of using MEG are that, compared to many other brain imaging tools (e.g. MRI), it is silent and participants are not confined within a tube, which naturally improves comfort levels and compliance. Depending on the MEG system available, participants can opt to lie down or sit up with only their heads inside a helmet. MEG is also useful for research questions on lateralisation of brain function. Magnetic fields do not get distorted by the scalp and skull like in other methods (e.g. ERPs), resulting in clear signals recorded from both hemispheres. However, this method requires participants to keep their heads still during testing, which may be difficult for individuals with more complex needs. It is also not portable, which excludes participants who are not able to travel to the few sites that house these systems. The MEG and its magnetically shielded room is also very expensive to build and maintain.

MEG studies have been successful in investigating auditory or visual processing in the brains of those with high-functioning ASD (Bailey et al., 2005, Gage et al., 2003; Roberts et al., 2010). Our experiences using MEG and ERPs in children with ASD, including those who are low functioning and nonverbal, have been positive. In Yau et al. (2015) and Yau et al. (2016), we used modified MEG protocols and portable EEG (see Figure 19.1) to test auditory processing of social and non-social sounds in a sample of children with ASD aged 6 to 14. We used a passive listening paradigm, and tested children with varying degrees of autism, from minimally verbal/low functioning to high functioning. We observed that modifying test protocols to fit more complex

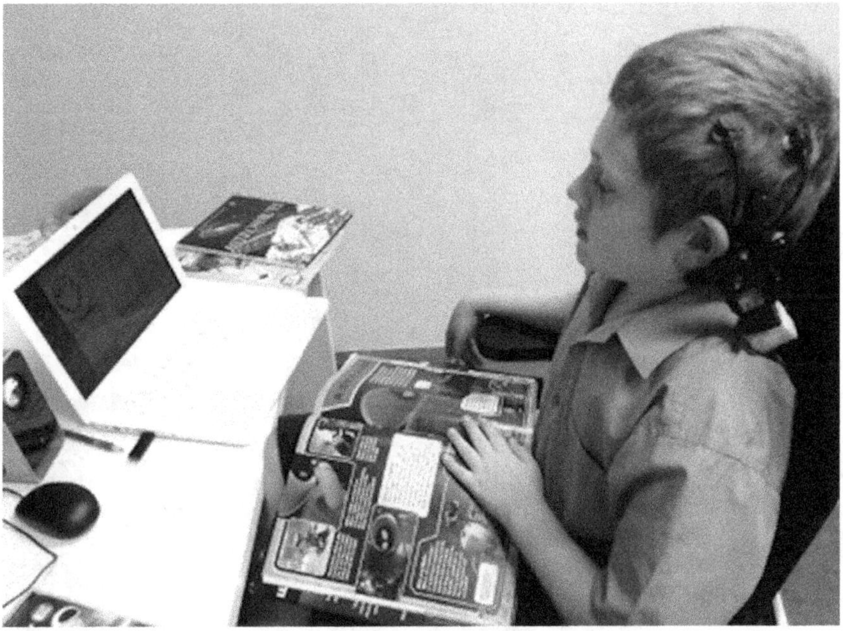

Figure 19.1 Portable electroencephalography (EEG) set up on a child, from Yau et al. (2015)

needs, such as multiple de-sensitising visits, and the use of weighted blankets and engaging videos, improved compliance and reduced head movements. Our findings suggest that auditory processing was generally impaired, showing signs of a maturational delay in the auditory cortex. This perceptual impairment was correlated to degree of language impairment in children with ASD. Additionally, a minimally verbal child with profound autism who became our case study showed a unique pattern of dissociation between social and non-social sounds. Specifically, non-social sounds elicited strong and early brain responses, while brain responses to social sounds were almost absent. We are now extending on this work using modified functional magnetic resonance imaging (fMRI) protocols and scan sequences to make testing sessions more comfortable.

Eye-tracking technology is another promising avenue useful in the study of visual preferences and looking behaviours in autism (Chawarska et al., 2012; Pelphrey et al., 2002). An experiment by Skwerer et al. (2016) used eye-tracking to test word comprehension as part of their multi-method study in minimally verbal children with ASD. Using a range of tests including standardised language tests, caregiver reports, a word-image pair paradigm and a word comprehension test on touch-screen, they found vast heterogeneity in receptive language abilities within this group of participants and across the tests. Similarly, Edelson et al. (2008) used eye-tracking to test for receptive language in 2- to 6-year-old children with ASD and found that looking times are longer in minimally verbal children for pictures for words they know but not for words they did not understand.

A more recent development is the use of eye-tracking within a virtual reality set-up (see Figure 19.2). In Caruana et al. (2017), adults with ASD were tested in an interactive game with a pre-programmed avatar who initiates or responds to joint attention bids. Joint attention is important in language and social skills development, with impairments or delays often being an early diagnostic indicator (Charman, 2003; Mundy et al., 1990). They found that their

Figure 19.2 Virtual reality research using eye-tracking and an interactive paradigm at Macquarie University
Source: Picture courtesy of Nathan Caruana

participants with ASD were slower to respond to the avatar's cues, and had difficulty using eye-gaze information. This is corroborated by subjective reports given by participants who found it difficult to communicate using eye gaze in social situations.

Issues in matching

In order to elicit useful comparisons in special needs and ASD research, typically a target group is compared to a separate population matched on one or more crucial variables. Whether to match and precisely how groups should be matched is an issue of some debate (Burack et al., 2002; Jarrold & Brock, 2004; Mottron, 2004; Mervis & Klein-Tasman, 2004). Researchers have highlighted numerous methodological challenges (Charman, 2004; Tager-Flusberg, 2004) and conceptual issues (Burack et al., 2002) that arise during this process, and in conducting research in ASD in general.

Tager-Flusberg (2004) notes four methodological concerns when conducting research on language in ASD, including concomitant intellectual disability, heterogeneity, developmental change with age and limited sample sizes. Many children with ASD also have intellectual disability, estimated to be up to 70% of the spectrum (Fombonne, 2003), and it can be difficult to ascertain any differences which are specific to the autism, rather than autism with intellectual disability. Heterogeneity, as noted, poses challenges of generalisation and standardisation of testing materials. The developmental component of ASD should also not be overlooked; development changes as a result of the interaction between genetic predisposition and environmental actions (Karmiloff-Smith, 1998). This means that an individual's specific level of input in early years will affect their developing abilities and level of impairment in a future end state, in a positive or negative direction. Tager-Flusberg (2004) emphasises that researchers often include wide age ranges of participants and implicitly (and falsely) assume that performance on a language task is not influenced by developmental change. The final methodological concern she highlights plagues research of any syndrome or clinical population: limited sample sizes. Although no longer seen as a rare disorder (Baird et al., 2006; Hill et al., 2015), most studies of individuals with ASD report relatively few participants which also contributes to issues of generalisation and interacts with the heterogeneous nature of the condition.

Other issues that have been identified include the use of a control or comparison group. The strengths and weaknesses in ASD, also termed peaks and valleys of social and cognitive ability, are core to the diagnostic formulation of ASD and thus specific to the condition and not found in other populations (Burack et al., 2004). This makes comparison to others already uneven. Studies of broader autism phenotype, traits of the condition found in relatives that do not reach diagnostic threshold, are also problematic in the sense that sensitivity and specificity of measures may vary between comparison groups (Szatmari et al., 2004). Comparison groups are only helpful when considering the context of the particular research questions that are asked, including a consideration of a focus on either investigating normality or uniqueness (Burack et al., 2004). When comparison groups are implemented, how they are matched needs to be carefully considered.

Charman (2004) advocates the use of language as a matching variable in preschool children with ASD, given the central role of language and communication impairment across individuals across the spectrum. In very young children with significant language impairment, though, some tests may not be appropriate with children failing to establish basal levels. One common test of receptive language abilities, used as it requires children to point to pictures thus removing verbal language demands, is the British Picture Vocabulary Scale (BPVS-3) (Dunn et al. 2009). It contains norms for children aged 3–16, thus standardised scores would be unavailable for some children who present with significant language impairment; it also has been suggested to overestimate performance in ASD (Mottron, 2004). Charman (2004) advises that parent measures may provide an alternative but are met with their own challenges including over-estimation of ability, and low rate of agreement between parental report and structured language assessments for language comprehension (Charman et al., 2003). Using multiple assessments can provide a composite of ability and may better characterise a target population and individual differences.

Some researchers use multiple scales to provide different areas for matching. For instance, Gillespie-Smith et al. (2014) compare performance of children with ASD to three comparison groups, one matching on chronological age, a second on receptive language and a third on non-verbal ability. This method of matching provides one systematic way to tease apart effects of background cognitive abilities on performance. On a practical level, though, incorporating multiple measures may be difficult to achieve with limited testing time and attention levels that vary and can be challenging to sustain in target populations. Other criticisms of this approach have also been identified, including the difficulty using an average measure like verbal or non-verbal age, which masks the fact that IQ profiles are not flat in ASD and, as mentioned in the prior section, that non-verbal scores tend to be higher than verbal abilities in many individuals (Jarrold & Brock, 2004). To eliminate these confounds, Jarrold and Brock (2004) suggest that recruiting a large sample of typical participants can allow researchers to determine a normative relation between task performance and background cognitive measures. Performance against age or ability can then be regressed in this population and differences amongst individual members of the clinical group of interest can be determined by evaluating the discrepancy between observed and expected performance for their specific age and ability level. The researchers also suggest that using a task that is designed to match a multitude of non-central features of the main experimental measure, yet is also sensitive to variation in ability, is perhaps the best way to maintain control when matching groups (Jarrold & Brock, 2004).

How atypical research can inform typical development

Research into ASD is essential to provide data-grounded rationale for appropriate educational and behavioural interventions, to directly benefit children and adults with the condition (Schopler et al., 2001). One of the arguably most popular interventions, applied behaviour analysis (ABA), was investigated in a ground-breaking two-year study by Lovaas (1987) and remains heavily researched and influential. Other inventions follow from careful work on joint attention (Kasari et al., 2006; Jones & Carr, 2004), the potential for digital technology (Allen et al., 2016) and the extensive literature base on social skills in ASD (Gates et al., 2017). It is clear that research in ASD in the last several decades has advanced knowledge of the cognitive and neuropsychological differences and unique patterns of behaviour seen in those across the spectrum.

Research into atypical developmental trajectories and populations can inform not just specific disorders, but also typical development (Leslie & Thaiss, 1992). Pennington (2009) emphasises that 'we cannot understand clinical phenomena without a theory of normal function, but clinical phenomena sometimes force revisions in our theories of normal function' (p. 72), suggesting the need for parallel study and an interdisciplinary approach. Karmiloff-Smith (1992) was a key proponent of the importance of studying different trajectories alongside one another, using a framework of progressive modularisation of cognitive modules that applied both to neurodevelopmental disorders and typical development (D'Souza & Filippi, 2017). She argued that cross-syndrome dissociations are key and studying a disorder in isolation fails to capture important information about subtle developmental differences and interactions. One paradigmatic literature base in the typical domain that has been greatly enriched by the study of ASD in particular is theory of mind.

The ability to infer mental states such as desire, belief and want, and use such inferences to predict behaviour is a crucial foundation for effective human communication. In Premack and Woodruff's (1978) seminal paper, the authors first questioned whether chimpanzees have a 'theory of mind', thus giving rise to a burgeoning area of research across comparative, typical and atypical development. Early studies with preschoolers looked at when this ability develops and concentrated on points of failure. The classic 'false belief' test initiated by Wimmer and Perner (1983) demonstrated that children below the age of 5 provided realist errors when asked where a doll (Maxi) would look for his hidden chocolate, after it was moved by another doll (his mother). Subsequent adaptions of the task explicitly pointed out that the protagonist was absent when the object of interest changed location, and consistently identified a transition between age 3 and 4 from failure to success on the task (Wellman, 2017). False belief research dominated the theory of mind realm for years (Wellman et al., 2001), but it was not until theory of mind was considered as a core deficit in ASD that researchers began to consider the breadth of precursor theory of mind skills (e.g. joint attention, preference for human biological motion) and how this might be represented in the brain.

Leslie (1994) and Baron-Cohen (1997) endorsed a modular approach postulating that theory of mind was encapsulated, and this module was uniquely impaired in individuals with ASD (see also Baron-Cohen et al., 1985). Research that followed over the next decades documented the extent of theory of mind difficulties in individuals across the spectrum (Baron-Cohen, 2000), changing how the disorder was characterised. The impact of this proliferation of theory of mind research stretched to typical development, with new investigations into neural substrates (Saxe &

Kanwisher, 2003; Schurz et al., 2014), theory of mind processing in typically developing adults (Schneider et al., 2017) and differences between explicit and implicit processing (Kulke et al., 2017). The modular approach advocated by Baron-Cohen (1997) and Leslie (1994) also shed light on the developmental origins of social cognition and brain plasticity (Mundy & Neal, 2000; Scholl & Leslie, 1999).

Conclusion

Studying any population with special needs can be challenging, and ASD is no exception. Researchers need to consider the enormous heterogeneity of the condition in terms of cognitive and linguistic profiles, and develop appropriate testing methods for individual populations. Passive neuropsychological and neuroscientific methods are one promising means of testing individuals who are minimally verbal. Despite the challenges, research in ASD is important for informing atypical and typical development, as well as providing a data-driven evidence base to evaluate intervention outcomes.

References

Allen, M.L., Hartley, C. and Cain, K. (2016) iPads and the use of "apps" by children with Autism Spectrum Disorder: Do they promote learning? *Frontiers in Psychology* 7, 1305.

American Psychiatric Association (2013) *Diagnostic and statistical manual of mental disorders* (5th edition). Arlington, VA: American Psychiatric Publishing.

Bailey, A.J., Braeutigam, S., Jousmäki, V. and Swithenby, S.J. (2005) Abnormal activation of face processing systems at early and intermediate latency in individuals with autism spectrum disorder: A magnetoencephalographic study. *European Journal of Neuroscience 21* (9), 2575–2585.

Baird, G., Simonoff, E., Pickles, A., Chandler, S., Loucas, T., Meldrum, D. and Charman, T. (2006) Prevalence of disorders of the autism spectrum in a population cohort of children in South Thames: The Special Needs and Autism Project (SNAP). *The Lancet* 368 (9531), 210–215.

Baron-Cohen, S. (1997) *Mindblindness: An essay on autism and theory of mind.* Cambridge, MA: MIT Press.

Baron-Cohen, S. (2000) Theory of mind and autism: A fifteen year review. *Understanding Other Minds: Perspectives from Developmental Cognitive Neuroscience* 2, 3–20.

Baron-Cohen, S., Leslie, A.M. and Frith, U. (1985) Does the autistic child have a "theory of mind"? *Cognition* 21 (1), 37–46.

Betancur, C. (2011) Etiological heterogeneity in autism spectrum disorders: More than 100 genetic and genomic disorders and still counting. *Brain Research* 1380, 42–77.

Beveridge, S. (1999) *Special educational needs in schools.* New York: Psychology Press.

Burack, J.A., Iarocci, G., Flanagan, T.D. and Bowler, D.M. (2004) On mosaics and melting pots: Conceptual considerations of comparison and matching strategies. *Journal of Autism and Developmental Disorders* 34 (1), 65–73.

Burack, J.A., Iarocci, G., Bowler, D. and Mottron, L. (2002) Benefits and pitfalls in the merging of disciplines: The example of developmental psychopathology and the study of persons with autism. *Development and Psychopathology 14* (2), 225–237.

Caruana, N., Stieglitz Ham, H., Brock, J., Woolgar, A., Kloth, N., Palermo, R. and Mcarthur, G. (2017) Joint attention difficulties in autistic adults: An interactive eye-tracking study. *Autism: The International Journal of Research and Practice.* doi: 1362361316676204.

Charman, T. (2003) Why is joint attention a pivotal skill in autism? *Philosophical Transactions of the Royal Society B: Biological Sciences* 358 (1430), 315–324.

Charman, T. (2004) Matching preschool children with autism spectrum disorders and comparison children for language ability: Methodological challenges. *Journal of Autism and Developmental Disorders* 34 (1), 59–64.

Charman, T., Pickles, A., Simonoff, E., Chandler, S., Loucas, T. and Baird, G. (2011a), IQ in children with autism spectrum disorders: Data from the Special Needs and Autism Project (SNAP). *Psychological Medicine* 41, 619–627.

Charman, T., Jones, C.R., Pickles, A., Simonoff, E., Baird, G. and Happé, F. (2011b) Defining the cognitive phenotype of autism. *Brain Research* 1380, 10–21.

Chawarska, K., Macari, S. and Shic, F. (2012) Context modulates attention to social scenes in toddlers with autism. *Journal of Child Psychology and Psychiatry* 53 (8), 903–913.

Christensen, D.L. (2016) Prevalence and characteristics of autism spectrum disorder among children aged 8 years – autism and developmental disabilities monitoring network, 11 sites, United States, 2012. *Mmwr-Morbidity and Mortality Weekly Report* 65, 404–404.

Coleman, M. and Gillberg, C. (2012) *The autisms*. Oxford: Oxford University Press.

Courchesne, V., Meilleur, A.A.S., Poulin-Lord, M.P., Dawson, M. and Soulières, I. (2015) Autistic children at risk of being underestimated: School-based pilot study of a strength-informed assessment. *Molecular Autism* 6 (1), 12.

Damiano, C.R., Mazefsky, C.A., White, S.W. and Dichter, G.S. (2014) Future directions for research in autism spectrum disorders. *Journal of Clinical Child and Adolescent Psychology: The Official Journal for the Society of Clinical Child and Adolescent Psychology, American Psychological Association, Division 53* 43 (5), 828–843.

Darrou, C., Pry, R., Pernon, E., Michelon, C., Aussilloux, C. and Baghdadli, A. (2010) Outcome of young children with autism: Does the amount of intervention influence developmental trajectories? *Autism* 14 (6), 663–677.

D'Souza, D. and Filippi, R. (2017) Progressive modularization: Reframing our understanding of typical and atypical language development. *First Language* 37 (5), 518–529.

Dunn, L.M., Dunn, L.M. and Styles, B. (2009) *The British picture vocabulary scale* (3rd edition). GL Assessment.

Edelson, L., Fine, A. and Tager-Flusberg, H. (2008) Comprehension of nouns and verbs in toddlers with autism: An eye-tracking study. *International Meeting for Autism Research*, May.

Elsabbagh, M., Mercure, E., Hudry, K., Chandler, S., Pasco, G., Charman, T., Pickles, A., Baron-Cohen, S., Bolton, P., Johnson, M.H. and Team, B. (2012) Infant neural sensitivity to dynamic eye gaze is associated with later emerging autism. *Current Biology* 22, 338–342.

Field, C., Allen, M.L. and Lewis, C. (2016) Attentional learning helps language acquisition take shape for atypically developing children, not just children with autism spectrum disorders. *Journal of Autism and Developmental Disorders* 46 (10), 3195–3206.

Folstein, S.E. and Piven, J. (1991) Etiology of autism – genetic influences. *Pediatrics* 87, 767–773.

Fombonne, E. (2003) Epidemiological surveys of autism and other pervasive developmental disorders: An update. *Journal of Autism and Developmental Disorders* 33 (4), 365–382.

Fountain, C., Winter, A.S. and Bearman, P.S. (2012) Six developmental trajectories characterize children with autism. *Pediatrics* 129 (5), e1112–e1120.

Gage, N.M., Siegel, B. and Roberts, T.P. (2003) Cortical auditory system maturational abnormalities in children with autism disorder: An MEG investigation. *Developmental Brain Research*, 144 (2), 201–209.

Gates, J.A., Kang, E. and Lerner, M.D. (2017) Efficacy of group social skills interventions for youth with autism spectrum disorder: A systematic review and meta-analysis. *Clinical Psychology Review* 52, 164–181.

Geschwind, D.H. (2011) Genetics of autism spectrum disorders. *Trends in Cognitive Sciences* 15, 409–416.

Gillespie-Smith, K., Riby, D.M., Hancock, P.J. and Doherty-Sneddon, G. (2014) Children with autism spectrum disorder (ASD) attend typically to faces and objects presented within their picture communication systems. *Journal of Intellectual Disability Research* 58 (5), 459–470.

Great Britain Committee of Enquiry into the Education of Handicapped Children and Young People and Warnock, M. (1978) *Special educational needs: Report of the committee of enquiry into the education of handicapped children and young people*, HMSO. London.

Happe, F. (1999) Autism: Cognitive deficit or cognitive style? *Trends in Cognitive Sciences* 3, 216–222.

Happe, F. and Ronald, A. (2008) The 'Fractionable Autism Triad': A review of evidence from behavioural, genetic, cognitive and neural research. *Neuropsychology Review* 18, 287–304.

Hari, R. and Salmelin, R. (2012) Magnetoencephalography: From SQUIDs to neuroscience. Neuroimage 20th Anniversary Special Edition. *Neuroimage* 61, 386–396.

Hartley, C. and Allen, M.L. (2014a) Intentions vs. resemblance: Understanding pictures in typical development and autism. *Cognition* 131 (1), 44–59.

Hartley, C. and Allen, M.L. (2014b) Brief report: Generalisation of word – picture relations in children with autism and typically developing children. *Journal of Autism and Developmental Disorders* 44 (8), 2064–2071.

Hartley, C and Allen, M.L. (2015) Symbolic understanding of pictures in low-functioning children with autism: The effects of iconicity and naming. *Journal of Autism and Developmental Disorders* 45 (1), 15–30.

Hill, A.P., Zuckerman, K. and Fombonne, E. (2015) Epidemiology of autism spectrum disorders. In: *Translational approaches to autism spectrum disorder*. Cham: Springer International Publishing, 13–38.

Howlin, P. (2003) Outcome in high-functioning adults with autism with and without early language delays: Implications for the differentiation between autism and Asperger syndrome. *Journal of Autism and Developmental Disorders* 33 (1), 3–13.

Howlin, P., Mawhood and Rutter, M. (2000) Autism and developmental receptive language disorder – a follow-up comparison in early adult life. II: Social, behavioural, and psychiatric outcomes. *Journal of Child Psychology and Psychiatry and Allied Disciplines* 41 (5), 561–578.

Jarrold, C. and Brock, J. (2004) To match or not to match? Methodological issues in autism-related research. *Journal of Autism and Developmental Disorders* 34 (1), 81–86.

Jones, E.A. and Carr, E.G. (2004) Joint attention in children with autism: Theory and intervention. *Focus on Autism and Other Developmental Disabilities* 19 (1), 13–26.

Joseph, R.M., Tager-Flusberg, H. and Lord, C. (2002) Cognitive profiles and social-communicative functioning in children with autism spectrum disorder. *Journal of Child Psychology and Psychiatry and Allied Disciplines* 43, 807–821.

Karmiloff-Smith, A. (1992) *Beyond modularity: A developmental perspective on cognitive science*. Cambridge, MA: MIT Press.

Karmiloff-Smith, A. (1998) Development itself is the key to understanding developmental disorders. *Trends in Cognitive Sciences* 2 (10), 389–398.

Kasari, C, Brady, N., Lord, C. and Tager-Flusberg, H. (2013) Assessing the minimally verbal school-aged child with autism spectrum disorder. *Autism Research* 6, 479–493.

Kasari, C., Freeman, S. and Paparella, T. (2006) Joint attention and symbolic play in young children with autism: A randomized controlled intervention study. *Journal of Child Psychology and Psychiatry* 47 (6), 611–620.

Kasari, C. and Rotheram-Fuller, E. (2005) Current trends in psychological research on children with high-functioning autism and Asperger disorder. *Current Opinion in Psychiatry* 18, 497–501.

Keil, S., Miller, O. and Cobb, R. (2006) Special educational needs and disability. *British Journal of Special Education* 33 (4), 168–172.

Klintwall, L., Eldevik, S. and Eikeseth, S. (2015) Narrowing the gap: Effects of intervention on developmental trajectories in autism. *Autism* 19 (1), 53–63.

Kulke, L., Reiß, M., Krist, H. and Rakoczy, H. (2017) Implicit theory of Mind across the life span – anticipatory looking data. *Data in Brief* 15, 712–719.

Leslie, A.M. (1994) ToMM, ToBy, and agency: Core architecture and domain specificity. *Mapping the Mind: Domain Specificity in Cognition and Culture*, 119–148.

Leslie, A.M. and Thaiss, L. (1992) Domain specificity in conceptual development: Neuropsychological evidence from autism. *Cognition* 43 (3), 225–251.

Lord, C., Risi, S., Dilavore, P.S., Shulman, C., Thurm, A. and Pickles, A. (2006) Autism from 2 to 9 years of age. *Archives of General Psychiatry* 63, 694–701.

Lovaas, O.I. (1987) Behavioral treatment and normal educational and intellectual functioning in young autistic children. *Journal of Consulting and Clinical Psychology* 55, 3–9.

Mannion, A. and Leader, G. (2013) Comorbidity in autism spectrum disorder: A literature review. *Research in Autism Spectrum Disorders* 7, 1595–1616.

Mayes, S.D. and Calhoun, S.L. (2003) Ability profiles in children with autism: Influence of age and IQ. *Autism* 7 (1), 65–80.

Mcgovern, C.W. and Sigman, M. (2005) Continuity and change from early childhood to adolescence in autism. *Journal of Child Psychology and Psychiatry* 46, 401–408.

Mervis, C.B. and Klein-Tasman, B.P. (2004) Methodological issues in group-matching designs: α levels for control variable comparisons and measurement characteristics of control and target variables. *Journal of Autism and Developmental Disorders* 34 (1), 7–17.

Mottron, L. (2004) Matching strategies in cognitive research with individuals with high-functioning autism: Current practices, instrument biases, and recommendations. *Journal of Autism and Developmental Disorders* 34 (1), 19–27.

Mundy, P. and Neal, A.R. (2000) Neural plasticity, joint attention, and a transactional social-orienting model of autism. *International Review of Research in Mental Retardation* 23, 139–168.

Mundy, P., Sigman, M. and Kasari, C. (1990) A longitudinal study of joint attention and language development in autistic children. *Journal of Autism and Developmental Disorders* 20 (1), 115–128.

National Institute for Health and Clinical Excellence (NICE) (2011) *Autism: Recognition, referral and diagnosis of children and young people on the autism spectrum*'. Retrieved 30 June 2014 from www.nice.org.uk/guidance/CG128.

Norwich, B. 2013. Categories of special educational needs. *The SAGE Handbook of Special Education: Two Volume Set* 1, 55. London: Sage.

Ozonoff, S., Iosif, A.-M., Baguio, F., Cook, I.C., Hill, M.M., Hutman, T. and Sigman, M.A. (2010) A prospective study of the emergence of early behavioral signs of autism. *Journal of the American Academy of Child & Adolescent Psychiatry* 49 (3), 256–266.

Pelphrey, K.A., Sasson, N.J., Reznick, J.S., Paul, G., Goldman, B.D. and Piven, J. (2002) Visual scanning of faces in autism. *Journal of Autism and Developmental Disorders* 32, 249–261.

Pelphrey, K.A., Shultz, S., Hudac, C.M. and Vander Wyk, B.C. (2011) Research review: Constraining heterogeneity: The social brain and its development in autism spectrum disorder. *Journal of Child Psychology and Psychiatry* 52 (6), 631–644.

Pennington, B.F. (2009) How neuropsychology informs our understanding of developmental disorders. *Journal of Child Psychology and Psychiatry* 50 (1–2), 72–78.

Preissler, M.A. (2008) Associative learning of pictures and words by low-functioning children with autism. *Autism* 12 (3), 231–248.

Premack, D. and Woodruff, G. (1978) Does the chimpanzee have a theory of mind? *Behavioral and Brian Sciences* 4 (1), 515–526.

Rapin, I. and Dunn, M. (2003) Update on the language disorders of individuals on the autistic spectrum. *Brain and Development* 25, 166–172.

Roberts, T., Khan, S., Rey, M., Monroe, J., Cannon, K., Blaskey, L.W., Woldoff, S., Qasmieh, S., Gandal, M., Schmidt, G.L. (2010) MEG detection of delayed auditory evoked responses in autism spectrum disorders: Towards an imaging biomarker for autism. *Autism Research* 3, 8–18.

Ronald, A. and Hoekstra, R.A. (2011) Autism spectrum disorders and autistic traits: A decade of new twin studies. *American Journal of Medical Genetics Part B-Neuropsychiatric Genetics* 156B, 255–274.

Saxe, R. and Kanwisher, N. (2003) People thinking about thinking people: The role of the temporo-parietal junction in 'theory of mind'. *Neuroimage* 19 (4), 1835–1842.

Schneider, D., Slaughter, V.P. and Dux, P.E. (2017) Current evidence for automatic theory of mind processing in adults. *Cognition* 162, 27–31.

Scholl, B.J. and Leslie, A.M. (1999) Modularity, development and 'theory of mind'. *Mind & Language* 14 (1), 131–153.

Schopler, E., Yirmiya, N. and Shulman, C. (2001) *The research basis for autism intervention*. (Marcus, L.M., ed.). New York: Kluwer Academic/Plenum Publishers.

Schurz, M., Radua, J., Aichhorn, M., Richlan, F. and Perner, J. (2014) Fractionating theory of mind: A meta-analysis of functional brain imaging studies. *Neuroscience & Biobehavioral Reviews* 42, 9–34.

Seltzer, M.M., Shattuck, P., Abbeduto, L. and Greenberg, J.S. (2004) Trajectory of development in adolescents and adults with autism. *Developmental Disabilities Research Reviews* 10 (4), 234–247.

Siegel, D.J., Minshew, N.J. and Goldstein, G. (1996) Wechsler IQ profiles in diagnosis of high-functioning autism. *Journal of Autism and Developmental Disorders* 26, 389–406.

Skwerer, D.P., Jordan, S.E., Brukilacchio, B.H. and Tager-Flusberg, H. (2016) Comparing methods for assessing receptive language skills in minimally verbal children and adolescents with autism spectrum disorders. *Autism* 20, 591–604.

Szatmari, P., Zwaigenbaum, L. and Bryson, S. (2004) Conducting genetic epidemiology studies of autism spectrum disorders: Issues in matching. *Journal of Autism and Developmental Disorders* 34 (1), 49–57.

Tager-Flusberg, H. (2004) Strategies for conducting research on language in autism. *Journal of Autism and Developmental Disorders* 34 (1), 75–80.

Tager-Flusberg, H. and Caronna, E. (2007) Language disorders: Autism and other pervasive developmental disorders. *Pediatric Clinics* 54 (3), 469–481.

Tager-Flusberg, H. and Kasari, C. (2013) Minimally verbal school-aged children with autism spectrum disorder: The neglected end of the spectrum. *Autism Research* 6, 468–478.

Terzi, L. (2005) Beyond the dilemma of difference: The capability approach to disability and special educational needs. *Journal of Philosophy of Education* 39 (3), 443–459.

Warnock. M. (2005) *Special educational needs: A new look*. London: Philosophy of Education Society of Great Britain.

Warnock, M. and Norwich, B. (2010) *Special educational needs: A new look.* New York: Bloomsbury.
Wellman, H.M. (2017) The development of theory of mind: Historical reflections. *Child Development Perspectives* 11 (3), 207–214.
Wellman, H.M., Cross, D. and Watson, J. (2001) Meta-analysis of theory-of-mind development: The truth about false belief. *Child Development* 72 (3), 655–684.
Wimmer, H. and Perner, J. (1983) Beliefs about beliefs: Representation and constraining function of wrong beliefs in young children's understanding of deception. *Cognition* 13 (1), 103–128.
Wolff, J.J., Gu, H., Gerig, G., Elison, J.T., Styner, M., Gouttard, S., Botteron, K.N., Dager, S.R., Dawson, G., Estes, A.M. and Evans, A.C. (2012) Differences in white matter fiber tract development present from 6 to 24 months in infants with autism. *American Journal of Psychiatry* 169 (6), 589–600.
Yau, S.H., McArthur, G., Badcock, N.A. and Brock, J. (2015) Case study: Auditory brain responses in a minimally verbal child with autism and cerebral palsy. *Frontiers in Neuroscience* 9, 208.
Yau, S.H., Brock, J. and McArthur, G. (2016) The relationship between spoken language and speech and nonspeech processing in children with autism: A magnetic event-related field study. *Developmental Science* 19 (5), 834–852.

20

USING MIXED METHODS RESEARCH WITH YOUNG CHILDREN AND THEIR FAMILIES IN CULTURALLY, LINGUISTICALLY AND SOCIALLY DIVERSE COMMUNITIES

Jim Anderson, Ann Anderson, Ji Eun Kim and Marianne McTavish

Several years ago during an introductory doctoral seminar, a student in the first month of his graduate program commented that he had decided he would "be doing a qualitative study" for his dissertation. When asked what problem he had identified and which research questions his study would address, he indicated that he had not thought that far ahead but he "definitely would not be doing a quantitative study." Such intransigence is fairly common among educational researchers and the so-called *paradigm wars*, which presuppose the incommensurability of qualitative and quantitative research methods, are still very much alive and well in some quarters (Shannon-Baker, 2016). This state of affairs certainly applies to research in the area of literacy education which we focus on in this chapter.

Despite the omnipresent tension between these two research paradigms (e.g., Calfee & Sperling, 2010), a significant number of educational researchers employ mixed methods, believing that there are distinct advantages to be had by utilizing data gathering and data analysis techniques from each paradigm. Like Mesel (2013), we believe that "Empirical research . . . originates in challenges or problems posed in a specific field of practice. Researchers formulate research aims, define research questions, and choose methodologies in an attempt to answer these questions" (p. 750). That is, the research enterprise should be about solving significant education problems and/or finding answers to important questions and educational researchers need to employ the best inquiry tools available; to do so, we argue, sometimes necessitates mixed methods.

In this chapter, we first review the principles and tenets of mixed methods research (e.g., Creswell & Clark, 2011; Onwuegbuzie & Mallette, 2011) and its roots in eclecticism and pragmatism. As noted, the problem or issue and the emanating research question(s) will obviously influence the methods one utilizes in a study. However, given that the educational research milieu is evolving, we believe researchers will increasingly need to attend to other factors, such as who is expected to read (or listen to or view) the findings or results of a study, for whom or for what purpose(s) is the research being conducted, who will it serve, the epistemology(ies) undergirding the research and/or claims that can be made based on the findings, the ethical and moral responsibilities of researchers and the purposes that the research aims to fulfill. Proposing that such factors or issues need to be considered when designing and conducting empirical studies, we demonstrate through examples from our own research with young children and families from working class homes and with immigrant and refugee families, how we utilized mixed methods in what we considered to be culturally and socially appropriate ways. We write from the perspectives of researchers working in Canada, although we believe that the issues we raise, and the perspectives or positions we offer, are similar to those in many other countries.

Principles and tenets of mixed methods research

Background

Over time, various terms have been used to describe studies that employ both quantitative and qualitative methods but currently, the name *mixed methods research* is most common and conventional (Creswell & Plano Clark, 2007). Mixed methods research involves the intentional incorporation of both quantitative and qualitative approaches in "the philosophical or theoretical framework(s), methods of data collection and analysis, overall research design, and/or discussion of research conclusions" (Shannon-Baker, 2016, p. 321), to answer an inquiry that a single method cannot address.

Some scholars call the divide (and sometimes, antagonism) between researchers aligned with qualitative approaches and those who identify with quantitative methods as a *paradigm war*, (Creswell & Plano Clark, 2007; Tashakkori & Teddlie, 1998). However, over the years, some researchers and scholars (e.g., Howe, 1988; Yin, 2006) have recognized, and argued for, the compatibility of, and commonalities between, quantitative and qualitative research methods. For example, Howe (1988) argued that the major tenets of quantitative and qualitative research methods are compatible, so that both approaches can be mixed and should be used in research. Indeed, four characteristics that need to be satisfied to ensure rigor and quality are common to both quantitative and qualitative research. These are: inclusion of all evidence, recognition of rival explanations, focus on significant results with implications and "investigatory expertise about the subject" (Yin, 1994, p. 82). Furthermore, both quantitative and qualitative research traditions have "a common goal: to understand and improve the human condition" (Reichardt & Rallis, 1994, p. 11). In addition, scholars have pointed out that using mixed methods helps to overcome some of the limitations of utilizing only one research method (e.g., Erzberger & Prein, 1997; Reichardt & Rallis, 1994; Sechrest & Sidani, 1995) and that utilizing mixed methods is a means of triangulation. Some researchers tend to view mixed methods as a research process, for example, using quantitative measures to gain an *etic* or more global understanding or perspective of a problem or issue and then using qualitative research methods to garner an *emic* or more nuanced, particularistic understanding or view of the same issue. For example, in their two phase study, Reese et al. (2003) used qualitative methods to document and analyze reading styles in parent-child shared book reading and then used quantitative methods to determine the relationship between the three reading styles they identified and measures of children's early literacy knowledge. Of course, the process can be reversed. We next examine some of the conceptual backdrop informing mixed methods research.

Philosophical/theoretical underpinning

Pragmatism is a central paradigmatic foundation for mixed methods research. Pragmatism considers phenomena as encompassing "singular or multiple realities" (Creswell & Plano Clark, 2007, p. 24), allows for both objective and subjective points of view, recognizes researchers' biased and unbiased perspectives, acknowledges possible causal, but unfixed relationships between events and/or phenomena, and legitimizes both deductive and inductive logic (Tashakkori & Teddlie, 1998).

As noted, in response to the so-called paradigm war, some researchers and scholars have argued for the necessity of adopting pragmatic stances in conducting literacy research (e.g., Dillon et al., 2004; Stephens & Pearson, 1992). According to Dillon et al. (2004), pragmatism can provide alternative ways to solve current problems in literacy research, including what some scholars contend has been the minimal impact of findings from literacy research on curriculum and pedagogy, and the continued and troubling underachievement of some children and youth, particularly those from marginalized groups.

According to Onwuegbuzie and Mallette (2011), studies in the literacy field tend to provide partial interpretations of the phenomena investigated, because of the inherent constraints of both qualitative and quantitative studies. For example, Lonigan et al.'s (1999) quantitative study showed a significant relationship between dialogic, parent-child shared reading and children's early literacy development, but did not provide detailed descriptions of how parents and children co-constructed meaning through interactions during the reading. In contrast, Heath's (1983) foundational qualitative study provided detailed descriptions of how parents and children from different socio-cultural contexts interacted during shared reading and other literacy events, but did not establish a relationship between these interactions and children's literacy knowledge. Of course, it is important to point out that the studies had different research questions and were located within different disciplinary boundaries – Heath's within ethnography and socio-linguistics and Lonigan et al.'s within developmental psychology. Nevertheless, the two studies, while important, provided a somewhat limited understanding of the shared reading phenomenon.

Advantages of mixed methods research

Mixed methods allow researchers to take advantage of the strengths of quantitative and qualitative approaches and to gain a more complete understanding of phenomena (Creswell, 2010). Quantitative studies provide insights "describing, explaining and predicting human phenomena" by presenting associations or relations among different variables, while qualitative approaches allow researchers to establish reasons and paths/methods in an observed phenomenon by "exploring, discovering, describing, and constructing"(Onwuegbuzie & Mallette, 2011, pp. 301–302). As described in the previous section, Lonigan et al.'s (1999) study showed the association between the two variables (parent-child interactions and children's literacy development), while Heath's (1983) study described in detail the ways parents and children shared texts during literacy events in three socio-cultural communities. A mixed methods study would provide more in-depth and nuanced understandings of the relationships between the two phenomena. Of course, it is important to reiterate that these two individual studies generated invaluable knowledge and indeed, for some research questions and educational issues, mixed methods is inappropriate. Nevertheless, mixed methods, when appropriate, can contribute to understanding issues and phenomena at both macro and micro levels (Bronfenbrenner & Evans, 2000). Scholars have pointed out that studies that employ mixed methods offer three major advantages over single method approaches: (1) provision of answers to the research questions that cannot be answered by single method approaches, (2) provision of better/stronger inferences and (3) provision of "the opportunity for presenting a greater diversity of divergent views" (Tashakkori & Teddlie, 2003, p. 15).

Importantly, mixed methods enable researchers to answer questions that cannot be answered by mono-method research (Creswell & Plano Clark, 2007; Morse & Niehaus, 2016) and advance our understanding of "different aspects or levels of reality" (Erzberger & Prein, 1997, p. 144). That is, qualitative methods can provide exploratory understandings of phenomena while quantitative studies provide confirmatory understandings of them (Tashakkori & Teddlie, 2003). As mentioned, in practice, some researchers select and integrate different methods that can answer their inquiry and are not constrained or fettered by a single method or a particular paradigm or belief system or disciplinary boundaries (Mesel, 2013).

Mixed methods research allows researchers to examine social phenomena in more depth and in greater breadth (Yin, 2006) and thereby possibly provides more *accurate* inferences (Tashakkori & Teddlie, 2003). Moreover, Erzberger and Prein (1997) posit that convergent results of quantitative and qualitative approaches can increase the validity of the results, by providing complementarity (and serving a triangulation function), and thus allowing multiple inferences (Tashakkori & Teddlie, 2003). Indeed, some scholars propose that because mixed methods research involves various data sources and analyses, it might better explain social phenomena that occur in complex institutions and multifaceted realities, such as young children's language and literacy development in homes, schools and communities than can qualitative *or* quantitative studies alone (Calfee & Sperling, 2010; Creswell et al., 2003).

Another advantage of mixed methods is that "divergent findings" provide opportunities to make different inferences, reflecting different perspectives (Creswell & Plano Clark, 2007; Tashakkori & Teddlie, 2003). According to Erzberger and Kelle (2003), divergent findings promote the "re-examination of the conceptual frameworks and the assumption[s] underlying" studies (Tashakkori & Teddlie, 2003, p. 17). Erzberger and Kelle (2003) contend that such re-examination should provoke "further analyses of the data in the form of possible transformation of data types to each other, internal validity audits, and design of a new study or phase for further investigation" (p. 17). In other words, checks and balances are embedded in mixed methods, a characteristic which we see as especially important in educational research.

Despite the advantages just outlined, some caution is called for in mixed methods research. For instance, this type of research requires an array of research skills and knowledge of data gathering and analysis, in both qualitative and quantitative domains, and it often requires more time and resources (Creswell & Plano Clark, 2007). Researchers need to have an adequate understanding about, and experience with, both quantitative and qualitative methods when conducting mixed methods research (e.g., Creswell & Plano Clark, 2007; Tashakkori & Teddlie, 1998) and importantly, know how to combine and integrate both research methods (Tashakkori & Teddlie, 2003). Thus, even though mixed methods research has strengths, before conducting a study, researchers should consider possible challenges when deciding whether using mixed methods is realistic.

While we wish to reiterate that the educational issue or problem and the research questions that flow from it should determine the method(s) used, we propose that other contextual factors also affect and influence that decision. In keeping with the pragmatic foundations of mixed methods, researchers need to be mindful of the changing educational landscape, and of changes in the academy. For example, differing perspectives sometimes come into play during the peer review process for journal articles, research grant applications and conference papers, for instance, reviewers steeped in quantitative tradition can be dismissive of studies that are interpretive or that employ qualitative methods. Likewise, the culture of an academic department is also an important consideration in terms of career progress such as tenure and promotion, for instance, in some departments and units, there is a palpable disdain for quantitative methods.

Audience

Historically, "curiosity driven research" has been prominent in universities and in the case of educational research, the audience or readerships has consisted mainly of other researchers, policy makers, administrators and educators/teachers. In the main, researchers have published their findings in academic journals and books (and book chapters) and presented them at scholarly conferences. However, the research milieu is evolving rapidly as there is less funding available from granting agencies to support curiosity driven research. Consequently, educational researchers increasingly conduct research collaboratively with business, community, governmental and not-for-profit agencies and organizations. Moreover, many universities are promoting community engagement and asking researchers and scholars to work more collaboratively with the broader community. By necessity then, the audience for our work is changing, as oftentimes the issues and problems identified and the questions posed are local and particular to a specific context, and in some cases, mixed methods is essential in order to provide different "evidences" and to demonstrate the nuanced relationships among evidences (Calfee & Sperling, 2010) to more diverse audiences. For example, in a large study of a bilingual family literacy program done collaboratively with government departments, a not-for-profit agency, school districts and community groups, we needed to ascertain if the program made a difference to children's literacy learning, whether the program promoted social inclusion, and if and how families were becoming familiar with and comfortable in Canadian schools. Using mixed methods was essential to addressing these questions (Anderson et al., 2011) in ways that *spoke* to all stakeholders involved in the project in different capacities, as well as to others interested in family literacy programs and immigrant and refugee families.

Ethics

Of course, ethical principles such as causing no harm, ensuring confidentiality and obtaining informed consent from participants need to guide all research studies. However, we also believe that researchers have an ethical obligation to consider different perspectives and interpretations, especially when the studies potentially have a significant impact on people. We concur with Denzin (1978) that there are inherent biases in "any particular data source, investigator, and . . . method" (p. 14) and likewise agree that using mixed methods can help ameliorate this issue. Furthermore, as just noted, we foresee an increasing need for researchers to work closely and collaboratively with communities and other groups in identifying educational issues and problems that need to be addressed and the research questions that flow from them. Indeed, questions identified from an emic perspective helps ensure that findings will be relevant and address real issues and problems in practice. For example, leading international indigenous scholar Linda Tuhiwai Smith (1999) recommends working collaboratively with communities to identify research questions as an essential principle in conducting research with Indigenous people. Because research questions should determine the appropriate method(s) for answering them, we argue that researchers have an ethical responsibility to use methods that can best answer the questions at hand and meet the needs of the people who participate in research studies. And, not to oversimplify, but in some contexts and for some issues and problems that need more in depth understandings, mixed methods will be most effective.

Impact

Traditionally, research impact has been measured largely by citation counts, a circuitous situation, as it accounts for how much researchers cite each other. Although citation counts and such will likely continue to be used to measure research impact, there is increasing recognition of the limitations of such measures. For example, the Social Sciences and Humanities Research Council of Canada, one of three funding agencies supported by the Government of Canada, requires dissemination plans for funded projects that go beyond the traditional publishing venues, such as papers presented at academic and scholarly conferences, books and book chapters and journal articles. Mixed methods, we believe, provide data that can demonstrate impact in a number of ways that fit with evolving, broader notions of impact. For example, in an intergenerational literacy program with preschoolers and their parents from immigrant and refugee families, we used Normal Curve Equivalent pre and post scores on norm-referenced tests to demonstrate to the funders that the program was having a significant impact on the adults and children's literacy learning (Purcell-Gates et al., 2012). On the other hand, to show further impact, we used the extensive field notes and detailed, critically reflective journals that the teachers kept identifying challenges within the program, what "worked" for the families, the adjustments in curriculum and pedagogy that we needed to make and so forth (Anderson et al., 2012).

University graduates: Traditionally, university-based researchers have carried out a great deal of research in education, but this situation is changing due to several factors. First, many universities are hiring fewer faculty members in the research stream. For example, the Conference Board of Canada (2015) reported that while the number of PhD graduates had increased dramatically, relatively few of them were obtaining positions as researchers and scholars in universities. They reported, "More than three-fifths of PhDs are employed in diverse careers outside the academy – in industry, government, and non-government organizations – drawing on their skills as researchers and critical thinkers to improve policy, organizational performance, innovation, and economic and social well-being" (n.p.). This trend is predicted to continue and indeed, some people within academe are calling for "re-visioning" doctoral studies (e.g., University of British Columbia, 2016) and we speculate an emphasis on developing skill sets necessary to conduct mixed methods research will be a critical part of this renaissance. That is, it appears that researchers will increasingly work outside the academy and will need the knowledge and skills to address a range of questions posed by diverse communities and groups.

In summary then, there are ethical, logistical and practical reasons for using mixed methods in educational research. Next, we illustrate how we used mixed methods in our own research with young children and their families.

Using mixed method approaches

Having provided some background for using mixed methods research, we now turn to how we have employed this approach in our own work in collaboration with various organizations and communities. In this section, we argue using a compendium of strategies, carefully chosen to suit the research question(s), enables us to serve a multitude of important purposes significant to the people who live and work in their communities, and which also contribute to knowledge that can be mobilized in other contexts.

Observations and field notes

Observations, including general observations in the "field" and specific observations of participants, fall under one of the many qualitative, interpretive methods that enable the researcher to understand the culture and structure of individuals and/or the community s/he is researching. Taken together, observations and field notes offer the opportunity to gather rich and detailed data that enable an intense account "in situ" and a "fullness of understanding" (Fine, 2015, p. 530) of people, their communities and their activities. In the case of participant observation, the researcher can actively experience the motivation and dynamics of the behavior observed and effectively cross the boundaries between being an insider and an outsider.

Field observations are typically accompanied by field notes; that is, inscribed material or narrative offering "thick description" (Geertz, 1973, p. 6) of events within the context in which they occurred, so that others can interpret them as vividly as possible. These notes generally are first person accounts written from the invesitgator's perspective, but may also include third person accounts of what individuals in the research context saw, did or reacted to. In these thick descriptions, the reader is provided with views of the data from multiple vantage points (Silverman & Patterson, 2015).

Examples of using observations and field notes

As previously mentioned, we used field notes extensively during an action research project called Literacy for Life (LFL) (Purcell-Gates et al., 2012), conducted by two of the authors of this chapter. The family literacy program, delivered over two years, enabled us to work collaboratively with three different cohorts of immigrant and refugee families in western Canada. Our goal was to build the program around children's and parents' out-of-school literacy lives, honoring the parents' wishes to prepare their children for Canadian, English-speaking classrooms, to support the adults in their own English literacy learning, through engaging in socially situated, real-life literacy activities for both parents and children (see Anderson, Purcell-Gates, Jang, & Gagne, 2010; Anderson et al., 2012, for a more detailed description). Classes were held twice a week for two hours, and the early childhood classes were loosely structured so that we could take advantage of opportunities to *incorporate real-world, or authentic literacy activities* that were presented to us. In order to gauge the effectiveness of instruction and to explore the effects of engaging students in real-life literacy activity, the early childhood educators carefully observed the children as they participated in, and reacted to, the activities and events presented to them, and took extensive field notes during each session. The field notes, along with the teachers' reflections on each session, were subsequently circulated, commented on and discussed during the weekly meetings of the research group. The field notes provided rich data enabling us to make changes to upcoming instruction and to increase fidelity to the criteria that we had developed for "real-life" literacy activities. Here is an excerpt from the field notes recorded by one of the early childhood educators during a typical early childhood classroom activity with the three- and four-year-old children.

> *Making birthday party banners. This activity was planned but took on a spontaneous nature. We were waiting for others to arrive because I wanted as many children as possible to participate in the planned activities. The girls wanted to cut paper while we waited, so I gave them some old chart paper that had been folded and generally abused. While they were cutting we were talking about the birthday plans we had made last day, and how R's birthday was going to be tomorrow. As she was cutting, N reminded me that we had made a birthday supply list and that we were*

> *going to make decorations. Interestingly, she was cutting the paper in long strips, so we decided to make them into birthday banners. She kept cutting and I kept printing [the words and expressions that] . . . they wanted on the banners. It turned out we made a total of seven, one for each of us with a simple Happy Birthday _________ and the person's name. As we completed them, we taped them up and decorated them with stickers. I was amazed at how this project became their own, and how they kept going back and pointing to the words, trying to recognize their names from the others.*

At that week's meeting of our research group, we determined that this was a good example of an activity that involved self-motivation, language practice and emergent literacy, demonstrating these young children's increasing understanding of the intentionality of print – namely, the notion that print carries meaning (Purcell-Gates, 1996). These observations and the subsequent rich qualitative descriptions added immeasurably to the corpus of data we collected to address the research question of the effectiveness of the family literacy program, as well as the challenges and issues that arose as we developed and implemented it. For example, we analyzed the field notes and compared levels of participation and engagement with the results from the Test of Early Reading Ability-3 (Reid et al., 2001) and the literacy sub-tests of the Canadian Adult Achievement Tests (CAAT). This analysis provided a more nuanced understanding of what worked in the program, what factors seemed to contribute to literacy learning, as well as concerns and issues that we needed to address.

Interviews

Conducting interviews with research participants is another source of qualitative data that enables researchers to obtain deeply contextual accounts of the participants' experiences relevant to the research question and their interpretation of these experiences (Schultze & Avital, 2011). Of course, interviews can be analyzed quantitatively and we have done so in some of our analyses. Olson (2011) states that when interviews are used as a data collection strategy, the goal is to engage the participant in a particular type of conversation to ensure quality information is obtained. Immigrant and refugee family participants often require special accommodations as they may be considered "vulnerable" research participants. Vulnerable research groups are those who may have been subjected to crises with little or no resources or support, and are considered at-risk to the consequences of those experiences (Chambers, 1983). The researcher's main objective in the research interview is to think carefully and ethically about the participants' increased vulnerability to talk about experiences. Added layers we needed to consider in this complex task involved in interviewing young immigrant and refugee children included the following: conducting interviews through an interpreter who was familiar to and with the children and their families, ensuring that our questions were culturally appropriate and would not trigger memories of traumatic experiences that the children and families may have encountered, establishing trust and support and finding a suitable setting to conduct the interview to ensure privacy and comfort and to maintain the confidentiality that we had guaranteed all participants.

Examples of using interviewing

In our work, we have used interviews in several studies with young refugee and immigrant children and their families. Specifically, McTavish (2009) used an open-ended interview protocol to gain information on eight-year-old Rajan's information literacy practices at home and school. We also used similar interviewing techniques with the refugee mothers and preschoolers in the

LFL program (Purcell-Gates et al., 2012) to help us better understand their literacy practices in the countries prior to their arrival in Canada, their current literacy practices in their homes and communities and the literacy practices that they wanted to learn. In this case, with the assistance of interpreters, we were able to gain a richer understanding of what we needed to attend to in the program to meet the unique needs and desires of the families with whom we worked. This was important to this study as the families' attendance in the LFL program was voluntary, and we worked diligently to ensure they returned each week. Furthermore, it helped ensure that we were meeting the central aim of the program, which was to engage immigrant and refugee families in authentic or real-life literacy experiences.

Focus groups

Typically, focus groups involve five to ten people from a particular cohort with shared experiences (Riazi, 2016). The interviewer acts as a moderator and asks open ended or semi-structured questions. There are criticisms of this type of interviewing in that some people may dominate the conversation or unduly influence the group (Riazi, 2016). Thus, the moderator needs to play a key mediational role by ensuring all participants have equal opportunity to contribute and by probing responses which appear to have been influenced by what others previously have said. Focus groups tend to be more conversational, and in some ways less stilted than more formal interviews.

A variation of the focus group technique that is sometimes used in indigenous communities is the talking circle. Essentially, this process involves participants sitting in a circle, with each person taking a turn and commenting or elaborating on previous points. This is thought to be a more culturally appropriate approach to data gathering with First Nations (indigenous) people in Canada, for example (e.g., Hare & Anderson, 2010), and helps ensure a more equitable distribution of turn-taking and also discourages individuals from dominating the conversation.

Examples of using focus groups

Anderson and his colleagues employed focus groups in the *PALS in Immigrant Communities* project. They first generated a series of open-ended questions, based on their original research questions as to the efficacy of the programs and concerns and issues that arose, which they had recorded in field notes and reflective journals. This was a bilingual family literacy program, so the interviewer asked the questions in English, while the cultural worker in each community translated into the families' first language. The families usually answered in their home language and the cultural worker translated into English and the interviewer or moderator either acknowledged the response, and if necessary, invited further comment or elaboration or asked a supplementary follow-up question, before moving on to the next one. Focus group sessions were audio-recorded in their entirety, translated where necessary and then analyzed. As with the interviews described earlier, the focus group sessions provided families an opportunity to identify which aspects of the program were working well for them, which aspects were not working well or needed adjustment and concerns and issues they had. The interviews were also confirmatory in that our observations and field notes indicated that the families seemed to be enjoying the program, the children were displaying evidence of learning early literacy and the families were engaging in the activities we were providing. Taken together, the analysis of the field notes, the focus group sessions and the results of the normed test that we describe later, indicated that the program was having a positive impact on children's early learning, and that the families valued the program. But in the focus group sessions, the families also raised concerns and issues that had not previously surfaced and we recognized that there were aspects of the program that needed to modified to make it a better fit for families.

Artifacts

Collecting and using artifacts, or documentary materials, as a data source, is fundamentally not very different from observations, field notes or interviews (Merriam & Tisdell, 2015). Finding relevant materials to collect and analyze as artifacts is dependent on the research question(s) or inquiry, and requires a systematic procedure for collection. Artifacts include materials such as samples of an adult's writing from their homes or children's spontaneous nursery rhymes in the playground. Artifacts may also be generated by participants for the researcher to learn more about the events or situation under study, and are commonly used in action, or participatory, research. For example, a researcher might ask a participant to keep a diary or journal during the course of the study, or produce a piece of artwork in response to an experience or critical incident in their lives. Researchers sometimes collect auxiliary documents that supplement and support a research project but are not the sole focus of the investigation (Altheide & Schneider, 2013). For example, in a study we are currently conducting in a socially disadvantaged neighborhood of families' access to, and use of, digital tools at home, we are collecting and analyzing the messages about young children and digital technology found in community newspapers and on the websites of local organizations.

Examples of using artifacts

In the LFL study (Anderson et al., 2012), we collected artifacts as evidence of the children's emerging literacy behaviors over the course of the study in several different ways. For example, after initial modeling by the teachers, we asked at the beginning of each session that the children "sign in" on an attendance sheet. This served not only to indicate their presence in an authentic way; it served as a record of their growth in printing their name over time (a skill they would need to use later in a classroom). Similarly, the teachers collected writing and drawing samples and took photos of the children engaged in literacy activities. The teachers then added contextualizing information and dates to accompany the materials collected. In McTavish's (2009) study, writing samples, drawings, flow charts, projects and photographs were collected to document Rajan's literacy practices at school and at home. In both studies, artifacts served in triangulation with other data collected, to present an in-depth picture of the phenomena under study.

Standardized tests

Our work is grounded in a literacy as social practice perspective (e.g., Heath, 1983; Street, 1995); that is, how literacy is defined, its functions and purposes, how it is learned and taught and the value ascribed to it, vary across cultural and social contexts (Clay, 1993). However, we also recognize that funding agencies and organizations sometimes require "evidence" that reflects what Street called an "autonomous" view of literacy. For as Purcell-Gates et al. (2012) point out, this "construct of literacy has gained sufficient political traction that research into the teaching of reading and writing is funded, and the results accepted, primarily by the degree to which the research relies on such end-point measures of literacy ability" (p. 397).

Examples of using standardized tests

In the Parents As Literacy Supporters in Immigrant Communities (PALS), a bilingual literacy project in which we worked with more than 500 families from four linguistic groups (Anderson et al., 2011), we used the *Test of Reading Ability-2* (TERA-2) (Reid et al., 1989) to document children's emerging knowledge and understanding of print and how it works. The test is designed for children aged three to eight, and was therefore suitable for the three- to five-year-olds who participated in the program. We first determined that the TERA-2 was reliable and valid. The researchers and research assistants who administered the test had attended the sessions of the bilingual family literacy program, and therefore the children were familiar with them. Although the TERA-2 measures children's knowledge of English print literacy, a trained cultural worker from the children's communities who the children knew provided the directions and prompts in English, and then translated them into the children's home language. Because it was not feasible (or ethically justifiable) to have a control group or to utilize a delayed treatment design in the year long program, we used the Normal Curve Equivalent Scores, essentially comparing the average pre- and post-test scores of the children in the program with the average scores of children in the norming group (e.g., Grant & Leavenworth, 1988).

In combination with the qualitative data from our field notes, interviews with the parents, focus group sessions and so forth, the results of the TERA-2, which showed a large effect size or impact, reassured the program funders that the program was effective and it continues, funded by a governmental agency, nearly two decades after its implementation. Many of the families who were curious about their children's literacy development were reassured by the results, as were the program developers who were committed to delivering a program that made a difference in children's early literacy learning.

Discussion

As we have shared how we employed various data gathering techniques in studies with young children and their families in culturally, linguistically and socially diverse communities, it is important to reiterate that our analyses involved looking across the data sets, looking for patterns, confirmations and contradictions. The example just shared about how we used qualitative and quantitative data synergistically in the PALS in Immigrant Communities project, is illustrative of this process.

As we employed the various techniques in our studies, we always tried to ensure that we did so in a manner that reflected the cultural, linguistic and social context of the participants. For example, when we administered the TERA-2 in the PALS project, a person with whom the children were familiar and who knew them, provided the directions and the prompts in their home language and in English. Likewise, we conducted the focus groups in English and in the families' first language, translating when necessary and encouraging the participants to code-switch as necessary. Furthermore, we have modified techniques such as using the talking circle with First Nations families because it is a better fit with their practices, than the more free flowing, spontaneous focus group format.

We have also attempted to demonstrate how using mixed methods to address the needs of various audiences or consumers of research results. For example, we believe the results of the TERA-2 that demonstrated that the program had a large effect size (or impact) on children's early literacy knowledge played an important role in ensuring continued funding from the Government of Canada agency that initially funded the project. Alongside these results, the insights that we were able to provide based on the data from our field notes and the focus group sessions, provided a portrait of the program that was effective, but was also respectful of families who are sometimes quite vulnerable and responsive to their needs. Likewise, the families told us in the focus groups that while they intuitively "knew" that their children were acquiring or learning valuable knowledge and skills through participating in the program, they found the results confirmatory and reassuring. Meanwhile, other researchers and practitioners have become aware of both the positive results of the program, as well as some of the concerns and issues that arose, through publications in more traditional venues such as book chapters and journal articles. For example, a teacher from South America recently was in contact, buoyed by the positive impact as evidenced by the results of the TERA-2 but also querying how the slippage in promoting families' first language – a central goal of the program – that we had documented in our field notes, might be addressed.

It is also important to point out that at times, we integrated both qualitative and quantitative domains. For example, in the LFL study, we coded the teachers' field notes and their reflective journals and then quantified the categories and identified the challenges that the teachers had encountered according to their frequency. Likewise, in the PALS in Immigrant Communities project, we coded the children's artifacts, using the extant literature on young children's writing and representation (e.g., Ferreiro & Teberosky, 1982; Kress, 2005) to develop the categories. Again, we quantified the different categories, and, for example, were surprised that workbook pages were the second most frequent form of writing and representing in the sample (Anderson et al., 2017). In essence, we were quantifying the qualitative data and we propose that mixed methods research lends itself to this type of cross-over and integration.

Although we attempt to collect and analyze data and share results in a concurrent manner, that is sometimes not possible. For example, in the study just described, our field notes gathered through participant observation in the program sessions indicated that most of children's emergent literacy development was progressing well. However, because we were using gains in the Normal Curve Equivalent scores on the TERA-2 from the beginning of the program (early October) to the end (late May), we really could not compare and contrast that data with those from our field notes and the focus group sessions until the end of the program.

In conclusion, we propose that the evolving milieu in research will likely lead to greater prominence in educational research. With the examples we provided from our own studies, we have attempted to demonstrate how we used mixed methods in thoughtful ways, reflecting the contexts in which we conducted the research. Our hope is that we have also shown how we used data from the various methods in integrated, holistic ways, and that by doing so, we were able to present more in-depth and nuanced understanding of the phenomenon we were studying – the implementation of family literacy programs with young children and caregivers from immigrant and refugee families. We have also endeavored to show how mixed methods can broaden the ways in which we conceptualize impact.

References

Altheide, D. and Schneider, C. (2013) *Qualitative media analysis*. London: Sage.

Anderson, J., Anderson, A., Friedrich, N. and Teichert, L. (2017) *Parents As Literacy Supporters (PALS) in immigrant and refugee communities*. Paper presented at the 20th European Conference on Literacy, Madrid, Spain, July.

Anderson, J., Friedrich, N. and Kim, J. (2011) *Implementing a bilingual family literacy program with immigrant and refugee families: The case of Parents As Literacy Supporters (PALS)*. Vancouver, BC: Decoda Literacy Solutions. www.decoda.ca/wp-content/uploads/PALS-in-Immigrant-Communities-Research-Report-Feb-2011-2.pdf.

Anderson, J., Purcell-Gates, V., Jang, K. and Gagne, M. (2010) *Implementing an intergenerational literacy program with authentic literacy instruction: Challenges, responses, and results*. Ottawa, ON: Canadian Council on Learning.

Anderson, J., Purcell-Gates, V., Lenters, K. and McTavish, M. (2012) Real-world literacy activity in pre-school. *Community Literacy Journal* 8 (2) 75–95.

Bronfenbrenner, U. and Evans, G.W. (2000) Developmental science in the 21st century: Emerging questions, theoretical models, research designs and empirical findings. *Social Development* 9 (1), 115–125.

Calfee, R. and Sperling, M. (2010) *On mixed methods: Approaches to language and literacy research*. New York: Teachers College Press.

Canadian Adult Achievement Tests. Toronto, ON: Pearson Canada Assessment.

Chambers, R. (1983) *Rural development: Putting the last first*. Longman: London.

Clay, M. (1993) Always a learner: A fable. *Reading Today*, 3, 10.

Conference Board of Canada. (2015) Where are Canada's PhDs employed? www.conferenceboard.ca/topics/education/commentaries/15-01-06/where_are_canada_s_phds_employed.aspx.

Creswell, J.W. (2010) *Research design: Qualitative, quantitative and mixed methods approaches*. Thousand Oaks, CA: Sage Publications.

Creswell, J.W. and Plano Clark, V.L. (2007) *Designing and conducting mixed methods research*. Thousand Oaks, CA: Sage Publications.

Creswell, J.W. and Plano Clark, V.L. (2011) *Designing and conducting mixed methods research*. Thousand Oaks, CA: Sage Publications.

Creswell, J.W., Plano Clark, V.L., Gutmann, M.L. and Hanson, W.E. (2003) Advanced mixed methods research designs. In: Tashakkori, A. and Teddlie, C. (eds.) *Handbook of mixed methods in social behavioral research*. Thousand Oaks, CA: Sage Publications, 209–240.

Denzin, N.K. (1978) *The research act: A theoretical introduction to sociological methods*. New York: Praeger.

Dillon, D.R., O'Brien, D.G. and Heilman, E.E. (2004) Literacy research in the next millennium: From paradigms to pragmatism and practicality. In: Ruddell, R.B. and Unrau, N.J. (eds.) *Theoretical models and processes of reading*. Newark: International Reading Association, 1530–1556.

Erzberger, C. and Kelle, U. (2003) Making inferences in mixed methods: The rules of integration. In: *Handbook of mixed methods in social and behavioral research*, 457–488.

Erzberger, C. and Prein, G. (1997) Triangulation: Validity and empirically-based hypothesis construction. *Quality & Quantity* 31, 141–154.

Ferreiro, E. and Teberosky, A. (1982) *Literacy before schooling*. Exeter, NH: Heinemann Books.

Fine, G. (2015) Participant observation. In: Wright, J. (ed.) *International Encyclopedia of the social & behavioral sciences* (2n edition). Amsterdam: Elsevier, 530–534.

Geertz, C. (1973) *The interpretation of cultures*. New York: Basic Books.

Grant, E.S. and Leavenworth, R.S. (1988) *Statistical quality control, sixth edition*. New York: McGraw Hill.

Hare, J. and Anderson, J. (2010) Transitions to early childhood for Indigenous children and families in Canada: Historical and social realities. *Australian Journal of Early Childhood* 35 (2), 19–27.

Heath, S.B. (1983) *Ways with words: Language, life and work in communities and classrooms*. Cambridge: Cambridge University Press.

Howe, K.R. (1988) Against the quantitative-qualitative incompatibility theses, or dogmas die hard. *Educational Researcher* 1, 10–16.

Kress, G. (2005) *Before writing: Rethinking the path to literacy*. London: Routledge.

Lonigan, C.J., Anthony, J.L., Bloomfield, B.G., Dyer, S.M. and Samwel, C.S. (1999) Effects of two shared-reading interventions on emergent literacy skills of at-risk preschoolers. *Journal of Early Intervention* 22 (4), 306–322.

McTavish, M. (2009) 'I get my facts from the internet': A case study of the teaching and learning of information literacy in in-school and out-of-school contexts. *Journal of Early Childhood Literacy* 9 (1), 3–28. doi: 10.1177/1468798408101104.

Merriam, S.B. and Tisdell, E.J. (2015) *Qualitative research: A guide to design and implementation*. http://ebookcentral.proquest.com.

Mesel, T. (2013) The necessary distinction between methodology and philosophical assumptions in healthcare research. *Scandinavian Journal of Caring Sciences* 27, 750–756.

Morse, J.M. and Niehaus, L. (2016) *Mixed method design: Principles and procedures*. New York: Routledge.

Olson, K. (2011) *Essentials of qualitative interviewing*. Walnut Creek, CA: Left Coast Press.

Onwuegbuzie, A.J. and Mallette, M.H. (2011) Mixed research techniques in literacy research. In: Duke, N.K. and Mallette, M.H. (eds.) *Literacy research methodologies*. New York: Guilford Press, 301–330.

Purcell-Gates, V. (1996) Stories, coupons and the *TV Guide*: Relationships between home literacy experiences and emergent literacy knowledge. *Reading Research Quarterly* 31 (4), 406–428.

Purcell-Gates, V., Anderson, J., Jang, K., Gagne, M., Lenters, K. and McTavish, M. (2012) Measuring situated literacy activity: Challenges and promises. *Journal of Literacy Research* 44 (4), 132–141.

Reese, E., Cox, A., Harte, D. and McAnally, H. (2003) Diversity in adults' styles of reading books to children. In: van Kleeck, A., Stahl, S.A. and Bauer, E.B. (eds.) *On reading books to children, parents and teachers*. Mahwah, NJ; Lawrence Erlbaum Associates, pp. 37–57.

Reichardt, C. S. and Rallis, S. F. (eds.) (1994) The qualitative-quantitative debate: New perspectives. *New Directions for Program Evaluation*, 61. San Francisco: Jossey-Bass.

Reid, D., Hresko, W. and Hammill, D. (1989) *Test of early reading ability-2*. Austin, TX: PROED.

Reid, D., Hresko, W. and Hammill, D. (2001) *Test of early reading ability-2*. Austin, TX: PROED.

Riazi, A.M. (2016) *The Routledge encyclopedia of research methods in applied linguistics*. Abingdon: Routledge.

Schultze, U. and Avital, M. (2011) Designing interviews to generate rich data for information systems research. *Information and Organization* 21 (1), 1–16. doi: 10.1016/j.infoandorg.2010.11.001.

Sechrest, L. and Sidani, S. (1995) Quantitative and qualitative methods: Is there an alternative? *Evaluation and Program Planning* 18 (1), 77–87.

Shannon-Baker, P. (2016) Making paradigms meaningful in mixed methods research. *Journal of Mixed Methods Research* 10 (4), 319–334.

Silverman, R.M. and Patterson, K.L. (2015) *Qualitative research methods for community development* (1st edition). New York: Routledge. doi: 10.4324/9781315797762.

Smith, L.T. (1999) *Decolonizing methodologies: Research and indigenous peoples*. London: Zed Books.

Stephens, D. and Pearson, P.D. (1992) Multiple perspectives on multiple perspectives. In: Beach, R., Green, J.L., Kamil, M.L. and Shanahan, T. (eds.) *Multidisciplinary perspectives on literacy research*. Urbana, IL: National Conference on Research in English, pp. 343–363.

Street, B. (1995) *Literacy in theory and practice*. Cambridge: Cambridge University Press.

Tashakkori, A. and Teddlie, C. (1998) *Mixed methodology: Combining qualitative and quantitative approaches*. Thousand Oaks, CA: Sage Publications.

Tashakkori, A. and Teddlie, C. (2003) Major issues and controversies in the use of mixed methods in the social and behavioral sciences. In: Tashakkori, A. and Teddlie, C. (eds.) *Handbook of mixed methods in social behavioral research*. Thousand Oaks, CA: Sage, 3–50.

University of British Columbia (2016) *2016 Ph. D. Career outcome survey*. Vancouver, BC: Faculty of Graduate Studies. www.grad.ubc.ca/about-us/news/ubc-phd-career-outcomes-report-website-now-available.

Yin, R.K. (2006) Mixed methods research: Are the methods genuinely integrated or merely parallel? *Research in the Schools* 13 (1), 41–47.

21

STUDENT GENERATED VISUAL NARRATIVES

Lived experiences of learning

Narelle Lemon

Introduction

It is an exciting time to consider how digital technology can enhance learning experiences in the early years context. It is important though, to acknowledge digital technology must be planned for with explicit goals and learning objectives. Also key is the discussion around technologies and the place they have in education being closely connected to equity, availability, skill set, capabilities and possibilities, and how they can enable transformative learning (The Australian Human Rights Commission, 2014; United Nations, 2017; U.S Department of Education, 2017). The Australian Human Rights Commission (2014) policy 'Supporting young children's rights: Statement of Intent (2015–2018)' highlights this with the need to:

> promote and develop resources for educators, professionals working with young children, children and the community to promote children's personal safety, particularly in relation to digital technology . . . [and] provide support to children, and their families, to promote children's privacy and personal safety particularly in relation to digital technology used in the early learning environment, services for young children and at home.
>
> *(p. 13)*

Underpinning this work is the need to scaffold and support young people with their digital technology use. That is, developing their digital literacy skills and confidence, while also illuminating how they are capable, have a voice, and can be trusted. What is present is an opportunity to now learn with and alongside young people in the learning process of learning about integrating technology in their learning opportunities.

When children are viewed as capable learners and knowledge experts of their own lives some feel that a postmodern perspective is held as they are empowered to be powerful members of society (Dahlberg et al., 1999; Einarsdottir, 2006; Garvis et al., 2015). From this stance, children are viewed in the study shared in this chapter as capable digital image makers of their lived experiences (Lemon, 2016, 2015, 2014, 2008, 2007). That is, they are capable of using a digital camera to capture their learning experiences and generate visual narratives to highlight stories of importance to them. When used in a way that includes young people, what emerges is a meaningful way to hear their voice and to support agency (Castelle, 1990; Clandinin et al.,

2016; Curts & Carter, 2000; Einarsdottir, 2006; Hall et al., 2015; Kellet & Ding, 2004; Lemon, 2008; Mac Naughton, 2003; Mauthner, 1997).

The digital camera supports the generation of photographs of lived experiences. These photographs, or still images as referred to in this chapter, support the documentation and recording of learning experiences. And in this case the learning experiences of young people by young people, rather than traditional models of practice that often see a teacher document learning through photography. For the young people discussed in this chapter, the digital camera was a way for them to become digital image makers. It allowed them to capture fragments that have no specific beginning or ending. The photographer – the generator of the image – captures a moment in time that, in the education field, has the power to allow for ongoing reflective practice, viewing over time and establishing and re-establishing meaning or meanings (Lemon, 2008, 2014).

"Images created with photographs thicken ways of seeing" (Bach, 2001a, p. 1). These photographs assist in marking a memory in our time, a memory around which we "construct stories" (Clandinin & Connelly, 2000, p. 114). When the photographs are paired with text (spoken or written), a visual narrative is formed. Visual narratives produced digitally promote a portable digitised environment that makes for 'anytime' and 'anywhere' teaching and learning possibilities (Groundwater-Smith et al., 2007; Halverson & Gibbons, 2008; Lemon, 2008, 2014, 2016).

This is where digital technology has the advantage of supporting young children to share their experiences by allowing them to be digital image makers (Dillner, 2001; Lemon, 2016, 2015, 2014, 2008, 2007; Leu & Kinzer, 2000). In generating visual narratives, it is the conversations that occur during and after the creation of images that can provide opportunities for young learners to move beyond simply writing about the photograph. Working within a constructivist framework (Denzin & Lincoln, 2000; Guba & Lincoln, 1985), young children's visual narratives are understood to reveal insights into their lived experiences and their existing schemas of knowledge and understanding. Seeing young people as capable photographers and documenters of their learning experiences supports their journey of meaning making and understanding the world (Lemon, 2015; Sairane & Kumpulainen, 2014).

The visual method I designed and share in this chapter shows how it is possible to include the children with(in) the research process. The case shared is an example of how a teacher can work with children in the classroom to include the visual cultures of both the teacher and individual students to enhance and extend their learning possibilities. My personal interest in the visual arts, and particularly photography, was transferred into the early childhood classroom. Integral to my practice is the belief that "teachers are viewed as learners" (Kincheloe, 2003, p. 18). It was my intention to learn from the students as much as they were going to learn from me. I believe the inclusion of children's voices is essential to the research process *and* to the further development of my teacher identity and professional knowledge.

Photography is not about a flat or linear view of the world, rather photography depicts and allows for a sharing of perspective and insight into life; lived experiences that can be interpreted and represented on multiple levels. The digital camera as a technology gives easy access to visually produced data. A strength of working visually in education is the capacity that digital technology makes available for the teacher-researcher, a method to *slow down* and *repeat observations* (Prosser, 1998) of learning environments. These movements allow multiple opportunities for deeper reflection, different perspectives, interruptions, questions, inquiries, and the complexities that occur in the learning environment to be noticed. Using student generated images is an essential contribution to the design of this research, and importantly, this emphasis allowed participants to identify their learning needs and to take increasing responsibility for greater independence. In particular, the visual narratives that the children produce in this research draw from and extend the idea of learning stories promoted by New Zealand researcher Margaret Carr.

Learning stories have traditionally been generated by the teacher to reveal children's strengths and interests and are a combination of written word and photographs (Carr, 2001). Currently the method is being used in the New Zealand and Australian early childhood contexts for the improvement of assessment practices. This chapter presents student generated visual narratives that build from the concept of a learning story, especially the three elements: a story of something a child achieved or did; an analysis of the learning associated; and suggestions for future possibilities or opportunities (Hatherly, 2006). From the perspective of five- and six-year-olds, the student generated visual narratives also disrupt the notions of learning being one way, and invite the educator, adults, and other young people to also engage with the learning stories as a way to enact reflective practice. Thus, visual narratives constructed by young people also could be viewed as learning stories in that they highlight strengths-based and interest-based learning in the natural setting (Williamson et al., 2006).

Throughout the chapter I invite you as the reader to consider the questions:

How can children's voices be included in learning and teaching?
How can digital technology assist children to share their voice?
What opportunities become available when young people generate visual narrative to share their lived experiences of learning?
How can young people be honoured as co-researchers?

Visual narratives

Narrative provides meaning and belonging in human lives because every human experience is a lived story, and a storied experience (Curtis & Carter, 2000; Wong, 2003). Connelly and Clandinin (1988) define narrative inquiry as "the study of how humans make meaning of experience by endlessly telling and retelling stories about themselves that both refigure the past and create purpose in the future" (p. 21). Most importantly working as a narrative inquirer is seen as "providing opportunities and spaces for research participants as well as researchers" (Bathmaker & Harnett, 2010, p. 3) which is an action as Riessman (2008) suggests that encourages and supports people to tell their stories and thus allows participants to negotiate their identities and meaning making of their experiences. The untold and *unsayable* stories (Leitch, 2008), evaded (Bach, 1998) and those with covers (Clandinin & Connelly, 1995) can be shared. As Clandinin and Connelly (1995) share the telling, retelling and reliving of stories assist in the exploration of meaning and meaning making of our lives, experiences, and thoughts. Sharing also allows for others to consider, reconsider, and ponder.

Research has advocated for the honouring of voice and narrative as a way to explore and represent lived experiences (Barnett & Nores, 2012; Castelle, 1990; Clandinin et al., 2016; Curts & Carter, 2000; Hall et al., 2015; Kellet & Ding, 2004; Lemon, 2008; MacNaughton, 2003; Mauthner, 1997). The use of narratives may provide early childhood educators with an alternative resource for understanding and considering the experiences of young people (Åkerman, 2012; Prior & Niesz, 2013).

Visual methods are significant and growing in the social science field (Moss, 2008, 2013; Moss & Pini, 2016; Prosser, 1998). The take up of these methods by educators is beginning to emerge, particularly in Australia and the United Kingdom. However, photographs and visual narratives have been used for the construction of social narratives for centuries (Bach, 1998; Clandinin & Connelly, 2000; Moss, 2003) – archives at museums, family history collections, or even memory boxes. "Visual narrative enables the researcher to work in a number of ways" (Moss, 2003, p. 5). Images can be collected in the forms of drawings, photographs, video, and digital photography. As Bach (2001a) comments, "images created with photographs thicken ways of seeing" (p. 1). Photographs mark a memory in our time, a memory around which we "construct stories" (Clandinin & Connelly, 2000, p. 114) and which show fragments that have no specific beginning or ending.

Visual narrative research draws upon the use of photography to evoke memory in our lives. Memory can be used to construct and reconstruct stories. Visual narrative, I assert, is not complete without narrative support through dialogue and language. Photographs can be used as a way to preserve the appearance of an event or a person and as a metaphor of an experience that has been closely associated with an initial idea or relationship (Bach, 1998, 2001b). But it is the construction of visual plus narrative that makes visible the different parts or narratives of a story, as well as enabling opportunities to explore different positions within a dynamic environment or situation. Photographs themselves do not preserve meaning (Bach, 2001b; Wood, 2000), they simply offer appearances that a narrator can make us understand, and provide the prospect to reflect and grow from our experiences.

The use of visual narrative as a means for providing opportunities for students to "photograph their world inside and outside of school" is discussed in relation to working with students in an educational setting (Bach, 2001b, p. 1). In Bach's work, she foregrounds the curiosity of the 'evaded' curriculum (Bach, 1998); that is, the experiences that are not seen and that can be ignored in both students' and teachers' lives. As Bager-Charleson (2004) note, an opportunity is created though visual narratives to connect learning and meaning to the images, and to create relationships that can connect to sub-cultures "uncovering the unrecognizable, unacknowledged or *unsayable* stories" (Leitch, 2008, p. 37).

Voice

When we are looking at working with young people, representing young people, and thus honouring young people, there are various frameworks internationally that maintain that children and childhood are important in their own right (Christensen, 2017; Parnell & Iorio, 2015; Tayler, 2012; Tayler et al., 2008). The Australian National Early Years Learning Framework, for example, builds on the United National Convention on the Rights of the Child. This framework builds from principles and practices for children and argues that children:

- Have a strong sense of identity;
- Are connected with and contribute to their world;
- Have a strong sense of wellbeing;
- Are confident and involved learners; and
- Are effective communicators.

Fielding (2002), for example, suggests a refocusing on the centrality of relationships in education, collaborative learning spaces, and opportunities for collective dialogue. He contends that the challenge is to build relationships and environments that support and sustain both student and teacher voice. Fielding recognises a move towards constructing practices that create new spaces for teachers and students to make meaning both individually and collectively, stating that:

> the voices of students, teachers and others are acknowledged as legitimately different and of equal value, the necessary partners in dialogue about how we learn, how we live and the kind of place we wish our community to become.
>
> *(p. 13)*

Using student voice is not only an instructional method for enhancing learning and motivation but also a way to enhance practice-orientated analytical approaches (Hadfield & Haw, 2001). As Britzman (1990), Clark and Moss (2001), and Christensen and James (2017) note, there is a need to acknowledge authenticity with regard to a child's voice, and it is important to recognise that voice is meaning which resides in the individual and enables the individual to participate in a community. This is key to recognise when working with contemporary research practices with children Christensen and James (2017).

Dennis Harper (2002) reiterates that listening to children in meaningful partnerships with adults, for example teachers, is foundational for addressing issues central to the empowerment of young people and for changing many system inequities and failures. This argument is endorsed by Hadfield and Haw (2001) who write:

> 'Voice' is now used in a wide variety of projects and policies from advocacy to consumer rights and citizenship education. The 'voice' of young people is being increasingly sought as part of the general move towards social inclusion.
>
> *(p. 485)*

Cook-Sather (2002) and Christensen and James (2017) concur and claim that children not only have the knowledge and position to shape what counts in education but they can help change power relationships and create new forums about learning through their active engagement in research processes. It is from this perspective that this chapter sees young people as co-researchers (Christensen & James, 2017; Clark & Moss, 2001; Egg et al., 2004; MacNaughton, 2005) of their learning environment through the generation of their visual narratives. This viewpoint believes that very young children can competently contribute to some of the research process and be involved in the discussions about the research process, questions, data, and analysis upon establishment of clear and ethical guidelines (Parnell & Iorio, 2015).

Foregrounding the research design

This qualitative mixed-methods case study (Mason, 2006), grounded in a constructivist paradigm, supports the notion that children can be both participants and researchers. Still digital photographs and resulting visual narratives that they create highlighted the enactment of a research method that was transparent and innovative, and provided a tangible experience for young people. As Egg et al. (2004) attest, working in this way involves "children immediately in collecting, interpreting, and using information without the need for extensive training, understanding of theory or knowledge of the research literature" (p. 11). The visual narratives created by the young people in this case study communicated new insights into teaching and learning that challenged beliefs and assumptions about their capability to engage with reflective and metacognitive thinking. The integration of technology in the early years learning environment demonstrates how a sense of belonging and self can be enhanced for individuals. The process of generating images, as well as sharing their voice, embodies trust, mutual respect, and the valuing of emotional and social development (see Figure 21.1).

The underlying principles of this study were to provide the young people with the opportunity to take photographs using a digital camera as a way to have their voices heard and to develop reflective skills as part of regular interaction in the learning community, and to support curriculum documents. It was important in establishing a learning community that all the voices of the classroom were heard, thereby changing the traditional power notions of a classroom

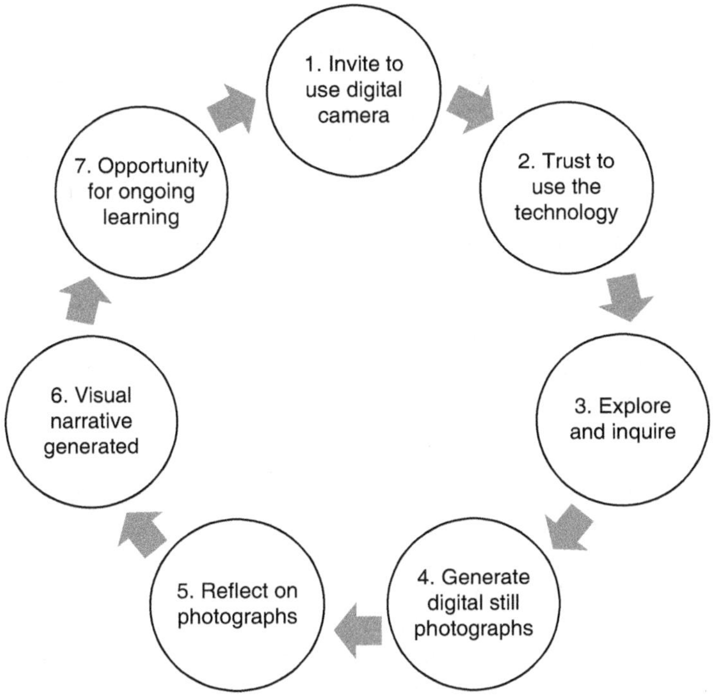

Figure 21.1 The process of student generated visual narratives in the classroom

where the teacher directs the learning and discussion to one where all were learners, acknowledging that the role of 'teacher' could be transferred amongst all in the classroom. With this study, the children were asked to firstly participate in classroom activities as usual. Secondly, they were invited to use a digital camera as another way for them to reflect on their learning and to share their voice. This is an illustration where photographs were being used as a way to preserve the appearance of an event or a person (Bach, 1998; Bach, 2001a). It is a method that allows for and makes visible the different parts or narratives of a story, as well as enabling opportunities to explore different positions within a dynamic environment or situation. Close links were made between this and reflection, whereby the student generates photography with text provided by a child photographer to form a visual narrative.

One digital camera was used, and a rotation system was set up for the children to use the camera one at a time. This rotation process allowed students to use the digital camera at different times during the day and over the week at 30 minute intervals. The camera was kept on the teacher's desk at the side of the room for easy access and for safety. In using the camera, the following instructions were agreed upon by all participants (see Lemon, 2008 for further discussion about specific methodological steps):

- When the camera was in use, no one should look at the camera or pose for the photographer as the natural occurrences in the classroom were wanting to be captured;
- It was the choice of each child if they wanted to use the digital camera in their scheduled time. If a child chose not to use the digital camera then it would remain on the teacher's desk with the opportunity for another to use it if they wished;

- No limit was set as to how many images were to be taken;
- When using the digital camera, the cord attached must be around the wrist of the photographer in case of an accident where one might trip over or drop the camera;
- After taking the photographs, the child photographer would reflect about the images either through conversation with the teacher and/or peer(s) or via reflection using sentence starters provided (e.g., What does your photograph tell us? What did you want to show to the viewer of your photograph? What is important to you in this photograph?) or a graphic organiser (e.g., mind map, concept map, etc.). This builds on the notion of photo self-elicitation (Harper, 2002); and,
- Photographs once taken were downloaded onto the teacher's laptop for storage and viewing enabling the photographs to be immediately deleted from the digital camera and for another child to use the digital camera. It should be noted a laptop was used to enable movement of the device to different locations. Once the photographs were on the laptop they could be viewed or printed off according to the choice of the child as to how they were going to reflect. For conversations, the photographs were viewed on the laptop screen. For written reflection and graphic organising, the child photographer would select the image(s) of choice to be reflected upon and then they would be printed.

This study draws on the sociological and anthropological uses of photo self-elicitation (Harper, 2002) and elements of photo elicitation (Collier, 1957). Uniquely, this study focuses on the conversations and reflections that are generated from the still digital photographs taken by participants (photo self-elicitation), not from photographs generated by someone else (photo elicitation).

Photo self-elicitation, in this study, involves the early childhood children generating their own digital images and additionally sharing their stories through written, oral, and visual reflections. Reflections with young people can occur in conversation or through written form using strategies such as graphic organisers, graffiti walls, and writing activities. Children capture images that are meaningful to them (Bach, 1998; Carr, 2001). A narrative connects events, actions, and experiences and moves them through time (Daiute & Lightfoot, 2004; Kramp, 2004), structuring and framing relationships. As Prosser (1998) suggests, visual narrative is a specific mode of constructing and constituting reality and prompts a re-examination of reflection and the role of language in the reflection process.

Visual narratives constructed by young children also could be viewed as learning stories in that they highlight strengths-based and interest-based learning in the natural setting (Williamson et al., 2006). Significantly, the narratives in this study, developed from the photo self-elicitation process, are different from learning stories in two ways. First, the student voice is not always highlighted during a learning story. Second, learning stories that include photographs do not include student generated photographs, rather they are photographs that record an action or piece of work taken by a teacher or teaching assistant. This research has established connections between visual narratives, learning stories, and photo self-elicitation. Figure 21.2 shows how, by combining visual narratives with learning stories, children are able to follow their interests and hence become more engaged in their learning (Williamson et al., 2006).

As Figure 21.2 shows, the narrator's (child's) interpretations are interspersed throughout the narrative, rather than those of the teacher or researcher. Importantly, the sequence of photos (visual narrative) and the text provided through the reflective conversations and written reflections represent their lived experiences of teaching and learning, and honour the voice of the child.

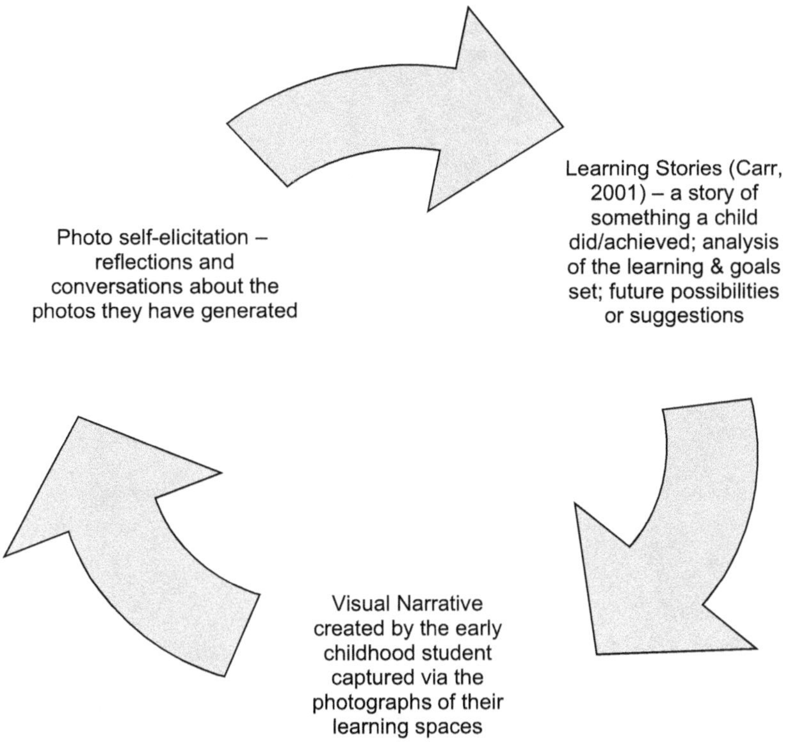

Figure 21.2 Relationship between visual narratives, photo self-elicitation, and learning stories

Using the digital camera for the first time

An introductory task was designed to support the introduction of the digital camera to the early years classroom. This were initiated with the macro aim of stimulating children to talk about their images. Initially children were asked to reflect on their images through written responses to avoid overwhelming them with too much choice during the introductory phase of familiarising the children with taking their own photographs and using the equipment. A set of questions were devised to trigger responses to their experiences when using the camera. Figure 21.3 shows a sample copy of these questions in the form of a worksheet.

What's so good about taking photos?

When asked about the good things associated with using a camera to remember their learning experiences the children replied in ways that displayed their understanding of using visual narrative as a form of reflection. Their responses frequently focused on remembering the past:

If I took photos long ago I would remember things (Celia)
Sometimes you can't remember what you did a long time ago (Cameron)
You can remember what you did a long time ago (Charles)
If I took photos I would remember things (Irene)
If you couldn't take pictures you would have to write it down (Hannah)

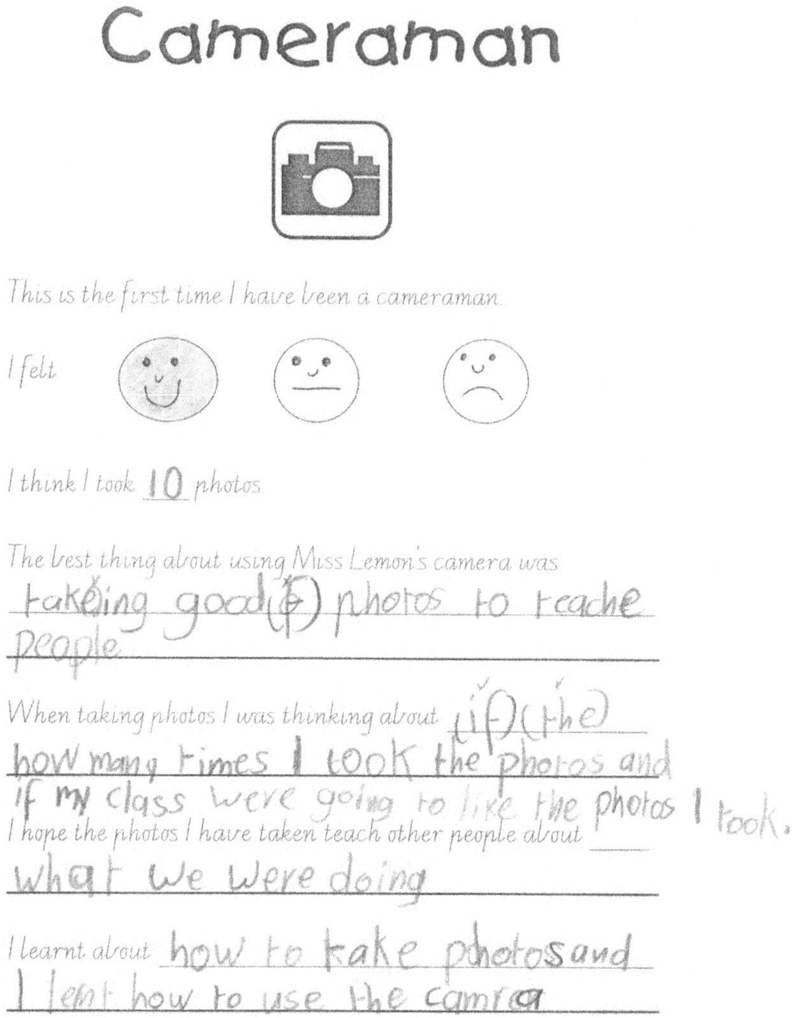

Cameraman

This is the first time I have been a cameraman.

I felt

I think I took 10 photos.

The best thing about using Miss Lemon's camera was takeing good photos to teache people

When taking photos I was thinking about how many times I took the photos and if my class were going to like the photos I took.

I hope the photos I have taken teach other people about what we were doing

I learnt about how to take photos and I lent how to use the camra

Figure 21.3 Document used for reflection after taking photographs for the first time

Some children applied their understanding of using photos to reflect further on the past by referring to specific examples:

If I went on a holiday and did not have a camera I would forget about my holiday (Olive)

If I was taking the photos of doing mathematics and I did not remember what they were about I could look at them again (Rose)

If you look at a photo you can go, 'Ahh, I remember that' but if you look at your writing you might not get it. So photos are better (James)

If I had a friend and she moved I should take a picture to remember her because if I didn't I won't remember (Gemma)

Children were asked about the possibility of never being able to use a camera to remember experiences, which provoked the following responses:

I would rewind and think what I did and then I would write it down on a piece of paper (Irene)
You would have to have a good memory to remember what you did (Mark)
You would have to think really hard about what you have done (Gemma)

The children clearly understood the role of a camera as a recorder of experiences, from exposure to its use by family members and the media. There was overwhelming agreement on the benefits of having a camera to help 'remember what you did.' This understanding of the role of a camera meant that children already viewed it as a positive resource in the classroom (Clark-Ibanez, 2007; Ewald & Lightfoot, 2001; Lemon, 2007). The openness of the children to using photos for remembering what they did allowed for reflective practices to extend beyond just written reflections. The children were prompted by requests to 'write down what you did today' or 'tell me how you felt about that activity,' to using other reflective techniques/options. The students' responses imply the need for teachers to approach reflection more creatively and with the possibility of using photos of the students in action for reflection purposes. The potential of the digital camera to enhance teaching and learning (Gee, 2003; Rickard, 2003; Swan et al., 2005) is also illustrated.

Engaging with new skills: first time using the digital camera

When asked the question 'What was the best thing about using the camera?,' the children's responses generally reinforced the enjoyment that they had in being able to use the digital camera. Written responses about what they enjoyed included:

Taking good photos to teach people (Rose)
I love it (Claire)
When I took a photo of my class (Hannah)
I was a risk taker because it was the first time I've done it (Rachel)
Taking the photos and enjoying myself (Gemma)

There was an overriding sense of enjoyment and excitement, as indicated by Claire saying simply, 'I love it.' The trust and support given to the children in using the technology was shown in their enthusiasm to make their thinking visible (Perkins & Ritchhart, 2008). For differentiating learning for students with special needs and English as Additional Language the excitement of being trusted to use the digital camera was evident with comments such as 'I really enjoyed using *the big button*' (Charles) and 'I was really happy' (Max). For several children, for example Mark and James, there was the valuing of being included in the same way as their fellow classmates. I did not want this to be an alternative activity for students with special needs or restricted to the more able students in the class. It was intended as an activity in which all children could participate, one that celebrated diversity (Sapon-Shevin, 2007) in its approach to the use of the camera, the generation of digital photographs, and the sharing of lived experiences.

To use technology freely and with the blessing of their teacher was appreciated by the children. Previously they had not been allowed to use this technology at school or at home as the digital camera had been labelled 'expensive' and it was feared that they may 'break it.' All students focused on the instructions about how to use the camera with no one student forgetting instructions or requiring further clarification. At no point did any child come close to having the camera confiscated for what could be deemed by some as 'incorrect' or 'unsafe' use. The excitement generated positive energy and this was used in a way that reciprocated my trust and created a productive working relationship between myself and the children. This philosophy and approach was central to us becoming a community of learners, and co-researchers of lived experiences of learning and teaching, whose members were willing to investigate the possibilities of reflection through visual narrative.

Co-researchers' lived experiences: what do they see?

Photographs can be a tool for learning, reflecting, and growing from lived experiences. In the classroom context, photographs can depict celebrations, personal achievements, actions, and interactions, and can assist in exploring recurring stories (Spence, 1986; Bach, 2001a).

The learning community created as part of this study provided access to resources that enhanced children's participation in class activities. In doing so, this opened up new possibilities for the children to put themselves on learning paths that they could identify with, and involved them in actions, discussion, and reflections that led to a valuing of the community's practices (Wenger, 1998). Figures 21.4 to 21.8 present visual narratives created by Claire about the learning community's space outside of the classroom. Taken by Claire (Week 5, Term 4), they are examples of a visual narrative showing knowledge and awareness of other parts of the school that make up the learning community. Claire reveals some meaningful links to spaces that are relevant to her outside of the classroom, but within the school context, through her visual narrative about the learning community.

Figure 21.4 'I took the photo of the computer lab because it helps us find out things. And it . . . we ummmm do games and maths with them.' (Claire)

Figure 21.5 'I took this photo because it helps the teachers have lunch and have a break and spend some time with the other teachers. And they have lunch there. I have after school there sometimes.' (Claire)

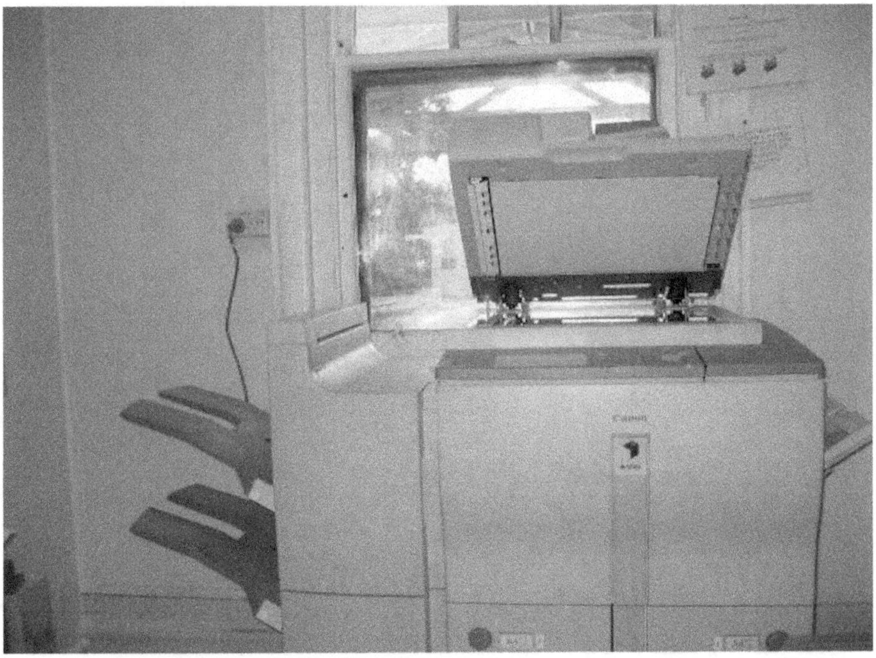

Figure 21.6 'I took . . . well this photo. . . . I took this because it helps us photocopy things if we don't have enough sheets.' (Claire)

Figure 21.7 'I took this photo because it's the art class. We have the art class there to teach us to do good drawings and paintings and ummm it will help us do clay.' (Claire)

Figure 21.8 'Classrooms, we'd have to work outside if we didn't have. . . . We can keep our writing neat and put our pencils and glue somewhere.' (Claire)

Conclusion

This chapter presents an example of how a digital camera can be integrated into the early years context to support the documentation of learning. The young people's initial experiences with the digital camera is shared to highlight their understanding and to support the place of student voice and agency in the classroom. The value of the digital camera as a resource for teaching and learning is established. The student generated digital images display the young people's capacity to construct meaning of everyday classroom experiences in a visual way (Bach, 1998; Miles & Kaplan, 2005). The visual narratives the children generated revealed their engagement with digital technology and reflective and metacognitive actions, and reinforced the potential of visual narratives to:

- promote reflection in the early childhood classroom;
- include child voice and encourage conversations and dialogue that are student centred;
- value reflective practice in and on action while looking at the lived experiences of teaching and learning; and
- develop children's metacognitive skills, particularly the element of self-evaluation.

Tips

Tips for using student generated visual narratives for educators are:

- Be open to student-centred discovery and the lived experiences they share through their visual narratives.
- Technology introduction is empowering. Scaffold and support use.
- The telling and retelling of stories allows for reflective and metacognitive thinking to be developed. Revisiting photographs and visual narratives provides opportunity for young people to retell their story over time; as there is more than one story in a photograph and always more than one layer to a story to be told.
- Be open to how the sense of belonging in the classroom can shift when young people are honoured for their capacity to record what is happening around them, and for the ways in which this can lead to new ways of understanding one's self, seeing each other, and developing relationships and leadership qualities in themselves. Most importantly the impact of sharing one's voice enhances the sense of self and wellbeing. This can be especially visible in students, young people, who previously had not had an opportunity to share their perspectives voice, and sense of belonging.
- When young people are seen as co-researchers of their learning environment through the generation of their visual narratives, data is produced that supports the opening up of conversations about learning and teaching, and impact on teacher reflective practice.

References

Åkerman, E. (2012) Children's systems telling and the story of a meatbal.'s social-ecological system: A narrative approach to systems thinking in early childhood education for sustainable development. http://urn.kb.se/resolve?urn=urn:nbn:se:su:diva-79240.

Australian Human Rights Commission (2014) Supporting young children's rights STATEMENT OF INTENT (2015–2018). www.humanrights.gov.au/sites/default/files/supporting_young_children_rights.pdf.

Bach, H. (1998) *A visual narrative concerning curriculum, girls, photography etc.* Edmonton, AB: Qual Institute Press.

Bach, H. (2001a) The place of the photography in visual narrative research. *Afterimage* 29 (3), 7.
Bach, H. (2001b) The place of the photograph in visual narrative research – project statement. Retrieved 3 January 2018 from www.findarticles.com/p/articles/mi_m2479/is_3_29/ai_80757500/print.
Bager-Charleson, S. (2004) The parents' school? Narrative research about parental involvement in schools. Retrieved 3 January 2018 from www.lse.ac.uk/Collections/genderInstitute/events/postgraduateSeminars/January.html.
Barnett, W.S. and Nores, M. (2012) *Investing in early childhood education: A global perspective. National Institute for Early Education Research.* New Brunswick, NJ: Rutgers, The State University of New Jersey.
Bathmaker, A.M. and Harnett, P. (2010) *Exploring learning identity and power through life history research.* Abingdon: Routledge.
Britzman, D. (1990) *Practice makes practice.* New York: SUNY Press.
Carr, M. (2001) *Assessment in early childhood settings: Learning stories.* London: Paul Chapman Publishing.
Castelle, K. (1990) *In the child's best interest: A primer on the U.N. Convention on the Rights of the Child.* East Greenwich, RI: Plan International.
Christensen, P. and James, A. (2017) *Research with children: Perspectives and practices.* London: Taylor & Francis.
Clandinin, D.J., Caine, V., Lessard, S. and Huber, J. (2016) *Engaging in narrative inquiries with children and youth.* London: Routledge.
Clandinin, D.J. and Connelly, F.M. (1995) *Teachers' professional knowledge landscapes.* New York: Teachers College Press.
Clandinin, D.J. and Connelly, F.M. (2000) *Narrative inquiry: Experience and story in qualitative research.* San Francisco, CA: Jossey-Bass.
Clark, A. and Moss, P. (2001) *Listening to young children: The Mosaic approach.* London: National Children's Bureau.
Clark-Ibanez, M. (2007) Inner-city children in sharper focus: Sociology of childhood and photo elicitation interviews. In: Stanczak, G.C. (ed.) *Visual research methods.* Los Angeles, CA: Sage, 167–196.
Collier, J. (1957) Photography in anthropology: A report in two experiments. *American Anthropologist* 59, 843–859.
Connelly, F.M. and Clandinin, D.J. (1988) *Teachers as curriculum planners: Narratives of experience.* New York, NY: Teachers College Press.
Cook-Sather, A. (2002) Authorizing students' perspective: Toward trust, dialogue, and change in education. *Educational Researcher* 31 (4), 3–14.
Curtis, D. and Carter, M. (2000) *The art of awareness: How observations can transform your teaching.* St Paul, MI: Redleaf Press.
Dahlberg, G., Moss, P. and Pence, A.R. (1999) *Beyond quality in early childhood education and care: Postmodern perspectives*, London: Falmer Press.
Daiute, C. and Lightfoot, C., eds. (2004) *Narrative analysis: Studying the development of individuals in society*, Thousand Oaks, CA: Sage.
Denzin, N.K. and Lincoln, Y.S. (eds.) (2000) *Handbook of qualitative research.* Thousand Oaks, CA: Sage.
Dillner, M. (2001) Using media flexibly to compose and communicate. *Reading Online* 5 (1), 85.
Egg, P., Schratz-Hadwich, B., Trubswasser, G. and Walker, R. (2004) *Seeing beyond violence: Children as researchers.* SOS-Kinderdorf: Hermann Gmeiner Akademie.
Einarsdottir, J. (2006) Playschool in pictures: Children's photographs as a research method. *Early Child Development and Care* 175 (6), 523–541.
Ewald, W. and Lightfoot, A. (2001) *I Wanna Take Me a Picture – Teaching Photography and Writing to Children.* Boston, MA: Center for Documentary Studies (in association with Beacon Press).
Fielding, M. (2002) Beyond the rhetoric of student voice: New departures or new constraints in the transformation of 21st century schooling? *Forum* 43 (2), 100–109.
Garvis, S., Eriksen Ødegaard, E. and Lemon, N. (2015) *Beyond observation: Narrative methods with young children.* Amsterdam: Sense.
Gee, J.P. (2003) *What video games have to teach us about learning and literacy.* New York: Palgrave Macmillan.
Groundwater-Smith, S., Ewing, R. and Le Cornu, R. (2007) *Teaching: Challenges and dilemmas.* South Melbourne: Thomson.
Guba, E. and Lincoln, Y. (1985) *Naturalistic inquiry.* Beverly Hills, CA: Sage Publications.
Hadfield, M. and Haw, K. (2001) 'Voice', young people and action research. *Educational Action Research* 9 (3), 485–499.
Hall, M., Pahl, K. and Pool, S. (2015) Visual digital methodologies with children and young people: Perspectives from the field. In: Stirling, E. and Yamada-Rice, D. (eds.) *Visual methods with children and young people. Studies in childhood and youth.* London: Palgrave Macmillan, 164–185.

Halverson, E. and Gibbons, D. (2008) *Digital literacy as production: Youth participation in media arts learning environments.* Paper presented at the Annual Conference of American Educational Research Association, New York City, March 24–28.

Harper, D. (2002) Talking about pictures: A case for photo elicitation. *Visual Studies* 17 (1), 14–26.

Hatherly, A. (2006) The stories we share: Using narrative assessment to build communities of literacy participants in early childhood centres. *Australian Journal of Early Childhood* 31 (1), 27–34.

Kellett, M. and Ding, S. (2004) Middle childhood. In: Fraser, S., Lewis, V., Ding, S., Kellet, M. and Robinsons, C. (eds.) *Doing research with children and young people.* London: The Open University, 161–174.

Kincheloe, J.L. (2003) *Teachers as researchers: Qualitative inquiry as a path to empowerment.* London: Routledge Falmer.

Kramp, M.K. (2004) Exploring life and experience through narrative inquiry. In: DeMarrais, K.B. and Lapan, S.D. (eds.) *Foundations for research: Methods of inquiry in education and the social sciences – Inquiry and pedagogy across diverse contexts.* Mahwah, NJ: Lawrence Erlbaum Associates, 104–121.

Leitch, R. (2008) Creatively researching children's narratives through image and drawings. In: Thompson, P. (ed.) *Get the picture: Visual research with children and young people.* London: RoutledgeFalmer, 35–58.

Lemon, N. (2007) Take a photograph: Teacher reflection through narrative. *Journal of Reflective Practice* 8 (2), 177–191.

Lemon, N. (2008) Looking through the lens of a camera in the early childhood classroom. In: Moss, J. (ed.). *Research education: Visually-digitally-spatially.* Rotterdam: Sense Publishers, 21–52.

Lemon, N. (2014) Image making as a way to build a sense of belonging and wellbeing in young people. In: Garvis, S. and Pendergast, D. (eds.). *Health and wellbeing in the early years.* Melbourne: Cambridge University Press, 206–221.

Lemon, N. (2015) Narratives by children. In: Garvis, S., Eriksen, S., Ødegaard, E. and Lemon, N. (eds.). *Beyond observation: Narrative methods with young children.* Rotterdam: Sense, 83–104.

Lemon, N. (2016) Young children photographing their learning to share their lived experiences of the learning environment. In: Garvis, S. and Lemon, N. (eds.) *Understanding digital technologies with young children: An international perspective.* London: Routledge, 46–59.

Leu, D.J. and Kinzer, C.K. (2000) The convergence of literacy instruction with networked technologies for information and communication. *Reading Research Quarterly* 35 (1), 109–127.

MacNaughton, G. (2003) Eclipsing voice in research with young children. *Australian Journal of Early Childhood Education* 28 (1), 36–42.

MacNaughton, G. (2005) *Doing Foucault in early childhood studies: Applying poststructural ideas.* London: Routledge.

Mason, J. (2006) Mixing methods in a qualitatively driven way. *Qualitative Research* 6 (1), 9–25.

Mauthner, M. (1997) Methodological aspects of collecting data from children: Lessons from three research projects. *Children and Society* 11, 16–28.

Miles, S. and Kaplan, I. (2005) Using images to promote reflection: An action research study in Zambia and Tanzania. *Journal of Research in Special Educational Needs* 5 (2), 77.

Moss, J. (2003) *Picture this: Visual narrative as a source for understanding diversity in our classrooms.* Melbourne: Festival against Racism in Education.

Moss, J. (ed.) (2008) *Educational researchers working – visually-digitally-spatially.* Rotterdam: Sense.

Moss, J. (2013) Visual research methods in education: In between difference and indifference. *International Journal on School Disaffection* 10 (2), 63–77.

Moss, J. and Pini, B. (2016) *Visual research methods in educational research*, London: Palgrave Macmillan.

Parnell, W. and Iorio, J.M. (eds.) (2015) *Disrupting early childhood education research: Imagining new possibilities (Changing images of early childhood).* London: Routledge.

Perkins, D. and Ritchhart, R. (2008) Making thinking visible. *Association for Supervision and Curriculum Development* February 2008, 57–61.

Prior, M.A. and Niesz, T. (2013) Refugee children's adaptation to American early childhood classrooms. *A Narrative Inquiry* 18 (39), 1–17.

Prosser, J. (ed.) (1998) *Image-based research: A sourcebook for qualitative researchers.* London: Falmer Press.

Rickards, T. (2003) Technology-rich learning environment and the role of effective teaching. In: Khine, M.S. and Fisher, D. (eds.) *Technology-rich learning environment: A future perspective.* New Jersey: World Scientific, 115–132.

Riessman, C.K. (2008) *Narrative methods for the human sciences.* CA, USA: SAGE Publications.

Sairanen, H. and Kumpulainen, K. (2014) A visual narrative inquiry into children's sense of agency in preschool and first grade. *International Journal of Educational Psychology* 3 (2), 141–174.

Sapon-Shevin, M. (2007) *Widening the circle: The power of inclusive classrooms.* Boston, MA: Beacon Press.

Spence, J. (1986) *Putting myself in the picture: A political, personal and photographic autobiography*. London: Camden Press.

Swan, K., van 't Hooft, M., Kratcoski, A. and Unger, D. (2005) Uses and effects of mobile computing devices in K-8 classrooms. *Journal of Research on Technology in Education* 38 (1), 99–113.

Tayler, C. (2012) Learning in Australian early childhood education and care settings: Changing professional practice. *Education 3–13: International Journal of Primary Elementary and Early Years Education* 40 (1), 7–18.

Tayler, C., Ure, C., Brown, R, Deans, J. and Cronin, B. (2008) *Victorian early years learning and development framework and the Victorian essential learning standards*. Melbourne: University of Melbourne.

United Nations. (2017) *Convention on the right of the child*. Retrieved 3 January 2018 from www.ohchr.org /EN/ProfessionalInterest/Pages/CRC.aspx.

U.S Department of Education. (2017) *National education technology plan*. Washington DC: American Institutes for Research.

Wenger, E. (1998) *Communities of practice: Learning, meaning and identity*. New York: Cambridge University Press.

Williamson, D., Cullen, J. and Lepper, C. (2006) Checklists to narratives in special education: Learning stories used for early childhood teaching. *Australian Journal of Early Childhood* 31 (2), 20–30.

Wood, D.R. (2000) Review of narrative inquiry: Experience and story in qualitative research. Retrieved 17 November 2018 from http://www. aaanet.org/cae/aeq/br/clandinin.htm

Wong, S.S. (2003) A narrative inquiry into teaching of in-service kindergarten teachers: Implications for re-conceptualizing early childhood teacher education in Hong Kong. *Early Child Development and Care* 173 (1), 73–81.

22
ARTS-BASED METHODS

Linda Knight

Children's digital media productions in early childhood

The mass availability of digital media in homes and educational sites across the globe has offered new possibilities for play, and for learning. Digital media appears in many of the spaces children inhabit, including formal learning spaces such as schools, kindergartens and day-care centres. Very young children learn basic skills such as reading, writing, music, drawing, numeracy and science concepts through digitally based educational toys, they participate in digital media play and learning sessions, and young children learn coding through robotics tasks. For children who have access, digital media can come to form a large part of their daily activity, especially when schooling embeds digital media use in teaching and learning activities.

This new vision of childhood is both exciting and terrifying, and full of possibility for researchers to assess the impacts and effects of children's access and use of digital media in their everyday lives. The rapid change that digital media and technologies more broadly have brought to children's lives in a very short time, mean there is uncertainty about the many impacts this exposure may have and how they will emerge in the long term. Research into digital media in early childhood recognises that 'digital technologies have a role to play in developing children's identity as effective learners in the classroom' (Flewitt et al., 2015, p. 305), however more research is needed to understand the impact digital media use is having on young children across their lives and learning. Children's digital media use is a new and growing area of research, and researchers are keen to examine its use by young children in different contexts. Researchers are also keen to use innovative and creative methods and procedures for undertaking their investigations to allow for more nuanced data types, and more nuanced findings and outputs.

This chapter examines the potential of arts-based methods for researching the uses of digital media by young children. The chapter will assert the difference between research that looks at children's digital art, and research that uses arts-based methods to investigate a wide range of topics. Recent research into children's digital media use is initially discussed to highlight some of the main issues and phenomena researchers focus on, and the methods that are commonly used. This is followed by one articulation of how a research project might extend on the usual methods and employ arts-based methods in digital media research, and how arts-based research can produce useful and meaningful data that can be used singly, or in combination with other forms of data.

I suggest that arts practices offer methodological opportunities for research into digital media in early childhood because they are able to accommodate complex and theoretically rich research questions and projects. Arts practices in research are variously described, and include arts-focused research and arts-led research (Knowles & Cole, 2008). This chapter specifically focuses on how arts-based research offers rich methodological potentials for investigating digital media in early childhood. Arts-based methods can be highly effective in attending to research projects that are multidimensional, that might be investigating and wanting to observe and record multiple things such as social interactions, physical use, posture, conversation, media activity, digital production and more.

Understanding the valorisations attached to young children's digital media making, and how this impacts on arts-based research into digital media in early childhood

In addition to researchers refining their understandings of their own arts-based data generating and data gathering practices, it is important for researchers to address normalising attitudes that surround the digital media that young children produce, and how such attitudes can have a limiting effect on project ideas. Being critically aware of the social and cultural valorisations attached to children's art can offer more expansive possibilities to researchers of what can be counted as child-produced, arts-based data.

Cultural valorisations are hard to dilute. I've had heated discussions with my own undergraduate students about whether all children's drawings are art, especially after I suggested that mostly young children's drawings were not art, but visualisations of ideas and concepts. I suggested that the child's intention to draw might often not be to create art, but to create an account of what happened at the weekend, their favourite sport, or it might be to figure out the workings of an aircraft, or what outer space might look like. My students were certainly shocked to hear their expert lecturer say such things! Clearly, ideas about what is children's art are socially and culturally constructed and upheld, and these ensure that certain images are read through schema commonly thought to define the work as art.

There is not enough space in this chapter to discuss how valorisations around children's art emerge, however as I have asserted elsewhere (Knight & Dooley, 2015), ideas about children's art are closely tied to developmental theories and Western theories of aesthetics. Two things happen because of this association: children's visual and performance productions are recognised, organised and classified due to particular schema, which means many productions by children that may actually be closer to an artistic intention are ignored or discarded, because they fall outside the schema. Two examples help to illustrate my point: a child's drawing of a battle scene and a child's collection of photographs. A child has made a drawing of a battle. It is created on paper using water-based markers and pencil. The scene is animated and contains figures in action firing weapons and various vehicles flying and exploding/combusting. Dotted lines trailing across the page suggest that ammunition is being fired. Drawings like these are familiar, and it is likely that many early childhood educators have seen children produce these types of drawings. Commonly this work might be described as art, but I suggest that the child's intention is not to create art but to explore live action, noises, engineering, power, speed, popular films and stories through the specifics of a battle event. This drawing visually experiments with conveying speed, movement and sequence, and also explores ways to visualise non-solid objects such as bullet trajectories, flames and smoke, however, these are within the intentions of creating a battle scene. Such a drawing has a singular focus with all components fixed on exploring a specific task.

Example two is a collection of photographs a child has taken using a smartphone (Figures 22.1A–D). The photographs were taken in quick succession and attend to the event of being out to dinner.

Figures 22.1A–D Photographs, taken with iPhone

Credit: Hannah Rayner

The photographs experiment with close-ups and the composition in the frame of objects on the table. The child has noticed details such as the effects of condensation on the glass, the light in and around the glass, the placement of cutlery on a napkin and plate and the numbers on the table sign. Spontaneous and emergent, each photograph attends to different observations and speculations. Different arrangements are noticed and captured and there is a focus on how distance affects the composition of the image and how light plays on surfaces. The photographs as a collection examine the notion of eating out. The child is not telling a story here though, they are standing back and looking at the occasion of eating out through photography. Different things are being thought about simultaneously, and these are build into the collection of images taken.

It is intention over end product that defines the work as art. Photographs and drawings are not automatically artworks, it is the intention and purpose that make them so. In focusing on only the finished product, the diverse reasons why children produce visual works can be missed. Hopefully the examples cement how important it is for researchers to understand children's diverse intentions for making, and that to fixate on specific reasons for children's productions generates a dualistic belief that all the visual materials created by children is art, and that conversely, children are not capable of making different types of art, including political or conceptual art. The photographs included here are an example of digital media art that is primarily conceptual and abstract in its intention.

Children's digital media use: recent research

Research into children's exposure to digital media emerged soon after the new millennia, at a time when digital technologies began appearing in learning sites such as classrooms and kindergartens (Brooker & Siraj-Blatchford, 2002; Marsh, 2005; Plowman & Stephen, 2005). As digital media has become more commonly available in schools and kindergartens, recent studies have moved beyond a fascination with the technology to focus on conceptual ideas about children's uses of devices and their impact on childhoods (Dale & Latham, 2014; Gibbons, 2016; Lafton, 2015; Laidlaw & Wong, 2016).

Children's media use through play is a key focus for contemporary research. Generally, researchers see that play can positively influence media use. Wohlwend (2017) observes how introducing toys and materials that reference popular media (such as commercial film characters, or toy franchise characters) can help children to gain cultural currency and social inclusion in social group dynamics. She reports on a previous study (Wohlwend, 2013) where children referenced popular media to create digital videos that allowed them to explore play narratives and create social connections with others, observing how the digital play initiates participatory literacies between children who might not socialise together otherwise. Similarly, Edwards (2016) and Eckhoff (2017) looked at the influence of culture on young children's digital play and the ways technologies shift conceptions of children's play. Eckhoff (2017) used a participatory design method to examine the use of digital media by young children as they encounter outdoor play spaces whilst attending school, and the photographic imagery young children create when undertaking free play in outdoor environments. In each study digital media is used ethnographically and as a resource in partnership with 'traditional' resources, to observe how young children negotiate and develop social skills.

The socio-material effects of digital devices extends on a focus on play, with theories and critiques providing a framework to examine interrelationalities between digital and physical materials, ideas and identities of young children. Laidlaw and Wong (2016) applied complexity thinking to push concepts around multiliteracy practices, and Dubé and McEwen (2017) used communication theory to articulate a framework around kindergartener's interactions with digital tablets. In each case, critical theories became part of the methodologic apparatus, helping to gather data on the encounters between children and digital devices.

Critical theory has been used to interrogate the socio-material impacts of digital media on early childhood teaching and pedagogy. Jordan (2016) considered the global shift towards the digital, asking 'Does media define the experience of childhood?' (p. 879). Jordan theorised that childhood is not a fixed notion but 'reflect[s] the familial, economic, social, political' (p. 879) aspects of its life and culture, and that these impact on how children encounter digital devices. Similarly, Lafton (2015) theorised that early childhood professional practices are shaped by social influences and these intertwine with the materiality of equipment and devices. Lafton applied a poststructural reading of practices of using digital devices to learn about events outside the classroom, and how the diverse characters featured on the screen 'challenge notions of agency when non-humans are understood as actors' (p. 142) in helping children to forge relationships and connections with world issues. For many researchers, theory acts methodologically and conceptually to help process the multiple, fast-paced changes occurring in early childhood, as digital media becomes a larger part of the learning landscape.

Research can foreground digital media, making it both the focus and the methodologic tool of the research. Green (2016) used wearable cameras with young children to gather data in different ways and to capture very close recordings of children's lived experiences of nature. Green considered how using digital media to conduct participatory phenomenological research might 'provide adult researchers with a deeper insight of children's experiences of "being-in-the-world"' (p. 281). For Green, giving children digital media to collect and direct data revealed how 'children see, interpret, and interact with their environments' (2016, p. 292).

As digital media becomes more prevalent in contemporary learning spaces, and as children and educators find new ways to use technologies in their daily activities, researchers are turning to diverse critical and methodologic practices to investigate and record the effects and impact of these interactions. Researchers' willingness to methodologically innovate and experiment means that arts-based methods can make a valuable contribution to research into digital media in early childhood.

It is particularly important that research with young children and media (that can record and capture personal images and recordings) is ethical. Arts-based methods are particularly ethical because the arts are highly subjective, being an individual expression and personal interpretation of the world. Rather than seeing the individual nature of art as an inconsistency or a weakness, arts-based methods can effectively and sensitively attend to the issues of ethics, including the growing sensitivity about power dynamics between researcher and researched (Deppeler et al., 2008; Banks, 2007; Matapo & Roder, 2018), as well as giving children an independent voice in the research process. Some of the ethical issues and concerns about researching with digital media and young children, and issues of protection of the data that is produced, are now discussed briefly to emphasise the benefits of using arts-based methods in digital media projects with children.

Arts-based research as an ethical practice

After a period of 'mesmerisation' with digital technologies per se, researchers are attending to issues of ethics in relation to children's exposure to digital technologies and media. In their systematic review of children's uses of technology in learning, Hsin et al. (2014) concluded that technology exposure had generally a positive effect on learning, particularly on children from low socioeconomic status families, however more research is needed in terms of children's roles as creators of technology, rather than focusing on children as digital consumers. Dale and Latham (2014) also considered the ethical implications of young children having a large amount of exposure to digital technologies. The authors propose that recognition of the impact on children of using a networked device, is needed. Grimes and Fields (2015) likewise suggest that children's familiarity with media creation prior to the availability of digital technologies does not necessarily guarantee a smooth transition into their use of networked media creation tools.

There are both opportunities and challenges to ensure equitable research practices into children's uses of online DIY media. Introducing children to networked devices raises issues around cultural rights and children's privacy and authorship, so calls for platforms that 'effectively and sustainably foster a rights-based, inclusive, child-centric approach' (Grimes & Fields, 2015, p. 115) to digital participation provide great opportunities for experimental and responsive methods like arts-based research to be used. For example, researching as well as designing high quality research tools, such as 'richly designed websites' (Grimes & Fields, 2015, p. 120) can use arts-based research methods to ethically investigate children's creative ideas and their expressions and responses to big questions, in ways that respect their cultural and personal rights. Arts-based research requires the child to have agency in the research process, and this creatively pushes the field of digital research in early childhood forward.

As digital research evolves, so should the nuanced understanding of children's everyday use of digital and technological media include attention to the ethical, pedagogic and social impacts of young children's digital exposure. Arts-based methodologies can accommodate the peculiarities of digital media technologies and their uses by children, and in the different contexts children encounter digital media, in responsive and ethical ways. This is because arts practices rely upon personal interpretations and productions, and participatory practices. Arts-based, participatory research methods are effective for researching with groups of children, parents, educators and digital devices and to attend to the changing contexts for research, and the changing nature of the digital phenomenon.

Digital media in early childhood education as an emerging research field, opens up opportunities for experimental methodologies to refine conceptual and theoretical thinking about digital media use by young children. Flick (2007) asserts that a good research question is equally about theory and methodology, because 'methods and theories should be appropriate to what is studied' (Flick, 2007, p. xi). A double attendance to methods and theories thinks sensitively about the complexities and details of cultures, children's lives, individual identities and subjectivities and livelihoods (Knight, 2016). Expansive understandings and theorisations about the environments, materials and contexts for education facilitate creative and ethically minded projects that can genuinely expand knowledge about education in respectful and egalitarian ways.

The importance of rigour in arts-based research

As early childhood knowledge becomes more refined and attuned and entwined in philosophy and theory, researchers can hone in on very specific questions about situations that are only just becoming visible, such as the use of digital media by babies and the development of iPad apps aimed specifically to be used by pets such as cats, dogs, birds and reptiles (Bart, 2013; Peachman, 2014). As an example, the recent rise in speculative and posthuman readings of early childhood education (Andersen & Otterstad, 2014; Jones et al., 2014; Pacini-Ketchabaw & Kummen, 2016) ethically gaze beyond the child/educator binary and take notice of the agentic presence and impact of humans, animals, politics, environments, materials, cultures, powers and beliefs. New, complex theorisations of early childhood education and care present significant conceptual and practical challenges to the field, so theoretically informed research projects can benefit from 'responsive and responsible' methodologies that enable results which are accessible and as closely connected and relevant to the research topic/question as possible.

Methodological innovation must demonstrate excellent responsivity and be highly effective in exploring the curiosities of the researcher, as well as translate theoretically difficult research to different audiences. Methodological complexity and elasticity accommodates multidimensionality and is utterly responsive to these shifting dimensions, while also effectively translating those into findings and outcomes. Learning to use new or experimental methodologies (which may include arts-based methods) can mean researchers take extra care in learning new processes to ensure quality and rigour while respecting participant involvement.

Applying methodological innovation in digital media research generates insightful ways of thinking through new theories about contexts (such as early childhood education) as well as speculating and experimenting with the process of researching. For example, the rise in infographics and data visualisation (Cruz et al., 2017; Verhoeven, 2016) has allowed for innovative ways for interpreting theories into images, tracking, ordering and reporting on data through schematics and graphics, and translating complex ideas via symbols, icons and animations to audiences.

Arts-based methods differ to other methods that rely upon set procedures and unwavering sequences that present particular types of data for specific purposes. Arts-based research works with intentions and expectations that are fluid and that move with the project, and produces findings that are responsive to difference, rather than seeking out regularity or aspects that can be grouped and coded (Eisner, 2008). Fluidity does not mean carelessness or a *laissez-faire* approach to research however; arts-based research must be highly rigorous, careful and skilful. As with all research methods, arts-based research can be badly applied or executed if there is a lack of understanding about processes and procedures and how theories and methods interrelate. Poorly theorised and poorly executed arts-based projects can also be accepted for publication because the journal and review team might not have the skills and understandings to rigorously critique it (Barone, 2008). Such papers then present a skewed idea of good arts-based research, and thus a downward cycle of quality can occur.

Finally, projects can confuse arts-based methods:

- the topic of investigation might not be related to, or focus on the arts, but arts practices form the data gathering method; or
- data is analysed through arts practices, and/or data results are translated into arts works.

With arts-focused research:

- the topic of investigation is about the arts, however other methods are used to gather data, analyse data and report on the data; or
- the project includes or promotes the arts in some way (such as a project that explores the different ways children learn to read, and comments on the use of picture books as one useful resource).

These confusions have a detrimental impact on the clarity and rigour of arts-based research. I now provide examples to help explain the different ways the arts appear in research into children's use of digital media, and to identify rigorous, arts-based research. The examples show the differences between arts-focused and generally focused projects, and that these approaches should not be confused with arts-based methods.

Arts-focused and arts-based methods in digital media research

Although an excellent study that has relevance to digital media education research, Doyle & Dezuanni's (2014) project is an example of a research investigation that is not arts-based but arts focused. Doyle & Dezuanni looked at the ways media arts teaching could enhance science learning in primary education. The authors found that digital media enhanced children's participation and communication in specific ways, and this assisted in their science learning. Doyle & Dezuanni claim that 'digital media production has the potential to make science more accessible' (2014, p. 42). The authors used video production to explore key science concepts, because making videos 'provided a multimodal means of communication' (p. 51). Video production is seen as arts-focused learning because it involves storyboarding, understanding of sequential imagery, cinematography, and the coding of moving images for specific purposes (in this case a procedural video). Through media arts experiences the children learnt about how digital media exposed them to 'participation in school science not provided by print literacy practices' (p. 53). Importantly, Doyle & Dezuanni (2014) worked critically with the artistic and design nuances of filmmaking by foregrounding these aspects with the participants. Their project was deeply concerned with 'the positive potential of linking media arts and science pedagogy' (p. 53).

Additional examples of research that is not arts-based include Eckhoff's (2015) study into informal play and Rowe and Miller's (2016) research into bilingual eBooks. Each of these projects is generally focused and promotes arts in early childhood education, but do not employ arts-based methods. Eckhoff (2015) considered the ethics of working with young children and their media-based informal play productions. Eckhoff positioned the young children as collaborating artists, researchers and documenters, through a sociocultural theorisation that proposed children make worlds through their play. Eckhoff (2015) regarded the children as 'competent individuals capable of engaging in effective participatory research' (p. 1617) using a variety of media-based resources. The positioning of the children as artists is respectful and promotes the place of media arts in children's learning, however what is foregrounded in this research are the subtle ways that young children devise their own play activities. Rowe and Miller (2016) conducted a two-year project into the eBooks that bilingual/biliteral young children produced. The authors focused on eBooks produced on iPads that integrated photos, voice recordings, print and drawings, to consider their effectiveness in connecting home-based and school-based learning, for families not typically able to access new generation digital technologies. A design-based research method was used which involved combing visual and audio recordings to create texts 'through non-linguistic means of creating and sharing meaning' (2016, p. 446). Rowe and Miller saw how these components had a fundamental role in helping to devise the eBooks, and they discussed how the children demonstrated high levels of excitement and interest in taking photographs for their eBooks. The project promoted the inclusion of visual materials on children's learning of other languages; however, the design research method focused on the emergence of participant-curated eBooks, of which visual materials form a part.

I will now use two fictional project examples to help explain and elucidate on arts-based methodological practices. It is hoped the examples help to conceptualise how arts-based methods might take form in a research project into digital media in early childhood. The two examples help to assert how arts-based research may not be focused on the arts but uses arts practices in the generating, analysis and reporting of research data. This might include using performance arts, drawing and arts installations as data, analysing data through the production of play scripts and exhibition works and disseminating on data finding through sculptural forms, dance, music compositions and conceptual art collaborations.

Arts-based research: two examples

Example one: a research project that investigates children's engagement with non-arts curriculum subjects. The project is driven by a curiosity about the ways digital tablet-created arts can aid early childhood learning about different subject matter. There is a desire to use something methodologically different to guided interviews, questionnaires or video observations to record and generate the data; there is a desire to use arts-based methodologies not only to generate other sorts of data, but to apply a method that thinks about a research question, and thinks about research itself, differently.

The project involves the teacher delivering regular curriculum learning content to students. The children produce regular types of school work in response to that curriculum. The arts-based methods will enable the children and teacher to produce 'other kinds' of responses to that content also. The tablets are loaded with a specific cache of apps and features which include the camera function, voice memo function, a cloud-based presentation tool and an image editing app. The choice of apps is significant: the apps require participants to make artistic productions using their own ideas and plans. The apps can be used alone or in combination. How or whether this happens is up to each child. Likewise, each child is free to direct how they create responses with the apps. Importantly however, the art making is a foregrounded aspect of the project. The children are working through artistic production primarily, and the curriculum content secondarily. The children use the camera and/or voice memo app to process and respond to content learning through photography and/or sound recordings. These are loaded into the image editing tool and individual multimedia works are created. The teacher and children then collaborate and curate their multimedia works into the cloud-based presentation tool, to create a class collection/portfolio of individual responses. The research project regards the sound files, photographs, multimedia works and class collection as different clusters of research data. The example project foregrounds arts processes and arts thinking, enacted through media-based materials, to learn about non-arts curriculum content.

Example two: a research project that investigates children's understandings of citizenship. The children are exploring notions of citizenship. The class is working with a multimedia artist who helps the children to think critically about the idea of citizenship through key concepts which include being a member of a community, belonging to a group, having identity and living somewhere new or strange. The artist brainstorms the concepts with the children and helps them to devise and create a series of multimedia projection works. The projection works are launched via a special event for the school, and the images are projected over the outside walls of the school at the end of each day. The project treats each of the projection works as the research data and part of the research outputs.

A key factor articulated in the two examples is that the production of artworks occurs but is not the topic focus of the research. Creating art does not automatically make a project about the arts. Projects that include arts productions as a major or minor aspect might be assumed to be about the arts (arts-focused), however these two examples are focused on curriculum engagement and understandings of citizenship respectively. The examples show how art-based methods initiate ways of working and types of information/participant responses that work to these two foci in ways that are different to undertaking questionnaires, guided interviews or ethnographic observations.

Art is made through motivations and intentions that inform physical and material procedures. Although the physical and material procedures might in themselves be mundane (such as sawing wood, using a camera, jumping, using a pencil), the motivations and intentions and the ways in which mundane procedures are utilised are what turn them into arts methods and arts works. Using arts as a research method will produce data from and of those unique processes and creative motivations, *as they have been applied within an arts intention*. In other words, even if those mundane procedures were to be used methodologically, they will not of themselves produce arts-based research data. Arts-based methods produce data that is not achievable by other investigative means. It is essential that researchers hone their understandings of the arts to expand their methodological repertoires so they might generate high quality data.

The intentions and intellectual drivers for making art are at the heart of arts-based research, however nuanced understanding of the diversity of practices and processes of different arts productions can be difficult to learn by researchers who are learning about arts-based methods. In the next section I will illustrate how diverse arts practices can occur. This is essential to understand that there is not 'one model' for identifying arts-based methods, because there is not 'one way' for making art – and, crucially it is essential to remind the reader about the difference between arts-focused research (the topic of investigation is about the arts, however other methods are used to gather data, analyse data and report on the data) and arts-based research (the topic of investigation might not be related to, or focus on the arts, but arts practices form the data gathering method, data is analysed through arts practices and/or data results are translated into arts works).

As I address issues when conducting research into digital media in early childhood, I will revisit the two examples to help illustrate problems and good practices around applying arts-based methods to such research projects. This is not to suggest that arts-based methods have a specific canon; the examples hopefully make clear how differently arts-based methods can attend to complex project ideas, and attempt to address the research question.

It is important to understand the difference between children creating visual records of their non-art learning (such as the engineering thinking of the battle scene drawing discussed at the beginning of the chapter) and their creation of art through exploration of artistic processes and concepts. This is the case even if the research focuses on topics not relating to children's art/art education. If researchers do not acknowledge there is difference in children's art, then the ability to plan good and useful arts-based research into children's digital media use is adversely affected. There is a danger that children will be encouraged to produce images with little content or meaning, and that these will not provide researchers with rich information to respond to their research questions. Children create artistic works about all manner of topics and ideas, so good quality arts-based methods can produce high quality findings about them. Researchers must take the time to learn about the ways the arts work for children, to fully grasp how arts-based methods can work coherently in a project that involves children's digital media productions.

Similarly, children's digital media use can be misinterpreted. Just as children enjoy undirected or unfocused play with paints, musical instruments, clay and costumes, children also enjoy using digital media in an unfocused way. It is easy to think that children are just messing about with arts materials, a smartphone or tablet, but it is important to understand what is going on when children want to persistently use the drum, the play dough, the camera, the microphone or various apps. This persistent and deeply immersed use shows how children are learning artistic practices and gaining and refining their understandings of all the functions and possibilities of the material. Children demonstrate their researching and experimenting skills through this repeated and intense play.

It takes a lot of practice to use digital apps to make images, recordings, movies, animations and more. Just as children's hand drawn images can be misread for their meanings and intentions, or their instrumental play as noise, so children's digital media productions can be misunderstood as 'gaming' or boredom busters, instead of seriously researched and carefully planned experimental digital/media/artworks.

Conventional valorisations about children's art and digital media practices directly impact on the rigour of arts-based investigations into children's digital media. Young children are capable of being sophisticated digital media users; however misconceptions about their capabilities can direct how researchers design projects. Similarly, misconceptions about what is accepted as early childhood digital arts and media, coupled with an 'ambivalence towards the incorporation of new technologies' (Flewitt et al., 2015, p. 290), can also affect the quality of the arts-based methods used.

How might this play out? In returning to the examples, project one investigates how teachers use digital tablets to initiate non-arts curriculum learning via the media works children produce. Misconceptions about children's media works might mean that data would be gathered on the basis of appearance rather than being attuned to the intention and purpose of those works, and this is likely to have a negatively impacting effect on the validity of the project. Because example two involves a multimedia artist working with child participants to investigate their understandings of citizenship, it is less likely that the artworks produced are not regarded as artworks, however care must be taken to read the works properly to understand the relationship of the works to the research question.

Logistics of arts-based research into children's use of digital media

The practicalities of planning and conducting arts-based research are not vastly different to the planning and implementation of other research projects. I am reluctant to present a step-by-step guide to arts-based research; though it is prudent to identify the key things researchers should attend to when doing this type of investigation. In conclusion, and to reiterate points raised throughout the chapter, the following logistics should be attended to:

- Understand whether the project is arts-based or art-focused. Adjust and refine the ideas for data production and analysis, if needed.
- Consider the expertise of the researcher/s. It is not necessary to be a practicing media artist, but a refined understanding of media arts is essential. Extensive reading and exposure to media arts is vital, prior to commencing the project.
- Consider how the arts will be produced, and who will facilitate that. The research team may wish to work with a digital media artist as a 'methodological expert' to ensure high quality data is generated.
- Ensure the design of field work is receptive and appropriate for arts-based research. This means giving time for good arts practices to be used, and for children to experience authentic digital media making.
- Pay attention to what data will be produced and how that will be analysed. Will it provide information that carefully attends to the research question? What tools of analysis can be used for that work, and does that analysis align with the conceptual frame being used for the project?
- Consider how the data might work as part of other data being gathered during the project. If the project is using a mixed methods approach, consider how the arts-based data contributes and aligns with other data.

Arts-based methods and research reporting

Finally, an advantage of arts-based research is the potential for high-impact dissemination of research projects and their findings. Not all data produced within an arts-based digital media research project will be appropriate for public dissemination. However, in the main, the highly visual nature of the data can help to support the research to generate impactful outcomes with large and diverse audiences (including the children and artists involved). Dissemination options for arts-based research projects include the traditional modes of conference papers, journal articles and books, and can also include:

- Exhibitions. Commercial galleries, university libraries, school spaces and community spaces all make excellent physical venues. Virtual exhibitions can also take place via digital arts spaces, including university webpages, galleries and other organisations.
- Collaborations. Depending on the arts-based data produced during the project, it is possible for the work to continue after the project by working with new collaborators who may be artists, children, audiences, institutions and other researchers. Subsequent work may not be counted as data, but be seen as art work in its own right.
- Living archives. The nature of digital media art allows it to continue to evolve after the end of the project. The work can shift and morph and continue to change long after the project has concluded. The work can continue to have currency and relevance long after the project ends.

References

Andersen, C.E. and Otterstad, A.M. (2014) Researching the assemblage of cultural diversity in Norway. *International Review of Qualitative Research* 7 (1), 93–110.

Banks, M. (2007) *Using visual data in qualitative research*. Los Angeles, CA: Sage.

Barone, T. (2008) Going public with arts-inspired social research: Issues of audience. In: Cole, A. and Knowles, G. (eds.) *Handbook of the arts in social science research*. Thousand Oaks, CA: Sage, 485–492.

Bart, P. (2013) Pay TV and mobile apps take aim at doggie demo: As more and more media target the pet market, will even Fido start texting? *Variety* 321 (12), 43.

Brooker, L. and Siraj-Blatchford, J. (2002) 'Click on miaow!': How children of three and four years experience the nursery computer. *Contemporary Issues in Early Childhood* 3 (2), 251–273.

Cruz, E.G., Sumartojo, S. and Pink, S. (eds.) (2017) *Refiguring techniques in digital visual research*. Berlin: Springer.

Dale, K. and Latham, Y. (2014) Ethics and entangled embodiment: Bodies-materialities-organization. *Organization* 22 (2), 166–182.

Deppeler, J., Moss, J. and Agbenyega, J. (2008) The ethical dilemmas of working the visual and digital across space. In: Moss, J. (ed.) *Researching education visually – digitally – spatially*. Rotterdam: Sense, 209–227.

Doyle, K. and Dezuanni, M. (2014) Children participating in science through digital-media literacies. *Literacy Learning: The Middle Years* 22 (3), 42–54.

Dubé, A.K. and McEwen, R.N. (2017) Abilities and affordances: Factors influencing successful child – tablet communication. *Educational Technology Research & Development* 65 (4), 889–908.

Eckhoff, A. (2015) Ethical considerations of children's digital image-making and image-audiencing in early childhood environments. *Early Childhood Development and Care* 185 (10), 1617–1628. doi: 10.1080/03004430.2015.1013539.

Eckhoff, A. (2017) Images of play experiences through a child's lens: An exploration of play and digital media with young children. *International Journal of Early Childhood* 49, 113–129. doi: 10.1007/s13158-017-0181-9.

Edwards, S. (2016) New concepts of play and the problem of technology, digital media and popular-culture integration with play-based learning in early childhood education. *Technology, Pedagogy and Education* 25 (4), 513–532. doi: 10.1080/1475939X.2015.1108929.

Eisner, E. (2008) Persistent tensions in arts-based research. In: Cahnmann-Taylor, M. and Siegesmund, R. (eds.) *Arts-based research in education: Foundations for practice*. New York: Routledge, 16–27.

Flewitt, R., Messer, D. and Kucirkova, N. (2015) New directions for early literacy in a digital age: The iPad. *Journal of Early Childhood Literacy* 15 (3), 289–310. doi: 10.1177/1468798414533560.

Flick, U. (2007) *Managing quality in qualitative research*. Los Angeles, CA: Sage.

Gibbons, A. (2016) Do 'we' really live in rapidly changing times? Questions concerning time, childhood, technology and education. *Contemporary Issues in Early Childhood* 17 (4), 367–376. doi: 10.1177/1463949116677921.

Green, C. (2016) Sensory Tours as a method for engaging children as active researchers: Exploring the use of wearable cameras in early childhood research. *International Journal of Early Childhood* 48, 277–294. doi: 10.1007/s13158-016-0173-1.

Grimes, S. and Fields, D.A. (2015) Children's media making, but not sharing: The potential and limitations of child-specific DIY media websites. *Media International Australia* 54, February 2015, 112–122.

Hsin, C.-T., Li, M.-C. and Tsai, C.-C. (2014) The influence of young children's use of technology on their learning: A review. *Educational Technology and Society* 17 (4), 85–99.

Jones, L., Osgood, J., Urban, M., Holmes, R. and MacLure, M. (2014) Eu(rope). *International Review of Qualitative Research* 7 (1), 58–79.

Jordan, A.B. (2016) Presidential address: Digital media use and the experience(s) of childhood: Reflections across the generations. *Journal of Communication* 66, 879–887. doi: 10.1111/jcom.12265.

Knight, L. (2016) Persistence is fertile: Pushing methodological potentialities in education research. In: Cole, D.R. and Woodrow, C. (eds.) *Super dimensions in globalisation and education*. Berlin: Springer, 173–188.

Knight, L. and Dooley, K. (2015) Visual arts learning with iPads. In: Dezuanni, M., Dooley, K., Gattenhof, S and Knight, L. (eds.) *iPads in the early years: Developing literacy and creativity*. London: Routledge, 103–122.

Knowles, J.G. and Cole, A.L. (2008) *Handbook of the arts in qualitative research: Perspectives, methodologies, examples and issues*. Los Angeles, CA: Sage.

Lafton, T. (2015) Digital literacy practices and pedagogical moments: Human and non-human intertwining in early childhood education. *Contemporary Issues in Early Childhood* 16 (2), 142–152. doi: 10.1177/1463949115585657.

Laidlaw, L. and Wong, S.S. (2016) Literacy and complexity: On using technology within emergent learning structures with young learners. *Complicity: An International Journal of Complexity and Education* 13 (1), 30–42.

Marsh, J. (2005) The techno-literacy practices of young children. *Journal of Early Childhood Research* 2 (1), 51–66.

Matapo, J. and Roder, J. (2018) Affective pedagogy, affective research, affect and becoming arts-based-education-research(er). In: Knight, L. and Lasczik Cutcher, A. (eds.) *Arts-research-education: Connections and directions*. Cham: Springer, 185–202.

Pacini-Ketchabaw, V. and Kummen, K. (2016) Shifting temporal frames in children's common worlds in the Anthropocene. *Contemporary Issues in Early Childhood* 17 (4), 431–441. Doi: 10.1177/1463949116677930.

Peachman, R.R. (2014) Keeping pets app-y. *Scholastic Parent & Child* 21, Feb, 100.

Plowman, L. and Stephen, C. (2005) Children, play and computers in preschool education. *British Journal of Education Technology* 36 (2), 145–157.

Rowe, D.W. and Miller, M.E. (2016) Designing for diverse classrooms: Using iPads and digital cameras to compose eBooks with emergent bilingual/biliterate four-year-olds. *Journal of Early Childhood Literacy* 16 (4), 425–472. doi: 10.1177/1468798415593622.

Verhoeven, D. (2016) Visualising data in digital cinema studies: More than just going through the motions? *Alphaville: Journal of Film and Screen Media* 11, 92–104.

Wohlwend, K.E. (2013) Literacy playshop: New literacies, popular media, and play in the early childhood classroom. New York: Teachers College Press.

Wohlwend, K.E. (2017) Who gets to play? Access, popular media and participatory literacies. *Early Years: An International Research Journal* 37 (1), 62–76. http://dx.doi.org/10.1080/09575146.2016.1219699.

23

SUPPORTING CHILDREN'S LEARNING AT HOME THROUGH SMARTPHONE APPS FOR PARENTS

Fiona Jelley, Kathy Sylva and Valeria Ortiz Villalobos

Supporting children's learning at home through smartphone apps for parents

This chapter begins with an exploration of the powerful means by which families can support their children's development. After a brief review of the literature, it focuses squarely on the development and use of two apps: EasyPeasy and Exploring Books Together (EBT). The apps are used as examples to delineate two different approaches by which smartphones can (1) lead to exciting parent-child play that stretches the child's imagination and concentration, and (2) be used for more 'instructional' support by parents of young readers when reading a school book at home. The first sends videos to parents to provide ideas for 'real-life' parent-child play (in the absence of the phone). The second provides in-the-moment support while listening to the child read at home (with the phone at hand).

The home learning environment

The important contribution of the Home Learning Environment (HLE; Sylva et al., 2010) to children's development, learning, and academic achievement has been documented by a growing body of literature in the field of child development and education (e.g. Burgess et al., 2002; Sénéchal & LeFevre, 2002; LeFevre et al., 2009; Anders et al., 2012). Most widely studied has been the contribution of the HLE to children's early literacy and reading skills (e.g. De Jong & Leseman, 2001; Melhuish et al., 2008; Sénéchal & Young, 2008). Individual differences in the family HLE have been linked to differences in children's vocabulary and emergent literacy skills, such as letter and word identification, knowledge about the alphabet and print-conventions, and phonological awareness (e.g. Storch & Whitehurst, 2001; Burgess et al., 2002; Bracken & Fischel, 2008; Baroody & Diamond, 2012). However, the contribution of the HLE (and parental involvement more generally) is not limited to children's language and literacy development; it is also important for the development of numeracy as well as children's socio-emotional and self-regulation skills (Sammons et al., 2003; Mcwayne et al., 2004; Foster et al., 2005; LeFevre et al., 2009; El Nokali et al., 2010; Kleemans et al., 2012; Huntsinger et al., 2016; Rose et al., 2018).

Furthermore, the HLE has been shown to have a larger impact on children's development and educational attainment than other family factors such as family socioeconomic status

(SES), commonly measured as family income, parental education, and/or parental occupation (see Sylva et al., 2004; Gutman & Feinstein, 2007; Melhuish et al., 2008). However, it is now known that the HLE can act as the link between SES and children's school readiness and subsequent academic attainment (e.g. Davis-Kean, 2005; Foster et al., 2005; Dearing et al., 2006). Therefore, helping parents improve the quality of home learning support has become a vital component of preschool and school programmes, specific interventions, and government initiatives (e.g. Sure Start), especially for children from disadvantaged backgrounds (Hunt et al., 2011).

Supporting parents of preschool children

Supporting parents with their children's learning at home begins in the early years and continues through the school years. During the preschool years, parents can benefit from help in supporting their child to develop the skills that predict later success at school. The most important of these "school readiness skills" are language and early literacy skills, mathematical skills, and socio-emotional skills such as self-regulation.

'Literacy' programmes and interventions are mainly focused on developing children's oral language and emergent literacy skills such as phonological awareness. Some examples of family literacy programmes are Project EASE in the US (Jordan et al., 2000) and in England, the Making It REAL (Raising Early Achievement in Literacy) programme, originally developed at the University of Sheffield (Hannon et al., 1991; Nutbrown et al., 2005). Many interventions have been carried out across the world that feature shared reading and dialogic reading (Loningan et al., 1999; Hargrave & Sénéchal, 2000; Zevenbergen et al., 2003; Mol et al., 2008; Sénéchal et al., 2008; Huebner & Payne, 2010; Lever & Sénéchal, 2011) in which parent and child read a book together while the parent 'scaffolds' the child's growing competence at reading on their own.

A well-known programme in the UK providing parental support for children's development in the early years is the Peep Learning Together Programme. It helps parents engage with their children's learning through play activities involving games, songs, rhymes, and stories (Evangelou & Sylva, 2003). The programme supports five strands of learning, broadly based on the Early Years Foundation Stage curriculum in England: Personal, Social, and Emotional; Communication and Language; Early Literacy; Early Maths; and Health and Physical Development. The programme has a good evidence base (Evangelou et al., 2007) and is offered to families with children from birth to the year before school entry to help parents foster positive development in all areas.

Supporting parents of school-age children

Support offered to parents of school-age children often specifically targets the development of language and/or academic school skills such as reading. To support children's reading during the school years, parents can be taught strategies to use when listening to their child read aloud. Two examples of school-age interventions providing support to parents with their children's reading are the SPOKES (Supporting Parents on Kids' Education in School) programme in the UK (Sylva et al., 2008) and the "Words to Go" home literacy programme in the US (Reutzel et al., 2006).

SPOKES is a preventive programme aimed at tackling behaviour and literacy problems at the beginning of school (Sylva et al., 2008). The reading programme in Year 1 (5–6-year-olds) consists of a 10-week intervention designed to teach parents strategies to use while their child reads with them at home (Sylva et al., 2008). Words to Go offers support to parents with their children's decoding skills. Parents are trained throughout the school year to support decoding in addition to reading aloud techniques. As part of the training, parents are provided with instructional material, such as reading books with scripted lessons to be carried out with children at home (Reutzel et al., 2006). Both programmes have been shown to be effective in improving children's reading (Reutzel et al., 2006; Sylva et al., 2008).

There are other home-based tutoring strategies for parents to provide support to children with identified reading problems. Parents are typically trained to deliver tutoring sessions to their children, which usually last between 15–20 minutes and are repeated up to five times a week (e.g. Powell-Smith et al., 2000; Persampieri et al., 2006; Gortmaker et al., 2007; Kupzy & Daly, 2017).

In the next section, the main modes that have traditionally been used for delivering parental support are summarised in terms of location (i.e. where the training takes place), and means and resources employed (e.g. face-to-face, telephone-based, printed manuals and guides).

Traditional modes for delivering parental support

Although the theoretical models, techniques, and strategies taught to parents may vary among programmes according to their different aims and targeted ages, the pedagogical resources and methods traditionally employed to train parents are often very similar.

The pedagogy for parent support depends on whether the training is provided in person or through resources that facilitate self-learning, such as instructional guides, videos, or reading material. Face-to-face training sessions are generally carried out at schools or centres and can take the form of one-to-one tutorials (e.g. Gortmaker et al., 2007) or parents' groups or workshops (e.g. Evangelou & Sylva, 2003; Jordan et al., 2000). Teaching methods used in these sessions include group discussions, modelling (by tutors or video support), role playing, practice time with feedback, instructional videos, and question and answer sessions (e.g. Powell-Smith et al., 2000; Sylva et al., 2008; Kupzy & Daly, 2017). These trainings are usually supported by printed material such as manuals, guides, children's reading books, and progress sheets that are given to parents to take home (e.g. Jordan et al., 2000; Evangelou & Sylva, 2003; Reutzel et al., 2006; Sylva et al., 2008).

Home-based training may include printed material, plus home visits and/or telephone calls (e.g. Hannon et al., 1991; Sylva et al., 2008). The length of the training varies according to the programme. Erion (2006) distinguished the following methodological features as quality indicators: training length, availability of written instructions, modelling of treatment, supervised practice, availability of consultation, and monitoring.

Digital media: a new platform to support parents

Due to the increasing use of technological devices such as smartphones, tablets, and computers by people of all ages (Gray et al., 2017), a new platform for providing support to parents has gained popularity: *technology-based support*. This type of support does not require face-to-face interaction and therefore no specific physical location is required. Digital media offers parents access to mobile apps to engage their children in learning activities (e.g. Vroom, Learning Potential, Bubl Draw, Cookie Next Door), websites providing information, educational resources, and parenting advice on various topics such as literacy (e.g. National Literacy Trust, Reading Rockets, The Oxford Owl), and educational television shows (e.g. Sesame Street, CBeebies, Dora the Explorer).

A number of technology-based programmes have been developed to provide parental support to preschool and school children. READY4K! is a text messaging programme implemented in the US which aims to support parents of preschoolers (4-year-olds) with their children's literacy, mathematics, and socio-emotional development (York & Loeb, 2014). The programme consists of sending weekly text messages over an 8-month period to parents suggesting short, simple activities related to early learning skills to engage in with their children at home. Messages are sent over a period of eight months. A randomised controlled trial (RCT) evaluating the effectiveness of the intervention showed that after taking part in the intervention, parents from the treatment group (receiving the messages) engaged more frequently in home literacy activities with their children than parents from the control group (d = .22 to .34 for a range of literacy outcomes), and were more often involved with the school than parents from the control group (d = .13 to .19 for a range of types of involvement). Furthermore, the increased parental involvement was related to children's literacy gains (d = .21 for alphabet knowledge and .34 for letter recognition; York & Loeb, 2014).

Following a similar design, Kraft and Monti-Nussbaum (2017) conducted a field experiment to evaluate whether sending text messages to parents over the summer could reduce the commonly found "summer reading loss" in which children's reading achievement declines during the summer holidays (Kraft & Monti-Nussbaum, 2017). Text messages contained ideas for specific literacy activities for parents and children to do at home together, and information about the relevance of those activities for children's reading. The results showed positive effects for third and fourth graders on two reading comprehension measures (d = .21 and .29 respectively) but not for first and second graders (Kraft & Monti-Nussbaum, 2017).

Another example of a technology-based intervention fostering children's literacy development is Parents And Children Together (PACT; Mayer et al., 2015). The intervention was aimed at parents of 3–5-year-old children in the US and aimed to increase the amount of time parents read to their children at home using a reading app. The app contained books in English and Spanish, and was accessed on a tablet lent to the participating families for a 6-week period. The intervention made use of behavioural strategies to promote app use among parents. At the beginning of each week, parents were asked to set a goal of how much time they aimed to spend reading to their child (commitment), and if their goal was achieved by the end of the week, they would receive a text message congratulating them (social incentive). Finally, reminders to get involved with reading were sent to parents weekly via text messages. An RCT demonstrated that parents from the treatment group (app + behavioural strategies) read on average 88.3 minutes more than parents in the control group (app only) over the 6-week period (d = .92; Mayer et al., 2015).

Interventions aimed to enhance children's socio-emotional development have also included technology devices as the main mode for delivering parental support. Infant-Net is an internet-based adaptation of the Play and Learning Strategies programme (Landry & Smith, 1996) focused on increasing sensitive and responsive parenting and improving child social-emotional behaviour. It is targeted to low-income families and includes parental skills instruction and coaching via online training videos for six months (Baggett et al., 2010). An RCT comparing Infant-Net with basic online parenting resources revealed that children in the treatment group had a greater increase in infant functioning than children in the control group (d = .69; Baggett et al., 2010).

From reviewing these studies, a number of conclusions can be drawn. First, the limited literature available on evaluations of technology-based interventions is only recent (mainly from the last 5 years), and comes principally from the United States. Second, technology was mostly used as a means to provide information and remind/encourage parents to become involved with their children's learning, and not as a resource itself to promote 'joint media engagement' between parents and children. Finally, results from the interventions described in this section suggest that internet- and smartphone-based interventions can be effective in implementing parenting programmes and can reach a wider range of participants at lower cost compared with traditional modes.

In the following sections, two apps developed to support parents with their children's learning at home through play and reading activities are described.

EasyPeasy app

This app for parents of preschool children provides examples of innovative and fun ways parents and children can play together in a way that should promote children's self-regulation, concentration, perseverance, and listening.

The examples consist of a number of video clips of games modelled by real families. Videos are about 1–3 minutes long and include brief text instructions. The app also includes snippets of information on child development and tips on how to interact during the games. Parents are initially invited to access the app through a personalised text message from their child's preschool practitioner or teacher. Once they join, they are able to explore a bank of videos from a personal dashboard and communicate with teachers or practitioners as well as other parents using the app. EasyPeasy sends reminders, encouragement, and tailored prompts to parents to promote regular use and create positive play habits at home. The content of the videos and information provided is aligned with the UK Early Years Foundation Stage (EYFS; Department for Education, 2017) curriculum.

EasyPeasy evaluation

EasyPeasy was evaluated by a team at the University of Oxford in two small-scale studies (Jelley et al., 2016; Jelley & Sylva, 2018). They studied its use by families living in disadvantaged communities in two English local authorities. In one area, Bournemouth (a coastal town in the UK), an individual-level RCT was carried out in which half the parents were given access to the app for 18 weeks while the remaining families were on a waiting list to receive the app when the trial was over. Staff in the children's centres from which the families were recruited coordinated the delivery of the games via their dashboard, but didn't play a role in face-to-face interaction with the families. In the second trial, conducted in Newham (an East London borough), families were randomised at the centre level (cluster-randomised). Each children's centre had a 'pod coordinator', a member of centre staff, who not only encouraged parents to use the app, but also held face-to-face sessions to demonstrate the games to families. The two evaluations had different designs but led to very similar conclusions about the benefits of parental use of the app on children's development.

In Bournemouth, a two-armed RCT was carried out in eight children's centres. A total of 144 families with a child aged 2–6 years were recruited and individually randomised to intervention or waiting list control group. Parents completed pre- and post-test measures on parenting self-efficacy and parenting stress, and rated their child's self-regulation. Parents in the intervention group had access to the app for 18 weeks. At post-test, after controlling for pre-test, child's age and gender, and the children's centre, there were significant differences in favour of the intervention group on parent-reported child cognitive self-regulation (Hedges' g = .44) and parents' self-efficacy regarding discipline and boundaries (g = .51) (Jelley et al., 2016).

In Newham, the effects of EasyPeasy on parents and children were found to be very similar. A cluster design was adopted in this site, which allowed for recruitment to the intervention to include all the families in a centre (in contrast to Bournemouth in which the intervention and control families came from the same centre). Eight children's centres were involved in the trial and recruited a total of 302 eligible families. The centres were then randomised to intervention or matched control group. Parents completed the same measures as described above, that is, rating their child's self-regulation and their own parenting self-efficacy and parenting stress. Following examination of potential clustering effects, analyses showed that the intervention group had significantly higher scores than the control group on two of the measures: parent-reported children's cognitive self-regulation (g = .35) and parental sense of control (g = .26) (Jelley & Sylva, 2018).

Parents' experiences using EasyPeasy

As part of EasyPeasy's work with families, parents posted comments in the app itself. The following anonymised comments were taken from an internal EasyPeasy report (Li, 2018), and demonstrate that the app was useful for parents and children, particularly in four different aspects: (1) building and strengthening relationships; (2) fostering parenting skills; (3) building children's developmental skills and knowledge; and (4) encouraging parents' and children's engagement in enjoyable educational activities.

Building and strengthening relationships

Since the games are designed to be played by parents and children together, using the app provides opportunities for families to spend time together doing fun activities, which in turn can encourage positive parent-child interactions and help create stronger bonds. As one parent said, "*This was a great tool for bonding with my son from an early age (. . .) My son at 1 would shout if I did it unacceptably. I recommend this as it really does build and strengthen bonds*". Another example of the potential of the app for getting families together is seen in the following quote: "*My little boy got the whole family involved in this one (. . .) He even roped in daddy on the guitar and mummy on keyboard and his sister on ukulele, fun game, will be playing again*". The app games were a tool not only for sharing with members of the immediate family but also with members of the extended family (e.g. *"She's taught her cousins how to play and uses every opportunity to play this when she can"*; "*Loves doing this at grandma's as she loves laughing at grandma's response to the noise metal spoons make in colanders*"), and even with friends. As one of the parents stated, the games were useful not only for families to interact with their children but also for children to interact with adults and peers in general, "*It helped X interact with people*".

Furthermore, the games seemed to enhance parent-child communication. For example, as one mother expressed, *"This was really good, my daughter talked about what makes her angry and sad (. . .) But she said she gets better quickly if you leave her alone for a little bit. Which is very good to know"*. Similarly, another parent referring to the same game said, "(. . .) *we used and learn new vocabulary, so surprised how well my daughter can read emotions, much better than myself!*". Thus, playing the games appeared to be revealing for some parents, who learnt new things about their children by playing and communicating with them, which in turns leads to a better understanding of each other, and ultimately to a stronger parent-child relationship.

Fostering parenting skills

The games appeared to be a great context for parents to make use of positive parenting skills such as giving praise (e.g. *"I've tried this with my goddaughter she loved the challenge (. . .) I gave her lots of positive encouragement and praise as we played the game")* or allowing the child to take the lead (e.g. *"We made musical gingerbread men (. . .). Really successful (. . .) giving them leadership was really appreciated I think. Great idea for building confidence").* It also provided parents with new ideas to teach children about different matters and so develop new parenting skills. For example, one parent found the game of organising the laundry clothes together as an opportunity to discuss an important matter, "*My daughter loves putting the washing into the machine & the detergent & I use it as an opportunity to discuss safety. She understands that we only touch these things together & never alone. She also feels empowered through helping*". Another parent found the same activity very useful for another purpose, "*It's so simple and such a good idea to explain to them about why and how we do things but in the hustle and bustle of family life and trying to get things done I sometimes don't do that – so it has been a good prompt for me to do that!*". Some other examples showing parents' new skills include supporting vocabulary development (e.g. "*I've made a role play with the sock to try and encourage him to say the correct vocabulary*"), and explaining the meaning of time (e.g. "*What a fantastic idea to explain your child the meaning of one minute!*").

Building children's skills and knowledge

Among the parents' comments, multiple examples were found referring to children's acquisition of new skills and knowledge through the games. This is not surprising since the main aim of EasyPeasy is to foster children's skills, especially self-regulation, concentration, persistence, and listening.

Sorting objects according to specific characteristics, such as colour, constitutes a good example of a skill fostered by the games (e.g. *"He picks up one ball at a time, call out its colour, then place it on its respective colour pile"; "My daughter knew exactly what to do here. She helps me regularly sorting her own and her baby sister's clothes into different piles and switching on the machine").* One child even went further and created a new classification for sorting the clothes (other than colour suggested by the game), "*when we started to put the clothes into the coloured and white piles she started doing really well and got it right most of the time. But then she realised that my clothes and her clothes were mostly white (light coloured) and that Daddy and her Brothers clothes were mostly dark and she switched her piles into the 'girls pile and boys pile'*". In these examples children are not only developing the ability to classify objects in a flexible way, but also learning about colours and expanding their vocabulary.

Several games targeted children's listening and imitation skills. Playing the games was good practice for children to get better in these skills. For example, one parent commented, "*She even began tapping out a short pattern for dad to copy on the pots and pans. Noisy but great to encourage keen listening skills*". It also fosters concentration since children have to pay attention in order to be able to imitate either a sound or an action (e.g. *"Did this with my daughter & she copies really well & understands the difference in speeds & volume. She listens well & watched intently to copy"; "(. . .)when I described what I was doing my little one managed to copy without seeing me every time!"*).

Parents also reported their children becoming more patient (e.g. waiting for 4 minutes to eat a strawberry instead of 1 minute as suggested by the game), and developing prosocial behaviours such as sharing and taking turns (e.g. "(. . .) *I was surprised that she quickly wanted to share leading, taking turns. I expected her to want to be the leader"; "Last night he played pass with his father using his favourite toy (the London bus) that he never shares with anyone!").*

Encouraging parents' and children's engagement in enjoyable educational activities

Parents' shared experiences of playing the different games showed that both parents and children enjoyed the time they spent together (e.g. "*Wow! I can't believe how much fun this was as it developed and how clever my little girl actually is"; "This activity is X's favourite so much so that she plays it with her siblings and even on her own. The smile on her face when she finds each treasure is so heart-warming and can see the look of success at the end that she tells everyone in the house"; "Me and my son loved this game").* Children really engaged with the games and were motivated to keep playing, some families even extended the games to make them more challenging (e.g. "(. . .) *he found 1 minute easy to wait. We tried 2 mins, he distracted himself by counting and singing. He then asked to do 4 minutes, that was really hard for him"),* or to make it more interesting for the child (e.g. "*We've adjusted the game to what he enjoys – adding 100 multicoloured playpen balls in the bathtub when he takes his bath").* Children's motivation to get other people involved in playing the games also demonstrates their enjoyment and engagement with the games. Finally, the large number of comments posted by parents evidenced their motivation to keep playing and extending the games.

These findings extend those from the randomised controlled trials described in the previous section by including parents' experiences playing the games and perceptions about the usefulness of the app. The findings shed light on the mechanisms through which the app is able to foster children's development and suggest new possible outcomes to be evaluated in future studies.

Exploring Books Together (EBT) app

Although a large number of apps intended for children's use are available, very few offer exclusive parental instruction on how to listen to and support their child reading books at home. Exploring Books Together (EBT) is a prototype mobile app developed at the University of Oxford to support parents with their child's reading of school books at home, targeting Reception (age 5), Year 1, and Year 2 children and their parents. It provided guidance for parental support of children's reading of specific school books sent home by the teacher.

In order to promote children's reading at home, children in the UK take a book home each day to read with their parents. Parents are asked to read the book (or part of it) with their child, complete a reading record/log reporting the child's progress as well as any relevant comment, and return it to the school teacher. However, this activity is frequently perceived by busy parents, or those who are reluctant readers themselves, as a challenging activity. Parents do not necessarily do it every day, they are often not sure how to use the reading record or what they are supposed to do to help their child, and sometimes the lack of motivation and confidence in their role can affect the reading task. EBT was developed in an effort to transform this frequently challenging task into a more motivating, educational, and exciting activity for both children and parents by providing a new platform (mobile app) to support parents' interactions with their children when reading school books together. The EBT app aimed to support parents by creating an interactive interface in which reading guidance could be directly linked to the content on specific pages of school books.

The app included two main elements: (1) guidance on what the parent might say or do on each page of the book, and (2) a reading record/communication link with the child's teacher. The guidance was tailored to named books sent home with the child. During a reading session, the child read a copy of the book (printed or eBook), while the parent followed the reading page by page with the app on their mobile phone. Prompts related to the book appeared on the mobile screen with guidance to scaffold the child's learning. Parents could choose the intensity of support desired by selecting how many 'tips' were required during the reading session (i.e. 'Just a few', 'A few more', or 'Quite a lot').

The tips consisted of a variety of features that the parent could choose to use during the reading session. The features included: new words (for pointing out potentially tricky or unfamiliar words); audio cues (to listen to certain words read aloud); questions related to understanding (suggested questions about the plot); talking points (suggested themes for initiating discussions); and follow-up activities (suggestions of fun activities to do after reading the book). The reading record allowed the parent to tick whether the child had read on a particular day and which pages. Further multiple choice questions about the reading session were optional for the parent to answer. These questions included the duration of the session, whether the child enjoyed the book, how easy the book was for the child, what the child was able to do (e.g. sound out and blend words, understand the story), and the option to add a comment.

Field-test study

A research team at the University of Oxford led a field-test study of the prototype EBT app. The aim of this exploratory study was to identify the potential benefits (or drawbacks) of using the app to (1) enhance parents' ability to support their children's reading (i.e. planning and motivation for reading, confidence, and skills); (2) engage children with reading; and (3) facilitate home-school communication.

This qualitative study included 32 parents of children in Reception, Year 1, or Year 2 of primary schools in Oxfordshire. A total of six schools participated in the study. Parents ranged in terms of socioeconomic status and language background. However, the majority were native English speakers or had fluent English proficiency. Data were collected through a one-to-one semi-structured interview carried out with each of the participating parents on the telephone. To start using the app, parents were provided with a link to open it in their mobile device's browser, an instruction card, and a copy of the relevant print book for their child to read.

Results of the field-test study showed that parents' perceptions of their experiences using the app were mostly positive. The app appeared to be helpful, especially for providing resources (such as prompts, audio cues, discussion points) to transform a regular reading session (mainly focused on reading the text in the book) into a longer, richer, and more enjoyable learning experience. For example, one of the parents expressed, "*I don't normally ask questions and I was so surprised that he could talk about the story. We were so much more engaged with the reading*".

Although some parents already felt very confident in their ability to support their child, they recognised the app's potential to support parents who "*struggle to know what to do*", who are less experienced in reading or are non-native English speakers, and parents who find it difficult to engage their child with reading books. Interestingly, three parents whose children had attention difficulties or special needs found the app particularly helpful and reported that it "*changed their reading experiences*".

In the following sections, the main findings regarding the capability of the app to enhance (1) parents' ability to support their children's reading; (2) children's engagement with reading; and (3) home-school communication are discussed.

Capacity to support children's reading

The app included two features involving prompts: 'Understanding questions' (specific questions related to features in the story) and 'Talking points' (suggested points of discussion related to the story). These two features seemed to be helpful for parents, particularly for discussing and extending the reading sessions, as one of the parents stated, "*It made us talk for longer about the book which was really helpful*".

Furthermore, parents found it useful in identifying skills and potential areas of improvement in their children (e.g. "*Really good to have the questions to prompt me to check X does understand what he's reading, whereas I might just have read the book and not followed things up*"), or as another parent said, it was helpful "*to consolidate his knowledge*". For some parents it was both revealing and satisfying to discover what their children could and couldn't do (e.g. *"He hadn't read between the lines so it was good to discover this"; "When I asked the questions he knew what he'd read"*).

Supporting children's phonics skills can be challenging for some parents. The 'Audio cues' feature of the app (words read aloud) was reported to be a useful tool in this respect, for example, for checking the pronunciation of difficult words. It also seemed to help in supporting non-native speaker parents who struggled with pronunciation of some words. Moreover, highlighting words in the app inspired a few parents to do extra, spontaneous activities such as word games (e.g. looking for words with the same number of syllables) or engage in deeper discussions about particular themes in the book.

Finally, one of the aims of the app was to help parents develop confidence in their abilities to support their children's reading. Although most of the parents expressed feeling quite confident supporting their children, for many parents, using the app reinforced their strategies and confidence by confirming they were on the right track (e.g. *"We do a lot of the things anyway, it was nice to see that this was good to do"; "You always feel better if you know you're doing the right thing").*

Children's engagement with reading

According to the parents, children's increased engagement with reading was demonstrated by the amount of time they spent reading the book (with the app) together, which was longer than normal (e.g. "*He's one of the youngest in his year [and often struggles to engage for a long time], but with this he was so engaged . . . normally after 5 minutes he wants to stop*"; "*More in-depth [experience] and engaged much more with the book than normal*"). It seemed that the app worked well to engage children who were not ordinarily keen readers. Children's engagement was also demonstrated by their enjoyment of the reading sessions (e.g. "*She was engrossed with the book*"; "*I don't normally ask questions and I was so surprised that he could talk about the story and we were so much more engaged with the reading*").

Home-school communication

The traditional reading record is a log book that the child brings home from school along with a reading book. Parents are asked to fill it in with observations regarding any reading that happens at home. The EBT app included a reading record and communication feature that extended the traditional model by gathering more specific information about the child's frequency of reading and their progress, and of course, by being an electronic means of communication. Parents considered the electronic reading record a valuable tool and a promising means to enhance home-school communication (e.g. "*Online or digital reading record would be fantastic*"). The majority (18 parents) agreed that they would be more inclined to complete an electronic record than a printed one.

Most of the parents found the electronic reading record a potentially useful resource for three main reasons. First, it was easy to use, and was quicker and more convenient than a paper one (e.g. "*It's open and there in your hand, it's so convenient – I'd definitely use the reading record more if it was on an app*"). The ease of use of the reading record could result in more immediate feedback on the reading session, minimising the chance of forgetting key points, which some parents reported to be an issue.

Second, including prompts in the reading record made it easier to complete, as some parents expressed feeling confused about exactly what they should share in the traditional reading record (e.g. *"It was good that it asked specific questions – I'm not always sure what type of things to write"; "I struggle to know what or how much to include and know what the teachers are doing too"*). Third, its potential to enhance home-school communication made it a very appealing app feature (e.g. *"I really like having dialogue from school"; "This would be great and useful to see the school dialogue"*).

Lastly, some parents suggested extending the electronic reading record by (1) allowing other family members, such as grandparents, to share their feedback, (2) including children's comments, (3) showing progress over time, for example by keeping track of books read, and (4) giving children rewards or incentives for goals achieved.

Future directions for EBT

Although the majority of parents found the app useful and enjoyed using it to read with their child, for a few parents using the app was more of a hindrance than a help, and for others, it just didn't make any difference. Those who thought it didn't make any difference said it was because they already did what the app suggested (e.g. "*I wasn't being provided with anything extra or things I wouldn't have ordinarily done*"). Thus, motivated and skilled parents pose a new challenge for the app developers on how to offer them support that goes beyond what they normally do.

A few parents perceived the app to be more of a hindrance. This was mainly because they felt it was a distraction for the child (e.g. "*Using the app was distracting for my son – he was more interested in the app than the book*") or that it was too difficult to keep track of the book and the app simultaneously, which made them feel somehow 'disjointed' with the child (e.g. "*It didn't engage me with his reading as it felt like we were doing separate things which was frustrating and put me off*"). However, strategies could be employed to solve this, for example, one of the parents showed the child the app before starting to read so it didn't disrupt the reading.

Despite the few negative experiences, the overall perception of the usefulness of the app was positive. For the majority of parents, using the app enhanced their reading sessions. It encouraged many parents to go beyond the text and engaged both children and parents in deeper discussions related to the book, and even in extended activities that were directly triggered by the app prompts. Furthermore, the app appeared to help increase children's interest and concentration.

This qualitative study shows promising results for the use of apps to support parents with their children's reading at home. Parents' participation in the study demonstrated a willingness to incorporate technology into their children's learning and an openness to new alternatives to what has been done traditionally. However, parents' positions regarding technology were paradoxical. While some parents recognised the major role of technology and its potential benefits (e.g. "*Technology will be a big part of his life so supporting him is so important*"), others were worried about the amount of time parents and children are currently exposed to technology (*"Parents spend too long already looking at their phones"; "I like to limit how much technology use my child has"*).

Finally, in order to achieve the goals any learning device has, its purposes and instructions on how to use it must be clear for the users. Furthermore, positive results are only possible to the extent that parents are involved and committed to using the devices. As one parent stated when referring to the reading record, "*It would be fantastic to have this on an app. However, it's only as good as the people involved, if they take the time to leave an entry*".

Conclusion

With widespread access to the internet, inviting and exciting interfaces, and user-friendly designs, smartphone apps offer a practical tool for parents to receive support with their children's learning – at a time and place most convenient for them. This seems especially true for today's 'busy parent' for whom face-to-face workshops can be difficult to schedule, or the 'shy parent' who finds group meetings challenging. Moreover, the type of app support illustrated in this chapter is the kind that encourages parents' and children's joint engagement in fun learning activities, rather than the child's (or parents') own engagement in 'screen time'. This is important since it is through rich adult-child interactions and parental scaffolding that change is most likely to be triggered. Although more research is needed, results from the EasyPeasy evaluation, as well as parents' experiences using both apps, demonstrate the potential of well-designed smartphone apps to foster children's skills. Therefore, we argue that technological resources can serve educational purposes and enhance children's learning through enjoyable experiences with parents at home.

Acknowledgements

We are grateful to the Sutton Trust who supported the evaluation of the EasyPeasy parent app, and also Character Counts who made the parents' views on their use of the app at home with their children available. Drs. Arjette Karemaker and Charlotte Clancy contributed to the interview study of Exploring Books Together and we are grateful for their insights. A big vote of thanks must go to the many parents who used the apps to extend their children's learning through just having fun!

References

Anders, Y., Rossbach, H.G., Weinert, S., Ebert, S., Kuger, S., Lehrl, S. and von Maurice, J. (2012) Home and preschool learning environments and their relations to the development of early numeracy skills. *Early Childhood Research Quarterly* 27 (2), 231–244.

Baggett, K.M., Davis, B., Feil, E.G., Sheeber, L.L., Landry, S.H., Carta, J.J. and Leve, C. (2010) Technologies for expanding the reach of evidence-based interventions: Preliminary results for promoting social-emotional development in early childhood. *Topics in Early Childhood Special Education* 29 (4), 226–238.

Baroody, A.E. and Diamond, K.E. (2012) Links among home literacy environment, literacy interest, and emergent literacy skills in preschoolers at risk for reading difficulties. *Topics in Early Childhood Special Education* 32 (2), 78–87.

Bracken, S.S. and Fischel, J.E. (2008) Family reading behaviour and early literacy skills in preschool children from low-income backgrounds. *Early Education and Development* 19 (1), 45–67.

Burgess, S., Hecht, S. and Lonigan, C. (2002) Relations of the home literacy environment (HLE) to the development of reading-related abilities: A one-year longitudinal study. *Reading Research Quarterly* 37 (4), 408–426.

Davis-Kean, P.E. (2005) The influence of parent education and family income on child achievement: The indirect role of parental expectations and the home environment. *Journal of Family Psychology* 19 (2), 294–304.

Dearing, E., Kreider, H., Simpkins, S. and Weiss, H.B. (2006) Family involvement in school and low-income children's literacy: Longitudinal associations between and within families. *Journal of Educational Psychology* 98 (4), 653–664.

De Jong, P.F. and Leseman, P.P. (2001) Lasting effects of home literacy on reading achievement in school. *Journal of School Psychology* 39 (5), 389–414.

Department for Education. (2017) *Statutory framework for the early years foundation stage*. London: Department for Education.

El Nokali, N.E., Bachman, H.J. and Votruba-Drzal, E. (2010) Parent involvement and children's academic and social development in elementary school. *Child Development* 81 (3), 988–1005.

Erion, J. (2006) Parent tutoring: A meta-analysis. *Education and Treatment of Children* 29 (1), 79–106.

Evangelou, M., Brooks, G. and Smith, S. (2007) The Birth to School Study: Evidence on the effectiveness of PEEP, an early intervention for children at risk of educational under-achievement. *Oxford Review of Education* 33 (5), 581–609.

Evangelou, M. and Sylva, K. (2003) *The effects of the Peers Early Education Partnership (PEEP) on children's developmental progress*. Department for Education and Skills Research Brief No. RB489.

Foster, M.A., Lambert, R., Abbott-shim, M., Mccarty, F. and Franze, S. (2005) A model of home learning environment and social risk factors in relation to children's emergent literacy and social outcomes. *Early Childhood Research Quarterly* 20, 13–36.

Gortmaker, V.J., Daly, E.J., McCurdy, M., Persampieri, M.J. and Hergenrader, M. (2007) Improving reading outcomes for children with learning disabilities: Using brief experimental analysis to develop parent-tutoring interventions. *Journal of Applied Behavior Analysis* 40 (2), 203–221.

Gray, C., Dunn, J., Moffett, P. and Mitchell, D. (2017) *Mobile devices in Early Learning*. Research Report Stranmillis University College. Retrieved October 02, 2017 from www.stran.ac.uk/media/media,756133,en.pdf.

Gutman, L.M. and Feinstein, L. (2007) *Parenting behaviours and children's development from infancy to early childhood: Changes, continuities, and contributions*. Centre for Research on the Wider Benefits of Learning Research Report No. 22. Retrieved 18 November 2018, from http://discovery.ucl.ac.uk/10005976/1/Morrison2006Parenting.pdf

Hannon, P., Weinberger, J. and Nutbrown, C. (1991) A study of work with parents to promote early literacy development, *Research Papers in Education* 6 (2), 77–97.

Hargrave, A. and Sénéchal, M. (2000) A book reading intervention with preschool children who have limited vocabularies: The benefits of regular reading and dialogic reading. *Early Childhood Research Quarterly* 15 (1), 75–90.

Huebner, C.E. and Payne, K. (2010) Home support for emergent literacy: Follow-up of a community-based implementation of dialogic reading. *Journal of Applied Developmental Psychology* 31 (3), 195–201.

Hunt, S., Virgo, S., Klett-Davies, M., Page, A. and Apps, J. (2011) *Provider influence on the early home learning environment (EHLE)*. Department for Education Research Report DFE-RR142.

Huntsinger, C.S., Jose, P.E. and Luo, Z. (2016) Parental facilitation of early mathematics and reading skills and knowledge through encouragement of home-based activities. *Early Childhood Research Quarterly* 37, 1–15.

Jelley, F., Sylva, K. and Karemaker, A. (2016) *EasyPeasy parenting app: Findings from an efficacy trial on parent engagement and school readiness skills*. London: The Sutton Trust.

Jelley, F. and Sylva, K. (2018) *EasyPeasy evaluation in Newham: Findings from the Sutton Trust Parental Engagement Fund (PEF) project*. London: The Sutton Trust.

Jordan, G.E., Snow, C.E. and Porche, M.V. (2000) Project EASE: The effect of a family literacy project on kindergarten students' early literacy skills. *Reading Research Quarterly* 35 (4), 524–546.

Kleemans, T., Peeters, M., Segers, E. and Verhoeven, L. (2012) Child and home predictors of early numeracy skills in kindergarten. *Early Childhood Research Quarterly* 27 (3), 471–477.

Kraft, M.A. and Monti-Nussbaum, M. (2017) Can schools enable parents to prevent summer learning loss? A text-messaging field experiment to promote literacy skills. *The ANNALS of the American Academy of Political and Social Science* 674 (1), 85–112.

Kupzy, S.S. and Daly, E.J. (2017) Teachers engaging parents as reading tutors. *Contemporary School Psychology* 21 (2), 140–151.

Landry, S. and Smith, K. (1996) *Playing and learning strategies – I*. Houston, TX: University of Texas – Houston Health Science Center.

LeFevre, J., Skwarchuk, S., Smith-Chant, B., Fast, L., Kamawar, D. and Bisanz, J. (2009) Home numeracy experiences and children's math performance in the early school years. *Canadian Journal of Behavioural Science/Revue canadienne des sciences du comportement* 41 (2), 55.

Lever, R. and Sénéchal, M. (2011) Discussing stories: On how a dialogic reading intervention improves kindergartners' oral narrative construction. *Journal of Experimental Child Psychology* 108 (1), 1–24.

Li, R. (2018) *A summary of parent feedback using the EasyPeasy App between 2016 and 2018*. Unpublished document: Character Counts.

Lonigan, C.J., Anthony, J.L., Bloomfield, B.G., Dyer, S.M. and Samwel, C.S. (1999) Effects of two shared-reading interventions on emergent literacy skills of at-risk preschoolers. *Journal of Early Intervention* 22 (4), 306–322.

Mayer, S.E., Kalil, A., Oreopoulos, P. and Gallegos, S. (2015) *Using behavioral insights to increase parental engagement: The parents and children together (PACT) intervention* (No. w21602). National Bureau of Economic Research.

McWayne, C., Fantuzzo, J., Cohen, H.L. and Sekino, Y. (2004) A multivariate examination of parent involvement and the social and academic competencies of urban kindergarten children. *Psychology in the Schools* 41 (3), 363–377.

Melhuish, E.C., Phan, M.B., Sylva, K., Sammons, P., Siraj-Blatchford, I. and Taggart, B. (2008) Effects of the home learning environment and preschool center experience upon literacy and numeracy development in early primary school. *Journal of Social Issues* 64 (1), 95–114.

Mol, S.E., Bus, A.G., De Jong, M.T. and Smeets, D.J. (2008) Added value of dialogic parent – child book readings: A meta-analysis. *Early Education and Development* 19 (1), 7–26.

Nutbrown, C., Hannon, P. and Morgan, A. (2005) *Early literacy work with families: Policy, practice and research.* London: Sage.

Persampieri, M., Gortmaker, V., Daly, E.J., Sheridan, S.M. and McCurdy, M. (2006) Promoting parent use of empirically supported reading interventions: Two experimental investigations of child outcomes. *Behavioral Interventions* 21 (1), 31–57.

Powell-Smith, K.A., Shinn, M.R., Stoner, G. and Good, R.H. (2000) *School Psychology Review*, 29, 5–27.

Reutzel, D.R., Fawson, P.C. and Smith, J.A. (2006) Words to go! Evaluating a first-grade parent involvement program for "making" words at home. *Reading Research and Instruction* 45, 119–159.

Rose, E., Lehrl, S., Ebert, S. and Weinert, S. (2018) Long-term relations between children's language, the home literacy environment, and socioemotional development from ages 3 to 8. *Early Education and Development* 29 (3), 342–356.

Sammons, Sylva, Melhuish, Siraj-Blatchford, Taggart and Elliot (2003) *Measuring the impact of pre-school on children's social/behavioural development over the pre-school period* (Technical paper 8b). London: Institute of Education, University of London.

Sénéchal, M. and LeFevre, J.A. (2002) Parental involvement in the development of children's reading skill: A five-year longitudinal study. *Child Development* 73 (2), 445–460.

Sénéchal, M., Pagan, S., Lever, R. and Ouellette, G.P. (2008) Relations among the frequency of shared reading and 4-year-old children's vocabulary, morphological and syntax comprehension, and narrative skills. *Early Education and Development* 19 (1), 27–44.

Sénéchal, M. and Young, L. (2008) The effect of family literacy interventions on children's acquisition of reading from kindergarten to grade 3: A meta-analytic review. *Review of Educational Research* 78 (4), 880–907.

Storch, S.A. and Whitehurst, G.J. (2001) The role of family and home in the literacy development of children from low-income backgrounds. *New Directions for Child and Adolescent Development* 2001 (92), 53–72.

Sylva, K., Melhuish, E., Sammons, P., Siraj-Blatchford, I. and Taggart, B. (2004) *The Effective Provision of Pre-School Education (EPPE) project: Final report.* London: DfES/Institute of Education, University of London.

Sylva, K., Melhuish, E., Sammons, P., Siraj-Blatchford, I. and Taggart, B. (2010) *Early childhood matters.* Evidence from the Effective Pre-school and Primary Education project. Abingdon: Routledge.

Sylva, K., Scott, S., Totsika, V., Ereky-Stevens, K. and Crook, C. (2008) Training parents to help their children read: A randomized control trial. *British Journal of Educational Psychology* 78, 435–455.

York, B.N. and Loeb, S. (2014) *One step at a time: The effects of an early literacy text messaging program for parents of preschoolers.* (No. w20659). National Bureau of Economic Research.

Zevenbergen, A., Whitehurst, G. and Zevenbergen, J. (2003) Effects of a shared-reading intervention on the inclusion of evaluative devices in narratives of children from low-income families. *Journal of Applied Developmental Psychology* 24 (1), 1–15.

24

WHEN TECHNOLOGY MET REAL-LIFE EXPERIENCES

Science curriculum project with technology for low-income Latino preschoolers

Lena Lee

Introduction

The number of ethnic minority children in the United States has grown consistently for the past several decades. In 2014, minorities became the majority in American public schools for the first time (Hussar & Bailey, 2013), and by 2050 more than half of American school children are expected to be from a minority group (Colby & Ortman, 2015; U.S. Department of Education & White House Initiative on Education Excellence for Hispanics, 2011). At present, English-Language Learners (ELL) are 9.3% of American K-12 students (U.S. Department of Education & National Center for Education Statistics, 2016).

Looking specifically at Latino children, their number almost doubled from 1997 to 2013 (Hussar & Bailey, 2013). By 2012, 25% of newborn American babies were Latino, and now these children are one of every five students in public kindergarten enrollment in 17 states (Krogstad & Lopez, 2014; U.S. Census Bureau, 2012). Among these ELL students, 71% speak Spanish as their first or home language (Soto et al., 2015). Despite these facts, however, the teacher population in the United States has not changed as much, as the majority of all public school teachers are non-Hispanic Whites (82%) and females (76%) (Goldring et al., 2013).

As the U.S. Department of Education and White House Initiative on Education Excellence for Hispanics (2011) poignantly indicated, Latino children are not always enrolled in a center-based early childhood education program, despite the fact that they are the largest segment of the American early childhood population. Moreover, there are significant gaps in cognitive skills, such as reading and math, between White and Latino children. However, if the variable of children's social class is added, the gaps are even wider (Garcia, 2015; Garcia & Weiss, 2015).

These demographic changes require that the American educational system more attentively meet the various needs of Latino children, and be more responsive to their cultures and values. One of the important reasons for this requirement is the academic achievement gaps between Latino children and their White counterparts (e.g., Fortuny et al., 2010; Garcia & Weiss, 2015; Reardon & Galindo, 2009). Differences in skill formation emerge early in children's lives, and they are mostly likely to continue over their lifetimes (Heckman, 2008). The project discussed in this chapter is motivated by numerous studies that emphasize high-quality early learning as a critical and effective recommendation for supporting Latino children and their success in education.

Many children in this research project were not only racial minorities, as recent Latino immigrants, but also had a lower socioeconomic status and, therefore, they mostly had more disadvantages due to these dual factors. Their status and circumstances are most likely to cause their parents to participate less in, or engage less with, their school and educational activities because of their work schedules, financial resources, unfamiliarity with the education system, different language, and cultural values and expectations (e.g., Farkas et al., 1990; Hill & Taylor, 2004; McWayne & Melzi, 2014; Suarez-Orozco et al., 2009; Wong & Hughes, 2006). Therefore, it is critical to recognize that these children's experiences, previous learning, interests, and educational goals can vary. That is why this chapter discusses a project that I initiated with the instructional approach of using technology to enhance the learning of Latino preschoolers who were from low-income families or schools. Moreover, the project is a practical venture to inquire how to make these low-income, minority children's learning experiences more effective through a technology-enhanced curriculum in which real-life experiences were involved. As a result, this chapter provides the detailed project procedure, which can encourage early childhood teachers to effectively adopt it in their classrooms.

Theoretical framework

This research project has been grounded in Bourdieusian theories of cultural capital and critical race theories (CTR), as well as the notion of a digital divide in early childhood education.

Cultural capital and critical race theories (CTR)

In early childhood education in the United States, developmental theories and practices have been prevalent for several decades. In particular, developmentally appropriate practices (DAP) have been considered as curriculum guidelines for programs. The DAP, developed by the National Association for the Education of Young Children (NAEYC), had three editions (Bredekamp & Copple, 1986, 1997, 2009). Although DAP was revised, it still did not have enough curriculum discussions and implementations of culturally relevant practices for children who are often marginalized in society, particularly Latino immigrant children. The examples and the assumptions the DAP presented were often based on typical mainstream children who have no issues cognitively, mentally, or socio-emotionally (Cannella, 1997; Cortazar & Herreros, 2010; Viruru, 2001).

By assuming one type of childhood as universal, the DAP embedded specific social values and cultural capital (Bourdieu, 1986) with insufficient implications of, and attention to, a wealth of knowledge and caring, culturally responsive teaching, and pedagogy for the students who do not have these values and capital in common (e.g., Gay, 2000; Ladson-Billings, 1995; Moll et al., 1992; Soto, 2005). Social values and cultural capital can be constructed through 'the processes and practices of everyday life' (Morrow, 1999, p. 746).

According to Bourdieu (1973, 1986), cultural capital is often obtained through *habitus*, which are predispositions and values formed from children's experiences and environments in their early years. For instance, children acquire cultural capital from their parents and merge it into their knowledge, language, and behaviors, including interaction patterns. While the degree of cultural capital varies with social class, the educational system assumes everyone has cultural capital in common, and as their standards (Bourdieu 1973, 1986). As a result, if children have less familiarity and abilities to understand and use 'educated' language and learning experiences in school that came from the dominant culture in society, there is a significant possibility for them to have fewer advantages and successes in an education system (Bourdieu, 1977). Several studies have indicated children's cultural capital positively correlated with their academic performances in education (e.g., Ball, 2003; Cheadle, 2008; DiMaggio, 1982; Gaddis, 2013; Gillborn, 2005; Raffo et al., 2010; Rothstein, 2004; Strayhorn, 2010; Sullivan, 2001; van de Werfhorst & Hofstede, 2007).

As critical race theory emphasizes, the experiences of marginalized students, including Latino children, challenge the discourses that discount their cultures and their schooling, that function to maintain the hierarchical social and economic powers (e.g., Ladson-Billings, 1995; McLaren, 1994). Therefore, it is important to present a more comprehensive challenge to traditional curricular structures, processes, and discourses that often isolate diverse students by developing a curriculum from knowledge that originates from the various groups of people (e.g., Matsuda, 1991; Solórzano, 1997; Yosso, 2010). Social experiences and realities vary, depending on each individual, and many minority students' experiences and realities in education and society have been ignored (Delgado, 1989; Delpit, 1988). The school experiences and curricula, which often do not include the minority students' educational goals, knowledge, and culture, make the students socially, politically, and economically marginalized, while their counterparts are preparing to assume mainstream power (Cookson & Persell, 1985).

This research project has sought to reflect some of the major principles of a critical race-based curriculum in developing a science curriculum for Latino preschoolers that recognizes the centrality and intersectionality of race and inequality in education, challenges dominant ideology, has a commitment to social justice, and centralizes diverse students' experiential knowledge (Freire, 1970; hooks, 1987, 1992; McIntosh, 1989; Nieto, 1992; Sleeter & McLaren, 1995; Solórzano & Delgado Bernal, 2001).

Digital divide

As is well-known, many children increasingly use technology and digital media in contemporary society. However, young children from low socioeconomic status (SES) families, minority children, and children whose parents have a lower level of educational attainment have a lower likelihood of having a computer at home (Rideout & Hamel, 2006). This phenomenon is the so-called digital divide (U.S. Department of Commerce, 2000). Children from low-income families and different ethnic groups, such as Black and Hispanic groups, obtain fewer advantages from technology use at home than their counterparts for two main reasons: (1) lack of good technological resources, including parental support and schools, and (2) insufficient knowledge of appropriate use (Attewell & Battle, 1999; Lee, 2015; Vigdor & Ladd, 2010). These challenges to learning with technology at home and in schools tend to lead to learning gaps between these children and children from high-SES schools and families (Wenglinsky, 2005).

Given the fact that low-income children may have little or no access to the latest technologies in their homes, early childhood settings, schools, or communities, educators should consider that this digital divide can cause the early discrepancy of academic and social experiences between these children and their counterparts. Moreover, high-quality interactive uses of technology can bring forth learning and creative advantages for children who were born in the technology era. When technology is combined with skillful teaching and complementary curriculum resources, this combination can accelerate learning and narrow the achievement gaps between children from low-income families. More effective technology use can also offer extra motivation for students to concentrate on their tasks throughout science content learning because of their excitement and engagement with the tablets, which they love to use. Many students do not view this as tedious learning; instead, they viewed it as playing (Lee, 2012). As a result, using technology was helpful, particularly for the low-achieving students who often failed in such traditional instructional tasks as worksheets and paper-and-pencil tests (e.g., Darling-Hammond et al., 2014; Flumerfelt & Green, 2013; Ortman, 2016). As the children were encouraged to work with digital media, this project aimed at improving their initiative in learning and, eventually, success.

Developing an authentic, early childhood, technology-supported curriculum is important, because it can be a means for promoting social justice and equity in education by opening some possibilities for these children to overcome the digital divide and achieve their educational goals (e.g., Lemke et al., 2009; Melhuish & Falloon, 2010; Ritchie & Gutmann, 2014). The project the chapter discusses was an attempt for social justice by highlighting the need for developing a curriculum for Latino immigrant children. As a result, the rationale underlying the project was to support minority, low-income preschoolers who often do not have sufficient opportunities and resources to participate in the same range of community and world experiences. Moreover, the rationale underscored the significant influence of cultural capital on children's learning in that this author is keenly aware that the minority, low-income, preschool children's range of richness in their academic and experiential learning is not comparable at formal school entry and through their lives as their counterparts, particularly their White peers.

Science curriculum project for low-income Latino preschool children

Contexts

This project was conducted in low-income preschool programs (ages three to five) in a Midwestern urban school district. The project had two sites with Head Start Programs (12 classes with three main teachers) and one public school preschool site (four classes with two main teachers) in which many students were ELL children, special-needs children, or children with behavioral issues.

Each class was a half-day program with 15 to 17 students. One Head Start site had two classes with only Latino children (100%) whose families were recent immigrants. Some of them (20% to 25%) had undergone or were undergoing the process of the Individual Education Program (IEP), and the other Head Start site had some ELL students (15% to 20%) and some students with behavioral issues (20% to 25%). The public school preschool site had fewer ELL students (15%) than the Head Start sites and more students with IEPs (25% to 30%). Most parents of the ELL students had limited English-language proficiency. This chapter focused on the two classrooms with all Latino children (100%) whose families were recent immigrants.

Project description

This project is part of a larger project exploring low-income families' children and their learning, and has been conducted since 2014. The project's curriculum approaches and ideas have evolved since the project started with continual attempts to create a more meaningful and effective curriculum for the children to the greatest extent possible. This chapter discusses the curriculum of a classroom for Latino children's science learning with technology and experiential learning for a year. In the project, one pre-service teachers participated to support me. I visited the classroom two to three times per week through the year and spent a couple of hours there per visit. The main teacher and the assistant teacher of these classes had bachelor's degrees in education or child development associate (CDA) credentials, and the main teacher was fluent in Spanish. Their level of teaching experience ranged from four to six years, and they were both female. Each class had 17 students.

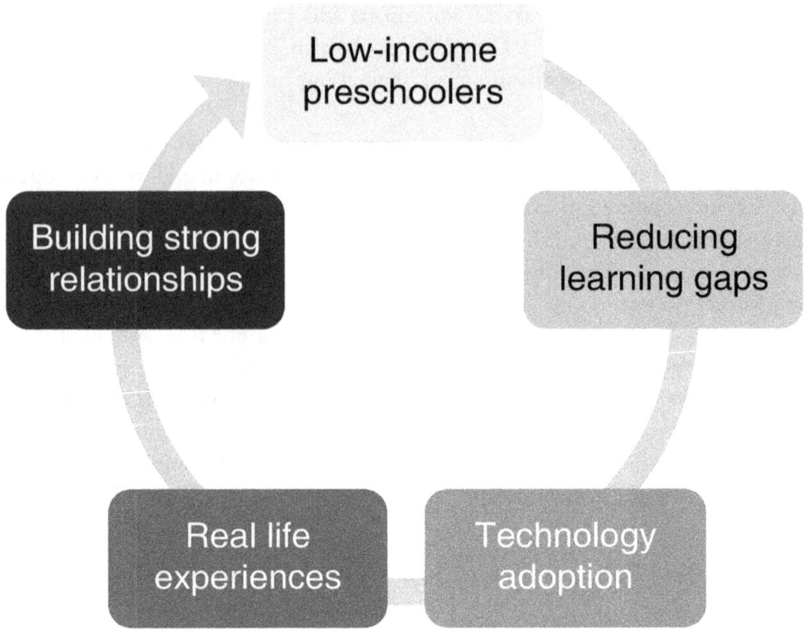

Figure 24.1 Project's rationale

The project had two practical objectives and the activities were set up to reflect the project's rationale of technology-enhanced science curriculum with real-life experiences (see Figure 24.1):

1 To support technology-enhanced experiences that improve children's learning interests, scientific understanding, and social knowledge and skills.
2 To provide socio-cultural knowledge-based learning to foster the educational experiences of children and connect their learning with technology and real-life experiences.

Both objectives and their implementation are discussed in the next section.

Project objectives and details

Supporting technology-enhanced experiences

I used digital media, iPads in particular, in the project. I visited the classroom with a pre-service teacher, and played a series of game applications that dealt with scientific concepts during the learning center time. Starting with the iPad application games, I aimed to keep young children engaged with their learning and to promote the interactive element with my pre-service student. This pre-service teacher played an assistant role to support children's learning with me by facilitating a small group and paying sufficient attention to each child. In using the iPad games, I took a social development approach and could scaffold each student as a More Knowledgeable Other (MKO) Vygotsky (1998) indicated in his work (Lee & Tu, 2016). Meaningful learning occurs best when young children actively interact with an MKO, who can model and offer appropriate guidance for solving problems when they are in the Zone of Proximal Development (ZPD). Therefore, the role of the MKO is critical for children not only to acquire and explore knowledge and information with the iPad games, but also to be supported in an encouraging learning environment (Vygotsky, 1998).

Moreover, TeachSmart®, a smartboard for young learners, was used in this class. This board was used not only for teaching science concepts with music and movements, but also for building emergent literacy with the science content. For instance, when I taught a science concept, plants and planting, I used several web-based sources such as educational animation shows and music from YouTube that dealt with the plant and planting to make their learning more fun and visualized. While I was playing the shows through the smartboard with the pre-service teacher, I could also assess the children's learning very effectively by pausing the shows and letting them recall what they have learned. Furthermore, I used this smartboard for early literacy development. From the beginning of the semester, all children who attended wrote their names every day on the classroom attendance sheet. This format of the attendance sheet became virtual on the smartboard as the semester went and their writing ability was more stable. Because they could erase what they wrote and rewrite on the smartboard, many children were not afraid of their misspellings or emergent handwriting skills. Writing their names from the paper to the smartboard allowed them to use a different medium for early literacy. Children could also easily see their progress throughout the semester, as could parents, because I saved their writings on the computer and printed out whatever was needed.

Providing socio-cultural knowledge-based learning

In the aforementioned discussion, cultural capital of children can be formed from their early experiences and environments, and provide rich contexts of learning as socio-cultural knowledge is critical for young children (Bourdieu, 1986). Given the importance of contextually based learning, I implemented the content knowledge of science – in particular, plants and planting – into relevant class activities. This implementation also aimed to connect the children's classroom learning with printed materials (i.e., books) and technology, to hands-on, real-life experiences. Following this process, the children could adopt the 5E Instructional Model: Engage, Explore, Explain, Elaborate, and Evaluate (Bybee, 1997; Bybee & Landes, 1990). They could connect their learning from technology to that of real-life experiences in various settings, by recognizing there are multiple ways of learning science concepts, and applying them.

Engage

This stage had started as they learned the basic information about plants and planting by using printed materials and technology. However, I wanted them to be more motivated and curious in developing their interests, and to learn more about actual planting. I asked the children, 'What do you think we will need to plant actual seeds in a pot?' and they discussed and asked more questions among themselves, and to me. The class made a list of things for planting (e.g., seeds, soil, water, trowels, pots, etc.) and offered some other comments, questions, or concerns, such as, 'Can I paint the pot?', 'What seeds do we need?', and 'Where should we keep them?'. After the discussion, the class decided on pot painting, chose pea seeds to plant, and found a sunny corner in class to keep the pots.

Explore

After the initial discussions, the children started to plant their seeds. Each child had his/her small pot and painted it, and then planted their seeds. I divided the class into three groups. I modeled each step of planting and each group followed the steps. Whenever extra support or questions arose, I, or the pre-service teacher, helped or answered. Since this activity was collaborative, each group of children needed to be patient, attentive, and supportive of one another. In addition, they commented on each other's pot designs or discussed with their peers what step they needed to do. When they finished planting, the children moved all pots to the sunny classroom corner. Two child volunteers and I watered the plants.

Explain and elaborate

Every morning after the children came into the classroom, they noticed their plants in the corner and naturally went to observe if the seeds had sprouted or the plants had become taller or bigger. The children took turns in the role of 'plant keeper' and watered them regularly with the teachers' or my support. They offered a brief weekly report on how the plants were progressing during their morning circle time. During this report time, they often described their understanding of planting stages and the parts of the plant (e.g., plants, seeds, leaves, stems, and peas) in Spanish (e.g., *plantas, semillas, hojas, tallos*, and *arvejas*). Then, I told each word in English with the English vocabulary card I created to make it easy for them to associate their Spanish vocabularies to those in English. These words, with corresponding photos, were also posted on a whiteboard. Therefore, a child who might not remember them could use this as a reference.

In addition, several children posed questions about the plants they had been exploring. For instance, they had a new question of why one plant was smaller than the others, or why some seeds took more time to bud by comparing and contrasting their plants to their peers' plants. When they were asking questions, they checked every component for a plant and thought carefully about what made each plant grow at a different pace. The children also shared information and ideas with their peers and their teachers. At the end of the planting process, they went on a field trip to a farm where they saw various plants, trees, and fruits. There, they tried to apply their knowledge and learning from the seed growing experience to the trees and flowers.

Evaluation

When the children talked about the plants based on their observations and learning experiences through using digital media, the hands-on activities, and the field trip, their understanding of the planting process was assessed effectively. The assessment was not done only once after completing all lessons. Instead, it happened frequently while they were learning, without them noticing it. As a result, the assessment was a continual and fun process in which both the students and I got involved. For example, when I used a YouTube video of a plant through TeachSmart, I stopped it at certain points to pose a question about their understanding. By using this non-formative form of assessment, I gathered more meaningful and individualized evidence of each child's learning process.

Conclusion

This chapter discussed a project for a comprehensive science curriculum design with technological and hands-on activities. Considering the increasing number of Latino children in the United States, the project was developed for Latino preschool children whose families were not only racial minorities as recent Latino immigrants but also had a lower SES. The project was driven by a serious effort to meet the educational needs of these young Latino children and be more attentive and culturally responsive to their learning. The project endeavored to connect to their improvement in academic learning and offer more opportunities to have experiential learning.

One meaningful evaluation of the children's improvement was shown when I conducted a parent survey written in English and Spanish. They mentioned how much they appreciated all the work I did. They said, 'My son talked about science a lot!', 'She kept asking if I knew a plant grows every day little by little', 'She has had a lot of questions about the environment lately!', and 'He [her son] wanted to get some more books about science'. Similar comments were in a parent survey I conducted at the end of the semester. They even mentioned the children's improved English vocabulary when they talked about science-related topics. Due to this, they said, 'I studied English as well with them'. Many families talked about 'school stuff' at home, which was related to one of the project's goals of 'providing socio-cultural knowledge-based learning to foster the educational experiences of children' with learning through digital media that was relevant to real-life experiences.

As mentioned earlier in this chapter, given the importance of cultural capital, culturally relevant teaching approaches, and the digital divide in developing a curriculum for Latino immigrant children, it is important to reflect on, and include, their experiences, previous learning, and interests into their educational goals. Therefore, the project was an attempt to understand how to make these low-income Latino preschoolers' learning experiences more meaningful and effective through technology and hands-on experiences.

By applying a comprehensive curriculum with the use of digital media as a part of the everyday classroom, I certainly recognized effective and successful science improvements. The young children's active participation with the instructions, high level of independence, and ownership of learning in the classes were clearly evidenced. The teachers in these classrooms told me that these students' academic performance for the year improved more than many other classroom children in the area on the Brigance, which is one of the assessment instruments for children in the Head Start programs.

I strongly believe that the technology-enhanced curriculum with meaningful hands-on activities can lead young children into having a more active engagement in, and responsibility for, their learning. Despite its short time and small student number, this project was a great example in showing this possibility. I aspire to make this curriculum development project a practical example to support low-income minority children so that early childhood classrooms become a crucial place to provide educational activities that obtain equity and social justice for all.

References

Attewell, P. and Battle, J. (1999) *The Atlantic century: Benchmarking EU & U.S. innovation and competitiveness*. Washington, DC: Information Technology and Innovation Foundation.

Ball, S.J. (2003) *Class strategies and the educational market: The middle class and social advantage*. London: Routledge Falmer.

Bourdieu, P. (1973) Cultural reproduction and social reproduction. In: Brown, R. (ed.) *Knowledge, education, and cultural change*. London: Tavistock, 71–112.

Bourdieu, P. (1977) *Outline of a theory of practice*. Cambridge: Cambridge University Press.

Bourdieu, P. (1986) The forms of capital. In: Richardson, J. (ed.) *Handbook of theory and research for the sociology of education*. New York: Greenwood, 241–258.

Bredekamp, S. and Copple, C. (eds.) (1986) *Developmentally appropriate practice for early childhood programs*. Washington, DC: National Association for the Education of Young Children.

Bredekamp, S. and Copple, C. (eds.) (1997) *Developmentally appropriate practice for early childhood programs*. Washington, DC: National Association for the Education of Young Children.

Bredekamp, S. and Copple, C. (eds.) (2009) *Developmentally appropriate practice for early childhood programs*. Washington, DC: National Association for the Education of Young Children.

Bybee, R.W. (1997) *Achieving scientific literacy: From purposes to practices*. Portsmouth, NH: Heinemann.

Bybee, R. and Landes, N.M. (1990) Science for life and living: An elementary school science program from Biological Sciences Curriculum Study (BSCS). *The American Biology Teacher* 52 (2), 92–98.

Cannella, G.S. (1997) *Deconstructing early childhood education: Social justice and revolution*. New York: Peter Lang.

Cheadle, J.E. (2008) Educational investment, family context, and children's math and reading growth from kindergarten through the third grade. *Sociology of Education* 81 (1), 1–31.

Colby, S.L. and Ortman, J.M. (2015) *Projections of the size and composition of the U.S. population: 2014 to 2060*. Washington, DC: U.S. Census Bureau.

Cookson, P.W. Jr. and Persell, C.H. (1985) English and American residential secondary schools: A comparative study of the reproduction of social elites. *Comparative Education Review* 29 (3), 283–298.

Cortazar, A. and Herreros, F. (2010) Early attachment relationships and the early childhood curriculum. *Contemporary Issues in Early Childhood* 11 (2), 192–202.

Darling-Hammond, L., Zielezinski, M.B. and Goldman, S. (2014) Using technology to support at-risk students' learning. *Stanford Center for Opportunity Policy in Education*. https://edpolicy.stanford.edu/sites/default/files/scope-pub-using-technology-report.pdf.

Delgado, R. (1989) Storytelling for oppositionists and others: A plea for narrative. *Michigan Law Review* 87 (1), 2411–2441.

Delpit, L.D. (1988) The silenced dialogue: Power and pedagogy in educating other people's children. *Harvard Educational Review* 58 (3), 280–298.

DiMaggio, P. (1982) Cultural capital and school success: The impact of status culture participation on the grade of U.S. high school students. *American Sociological Review* 47 (2), 189–201.

Farkas, G., Grobe, R.P., Sheehan, D. and Shuan, Y. (1990) Cultural resources and school success: Gender, ethnicity, and poverty groups within an urban school district *American Sociological Review* 55 (1), 127–142.

Flumerfelt, S. and Green, G. (2013) Using lean in the flipped classroom for at risk students. *Journal of Educational Technology & Society* 16 (1), 356.

Fortuny, K., Hernandez, D.J. and Chaudry, A. (2010) *Young children of immigrants: The leading edge of America's future (Brief No. 3)*. Washington, D.C: The Urban Institute.

Freire, P. (1970) *Pedagogy of the oppressed*. Ramos, M.B. (trans.) New York: Continuum, 65–80.

Gaddis, S.M. (2013) The influence of habitus in the relationship between cultural capital and academic achievement. *Social Science Research* 42 (1), 1–13.

Garcia, E. (2015) *Inequalities at the starting gate: Cognitive and noncognitive skills gaps between 2010–2011 kindergarten classmates*. Washington, DC: Economic Policy Institute.

García, E. and Weiss, E. (2015) Early education gaps by social class and race start U.S. children out on unequal footing: A summary of the major findings. In: *Inequalities at the Starting Gate*. Washington, DC: Economic Policy Institute. www.epi.org/publication/early-education-gaps-by-social-class-and-race-start-u-s-children-out-on-unequal-footing-a-summary-of-the-major-findings-in-inequalities-at-the-starting-gate/

Gay, G. (2000) *Culturally responsive teaching: Theory, practice, & research*. New York: Teachers College Press.

Gillborn, D. (2005) Education policy as an act of white supremacy: Whiteness, critical race theory and education reform. *Journal of Education Policy* 20 (4), 485–505.

Goldring, R., Gray, L. and Bitterman, A. (2013) Characteristics of public and private elementary and secondary school teachers in the United States: Results from the 2011–12 schools and staffing survey (NCES 2013–314). In: *U.S. Department of education*. Washington, DC: National Center for Education Statistics. http://nces.ed.gov/pubsearch.

Heckman, J.J. (2008) The case for investing in disadvantaged young children. *CESifo DICE Report* 6 (2), 3–8.

Hill, N.E. and Taylor, L.C. (2004) Parental school involvement and children's academic achievement: Pragmatics and issues. *Current Directions in Psychological Science* 13 (4), 161–164.

hooks, b. (1987) Feminism: A movement to end sexist oppression. In: hooks, b. (ed.) *Feminist theory: From margin to center*. Boston, MA: South End Press, 62–76.

hooks, b. (1992) *Yearning: Race, gender, and cultural politics*, Boston, MA: South End Press.

Hussar, W.J. and Bailey, T.M. (2013) Projections of education statistics to 2022 (NCES 2014-051). In *U.S. Department of Education*. Washington, DC: National Center for Education Statistics.

Krogstad, J.M. and Lopez, M.H. (2014) *Hispanic nativity shift: U.S. births drive population growth as immigrant stalls*. Washington, DC: Pew Research Center. www.pewhispanic.org/2014/04/29/hispanic-nativity-shift/.

Ladson-Billings, G. (1995) Toward a theory of culturally relevant pedagogy. *American Educational Research Journal* 32 (3), 465–491.

Lee, L. (2012) A learning journey for all: American elementary teachers' use of classroom wikis. *Journal of Interactive Online Learning* 11 (3), 90–102. www.ncolr.org/jiol/issues/pdf/11.3.1.pdf.

Lee, L. (2015) Young children, play, and technology: Meaningful ways of using technology and digital media. In: Fromberg, D.P. and Bergen, D. (eds.) *Play from birth to twelve: Contexts, perspectives, and meanings* (3rd edition), New York: Routledge, 217–224.

Lee, L. and Tu, X. (2016) Digital media for low-income preschoolers' effective science learning: A case study of iPads with a social development approach. *Computer in the Schools* 33 (4), 1–14.

Lemke, C., Coughlin, E. and Reifsneider, D. (2009) *Technology in schools: What the research says: An update.* Culver City, CA: Cisco Systems. www.cisco.com/web/strategy/docs/education/TechnologyinSchools Report.pdf.

Matsuda, M.J. (1991) Voices of America: Accent, antidiscrimination law, and a jurisprudence for the last reconstruction. *Yale Law Journal* 100 (5), 1329–1407.

McIntosh, P. (1989) White privilege: Unpacking the invisible knapsack. *Peace and Freedom* 10–12.

McLaren, P. (1994) White terror and oppositional agency: Towards a critical multiculturalism. In: Goldberg, D.T. (ed.) *Multiculturalism: A critical reader.* Cambridge: Blackwell, 45–74.

McWayne, C. and Melzi, G. (2014) Validation of a culture-contextualized measure of family engagement in the early learning of low-income Latino children. *Journal of Family Psychology* 28 (2), 260–266.

Melhuish, K. and Falloon, G. (2010) Looking to the future: M-learning with the iPad. *Computers in New Zealand Schools* 22 (3), 1–16.

Moll, L., Amanti, C., Neff, D. and Gonzalez, N. (1992) Funds of knowledge for teaching: Using a qualitative approach to connect homes and classrooms. *Theory into Practice* 31 (2), 132–141.

Morrow, V. (1999) Conceptualising social capital in relation to the well-being of children and young people: A critical review. *Sociological Review* 47 (4), 744–766.

Nieto, S. (1992) *Affirming diversity: The sociopolitical context of multicultural education*, New York: Longman.

Ortman, L.M. (2016) *Creating an equitable educational technology plan for elementary Hispanic English language learners in rural California communities* (Published master's project). San Francisco, CA: University of San Francisco.

Raffo, C., Dyson, A., Gunter, H., Hall, D., Jones, L. and Kalambouka, A. (eds.) (2010) *Education and poverty in affluent countries.* London: Routledge.

Reardon, S.F. and Galindo, C. (2009) The Hispanic-White achievement gap in math and reading in the elementary grades. *American Educational Association Journal* 46 (3), 853–891.

Rideout, V.J. and Hamel, E. (2006) *The media family: Electronic media in the lives of infants, toddlers, preschoolers and their parents.* Menlo Park, CA: Kaiser Family Foundation.

Ritchie, S. and Gutmann, L. (eds.) (2014) *FirstSchool: Transforming preK-3rd grade for African American, Latino, and low-income children.* New York: Teachers College Press.

Rothstein, R. (2004) *Class and schools: Using social, economic and educational reform to close the black-white achievement gap.* Washington, DC: Economic Policy Institute.

Sleeter, C.E. and McLaren, P.L. (eds.) (1995) *Multicultural education, critical pedagogy, and the politics of difference.* Albany, NY: SUNY Press.

Solórzano, D.G. (1997) Images and words that wound: Critical race theory, racial stereotyping, and teacher education. *Teacher Education Quarterly* 24 (3), 5–19.

Solórzano, D.G. and Delgado Bernal, D. (2001) Examining transformational resistance through a critical race and latcrit theory framework: Chicana and Chicano students in an urban context. *Urban Education* 36 (3), 308–342.

Soto, A.G.R., Hooker, S. and Batalova, J. (2015) *Top languages spoken by English language learners nationally and by state.* Washington, DC: Migration Policy Institute. www.migrationpolicy.org/research/top-languages-spoken-english-language-learners-nationally-and-state.

Soto, N.E. (2005) Caring and relationships: Developing a pedagogy of caring. *Villanova Law Review* 50 (4), 859.

Strayhorn, T.L. (2010) When race and gender collide: Social and cultural capital's influence on the academic achievement of African American and Latino males. *The Review of Higher Education* 33 (3), 307–332.

Suarez-Orozco, C., Rhodes, J. and Milburn, M. (2009) Unraveling the immigrant paradox: Academic engagement and disengagement among recently arrived immigrant youth. *Youth and Society* 41 (2), 151–185.

Sullivan, A. (2001) Cultural capital and educational attainment. *Sociology* 35 (4), 893–912.
U.S. Census Bureau (2012) *Profile America: Facts for features*. Washington, DC: U.S. Census Bureau. www.census.gov/newsroom/releases/archives/facts_for_features_special_editions/cb12-ff19.html.
U.S. Department of Commerce (2000) *Falling through the net: Toward digital inclusion*. Washington, DC: U.S. GPO.
U.S. Department of Education & National Center for Education Statistics (2016) *The condition of education 2016: English language learners in public schools (NCES 2016–144)*. Washington, DC: U.S. Department of Education, Institute of Education Sciences. https://nces.ed.gov/fastfacts/display.asp?id=96.
U.S. Department of Education & White House Initiative on Education Excellence for Hispanics (2011) *Winning the future: Improving education for the Latino community*. Washington, DC: U.S. Department of Education. https://www2.ed.gov/about/inits/list/hispanic-initiative/winning-the-future-improving-education-latino-community.pdf.
Van de Werfhorst, H.G. and Hofstede, S. (2007) Cultural capital or relative risk aversion? Two mechanisms for educational inequality compared. *The British Journal of Sociology* 58 (3), 391–415.
Vigdor, J.L. and Ladd, H.F. (2010) *Scaling the digital divide: Home computer technology and student achievement (Working Paper No. 16078)*. National Bureau of Economic Research. www.nber.org/paper/w16078.
Viruru, R. (2001) Colonized through language: The case of early childhood education. *Contemporary Issues in Early Childhood* 2 (1), 31–47.
Vygotsky, L. S. (1998) The problem of age. In R.W. Rieber (ed.) *The collected works of L. S. Vygotsky, Volume 5: Child psychology*. Trans. by M. J. Hall. New York, NY: Plenum Press, 187–205.
Wenglinsky, H. (2005) *Using technology wisely: The keys to success in schools*. New York: Teachers College Press.
Wong, S.W. and Hughes, J.N. (2006) Ethnicity and language contributions to dimensions of parent involvement. *School Psychology Review* 35 (4), 645–662.
Yosso, T. (2010) Towards a critical race curriculum. *Equity and Excellence in Education* 35 (2), 93–107.

25

READING IN THE DIGITAL AGE

Lessons learned and future opportunities

Rebecca A. Dore, Jennifer M. Zosh, Brenna Hassinger-Das, Roberta Michnick Golinkoff and Kathy Hirsh-Pasek

Technology is ubiquitous. It now pervades early childhood in ways that were unimaginable even five years ago. From the roughly two hours a day children under the age of eight spend using screen media (Common Sense Media, 2017), to the recent report that most children have their own devices by the age of four (Kabali et al., 2015), children's first-hand experience with technology has changed dramatically over the last decade. Indeed, even parent-child interaction has undergone a remarkable transformation with one observational study finding that 40 out of 55 caregivers used a mobile device during a family meal at a fast food restaurant (Radesky et al., 2014). These devices are changing the landscape of childhood.

One specific area in this "digital landscape" of particular importance is the use of e-books. When we refer to e-books, we include a variety of formats in which books are consumed digitally, including those that are read on computers, consoles, and tablets. The term "e-books" is an umbrella term inclusive of all of these formats. Similarly, the term e-book includes both interactive and non-interactive reading experiences. This wide variability may account for some of the divergent findings in this literature. However, to be comprehensive we include all of these formats in our review.

By 2014, 62% of two- to ten-year-olds had access to either a tablet or a dedicated e-reader for electronic reading at home, and parents reported that half of those children regularly engaged in electronic reading (Rideout, 2014). Even pre-literate children use this technology: two- to four-year-olds clock in at rates similar to those of older children (Rideout, 2014). E-book reading is common for children of all SES backgrounds: Parents of four-year-olds in a low-income sample, for example, report that 46% of children read or looked at e-books at home at least once per week (Pasnik et al., 2015).

As e-books proliferate, researchers rush to keep up with the rapidly evolving technology. Admittedly, research in this area is still in its infancy. However, scientists have already provided valuable insights into the role of e-book technology in children's learning. In this chapter, we highlight a number of important "lessons learned" over the past decade. These lessons reflect both current challenges and future opportunities.

Lesson 1: it is vital for research to keep up with rapidly changing technology

One unique challenge in studying e-book reading is the rapidly changing technology in the way e-books work. For example, early e-book research used CD-ROM storybooks that children interacted with through a desktop computer (de Jong & Bus, 2002; Kim & Anderson, 2008; Korat & Shamir, 2007; Lauricella et al., 2014; Moody et al., 2010). Since the advent of smartphones and tablets, computer-based e-books have taken a nosedive. Similarly, one study conducted in our labs (Parish-Morris et al., 2013) used a console-based e-book which allowed users to insert a paper book along with a matching cartridge that resulted in touch-activated pictures, sound effects, and games. These talking book consoles were popular when the study was originally designed and conducted, but by the time it was published, iPads were common and e-books on tablets commanded the marketplace. By the time results are published, the technology used in the study has often given way to newer developments.

Children's engagement and learning may also differ across formats, and these differences may be important for interpreting research using now-outdated technologies. For example, different levels of materiality – or the ability to touch and physically interact with the book – across formats play a role in engagement and pleasure during reading (Kucirkova, 2017). In short, the pace of scientific discovery does not compete well with the pace of technological delivery.

Changes in technology can also affect the research itself. A recent study in our labs, for example, set out to test features of e-books and traditional books that might affect parent-child interaction and child story comprehension (Hassinger-Das, 2017). The study used an app downloaded from the web called *Storia* by Scholastic, and was showing interesting preliminary results: book format did not seem to have a large impact on children's story comprehension. However, a particular aspect of parent talk – connecting the story to the child's life – predicted comprehension across platforms. Partway through data collection, however, the Storia app was discontinued and because the app was no longer functional, additional participants could not be tested using the e-book versions of the story. Although the research team presented the preliminary results at several conferences, these presentations do not contribute to the field in the same way that a peer-reviewed publication would. As this example shows, even ongoing data collection can lag behind the rapidly changing digital world.

Diverging timelines of research and technology call for innovation in making our work timely and relevant. It may be valuable for the field to consider alternative models of collecting data, such as rapid cycle studies in which teams develop and share materials for studies that are run by a network of multiple research labs simultaneously (Hassinger-Das, 2017). By distributing data collection responsibilities across sites, timely studies can be conducted quickly, resulting in knowledge dissemination while the data are relevant and useful. One should also be in front of rather than behind the curve by using the newest technology as soon as it is available, rather than designing studies based on last year's models. It is not always clear what new fad will dominate the marketplace and which will wilt, but researchers can attempt to keep up with tech news. The field may also benefit from considering funding and publishing practices that move more quickly so that the pace of research closely matches the pace of technology. Another alternate and promising approach is to encourage collaborations between researchers and designers so that designers are familiar with the latest research and scientists are doing relevant research on next generation products.

Lesson 2: balancing the wide variety of e-book features and creating generalizable findings is a challenge

Another challenge is that "e-books" are not all created equal. Our cumulative knowledge is based on studies using a variety of e-book types, yet, different types of e-books have unique effects on how children interact with and learn from them. Some of the mixed findings in this literature may result from the different forms (computer, console, tablet) being lumped together under the umbrella of "e-book."

Even tablet-based e-books vary drastically in the amount and type of their interactivity. Some are simply picture books mapped into an electronic format, whereas others include "bells and whistles," like hotspots, sound effects, and games. Some studies suggest that interactive features can inhibit parent-child interactions as well as children's learning (Parish-Morris et al., 2013; Reich et al., 2016), whereas others indicate that high-quality multimedia or interactive features closely related to the story content may improve learning (Moody et al., 2010; Smeets & Bus, 2014; Takacs et al., 2014; Walker et al., 2017; Zucker et al., 2009). Still others show no influence of interactive or animated features on story comprehension compared to non-interactive e-books or print books (Karemaker et al., 2017; Rvachew et al., 2017; Zipke, 2017). When researchers study e-book reading, they have to make principled decisions, depending on their research question, about which e-book type to use. A recent study in our lab (Dore et al., 2018) favored a simple e-book based on the research suggesting that "bells and whistles" can be distracting (Hirsh-Pasek et al., 2015). Many e-books include these interactive features, so when researchers draw conclusions based on simpler books, they may not generalize to the types of e-books that are likely more prevalent. Gathering survey data would be beneficial to give researchers more accurate information about the types of e-books being used in homes and how different features are used and evaluated by parents. Further, the differences in format and in results make it imperative that researchers fully identify which kind of formats they are using and hypothesize about how they think the features of that format should or will impact the outcome of interest.

Once a researcher decides whether to include interactive features, like hotspots and games, the content of the e-book needs to be considered. First, researchers must decide whether to use a commercially available e-book or one they create. Ultimately, this decision needs to be based on what research question the researchers are attempting to study. If a researcher is interested in "real world" experiences, they are more likely to turn to commercially available books given that they increase ecological validity and reflect what families actually have access to in everyday life (Kelley & Kinney, 2017; Korat & Or, 2010; Lauricella et al., 2014; Parish-Morris et al., 2013; Richter & Courage, 2017; Ross et al., 2016; Yuill & Martin, 2016). However, when researchers want to closely control aspects of e-book reading, they might need to use experimenter-created materials. For example, Strouse and Ganea (2016) used an e-book created to teach preschoolers about camouflage, and Strouse and Ganea (2017) created an e-book with photographs of novel objects (i.e. a citrus reamer) to test toddlers' learning of new labels. This approach allows researchers to provide specific information and to manipulate different features. Indeed, Etta et al. (2017) manipulated both electronic versus print format and interactive versus non-interactive features using an experimenter-created book. Studies using both types of materials are valuable and future research might consider ways to use these approaches together when possible to provide stronger conclusions.

Lesson 3: context and previous experience matter

When studying e-book reading in the laboratory setting, researchers are implicitly providing a certain context for the reading activity. Most often, researchers tell parents to read with their child as they would at home. In one recent study in our lab we told parents, "I have an eBook for you to read to your child! Just read how you normally would at home" (Dore et al., 2018). Likewise, a previous study in our lab told parents to "Do what you normally do with books" (Parish-Morris et al., 2013). Other lab-based experimental studies have used similar instructions (e.g., Korat & Or, 2010; Krcmar & Cingel, 2014; Yuill & Martin, 2016). The goal of these instructions is to make reading in the lab as similar as possible to the book-reading experience in children's everyday lives. However, to our knowledge, no one has tested whether these instructions are necessary or whether different instructions would skew results in a different direction. Although directives to behave normally have strong face validity, it would be useful for future research to vary instructions to assess whether more sparse instructions (e.g., "Please read this book with your child") or more direct instructions (e.g., "Please read this book to help your child learn the names of the animals in the book") would result in behaviors that may be more reflective of everyday home experiences. This is an area ripe for future investigation.

A second way to facilitate ecologically valid reading experience is through the physical environment. Some studies that use experimental methods are conducted in the child's home. For example, Korat and Or (2010) had mother-child dyads choose a place in the home for reading (i.e., the living room, the child's room, or the kitchen), and both Lauricella et al. (2014) and Yuill and Martin (2016) had participants read in their living room. Indeed, some findings from the clinical literature suggest that observations of parent-child interaction made in lab settings may result in different behaviors than those conducted in more natural home environments, suggesting that testing families in their homes may be ideal when possible (Gardner, 2000) even if this lessens the control of alternate variables such as distraction. However, in studies that must take place in the lab, researchers typically attempt to design a home-like naturalistic setting. In a recent study in our lab, parents and children sat next to each other in child-sized chairs (Dore et al., 2018). However, few reports describe how the physical set-up of the room and families' comfort level with the physical space may affect findings.

The placement of a camera for recording the testing session is also essential. In one of our labs, webcams are placed unobtrusively in a corner of the testing room near the ceiling so that an obvious camera will not distract children and parents. When such a set-up is not possible, researchers try to avoid drawing parent and children's attention to cameras by preparing equipment ahead of time and placing it as inconspicuously as possible. Although this is true to some extent for all child development research, adults' behavior may be more influenced by camera presence than children, especially in a situation in which they may think their parenting is being evaluated. Balancing informed consent of videotaping while concurrently trying to make the experience as unobtrusive as possible is a challenge, but not one that should be overlooked. One way to help ameliorate parent concerns about evaluation is for the researcher to emphasize that the goal is to understand how families in general interact, rather than focusing on an individual parent's teaching practices.

Researchers should also consider families' experience with e-books outside of the laboratory setting as it may influence children's responses to e-books during studies. Given the increasing popularity of e-books, it will be valuable for future research to more consistently obtain survey data about children's experience with e-books at home. For example, in the console e-book study (Parish-Morris et al., 2013), questionnaire data revealed that the majority of the families in the study reported having electric console books in the home and so were familiar with the format (Parish-Morris et al., 2013). The precise questions asked have varied across studies. Krcmar and Cingel (2014), for instance, focused on *duration*, asking parents how long children spent reading on an iPad, whereas Yuill and Martin (2016) queried mothers and children about their *access* to tablets at home and whether children used a tablet device for reading either at home or at school. Ross et al. (2016) similarly asked about the availability of e-books in the home, but also about frequency, or how often children read e-books. Notably, even when such data is collected, results are often not reported or reported only descriptively, and researchers do not use the data to address questions such as whether children with more home e-book experience learn more from e-books in laboratory settings.

Given children's varied experience with e-books, measures of prior experience may explain differences in dependent variables both within and between studies. For example, e-books may be distracting when families are unfamiliar with the technology, but not when families are comfortable with it. This might explain why some early studies found differences between e-books and traditional books in parent-child interaction and learning (Krcmar & Cingel, 2014; Parish-Morris et al., 2013), whereas more recent studies have not always indicated such a stark contrast (e.g., Hassinger-Das, 2017) or have even shown advantages for e-books (Courage et al., 2017; Etta et al., 2017; Strouse & Ganea, 2017). Perhaps using technology increases cognitive load when it is new but as this technology becomes more familiar, parents are better able to effectively scaffold the interaction and children are better able to learn.

Information about children's overall screen experience may also be relevant. Strouse and Ganea (2017) found that toddlers who watch passive video (e.g., TV, movies, YouTube) more than they use screen interactive media (e.g., Skype, digital games, etc.) were less likely to transfer learning from an e-book to real-world objects. The authors suggest that because these children are used to passive video that has no clear relevance for the real world, they do not see the touch-screen as a contingent, learning activity (see also Sheehan & Uttal, 2016). Future research would do well to include measures, ideally measures that researchers could create and standardize so they can be compared across studies, to assess parents' and children's experience with e-books, as well as with other types of screen media. For example, standardized measures about past use, duration of past and current use, types of experiences, co-viewing practices, frequency, availability, and even attitudes towards e-books versus traditional books would help provide insight into today's families. When these measures are included, researchers may uncover explanations for divergent findings across studies, as well as individual differences within studies. Additionally, the ability to examine large sets of data that account for factors like previous technology use may help give the field a more nuanced and representative understanding of technology's impact on reading practices. However, researchers should carefully consider which variables they hypothesize should relate to outcomes in their particular study, rather than indiscriminately including as many measures as possible.

In addition to familiarity and experience with e-books as a format, researchers should also be cognizant of families' familiarity with the particular book used in the study. Lauricella et al. (2014), for example, used books that were relatively novel. Parents reported that they were either "not at all" or "a little bit" familiar with the books. Similarly, Krcmar and Cingel (2014) reported that only 2 out of their 70 participants had previously read the book used in their study and Ross et al. (2016) chose storybooks that were not best sellers and found that, as expected, none of the children in their study had previously read them. It is often desirable for families to be unfamiliar with the e-books used in the study because parental interactions and children's story comprehension may differ for books that they know. However, a drawback to this approach is that using unfamiliar books in lab studies for experimental control may lead to lower ecological validity, because although children may struggle to understand an e-book after a first reading, comprehension may improve with repeated reading. In home settings, children often request to read the same books repeatedly, so lab studies with unfamiliar books may not be reflective of most of children's everyday experiences. Future studies might test whether parent-child interaction differs around familiar versus novel e-books.

Lesson 4: there is a need for innovative methods for quantifying language, behavioral/emotional engagement, and caregiver-child interaction

Researchers studying parent-child interaction around e-books in the lab have to decide how to best capture that experience in quantifiable data (e.g., determining what speech and behavior is critical to code). Parish-Morris et al. (2013) coded for behavior-related utterances such as "Can you push the button?" versus story-related utterances such as "Look at what Clifford did!" Other studies used similar categories to distinguish between comments about book format or technology and those that focus on story content (e.g., Krcmar & Cingel, 2014; Lauricella, Barr, & Calvert, 2014; Moody et al., 2010). Researchers often also code for the types of verbalizations such as whether each verbalization was a question or a comment (e.g., Parish-Morris et al., 2013), or a directive, corrective, affirmation, or an answer to a child's question (Krcmar & Cingel, 2014). Some researchers have coded for dialogic reading strategies, like distancing prompts, which connect the story to the child's life (Parish-Morris et al, 2013; Hassinger-Das et al., 2017) and talk that expands on the book's meaning (Korat & Or, 2010). These different approaches provide unique insights into the parent-child reading interaction. It will also be valuable for researchers to innovate and develop categorizations that consider more complex dyadic interactions like the sophisticated scaffolding that parents might provide to support children's comprehension.

Although coding for specific types of extra-textual talk is more common, some research has also focused on measures of attention or engagement during e-book reading. Attention and engagement in e-books may promote learning and increase children's interest in reading in general. Some studies have coded children's visual attention to the e-book (Lauricella et al., 2014), or to the e-book versus the adult or elsewhere in the room (Richter & Courage, 2017). Others have attempted to quantify children's engagement more broadly: Moody et al. (2010), for instance, used a modified version of the Minnesota Teaching Task to code children's persistence, enthusiasm, and compliance, each on a seven-point scale, while engaged with a book. Persistence was based on indicators like points to the book, turning pages, positive commenting, and asking questions. Enthusiasm was coded when the child smiled or laughed, turned pages, commented positively, and showed excitement, whereas compliance was demonstrated by the child staying seated, following direction, and responding to questions. Similarly, Yuill and Martin (2016) used a coder's rating of overall child engagement, based on visual attention, gesture, expression, and verbalization, for each minute of reading on a scale from one to five. Despite the focus on e-books for education and learning, researchers should also consider children's reading for pleasure and how e-books can foster different facets of reader engagement (Kucirkova et al., 2017).

In addition to the cognitive benefits of joint reading, children and parents may gain emotional benefits, such as joy and intimacy, from reading together. Several recent studies have begun to investigate child and parent emotional engagement during e-book reading. Ross et al. (2016), for instance, coded for both mother and child's positive, neutral, and negative emotion during reading. Positive emotion was coded when smiling, laughter, or surprise was exhibited, whereas negative emotion was coded when dyads exhibited boredom, frustration, confusion, anger or anxiety, and neutral emotion was coded when participants were calm and attentive. Relatedly, Yuill and Martin (2016) used a coder's rating of interaction warmth adapted from a validated measure (Parent-Child Interaction System; Deater-Deckard et al., 1997) to code for positive affect on a scale from one to five for each minute of the reading activity. Although inter-observer reliability for these codes was high, to support replication and expansion of findings, it would be helpful if detailed instructions for these coding schemes were documented and made available to other researchers. Technology will also increasingly make it possible to automate this kind of emotion coding. Indeed, researchers are working to create programs that can classify emotional facial expressions in still images (Baker et al., 2017), a tool that could soon be extended to dynamic videos. It will also be valuable for researchers to consider other avenues for assessing emotional engagement, such as physiological measures. In ongoing work in our lab, for example, we are investigating the use of heart rate and galvanic skin response as potential measures of the effect of e-book reading on parent and child emotion. Finally, qualitative and multimodal measures of emotion and reading engagement may also prove useful in understanding children's interactions with e-books (Kucirkova et al., 2013; Laidlaw & O'Mara, 2015; Rvachew et al., 2017).

Lesson 5: using multiple measures helps capture multiple facets of learning

The ultimate goal of measuring parent-child interaction during e-book reading is typically to assess how these exchanges affect children's story comprehension and learning. Story comprehension focuses on children's understanding of and memory for the content of the e-book. Learning measures typically assess whether children learned novel, generalizable information. Both types of outcomes can be measured in a variety of ways.

Story comprehension is often measured through specific questions designed to assess whether children understood important aspects of the e-book content. In our lab, we have asked preschoolers forced-choice questions about the story with two response options (Dore et al., 2018; Parish-Morris et al., 2013). For example, one question was "How did the beaver get better at saying 'I'm sorry?' A) He read a book about it. B) He practiced in the mirror." In a similar study, Lauricella et al. (2014) used a procedure based on Calvert et al. (2007) to choose three-option multiple-choice questions by generating questions and having adults rate them for their centrality to the plot and retaining only questions with at least 70% centrality rating. A more systematic approach like this one using adult raters may ensure that the assessment of children's comprehensions aligns with the central themes of the story.

Forced-choice questions are commonly used with preschoolers for several reasons. First, open-ended questions may be difficult for children with limited verbal abilities. Second, open-ended questions are more time-intensive to code, and judging whether the response is correct or incorrect can be subjective. However, creating and using multiple-choice questions has its own complications. First, it is vital to ensure that response options are clear and that even the youngest participants can comprehend them and make a meaningful choice. Part of this issue is related to inconsistencies in limiting the number of options children have to choose from. In our lab, we have had success with two choices (Dore et al., 2018), whereas others have used three (Lauricella et al., 2014) or even four (Richter & Courage, 2017). When using several response options, it can be useful to pilot with simple, non-story-related questions to ensure that children understand the procedure. Few publications report methods for validating these procedures, making null results difficult to interpret.

Another potential issue is that younger children's lower working memory and inhibition skills may lead them to choose the most recent of multiple response options. If options are given in a fixed order, some answers may be chosen more often than chance simply because of their placement. To avoid this confound, researchers often counterbalance the order of response options across children (e.g., Dore et al., 2018). In this way, we can identify how easy or difficult the questions are independent of the order of response options.

Other researchers have asked questions beyond simple multiple-choice questions to assess comprehension. Richter and Courage (2017), for instance, used a funneling procedure with preschoolers by starting with open-ended questions and then providing four multiple-choice response options if children did not recall the answer independently. Responses were scored according to strict versus lenient criteria and analyzed separately. In addition to multiple-choice questions, Parish-Morris et al. (2013) used a chronology task in which preschoolers had to temporally order four pictures by the sequence in which they occurred in the story. With older children (six- and seven-year-olds), Ross et al. (2016) used several different types of questions including picture-based, short-answer, true/false, and fill-in-the-blank, along with typical multiple-choice questions (see also Korat, 2010). Research comparing different types of questions and assessing their appropriateness for different age groups will be valuable moving forward.

Multiple-choice questions and similar measures assess children's understanding of specific aspects of the e-book content, but another common assessment is to have children retell the story. We have used a page-by-page retell measure in which the researcher shows children the pictures from the book and asks them to retell what happened on each page (Dore et al., 2018). The experimenter provided an initial prompt (i.e., "I'll get you started. . . . There once was a . . .") and additional generic prompts (e.g., "What happened here?") if needed to encourage children's storytelling throughout the task, but did not include any specific information or give any feedback. Responses were coded by counting how many of a predetermined set of possible elements children recalled from the story. Elements were determined by breaking down the story text into fundamental discrete ideas. For example, for the part of the story when the main character makes a vase for his friend Bear, children could receive one point for "made/gave," one point for "Bear," and one point for "vase." Synonyms and closely related words were also accepted (e.g., flower pot for vase). This procedure attempts to give children credit for as much of the storyline as they can recall without penalizing them for not remembering precise wording or order. Incorrect inclusions (providing incorrect details) were not coded. Notably, we also used a free recall task without the support of pictures and found that it was too difficult for the four- and five-year-olds in our sample, resulting in floor effects.

Although story retell measures typically have more variability than multiple-choice questions, they are time-intensive to code and require careful calibration to achieve high reliability. However, story retell assessments result in rich datasets that can be analyzed in a variety of ways. Yuill and Martin (2016) had coders read children's free recall responses and rate them for richness of descriptive detail and narrative coherence, both on three-point scales. McCabe and Peterson (1984) showed that children's narratives can be analyzed using scoring systems that focus on story grammar or structure. To our knowledge, these approaches have yet to be used with children's retelling of e-book stories. Other tools, like the online program Coh-Metrix (Graesser et al., 2011) allow for computer-based analysis of text and provides measures of basic features like parts of speech and sentence structure, as well as more holistic measures based on linguistic analysis, like narrativity, or the extent to which the text conveys a story, and cohesion, or the extent to which the text forms a coherent whole. Although these tools have been used more commonly with authored works like textbooks, they have strong potential for use with spontaneous storytelling transcriptions.

Although much e-book research focuses on story comprehension, some studies also assess children's learning of novel information, such as new vocabulary. For example, Korat and colleagues asked children multiple-choice questions about word meanings, using either oral definitions or picture options (Korat & Shamir, 2007; Korat, 2010; Shamir et al., 2012, see also Kucirkova et al., 2014). In a study with toddlers, Strouse and Ganea (2017) tested children's learning of labels for novel objects named in an e-book they were read. Children were tested with both images of the exact objects they had seen in the e-book and with images of objects similar in shape but different in color to determine whether children generalized the label to other objects in the same category. Some studies also use vocabulary measures that go beyond receptive language. Kelley and Kinney (2017) used two measures of expressive vocabulary knowledge: one in which children had to provide a definition ("What does 'daft' mean?"), which was coded as incorrect, partial, or complete, and a measure adapted from Beck and McKeown (2007) in which children had to answer four yes/no questions related to word meaning (e.g., "If you wore shoes on your hand, would that be daft?"). These different types of measures all provide valuable information, potentially assessing different aspects of children's word learning from e-books.

Other studies assess how children learn new facts from e-books. Strouse and Ganea (2016), for example, used an e-book that teaches preschoolers about camouflage and then asked multiple-choice questions to assess children's understanding. They also asked for justifications and coded for whether children used camouflage reasoning to explain their answers. Few studies have assessed children's learning of facts from e-books, but it would be useful for future research to adapt measures from studies of traditional books (Geerdts, 2015; Walker et al., 2015; Waxman et al., 2014) to assess how well children learn this kind of information from e-books. It will also be valuable to consider whether children are simply repeating information from the e-book or whether they transfer those novel facts to the real world. For instance, studies by Richert and colleagues (Richert et al., 2009; Richert & Smith, 2011) using traditional books ask children to transfer a problem solution from a book to a real-world situation, showing that factors like fantasy content influence level of transfer. Researchers studying e-books may want to consider using measures that assess this kind of application as well as recall of facts. Future studies would also do well to test children again after a delay to assess long-term learning.

More broadly, it would be useful for the field to both be more specific about what we mean by the terms we use, such as "comprehension" and "learning," and to combine different types of measures into one study. Many of the studies assessing fact learning, for example, used experimenter-created e-books whereas most studies of comprehension used commercially available e-books, making it difficult to determine the role these different factors play in their results. It will be valuable for future research to use comparable materials and methods across different studies, as divergent findings in this literature may depend on the type of materials and assessments used.

Conclusion

Just as childhood has undergone a dramatic shift in the digital age, so too, must our approach to studying the technology and its impact on children. We described five of the key lessons we learned over the last decade about conducting experimental research on e-book reading during childhood. Although this is not an exhaustive list of methodological issues, we highlighted some of the most salient issues we have encountered and seen addressed in the literature in this area. There are many significant challenges, but also exciting opportunities for future research.

Our first lesson noted that research needs to keep up with the rapid pace of technology. As technology is changing, so must the methods we use and the publishing process. We recommend that researchers move towards rapid cycle studies and investigate opportunities for making research findings available to scholars and the broader public more quickly. Measures to assess interaction and learning must also change with advancing technology. For example, we recommend moving towards using automated tools for coding emotional expressions (Baker et al., 2017) and for analyzing children's story retell responses (Graesser et al., 2011). These new directions represent exciting opportunities for moving this field forward and making important advancements in our knowledge base.

Second, we highlighted the challenge of creating generalizable findings, given the many types of e-book features available. It is vital for the field to consider the balance between experimental control and ecological validity. This is a recurring issue in the existing research, for example, with researchers studying reading using experimentally controlled materials and procedures but asking parents to read as they would at home. However, there are many opportunities to further balance these needs across different types of studies in future research. For instance, we recommend that researchers try to forge partnerships with e-book publishers to create high-quality, professional e-books that can meet researchers' needs for experimental design. Such partnerships would allow researchers to answer significant empirical questions while also creating benefit for the publishers by providing valuable evidence-based claims about the efficacy of their products (Hirsh-Pasek et al., 2015; Kucirkova et al., 2017). This approach would help researchers keep up with the newest technology and open up opportunities to conduct increasingly meaningful and useful research for families and society. Furthermore, when research aligns with current technology, it can feed into public engagement and allow parents and teachers to learn from and contribute to translational efforts (e.g., Kucirkova & Cremin, 2017).

Our third lesson speaks to the context for the reading interaction, including what happens before the child steps into the lab. We recommend that the field move towards considering families' prior experience with e-book technology and screen media generally. Incorporating these data into our analyses in meaningful ways may at least partially explain divergent findings, as well as individual differences between children within studies. These types of analyses will be vital to distinguishing between effects due to technological novelty and issues that are more fundamental to particular devices. Notably, e-book technology cannot be examined in a vacuum: broader patterns of children's media may influence children's interactions with e-books in complex ways. By using a wide-angle lens on families' experiences, we will better understand e-books in the larger context of today's digital childhood. Taking the context into account will allow us to answer more complex questions and advance our knowledge about potential moderating effects of individual differences among families and children.

Lessons 4 and 5 focused on the methods and measures we use to assess the experience of e-book reading and children's learning. As in any area of research, measurement matters. Different types of interaction and learning measures may result in substantially different outcomes. We recommend that researchers combine different types of methods and measures to best understand the complex phenomenon of e-book reading. Given the discrepant findings in this area and the ever-changing landscape of e-book technology, being transparent about our methodology and using multiple measures in each study will be important to move the field forward. Extending the methods we use and collaborating across labs will give researchers the opportunity to understand e-book reading from a variety of perspectives.

Although we have described the formidable challenges in lab-based e-book studies, we also note the valuable insights gleaned from the existing literature and highlight exciting opportunities for future research. Given the wealth of evidence supporting the value of traditional book-reading for children's learning both at home and in school settings, it is clear that e-books have great potential for education in today's tech-focused childhood. Researchers studying these issues have the opportunity to collaborate to create generalizable and useful knowledge about how parents and children interact with and learn from e-books. Further, we would do well to be flexible and creative in our thinking and innovate new models of research to keep pace with how today's digital-native children experience and learn from technology.

Acknowledgements

This research was supported by Institute of Education Sciences training grant #R305B130012 supporting fellow RAD, awarded to the fourth author, N. Jordan, and H. May, Institute of Education Sciences Grant #R305A150435 awarded to the fourth author, fifth author, and D. Dickinson, and Institute of Education Sciences Grant #R324A160241 awarded to the fourth author, fifth author, J. de Villiers, and A. Iglesias.

References

Baker, L.J., Lobue, V., Bonawitz, E. and Shafto, P. (2017) Towards automated classification of emotional facial expressions. In: *Proceedings of the 39th Annual Conference of the Cognitive Science Society*. London: Cognitive Science Society.

Beck, I.L. and McKeown, M.G. (2007) Increasing young low-income children's oral vocabulary repertoires through rich and focused instruction. *The Elementary School Journal* 107 (3), 251–271. https://doi.org/10.1086/511706.

Calvert, S.L., Strong, B.L., Jacobs, E.L. and Conger, E.E. (2007) Interaction and participation for young hispanic and caucasian girls' and boys' learning of media content. *Media Psychology* 9 (2), 431–445. https://doi.org/10.1080/15213260701291379.

Common Sense Media. (2017) *The Common Sense consensus: Media use by kids age zero to eight*. www.commonsensemedia.org/research/the-common-sense-census-media-use-by-kids-age-zero-to-eight-2017.

Courage, M.L., Waring, S. and Flynn, K. (2017) *E-storybooks for preschoolers: It's not all about the books*! Poster presented in invited session at SRCD pre-conference on Poverty-related Disparities in Children's Early Language Experience and Language Development: Prevention, Intervention, and Policy, Austin, TX.

de Jong, M.T. and Bus, A.G. (2002) Quality of book-reading matters for emergent readers: An experiment with the same book in a regular or electronic format. *Journal of Educational Psychology* 94 (1), 145–155. https://doi.org/10.1037/0022-0663.94.1.145.

Deater-Deckard, Pylas, K. and M.V. Petrill, S.A. (1997) *Parent-Child Interaction System (PARCHISY)*. London: Institute of Psychiatry.

Dore, R.A., Hassinger-Das, B., Brezack, N., Valladares, T., Paller, A., Vu, L., Golinkoff, R.M. and Hirsh-Pasek, K. (2018) The parent advantage in fostering children's e-book comprehension. *Early Childhood Research Quarterly* 44, 24–33.

Etta, R.A., Kirkorian, H.L. and Choi, K. (2017) *Preschoolers' learning from children's books: Effects of platform and interactivity*. Poster presented at the biennial meeting of the Society for Research in Child Development, Austin, TX.

Gardner, F. (2000) Methodological issues in the direct observation of parent–child interaction: Do observational findings reflect the natural behavior of participants? *Clinical Child and Family Psychology Review* 3 (3), 185–198.

Geerdts, M.S. (2015) Learning about real animals from anthropomorphic media. *Imagination, Cognition, and Personality and Personality*, 36 (1), 5–26.

Graesser, A.C., McNamara, D.S. and Kulikowich, J.M. (2011) Coh-Metrix: Providing multilevel analyses of text characteristics. *Educational Researcher* 40 (5), 223–234. https://doi.org/10.3102/0013189X11413260.

Hassinger-Das, B. (2017) The pace of digital media development and academic research. http://bold.expert/the-pace-of-digital-media-development-and-academic-research/.

Hassinger-Das, B., Mahajan, N., Metz, R., Ramsook, K.A., Margulis, K., Hirsh-Pasek, K., Golinkoff, R.M. and Parish-Morris, J. (2017, June) Reading in the digital age: Investigating differences between traditional and electronic books. In: Hassinger-Das, B., Dore, R. and Golinkoff, R.M. (Chairs) *Taming technology: Making evidence-based decisions regarding digital media*. Symposium conducted at the annual meeting of the Jean Piaget Society, San Francisco, California.

Hirsh-Pasek, K., Zosh, J.M., Golinkoff, R.M., Gray, J.H., Robb, M.B. and Kaufman, J. (2015) Putting education in "educational" apps: Lessons from the Science of Learning. *Psychological Science in the Public Interest* 16 (1), 3–34. https://doi.org/10.1177/1529100615569721.

Kabali, H.K., Irigoyen, M.M., Nunez-Davis, R., Budacki, J.G., Mohanty, S.H., Leister, K.P. and Bonner, R.L. (2015) Exposure and use of mobile media devices by young children. *Pediatrics* 136 (6), 1044–1050. https://doi.org/10.1542/peds.2015-2151.

Karemaker, A., Jelley, F., Clancy, C. and Sylva, K. (2017) The effects on children's literacy skills of reading e-books with different features: Are 'bells and whistles' over-rated? *International Journal of Child-Computer Interaction* 12, 30–36. https://doi.org/10.1016/j.ijcci.2017.01.004.

Kelley, E.S. and Kinney, K. (2017) Word learning and story comprehension from digital storybooks: Does interaction make a difference? *Journal of Educational Computing Research* 55 (3), 410–428. https://doi.org/10.1177/0735633116669811.

Kim, J.E. and Anderson, J. (2008) Mother–child shared reading with print and digital texts. *Journal of Early Childhood Literacy* 8 (2), 213–245. https://doi.org/10.1177/1468798408091855.

Korat, O. (2010) Reading electronic books as a support for vocabulary, story comprehension and word reading in kindergarten and first grade. *Computers and Education* 55 (1), 24–31. https://doi.org/10.1016/j.compedu.2009.11.014.

Korat, O. and Or, T. (2010) How new technology influences parent-child interaction: The case of e-book reading. *First Language* 30 (2), 139–154. https://doi.org/10.1177/0142723709359242.

Korat, O. and Shamir, A. (2007) Electronic books versus adult readers: Effects on children's emergent literacy as a function of social class. *Journal of Computer Assisted Learning* 23 (3), 248–259. https://doi.org/10.1111/j.1365-2729.2006.00213.x.

Krcmar, M. and Cingel, D.P. (2014) Parent–child joint reading in traditional and electronic formats. *Media Psychology* 17 (3), 262–281. https://doi.org/10.1080/15213269.2013.840243.

Kucirkova, N. (2017) Pop-ups and pull-outs : How digital books offer children an experience of 'materiality.' http://blogs.lse.ac.uk/parenting4digitalfuture/2017/07/05/pop-ups-and-pull-outs-how-digital-books-offer-children-an-experience-of-materiality/.

Kucirkova, B.N. and Cremin, T. (2017) Digital books supporting reading for pleasure. https://digilitey.wordpress.com/2016/07/28/digital-books-supporting-reading-for-pleasure/.

Kucirkova, N., Littleton, K. and Cremin, T. (2017) Young children's reading for pleasure with digital books: Six key facets of engagement. *Cambridge Journal of Education* 47 (1), 67–84. https://doi.org/10.1080/0305764X.2015.1118441.

Kucirkova, N., Messer, D. and Sheehy, K. (2014) Reading personalized books with preschool children enhances their word acquisition. *First Language* 34 (3), 227–243. https://doi.org/10.1177/0142723714534221.

Kucirkova, N., Messer, D., Sheehy, K. and Flewitt, R. (2013) Sharing personalised stories on iPads : A close look at one- parent-child interaction. *Literacy* 47 (3), 115–122.

Laidlaw, L. and O'Mara, J. (2015) Rethinking difference in the iWorld: Possibilities, challenges and "unexpected consequences" of digital tools in literacy education. *Language and Literacy* 17 (2), 59–74.

Lauricella, A.R., Barr, R. and Calvert, S.L. (2014) Parent–child interactions during traditional and computer storybook reading for children's comprehension: Implications for electronic storybook design. *International Journal of Child-Computer Interaction* 2 (1), 17–25. https://doi.org/10.1016/j.ijcci.2014.07.001.

McCabe, A. and Peterson, C. (1984) What makes a good story? *Journal of Psycholinguistic Research* 13 (6), 457–480.

Moody, A.K., Justice, L.M. and Cabell, S.Q. (2010) Electronic versus traditional storybooks: Relative influence on preschool children's engagement and communication. *Journal of Early Childhood Literacy* 10 (3), 294–313. https://doi.org/10.1177/1468798410372162.

Parish-Morris, J., Mahajan, N., Hirsh-Pasek, K., Golinkoff, R.M. and Collins, M.F. (2013) Once upon a time: Parent-child dialogue and storybook reading in the electronic era. *Mind, Brain, and Education* 7 (3), 200–211. https://doi.org/10.1111/mbe.12028.

Pasnik, S., Hupert, N., Silander, M., Moorthy, S., Llorente, C. and Dominguez, X. (2015) *Supporting parent-child experiences with PEG + CAT early math concepts: Report to the CPB-PBS Reading To Learn initiative.*

Radesky, J.S., Kistin, C.J., Zuckerman, B., Nitzberg, K., Gross, J., Kaplan-Sanoff, M., . . . Silverstein, M. (2014) Patterns of mobile device use by caregivers and children during meals in fast food restaurants. *Pediatrics* 133 (4), e843–849. https://doi.org/10.1542/peds.2013-3703.

Reich, S.M., Yau, J.C. and Warschauer, M. (2016) Tablet-based eBooks for young children: What does the research say? *Journal of Developmental and Behavioral Pediatrics* 37 (7), 585–591.

Richert, R.A., Shawber, A., Hoffman, R. and Taylor, M. (2009) Learning from fantasy and real characters in preschool and kindergarten. *Journal of Cognition and Development* 10 (1), 41–66. https://doi.org/10.1080/15248370902966594.

Richert, R.A. and Smith, E.I. (2011) Preschoolers' quarantining of fantasy stories. *Child Development* 82 (4), 1106–1119. https://doi.org/10.1111/j.1467-8624.2011.01603.x.

Richter, A. and Courage, M.L. (2017) Comparing electronic and paper storybooks for preschoolers: Attention, engagement, and recall. *Journal of Applied Developmental Psychology* 48, 92–102. https://doi.org/10.1016/j.appdev.2017.01.002.

Rideout, V. (2014) Learning at home: Families educational media use in america. *The Joan Ganz Cooney Center* (January).

Ross, K.M., Pye, R.E. and Randell, J. (2016) Reading touch screen storybooks with mothers negatively affects 7-year-old readers' comprehension but enriches emotional engagement. *Frontiers in Psychology* 7. https://doi.org/10.3389/fpsyg.2016.01728.

Rvachew, S., Rees, K., Carolan, E. and Nadig, A. (2017) Improving emergent literacy with school-based shared reading: Paper versus ebooks. *International Journal of Child-Computer Interaction* 12, 24–29.

Shamir, A., Korat, O. and Fellah, R. (2012) Promoting vocabulary, phonological awareness and concept about print among children at risk for learning disability: Can e-books help? *Reading and Writing* 25 (1), 45–69. https://doi.org/10.1007/s11145-010-9247-x.

Sheehan, K.J. and Uttal, D.H. (2016) Children's learning from touch screens: A dual representation perspective. *Frontiers in Psychology* 7. https://doi.org/10.3389/fpsyg.2016.01220.

Smeets, D.J and Bus, A.G. (2014) The interactive animated e-book as a word learning device for kindergartners. *Applied Psycholinguistics*, 1–22. https://doi.org/10.1017/S0142716413000556.

Strouse, G.A. and Ganea, P.A. (2016) Are prompts provided by electronic books as effective for teaching preschoolers a biological concept as those provided by adults? *Early Education and Development* 27 (8), 1190–1204. https://doi.org/10.1080/10409289.2016.1210457.

Strouse, G.A. and Ganea, P.A. (2017) Toddlers' word learning and transfer from electronic and print books. *Journal of Experimental Child Psychology* 156, 129–142.

Takacs, Z.K., Swart, E.K. and Bus, A.G. (2014) Can the computer replace the adult for storybook reading? A meta-analysis on the effects of multimedia stories as compared to sharing print stories with an adult. *Frontiers in Psychology* 5 (December), 1–12. https://doi.org/10.3389/fpsyg.2014.01366.

Walker, C.M., Ganea, P.A. and Gopnik, A. (2015) Learning to learn from stories: Children's developing sensitivity to the causal structure of fictional worlds. *Child Development* 86 (1), 310–318.

Walker, E., Adams, A., Restrepo, M.A., Fialko, S. and Glenberg, A.M. (2017) When (and how) interacting with technology-enhanced storybooks helps dual language learners. *Translational Issues in Psychological Science* 3 (1), 66–79.

Waxman, S.R., Herrmann, P., Woodring, J. and Medin, D. (2014) Humans (really) are animals: Picture-book reading influences five-year-old urban children's construal of the relation between humans and non-human animals. *Frontiers in Psychology* 5 (172). https://doi.org/10.3389/fpsyg.2014.00172.

Yuill, N. and Martin, A.F. (2016) Curling up with a good e-book: Mother-child shared story reading on screen or paper affects embodied interaction and warmth. *Frontiers in Psychology* 7. https://doi.org/10.3389/fpsyg.2016.01951.

Zipke, M. (2017) Preschoolers explore interactive storybook apps: The effect on word recognition and story comprehension, 1695–1712. https://doi.org/10.1007/s10639-016-9513-x.

Zucker, T.A., Moody, A.K. and McKenna, M.C. (2009) The effects of electronic books on pre-kindergarten-to-grade 5 students' literacy and langauge outcomes: A research synthesis. *Journal of Educational Computing Research* 40 (1), 47–87. https://doi.org/10.2190/EC.40.1.c.

26

HEAD MOUNTED, CHEST MOUNTED, TRIPOD OR ROAMING?

The methodological potentials of a GoPro camera and ontological possibilities for doing visual research with child participants differently

Lucy Caton and Abigail Hackett

Preamble

This chapter shares experimentation and analysis of the different configurations of a GoPro camera, the sorts of intra actions and videos produced through these configurations and how the videos can take on a life of their own in research with children and digital media. We argue that in a context in which the choices researchers have about how to use video and the quantities of video produced are both increasing, there is a need to further theorise the visual ontologies that underpin these choices and this production. Drawing on the scholarship of the ontological turn, which critiques the separation between being and knowing, we highlight the importance for visual researchers to think through these ideas and resist the lure of 'naive empiricism' (Elwick, 2015). In particular, we put to work notions of life lived along lines (Deleuze & Guattari, 1987; Ingold, 2007) to re-think visual methods that render both 'data' and 'researcher' in particular ways. Instead of offering a recipe, our analysis prompts researchers to question how the camera and video also have agential power and to interrogate child and researcher positions that do not necessarily produce predictable or similar results for others.

In a context in which researchers are experimenting with the fast-developing potentials of ever smaller and more sophisticated video cameras, that can be worn, mounted or incorporated into the action in a number of ways, this chapter has two aims. Firstly, we will share experiences from the first author's fieldwork, in which GoPro cameras were used in an after-school computer club and in a number of different ways, over the course of a year; head mounted, chest mounted, on a tripod and 'roaming'. This gives a starting point for considering the unique affordances and constraints of each of these options. Further, we consider what an ontological conceptual framework can contribute to understandings of exactly what is taking place when cameras, children and researchers come together in this kind of scenario.

Methodological possibilities have never been more wide ranging for researchers wanting to provide an account of children's engagement and improvisation with creative digital media. The increasing availability of small, affordable video cameras for educational research has dramatically changed the field over the course of the last 20 years (Flewitt, 2006; Rose, 2010; Wilson, 2017) in a number of different directions. For example, participatory approaches have embraced video as a way for children to tell their own stories or communicate their own perspectives (Lomax et al, 2011; Pahl & Pool, 2011; Mills et al., 2014), including across different contexts or whilst 'on the move' (Christensen & Cortés-Morales, 2015; Kullman, 2012; Powell, 2017). More naturalistic or ethnographic video data has undergone fine grained analysis to understand the role of the body in children's communication (Flewitt, 2006; Hackett, 2014) and wearable cameras enabling an 'automatic' capturing of still or moving images over longer periods of time have generated large datasets (Wilson, 2017). All of these changes in research methodologies have taken place in a context in which the visual mode seems to have an increasing significance in children's lives (Rose, 2016; Stirling & Yamada-Rice, 2015) and digital technologies have become an everyday and ordinary aspect of daily life (Riviere, 2005; White, 2009).

Key debates within the methodological literature on use of video in educational research tend to focus on the impact of video recording, the extent to which video data can be considered naturalistic and the partiality of video as an account of the field (see Jewitt, 2012 for a summary). In terms of research with children, debates centre on levels of children's participation and agency within this kind of research, along with the ethical issues implicated (Robson, 2011). However, also important are considerations about the visual ontologies that lie behind the making and viewing of video data in educational research. As video footage becomes increasingly commonplace, and easily obtained during fieldwork, researchers need to be cautious about "the risk of naïve empiricism" (Elwick, 2015, p. 325); it is all too tempting to consider video footage as either comprehensive record of the field, or as-comprehensive-as-possible (hence debates around partiality of video data). As de Freitas points out, this is reflected in dominant approaches to dealing with video in educational research, which tends to focus on "viewing the video attentively, describing the data, identifying critical events, transcribing, coding, constructing a storyline, and composing the narrative" (2016, p. 413). Elwick (2015) recommends a focus on the intersection between participants, images and audiences in order to avoid video as empiricism. As Harwood and Collier (this volume) also point out, there is a need to consider both the agency of the video camera and the resultant video data itself. Video data is not just reality captured in a more efficient and convenient format. Video data itself takes on a life of its own; it can evoke the emotions of the field (Pink, 2009), or grab the researcher with an intensity and affect (Rautio & Millei, 2017). Describing a research team viewing video data from a school-based ethnography, MacLure (2010, p. 282) writes

> [S]ome detail – a fieldnote fragment or video image – starts to glimmer, gathering our attention. Things both slow down and speed up at this point. On the one hand, the detail arrests the listless traverse of our attention across the surface of the screen or page that holds the data, intensifying our gaze and making us pause to burrow inside it, mining it for meaning. On the other hand, connections start to fire up: the conversation gets faster and more animated as we begin to recall other incidents and details in the project classrooms, our own childhood experiences, films or artwork that we have seen, articles that we have read.

Visual ontologies in an after-school computer club

These issues of visual ontology, the need for theorising video as an encounter between participants, technology and researchers, seem to be becoming ever more pressing in current contexts of educational research. For example, researchers have more choices to make from a greater range of possibilities for how cameras could or should be used during fieldwork. Quantities of video data produced during educational research are increasing, and these quantities need to be dealt with in a rationalised and practical way. Additionally, in a context in which research is increasingly likely to be inter-disciplinary, researchers may not share ontologies with regards to video data (Leder-Mackley & Pink, 2013).

We draw on data from the first author's forthcoming PhD thesis, located in a primary school digital skills club based in the North West of England, where the action was filmed using distinct GoPro camera perspectives (head harness, chest mounted, roaming camera and static).[1] The cameras used during the fieldwork were GoPro Hero HD®, designed mainly for the extreme sports market on account of their curved aperture and wide field of view, but selected here due to their small size, rugged design, rubber waterproof casing, variable mountable configurations and high definition output. We challenge the dominant realisms that continue to regulate educational video research and to theorise video that is co-curated through child and camera entanglements. Video data was collected during 11 months of participant observation in an after-school digital skills club. The children played with Little Bits Technology, which is a simple, battery operated electronic circuit, consisting of brightly coloured blocks that clip together in order to operate various bells, lights, counters and switches as part of the circuit. The pilot study preceded the main study and took place over a four-month period at the same location. Table 26.1 summarises when the fieldwork took place, and which of those months the GoPro camera was used in a particular way (head harness, chest harness, static and roaming device). Highlighting the patterns, routine and changing use of the camera is important to provide a sense of the developing nature of the research design, influenced entirely by the children's changing needs and desires.

Living life along lines: ontological theory and video-based research

By the ontological turn, we refer to a diverse and burgeoning body of scholarship rejecting a Cartesian division between being and knowing, that pushes the limits of how to understand 'humanness' and more specifically the ideas of subjectification. For example, is it possible to think about the world beyond normativity by exceeding established practices, patterns and ways of thinking about the human. In this chapter we draw on the philosophies of Deleuze

Table 26.1 Summary of types of cameras

Fieldwork (Dates)	*Head Harness*	*Static (tripod)*	*Chest Harness*	*Roaming Camera*
Pilot Study April 2016–July 2016		X		
Main Study Sept 2016–Oct 2016	X	X		
Oct 2016–March 2017		X	X	
April 2017–June 2017		X		X
June 2017–July 2017				X

and Guattari (1987), in which the notion of the human as a singular, independent and bounded entity is contested. Additionally, we draw on post-human theoretical work which understands a 'flat ontology' in which discourse does not sit above matter; rather, the two are mutually implicated (Barad, 2007; MacLure, 2013). Methodological implications of the ontological turn are wide ranging, and include a critique of the researcher as capable of standing outside of data/method, in order to collect, survey and answer an autonomous research question (Lather & St Pierre, 2013; Springaay & Truman, 2017) and a critique of data as static, readable or in any way separate from the world (Holmes & Jones, 2013).

De Freitas (2016, p. 555) argues that one of the greatest tensions in video-based educational research is its interest in temporal chunking, in halting time in order to make "'an instant' visible and analysable". She traces this "tension between his aim to capture the continuous flow of movement and his desire for a legible record of the event" (2016, p. 558) from the origins of cinematic practices in the 19th century. Responding to these tensions, we turn to Deleuze and Guattari's (1987) and Tim Ingold's (2007, 2008) theorisations life as lived along lines. This notion of lines, which are ongoing, in constant movement and entangled, sits in opposition to conceptualisations of life as a series of fixed temporal or spatial points, and thus helps us interrogate visual ontologies during video-based educational research.

Ingold (2007) conceptualises life as lived along a series of lines, setting out his thesis for an anthropology of the line thus:

> As walking, talking and gesticulating creatures, human being generate lines wherever they go. It is not just that line-making is as ubiquitous as the use of the voice, hand and feet – respectively in speaking, gesturing and moving around – but rather than it subsumes all these aspects of everyday human activity and, in doing so, brings them together into a single field of inquiry.
>
> *(Ingold, 2007, p. 1)*

Lines are also an important conceptual tool for Deleuze and Guattari in their book *A Thousand Plateaus*. "Individual or group", they write (1987, p. 223), "we are composed of lines . . . or rather, bundles of lines". There are lines of life, lines of writing, lines productive of variation in lines of life or writing, lines of luck and misfortune and so on (1987, p. 215). Deleuze and Guattari (1987) explain the 'molar line' is a line that holds in place the status quo. We might understand the 'molar line' as a physical structure of some kind that is recognisable through its associated signs, regimes and symbols. For example, an institutional structure, such as a university, is characterised by student timetables, assessment schedules and professional academic hierarchy. Molar lines might also form internalised discourses (for example, what it means to carry out good/bad research practices in certain academic fields). Ways of 'doing' visual research with child participants are often constrained by 'molar lines' which tend to inhibit ways of 'seeing' and thinking outside of the status quo. Some of these 'molar lines' are at the level of the academic institutions, where there might be a lack of resources restricting the work of specific research pursuits. Other 'molar lines' are those that visual researchers internalise, such as deep set beliefs regarding ideas of object and subject. These internal beliefs are often grounded in human-centric notions that render visual 'data' as something that transmits information (the object), often used as evidence for the researcher (the subject). Navigating these internal/external constraints means that much visual research consists of these day to day practices, and thereby supports the status quo or the 'molar line'. This in turn creates visual research that is characterised solely by the researcher's interpretations and conceptual understandings, often driven by external research aims and desires.

Lines of flight

Deleuze and Guattari (1987) also describe, interchangeably, 'lines of flight' and 'lines of becoming', viewing these interwoven lines as a 'rhizome' where boundaries are never absolute and nothing is ever contained or modular. There are unpredictable 'lines of flight' that serve to disturb or 'deterritorialize' (Deleuze & Guattari, 1987) those 'molar lines'. As we will outline in this chapter, the chest mounted camera and the roaming camera both served at times to initiate break out points from the 'molar line'. 'Lines of flight' are incited, within those child-led moments of improvisation with the camera. For example, the film produced by the chest mounted and roaming camera, are both characterised through a series of different types of non-linear shots, serving to disrupt the hierarchical visual researcher gaze. This intimate perspective onto the action joins in conversation with Hultman and Lenz Taguchi (2010) and Millei and Rautio (2017), who highlight the importance of thinking about the agency of the material object within our visual practices.

Ingold's (2007) theory of life lived along lines complements Deleuze-Guattarian notions as discussed earlier. From the point of view of video research with children, two aspects of Ingold's conceptualisation seem particularly significant. Firstly, lines of walking, talking and gesticulating always occur in place, and further, play a part in the making of place. For Ingold (2007), place is conceptualised not as dots or circles on a map, but as points where many lines of movement come together and are concentrated. Ingold (2007) proposes the notion of a 'meshwork' consisting of lines, quite often referred to as threads or paths that are interwoven.

> A world that is occupied, I argue, is furnished with already-existing things. But one that is inhabited is woven from the strands of their continual coming-into-being
>
> *(Ingold, 2008, p. 1797)*

Thus, understandings of life as lived along lines, and a use of video within educational research as a component of this meshwork, offer a conceptual way forward for thinking about our practices of collecting, watching and interpreting video data. De Freitas (2016) suggests that video data is now the dominant form of data in classroom research, in archiving the body of both the teacher and the student. She argues that we know very little about our own practices and often proceed to use such data without examining the ways that video structures the research we do. Understanding her research in mathematics classrooms, within the genre of 'scientific cinema', de Freitas highlights how early sets of conventions 'used in the capitalist over coding of the human body' (2016, p. 554) during the industrial age, still dominate our understanding of the human body. The philosophy of lines we outline here complements De Freitas's argument in thinking about dominant understandings of the human body as mechanically represented. De Freitas argues for new visual methodologies that move beyond the inherited ways that serve particular kinds of learning theories and perceptions of the human body.

Head, chest, roaming, static: the different configurations of the GoPro camera during this research

In this next section, we describe the use of the GoPro camera in different configurations across the course of the fieldwork, as well as the process whereby the GoPro camera moved from head to chest to hands. In the pilot, children sometimes wore the camera attached to a head harness with the intention of bringing the camera close to the participant's field of view. This was an alternative procedure also achieved by others using cameras fitted to infants' headwear (Elwick et al., 2014; Elwick, 2015), but proved unfeasible due to the children's complaints about the harness causing discomfort. The head harness was also discarded due to its clumsy intrusion, and because when the children ran around, the resulting film made for unpleasant viewing. Once the main study had commenced, the chest harness was the preferred approach for collecting video footage. This provided a much more stable film to watch. The chest harness allowed the children to wear the GoPro camera on the upper torso using a system of interconnected, elasticated straps that adjusted to fit the children's shapes and sizes. The children who attended the primary school, were mixed sex and aged between seven and eleven.

School computer club: an introduction

> It must be a somewhat peculiar sight for the children to see me clunking and clattering my way into the school computer club, my arms filled with camera equipment, boxes and a rucksack hanging off each shoulder. I have done this many times now, and for a few of the children, my arrival signals something special. I'm the camerawoman, the researcher, the one who brings fun technology to play with. I busily go about setting up the GoPro cameras; one fixed to a tripod on the central table and the other fixed in a chest harness, which ultimately makes its way around various child participants, during the course of the session. My role involves helping the children to adjust the harness strap depending on which child wishes to film with it.
>
> – *Fieldnotes, Caton (October, 2016)*

Chest mounted camera

In the next section, we draw on the first author's field notes in order to offer a glimpse into the types of behaviours the children began to demonstrate, whilst taking part in filming activities. The children were happy to participate in the filming process, demonstrated through their willingness to wear and exchange the chest mounted camera, albeit for around 10 minutes each, before making it quite clear they were 'tired' or 'bored'. Filming with the chest mounted camera, lasted for approximately six months, however, I was confident that the children and I had formed a relationship where they were able to draw attention to any discomfort whilst wearing the device, or highlight any anxiety towards their ongoing participatory role. I remained attentive to those ongoing nuances in the children's behaviour, firstly in relation to a pragmatic and ongoing ethical awareness and secondly to remain mindful of my researcher position within this experimental yet speculative methodology. Filming with the children in computer club in this manner of experimentation required an ethics that took place through a politics of listening, experimentation and potentiality, with an ongoing care for belonging.

Roaming camera

After approximately six months, it became apparent that the children's interest in wearing the chest mounted camera began to wane and they stopped using it, as discussed earlier. Thereafter, the camera transformed into a device that could be freely passed around in an improvisatory manner. Together, the children and I coined the device 'roaming cam' to help differentiate use between the chest mounted and the static devices. The approach to using the camera as a roaming device had not been planned and came about as a 'happy accident' in a moment of improvisation. The research shifted to acknowledge a new type of child and camera entanglement; one that did not involve my researcher physical presence to manipulate its operation. I later discuss the implications for this change.

Static camera

The static camera served as a permanent piece of apparatus throughout the project. In the early weeks of the study, I spent time finding the best possible vantage point in the classroom, in order to set up the static, third eye camera. At this point, I became more involved with the filming process than originally intended as I moved the device around according to the livelier sequences of action that were aligned with my adult-centric viewpoints. I suggest this rendered the children both physically and ontologically according to my adult pre-fixed ways of knowing, which I initially aimed to trouble. This was a stark move away from the original plan to use the static device as an objective, third eye view over the action that filmed from one set position. I wondered if a handheld, mobile camera would have been more suitable to follow the action around the room. However, I conceded that the process of filming with a handheld device was too physically intrusive, due to the practicalities of weaving my adult body around the children's personal space.

The children seemed comfortable with the camera's presence, yet their inquiries about the device were extremely rare; little did they tamper with the device or attempt to manipulate it in any way. I had made explicit attempts to verbally inform the children about the aims, purpose and intentions for the study, and I also disseminated child-friendly reading material to take home. However, it was only in the concluding weeks of the study that the children began to show a real interest in relation to what the films were actually for and how their involvement aided this process. One child, asked if his images were going to be 'put in a book', to which I replied yes, 'if that is still ok with you'? The children deemed the physical camera device mine and not theirs, in so far as they knew that the Manchester Metropolitan University owned the device, as I had explained this to them at the start. Yet, ownership of the digital 'data' created by the children themselves and that included their images, was an ambiguous ethical area. The research helped to trouble ideas of ownership and what this actually meant within a speculative ontology, where entities (children, camera, digital image, researcher) worked in co-existence, and agency was distributed through the flows and materials that moved in relation to one another.

Troubling underpinning visual ontologies: chest mounted camera

> The image [Figure 26.1] forces us to suspend our 'gaze' for that second longer, drawing our attention to an intimate and dynamic perspective of the child and their material world. We are presented with a view of the child's hands as he manipulates a long, white plastic light that forms part of the electronic circuit. The image captures the boy's attempts at manipulating the light, in order for it to successfully operate. We see a red light (bottom right of image) indicating that the battery within the circuit is working. The circuit is therefore complete yet, the light does not work. We are invited to observe the boy as he uses his hands to improvise, problem solve in co-existence with the materials. Together the child and camera move in a manner, creating a space that foregrounds the material objects in shot. We are coerced into focusing on the finer details that include the textures, materials, size and shapes of the various objects and how they work with and against the child's body, from an alternative perspective. The human figure pales into the background, as we are invited to take a closer look.
>
> – *(Caton Notes, Dec, 2016)*

Theorising life as lived along lines, serves to 'push' against traditional visual ontologies that persist in ascribing greater agency and therefore value to human movement. The image presented

Figure 26.1 Child's perspective

creates 'lines of flight' troubling how we have traditionally come to 'see' children within participatory educational video, as the object. The chest-mounted images open a conduit to help deconstruct the notion of the human being as a discrete, bounded entity that is set in an environment (Ingold, 2008). Instead we can think about the human hands within the image as entwined within the flows and materials that share the space, breaking down subject and object dichotomies and troubling ideas of agency within the action.

The 'molar line' often renders the image as something that transmits information, perpetuating such object and subject dichotomies. Theorising life lived along lines invites us to view the world from an alternative angle, where we too have to adjust mentally and physically in order to appreciate and experience a new reality. The image (Figure 26.2), which is also filmed on the chest mounted camera, incites 'lines of flight' as the spectator is drawn to noticing the size, shape, colours and textures of the material components that scatter across the table, bringing the material into the foreground. This perspective opens up the opportunity to experience life according to a child's individual height perspective, which immediately dislodges the spectator from their adult-centric view point of the world. A 'line of flight' takes shape within the 'meshwork' of relations. The spectator is forced from their position within the status quo and from their fixed adult-centric view point. Therefore, those 'molar lines' are disturbed as the spectator is forced to 'see' the world from a new height perspective that may be unfamiliar to them. New 'lines of flight' are incited as the spectator is forced to attune differently to the world in digital skills club in relation with the child, the image and the camera.

Engaging with the world from a new height perspective, it becomes clear that tables, chairs, equipment and adult bodies in shot may serve as obstructions as well as aids and supports. We are not entirely sure what the child is looking at or physically doing with their limbs as they film the action. The image offers a challenge to the dominant human-centric gaze, with which researchers tend to approach visual data (Harwood and Collier, this volume; Hultman and Lenz Taguchi, 2010). This new entanglement forces an active rather than a passive encounter, as the spectator is coerced into suspending their gaze for that second longer in order to make sense of a new aesthetic on screen. The aesthetic affect is created within the frame of shot, as the child manoeuvres, adjusts and navigates the space in co-existence with the digital device. This framework helps to think about how the human figure works as part of the 'mesh work' (Ingold,

Figure 26.2 Within the action

2008) of child, environment and researcher, troubling dominant understandings of the human body as mechanically represented within educational visual research (see Figure 26.3).

From chest camera to roaming camera

As discussed, the chest camera was discontinued after approximately six months, due to the children's lack of interest. The harness was restrictive and uncomfortable, according to the children. Often the children would avoid contact with me for fear of being asked to wear it and I felt this began to hinder our relationship. Ethically, I did not want to manipulate or cajole the children into wearing it and so the process of filming in this particular manner came to a natural end. The camera thereafter was used as a 'roaming device' that was freely passed around by the children in an improvisatory manner. At this point in the filming, I had very limited control over the content of the film as the children took complete charge of the curation process. I allowed my initial researcher anxieties to wane and instead took comfort in thinking about what potentialities lay ahead.

> The children playfully, navigate their way around the space of club whilst manipulating the 'roaming camera' with great dexterity. They seem fairly proficient and familiar with the task of filming. I provide minimal instruction other than to go ahead and improvise with the camera. I watch as the device is passed around, the children act with an equal measure of gusto and carefulness, talking excitedly about the possibility of creating their own 'vlogs'. I opt to sit to one side, feeling a sense of redundancy as the children take the lead in the camera's operation. I begin to lose track of the camera's location as it is passed around the room. I attempt to limit my researcher anxieties as I wait with apprehension and excitement for the resulting film.
>
> *(Field notes, Caton, April, 2017)*

The images capture a range of emotions and behaviours (joy, surprise, intrigue, cheekiness). When the camera became a 'roaming camera' (Figure 26.4) the size of the GoPro meant that the children were physically able to hold and manipulate the small device in the palm of their hand with relative ease. This is an example of the material device working in co-existence with the child. This ease of use afforded some of the more obscure camera angles, and therefore the playful behaviour that the children exhibited whilst filming. The children often decided to place the camera on the table top or at the back of the computer monitor, still filming as they busied themselves with other activities, for example, talking to a friend or playing on a computer game.

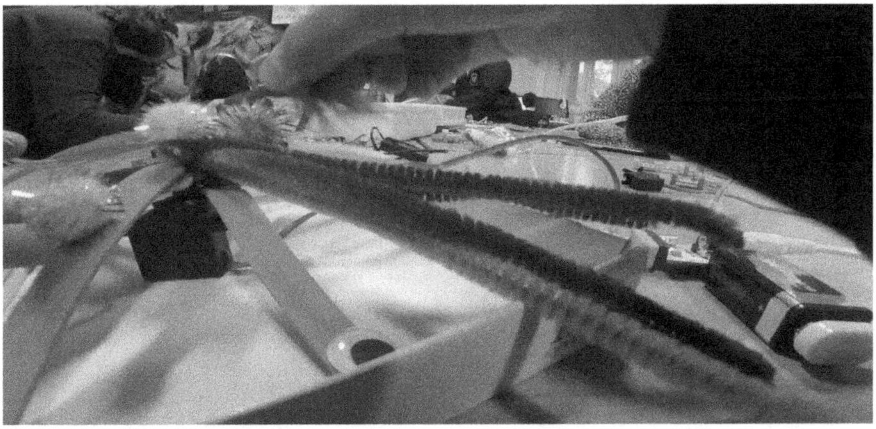

Figure 26.3 Mechanical representations

Figure 26.4 Child's perspectives

We can see the filming process became entirely child led, as the device grew more independent of researcher involvement to operate it. The children quickly became familiar with the process of filming with the roaming camera. The camera operated as an extension to the body, as I noticed many children forgetting they had hold of the camera, evident in some of the floor and ceiling shots that thread through the video.

Creating vlogs with the 'roaming camera': rethinking agency within participatory research with children

In stark contrast to the chest harness camera, the camera used as a roaming camera was enthusiastically received by the children. Filming in this manner slowly opened up the opportunity for the children to create individual 'vlogs'.[2] Some children explained they had their own vlogs, which generally involved filming themselves, in their home environment, talking about, in most cases, their love of computer games. As filming with the roaming camera continued, the children began to appropriate the camera as a device to create their own vlogs in computer club. The following vignette navigates through a short sequence of film made by one of the children, in attempt to make their own computer club vlog.

> The boy playfully carries the camera around. He turns the camera around to greet his virtual audience and then proceeds to point it at various objects, bodies, materials that catch his eye. The sequence catches those fleeting, momentary interactions that invite the spectator to join and explore the lively ecologies of computer club. We are coerced into noticing the textures, the materials, the bodies, the sounds and shapes that leave us curious of those hidden places that are not always in frame. The camera moves so swiftly, teasing, as we quickly glimpse one form to the next, the interludes too brief to offer any sense of stability. The film is dizzying and the collapse of the physical surrounding space is jolted in favour of irregular, blurred shots that incite a sense of claustrophobia.
>
> *(Caton, Field notes, June 2017)*

In the images (Figure 26.5) the boy points the camera towards his face, seemingly confident as he addresses the spectator. The spectator and the boy are connected through the camera, so we already have an interaction between human being and a material object. Expressive qualities are incited through the nuanced movements of the child and camera which serve to highlight the fleeting nature of the whole experience; Ingold (2013, 2015) stresses the unfolding nature of these interactions, rather than a designed and intentionally created product. Even videos such as this one, which feel quite curated, necessarily emerge in the moment, and are realised in unpredictable ways.

We can also note that the roaming camera film differs from early footage recorded with the chest harness, due to the child having complete physical control over the device. The roaming camera offers a new kind of mobility due to its small size, square shape and rubber textured coating, each of the physical qualities improved the child's dexterity whilst handling the camera. The sequence of film moves at such a pace that the spectator is unable to rest their gaze on any one object for a prolonged period of time in stark contrast to the fixed position chest mounted camera, which offers a more intimate perspective of the action, often at a much slower pace.

A couple of the children mentioned that they had created their own personal vlogs at home, in which they uploaded videos of themselves onto various social networking sites, discussing the

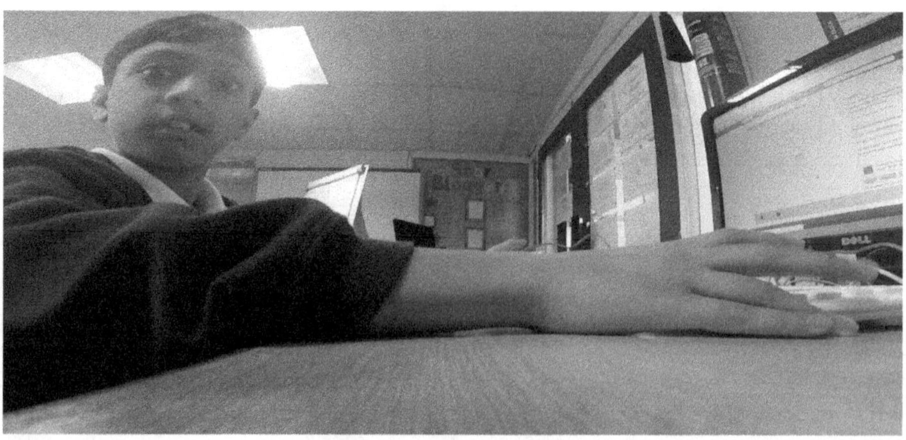

Figure 26.5 A boy points camera towards his face

merits of computer games to other online users. I began to consider and link the idea of vlogging to the young boy in the images (Figure 26.5), who competently navigates his surroundings, whilst providing a narration into the camera. This, I suggest, emulates a popular mode of address on many social networking videos and however mundane the film commentary may seem to an adult-centric view, the boy offers us a rare glimpse of his thoughts and feelings as he competently commands the small classroom space. The boy invites the audience to meet his peers as he excitedly shouts 'introduce yourself to the people' and then simultaneously draws us into conversations asking his peers 'what are you doing in club today?'.

Those fleeting moments between the boy and his friends can be worked through a theorisation of lines that force us to attune to those behaviours, conversations and nuances in movements that often get overlooked in classroom narratives. I am therefore, attuned to 'slowing down' (Horton & Kraftl, 2006, Millei & Rautio, 2017) my observations. In 'slowing down' research observation and taking time to consider the 'mundane' and 'irrelevant', I am able to consider a range of competencies that include communication, questioning and listening and negotiation, that could be overlooked as 'educationally irrelevant' exchanges between the boy and his friends. Instead, new insights can be brought to such exchanges.

Roaming camera and researcher: viewing, jamming and breaking

> At home I unpacked the cameras, charged the batteries, downloaded the video onto hard drives and selected time-sampled sequences from the footage in order to 'mull' over. As I watched the footage at home in my office temporally separated from the event, by one week and spatially separated by fifteen miles, I begin to wonder about ideas of 'agency', particularly in relation to my participant researcher role. Was I (researcher) the agent, having decided to bring the cameras into the children's environment whilst also taking charge of the editing process? Or more controversially, was the camera the agent? Equally, is there an argument to suggest there was a dispersal of agency across all entities, through the relations of researcher, child, camera and spectator? Were we all part of the mangle?
>
> *(Caton, research notes, July 2017)*

In her discussion of viewing data through two different cameras (fixed and head mounted), Elwick (2015) argues that engaging in viewing different kinds of video data helps the viewer to

Figure 26.6 Conversation with the teacher

acknowledge the embodied nature of viewing video footage, and the role of the video camera in mediating this. This is evident in the next moment, as we witness a 'jam or break' to the action-oriented schemata. Deleuze argues a different kind of image appears – a non-metaphorical image of the 'thing in itself' in its intolerable 'excess of horror or beauty' (Deleuze 1987, p. 20). The disruption to the action is momentarily disturbed, due to the presence of a teacher who enters the room. The child immediately hides the camera out of view. Consciously or unconsciously, the child continues to film the ongoing conversation with the teacher (see Figure 26.6).

This 'jam or break' in the action incites a new set of relations between the child, camera and spectator as the child plunges the camera towards the floor; this movement renders the spectator voyeur within the action that takes place in Figure 26.6. Those corresponding 'molar lines' and 'lines of flight' (Deleuze & Guattari, 1987) within the event help to create new meaning. The spectator is immediately forced to consider their position within the action, as the child continues to film his private student and teacher conversations. I argue, by using a post-structural theoretical framework to deconstruct these seemingly irrelevant, 'out take' shots that are often overlooked as disruptions, the images actually open up potentials within mundane events. Maclure (2013) argues that classroom video such as this is often considered as 'junk' or 'off task', and such nonsense is seen as 'educationally worthless'. However, Maclure argues that these seemingly mundane classroom episodes are worthy of attention, in order to understand how language and learning emerge out of the movements and rhythms of bodies, formlessness and chaos.

I suggest, persisting in the mess of an ontological struggle, yet consciously engaged in the process, gives such post-human research both ethical rigour and validity in the face of other more scientific enquiries. As such, concerns about ownership, data, bodies, knowledge and permissions are each imperative within the ongoing ontological research encounter. However, notions of 'reflexivity' are problematic in an ontological paradigm because they assume bounded individuals with agency making autonomous and informed choices about what transpires.

Reflection: visual ontologies, GoPro cameras and life along lines

The chapter draws on Gilles Deleuze, Felix Guattari and Tim Ingold and their theoretical synergies of life lived along lines. We attempt to do this in the context of child participatory visual research in order to theorise the video data that is created through two distinct camera perspectives (chest mounted and roaming camera). A common thread through the chapter is the need for visual researchers to question their own visual ontologies, rendering normative ideas about children within participatory educational video. What we have emphasised in our experiments is the usefulness of philosophies as conceptual tools that enable us to say something more about children's lives and in doing so, giving young people a somewhat 'better' position within an educational context.

Notes

1 Throughout the discussion of fieldwork, methodological decisions and analysis in the chapter, 'I' refers to first author Lucy Caton.

2 A vlog is a blog that contains video content and the children explained that some online vloggers had millions of followers worldwide, which they were familiar with.

References

Barad, K. (2007) *Meeting the universe halfway: Quantum physics and the entanglement of matter and meaning*. Durham, NC: Duke University Press.

Caton, L. (forthcoming) *Rethinking visual methodologies in child participatory research: A study involving wearable action cameras in an after-school club*. PhD thesis, Manchester Metropolitan University, Manchester, UK.

Christensen, P. and Cortés-Morales, S. (2015) Children's mobilities: Methodologies, theories, scales. In: Laoire et al. (eds.) *Movement, mobilities and journeys*. New York: Springer, 13–44.

de Freitas, E. (2016) The moving image in education research: Reassembling the body in classroom video data. *International Journal of Qualitative Studies in Education* 29 (4), 553–572.

Deleuze, G. and Guattari, F. (1987) *A Thousand Plateaus*. Massumi, B. (trans.) London: Continuum.

Elwick, S. (2015) 'Baby-cam' and researching with infants: Viewer, image and (not) knowing. *Contemporary Issues in Early Childhood* 16 (4), 322–338.

Elwick, S., Bradley, B., and Sumsion, J. (2014) Infants as Others: Uncertainties, difficulties and (im)possibilities in researching infants' lives. *International Journal of Qualitative Studies in Education* 27 (2), 196–213.

Flewitt, R. (2006) Using video to investigate preschool classroom interactions: Education research assumptions and methodological practices. *Visual Communication* 5 (1), 25–50.

Hackett, A. (2014) Zigging and Zooming all over the place: Young children's meaning making and moving in the museum. *Journal of Early Childhood Literacy* 14 (1), 5–27.

Holmes, R. and Jones, L. (2013) Flesh, wax, horse skin, and hair: The many intensities of data, *Cultural Studies ↔ Critical Methodologies* 13 (4), 357–372.

Horton, J. and Kraftl, P. (2006) What else? some more ways of thinking and doing 'Children's Geographies'. *Children's Geographies* 4 (1), 69–95.

Hultman, K. and Lenz Taguchi, H. (2010) Challenging anthropocentric analysis of visual data: A relational materialist methodological approach to educational research. *International Journal of Qualitative Studies in Education* 23 (5), 525–542.

Ingold, T. (2007) *Lines: A brief history*. Abingdon: Routledge.

Ingold, T. (2008) Bindings against boundaries: Entanglement of life in an open world. *Environment and Planning* 40, 1796–1810.

Ingold, T. (2013) *Making: Anthropology, archaeology, art and architecture*. London: Routledge.

Ingold, T. (2015) *The Life of Lines*. Abingdon: Routledge.

Jewitt, C. (2012) An introduction to using video for research – NCRM EPrints Repository. http://eprints.ncrm.ac.uk/2259/4/NCRM_workingpaper_0312.pdf.

Kullman, K. (2012) Experiments with moving children and digital cameras. *Children's Geographies* 10 (1), 1–16.

Lather, P. and St. Pierre, E. (2013) Post-qualitative research. *International Journal of Qualitative Studies in Education* 26 (6), 629–633.

Leder Mackley, K. and Pink, S. (2013) From emplaced knowing to interdisciplinary knowledge: Sensory ethnography in energy research. *The Senses and Society* 8, 335–353.

Lomax, H. Fink, J. Singh, N. and High, C. (2011) The politics of performance: Methodological challenges of researching children's experiences of childhood through the lens of participatory video, *International Journal of Social Research Methodology* 14 (3), 231–243.

MacLure, M. (2010) The offence of theory. *Journal of Education Policy* 25 (2), 277–286.

Maclure, M. (2013) Researching without representation? Language and materiality in post qualitative methodology. *International Journal of Qualitative Studies in Education* 26 (6), 658–667.

Millei, Z. and Rautio, P. (2017) 'Overspills' of research with children: an argument for slow research, *Children's Geographies*, 15(4), 466–477. DOI: 10.1080/14733285.2016.1277182.

Mills, K., Unsworth, L., Bellochi, A., Yong Park, J. and Ritchie, S. (2014) Children's emotions and multimodal appraisal of places: Walking with the camera. *Australian Journal of Language and Literacy* 37 (3), 171–181.

Pahl, K. and Pool, S. (2011) Living your life because it's the only life you've got: Participatory research as a site for discovery in a creative project in a primary school in Thurnscoe, UK. *Qualitative Research Journal* 11 (2), 17–37.

Pink, S. (2009) *Doing sensory ethnography*. London: Sage.

Powell, K. (2017) StoryWalking: Place-based narratives of identity, history and interculturality in San Jose Japan town, USA. In: Burnard, P., Ross, V., Mackinlay, E., Powell, K., Dragovic, T. and Minors, H.J. (eds.) *Building interdisciplinary and intercultural bridges: Where practice meets research and theory*, 142–149. E-book, open access Online Publication by BIBACC available through www.bibacc.org.

Riviere, C. (2005) Mobile camera phones: A new form of 'being together' in daily interpersonal communication. In: Ling, R. and Pederson, P.E. (eds.) *Mobile communications: R-Negotiation of the social sphere*. London: Springer, 167–186.

Robson, S. (2011) Producing and using video data in the early years: Ethical questions and practical consequences in research with young children. *Children and Society* 25, 179–189.
Rose, G. (2010) *Visual methodologies: An introduction to the interpretation of visual materials.* (2nd edition.), London: Sage.
Rose, G. (2016) *Visual methodologies: An introduction to researching with visual materials* (4th edition). London: Sage.
Springaay, S. and Truman, S (2017) On the need for methods beyond proceduralism: Speculative middles, (In)Tensions, and response-ability in research. *Qualitative Inquiry* 24 (3), 203–214.
Stirling, E. and Yamada-Rice, D (2015) *Visual methods with children and young people.* London: Palgrave.
White, M.L. (2009) Ethnography 2.0: Writing with digital video. *Ethnography and Education* 4 (3), 389–414.
Wilson, G. (2017) Examining the differences between the use of wearable cameras and traditional cameras in research – A research note. *International Journal of Social Research Methodology* 20 (5), 525–532.

27

CRITICAL VISUAL DISCOURSE ANALYSIS

Peggy Albers, Vivian Maria Vasquez, and Jerome C. Harste

Introduction

To situate the studies in this chapter, we recognize image as a communicative event, one that elicits and invites viewers to participate (or not) vicariously in the lived worlds of those represented or objects featured. Informed by Gee's (2005) discourse analysis, critical visual discourse analysis (CVDA) is grounded in several semiotic and critical principles (Albers, Vasquez, & Harste, 2011). First, visual language is reflexive in that it has the capacity both to create and to reflect the context and reality in which it was created. The viewer is implicated to the degree of her or his familiarity with the context, as well as visual messages sent and interpreted by the viewer. Second, visual language creates opportunities for situated meanings. That is, interpretations and productions of visual data are produced in a given context and based upon previous experiences. Third, language is composed of many different social languages (Bakhtin, 1981), and visual designers and artists use different tools or media through which to communicate or carry out their intended message. Fourth, there are units of analysis within visual texts, including graphic, structural, semantic, pragmatic, and tactile (Albers, 2007), that focus attention on how art elements and principles of design operate in visual images, and which make visible discourses that become evident in the artwork.

Why CVDA

As critical literacy educators, we are very interested in how arts-based pedagogy intersects with critical literacy practices, and understand how images come to mean in print-based (e.g., magazines, billboards, posters, etc.) and digital spaces (e.g., pop-ups, forced viewings of ads, YouTube videos, etc.) (Albers, Vasquez, & Harste, 2017). Our work has increasingly argued for the systematic study of images as integral to critical knowing, and encourage participants to use art as a way to interrogate the everyday images and language we encounter, to understand the relationship between image and language, offer a lens through which to analyze images – both published and student-generated – and consider how art can be used to speak to and against social injustices. Theoretically, we have argued that images, like written texts, are embedded in an ideology of visibility (Albers et al., 2017; Johnson-Roullier, 2009–2010). Across our work, we have argued that visual language is marked with ideologies, beliefs, and practices (both producer and viewer) around which it is used, read, and applied. We position CVDA as both a theory and a method that drives analysis of visual data.

The phrase "What we see is what we get" implies nothing is hidden in what is seen. Yet, in an ideology of visibility, argues Johnson-Roullier (2009–2010), the self and other necessarily are in a "tangled maze of representations" (p. 28) in which what is "'real' becomes only that which can be seen, whether or not what is seen is the same as what actually is" (p. 28). Van Winkel (2005) argued that regimes of visibility seep through all aspects of culture, and the most "diverse forms of cultural production have reduced themselves (or allowed themselves to be reduced) to a number of visually mediatable aspects" (p. 1). For example, in digital spaces, we have discussed how pop-up advertisements work both as ideology and regime. In a simple search on *The New York Times* site for information, a viewer's interest in the top stories is interrupted by banners, not of headlines, but of advertisements for products and/or services. Further, before viewers can access a complete article, often they must view an ad or a sequence of ads – not by choice – but determined through a search engine's complex algorithms targeted personally to a viewer. There is little choice for a viewer in digital spaces to simply access information (e.g., news story) as they can in print-based texts. Readers are forced into viewing information they may not wish to read. Thus, viewers' desire to read the news online is entangled in a web of visual representations, both still and moving, which, as Fuchs (2016) argued, engenders a "colonization of societies and human spaces to open up new spaces of commodification and capital accumulation" (p. 62). Further, an unrelenting barrage of these visual ads becomes a regime of visibility, a systematic imposition of ads – mediatable aspects – targeted to a viewer's searches by search engines like Google, Yahoo, Bing, etc. We argue that attention to the visual mode is significant and critical, especially with young children who also are barraged with similar visual information. We suggest that CVDA provides analysts with a way to work through mazes of representations and regimes of visibility to understand ideologies and how they act on viewers to engage in particular practices, develop particular beliefs, and act in particular ways (Shannon, 2011).

As CVDA analysts, we acknowledge that all written texts reside in other texts, just as all readings of images reside in past readings. Thus, our aim in CVDA is to understand which art elements, structures, and discourses in commercially designed images inform teacher- and student-generated visual representations and their interpretations, and to what extent they are redesigned and/or reproduced in these texts. Said another way, we attempt to understand the mazes of representation that emerge in participants' visual productions. Questions that drive CVDA include the following (Vasquez, 2004):

- How do texts work?
- How do texts do what they do in constructing readers and viewers?
- How do we understand what texts attempt to do in the world and to people?
- Whose story is this? Who benefits from this story? Whose voices are heard and whose are not?
- Whose story is missing from this text? Whose story dominates this text?
- What modal and design choices do textmakers produce, and what ideologies/discourses underpin these choices?
- How do these modal and design choices position the viewer to read and respond to the image in particular ways?
- What alternative perspectives might be offered in reading/viewing between the lines/elements?
- How do we move students to take active stances with texts as a means to de-construct and re-construct the social spaces in which they live?

- How can students and teachers together see how texts work to construct their world, their cultures, and their identities in ideological ways?
- How can students and teachers come to know how they use texts and images in particular ways to put on offer particular ways of thinking, doing, or being?
- How can texts be used as social tools for re-constructing identities, cultures, and worldviews?

Using CVDA

We offer an example of CVDA from a study that we conducted in 2012 regarding teachers' critical work with advertisements. The purpose of this study was to understand how ads worked on participants as viewers and consumers, and the extent to which teachers, engaged in a critical literacy curriculum, learned the visual language with which to talk back to discourses of consumerism, especially through their construction of counter ads. In particular, we studied: (1) What messages do teachers speak to when they read and analyze advertisements? (2) How do teachers critically redesign a common advertisement through their production of counter ads? and (3) What can be learned from these counter ads for creating curriculum for young children? To situate their reading within a CVDA perspective, teachers learned and applied the grammar of visual design (orientation, vectors, colors, size, weight of object, etc.) to study the modal and design choices in advertisements, and critically studied the discourses that underpinned visual elements and messages conveyed (Harste & Albers, 2013). We then invited teachers to study commercially generated advertisements found in magazines, home improvement stores, and the internet, and to interpret and discuss discourses and messages they saw operating in these ads. Specifically, they responded to the following questions: What do you think the designer of this advertisement is selling? How are they selling this product/concept/idea? After these experiences, teachers in small groups chose one ad and redesigned it from a critical perspective (Harste & Albers, 2013).

Participants created a range of different counter ads, one of which was Figure 27.1. We present how we analyzed this image using CVDA. One group of participants chose the popular McDonald's Big Mac ad with the tag line, "the only cure for a Big Mac Attack, Attack, Attack, Attack, Attack" (each of the Attacks increases in size and shifts color, with a large photo of a Big Mac superimposed over the bottom two Attacks) (www.pinterest.com/redbeard1983/mcds/?lp=true). In the original ad, the viewer is compelled to engage in the visual appeal of the Big Mac, initiating a relationship between the viewer and the product in which the product is needed and used by the consumer. In the ad, the consumer's hunger attack becomes greater as it nears the Big Mac, symbolized by the increasing font size of the word "Attack." Stavrakakis (2006) argued that there is a challenge to "lessen the ideological grip of advertising fantasies" (p. 87); viewers are constructed as consumers who engage in the visual elements mediated as fantasy. While consumers of this product may think this product is good, because the Big Mac is an ATTACK on hunger, McDonald's is the clear financial beneficiary of engaging viewers in the fantasy of consuming, knowing that their product may result in health issues.

The group of teachers who created this counter ad deconstructed the original ad by first reading with the text to understand the relationship between one's health and food being constructed in order to read/speak against the discourses in place regarding this relationship. To do this, they use a similar design as the original ad. Structurally, the Big Mac remains at the lower center of the ad except that, in the new ad, ingredients symbolic of death have been added: five sets of skull and crossbones, electrocardiogram readouts, and RIP (rest in peace) repeated eight times. Written in bold black and red permanent markers, the text "Have YOU had a Mac Attack LATELY?" is an ironic response to the "only cure," the sandwich itself. The words "Mac

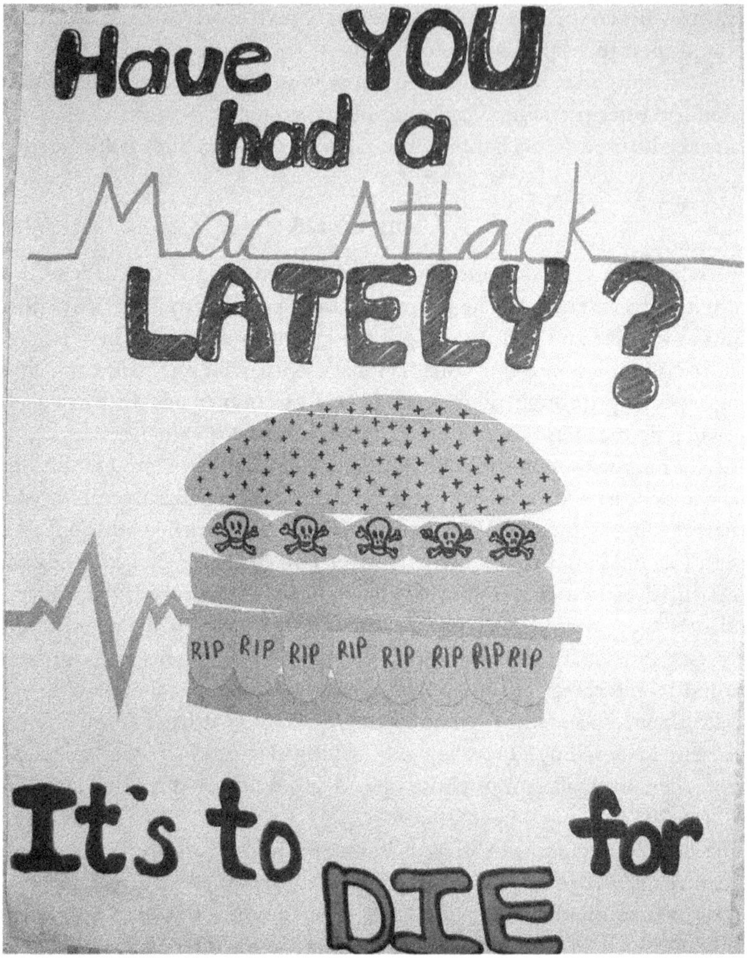

Figure 27.1 "Mac Attack" counter ad created by teachers in response to a McDonald's ad

Attack" are written as an electrocardiogram tape reading that represents heartbeats with the letter "k" in "attack" being drawn out into a flat line. The "attack" is not "a cure," but the cause of a lethal heart attack.

As a viewer, there is an immediate attraction to the image of the sandwich itself, which reveals a deeper message: discourses around eating fast food and health. Symbolized by repeated RIPs and skull and crossbones, these mediatable aspects of the counter ad are emphasized through repetition, and make visible possible lethal results of repeated consumption. Like the original ad, this group of teachers drew upon desire to engage the viewer in the fantasy of consuming this product. The product carries the weight of the ad, surrounded by large blocked fonts and use of vibrant colors of yellow, black, red, sky blue, and lavender colors, with words written in heavy black marker demanding viewers' attention (Kress & van Leeuwen, 2006). The word "DIE," written as a subscript in red and outlined in black, rests visibly at the bottom of the text, symbolic of – figuratively and literally – "six feet under," the final resting place for those who overly consume this product. While not visible, this group of teachers invited viewers into inquiry: What about this product may cause eventual death with overconsumption?

Metaphorically and literally, the teachers repackaged the ad to send a message that is critically clear: The Big Mac, "It's to DIE for."

The desire that advertisements creates, argued Stavrakakis (2006), is a nexus of consumer desire, lure of advertising fantasies, and identification with the product. Viewers are positioned in a consumer culture, one in which practices of desire and consumption are ideologically, physically, and emotionally embodied. Desire as a discourse has an authoritative hold on consumers. According to Jhally (1990), there must be a material-symbolic relationship between consumer and object. People's use of the object is the minimal starting point for the discourse concerning products/objects. In this counter ad, teachers have created this relationship. Like the original ad, they have repackaged the product in similar ways. Using the layered beauty of the sandwich itself, from the sesame seed bun to the tomato (skull and crossbones) and lettuce (RIPs), teachers produced a visual material-symbolic relationship with viewers, with the message of danger clearly evident in the product's use. At once, while teachers repackaged and questioned the original ad, they also organized their counter ad drawing upon those same aspects of desire (color, message, organization of objects, etc.). The advertising industry – and the companies who employ them – enjoy a "passive legitimization that adds to its hegemonic hold" (Stavrakakis, 2006, p. 87). By studying counter ads through CVDA, we identified which aspects of the original ad teachers chose to repackage, how they repackaged them, in terms of which modes and how they represented through these modes, and the extent to which they were able to offer alternative perspectives on a popular product. Studies that we have undertaken that involve CVDA, we suggest, provide researchers, teachers, and teachers of young children with an analytical tool to study the discourses that underpin the attractive designs in texts, like advertisements, that seduce consumers – including young children – with slick taglines and deliberate placement of objects. Awareness of messages, both those we see and those we and others create, we argue, is what makes democracy possible.

Rationale for using CVDA

Critical methods of reading and analyzing images and discourses that underpin them within and across different types of texts, for example, picturebooks, advertisements, public service announcements (PSAs), and video, have become more visible in literacy research (Albers et al., 2013). Scholars have outlined a range of analyses that have illuminated pathways into understanding how discourses emerge in image-based work and in different contexts. We articulate two reasons why studying image and how they act on young and older viewers are important. First, using CVDA demonstrates the importance that educators and researchers become consciously aware of how arts-based images, media, and digital texts work. Awareness of material-symbolic relationships between viewer and object positions viewers to read images more critically. In that way, CVDA allows for the development of a set of new media skills that enable researchers, teachers, and their students alike to interrogate and critically analyze media texts such as advertisements, YouTube videos, website images, and so on, and participate more fully and democratically in a media-rich world. Second, of critical importance is knowing, studying, and understanding the role of structures, elements, and discourses that play out in all types of visual texts. Visual language, like written language, can become a language of critique. Viewers learn this language that allows them to understand and question how images mean and how they encourage particular beliefs and social practices, especially as they encounter messages that financially benefit large corporations and their own interests (Albers et al., 2008).

We have studied the visual, media, and digital texts of hundreds of participants, from young children to pre- and in-service educators and administrators. We have used children's literature, advertisements, digital devices, and electronics (among others) in our studies to understand and adopt critical stances towards research and education. Our work with young children and teachers of young children has led us to understand that images shape the mindsets, identities, and practices of young children both at home and at school. Our studies have produced significant insights into why CVDA is an important tool in the classroom and in research. First, children have the capacity to engage in deep thinking and analytical understandings of a range of texts, and ask sophisticated questions about everyday texts, like cereal boxes, candy wrappers, and school/class posters. Second, young children who grapple with social issues (e.g., gender, poverty, religion, translanguaging) can learn how to speak against the inequalities that exist in their lives. Third, children speak visibly through their images. Teachers who read images with intentionality and systematically can address issues that children present in their drawings. Fourth, teachers who are knowledgeable about image analysis can create curriculum for young children that opens up what literacy looks like, and the many ways in which communication can be expressed.

Examples of studies analyzing data through CVDA

Across our professional lives, we have conducted a number of studies with young children and teachers of young children that involved the use of CVDA. We suggest that researchers can work with a range of data when using CVDA. For example, in one study (Fisher et al., 2014), we examined the images of a six-year-old boy, John, who drew how he misbehaved and how he would "make a better choice" on school behavioral forms. As his primary mode of written communication and over time, John's images evolved from active participation in class to images of anger, violence, and power, to images of isolation and hopelessness (Figure 27.2)

CVDA forced us to problematize the use of visual imagery as a punitive endeavor in literacy, and to interrogate how art was used to reify concepts of "good children" versus "bad children." We argued educators must study all communicative forms of children, including those on behavior forms that may seem benign, to understand how children's images communicate their social practices, motivations, origins, and destinations. In another study with grade three children (Albers et al., 2009), we investigated how children visually interpreted and represented gender. After studying and discussing gender stereotypes in fairy tales in a six-week unit on gender and how women and men can take on alternative roles, we asked girls to represent the activities they thought boys liked, and asked boys to represent the activities they thought girls liked. Despite discussions of stereotypes, all but several children represented women/girls and men/boys in traditional gender roles.

In the next section, we present a more in-depth discussion of other studies in which we have used advertisements, picturebooks, word clouds, and technology devices as data.

Using CVDA to analyze illustrations in children's literature

In our article (Albers et al., 2011) "Interrupting Certainty and Making Trouble: Teachers' Written and Visual Responses to Picturebooks," we studied both the visual and written responses of two groups of teachers, one from the US and one from Canada (N=41), to three picturebooks we saw as conveying social issues, *Willy & Hugh* (Browne, 2000), *Sister Anne's Hands* (Loribecki, 2000), and *Into the Forest* (Browne, 2005). Teachers in the US primarily conveyed their understanding of these picturebooks through image while the Canadian teachers responded through written and voiced reflections. We wanted to know to what extent two different groups of participants were growing in their ability to identify explicit (easily seen images/words) and implicit (hidden/subtext) visual and/or written messages in these books.

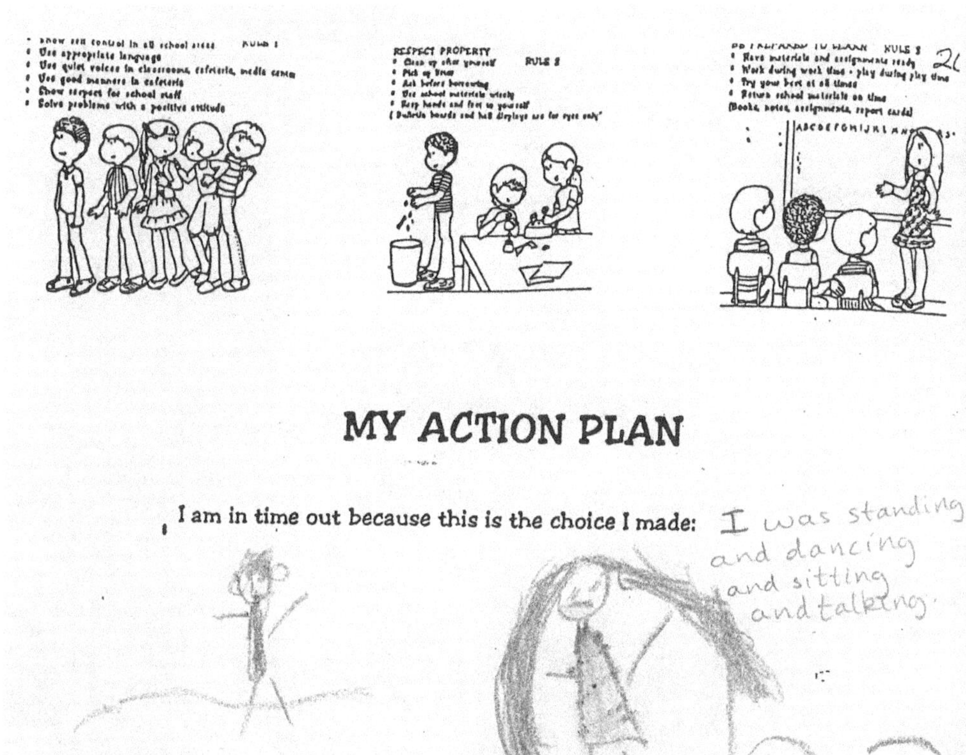

Figure 27.2 Series of three drawings by John

MY ACTION PLAN

I am in time out because this is the choice I made:

Next time I will make a better choice by........

Name Date

Parent Signature Date

Figure 27.2 (Continued)

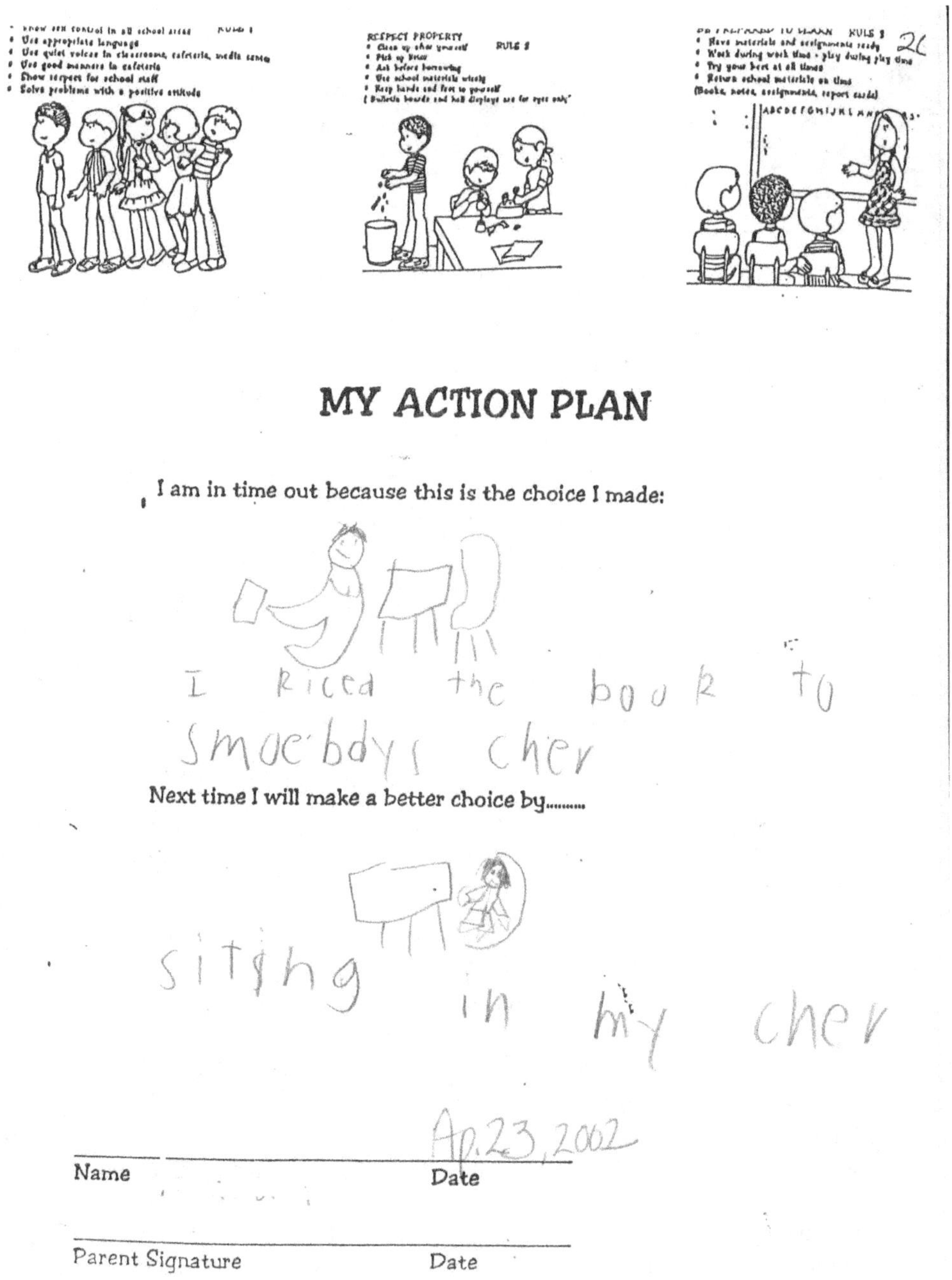

Figure 27.2 (Continued)

We used critical discourse analysis (Rogers, 2013) to study written responses and CVDA to study visual responses (Albers, 2007). We looked at both groups and how they represented their understanding of these picturebooks, and developed a table to analyze how image and word across groups expressed discourses that emerged. Canadian teachers as a group were much better

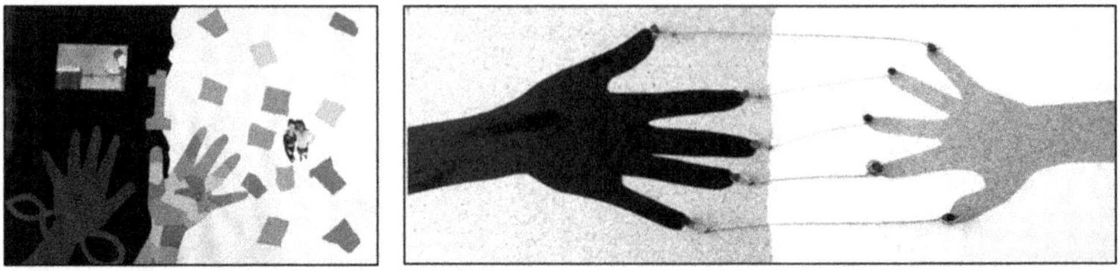

Figure 27.3 Single discourse represented visually, using common symbols

at identifying explicit messages in text (those signed by either words or pictures) than they were at identifying implicit messages.

They seemed better able to articulate verbally their critiques of books than write about them. In the US group, teachers drew upon their knowledge of the grammar of visual design (Kress & van Leeuwen, 2006) and visual discourse analysis (Albers, 2007, 2013) to represent the complexity of discourses they saw operating in these picturebooks. They often saw only a single discourse emerge to visually render a solution to the issue, like bullying (*Willy & Hugh*). Significant to this study, CVDA enabled us to see how easily common assumptions about issues (bullying, racism, traditional family units) are visually (and easily) reproduced as dominant discourses. After reading *Sister Anne's Hands*, participants visually represented racism, for example, through iconic symbols and multi-colored objects (hands, squares), with race visually and metaphorically separated by line. Race was treated as an issue of equality rather than an issue of dominance, access, diversity, or desire (Janks, 2010) (Figure 27.3). By opening up spaces to understand regimes of visibility (van Winkel, 2005) and engaging participants in discussions of how discourses become internalized and reproduced in their own images, they became more critically aware of how and which images acted on them, and the cultural – and hegemonic – hold that these symbols had on how they represent dominant discourses.

Using CVDA to study word clouds

In their book, *Technology and Critical Literacy in Early Childhood* (Vasquez & Felderman, 2012), Vivian writes about an inquiry that she and her son TJ led with a group of young children (aged five to six years) in a co-op class and their parents just outside Washington, DC., in which they planted tomatoes, a study that Vivian called the "Tomato Trials" (p. 65–75). Vivian used Wordle, a word cloud software program, to study an inquiry project on planting, specifically tomatoes, which was part of the early childhood curriculum. This group of young children and adults used the tools of technology not just to seek information, but as a tool for critically analyzing the information they would gather on planting. The group analyzed a TV commercial, the Topsy Turvey Tomato Planter, which was available on YouTube. Children studied the commercial designer's use of black and white and color video. The children noticed that black/white video was used to convey "back-breaking work" of planting tomatoes and featured a man. When the Topsy Turvey Tomato Planter was introduced, the commercial turned to color featuring a woman effortlessly planting tomatoes. Children discussed the overt message that only men can do back-breaking work, with the implicit message suggesting that women cannot. Children also compared two websites, Topsy Turvey and a Vegetable Garden site, using Wordle. Wordle gave prominence to the frequency in which particular words appeared in the online article. In the Vegetable Garden site, children identified which words in the word cloud were the largest, like "tomatoes," "grow," "plant," and "garden," important words about planting tomatoes. They then analyzed the Topsy Turvey site, and noticed that the most frequent words used were "Topsy Turvy," "order," and "step," important words about ordering this product. Children generated multiple uses and functions for Wordle: (1) analysis: to compare/contrast website articles to see which words are more frequently used and how readers/viewers are positioned, for example, gardeners or consumers; (2) editing: studying which words are used too frequently in a written text; (3) promoting and advertising: generating words to promote what a text might be about; and (4) art: to see Wordles as shapes, colors, metaphors, and symbols that can be overlaid onto photographs and other artworks.

Using CVDA to analyze teacher-generated paintings

Jerry conducted a series of workshops with teachers working with the paintings of artist Jacob Lawrence, an African American Harlem Renaissance painter (Harste et al., 2007). Teachers identified a critical issue they felt strongly about, and used any element of Jacob Lawrence's artwork that they wanted to produce a painting that addressed this issue. Jerry introduced teachers to Jacob Lawrence by showing them some of his artwork, and talked about how Jacob Lawrence, single-handedly almost, alerted the world to what the black experience meant to African Americans growing up in the United States. He also showed the video *Jacob Lawrence: The Glory of Expression* (Freeman, 1999), after which he invited participants to try to take a critical stance for themselves on some aspect of literacy they felt strongly about. They wrote short reflections on what they were trying to say in their artwork and distilled their reflections into four-line poems that captured their intent and accompanied their paintings. In these studies, Jerry had done all this work analyzing these texts using ongoing critical literacy methods of analysis (Harste et al., 2007). However, when we reanalyzed these texts together and applied CVDA, we were surprised at what we found. Using CVDA allowed us to consider how teachers as artists positioned the people, objects, and their understanding of literacy in their paintings. The significance of this analysis was a breakthrough for us in terms of what it meant to be critical. How teachers viewed literacy, who gets to participate in literacy, and how they participate became much clearer in their paintings and four-line poems. We saw, for example, in Figure 27.4, how teachers understood and valued literacy in the traditional sense of reading (the book) and writing (book's content), visually representing literacy as knowing how to read and write. The poem also clearly represented this understanding, "Open wide this book/and enter in." This research allowed us to understand that despite all of what researchers at the time were doing to analyze data, they were not necessarily taking a pragmatic approach. Rather, they attended more closely to the semantic and syntactic systems of meaning operating in texts (Vasquez et al., 2017).

Using CVDA to analyze critical redesigning with technology

In 2016, we taught a summer institute focused on critical redesign and making with teachers and administrators (Vasquez et al., 2017) working with wet media, clay, and technology. We studied how knowledge of these modes could support children's reading and production of images. Questions we asked included the following: Is making different from inquiry? What is the relationship between making and critical literacy? What role does critical literacy play in making? We were interested in how teachers used modes (visual, spatial, digital, written, among others) to represent a social issue. In Vivian's technology workshop, institute participants created satirical art, from a critical literacy perspective, using a discarded piece of technology. The redesigned objects and their titles were data, alongside the discussion that accompanied these

Figure 27.4 Teachers drew upon Jacob Lawrence to make visual and written statements on critical literacy issue

projects. We studied teachers' processes of redesign, the critical response to their project, and the extent to which they conveyed a message that positioned viewers and makers to take social action and/or be aware of the social issues that underpinned this redesign.

Where CVDA gets us

Activist, author, and conservationist Terry Tempest Williams (Toms & Williams, 2006) argued for the importance of an ethical stance towards life. She stated, "I think that, as children, the art that we are raised with seeps into our blood stream. It becomes part of our DNA." We suggest that CVDA enables us to understand, to some extent, participants' DNA – the origin(s) of their representations and the discourses that underpin these representations. Further, CVDA enables us to engage participants of all ages in critical discussions and reflections on how texts – theirs and others – work in terms of modes, art elements, structural organization of objects, etc. We pose that the significance of CVDA lies in the reading, production, and analysis of visual and digital texts, texts that continually shape our "DNA," and help us understand how we, as researchers, can build a more critically aware citizenry.

First, critical literacy provides children with another set of media skills to understand how power and language operate within texts. Discourse analysis and critical discourse analysis are often applied to print-based and/or written texts, while visual discourse analysis is applied to school-generated and commercially generated visual texts. In combinatorial relationship, CVDA enables us to more systematically apply structural and discursive analyses to a range of visual and digital texts. As texts become increasingly modally mixed and complex, we suggest that CVDA provides a tool of analysis that can be applied to these intricate texts.

Second, as teacher educators and researchers, we invite young children and teachers to engage in practices driven by visual and digital modes and represent across modes, such as Wordles, paintings, and podcasts (Vasquez & Felderman, 2012), among others. CVDA positions us well to study how modes operate, the relationship between and among material-symbol-textmaker, and discourses that are culturally and linguistically embedded in representations. While we are well versed in conventional methods of qualitative analysis and have together authored a number of research studies, we also turn to other disciplines to build upon our work with CVDA. For example, we draw specifically upon art as a discipline to help us as researchers to respond to the function and value of art, both as an aesthetic object and as an object created from social practices, and to understand the role of the arts in making life meaningful. When this happens, new understandings are made in experience, and new ways of working in the world are opened (Greene, 2001). For example, texts like word clouds are not mere linguistic arrangements of words, but highlight the discourses that underpin written text through visual means. In essence, then, visually representing as a social practice involves understanding how art is a way of doing things in the everyday. Critical visual discourse analysis enables us to understand the social practices around which visual texts are produced – the mazes of representation, how different texts operate on viewers, and how participants represent others and objects in their own texts – and interpret the "DNA" or origins of these representations through discursive and structural approaches.

Practical application and future of CVDA

Maxine Greene (1995) argued that the ethical, the political, and the social cannot be separated from the imagination. We concur and argue that CVDA provides both a theory and method through which imagination in research is inextricably connected to the ethical, the political, and the social, and positions us as researchers to understand new possibilities in data. In this section, we offer some practical applications and the future of CVDA.

1. When research involves visual representations (print-based and/or digital), remixed texts, children's literature, graphic novels, etc., we argue that the researcher must have a mindset that art as a discipline is amenable to analysis, and does not always necessitate a textmaker's interpretation of her/his text. The humanities are filled with scholarly interpretations of classic artworks, classic literature, sculptures, and so on, and have been read, studied, and analyzed through a range of different lenses (critical, political, artistic, religious, etc.) with conclusions drawn and supported by disciplinary principles that guide this analysis. Critical visual discourse analysis is an approach to reading visual representations that systematically draws upon a number of disciplines including literacy, art, sociology, semiotics, among others to understand phenomena. Our analysis of a counter ad presented earlier demonstrates the complexity of CVDA which necessitates structural, discursive, and disciplinary understandings.
2. Research that involves analysis of visual representations should start from an inquiry perspective. For example, Vivian's work with the Tomato Trials shows that young children ask sophisticated questions when viewing infomercials to understand gendered roles and particular work, and techniques, like color, emphasize these roles. Peggy's work with children's

drawings signals the importance of looking at children's images across time and discursively to better understand how to support them, and to understand how young children easily reproduce gender stereotypes despite sustained discussions on alternative roles. Jerry's work with teachers' representations of literacy and how people and objects are positioned in paintings encourages all of us to critically look at how we have had our hands in the cookie jar, despite our good intentions, and how we might reposition ourselves more ethically in the world. We suggest, then, that work with CVDA enables people to learn to read image and discern ideologies and regimes of visibility that underpin these images.

3 If researchers are interested in CVDA, studies can be designed around visual representations that participants read, interpret, and reproduce. Our study of children's literature was designed with two clear representational modes in mind: written reflection/interpretation and visual representation. We wanted to understand how messages in children's literature are communicated, how participants responded to the systems of meaning in these picturebooks, and to what extent critical literacy informed their representations. By designing studies in this way, teachers can use CVDA with young children to read, interpret, analyze, and engage in sophisticated discussion of critical issues in children's literature.

Conclusion

Eisner (2003) argued that "not everything knowable can be articulated in propositional form" (p. 379). We suggest that CVDA is a move towards knowing across modes rather than within one mode – written language – which often prevails in literacy research. We also forward that CVDA involves risky readings of visual representations that address social issues (Harste et al., 2000). Said another way, we position our analyses to look intentionally and differently at visual elements that comprise participants' representations to understand what, where, and how underpinning discourses emerge and the practices around which representations are produced. In so doing, we lift the "lid of education" and see "the stuff inside . . . as the stuff of revolt" (Britzman, 1994, p. 276). That is, we take on critical researcher roles that imagine literacy education as something different – as something that signifies the importance of visual modes to communicate freshly – and which surprises itself through study findings. In working with CVDA, we recognize that art gives rise to ideas in studies that other systems of meaning may not, and allows us to imagine something different in data than what is often normalized and repressive.

Note

1 Hereafter called viewers.

References

Albers, P. (2007) Visual discourse analysis: An introduction to the analysis of school-generated visual texts. In: Rowe, D.W., Jimenez, R.T. Compton, D.L., Dickinson, D.K., Kim, Y., Leander, K.M. and Risko, V.J. (eds.) *56th Yearbook of the National Reading Conference*. Oak Creek, WI: NRC, 81–95.

Albers, P. (2013) Visual discourse analysis. In: Albers, P., Flint, A.S. and Holbrook, T. (eds.) *New methods of literacy research*. New York: Routledge, 85–98.

Albers, P., Flint, A.S. and Holbrook, T. (2013) *New methods of literacy research*. New York: Routledge.

Albers, P., Frederick, T. and Cowan, K. (2009) Features of gender: A study of the visual texts of third grade students. *Journal of Early Childhood Literacy* 9 (2), 243–269.

Albers, P., Harste, J.C. and Vasquez, V. (2011) Making trouble and interrupting certainty: Teachers' critical and visual responses to children's literature. In: Dunston, P.J., Gambrell, L.B., Fullerton, S.K., Gillis, V.R., Headley, K. and Stecker, P.M. (eds.) *60th Yearbook of the Literacy Research Association*. Oak Creek, WI: LRA, 68–83.
Albers, P., Vasquez, V.M. and Harste, J.C. (2008) A classroom with a view: Teachers, multimodality and new literacies. *Talking Points* 19 (2), 3–13.
Albers, P., Vasquez, V. and Harste, J.C. (2011) Making visual analysis critical. In: Lapp, D. and Fisher, D. (ed.) *The handbook of research on teaching the English language arts* (3rd edition). New York: Routledge, 195–201.
Albers, P., Vasquez, V.M. and Harste, J.C. (2017) Critically reading image in digital times. In: Mills, K., Pandya, J., Stornaiuolo, A. and Smith, A. (eds.) *Handbook of writing, literacies and education in digital culture*. New York: Routledge, 223–234.
Bakhtin, M.M. (1981) *The dialogic imagination: Four essays*. Austin, TX: University of Texas.
Britzman, D.P. (1994) Reconsideration: "On doing something more." [Review of the book *The public school and the private vision: A search for America in education and literature* by Maxine Greene]. *Educational Studies* 25 (4), 273–282.
Browne, A. (2000) *Willy and hugh*. Sydney, AU: Red Fox.
Browne, A. (2005) *Into the forest*. London: Walker Books Ltd.
Eisner, E.W. (2003) The arts and the creation of mind. *Language Arts* 80, 340–344.
Fisher, T., Albers, P. and Frederick, T. (2014) When pictures aren't pretty: Deconstructing punitive literacy practices. *Journal of Early Childhood Education* 14 (3), 291–318.
Freeman, L. (Director/Producer). (1999) *Jacob Lawrence: The glory of expression* [Motion Picture]. USA. L&S Studios.
Fuchs, C. (2016). *Social media: An introduction*. Thousand Oaks, CA: Sage Publications, Inc.
Gee, J. (2005) *An introduction to discourse analysis: Theory and method* (2nd edition). Abingdon: Routledge.
Greene, M. (1995) *Releasing the imagination: Essays on education, the arts, and social change*. San Francisco, CA: Jossey-Bass.
Greene, M. (2001) *Variations on a blue guitar: The Lincoln Center Institute lectures on aesthetic education*. New York: Teachers College Press.
Harste, J.C. and Albers, P. (2013) "I'm riskin' it": Teachers take on consumerism. *Journal of Adolescent and Adult Literacy* 56 (6), 1–10.
Harste, J.C., Leland, C.H., Grant, S., Chung, M.H. and Enyeart, J.A. (2007) Analyzing art in language arts research. In: Rowe, D.W., Jiménez, R.T., Compton, D.L., Dickinson, D.K., Kim, Y., Leander, K.M. and Risko, V.J. (eds.) *56th yearbook of the National Reading Conference*. Oak Creek, WI: National Reading Conference, 254–265.
Harste, J., Vasquez, V., Lewison, M., Beau, A., Leland, C., & Ociepka, A. (2000). Supporting critical conversation in classrooms: A review of more than 50 picture books and young adult novels. In: K. M. Pierce (Ed.). *Adventuring with books* (4th ed.). Urbana, IL: National Council of Teachers of English, pp. 507–544.
Janks, H. (2010) *Literacy and power*. New York: Routledge.
Jhally, S. (1990) *The codes of advertising*. New York: Routledge.
Johnson-Roullier, C. (2009–2010) 'Blackness', modernity, and the ideology of visibility in the Harlem Renaissance. *Review of International America Studies* 4 (2–3), 25–29.
Kress, G. and van Leeuwen, T. (2006) *Reading images: The grammar of visual design* (2nd edition). New York: Routledge.
Loribecki, M. (2000) *Sister Anne's hands*. New York: Puffin Books.
Rogers, R. (2013) Critical discourse analysis in literacy education. In: Albers, P., Flint, A.S. and Holbrook, T. (eds.) *New methods of literacy research*. New York: Routledge, 19–39.
Shannon, P. (2011) *Reading wide awake: Politics, pedagogies, and possibilities*. New York: Teachers College Press.
Stavrakakis, Y. (2006) Objects of consumption, causes of desire: Consumerism and advertising in societies of commanded enjoyment. *Gamma* 14, 83–106.
Toms, M. and Williams, T.T. (2006) The transformative power of art: An interview with Terry Tempest Williams. In: Austin, M. (ed.) *Voice in the Wilderness*. Boulder, CO: University Press of Colorado, 115–130.
van Winkel, C. (2005) *The regime of visibility*. The Netherlands: NAi.

Vasquez, V. (2004) *Negotiating critical literacies with young children*. Mahwah, NJ: Lawrence Erlbaum Associates.

Vasquez, V., Albers, P., Harste, J.C. (2010) From the personal to the worldwide web: Moving teachers into positions of critical interrogation. In: Baker, E.A. (ed.) *The new literacies: Multiple perspectives on research and practice*. New York: Guildford Press, 265–284.

Vasquez, V.M. and Felderman, C. (2012) *Technology and critical literacy in early childhood*. New York: Routledge.

Vasquez, V.M., Harste, J.C. and Albers, P. (2017, Nov. 30). *Making literacies critical*. Paper Presented at the Annual Conference of the Literacy Research Association, Tampa, FL.

28

USING TABLET TECHNOLOGY IN PRESCHOOL AND EARLY KINDERGARTEN FOR THE IDENTIFICATION OF CHILDREN AT RISK FOR READING DIFFICULTIES

Sibylla Leon Guerrero, Ola Ozernov-Palchik, Michelle Gonzalez, Jennifer Zuk and Nadine Gaab

Introduction

In 2016, approximately 3.8 million children in the United States entered public school kindergartens (NCES, 2016), joining the estimated 656 million children of primary-school age worldwide (United Nations Department of Economic and Social Affairs, 2017), where they embarked on a journey of learning to read and write, skills that will carry them through high school and beyond. For up to 20% of these children across different languages and countries, this journey carries with it a risk of school failure due to an inability to learn to read as expected (Brunswick et al., 2010; Elliott & Grigorenko, 2014; Görker et al., 2017; Shaywitz et al., 1990; Ziegler & Goswami, 2005). Intervention research demonstrates that targeted, evidence-based programs in kindergarten and first grade can substantially improve reading outcomes for those children who require intensive intervention in order to become successful readers (e.g. Catts et al., 2015; Fricke et al., 2013; Hatcher et al., 1994; Hatcher et al., 2004; Torgesen, 2000; Vellutino et al., 2004). However, pre- and beginning readers are not routinely screened for risk in part due to the formidable logistical and financial challenges of providing millions of children with a full clinical assessment of the language and cognitive skills that are precursors to reading. One solution to the impracticality of administering a full diagnostic assessment to every child is a rapid screener that would identify children with an elevated risk of reading failure. Such a screener would provide a systematic and reliable basis for close monitoring and evidence-based instruction within a general education setting. Further, a screener that pointed to resources, teacher-training opportunities and evidence-based instructional strategies could aid parents, daycare providers and teachers to address weaknesses in the component skills of reading before or without formal diagnosis. In the following sections, we first describe the research on reading demonstrating that early screening is not only feasible but also necessary in order to prevent reading failure. Next, we outline the critical components of a high-quality screening tool for early reading risk and describe the unique supports and considerations that digital technologies, and in particular tablet apps, bring to bear on screening young children. We share our app development process as one example of the ways in which mobile technology can serve as a tool for the assessment of risk. Finally, we highlight potential clinical and educational implications of early screening.

Typical reading development

For individuals with typical reading development, reading may be an effortless and automatic activity. However, underlying skilled reading is a multifaceted network of competencies for both understanding language meaning and recognizing printed words (Rumelhart, 1994; Scarborough, 2001; Vellutino et al., 2007). General language competencies include knowledge of word meanings, facts and concepts, as well as mastery of grammar and the structure of language at the sentence, text and discourse levels (Flax et al., 2009; Hemphill & Tivnan, 2008; Scarborough, 2001). Word recognition requires skill with phonology, the sounds of a language and orthography, the written symbols associated with those sounds (Stanovich & West, 1989). In addition, the automatic recognition of familiar sight words is essential to fluent and rapid reading, particularly in languages such as English in which there are frequent exceptions to regular 'rules' for spelling and sound correspondence (Cunningham & Stanovich, 1997). Thus, children must learn both to understand a spoken system of language and also to decipher printed words corresponding to that oral language by recognizing patterns in sound and visual symbols in order to become successful readers.

Predictive indicators of general language and printed word-reading competencies can be found even before children have begun to read: *vocabulary knowledge* and *oral sentence comprehension* measure early oral language skills upon which later reading comprehension and reading fluency depend (Catts et al., 2016; Hulme et al., 2015). *Phonological awareness* and *phonological memory* are indicators of pre-readers' ability to perceive, remember and manipulate the sounds that distinguish words, and *rapid automatized naming* and *letter-sound* knowledge demonstrate pre-readers' ability to integrate oral and visual symbols in language. Remarkably, although these constructs do not directly involve reading words or text, in preschool and kindergarten these six constructs are good predictors of later reading success and failure (Catts et al., 2015; Gilger et al., 1996; Lyytinen et al., 2015; Pennington & Lefly, 2001; Scarborough, 1989; Snowling et al., 2003; Snowling & Melby-Lervåg, 2016; Torgesen, 2000).

Atypical reading development

Although individuals typically display a broad spectrum of ability in both reading and its precursor skills (Snowling et al., 2003), in this article we address the lower end of the spectrum, termed in the clinical literature 'specific learning disability in reading' or 'developmental dyslexia'. We understand this condition from a developmental perspective as an atypical, neurocognitive variation (Gilger & Kaplan, 2001), and one that bears profound consequences for children's educational success in a modern learning environment that heavily relies upon fluent, rapid reading. When individuals with such variation, which we call 'reading difficulties' in this article, do not receive appropriate intervention, the consequences can be devastating: children who do not learn to read in elementary school risk not only academic failure but also the social and psychological consequences of this failure that include poor self-esteem, anxiety and negative life outcomes (McArthur et al., 2016; Mugnaini et al., 2009; Quinn et al., 2001). These negative outcomes may be preventable as early differences in the component skills that are foundational for reading can be detected in preschool and kindergarten. Early detection of reading risk is especially important, as the earlier intervention occurs in a child's schooling, the more successful the intervention is likely to be (Hatcher et al., 1994; Wanzek et al., 2013).

Early timing of intervention is further supported by neurobiology research indicating that the development of networks of brain regions commonly associated with language and the integrative processing required in skilled reading is influenced by modifiable factors such as practice with language and literacy in addition to environmental factors such as socioeconomic status (e.g. years of parental education), and also genetics (Logan et al., 2013; Norton et al., 2015; Ozernov-Palchik et al., 2016; Taylor et al., 2010). Variations in reading abilities are associated with neurobiological differences that emerge early in brain development, particularly in left-hemispheric areas and networks related to reading (Ozernov-Palchik et al., 2016). Brain differences in these reading-related regions are already evident in infants (Leppänen et al., 2010; Langer et al., 2017) and pre-reading children (Raschle et al., 2012) who have a family history of reading difficulty, suggesting that atypical brain characteristics may predate reading failure and can be targeted even before children learn to read.

Although evidence from neurobiology, intervention research and clinical psychology supports the efficacy of early identification and intervention before children have begun to fail, in the U.S. children are often referred to clinical evaluation only after several years of failing to learn to read as expected, and the process of determining need for intervention is a lengthy one, often taking many months. In many schools, children do not receive intensive intervention until the third grade or later, when they have failed to learn to read and are also well past the optimal window for intervention (Ozernov-Palchik & Gaab, 2016). This late timing of intervention has limited efficacy: children who start out as below-average readers in first grade, on average, continue to show below-average performance in fourth grade (Juel, 1988) and on into high school (Landerl & Wimmer, 2008; Shaywitz, 1999).

Early identification and screening

As research demonstrates, early identification and instructional support can provide a viable alternative to reading failure (Hatcher et al., 1994; Torgesen, 2000; Wanzek et al., 2013). Based on the research discussed in the previous paragraph examining predictors of reading outcomes, we propose that an early screener for reading difficulties in preschool and early kindergarten should evaluate seven indicators: phonological awareness, phonological memory, rapid naming, letter-sound knowledge, vocabulary, oral comprehension and familial risk for reading difficulty. With such a screener, we might support individual needs and risk profiles within the home, community or general education context. In this way, early difficulties with language or other foundational skills that are crucial for skilled reading may be remediated through intensive and evidence-based responses to screening such that later clinical diagnoses are tempered or not required.

The idea that early support for reading development is efficacious and desirable is certainly not new: the importance of pre-reading literacy skills and kindergarten and pre-literacy intervention strategies that address those skills has also long been recognized in educational research and practice (Lonigan et al., 2011; Snow et al., 1998) and has resulted in numerous early literacy assessment tools. A large proportion of these rely upon word reading with the result that their predictive power depends upon previous exposure to decoding instruction. While fluent word reading in and after first grade does predict later reading outcomes, word-reading tasks are unable to distinguish children at risk for reading failure without prior instruction. Thus, for the purpose of pre-reader screening, we discuss in the next section only those early literacy assessments that do not rely on word reading. These measures can be divided into three general categories: composite batteries, curriculum-based formative assessments and rapid screeners.

Overview of existing early literacy screeners

Perhaps the most effective and widely available current screening batteries for pre-readers are composites of diagnostic standardized assessments that include all key component areas of phonological awareness, phonological memory, rapid automatized naming, letter (sound) knowledge, vocabulary and oral language comprehension. These largely non-digital assessments are conducted one-on-one by a professional with a child using visual stimuli in paper presentation books and/or recorded audio stimuli played on a recorder or MP3 player. While currently no single commercial battery encompasses all component areas, clinical or school evaluators and testing companies are able to compose 'packages' of assessments that are tailored for the screening of young children and generally include tasks that have been validated and nationally normed with young children. Children's performance is scaled on a normative distribution with the lowest quantiles as markers of risk (although many measures were normed on relatively small and non-representative samples). Composite batteries have high reliability and validity as well as predictive value demonstrated in scientifically validated research and are ideal for clinical diagnosis. However as screeners, composite batteries are extensive and often time-consuming, requiring anywhere from one to three hours to complete. Clinical batteries of standardized assessments require trained staff to administer tasks to children on a one-to-one basis, score children's responses and interpret the results for a lay audience. Most standardized assessments are costly and sold under requirement of extensive clinical or academic training at the graduate level, a staffing resource not available to most schools and clinics for screening all pre-readers. Thus, although composite batteries are effective and comprehensive diagnostic tools, they are not a feasible method of widely screening pre-readers for reading risk.

Pre-readers may also be screened through curriculum-based, formative early literacy assessments evaluating the child's progress in a sequence of curricular program objectives, levels or benchmarks. Often employed as program screeners, these formative assessments are less expensive and time-consuming than composite batteries, requiring from only four to sixty minutes to administer. Although many curriculum-based assessments are only available in paper-and-pencil format, others are digital and may even incorporate game-like elements such as animated characters, goals and rewards to motivate completion when measuring multiple, independent component skills. Intended for use on a large scale, potentially with all children in a classroom or entering a school, these tests are often more user-friendly than standardized batteries and may require little to no training to administer while providing automated scoring and interpretive reports. In addition, tools published by universities or education districts may have been reported in peer-reviewed forums and have passed through psychometric validation studies. However, formative assessments generally focus on proximal skills salient in the classroom environment, are oriented towards next steps for instruction in specific curricular programs and are criterion- rather than norm-referenced. Often not constructed to provide a normative testing distribution, they may lack sensitivity or specificity to accurately identify individual children who fall in a critically low quantile of the population as a whole (Catts et al., 2009; Jenkins et al., 2007; Johnson et al., 2009).

The third and rapidly growing category of reading screening tools comprises rapid screeners, defined as brief curriculum-independent assessments whose goal is a fast but sensitive and specific, categorical classification of children as at-risk or not for later reading failure (Johnson et al., 2009). Several screeners, though of uncertain efficacy, exist in questionnaire format. Most validated pre-reading screeners directly test one or more of the component skills of reading: those that assess multiple reading components have higher sensitivity and specificity than those that target a single skill (Jenkins et al., 2007; Ozernov-Palchik et al., 2017). There is currently not one screener that directly tests all seven optimally predictive components outlined earlier, and phonological awareness and/or letter-sound knowledge are the most common sub-skills evaluated. Many screeners are paper-based, though digital tests are increasingly available from private commercial entities or public initiatives by states and institutes of higher education. While some commercial screeners are costly, others, often online screeners, are easily accessible, available at low-cost and generally do not require extensive training to administer while providing automated scoring and score interpretation. Furthermore, digital technology has enabled some of these tools to incorporate creativity and imagination in engaging children through game-like tasks. For example, the need to evaluate multiple disparate component skills is well-served both by the content gamification of a meaningful story line and animated characters and also by structural gamification features such as a journey or quest, badges, points and levelled play (Deterding et al., 2011). However, the principal drawback of many commercial rapid online screeners is their lack of psychometric evaluation: only eight of the over fifty rapid pre-reader screeners we examined for the purpose of this paper have published peer-reviewed validation studies, all emerging from state or public institution screening initiatives. While rapid digital screeners hold great promise for the future of reading risk screening, it is critical that these tests be constructed in a valid and scientifically supported manner, provide a normative score indicating risk and encompass the pre-reading skills that have been demonstrated to predict later reading success (Glover & Albers, 2007). As there is no single screener that meets all of these criteria, at present a comprehensive reading screening initiative must employ several disparate tools for a comprehensive assessment of reading risk.

Developing a tablet screener

One way in which an optimal screening tool can be constructed to be resourceful, comprehensive and developmentally appropriate is through the incorporation of mobile digital technologies. Tablets and mobile apps incorporate features that are uniquely suited to the developmental capabilities of the young child: in 2013, an average of 72% of U.S. preschoolers engaged with mobile technology on a daily basis (Rideout et al., 2013). Touch technology accommodates young children's still-developing fine motor capacities by allowing simple gestures to convey complex intentions (Rust et al., 2014). Individualized feedback provides cognitive scaffolding through hints or cues and also affective scaffolding through verbal encouragement and other forms of extrinsic reward (Yelland & Masters, 2007). Advances in hardware technology allow devices to be constructed at a comfortable handling weight and size for young children (Petersen, 2015). While research is still inconclusive regarding best practices for integrating technology into children's learning in developmentally beneficial ways (Spektor-Levy et al., 2017), as the chapters by Sylva and Roberts and by Lee in this volume discuss, tablets and mobile apps are a highly accessible technology for young children facilitating not only entertainment, but also social interaction and educational content.

Beyond interaction and instruction, mobile technology is rapidly becoming an integral tool in clinical assessment. Digital formats allow item presentation to be highly standardized and precisely timed (Hadwin et al., 2005; Singleton, 2001). Internet server connectivity as well as local data storage in mobile devices permit both data retention and transfer avoiding data loss and enabling collection and sorting of large datasets for psychometric analysis and the creation of baseline norms (Santos-Febles et al., 2015). Secure cloud-based web services provide the capability to store and aggregate large-scale data compliant with health privacy laws facilitating updates of norms, stimuli and software. Mobile clinical testing apps can be especially useful in contexts in which full assessment in a clinic or hospital is simply not possible, overcoming the limitations of geographically remote or resource-restricted environments. As we have described, one such context in which clinical assessment is often sorely needed but infeasible using non-digital tools is that of preschool screening.

Consequently, we set out to construct a pre-reader screening tool that would be comprehensive and yet short, psychometrically valid yet not require extensive tester credentialing and efficient yet engaging and developmentally appropriate while keeping in mind the advantages and challenges of composite batteries, formative assessments and digital screeners. We envisioned a screening app as a cost-effective, mobile platform that could be readily accessed in a variety of settings. Designed as a thirty-minute interactive and engaging game, the app would screen for early indicators of atypical reading development. Free or low-cost, wide distribution would allow large data aggregation and a dynamic standardization process with norms updated on an ongoing basis and refined for validity with local populations. After screening, the supporting adult would receive a risk profile and a set of activities, downloadable curricula, illustrative videos, resource list and recommendations for next steps. These would be targeted specifically for educators, clinicians and parents as evidence-based strategies that would give all children the opportunity to reach their full reading potential (see earlier references).

Constructing a tablet-based risk screener ideally involves four phases: (1) task and stimulus design, (2) pilot testing and initial psychometric review, (3) validation and norming, and (4) development of evidence-based supports. We consider here the first design phase in which, based on prior research, we chose the five pre-reading components: phonological awareness, phonological memory, letter-sound knowledge, rapid naming and the family history of reading difficulty, and the two language components, vocabulary and oral language comprehension, that are most predictive of future reading abilities (see earlier discussion). For each of these components, we carefully examined the validated, standardized tasks used in composite batteries and peer-reviewed studies (e.g., Catts et al., 2005; Chiat & Polisenska, 2016; Norton & Wolf, 2012; Ozernov-Palchik et al., 2017; Pennington & Lefly, 2001; Scarborough, 1989).

For digital tools in particular, this first phase provides a crucial opportunity to consider the match (or mismatch) between ideal test design and technology implementation. We next provide three examples of the ways in which the benefits and constraints of the digital format are considered during design: in item selection, response modality and motivation.

Design examples

First, while each subtest of a psychometrically validated composite battery may consist of tens of items requiring up to forty-five minutes administration time, a useful rapid screener must assess all seven features of reading risk in a relatively short period of time without the presence of a trained evaluator. While digital formative measures can use computer-adaptive testing techniques to rapidly shift to items that match a child's skill level, for a normative assessment the psychometric requirements of item response theory require a consistent item set to be administered (Hadwin et al., 2005). Thus, instead of providing the full formative range of evaluation, a normative risk screener in development must be brief by focusing on a limited but consistent item set discriminating children at-risk from those not at-risk. In our app, we therefore included only items that bordered the divide between at-risk and average skill levels, eliminating very easy items that even at-risk children would be expected to get correct as well as very difficult items that only advanced children would be likely to master. Psychometric considerations thus did not allow us to avail of computer-adaptive capabilities while timing considerations required us to define a restricted and optimally discriminant item set.

The balance of digital capabilities with appropriate testing methodology is also reflected in choices regarding response modality that potentially impact the assessment's developmental suitability for the child. For example, vocabulary can be evaluated receptively by speaking the name of an object, such as an orange, and having the child point to (or touch) a picture of the object, or expressively by displaying an orange and asking the child for its name or for an alternate name if the child provides a broad category, such as 'fruit' instead of 'orange'. In a mobile app environment without a trained test administrator, speech recognition software would be required to record, score and potentially provide immediate feedback to a child's response in a productive task; this immediate feedback is not currently technically feasible. One drawback of receptive tasks, though, is that they are fundamentally multiple-choice activities. A child may pick a correct object simply by chance and the fewer choices presented, the higher the probability that the child receives a correct score. The common testing solution of providing many choices may be counterproductive as the visual and fine motor skills of preschoolers are still developing and may result in tapping errors when the correct response area is small (McKnight & Fitton, 2010). On the other hand, confirmatory gestures such as double-taps or object-dragging used for older children and adults may be difficult for young children (Dubé & McEwen, 2017; Vatavu et al., 2015).

Although computer-adaptive testing and speech recognition capabilities of the digital format might be unsuitable for shortening task length or for speech recognition of expressive vocabulary, in other cases digital technologies can facilitate resourceful screening, for example with rapid naming. Rapid automatized naming is an inherently expressive task: in the rapid object naming format, this task requires the child to name familiar objects in several rows of pictures as quickly as possible while the child's score is based upon the time required to complete all rows. Rapid automatized naming is the least commonly assessed component skill of reading in current digital screeners, perhaps in part due to the difficulty of capturing speech onset and offset times. However, rapid naming tasks are in fact good candidates for digital analysis because speech scoring is relatively simple: first, because there is a limited set of words the software must identify and second, because scores do not depend upon fine differences in pronunciation of the object names or computer feedback during the task. Although immediate scoring is not presently technologically feasible, voice recordings can be stored and transmitted online for later automated analysis and reporting. Whether or not the digital format supports a particular task or response modality therefore depends not simply upon the modality itself but also upon the task goal and response evaluation criteria.

In addition to item selection and response modality, user motivation provides a third example of balance between optimal test design and digital implementation. The engaging game play of many rapid digital screeners illustrates how an imaginative narrative in a gamified scene can keep children attentive to and engaged in tasks they often find boring or frustrating in traditional psychometric batteries (Brewer et al., 2013). Motivational principles such as novelty, e.g., in exploring a virtual world that can be interspersed with elements of surprise; reward, e.g., for completing tasks or staying engaged in the game; and social interaction and approval, e.g., from a virtual 'friend' (Dichev & Dicheva, 2017), engage children just as adults. For preschoolers, however, it is important to keep in mind potential developmental differences that impact their interaction with gamification elements. For example, in more demanding language-based tasks requiring inhibitory control, children do not begin to consistently demonstrate theory of mind, a construct that reflects a person's ability to understand another's point of view or imagine themselves in another's place, until around the age of three or four years old, even though they may possess this capacity as toddlers (Scott & Baillargeon, 2017). Participating in gamified role-play thus requires metacognitive skills and information-processing capacities that may be challenging for preschoolers. In addition, young children may be more easily distracted than older children or adults from the primary assessment task by excessive visual detail, extraneous sounds or challenging physical interactions such as dragging and dropping (Brewer et al., 2013). Further, they may not be able to decipher an ambiguous or complex screen interface (Dubé & McEwen, 2017; Masood & Thigambaram, 2015). An optimal interface for young children is thus relatively simple, well-guided and sparse, while retaining the basic motivational elements of novelty, reward and social interaction.

As the examples of item selection, response modality and motivation demonstrate, the first design phase of a tablet-based screening tool requires a fine balance among what is technologically feasible, psychometrically valid and developmentally appropriate. Although we do not describe these in detail for the purposes of this chapter, there are three additional phases equally critical for constructing an effective screener. First, stimuli must be pilot-tested and test items must be reviewed for psychometric properties. Second, validation, norming and standardization studies must be conducted and submitted for peer-review of results. Third, practitioner tools and references must be constructed so that skills flagged as needing support can be accompanied by practical and evidence-based resources. Only after all four phases are complete is a screener ready for public dissemination.

Clinical and educational implications

Our knowledge about the neurobiological origins of atypical reading development and the effectiveness of early intervention was made possible by neuropsychological studies and confirmed and refined in recent decades by brain imaging research. Complementary advances in child-friendly technologies such as tablets and mobile apps make the utilization of this knowledge for early universal reading risk screening feasible. Screening is crucial because early risk for reading difficulties is not deterministic: cognitive, perceptual, genetic and neurobiological factors interact with the home and educational environment to shape the child's developing brain and later reading ability (Peterson & Pennington, 2015). Providing schools, clinics and communities with a digital, cost-effective and efficient, scientifically validated tool for early risk identification can potentially impact positively upon the lives of thousands of children who would no longer be required to fail to learn to read in order to receive support to learn to read. We end with a caution, however, that an efficient screening tool will be of little use if children do not subsequently receive evidence-based supports through close monitoring, instruction and potentially, further diagnostic evaluation. In addition, the supports must target the specific reading components flagged in the screener (Glover & Albers, 2007), whether phonological awareness and memory, letter-sound knowledge, rapid naming, vocabulary or oral comprehension. If universal screening of pre-readers as well as evidence-based responses to screening for children found to have elevated risk are in place, early and customized remediation programs, ideally delivered through well-trained teachers within general education, may in the future be possible for all children. Such programs themselves may have a ripple-up effect in terms of resource savings and academic improvement as remediation in the early grades is more efficient and effective than in later years and leads to improved academic, psychological and social development for children formerly at risk of reading and thus academic failure.

References

Brewer, R., Anthony, L., Brown, Q., Irwin, G., Nias, J. and Tate, B. (2013) *Using gamification to motivate children to complete empirical studies in lab environments*. New York: ACM Press, pp. 388–391.

Brunswick, N., McDougall, S. and de Mornay Davies, P. (2010) *Reading and dyslexia in different orthographies*. Hove: Psychology Press, Taylor & Francis.

Catts, H., Petscher, Y., Schatschneider, C., Sittner Bridges, M. and Mendoza, Katherin. (2009) Floor effects associated with universal screening and their impact on the early identification of reading disabilities. *Journal of Learning Disabilities* 42 (2), 163–176.

Catts, H.W., Adlof, S.M., Hogan, T.P. and Weismer, S.E. (2005) Are specific language impairment and dyslexia distinct disorders? *Journal of Speech Language and Hearing Research* 48 (6), 1378.

Catts, H.W., Nielsen, D.C., Bridges, M.S., Liu, Y.S. and Bontempo, D.E. (2015) Early identification of reading disabilities within an RTI framework. *Journal of Learning Disabilities* 48 (3), 281–297.

Catts, H.W., Nielsen, D.C., Bridges, M.S. and Liu, Y.-S. (2016) Early identification of reading comprehension difficulties. *Journal of Learning Disabilities* 49 (5), 451–465.

Chiat, S. and Polišenská, K. (2016) A framework for crosslinguistic nonword repetition tests: Effects of bilingualism and socioeconomic status on children's performance. *Journal of Speech, Language, and Hearing Research* 59 (5), 1179–1189.

Cunningham, A.E. and Stanovich, K.E. (1997) Early reading acquisition and its relation to reading experience and ability 10 years later. *Developmental Psychology* 33 (6), 934.

Deterding, S., Dixon, D., Khaled, R. and Nacke, L. (2011) From game design elements to gamefulness: Defining gamification. In *Proceedings of the 15th international academic MindTrek conference: Envisioning future media environments*. New York: ACM Press, 9–15.

Dichev, C. and Dicheva, D. (2017) Gamifying education: What is known, what is believed and what remains uncertain: A critical review. *International Journal of Educational Technology in Higher Education* 14, 9.

Dubé, A.K. and McEwen, R.N. (2017) Abilities and affordances: Factors influencing successful child – tablet communication. *Educational Technology Research and Development* 65 (4), 889–908.

Elliott, J.G. and Grigorenko, E.L. (2014) *The dyslexia debate*. Cambridge: Cambridge University Press.

Flax, J.F., Realpe-Bonilla, T., Roesler, C., Choudhury, N. and Benasich, A. (2009) Using early standardized language measures to predict later language and early reading outcomes in children at high risk for language-learning impairments. *Journal of Learning Disabilities* 42 (1), 61–75.

Fricke, S., Bowyer-Crane, C., Haley, A.J., Hulme, C. and Snowling, M.J. (2013) Efficacy of language intervention in the early years. *Journal of Child Psychology and Psychiatry, and Allied Disciplines* 54 (3), 280–290.

Gilger, J.W. and Kaplan, B.J. (2001) Atypical brain development: A conceptual framework for understanding developmental learning disabilities. *Developmental Neuropsychology* 20 (2), 465–481.

Gilger, J.W., Lyytinen, H., Ahonen, T., Leiwo, M. and Lyytinen, P. (1996) A longitudinal study of Finnish families genetically at risk for developmental reading disorder: Preliminary data on the ability of parental variables to predict early infant ERP and motor skills. *Behavior Genetics* 26 (6), 585–585.

Glover, T.A. and Albers, C.A. (2007) Considerations for evaluating universal screening assessments. *Journal of School Psychology* 45 (2), 117–135.

Görker, I., Bozatli, L., Korkmazlar, U., YüCel Karadag, M., Ceylan, C., Sogut, C., . . . Turan, N. (2017) The probable prevalence and sociodemographic characteristics of specific learning disorder in primary school children in Edirne. *Nöro Psikiyatri Arşivi* 54 (4), 343–349.

Hadwin, A.F., Winne, P.H. and Nesbit, J.C. (2005) Roles for software technologies in advancing research and theory in educational psychology. *British Journal of Educational Psychology* 75 (1), 1–24.

Hatcher, P.J., Hulme, C. and Ellis, A.W. (1994) Ameliorating early reading failure by integrating the teaching of reading and phonological skills: The phonological linkage hypothesis. *Child Development* 65 (1), 41–57.

Hatcher, P.J., Hulme, C. and Snowling, M.J. (2004) Explicit phoneme training combined with phonic reading instruction helps young children at risk of reading failure. *Journal of Child Psychology and Psychiatry, and Allied Disciplines* 45 (2), 338–358.

Hemphill, L. and Tivnan, T. (2008) The importance of early vocabulary for literacy achievement in high-poverty schools. *Journal of Education for Students Placed at Risk* 13 (4), 426–451.

Hulme, C., Nash, H.M., Gooch, D., Lervåg, A. and Snowling, M.J. (2015) The Foundations of Literacy Development in Children at Familial Risk of Dyslexia. *Psychological Science* 26 (12), 1877–1886.

Jenkins, J.R., Hudson, R.F. and Johnson, E.S. (2007) Screening for at-risk readers in a Response To Intervention framework. *School Psychology Review; Bethesda* 36 (4), 582–600.

Johnson, E.S., Jenkins, J.R., Petscher, Y. and Catts, H.W. (2009) How can we improve the accuracy of screening instruments? *Learning Disabilities Research & Practice* 24 (4), 174–185.

Juel, C. (1988) Learning to read and write: A longitudinal study of 54 children from first through fourth grades. *Journal of Educational Psychology* 80 (4), 437.

Landerl, K. and Wimmer, H. (2008) Development of word reading fluency and spelling in a consistent orthography: An 8-year follow-up. *Journal of Educational Psychology* 100 (1), 150.

Langer, N., Peysakhovich, B., Zuk, J., Drottar, M., Sliva, D.D., Smith, S., . . . and Gaab, N. (2017) White matter alterations in infants at risk for developmental dyslexia. *Cerebral Cortex* 27 (2), 1027–1036.

Leppänen, P.H.T., Hämäläinen, J.A., Salminen, H.K., Eklund, K.M., Guttorm, T.K., Lohvansuu, K., . . . Lyytinen, H. (2010) Newborn brain event-related potentials revealing atypical processing of sound frequency and the subsequent association with later literacy skills in children with familial dyslexia. *Cortex* 46 (10), 1362–1376.

Logan, J.A., Hart, S.A., Cutting, L., Deater-Deckard, K., Schatschneider, C. and Petrill, S. (2013) Reading development in young children: Genetic and environmental influences. *Child Development* 84 (6), 2131–2144.

Lonigan, C.J., Allan, N.P. and Lerner, M.D. (2011) Assessment of preschool early literacy skills: Linking children's educational needs with empirically supported instructional activities. *Psychology in the Schools* 48 (5), 488–501.

Lyytinen, H., Erskine, J., Hämäläinen, J., Torppa, M. and Ronimus, M. (2015) Dyslexia – early identification and prevention: Highlights from the Jyväskylä Longitudinal Study of Dyslexia. *Current Developmental Disorders Reports* 2 (4), 330–338.

Masood, M. and Thigambaram, M. (2015) The usability of mobile applications for pre-schoolers. *Procedia – Social and Behavioral Sciences* 197 (Supplement C), 1818–1826.

McArthur, G., Castles, A., Kohnen, S. and Banales, E. (2016) Low self-concept in poor readers: Revalence, heterogeneity, and risk. *PeerJ* 4, e2669.

McKnight, L. and Fitton, D. (2010) Touch-screen technology for children: Giving the right instructions and getting the right responses. In *Proceedings of the 9th international conference on interaction design and children.* New York: ACM Press, 238–241.

Mugnaini, D., Lassi, S., Malfa, G.L. and Albertini, G. (2009) Internalizing correlates of dyslexia. *World Journal of Pediatrics* 5 (4), 255–264.

NCES. (2016) Digest of education statistics, 2016. https://nces.ed.gov/programs/digest/d16/tables/dt16_203.10.asp.

Norton, E.S., Beach, S.D. and Gabrieli, J.D. (2015) Neurobiology of dyslexia. *Current Opinion in Neurobiology* 30, 73–78.

Norton, E.S. and Wolf, M. (2012) Rapid automatized naming (RAN) and reading fluency: Implications for understanding and treatment of reading disabilities. *Annual Review of Psychology* 63, 427–452.

Ozernov-Palchik, O. and Gaab, N. (2016) Tackling the 'dyslexia paradox': Reading brain and behavior for early markers of developmental dyslexia. *Wiley Interdisciplinary Reviews: Cognitive Science* 7 (2), 156–176.

Ozernov-Palchik, O., Norton, E.S., Sideridis, G., Beach, S.D., Wolf, M., Gabrieli, J.D. and Gaab, N. (2017) Longitudinal stability of pre-reading skill profiles of kindergarten children: Implications for early screening and theories of reading. *Developmental Science* 20 (5), e12471.

Ozernov-Palchik, O., Yu, X., Wang, Y. and Gaab, N. (2016) Lessons to be learned: How a comprehensive neurobiological framework of atypical reading development can inform educational practice. *Current Opinion in Behavioral Sciences* 10, 45–58.

Pennington, B.F. and Lefly, D.L. (2001) Early reading development in children at family risk for dyslexia. *Child Development* 72 (3), 816–833.

Petersen, P. (2015) That's how much I can do: Children's agency in digital tablet activities in a Swedish preschool environment. *Nordic Journal of Digital Literacy* 10 (3), 145–169.

Peterson, R.L. and Pennington, B.F. (2015) Developmental Dyslexia. *Annual Review of Clinical Psychology* 11 (1), 283–307.

Quinn, M.M., Rutherford Jr, R.B. and Leone, P.E. (2001) *Students with disabilities in correctional facilities.* ERIC Digest. Washington, DC: U.S. Department of Education.

Raschle, N., Zuk, J., Ortiz-Mantilla, S., Sliva, D.D., Franceschi, A., Grant, P.E., . . . Gaab, N. (2012) Pediatric neuroimaging in early childhood and infancy: Challenges and practical guidelines. *Annals of the New York Academy of Sciences* 1252 (1), 43–50.

Rideout, V., Saphir, M., Pai, S. and Rudd, A. (n.d.) *Zero to eight: Children's media use in America 2013.* San Fransisco, CA: Common Sense Media.

Rumelhart, D.E. (1994) Toward an interactive model of reading. In: Ruddell, R., Ruddell, M. and Singer, H. (eds.) *Theoretical models and processes of reading,* (4th edition). Newark, DE: International Reading Association, 864–894.

Rust, K., Malu, M., Anthony, L. and Findlater, L. (2014) Understanding child-defined gestures and children's mental models for touchscreen tabletop interaction. *Proceedings of the 2014 Conference on Interaction Design and Children.* New York: ACM Press, 201–204.

Santos-Febles, E., Reigosa-Crespo, V., García-Liashenko, K., Echemendía, A., Plasencia, E., Pujols, G., . . . Eimil, E. (2015) A system to support regional screening programs to identify school-age children at risk of neurodevelopmental disorders. In: *World Congress on Medical Physics and Biomedical Engineering, June 7–12, 2015, Toronto, Canada*. Cham: Springer, 1469–1473.

Scarborough, H.S. (1989) Prediction of reading disability from familial and individual differences. *Journal of Educational Psychology* 81 (1), 101–108.

Scarborough, H.S. (2001) Connecting early language and literacy to later reading (dis)abilities: Evidence, theory, and practice. In: Neuman, S. and Dickinson, D. (eds.) *Handbook of early literacy research*. New York: Guilford Press, 97–110.

Scott, R.M. and Baillargeon, R. (2017) Early false-belief understanding. *Trends in Cognitive Sciences* 21 (4), 237–249.

Shaywitz, S.E., Fletcher, J.M., Holahan, J.M., Shneider, A.E., Marchione, K.E., Stuebing, K.K., . . . and Shaywitz, B.A. (1999) Persistence of dyslexia: The Connecticut longitudinal study at adolescence. *Pediatrics* 104 (6), 1351–1359.

Shaywitz, S.E., Shaywitz, B.A., Fletcher, J.M. and Escobar, M.D. (1990) Prevalence of reading disability in boys and girls: Results of the Connecticut longitudinal study. *JAMA* 264 (8), 998–1002.

Singleton, C. (2001) Computer-based assessment in education. *Educational and Child Psychology* 18 (3), 58–74.

Snow, C.E., Burns, M.S. and Griffin, P. (1998) *Preventing reading difficulties in young children: Committee on the prevention of reading difficulties in young children*. Washington, DC: National Research Council.

Snowling, M.J., Gallagher, A. and Frith, U. (2003) Family risk of dyslexia is continuous: Individual differences in the precursors of reading skill. *Child Development* 74 (2), 358–373.

Snowling, M.J. and Melby-Lervåg, M. (2016) Oral language deficits in familial dyslexia: A meta-analysis and review. *Psychological Bulletin* 142 (5), 498–545.

Spektor-Levy, O., Plutov, I., Israeli, N. and Perry, N. (2017) Integrating technology in preschool science and inquiry. In: *Digital tools and solutions for inquiry-based STEM learning*. Hershey, PA: IGI Global, 1–32.

Stanovich, K.E. and West, R.F. (1989) Exposure to print and orthographic processing. *Reading Research Quarterly* 402–433.

Taylor, J., Roehrig, A.D., Hensler, B.S., Connor, C. and Schatschneider, C. (2010) Teacher quality moderates the genetic effects on early reading. *Science* 328 (5977), 512–514.

Torgesen, J.K. (2000) Individual differences in response to early interventions in reading: The lingering problem of treatment resisters. *Learning Disabilities Research & Practice* 15 (1), 55–64.

United Nations, Department of Economic and Social Affairs (2017) World population prospects: The 2017 revision, key findings and advance tables. https://esa.un.org/unpd/wpp/Download/Standard/Population/.

Vatavu, R.-D., Cramariuc, G. and Schipor, D.M. (2015) Touch interaction for children aged 3 to 6 years: Experimental findings and relationship to motor skills. *International Journal of Human-Computer Studies* 74, 54–76.

Vellutino, F.R., Fletcher, J.M., Snowling, M.J. and Scanlon, D.M. (2004) Specific reading disability (dyslexia): What have we learned in the past four decades? *Journal of Child Psychology and Psychiatry* 45 (1), 2–40.

Vellutino, F.R., Tunmer, W.E., Jaccard, J.J. and Chen, R. (2007) Components of reading ability: Multivariate evidence for a convergent skills model of reading development. *Scientific Studies of Reading* 11 (1), 3–32.

Wanzek, J., Vaughn, S., Scammacca, N.K., Metz, K., Murray, C.S., Roberts, G. and Danielson, L. (2013) Extensive reading interventions for students with reading difficulties after grade 3. *Review of Educational Research* 83 (2), 163–195.

Yelland, N. and Masters, J. (2007) Rethinking scaffolding in the information age. *Computers & Education* 48 (3), 362–382.

Ziegler, J.C. and Goswami, U. (2005) Reading acquisition, developmental dyslexia, and skilled reading across languages: A psycholinguistic grain size theory. *Psychological Bulletin* 131 (1), 3–29.

INDEX

Note: Page numbers in **bold** indicate tables and page numbers in *italics* indicate figures.

3D Hummingbird-Gigi 128
3-dimensional (3D) habitat designs 128

AAC *see* alternative/augmentative communication (AAC) systems
ABA *see* applied behaviour analysis (ABA)
academic achievement 324
accidental ethnography/ethnographers 183, 184
after-school digital skills club 364
agency 19–21; and intra-actions in educational methods 19–21
agential realism 134
agentive intra-actions 19–21
Albers, Peggy 16, 377–392
Allen, Melissa L. 15
alternative/augmentative communication (AAC) systems 269
American educational system 338
Anderson, Ann 15
Anderson, Jim 15
Angry Birds 159
Antle, A.N. 241
applied behaviour analysis (ABA) 274
app scaffolding in parent-child-app learning assemblage 215
ARC-Discovery Grant 210
artifacts 289
artifactual literacies 221
artistic works 320
arts-based methods; *see also* children's art: children's digital media productions in early childhood 311–315; into digital media in early childhood 312–314; and research reporting 322
arts-based pedagogy 377
Ashton, Emily 27
assemblages 57
attitudes 312
atypical reading development 394–395
audience 284
audio-recording 53
audio recording apps 40
audio-visual representation 56
augmented reality (AR) 182
Australian Human Rights Commission 294
authentic data 41
autism spectrum disorder (ASD) 267; special educational needs 268–272
automatic anonymity 26

"back-breaking work" 386
Bakhtin, M. 82
Bakhtinian dialogic frame 82
Barad, K. 134, 164
barefoot, jabbing at screens 149–150
Barsalou, L.W. 241
Basil Bernstein (social stratification) 20
BBC (CBeebies) 158
B-Club 62
Before Writing 172
behavioral/emotional engagement 354–355
belongingness 83
below-average readers 395
bespoke display 33
Beveridge, S. 267
Bien, A.C. 63
Bigum, C. 197
bilingual/biliteral young children 318
bilingual eBooks 318
Bitou, A. 160
Blommaert, J. 221

Bloom's Taxonomy 35
body morphology 241
body movement (gross motor) 244
body sensors 167
Bolitho, R. 64
boredom busters 321
Born to Read 24
Bortolussi, M. 242
Bourdieu, P. 339
Bourdieusian theories of cultural capital 339
Brandt, D. 249
Brennan, K. 35
Brian Sutton-Smith (play and the imagination) 20
brief curriculum-independent assessments, literacy screeners 396
bright children 83
Bring Your Own Device (BYOD) 31
Brooker, L. 145
Brown, K.M. 55
Bruehel, Elisabeth Young 22
Brunswick Curriculum Framework 26
building blocks and construction toys 236
Burner, J. 144
Burnett, Cathy 13, 22, 143–153, 252
Bus, A.G. 240

cameraman 301–303
Camtasia 30
Canadian Adult Achievement Tests (CAAT) 287
Candy Crush Saga 159
Captivate 30
Cara and the Wizard 26
caregiver-child interaction 354–355
Carter, R. 64
Caton, Lucy 16, 362–376
CBeebies (general apps) 159
character-filled films 103
Charman, T. 273–274
chest camera to roaming camera 370–371
chest mounted camera 367–370, *369*
child-adult connections 19
child-audiences 96
child cognitive self-regulation 328
child-controlled practices 76
child-controlled school worlds 74
child cultures 85
child development associate (CDA) credentials 341
child/educator binary 316–317
child-friendly apps 210
child-friendly malleability 170
child-friendly reading material 368
childhood professional practices 315
childhoods across boundaries 107–108
childhood teaching and pedagogy 315
child-matter 12
child negotiations 80
children learning with grandparents and other elders 223–231; artifactual literacies 221; ethnographic lessons 231–232; ethnography and literacy 222–223; framing literacy 220; literacies and the material 220; literacies and the socio-cultural 220; literacy across generations 222; multimodal literacy 220–221; narrative framing of literacy 219; placed resources 221–222
children's art: artistic works 320; citizenship and 319; conventional valorisations 321; creators of technology 315–316; developmental theories and 312; as digital consumers 315–316; ethics of working 318; logistics of arts-based research 321; misconceptions 321; motivations and intentions 320; and research reporting 322; Western theories of aesthetics 312
children's comprehension 354
children's digital media 9; use 314–315
children's engagement and improvisation 363
children's language and literacy development 324
children's learning 351
children's learning at home through smartphone apps for parents: digital media 326–328; home learning environment 324–325; parental support delivering, traditional modes 326; parents of preschool children 325; parents of school-age children 325–326
children's literacy development and parental support 327
children's materialities and artifacts 21–22
children's media 314
children's motivation 331
children's personal space 368
children's perspectives on schooling 78
children's play and making 170–171; cutting across methods, multimodality, and materiality 171; digital cutouts 177–179; materiality 173–176, **176**; multimodality 172–173, 173–176, **176**; value to field of digital technologies 179–180
children's screen experience 353
children's skills and knowledge 330
children's socio-emotional and self-regulation skills 324–325
children's story comprehension and learning 355
children's technology 8; use **204**, 207–208
children's thinking (Piaget) 20
children's visual and performance productions 312, *313*
child's embodied textual play 88; collaborative play 89–90; data analysis 92–96; data collection methods 91–92; drawing maps 99–101; processes of production 98; production and reception 96–98; texts analysis 90–91, 102–104; theoretical approaches 89; writing books 101–102
child's handwriting 261
child social-emotional behaviour 327

child story comprehension 350
cholera 9
Cingel, D.P. 353
citizenship, children concept 319
clinical batteries 396
clips 148
cloud-based presentation tool 319
cloud-based web services 397–398
Cobb, P. 251
coder-agreement purposes 37
coder's rating, overall child engagement 354
coding 311
Coelho, E. 64
cognitive and emotional understandings of technologies 8
cognitive and language profile: special educational needs 269
cognitive scaffolding 216
Cole, M. 63
collaborative play 89–90
Collier, Diane 12, 24
commercial film characters 314
commercially generated advertisements 379
commercially generated visual texts 389
Communication and Language 325
Community Action Program for Children (CAPC) 27n2
complex entanglements and messy methods 191–192
compliance 354
composite batteries 396
compositional work 18
comprehension 357
computer-adaptive testing 399
computer-based e-books 350
connected play 157
console-based e-book 350
Constance Kamii (mathematical problem solving) 20
construction projects **91**
consumer culture 381
contemporary practice theory 76
content gamification, literacy screeners 397
conventional humanist qualitative inquiry 131
conventional valorisations 321
conversational context *109*
co-researchers lived experiences 304
Couldry, N. 166
counter ad 379, *380*
Courage, M.L. 355–356
covert surveillance 39
Cramer, F. 157
created books **91**
critical discourse analysis 385–386
critical literacy educators 377
critical literacy practices 377
critical race literacy 88
critical race theory 16
critical theory 315
critical visual discourse analysis (CVDA) 16, 389; analysts 378; in children's literature 382–386; critical redesigning with technology 387–388; practical application and future of 389–390; questions 378–379; rationale for using 381–382; significance 388–389; studies analyzing data through 382; teacher-generated paintings 387, *388*; using 379–381; word clouds 386–387
cross-sectional analyses 9
cultural amplification 65
cultural capital and critical race theories (CTR) 339–340
cultural contact zones 62
cultural currency and social inclusion 314
cultural valorisations 312
culture and ethnicity 222
Cummins, J. 64
cumulative knowledge 350–351
curriculum-based assessments, literacy screeners 396
curriculum teaching and learning 249
Cutting out 172–173
Cutting with 174, 178

DAP *see* developmentally appropriate practices (DAP)
data analysis 92–96, 102
data collection 10; methods 91–92
data interpretation 10
de Certeau, M. 172
decision-making strategies 41
deficit discourses 187
deficit framings of children in research methods 24–25
de Freitas, E. 365, 366
degrees of diverse cultures 76
Deleuze, G. 52, 57, 133, 137–138, 364–365, 366, 374
Deleuze, Gilles 211; philosophy 133; notions 137–138
demographic profiles 159
design-based experiments in teacher/researcher collaborations 248; cycle 1 254–257; cycle 2 257–258; cycle 3 258–262; design-based experiments 251–252; foregrounding text production 249–250; makerspace pedagogy 252–253; materiality and multimodality 253–254; methodology and conceptual thinking 250–251; reflection and conclusions 262–263; sociomateriality and literacies 252
design-based interventions 253
design-based models 6
design-based research: approaches 10; collective 252
de-territorialised pedagogies 262
developmental dyslexia 394

developmentally appropriate practices (DAP) 327
device-embedded recorder 32–33; display capture data, analysing 35–37; research context and studies 33; studies 33–35
Dezuanni, M. 318
Diagnostic and Statistical Manual (DSM-V) 268
dialogic and dual language reading 67
dialogic reading strategies 354
dialogue-based reading 238
diffractive seeing 53
digital and print literacies 92–93
digital camera, using 301
digital capabilities 398–399
digital cutouts 177–179
digital devices 143; socio-material effects 314–315
digital divides 24, 85, 182, 340–341
digital ethnographic methods 49–50; children to co-author video data 55–56; child's role, researcher positioning, and ethical issues 55; decentering the researcher 57–59; educators and researchers 59–60; GoPro as data generation tool 54–55; GoPro view of children's sociomaterial entanglements 56–57; researcher narrative 50–52; research project 52–53; theoretical framing and methods 53; visuals and video methods 53–54
"digital landscape" 349
digital literacy research 183
digitally based educational toys 311
digital media: art 314; arts-focused and arts-based methods in 318–319; children's privacy and authorship 316; in contemporary learning spaces 315; cultural rights 316; in daily activity 311; effective learners in classroom 311; mass availability of 311; parents, platform to support 326–328; in schools and kindergartens 314; socio-material impacts of 315
digital research 18
digital scraps *179*
digital spaces 378
digital tablet-created arts 319
digital technologies: growth of 3; literacy screeners 397
digital tools 248
digital world, researching in 182–183; comparative ethnografiction 186–187; complex entanglements and messy methods 191–192; ethnographers, accidental 184; iDollhouse in the iWorld 185–186; iPads at home in Canada and Australia 184–185; playground conversations to policy analysis 189–190; popular media and home perspectives 190–191; practices and possibilities 192–193; researching in other people's homes 187–189
discourse analysis and critical discourse analysis 388–389
disembodied grammar 82
Disney (general apps) 159
display recording software 30; changes and learning environment 31–32; in classroom 38; ethical considerations 38–41, 41–44; planning and introducing 37
diverse methods, multidisciplinarity 5
Dixon, Kerryn 13
Dixon, P. 242
'do-it-with-others' 252
dominant discourses 386
Dore, Rebecca A. 16, 349–361
Doyle, K. 318
drawing maps 99–101
drawings **91**
dual language books (DLBs) 12; and language awareness (LA) 65–66; program 66–67, 70–71
Dubit and Foundling Bird 158
Duckling gets a cookie, The 99
Dyson, Anne Haas 13, 89

Early, M. 64
early childhood education (ECE) 20
early childhood educators 312
Early Literacy programme 325
Early Maths programme 325
Early Years Foundation Stage (EYFS) 328
Early Years Foundation Stage curriculum in England 325
EasyPeasy app: children's skills and knowledge 330; cluster design 328–329; evaluation 328–329; parenting skills fostering 329–330; parents and children's engagement in enjoyable educational activities 330–331; parents' experiences 329; relationships, building and strengthening 329
e-books 318, 349; attention and engagement in 354; CD-ROM storybooks 349–350; child and parent emotional engagement 354; co-viewing practices 353; experimenter-created materials 351; features 350–351; hotspots and games features 351; in laboratory setting 351–352; and traditional books 350
Eckhoff, A. 314, 318
economic distress 9
ed apps 6
educated language 339
educational activities, parents and children's engagement 330–331
educational animation shows 343
educational assemblage 211
educational methods, agency and intra-actions in 19–21
educational research 5
educational television shows 326
education-related design-based approaches 252
Edwards, S. 197, 314
Egg, P. 298
embodied cognition 236, 240–241

emotional benefits and joint reading 354
emotional facial expressions 355
emotions and reading engagement 354–355
empathy 79
empirical representations 133
empiricism 50; and materialism 132
engineering thinking 320
English-Language Learners (ELL) 338, 341
English-language proficiency 341
enthusiasm 354
ephemeralities of literacy 144
epistemologies and ontologies 25–26
Erickson, F. 58
Erion, J. 326
error-plagued sentences 81
ethic-onto-epistemologies 130
ethico-onto-epistemological inspirations for multi- and digital literacies 139–140
ethico-onto-epistemology 134–135
ethics 284–285
ethnograficion 186–187
ethnographers, accidental 184
ethnographic lessons 231–232
ethnography 74–75; basics, dynamics of 81–83; belonging, challenges of 83–84; complexities of gaining entry 79; data analysis 81; diversity and childhood cultures 76–78; entering and documenting 78; gathering data inside children's worlds 80–81; joy and challenges 85–86; and literacy 222–223; in literacy research 89; positionality 79–80; privileging children's worlds 75–76; technology upside-down 85; vital importance 78
Etta, R.A. 351
event-related potentials (ERPs) 270
experimenter-created e-books 357
Exploring Books Together (EBT) app 331; children's engagement with reading 333; children's reading, capacity to support 332–333; field-test study 332; home-school communication 333–334; points for improvement 334
extra-textual talk 354
extreme liberalisation 9
extreme protectionism 9
eye-tracking 270

Facecam activation 33, *34*
face-to-face training sessions 326
Fairclough's model *97*
Falloon, Garry 12
family literacy practices: across boundaries 108–110; and adult-child interactions 110–112
family literacy programmes 325
family literacy project 23
family's heritage language 107; *see also* heritage language learning
Fielding, M. 297
field notes 53
filmmaking 318
Finding Nemo (Disney) 258
fine-grained analysis methods 43
fine-motor activity 244
flexible home visit organisation 203
flexible learning space 31, *31*
Flick, U. 316
foam stickers 102
forced-choice questions 355
foregrounding text production 249–250
Forest School 52
formal learning spaces 311
Foucault, M. 140; technology 172
Fragile X syndrome 269
framing literacy 220
Fredericton Regional Family Resource Centre 27n2
free play in outdoor environments 314
Frieson, Brittany 85
Frozen 21, 25
functional magnetic resonance imaging (fMRI) protocols 270, 271
'future-focused' pedagogy 31

Gaab, Nadine 393–403
Gallacher, L. 89
Gallagher, M. 89
gaming 321
Ganea, P.A. 351, 353, 356, 357
Garmann's Summer 239
gatekeeping of children and adults 26–27
Geertz, C. 85
George and the Blue Moon 10
gesture, pointing 243
give-and-take relationship 84
globalisation 9
global urban subculture 64
Golinkoff, Roberta Michnick 16, 349–361
Gonzalez, Michelle 16, 393–403
GoPro 53; data generation tool 54–55; view of children's sociomaterial entanglements 56–57
GoPro camera 12, 49, 54, 58, 164, 166; from chest camera to roaming camera 370–371; chest mounted camera 367–370; head, chest, roaming, static 366–367; lines of flight 366–374; ontological theory and video-based research 364–365; roaming camera 367, 373–374; school computer club 367; static camera 368; visual ontologies in an after-school computer club 364; vlogs creation 371–373; watching and interpreting video data 366
GoPro Hero HD® 364

GoPro video recording 55
Grandma's Saturday Soup 69–70
grandparents and other elders, children learning with 223–231; artifactual literacies 221; ethnographic lessons 231–232; ethnography and literacy 222–223; framing literacy 220; literacies and the material 220; literacies and the socio-cultural 220; literacy across generations 222; multimodal literacy 220–221; narrative framing of literacy 219; placed resources 221–222
Grant MacEwan Child Care Lab School 25
Green, C. 166, 315
Green, Leila 14
Greene, Maxine 389
Grosz, Elisabeth 22, 23
Grosz's onto-ethical way of being fits 22
Guattari, A. 52, 57
Guattari, F. 133, 137–138, 211, 365, 366, 374
Guerrero, Sibylla Leon 16, 393–403
Gutierrez, Kris 22, 63, 251

habits of seeing 53
habitual anthropocentric style of seeing 51
Hackett, Abigail 16, 362–376
Haddon, Leslie 14
'hard-done-by' child 96
Harste, Jerome C. 377–392
Harwood, Debra 12, 21, 24
Hassinger-Das, Brenna 16, 349–361
Hawking, Stephen 10
Health and Physical Development 325
Hepp, A. 166
heritage language learning: childhoods across boundaries 107–108; ethics of collecting video data 123–124; family literacy practices across boundaries 108–110; family literacy practices and adult-child interactions 110–112; multilingual children's literacy practices 122–123; WeChat, researching on 112–122
Heydon, Rachel 14
Hicks, Deb 20
hidden talent 22–23
hierarchical fix-its 81
high-quality education 3
hijab (dupatta) 68–69
Hirsh-Pasek, Kathy 16, 349–361
HLE *see* home learning environment (HLE)
Hoel, Trude 14
Hole, Stian 239
Holloway, Donell 14
home-based training 326
home-based tutoring: strategies and parental support 326
home learning environment (HLE) 324–325
home-school communication 332, 333
Hsin, C.-T. 315–316
Hultman, K. 58
human-centered theories 130
human/non-human assemblages 144
human-only designers 180
hundred languages 20

i, movie: i am your data 148–149
iDollhouse 185; in the iWorld 185–186
illustrative vignettes 74
image editing app 319
imaginative story-telling 25
immigrant families, children 107; *see also* heritage language learning
immigration, sociocultural impact of 3
impact 285
Incorporeal: Ontology, Ethics, and Limits of Materialism, The 22
individual differences and HLE 324
inequalities 382
inequality, contexts of 221
Infant-Net 327
Ingold, Tim 365, 374
inner-city multicultural community 201
inquiry-based approach 65
institutional structure 365
interdisciplinarity: body movement (gross motor) 244; embodied cognition 240–241; fine-motor activity 244; gesture, pointing 243; multisensory, embodied reading with books and apps 239–240; narratives and storytelling 236–238; need for 241–243; posture 243; sensorimotor contingencies 238–239; technologies, affordances and embodiment 235–236
interdisciplinary evidences 5
interdisciplinary juxtaposition of thinkers 20
interest 22–23
intergenerational communication on social media 107, 114
intergenerational Skype interaction 112
inter-human relations 22
international ethics 9
internet- and smartphone-based interventions 328
Internet of Toys 160, 165
internet server connectivity, tablet screener 397
interpretive analysis 54
interpretive anthropology 75
interviews and conversations **91**
in-the-moment be(com)ing of humans 130
in-the-moment decisions 135
intra-actional elements 211
intra-actions with tablet-based texts 21
intra-active entanglement 213–214, 263
Ionesco, T. 240
iPad 30, 32, 350, 352; Air 35; apps 316; embedded data system 12; at home in Canada and Australia 184–185

It's 'digital heroin' 190
iWorld 184, 185

'jam or break' in action 374
Janks, Hilary 13
Jayemanne, D. 157
Jean Piaget (children's thinking) 20
Jelley, Fiona 16, 324–337
Jellyfish-Nick 128–129
Jewitt, C. 242
Ji Eun Kim 15
Johnson, Jaye 14
Johnson-Roullier, C. 378
'joint media engagement' 328
joint reading 354
Jordan, A.B. 315

Kelley, E.S. 357
Kelly, C. 114
Kervin, L. 197
Kincheloe, J.L. 145
kindergarten 76
Kinney, K. 357
Knight, Linda 15, 311–323
knowing and thinking 137–138
knowledge co-creation 20
Korat, O. 352
Koro-Ljungberg, M. 130, 135
Kraft, M.A. 327
Krcmar, M. 353
Kress, G. 172, 220
Kuby, Candace R. 13, 21

Lafton, T. 315
Laidlaw, Linda 14, 314–315
laissez-faire approach 317
Lakoff, G. 241
language awareness (LA): and dual language books 65–66; and transculturalism 64–65
language-based methods 9
language competencies 394
language development 63
Lather, P. 223
Latino immigrant children 341
Latour, B. 174
Lauricella, A.R. 352–353
Law, J. 160
Lawrence, Jacob 387
learning 317; environments 7; multimedia or interactive features 351; sites 314
learning-sub-group researchers 8
Learning to write in the early years project (LWEY) 263n2
LeCompte, M.D. 223
Lee, Lena 16, 338–348
Leiter-R 270
Lemon, Narelle 15
Lenz Taguchi, H. 58
letter-sound knowledge, literacy screeners 394, 397
linear print-based reading and writing skills 64
lines of flight: from chest camera to roaming camera 370–371; chest mounted camera 367–370; head, chest, roaming, static 366–367; roaming camera 367, 373–374; school computer club 367; static camera 368; thinking 366; threads or paths 366; visual practices 366; vlogs creation 371–373; watching and interpreting video data 366
linguistic anthropology 80
Lion, the Witch and the Wardrobe, The 26
listening 20
literacy 326; across generations 222; constituents 219; data 250; and material 220; ontoepistemology 231; programmes and interventions 325; screeners 396–397; skills 325; as social practice 144; and socio-cultural 220; and transculturalism 62–63
literacy-based digital artefacts 33
literacy for life (LFL) 286
'literary documentary' tradition 145
Little Bits Technology 364
logical empiricism 131, 133
Lotherington, H. 63
low-income preschool programs 341
low-scoring children 81
Lynch, C. 41

"Mac Attack" counter ad 379–380, *380*
MacLure, Maggie 23, 133, 374
MacNaughton, Glenda 20, 23
magnetoencephalography (MEG) 270
makerspace pedagogy 252–253
Making do 172, 178
making much with shifts 179
Malaguzzi, Loris 20
Manchester Metropolitan University 368
Mangen, Anne 14
Mantra Lingua: collection 70; publisher 66
Marsh, Jackie 13, 22
Martin, A.F. 240, 352–353, 356
Martin, Jane Roland 22
mass immigration 9
Masters, J. 212
matching, issues: in special educational needs 272–274
material artifacts used in play **91**
material-discursive reality 217; of digital tool 216
material feminisms 53
materialist reframing 170–171; *see also* children's play and making
materiality 173–176, **176**
materiality and multimodality 253–254
material-symbolic relationship, consumer and object 381

mathematical problem solving (Kamii) 20
mathematical skills 325
McNiff, Jean 23
McTavish, Marianne 15
meaning makers 89
meaning making: small stories 19; technology 84, 85
media **91**; arts 321; tours 160
Merchant, Guy 13, 143–153
Merleau-Ponty, M. 240
mesmerisation 315–316
methodological complexity and elasticity 317
methodology and conceptual thinking 250–251
microgenetic movements 174
Miller, M.E. 318
Mills, Kathy 241
Minecraft 159, 203–204
Minnesota Teaching Task 354
minority children's learning experiences 339
misspellings 343
Mistry, Nilesh 68
MixCast VR 167
mixed methods research 281
mixed methods research with children 280–281; artifacts 289; audience 284; ethics 284–285; focus groups 288–289; impact 285; interviews 287–288; mixed methods research 282–284; observations and field notes 286–287; philosophical/theoretical underpinning 282; principles and tenets 281; standardized tests 289–290
MKO *see* More Knowledgeable Other (MKO)
molar lines 365
monodisciplinary approaches 5
monolingual learners 65
Monteney Primary School 158
Monti-Nussbaum, M. 327
More Knowledgeable Other (MKO) 342
Moser, Thomas 14
motivational principles, tablet technology 399
Mr. Phonics 33
multidisciplinarity 4; challenge of 4; diverse methods 5; diverse writing styles 4–5; one-sided policy 5–6; reality 6–7
multidisciplinary projects 9–10; empirical research 10–12
multi-level analyses 9
multilingual children's literacy practices 122–123
multilingual connections 65
multilingual immigrant children 110, 123
multiliteracies 128
multimodal analyses 170, 178; interactional strand of 171; video analysis 171
multimodal choices 80
multimodal curriculum documents 23
multimodal discourse analysis 6
multimodal improvisational work 18
multimodal interaction analysis framework 165
multimodality 172–173, 173–176, **176**; sociocultural interpretations 172
multimodal literacy 220–221
multiple-choice questions 355–356
multiple disparate component skills, literacy screeners 397
multisensory, embodied reading with books and apps 239–240
multisensory engagement 63
multisensory human-technology interaction 236

NAEYC *see* National Association for the Education of Young Children (NAEYC)
naive empiricism 362–363
Naqvi, Rahat 22
narratives 203; framing of literacy 219; parents and child 203–205; and storytelling 236–238; voice 145
Nason, Pam 20
National Assessment Program of Literacy and Numeracy (NAPLAN) 249, 253, 263n1
National Association for the Education of Young Children (NAEYC) 339
National Institute for Health and Care (NICE) 268
National Literacy and Numeracy week 256
National Research Council 131
neurobiological differences and reading abilities 395
Nick-Ella-Emily-Panda Bear Habitat-Be(com)ing 127
Nick-Jellyfish-Be(com)ing 127
No Child Left Behind 131
nomadic thinking 53
non-art learning 320
non-digital assessments 396
non-digital research 18
nonfiction writing projectss 130
nonfiction writing unit 128
non-human forces 51
non-native English speakers 332
non-representational logic 132–133
non-verbal modes of communication 110
Norwich, B. 267
numeracy development 324
Núñez, R.E. 241

OECD (Organisation of Economic Co-operation and Development) 31
official teacher-led practices 82
Olsson, L.M. 135
O'Mara, Joanne 14
on-device display recording 43
one-on-one interviews with parents 201
one-on-one talks 201
online program Coh-Metrix 356

online training videos and parental support 327
onto-ethical-temporal-spatial conversations over books 23–24
ontological entanglements 164
open-ended questions 355–356
opportunistic sampling method 112
Or, T. 352
oral language skills 394
"oral language" textbook 81
oral sentence comprehension measure 394
Orellana, M.F. 62, 63
Orlando, Joanne 14
Ortiz, Fernando 62
Our Story app 6
out-of-school environments 32, *32*
out-of-school learning events 164
Ozernov-Palchik, Ola 16, 393–403

PACT *see* Parents And Children Together (PACT)
page-by-page retell measure 356
Pahl, K. 102
Panda-Emily 129–131
paper cellphone 175–178
paradigm wars 280
parental involvement and children's literacy 327
parental scaffolding **116–120**
parental support delivering, traditional modes 326
parent-child-app learning assemblage 210–211, 213–214; app scaffolding 215–216; cognitive, affective and technical scaffolding 212; conceptual framework and research methods 211–212; parent/child/app instructional assemblage 214; parent scaffolding 213; parent scaffolding in the parent-child-app learning assemblage 213–214; research assemblage 213
parent-child interactions 6, 350–352; reading 354
Parenting for a Literate Community 23, 24; handbooks 23
parenting self-efficacy 328–329
parenting skills fostering 329–330
parenting stress 328–329
parents and children's engagement in enjoyable educational activities 330–331
Parents And Children Together (PACT) 327
parent scaffolding 213; in parent-child-app learning assemblage 213–214
parents of preschool children 325
parents of school-age children 325–326
parents' self-efficacy 328
partisan strategy 5
Paw Patrol 182
pedagogical shifts in 129
Peep Learning Together Programme 325
Penguins-Billy-Peers 129
Peppa's Paintbox 159
perceptual-sensory experience 56
persistence 354
Personal, Social, and Emotional 325
personal intentions 80
Peterson, R.L. 356
Pfister, Marcus 258
philosophical/theoretical underpinning 282
phonological awareness 394; literacy screeners 397
phonological memory 394
photographing artifacts 53
photographs and drawings 312–314
Pic Collage 33
Picture Exchange Communication System (PECS) 269
Pigeon and Duckling give the Princess something 99, *100*
Pigeon finds a hotdog, The 99
Pigeon goes to the beach 101
Pinyin 108
placed resources 221–222
play and imagination (Sutton-Smith) 20
Play and Learning Strategies programme 327
play-based makerspace activities 254
playground conversations to policy analysis 189–190
play tours 160–163
point-of-view (POV) cameras 164–166
Polkinghorne, D.E. 144
polysemous scraps 179
Popplet 33
popular media and home perspectives 190–191
pop-up advertisements 378
post-digital approach 157–158, 163
post-digital play 157–158; participatory methods 160; play tours 160–163; point-of-view cameras 164–166; technology and play study 158–160
post-humanism 21; thinking 22
post humanist turn 53
posthuman perspectives 9
post qualitative inquiry (PQI) 131–132
post-qualitative research 53
post-scholars theorize 133
poststructural and posthumanist theories 129, 130
post-typographic digital era 191
posture 243
practitioner tools and references, screener 400
Pratt, M.L. 62
pre-Facecam functionality 40
pre-literate children 349
pre-readers ability 394
pre-reader screening 395–396; tool 398
pre-reading children 395
preschoolers forced-choice questions 355
Price, S. 242
Prinsloo, M. 221
printed word-reading competencies 394
privacy implication 123
problem solving 41
processes of production 98

production and reception 96–98
Project EASE 325
public service announcements (PSAs) 381
PuppetPals 33

qualitative data analysis 81
qualitative inquiry 130
quantifying language 354–355

racial tensions 79
Rainbow Fish, The 258
randomised controlled trial (RCT), parental support 327–328
rapid automatized naming 394, 399
rapid naming tasks 399
reading activities, participation in 237
reading concepts and data through one another 138–139
reading development: tablet technology in preschool 394
reading difficulties 394
Reading Eggs app 213
reading in digital age: lesson 1: rapidly changing technology 349–350; lesson 2: e-book features 350–351; lesson 3: context and previous experience matter 351–353; lesson 4: quantifying language, behavioral/emotional engagement and caregiver-child interaction 354–355; lesson 5: multiple measures helps capture multiple facets of learning 355–357
Reading Lives 20
reading record/communication link 331
reading risk 394–395
reading screening tools 396
READY4K!, text messaging programme 327
reality, partial semblance of 58
REAL (Raising Early Achievement in Literacy) programme 325
Rebecca-Octopus-Be(com)ing 127–128
receptive language 357
recording information *see* device-embedded recorder
reflection 374
reflexive/affective engagement 152
reflexivity 50
Reggio Emilia 20
(re)imagining multiliteracies research: 3D Hummingbird-Gigi 128; diffracting 138–139; ethico-onto-epistemological inspirations for multi- and digital literacies 139–140; ethico-onto-epistemology 134–135; Jellyfish-Nick 128–129; knowing and thinking 137–138; methodologies without methodology 135–136; Nick-Ella-Emily-Panda Bear Habitat-Be(com)ing 127; Nick-Jellyfish-Be(com)ing 127; non-representational logic 132–133; Panda-Emily 129–131; Penguins-Billy-Peers 129; philosophical concepts 138; post qualitative inquiry 131–132; Rebecca-Octopus-Be(com)ing 127–128; resisting the binaries 132; subjectivity as assemblage and/or entanglement 133–134; theoretical concepts becoming method(s) 136–137; transcendental empiricism 132–133
relationality 19
relational materialism 53
relational materialist approach 51
relational moments 18–27
relationships with children 79
research collaborations 10
research designs employed in research literature **200**
researcher-child relationship 40
researching in other people's homes 187–189
research participants 202
resemiotization 172
resisting the binaries 132
Resnick, M. 35
resource-rich social context 103
(re)think empiricism 139
re-thinking 132
return 149–150
Richardson-Ngwenya, P. 53
'richly designed websites' 316
Richter, A. 355–356
rights holders 89
Rinaldi, Carlina 20
roaming camera 367, 373–374
Robert, Na'ima Bint 68
robotics tasks 311
Rowe, D.W. 318
Rowsell, Jennifer 12, 18–27, 102
ruling passions 22–23
Ryan, M.-L. 103

SAGE Handbook of Qualitative Research 131
Saxton, Juliana 184
scaffolding 212
Schensul, J.J. 223
scholarship 139
school computer club 367
school-generated visual texts 389
"school readiness skills" 325
schools and kindergartens, digital media in 314
science, technology, engineering, and mathematics (STEM) 252
science curriculum project, low-income Latino preschool children 341
Scratch Jnr. Coding 35
screen recording 30
screens that are stealing childhood, The 190
self-disclosure 203, 205–206
self-evaluation report 7
self-learning 326

self-portrait 74–75, 78
self-regulation 325
Selland, M.K. 63
SEN *see* special educational needs (SEN)
sensorimotor contingencies 238–239
Sensory Tours 164
Shah, Nisant 85
'shock machine' experiments 39
Shu Yau 15
single discourse 386, *386*
skillful communicators 89
Skype 157
'slowing down' research observation 373
small stories 19
Smart Board 67
Smith, Linda Tuhiwai 284
SnagIt 30
social and cultural valorisations 312
social class "deficits" 22
social-contextual model of family literacy 23
social institutions 23
social interactions 80, 85
social justice and equity in education 341
social-material-discursive spaces of educational care 21
social-material enactments 262
social media 108; intergenerational communication on 107, 114; multimodal 109; platforms 110
social networking sites 372–373
social networking videos 373
social practices 220
social stratification (Bernstein) 20
societies and human spaces, colonization 378
socio-cultural communities 282
sociocultural impact of immigration 3
socio-cultural insecurities 9
socio-cultural knowledge-based learning 342, 343
socio-cultural theories of literacy 89
socioeconomic status (SES) 324–325
socio-emotional capabilities 8
socio-emotional skills 325
sociomateriality and literacies 252
sociomaterial ways of thinking 248
socio-material worlds 54
Soja, Edward 77
Somerville, M. 58, 59
special educational needs (SEN) 267–268; autism spectrum disorder 268–269, 270–273; cognitive and language profile 269; matching, issues in 272–274; research 274–275
specific learning disability in reading 394
speech: and behavior 354; recognition software 399
Spitzer, Manfred 235
SPOKES (Supporting Parents on Kids' Education in School) programme 325–326
St. Pierre, E.A. 131–132
stacking stories 143–144, 146–150; *barefoot, jabbing at screens* 149–150; *i, movie: i am your data* 148–149; juxtaposition 143; in literacy research 145–146; as method 150–151; practical application 151–153; problem with representation 144; *return* 149–150; *The Three Little Pigs* (Nosy Crow) 147–148
standardized tests 289–290
static camera 368
Stavrakakis, Y. 379, 381
Stein, P. 63
Stevenson, Kylie J. 14
Stewart, K. 146
stimuli and screener 400
Storia app 350
stories, stacking *see* stacking stories
storybook reading 238–239
story comprehension 355
storying and re-storying 150–151
story-making events 83
story of the stolen crown, The 99, *100*
story-sharing 149
storytelling 76
Strouse, G.A. 351, 353, 356, 357
structural dynamics 76
student generated visual narratives 294–297; cameraman 301–303; co-researchers lived experiences 304; digital camera, using 301; foregrounding the research design 298–301; voice 297–298
student-generated visual representations 378
Students' writing performance 249
Studiocode 35
Studiocode window *36*, 37
stuff of literacy 220
subjectivity as assemblage and/or entanglement 133–134
"summer reading loss" 327
super diversity 62
Suzanna, So-Har Wong 14
Swirling Hijab, The 68–69
Sylva, Kathy 16, 324–337
symbolic interactionism 75
symbolic production 74

tablet-based e-books 351
tablet-based risk screener 398
tablet screener 397–398
tablet technology in preschool: atypical reading development 394–395; clinical and educational implications 400; design 398–400; early identification and screening 395; literacy screeners 396–397; reading development 394; tablet screener 397–398
Tager-Flusberg, H. 272–273
Taguchi, Lenz 51, 52, 134, 262
talking book consoles 350

Talking Tom 159
Taylor, Denny 23
teacher- and student-generated visual representations 378
teacher/researcher collaborations, design-based experiments in 248; cycle 1 254–257; cycle 2 257–258; cycle 3 258–262; design-based experiments 251–252; foregrounding text production 249–250; makerspace pedagogy 252–253; materiality and multimodality 253–254; methodology and conceptual thinking 250–251; reflection and conclusions 262–263; sociomateriality and literacies 252
teaching and digital divide 340
teaching methods and parental support 326
teaching sequence, planning and design of 66
TeachSmart 343, 344
technologies, affordances and embodiment 235–236
technologies and media 3
technology, materiality and embodiment 102
Technology and Critical Literacy in Early Childhood 386
technology-based intervention and parental support 327
technology-based programmes, parental support 327
"technology-based support," digital media 326
technology-driven initiatives 10
technology-enhanced curriculum 339
technology-enhanced experiences 342
technology-mediated practices, 122
technology met real-life: cultural capital and critical race theories (CTR) 339–340; digital divide 340–341; engage 343; evaluation 344; explanation and elaboration 344; explore 343–344; project description 341–342; science curriculum project for low-income Latino preschool children 341; socio-cultural knowledge-based learning 343; supporting technology-enhanced experiences 342–343
techno-tours 160
Temple Run 159
test-monitored curricula 76
Test of Early Reading Ability-3 287
Test of Reading Ability-2 292
text-mediated system 145
text messages and parental support 327
texts analysis 90–91
textual choreography 80
textual playgrounds 89
theoretical concepts becoming method(s) 136–137
theories of childhood 89
theories of embodiment 89
thinking, lines of flight 366
thinking with theory 136
three-dimensional albeit 172
Three Little Pigs, The (Nosy Crow) 147–148
Toca Boca 159
toddlers: passive video 353; learning 351
Toddlers and tablets: exploring the risks and benefits 0–5s face online 210
"Tomato Trials" 386
Topsy Turvey Tomato Planter 386
touch technology, tablet screener 397
toy franchise characters 314
trained test administrator 399
transcendental empiricism 132–133
transculturalism: defined 62; dual language book program 66–67, 70–71; *Grandma's Saturday Soup* 69–70; and language awareness 64–65; language awareness and dual language books 65–66; and literacy 62–63; practice 67; *Swirling Hijab, The* 68–69
transduction 173
translinguistic meaning-making repertoires 109
trusted adult friend 79

validation 400; and screener 400
valued literacy 387
value-laden activities 80
value to field of digital technologies 179–180
Vander Woude, J. 237
van Winkel, C. 378
Vasc, D. 240
Vasquez, Vivian Maria 377–392
Verenikina, I. 197
Vertovec, S. 62
video: in educational research 363; production 318
video-based educational research 365
video-based fieldwork 110, 111
video cameras: for educational research 363; ethnographic video data 363; types of **364**
video data: ethics of collecting 123–124; as fieldnotes 111
video-editing tools 180
video-recorded engagement 96
video recording methods 32
videotaping, informed consent 352
Villalobos, Valeria Ortiz 16, 324–337
virtual reality 166
virtual worlds 159
visual ads 378
visual discourse analysis 386
visual language 377–378, 381
visual methods 10, 54, 296
visual narratives *299*; *see also* narratives
visual ontology 364
visual-textual-digital form 26
visual works 314
vlogs creation 370, 371–373

vocabulary: development 330; knowledge 357, 394
Vossoughi, S. 63
Vygotsky's zone of proximal development 212

Walled Garden 32
Waller, T. 160
watching and interpreting video data 366
wearable cameras 315, 363
WeChat 107–108, 112–122
Wechsler Intelligence Scale for Children (WISC-IV) 270
Western theories of aesthetics 312
White House Initiative on Education Excellence for Hispanics (2011) 338
Whitty, Pam 12, 18–27
Wohlwend, Karen E. 14, 22, 314
Wong, S.S. 314–315
Woods, Annette 15, 22
word cloud software program 386
word recognition 394
"Words to go" home literacy programme 325–326
work as art 314
working memory and inhibition skills 355
working-with-theory-data 136
writing ability 343
writing books 101–102

Xiaoxiao Du 14

Yelland, N. 212
young children's home technology use 196–197; adult-only interpretations 197–198; build rapport and trust 203–206; context affects use 198; dangers of technology 198–199; designing research 207–208; family visits 201–203; flexible home visit organisational strategies 206–207; narratives 203–205; recruitment of participants 201; research design 199–200; self-disclosure 205–206; sensitive nature 199; technology use, play and learning 197
YouTube 122, 159; video 344
Yu, Q. 114
Yuill, N. 240, 352–353, 356

Zaidi, Rahat 12, 62–72
Zhao, Sumin 13, 107–124
Zone of Proximal Development (ZPD) 342–343
Zosh, Jennifer M. 16, 349–361
ZPD *see* Zone of Proximal Development (ZPD)
Zuk, Jennifer 16, 393–403

For Product Safety Concerns and Information please contact our EU
representative GPSR@taylorandfrancis.com
Taylor & Francis Verlag GmbH, Kaufingerstraße 24, 80331 München, Germany

www.ingramcontent.com/pod-product-compliance
Lightning Source LLC
LaVergne TN
LVHW080804011026
849160LV00015B/1529
* 9 7 8 1 1 3 8 3 0 8 1 9 0 *